Taxation

Incorporating the Finance Act 2018

37th edition 2018/19

Taxation

Incorporating the Finance Act 2018

Alan Combs BA, MSc, FCCA
Ricky Tutin BSc, FCA
Peter Rowes BSc(Econ), FCA, ATII

Taxation: Incorporating the 2018 Finance Act – 37th Edition 2018/2019

For more information visit: http://www.fiscalpublications.com

British Library Cataloguing-in-Publication Data

A catalogue record for this book is available from the British Library

Lecturer supplement and other materials are available from the Rowes 2018 website – see http://www.fiscalpublications.com/rowes/2018

ISBN 978 1 906201 41 8

Thirty seventh edition 2018

Cover design by FD Design Ltd

Printed in Great Britain by Antony Rowe Ltd., Chippenham, Wiltshire

Typesetting and production by P. K. McBride, Southampton

Contents

	Acknowledgements	vii
	Preface	viii
	Abbreviations and statutes	ix
	Summary of main changes 2018/19	xii
Part I: Introduction		**1**
1	Principles of taxation	2
Part II: Income Tax		**13**
2	General principles of income tax	14
3	Administration	28
4	Personal allowances and reliefs	38
5	Allowable payments and Gift Aid	44
6	Savings and investment income	49
7	Income from employment I – general principles	67
8	Income from employment II – PAYE	90
9	Income from UK land and property	95
10	Income taxed as trade profits I – general principles	107
11	Income taxed as trade profits II – basis periods	126
12	Income taxed as trade profits III – change of accounting date	138
13	Capital allowances	143
14	Relief for trading and capital losses	166
15	Partnership taxation	181
16	Personal investment – pensions	191
17	National Insurance contributions and social security	201
	End of section questions without answers	212
Part III: Corporation Tax		**219**
18	General principles of corporation tax	220
19	Computation of total profits	234
20	Capital allowances	258
21	Quarterly returns and qualifying charitable donations	265
22	Relief for losses	272
23	Groups	288
24	International aspects	302
	End of section questions and answers	316

Part IV: Taxation of chargeable gains 327
25 General Principles of taxation of chargeable gains 328
26 The basic rules of computation 343
27 Chargeable persons 352
28 Chargeable occasions 359
29 Land and chattels 366
30 Shares and securities 377
31 CGT special reliefs and CGs groups 395
32 Gifts and CGT holdover relief 416

Part V: Inheritance Tax 423
33 General principles of Inheritance Tax 424
34 IHT computations 436

Part VI: Value Added Tax 453
35 General principles of Value Added Tax 454
36 The VAT system in more detail 472

Part VII: Tax Planning 499
37 Elements of tax planning 500
38 Additional questions **523**

Index 567
Tax rates 2018/19 571

Acknowledgements

The authors would like to express thanks to the following for giving permission to reproduce past examination questions and forms:

Association of Chartered Certified Accountants (ACCA)

Chartered Institute of Management Accountants (CIMA)

Chartered Institute of Taxation (CIOT)

Controller of Her Majesty's Stationery Office

Many of the questions and answers in the 37th edition are from a bank of materials compiled by Jill Webb of the University of York and Dora Hancock of Birmingham City University. The use of these questions and answers is gratefully acknowledged. Stephanie Little shared authorship of the 29th to 33rd editions and Richard Andrews of the University of Hull shared authorship of the 25th to 28th editions. The authors gratefully acknowledge the contributions of their co-authors.

Preface

Aims of the book

1. The main aim of this book is to provide a thorough basic knowledge of UK taxation, covering Income Tax, Corporation Tax, Taxation of Chargeable Gains, Inheritance Tax, and Value Added Tax.

   It has been written for students of the following:

   Association of Chartered Certified Accountants
   Paper F6 (UK) Taxation
   Institute of Chartered Accountants in England and Wales
   Principles of Taxation
   Certified Accounting Technician
   Paper FTX Foundations of Taxation
   Association of Accounting Technicians
   Business Taxation
   Personal Taxation
   Association of Taxation Technicians
   All papers (introductory text)
   Association of International Accountants
   Module F Paper 16 Taxation and Tax Planning
   Universities and colleges
   Accounting and Business Studies Degrees – Taxation Modules

Approach

2. a) This book should provide the student with:

   i) A knowledge of the basic relevant statutory law

   ii) A knowledge of some of the case law developed to interpret statutory law.

   It should enable the student to apply these legal principles to practical problems and prepare the necessary computations, and to understand the importance of tax planning.

   b) Each of the areas of taxation is introduced by a general principles chapter which outlines the main features of each tax. Subsequent chapters develop the principles in detail with examples.

   c) Illustrative examples form an important feature of this text. At the end of each chapter there are questions with answers for student self-testing. Also provided are further questions, the answers to which are contained in a separate supplement which can be obtained direct from the publishers by lecturers recommending the manual as a course text.

This edition incorporates the provisions of the Finance Act 2018 in so far as it relates to the year 2018/19.

Alan Combs, Ricky Tutin and Peter Rowes, 2018.

Abbreviations and statutes

Abbreviations

AA	Automobile Association
A/C	Accounting (or Accounts)
ACCA	Association of Chartered Certified Accountants
AEA	Annual Exempt Amount
AIA	Annual investment allowance
AIM	Alternative investment market
ANI	Adjusted net income
AP	Accounting period
APA	Advance Pricing Agreement
AR	Additional rate
ATED	Annual Tax on Enveloped Dwellings
AVC	Additional voluntary contributions
BA	Balancing allowance
BBC	British Broadcasting Corporation
BC	Balancing charge
BEPS	Base erosion and profit shifting
b/f b/fwd	Brought forward
BP	Basis period
BPR	Business property relief
BR	Basic rate
CA	Capital allowance
CAA	Capital Allowances Act 2001
CASC	Community amateur sports club
CFC	Controlled foreign company
c/f c/fwd	Carried forward
CG	Chargeable gain
CG group	Capital gains group
CGT	Capital gains tax
Ch D	Chancery Division
CIHC	Close Investment Holding Company
CIMA	Chartered Institute of Management Accountants
CIS	Construction industry subcontractors' scheme
CLT	Chargeable lifetime transfer
CO_2	Carbon dioxide
CP	Civil partner
CPI	Consumer Prices Index
CSOP	Company share option scheme
CT	Corporation tax
CTA2009	Corporation Tax Act 2009
CTA2010	Corporation Tax Act 2010
CTAP	Corporation tax accounting period
CTF	Child trust fund
CTSA	Corporation tax self-assessment
CVS	Corporate venturing scheme
CY	Current year
CYB	Current Year Basis
DT	Death Transfer
DTR	Double taxation relief
ECA	Enhanced capital allowances
EEA	European Economic Area
EFRBS	Employer financed retirement benefit schemes
EIS	Enterprise investment scheme
EMI	Enterprise Management Incentive share scheme
ER	Entrepreneur's relief
ESSU	Employee shares and securities unit
ET	Earnings threshold
EU	European Union
EX	Exempt
FA 2018	Finance Act 2018
FHL	Furnished holiday letting

FICO	Financial intermediaries and claims office
FIFO	First in, first out
FY	Financial year
FYA	First year allowance
GAAP	Generally Accepted Accounting Principles (or Practice)
GAAR	General Anti-Abuse Rule
g/km	Grams per kilometre
GPPP	Group personal pension plan
GR	Group relief
HMRC	HM Revenue and Customs
HP	Hire purchase
HR	Higher rate
IA	Indexation allowance
IHT	Inheritance tax
ISA	Individual savings account
IT	Income tax
ITA	Income Tax Act 2007
ITEPA	Income tax (Earnings & Pensions) Act 2003
ITTOIA	Income Tax (Trading and Other Income) Act 2005
LEL	Lower earnings limit
LIFO	Last in, first out
LR	Loan relationship
LT	Lifetime Transfer
MCA	Married couples allowance
MV	Market value
n/a	not applicable
NGNL	No gain, no loss
NHS	National Health Service
NI	National insurance
NIC	National insurance contribution
NISA	New Individual Savings Account
NRB	(Inheritance Tax) Nil rate band
NRV	Net Realisable Value
NSI	National savings and investments
NTLR	Non-Trade Loan Relationship
OECD	Organisation for Economic Co-operation and Development
ONS	Office for National Statistics
ORI	Official rate of interest
p.a.	Per annum
PA	Personal allowance
PAYE	Pay as you earn
PET	Potentially exempt transfer
PIBS	Permanent interest bearing shares
POA	Payment on account
PPP	Personal pension plan
PPR	Principal private residence
PSO	Pension schemes office
p.u.	Private use
p/w	Per week
QBD	Queen's Bench Division
QCB	Qualifying Corporate Bond
QCD	Qualifying Charitable Donations
R&D	Research and development
RDE2	Real driving emissions step 2
RPT	Relevant property trust
RTI	Real time information
SAYE	Save as you earn
SEIS	Seed Enterprise Investment Scheme
SIP	Share incentive plan
SIPP	Self invested personal pension
SME	Small or medium sized enterprise
SMP	Statutory maternity pay
SR	Standard rated
SSE	Substantial shareholdings exemption
SSP	Statutory sick pay
STC	Simon's Tax cases
TIOPA	Taxation (International and Other Provisions) Act 2010
TC	Tax Cases
TCGA	Taxation of Chargeable Gains Act 1992
TDR	Total disposal receipts
TMA	Taxes Management Act 1970

TTP	Taxable total profits	VATA	Value Added Tax Act 1994
UEL	Upper earnings limit	VCT	Venture capital trust
UK	United Kingdom	WDA	Writing down allowance
UKUT	UK Upper Tribunal	WDV	Written down value
USM	Unlisted securities market	WHT	Withholding tax
VAT	Value added tax	ZR	Zero rated

Statutes

Income Tax	Income Tax Act 2007
Income Tax	Income Tax (Trading and Other Income) Act 2005
Income Tax	Income Tax (Earnings & Pensions) Act 2003
Income Tax	Finance Act 2018
Corporation Tax	Corporation Tax Act 2009, Corporation Tax Act 2010, Taxation (International and Other Provisions) Act 2010
Corporation Tax	Finance Act 2018
Capital Gains Tax	Taxation of Chargeable Gains Act 1992
Inheritance Tax	Inheritance Tax Act 1984
Value Added Tax	Value Added Tax Act 1994
Capital Allowances	Capital Allowances Act 2001

Summary of main changes 2018/19

Part II. Income tax and National Insurance Contributions

1. Personal reliefs

		2018/19	2017/18
		£	£
a)	Personal allowance	11,850	11,500
	Abatement of allowance where income exceeds	100,000	100,000
	Blind person's allowance	2,390	2,320
	Marriage allowance: Both born after 05-Apr-1935*	1,190	1,150
	Married couple's allowance: Born before 06-Apr-1935	** 8,695	** 8,445
	Minimum married couple's allowance	** 3,360	** 3,260
	Abatement of relief where income exceeds	28,900	28,000

Note that there is now a single main Personal Allowance, rather than different Personal Allowances dependent upon a taxpayer's age.

b) The allowance marked with an asterisk (*) allows a spouse or civil partner who is not liable to income tax, or not liable at the higher or additional rate, to transfer up to £1,190 of their personal allowance to their spouse or civil partner. The recipient must not be liable to income tax at the higher or additional rate. This relief is given at 20%. From 29 November 2017 claims may be made on behalf of a deceased spouse or civil partner, back dated up to four years.

c) The allowances marked with a double asterisk (**) allowed at the 10% rate are given as a deduction in computing the tax liability.

2. Income tax rates

	2018/19	2017/18
Starting rate - savings	0%	0%
- where savings income comprises taxable income up to	£5,000	£5,000
"Personal savings allowance" – nil rate	0%	0%
on savings income (not covered by PA or starting rate) up to:		
- for basic rate taxpayers	£1,000	£1,000
- for higher rate taxpayers	£500	£500
- for additional rate taxpayers	0	0
"Dividend allowance" – nil rate	0%	0%
on dividend income up to	£2,000	£5,000
Basic rate		
- non-savings, non-dividend income (except Scottish rates)	20%	20%
- savings income	20%	20%
- dividends ordinary rate	7.5%	7.5%
Higher rate – savings and non-savings (except Scottish rates)	40%	40%
- dividends upper rate	32.5%	32.5%
Additional rate – savings and non-savings (except Scottish rates)	45%	45%
- dividends additional rate	38.1%	38.1%

3. Taxable bands

UK taxpayers excluding Scotland

Taxable income	Band	**2018/19** Rate
£	£	%
0 – 34,500	34,500	20
34,501 – 150,000	115,500	40
150,001+		45

Taxpayers resident in Scotland

Taxable non-savings non-dividend income	Band	**2018/19** Rate
£	£	%
Personal allowance up to £11,850		0
11,851* – 13,850	2,000	19
13,851 – 24,000	10,150	20
24,001 – 43,430	19,430	21
43,431 – 150,000	106,570	41
150,001+		46

* Assuming a personal allowance of £11,850.

UK taxpayers

Taxable income	Band	2017/18 Rate
£	£	%
0 – 33,500*	33,500	20
33,501* – 150,000	116,500	40
150,001+		45

* For taxpayers resident in Scotland the basic rate band is from £0 to £31,500 for 2017/18.

4. Individual savings accounts

The Junior ISA limit for 2018/19 will be £4,260 (2017/18 £4,128).

5. Employment income

Benefits

- **Car benefit**

  Car benefit is based on a percentage of the list price of the car when new, graduated according to CO_2 emissions. The percentage ranges from 13% for cars emitting 0-50g/km of CO_2 to a maximum of 37%. See Chapter 7, section 14 for the full table. The diesel supplement is 4% in 2018/19 for cars which do not meet the Real Driving Emissions Step Two (RDE2) standard. Diesel cars meeting the RDE2 standard will not be subject to a supplement, (*unless they were registered before 1st September 2017, in which case the supplement still applies*).

- **Car fuel benefit**

2018/19	2017/18
CO_2 emissions % × £23,400	CO_2 emissions % × £22,600

- **Van benefit** £3,350 (increased from £3,230 in 2017/18).
- **Van fuel benefit** £633 (increased from £610 in 2017/18).

Payments in lieu of notice

From 6 April 2018 all payments in lieu of notice, including non contractual payments, will be taxable as earnings.

6. Income from UK land and property

Tax free allowance on property gives an exemption of up to £1,000 a year for individuals with income from property, 6th April 2017 onwards. Individuals with property income below £1,000 a year will no longer need to declare or pay tax on that income.

Since 6th April 2017 **tax relief on finance costs deductible from property income** have been restricted for individuals who are landlords of let residential properties. The restriction is phased in from 2017/18 onwards. In 2018/19 50% of finance costs will be allowed as a deduction from property income, while the remaining 50% will be given as a basic rate tax reduction, although this may not be used to create a tax refund.

Most unincorporated property businesses with turnover of less than £150,000 will be able to calculate taxable profits on a simplified cash basis.

7. Income from trading

Tax free allowance on trading gives an exemption of up to £1,000 a year for individuals with income from self-employment, casual services and hiring personal equipment, from 6th April 2017 onwards. Individuals with trading income below £1,000 a year will no longer need to declare or pay tax on that income.

8. Capital allowances – CO_2 emissions levels for cars

For cars purchased on or after 1 April 2018, the CO_2 emissions limit for "low-emission" cars eligible for the 100% enhanced capital allowance is reduced to 50g/km (previously 75g/km).

For cars purchased on or after 1 April 2018, the CO_2 emissions limit for cars eligible for 18% writing down allowance is reduced to 110g/km (previously 130g/km).

9. Class 1 National Insurance Thresholds

Weekly pay	2018/19 £	2017/18 £
Upper earnings limit	892	866
Earnings threshold (employee)	162	157
Earnings threshold (employer)	162	157
Lower earnings limit	116	113

As an incentive to employ and train more young people, different secondary Class 1 contribution bands apply for employees under 21 years old and for apprentices under 25 years old:

Employer "secondary" Class 1 contributions for ...

... Employees under 21:

Up to £116 a week – lower earnings limit	exempt
Up to £892 a week (UST, Upper Secondary Threshold)	0.0%
Over £892 per week	13.8%

... Apprentices under 25:

Up to £116 a week – lower earnings limit	exempt
Up to £892 a week (AUST, Apprentices UST)	0.0%
Over £892 per week	13.8%

10. Self-employed National Insurance

	2018/19	2017/18
Class 2	£2.95 per week	£2.85 per week

Liability for class 2 contributions for 2018/19 will arise at the end of each year by reference to profits used to calculate class 4 contributions. Where a taxpayer has profits below a small profits threshold of £6,205 for 2018/19 they may voluntarily choose to pay class 2 contributions to preserve their entitlement to contributory state benefits.

Class 4	2018/19	2017/18
Taxable band (£)	8,424 – 46,350	8,164 – 45,000
Rate of tax	9%	9%
Taxable band (£)	above 46,350	above 45,000
Rate of tax	2%	2%

Part III. Corporation tax

1. Rates

	FY 2018 y/e 31.3.2019	FY 2017 y/e 31.3.2018
Main rate	19%	19%

2. Loss relief reform

Losses arising on or after 1st April 2017 may be carried forward against profits from different types of income and profits of other group companies.

Companies or groups whose profits are above £5m are restricted in the amount of carried forward losses which are set against their profits. Profits arising on or after 1st April 2017 may not be reduced by more than £5m plus 50% of the excess profits above £5m for such companies.

3. Research and Development Expenditure Credit (RDEC)

For expenditure incurred from 1st January 2018, Research and Development Expenditure Credit (RDEC) increases to 12% (previously 11%).

4. Deductibility of interest expense

From 1st April 2017 a group's net interest deduction is restricted to a fixed 30% of earnings before interest, taxation, depreciation and amortisation (EBITDA) in the UK. A worldwide group ratio may be substituted, by election, for the 30% ratio. Existing debt cap legislation will be repealed, and replaced with a modified debt cap that ensures net UK interest deduction does not exceed the total net interest expense of the worldwide group.

Worldwide groups with net interest expenses of less than or equal to £2 million will not need to apply these rules.

5. Double taxation relief and permanent establishment losses

From 22nd November 2017 there will be a restriction on the amount of credit allowed, or deduction given for foreign tax suffered by an overseas establishment of a company, where the company has received relief in the foreign jurisdiction for the losses of the permanent establishment against profits other than those of the permanent establishment.

6. Chargeable gains indexation allowance

Indexation on chargeable gains will be frozen from December 2017.

Part IV. Capital gains tax

Rates and allowances

	2018/19	2017/18
Standard rate	10%	10%
Higher rate and trust rate	20%	20%
Surcharge on residential property *	+8%	+8%
Annual exemption		
For individuals, PRs and some trustees	£11,700	£11,300
For most trustees	£5,850	£5,650
Entrepreneurs' relief rate	10%	10%
Entrepreneurs' relief lifetime limit of gains	£10m	£10m
Investors' relief rate	10%	10%
Investors' relief lifetime limit of gains	£10m	£10m

Part V. Inheritance tax

Rates

For 2018/19, the IHT residence nil rate band is increased through the phasing in arrangements.

	2018/19	2017/18
Rate for estates	40%	40%
Reduced rate for estates leaving 10% or more to charity	36%	36%
Rate for chargeable lifetime transfers	20%	20%
Nil rate band	£325,000	£325,000
Residence nil rate band	£125,000	£100,000

Part VI. Value added tax

1. Registration

Registration levels are unchanged from those applicable from April 2017.

	£
Taxable turnover in previous 12 months	85,000
Taxable turnover in next 30 days	85,000

2. Deregistration

The annual limit for deregistration is £83,000, unchanged from April 2017.

Future tax changes

The government has proposed a number of tax changes which it intends to implement in the future. These include:

Income tax

The Conservative government has committed to raising the Personal Allowance to £12,500, and the higher rate threshold to £50,000. Note that the commitment to a £50,000 higher rate threshold refers to total income rather than taxable income; it corresponds to £37,500 of taxable income (i.e. after deducting the Personal Allowance).

Welsh income tax

From April 2019 taxpayers in Wales will be taxed through a Welsh income tax.

National insurance

The government intends to abolish Class 2 National Insurance Contributions, as a tax simplification measure.

Income from UK land and property

Finance costs (e.g. mortgage interest)

From 6th April 2017, there is phased implementation of a move towards allowing landlords to claim relief for finance costs only at basic rate:

- 2018/19: 50% of finance costs as expense in calculating property income; 50% as a basic rate tax reduction;
- 2019/20: 25% of finance costs as expense in calculating property income; 75% as a basic rate tax reduction;
- 2020/21: all finance costs as a basic rate tax reduction.

Corporation Tax

Corporation Tax rates

The government intends to reduce the rate of Corporation Tax to 17% for the tax year beginning 1st April 2020.

Timing of Corporation Tax payments

For Accounting Periods commencing on or after 1st April 2019, very large companies (those with profits above £20million) will be required to pay Corporation Tax by quarterly instalments at months 3, 6, 9 and 12 of a 12-month Accounting Period.

Inheritance tax

Residence Nil Rate Band

From 6th April 2017, there is a phased introduction of a main residence nil-rate band, in addition to the general nil-rate band. It will apply when a residence is passed on to a direct descendant, or when the taxpayer downsizes (or ceases to own a home) and passes assets of equivalent value to the direct descendant(s).

The proposal is to set the main residence nil rate band at:

- 2018/19: £125,000
- 2019/20: £150,000
- 2020/21: £175,000

thereafter rising in line with CPI. Any unused band on death will be transferred to a surviving spouse or civil partner.

There will be tapered withdrawal of the main residence nil-rate band for estates worth over £2million, at a rate of £1 for every £2 over that threshold.

Value added tax

From April 2019 VAT registered businesses will be required to use computer based VAT submissions under the "**Making Tax Digital**" development.

A reverse charge will be introduced from 1 October 2019 for labour supply chains in the construction industry. The recipient of services will become responsible for accounting for VAT, to combat fraud through the VAT paid being subsequently stolen.

Part I

Introduction

1 Principles of taxation

1.1 Definition of tax

Taxes are contributions levied on persons, property or business, for the support of national or local government[1].

1.2 Reasons for tax

'Taxes are what we pay for a civilized society'

Oliver Wendell Holmes, Jr, U.S. Supreme Court Justice

Broadly, we can identify the purposes of taxation as being:

- to fund **provision of "public goods"**, goods and services which would be under-provided if left to market forces due to the "free-rider" problem. These include national defence, the fire service and vaccination programmes;
- to fund **provision of "merit goods"**, goods and services which could in principle be provided by the market but which, as a society, we consider to be particularly valuable – even rights – such that we have collectively decided that the state ought to provide the items. Examples include provision of education (indeed, Article 26 of the Universal Declaration of Human Rights specifies education as a right, which must be available for "free, at least in the elementary and fundamental stages") and health care which, in the UK, is universally available and provided free at the point of use by the National Health Service;
- to fund **physical infrastructure** - such as road and rail networks;
- to fund what we might call "**organisational infrastructure**" to create conditions in which citizens and businesses may prosper, in such areas as environmental protection, justice and home affairs, foreign and security policy, and negotiations in – and defence of rights under – international treaties;
- to fund **social protection**, such as unemployment protection, disability benefits, maternity and paternity protection, family/child benefits and pensions;
- to discourage behaviour which gives rise to **negative externalities**. A negative externality is a cost imposed upon a third party by the actions of producers and consumers. Taxes on alcohol, tobacco and CO_2 emissions are examples of taxes which seek to discourage behaviour having negative externalities (conversely, tax incentives may encourage behaviour having positive externalities; generous allowances for investment in environmentally-friendly plant and machinery for example (sections 13.10-13.12));

- to achieve **redistribution** of income through the tax and benefits systems, to improve social outcomes and sustain long-term growth[2];
- to achieve **stabilisation** of the economy, smoothing out peaks and troughs of the economic cycle through high taxation in good years and low taxation in bad years.

1.3 Tax provides benefits

Tax is justified by the benefits it provides. In a society that tolerates free speech public spending is subject to intense scrutiny. One reason for this may be that if benefits are not being provided to the members of society, the reason for collecting tax is lost. Adverse comments, and civil disobedience, can also result where taxation is seen as unfair.

1.4 A balanced budget

The amount of money raised by taxation and the amount of public expenditure will not necessarily equal each other in a particular year. A 'budget deficit' arises in a year where public expenditure is more than the amount raised by taxation. The government can fund the extra expenditure by inviting people to lend it money, in the form of government securities or investments in National Savings. Years of 'budget surplus' where taxation exceeds public expenditure would give the opportunity for government borrowings to be repaid.

Early in the history of modern Western economics 'classical' economists, such as Adam Smith, formed a view that market forces would produce the most efficient allocation of resources of labour and financial capital[3]. If there were unemployment, for example, market forces would cause wages to fall, until lower wages encouraged employers to take on more workers. It was believed the wages received by the newly employed workers would stimulate demand for more goods and services, and a virtuous circle of growth would continue until equilibrium was reached when everyone was employed. The belief in efficient markets implied it was best for governments to intervene as little as possible in the economic choices made by people and businesses. This 'fiscal neutrality' would include running a 'balanced budget' where necessary public expenditure was financed by an equal amount of taxation.

'Keynesian' economists formed the view that equilibrium in the economy could be reached at points below full employment[4]. In times when market demand was low it would be beneficial for the government to use reflationary policies to stimulate demand, and start the cycle of growth. These policies might include[5]:

- increasing government expenditure;
- cutting direct or indirect taxation to encourage spending;
- cutting interest rates to discourage saving and encourage spending.

The first two techniques are 'fiscal' policies which directly affect public expenditure and tax revenue. Applying these policies could cause a budget deficit. Keynesian economics accepts a budget deficit in years when the market economy is in recession, providing it is matched by a budget surplus in years of high growth in the market economy. The deflationary policies available to achieve budget surpluses and restrain demand would be the opposite of the reflationary policies above. Budgets should still be balanced over the long term. Applying Keynesian economics to the government's budget would involve using changes in public expenditure and taxation to affect demand for goods and services[6], and so counteract the effects of the 'boom and bust' cycles in the market economy: 'counter-cyclical demand management policies'.

The UK Treasury predicted[7] total government receipts for 2018/19 of £769 billion and total managed expenditure of £809 billion. This is a budget deficit of £40 billion, with expenditure 5.2% more than receipts.

The UK government typically spends more than it receives, the extent of this depending upon economic conditions:

- from 1946 to 1972 the average deficit (as a percentage of government receipts) was 2.4%;
- from 1973 to 1978 (ie. following the 1973 oil crisis) it was 12.2%;
- from 1979 to 1991 (with a new Conservative government) it was 5.6%;
- from 1992 to 1996 (ie. following 'Black Wednesday' when the UK was forced to withdraw sterling from the European Exchange Rate Mechanism) it was 16.2%;
- from 1997 to 2007 (with a new Labour government) it was 4.2%.

When the global financial crisis hit in 2008, governments were forced to enact substantial fiscal stimulus packages. You can see from the following table (reading up from the bottom) what an impact that had on the deficit (measured as public sector net borrowing), which shot up to 35.5% of the amount of current receipts in 2009/10 and took until 2016/17 to get back to the level seen in 2007/08.

Year	Public sector current receipts, £m	Total managed expenditure, £m	Surplus/ (deficit), £m	Surplus/ (deficit), %
2017/18 (forecast)	745,400	795,300	(49,900)	(6.7%)
2016/17	726,534	785,874	(59,340)	(8.2%)
2015/16	684,115	770,737	(86,622)	(12.7%)
2014/15	659,872	766,422	(106,550)	(16.1%)
2013/14	635,605	763,995	(128,390)	(20.2%)
2012/13	610,972	769,472	(158,500)	(25.9%)
2011/12	601,146	755,892	(154,746)	(25.7%)
2010/11	580,187	754,226	(174,064)	(30.0%)
2009/10	541,923	734,251	(192,328)	(35.5%)
2008/09	548,179	694,581	(146,402)	(26.7%)
2007/08	563,552	609,544	(45,992)	(8.2%)
2006/07	533,915	571,778	(37,863)	(7.1%)
2005/06	504,809	546,251	(41,442)	(8.2%)
2004/05	470,734	516,861	(46,127)	(9.8%)
2003/04	438,674	477,373	(38,699)	(8.8%)
2002/03	405,732	437,619	(31,887)	(7.9%)
2001/02	399,803	403,997	(4,194)	(1.0%)
2000/01	394,375	378,083	16,292	4.1%
1999/2000	367,032	355,910	11,122	3.0%
1998/1999	344,183	342,936	1,247	0.4%
1997/1998	324,300	333,230	(8,930)	(2.8%)

Sources: HM Treasury Autumn Budget 2017;
Office for National Statistics Public Sector Finances time series dataset

1.5 Desirable characteristics of taxation

Adam Smith[8] proposed 'Canons of Taxation', which listed desirable features for a system of taxation. These may be restated in contemporary terms as equity, certainty, convenience and efficiency.

Equity means taxes should be fair. **Horizontal equity** would require justice and equality of treatment, so taxpayers having similar circumstances would be treated in a similar way by the tax authorities and have similar tax liabilities. **Vertical equity** would mean the burden of tax fell fairly across taxpayers with different circumstances. This requires a subjective value judgement about what is fair. Adam Smith believed fairness would link tax liabilities with the taxpayer's ability to pay, so taxpayers with high income and wealth would pay more tax than those with low income and little wealth. Another possible approach to fairness would be linking the amount of a taxpayer's liability with the value of benefits from public expenditure they receive.

Certainty means taxpayers should be able to establish how taxes will result from their economic decisions such as whether to work in return for income, save or spend their wealth, or deal in assets. This would mean the tax law and regulations would need to be clearly written, and not applied retrospectively.

Convenience would minimise the taxpayer's costs in complying with tax laws and regulations. A tax requiring only simple calculations by a taxpayer would satisfy this 'Canon of taxation' better than a tax requiring complex calculations based on records kept over many years.

Efficiency has two elements:

- **Administrative efficiency** means that the costs of collecting tax should be as low as possible in comparison with the revenue raised.
- **Economic efficiency** means that tax does not distort taxpayers' economic decisions, such as whether to work or take leisure, and whether to save or spend their income and wealth.

In working through this book, you will see that there are limits to which taxes in the UK achieve the ideals set out as the Canons of Taxation.

Indeed, some features of UK taxes are intended to influence taxpayers and have distorting effects on economic decisions. There is a current theme of encouraging spending on assets which help minimise environmental damage and discouraging spending on vehicles with high levels of carbon dioxide emissions.
Taxes with an intentional distorting effect are called 'corrective' taxes.

1.6 Tax bases

What to tax? The most basic form of tax is a poll tax, where every taxpayer has an equal liability. Such a tax is widely regarded as inequitable, because it is not related to ability to pay, or to benefits consumed. A form of poll tax was used for local taxation in the UK during the 1980s and 1990s. The tax was administratively inefficient because of widespread non-payment through lack of public acceptance and the impossibility of collecting tax from people without the ability to pay. The 'community charge' caused riots and the prime minister of the time was removed from office.

Major tax bases in modern economies are income, expenditure and wealth.

Taxing income or expenditure recognises transactions are taking place, and so it has some relationship to ability to pay.

Wealth may not be in the form of cash and so does not necessarily show an ability to pay. In the UK wealth taxes at the national level are usually linked to wealth being transferred by sale, gift or inheritance, on the basis that the existence of a transaction increases the likelihood of cash being available to pay tax.

In recent years, there has been discussion in the UK as to the desirability of a wealth tax in the form of a so-called 'Mansion Tax' on high-value residential properties; for example, at the Liberal Democrat conference in 2012 a motion was passed calling for 'an annual mansion tax on the excess value of residential properties over £2 million as a first step towards wealth taxation designed to reduce inequality'[9]. In their 2015 general election manifestos, the Labour Party committed to introducing such a tax[10] and the Scottish National Party committed to supporting it[11], while the Green Party promised a wider 'Wealth Tax' on citizens whose wealth exceeds £3million[12]. This has proved highly controversial, and was rejected by the Conservative Party, its position being that 'we are not going to have a mansion tax, or a new tax that is a percentage value of people's properties.'[13]

However, a notable departure from the principle of taxing wealth only when it is transferred is the new 'Annual Tax on Enveloped Dwellings' – a tax introduced as an anti-avoidance measure, charged on the value of property owned in some circumstances – see section 25.10.

1.7 Direct taxes

Direct taxes are related to a taxpayer's circumstances, for example income or wealth. The taxpayer in principle is personally responsible for making payments of tax directly to the tax authorities. However, for some types of income, including bank and building society interest and earnings from employment, an estimated (not the final) amount of income tax is deducted by the savings institution or employer before the taxpayer receives the income. The institution or employer pays this tax over to HM Revenue and Customs, and notifies the taxpayer. This is still direct tax, as the tax liability (which may require an adjustment at the end of the tax year) is directly related to the taxpayer's personal circumstances.

1.8 Indirect taxes

Indirect taxes are charged on a taxpayer, but with the effect that the cost of the tax is borne by another person or organisation. For example, retailers are responsible for paying Value Added Tax (VAT) to HM Revenue and Customs, but the tax is collected by the retailer from customers, who actually bear the cost.

1.9 Incidence of tax

The 'incidence' of tax may simply be described as the person or organisation obliged to pay the tax. Indirect taxes have a different 'formal incidence', the taxpayer legally responsible for making tax payments to the tax authorities, and 'effective incidence', the person or organisation whose wealth is actually reduced by the tax.

Direct taxes are more likely to have the same formal and effective incidence.

1.10 Hypothecated taxes

Hypothecated taxes are taxes collected to fund a particular service. Although in the UK hypothecation is rare, some government charges can be seen as akin to hypothecated taxes. For example, money collected from the UK television licence is used to pay for the television programmes of the BBC. In the same way, money collected from National Insurance contributions was originally matched against spending on State pensions and benefits, but Treasury accounts no longer reconcile income and outgoings. Thus UK National Insurance is now in effect a direct tax, although class 1, 2 and 3 NI contributions still earn entitlement to State Pension, and certain other social security benefits (see Chapter 17).

1.11 Excise duties

Excise duties are indirect expenditure taxes on goods such as alcohol, tobacco and fuel oil. They are unit taxes based on the quantity of the product. This distinguishes them from indirect taxes based on value, such as Value Added Tax and insurance premium tax.

1.12 Withholding taxes

Withholding taxes are deducted from certain types of income before a taxpayer receives it. Withholding taxes are in general used as a safeguard against certain types of income escaping tax. In states with developed self-assessment tax systems, they survive mainly as deductions imposed on certain payments of 'passive income' (i.e. interest, dividends, royalties and rents) which might otherwise escape tax, especially if paid to persons not resident in the state where the income source is located.

Until 5th April 2016, a form of withholding tax was the UK income tax at basic rate deducted by banks and building societies paying interest to individuals on deposit and savings accounts. However, such deductions at source are no longer made. Instead, HMRC includes any taxable savings income in the PAYE code (see Chapter 8 for how this operates).

Also, currently UK individuals must deduct 20% tax at source from patent royalty payments made, and account for it to HMRC on behalf of the royalty recipient.

This is a classic domestic (as opposed to cross-border) withholding tax. The person who deducted the tax pays it over to the tax authorities on behalf of the patent owner, who can later claim it back if they do not in fact owe any tax (e.g. because they had tax losses to set off).

1.13 Double taxation

If a taxpayer receives interest, royalty, rent or dividend income from foreign individuals or organisations, withholding tax may have been deducted in the foreign country. If domestic tax is also charged in the taxpayer's home country the same income has been taxed twice. Double taxation treaties between countries will arrange for some relief to be available against double taxation. There are various possibilities for the practical workings of double taxation relief, any of which may be specified in a tax treaty:

- income taxed in one country may be exempted from tax in another;
- withholding tax deducted, or other direct tax paid, in a foreign country may be credited against the taxpayer's tax liability in the home country;
- the proportion of the 'underlying tax' on a foreign company's profits that relates to dividend income distributed to the home country may be deducted from the taxpayer's liability in their home country;
- the net income, after any foreign tax, may be taken as the amount of income to be taxed in the home country.

The UK has an extensive network of double tax treaties. If a UK taxpayer has income from a source country with which no treaty exists, unilateral (non-treaty) double tax relief may be claimed by the 'credit method' (the second type above), but only up to a maximum of the UK tax due on the same income.

1.14 Imputation system of Corporation Tax

A problem of double taxation arises when a company distributes dividends to shareholders. The company pays corporation tax on its profits and gains. When dividends are received by a shareholder the profits being distributed may well be taxed a second time, as investment income.

In the UK this is avoided **for companies** by excluding all dividends received from their total of taxable income.

Individuals are taxed on dividend income but at a lower rate. Until 5th April 2016, individuals could claim a tax credit on the dividends received, as though some income tax had already been paid. This credit was for the tax the individual was 'imputed' to have paid when the company paid corporation tax on its profits.
However, the imputation tax credit was abolished with effect from 6th April 2016. Shareholders may now receive up to £2,000 of dividends tax-free; however, dividends they receive above that level are subject to income tax, and therefore this part of the profits distributed as dividends will be subject to double-taxation. That is, the profits will be taxed once in the hands of the company and a second time in the hands of the shareholder.

1.15 Evasion and avoidance

Tax evasion involves breaking the law to reduce tax paid. Examples could include failing to record income, falsifying accounting records, or failing to make any returns of income, gains, or taxes collected. Tax avoidance involves a taxpayer arranging their affairs so as to minimise the tax they legally have to pay. It has been an established principle for many years that a taxpayer should not be expected to pay more tax than they legally must. Indeed, some features of the tax system depend on a taxpayer making choices to reduce tax liabilities, for example encouraging taxpayers to choose a car with low levels of exhaust emissions. However, a view has started to be put forward from the Treasury and HM Revenue and Customs that tax avoidance can be either 'acceptable' or 'unacceptable'. Tax avoidance schemes which are considered unacceptable tend to be complex transactions which do not reflect the economic substance of the taxpayer's activities but have a reduction in tax liability as a leading motive, or the main motive, for the transactions undertaken. In recent years the UK and other governments have legislated against identified tax avoidance schemes, so that even where the arrangements are legally effective, they will not be effective in saving tax.

The UK government introduced legislation in the 2013 Finance Act planned to counteract advantages arising from abusive tax avoidance schemes: a 'general anti-abuse rule' (GAAR).

The 2015 Finance Act provided for a Diverted Profits Tax from 1st April 2015. The tax may be applied to arrangements that erode the UK tax base by the avoidance of a UK permanent establishment, or by transfer of profits to entities that pay low amounts of tax where there is a lack of economic substance. The rate of tax is 25% on the diverted profits. See section 25.16 for further details of this tax.

1.16 Tax gap

The 'tax gap' is a term used to describe the shortage of actual tax collected, compared to the total tax which should be collected if there was no non-payment through tax evasion, fraud and error. The Government reports annually on how much it estimates the UK tax gap to be. It is a necessarily hypothetical figure.

You may access the latest report at:
https://www.gov.uk/government/statistics/measuring-tax-gaps
There is controversy over how the 'tax gap' should be defined, and whether it should include tax avoidance.

1.17 'Stealth taxes'

Increases in taxation which are not the result of explicit changes in rates, allowances or methods of calculating tax, have come to be called 'stealth taxes' by the media.

Some UK tax limits have not been linked to inflation and the result is that over the years their real value has diminished. The consequence is that inflation 'drags' people into tax bands with higher rates – this is referred to as 'fiscal drag'. The Daily Telegraph newspaper[14] noted that Inheritance Tax generated £3.8bn of revenue in 2014/15 as compared to £2.7bn in 2010/11, the threshold of £325,000 and the rates of inheritance tax remaining unchanged during that time.

1.18 Recent changes

Recently (in the 2011 to 2018 Finance Acts), the income tax personal allowance has been increased by more than the rate of inflation, to help people with low incomes.

Questions without answers

1. What 'corrective' taxes, if any, might you introduce in the UK at present?

2. Discuss the extent to which taxes on income create disincentive effects.

3. What are the advantages of an indirect tax such as VAT compared with an income tax?

4. Evaluate the extent to which the budget deficit figures in section 1.4 indicate a 'Keynesian' policy approach by the UK government.

References

1 Sykes, J.B. ed., *Concise Oxford Dictionary of Current English*, Oxford University Press, 1976.

2 Cingano, F. (2014), "Trends in Income Inequality and its Impact on Economic Growth", OECD Social, Employment and Migration Working Papers, No. 163, OECD Publishing, Paris. http://dx.doi.org/10.1787/5jxrjncwxv6j-en

3 http://www.bized.co.uk/virtual/economy/library/theory/classical

4 Keynes, John Maynard, (1936), *General Theory of Employment Interest and Money*, Prometheus Books, Amherst, New York, 1997.

5 http://www.bized.co.uk/virtual/economy/library/theory/keynesian

6 Sheehan, Brendan, *Understanding Keynes' General Theory*, Palgrave Macmillan, Basingstoke, 2009.

7 HM Treasury, Autumn Budget 2017, available at https://www.gov.uk/government/uploads/system/uploads/attachment_data/file/661480/autumn_budget_2017_web.pdf

8 Smith, Adam, (1776), *The Wealth of Nations*, Penguin, Harmondsworth, 1999.

9 Policy Paper 107 'Tackling Inequality at its Roots', Liberal Democrats, Autumn Conference 2012

10 http://www.labour.org.uk/page/-/BritainCanBeBetter-TheLabourPartyManifesto2015.pdf (pages 10 and 33)

11 http://votesnp.com/docs/manifesto.pdf (pages 5 and 8)

12 https://www.greenparty.org.uk/we-stand-for/2015-manifesto.html

13 http://www.dailymail.co.uk/news/article-2213936/George-Osborne-Chancellor-pledges-NO-mansion-tax-NO-wealth-tax-FREEZE-council-tax.html

14 http://www.telegraph.co.uk/finance/personalfinance/tax/11576146/The-stealth-taxes-that-have-risen-by-up-to-80pc.html

Part II

Income Tax

2 General principles of income tax

2.1 Introduction

Income tax is a direct tax. Taxpayers contribute tax on some types of income directly to HM Revenue and Customs. For other types of income, including bank and building society interest and earnings from employment, the employer deducts income tax from the employment earnings then pays the tax over to HMRC. However, this tax payment is only an estimate. The taxpayer is still responsible for settling the final position with HMRC, if the tax already paid is not the final liability on the income.

In this chapter, we outline the main features of the income tax system, all of which we develop in detail in later chapters. We begin with some basic expressions. We then provide a summary of taxable income, its classification and basis of assessment. The remainder of the chapter deals with savings income, and non-taxable income. We give a summary of tax rates for tax year 2018/19 at the end of the chapter, and in the full reference tax tables at the end of the book.

Under the UK Tax Law Rewrite Project (*which lasted from 1998 to 2011*), the previous technical language of UK income tax, which dated from the nineteenth century, was rewritten in 'plain English'. Income tax law is now contained in the Income Tax (Employment and Pensions) Act 2003 (ITEPA), the Income Tax (Trading and Other Income) Act 2005 (ITTOIA) and the Income Tax Act 2007 (ITA), as amended by later Finance Acts.

2.2 Basic expressions

Tax Year 2018/19: This runs from 6th April 2018 to 5th April 2019. The Income Tax Act 2007 uses the term 'Tax Year' but the period from 6th to 5th April is still referred to elsewhere in law as the 'fiscal year'. Personal Self-Assessment Tax Returns are submitted for complete tax years.

Tax rates and the annual Finance Act. Rates of income tax for a tax year are determined annually in the Finance Act. It is a constitutional principle in the UK that income tax is an annual tax, requiring a new approval by Parliament for each tax year. Currently, the legislation continuing the existing tax and setting out any changes is published as a Finance Bill following the Autumn Statement.

Taxable persons. Income tax is charged on the income of individuals and trusts resident in the UK. Non-residents deriving any income from a UK source are also in principle liable to UK income tax, though the terms of a Double Tax Treaty may vary or remove this liability.

Taxable income. Income on which income tax is payable is known as taxable income. This consists of the sum of income from all taxable sources, as defined, less deductions for allowable payments, less personal allowances and reliefs (*other than allowances and reliefs given 'in terms of tax', that is as a deduction from tax liability rather than from income*).

Order of taxing income. The ITA 2007 requires income to be classified into three types: non-savings income (also called 'other income'), savings income and dividend income.

Allowable deductions and personal reliefs and allowances reduce total income in the following order: non-savings income first, then savings income, finally dividend income. This order is prescribed because dividend income is treated as the highest part of total income and savings income as the next highest part (section 16, ITA 2007).

The order in which the various sources of income are combined and the reliefs and allowances against total income are deducted is shown in the following summary:

Summary of Taxable Income 2018/19

	Non-savings, non-dividend income	Savings income	Dividends	Total income
	£	£	£	£
Employment income (i)	×			×
Property income	×			×
Social Security income	×			×
Trading profits (ii)	×			×
Miscellaneous income	×			×
Interest		×		×
Dividends			×	×
Total income	×	×	×	×
less Allowable payments	(×)			(×)
less Loss reliefs	(×)	(×)	(×)	(×)
less Personal Allowance (iii)	(×)	(×)	(×)	(×)
Taxable income	A	B	C	×
				£
Non-savings income:	£			
basic rate 20% ×	×			×
higher rate 40% ×	×			×
additional rate 45% ×	×			×
	A			

		£		
Savings income:				
starting rate 0% ×		×		×
'personal savings allowance'		×		×
basic rate 20% ×		×		×
higher rate 40% ×		×		×
additional rate 45% ×		×		×
		B		
Dividends:			£	
dividend allowance 0% ×			×	
ordinary rate 7.5% ×			×	
higher rate 32.5% ×			×	
additional rate 38.1% ×			×	
			C	×
Tax borne				×
less Tax allowances and reliefs	(v)			(×)
less PAYE deducted at source				(×)
add UK tax retained on payments	(vii)			×
Tax liability				×

Notes

(i) Income from employment is after the deduction of any expenses specifically allowable against employment income and includes taxable benefits in kind from employment. See Chapters 7 and 8.

(ii) Income from self-employment is the taxable profits of a trading business for the tax year, less capital allowances, and is measured using 'basis period' rules which mean the profit measurement period does not always match the tax year. See Chapters 10 to 15.

(iii) The Personal Allowance is available to most UK taxpayers but there are exceptions, and for the tax year 2018/19 it is gradually withdrawn for incomes over £100,000. See Chapter 4.

(iv) Under ITA 2007, allowable payments, loss reliefs and personal allowances reduce total income in the following order: non-savings, non-dividend income; then savings income; then dividend income.

(v) 'Tax allowances and reliefs' refers to items where the relief is given by way of a reduction in the tax liability, rather than a deduction used in calculating taxable income. Such items include:

- basic rate relief on 50% of the interest costs incurred by landlords in financing their properties (ie. the relief is calculated at 20% × 50% × the finance costs). See section 9.4;
- age-related married couple's allowance (10% relief);
- transferable personal allowance (20% relief);

- investment scheme reliefs *(Enterprise Investment Scheme; Seed Enterprise Investment Scheme; Social Investment Tax Relief).*

(vi) The Married Couple's Allowance is only available where one or both spouses or civil partners reached the age of 75 before 6th April 2010; relief is given at a 10% tax rate. See Chapter 4.

(vii) 'UK tax retained on payments' refers to UK tax retained by the payee when making a payment of rent to overseas-resident property owners and/or patent royalties.

2.3 The nature of income

Income for a tax year is measured by rules set out in the Income Tax (Earnings and Pensions) Act 2003 and the Income Tax (Trading and Other Income) Act 2005.

Nature of Income	Source
Employment income, pensions income, social security income	ITEPA 2003
Income taxed as trade profits Savings income Dividend income Property business income *(Income from UK land and property)* Foreign income Miscellaneous income	ITTOIA 2005

Details of the rules for measuring each type of income are contained in later chapters.

2.4 Tax rates and bands 2018/19

Broadly, to calculate income tax you must take the taxpayer's 'taxable income' *(after deducting their Personal Allowance)* and slice it into sections which are 'basic rate', 'higher rate' and 'additional rate'. Each section is then taxed at a different rate:

	Additional rate
£150,000	
	Higher rate
£34,500*	
	Basic rate
£0	

*£31,580 for Scottish Income Tax

However, there are complications in applying this:

- the percentages use for basic, higher and additional rate tax vary according to the type of income;
- there is a special '0% starting rate' for savings;
- there are some extra 'nil rates' for dividend income and for savings income; and
- the bands are extended where an individual makes a Gift Aid donation to charity.

We will now consider each of these complications.

First, the percentages used as basic, higher and additional vary according to the type of income:

Rate for non-savings and savings income				Rate for dividend income
45%		Additional rate		38.1%
	£150,000		£150,000	
40%		Higher rate		32.5%
	£34,500*		£34,500*	
20%		Basic rate		7.5%
	£0		£0	

*£31,580 for Scottish Income Tax

This necessitates rules about which income is treated as belonging to which band. The legislation requires that, in 'stacking up' a taxpayer's income, **non-savings income** must come first, then **savings income**, and then **dividend income** – see Chapter 6.

Second, there is a special **'0% starting rate for savings'**. This is not an extra band; rather, it is a band which 'overlaps' the taxable income shown above. If any savings income falls within a taxpayer's first £5,000 of taxable income, then that part of the savings income attracts a tax rate of 0% instead of 20%.

Third, there are some extra **'nil rates' for dividend income and for savings income**. As with the savings starting rate, these 'overlap' the taxable income shown above. They are not separate bands, nor does their use affect the calculation of taxable income. Rather unhelpfully, the savings income to which the nil rate *(as distinct from the 'starting rate')* applies is called a 'Personal Savings Allowance'. This sounds rather like the 'Personal Allowance', which might suggest that a portion of savings income is exempt from tax. However, that is not the case. Rather, it is subject to income tax but at a zero rate. That might sound like the same thing, but it is not. If some savings income were exempt from income tax, then it would not count within the calculation of income for the purposes of determining whether a taxpayer is basic, additional or higher rate. However, being subject to tax means that the part of savings income which is chargeable at nil rate, although it does not attract a positive tax charge, does build up a person's income for the purposes of determining how much tax they pay on the next slice of income.

The dividend nil rate band, called the 'dividend allowance', applies to the first £2,000 of dividend income a taxpayer has, irrespective of whether he or she is a basic, higher or additional rate taxpayer.

For the savings nil rate, there is a £1,000 'personal savings allowance' for basic rate taxpayers, a £500 'personal savings allowance' for higher rate taxpayers and no 'personal savings allowance' for additional rate taxpayers. The 'personal savings allowance' applies to any savings income not covered by the Personal Allowance or the 0% starting rate.

Fourth, the bands of £34,500 and £150,000 are extended where an individual makes a Gift Aid donation to a charity, as a mechanism for ensuring that the part of their income which they have put aside for the charity is taxed at basic rate *(since the charity will have reclaimed tax from the government on that basis)* – see Chapter 5 for details.

Example 1

For the tax year ended 5th April 2019, Asmita (who lives in England) has employment income of £19,850. What is her income tax contribution for the year?

Asmita's taxable income is £19,850 minus her Personal Allowance of £11,850 *(see section 2.9 for details of Personal Allowances)*; ie. £8,000. This is subject to tax at the basic rate of 20%, so her tax contribution for the year is £1,600.

Example 2

For the tax year ended 5th April 2019, Mohamed (who lives in Wales) has income of £19,850, comprising employment income of £13,850 and £6,000 of savings income. What is his income tax contribution for the year?

We apply Mohamed's Personal Allowance first to his non-savings income then to his savings income:

	Non-savings income	Savings income	Total income
	£	£	£
Employment income	13,850		13,850
Savings income		6,000	6,000
	13,850	6,000	19,850
Personal Allowance	(11,850)		(11,850)
Taxable income	2,000	6,000	8,000

First, we need to check whether Mohamed is entitled to the 0% starting rate of savings income. His first £2,000 of taxable income, going in the order set out by statute, is non-savings. Therefore, of his savings income of £6,000, only £3,000 falls within the 'overlapping' band giving entitlement to the 0% starting rate.

With £8,000 of taxable income, Mohamed is a basic rate taxpayer, and will qualify for the £1,000 'personal savings allowance'. His tax contributions for the year will therefore be:

	Non-savings income	Savings income		Total income
	£	£		£
Taxable income	2,000	6,000		8,000
	£	£		£
Non-savings	2,000		@ 20% =	400
Savings income:				
Starting rate		3,000	@ 0% =	-
Personal Savings Allowance		1,000	@ 0% =	-
Basic rate		2,000	@ 20% =	400
				800

So, despite having the same amount of taxable income as Asmita, Mohamed will pay £800 less tax for the year, because £4,000 of his savings income is covered by the starting rate and Mohamed's personal savings allowance.

Example 3

For the tax year ended 5th April 2019, Nazeh (who lives in Northern Ireland) has income of £19,850, comprising employment income of £11,850, £6,000 of savings and £2,000 of dividend income. What is his income tax contribution for the year?

	Non-savings income	Savings income	Dividends	Total income
	£	£	£	£
Employment income	11,850			11,850
Savings income		6,000		6,000
Dividends			2,000	2,000
Total income	11,850	6,000	2,000	19,850
Personal Allowance	(11,850)	-		(11,850)
Taxable income	-	**6,000**	**2,000**	**8,000**

	£	£	£
Savings income:			
Starting rate	5,000	@ 0% =	-
Personal Savings Allowance	1,000	@ 0% =	-
Dividend allowance		2,000	-
			nil

Therefore, despite having the same amount of taxable income as Asmita and Mohamed, Nazeh will pay no income tax at all. His employment income has been fully covered by his Personal Allowance, his savings income has been fully covered by his 'personal savings allowance' and the savings starting rate, and his dividends have been fully covered by the "dividend allowance".

Example 4

For the tax year ended 5th April 2019, Olivia (who lives in England) has income of £90,000, comprising employment income of £30,000, £30,000 of savings and £30,000 of dividend income. What is her income tax contribution for the year?

	Non-savings income	Savings income	Dividends	Total income
	£	£	£	£
Employment income	30,000			30,000
Savings income		30,000		30,000
Dividends			30,000	30,000
	30,000	30,000	30,000	90,000
Personal Allowance	(11,850)			(11,850)
Taxable income	18,150	30,000	30,000	78,150

With £78,150 of taxable income, Olivia is a higher rate taxpayer, and only qualifies for the £500 'personal savings allowance'.

	Non-savings income	Savings income	Dividends		Total income
	£	£	£		£
Taxable income	18,150	30,000	30,000		78,150
	£	£			£
Non-savings	18,150			@ 20% =	3,630
Savings income:					
Personal Savings Allowance		500		@ 0% =	-
Basic rate (34,500 – 18,150 – 500)		15,850		@ 20% =	3,170
Higher rate (30,000 – 15,850 – 500)		13,650		@ 40% =	5,460
		30,000			
Dividends:					
Dividend allowance			2,000		-
Higher rate @ 38.1%			28,000		10,668
			30,000		
Tax contribution					**22,928**

2.5 Basis of assessment and doctrine of the source

To ascertain an individual's assessable income for a tax year, it is necessary to identify all sources of income that existed in the year, and then measure the income under the statutory rules (ITEPA 2003 or ITTOIA 2005) for that income.

2.6 PAYE system

A substantial proportion of all income tax due on employment, pension and savings income is collected under the Pay As You Earn (PAYE) system. We describe the main features of this in Chapter 8.

2.7 Due dates for payment – 2018/19 Tax Year

A taxpayer whose tax liability is not substantially collected at source, and whose self-assessment tax payments exceeded set levels the year before, is required to make two payments-on-account of income tax before the self-assessment return is due for submission.

A third 'balancing' payment settles the remaining liability for the year and is due on the same date by which the self-assessment return must ultimately be with HMRC. The payment dates for 2018/19 income tax, under the payments on account system, are:

First payment on account	31st January 2019
Second payment on account	31st July 2019
Balancing payment	31st January 2020

Taxpayers whose income is largely or wholly received net of tax deducted at source do not have to make any income tax payments on account. The date for them to pay any balance of income tax due for a year is 31st January following the tax year end *(i.e. 31st January 2020 for tax year 2018/19)*. For an employee who pays tax by PAYE, there is an optional alternative of having any remaining 2018/19 income tax liability not exceeding £2,000 collected from employment income during the following year, by including the tax underpayment in the 2019/20 PAYE code.

Further details of the income tax payments-on-account system are in Chapter 3.

2.8 Non-taxable income

The following types of income are exempt from UK income tax:

(a) Certain NSI (Government-backed) savings products: Index-Linked Savings Certificates, Fixed Interest Savings Certificates, and Children's Bonus Bonds.

(b) Interest and bonuses on certified Save As You Earn (SAYE) schemes.

(c) NSI Premium Bond prizes.

(d) Interest on certain UK government securities held by non-residents.

(e) Payments for service in the armed forces relating to:
   - (i) wound and disability pensions
   - (ii) service grants, bounties and gratuities
   - (iii) annuities and additional pensions paid to holders of the Victoria Cross, George Cross and other gallantry awards.

(f) Certain social security income:
   - Armed forces independence payment
   - Attendance allowance
   - Bereavement payment (*but not bereavement allowance – see 7.34*)
   - Budgeting loan
   - Child Tax Credit
   - Christmas bonus

- Cold weather payment
- Discretionary housing payment
- Employment and support allowance - income-related
- Funeral payment
- Guardian's allowance
- Healthy start
- Help with health costs
- Housing benefit
- Income support
- Industrial injuries disablement benefit
- Maternity allowance (*but not statutory maternity pay – see 7.34*)
- Pension credit (*but not State Pension – see 7.33*)
- Personal Independence Payment
- Reduced earnings allowance
- Retirement allowance (*but not State Pension – see 7.33*)
- Sure Start maternity grant (*not statutory maternity pay – see 7.34*)
- Universal Credit
- Vaccine damage payment
- War disablement pension
- War widow's or widower's pension
- Winter fuel payment
- Working Tax Credit

Note that some types of social security income are taxable. We list these in Chapter 7 sections 33 and 34.

(g) Child Benefit is a social security payment. For taxpayers with income above £50,000 a tax charge progressively claws back the benefit (see 17.9).

(h) Free television licences for those aged over 75.

(i) Ex gratia compensation for loss of office/employment, up to £30,000, so long as it is not paid for services, and is not contractually promised (*which is what 'ex gratia' means*). See Chapter 7.

(j) Redundancy payments, statutory or contractual, within the same £30,000 limit.

(k) Job release allowances, if paid within one year of normal retirement age.

(l) Outplacement counselling paid for by a third party or an employer.

(m) Long service awards to employees, subject to certain limitations (*see Ch 7*).

(n) Interest payable on damages for personal injury or death.

(o) Gambling winnings (*including the National Lottery*) and competition prizes.

(p) Scholarship awards and other educational grants.

(q) Up to £7,500 p.a. of gross rent received on furnished lettings in the taxpayer's only or main residence (*'Rent-a-Room relief'- see Chapter 9*);

(r) other property income up to £1,000 (*see section 9.14*);

(s) trading income up to £1,000 (*see section 10.26*).

2.9 Income Tax Personal allowances

(For more details, see Chapter 4)

	Deducted from income	Relief at 10% rate
Personal Allowance	£11,850	
Income limit for Personal Allowance	£100,000	
Blind person's allowance	£2,390	
Marriage allowance	£1,190	
Married couple's allowance for those born before 5th April 1935		
Maximum amount of married couple's allowance		£8,695
Minimum amount of married couple's allowance		£3,360
Income limit for Married couple's allowance	£28,900	

Student self-testing questions

Question 2.1, Jules

In 2018/19 Jules (who lives in England) has the following income:	£
Income from employment (salary) - amount before tax	50,000
Bank deposit interest	9,000

Jules' personal allowance is £11,850 and he does not have any allowable deductions from income.

Required

Calculate the income tax contribution required by Jules for the tax year 2018/19 and, if £9,000 were deducted under PAYE, the tax remaining payable.

Solution to Question 2.1, Jules

	Non-savings	Savings	
Income	£	£	£
Salary/ bonus	50,000		50,000
Bank interest		9,000	9,000
Total income	50,000	9,000	59,000
Less Personal allowance	(11,850)		(11,850)
Taxable income	38,150	9,000	47,150
Tax on this income:			
Non-savings:	£	£	£
Basic rate @ 20% on	34,500		6,900
Higher rate @ 40% on	3,650		1,460
Savings:			
Personal Savings Allowance @ 0%		500	0
Higher rate @ 40%		8,500	3,400
Income tax borne on taxable income			11,760
Less: PAYE already paid			(9,000)
Remaining income tax, due 31st January 2020			2,760

Question 2.2, Jamie

During 2018/19 Jamie (who lives in Wales) has income from employment of £86,000 gross, from which PAYE of £34,400 has been deducted. He also received bank deposit interest of £14,000, and dividends from UK companies of £60,000.

Required

Show the income tax liability and tax remaining payable by Jamie in respect of 2018/19.

Solution to Question 2.2, Jamie

			Non-savings £	Savings £	Dividends £
Employment			86,000		
Interest				14,000	
Dividends					60,000
Total income		£160,000	86,000	14,000	60,000
Personal allowance		-	-		
Taxable income		£160,000	86,000	14,000	60,000

Income tax on taxable income:				£
Basic rate	Non-savings	34,500	@ 20%	6,900
Higher rate	Non-savings	51,500	@ 40%	20,600
		86,000		
	Savings	14,000	@ 40%	5,600
	Dividend nil rate	2,000	@ 0%	0
	Dividend higher rate	48,000	@32.5%	15,600
		150,000		
Additional rate	Dividends	10,000	@38.1%	3,810
		£160,000		

Income tax borne	£52,510
Less tax deducted under PAYE	(34,400)
Tax payable by self-assessment	**£18,110**

3 Income Tax: administration

3.1 Introduction

This chapter outlines the administrative features of the income tax system. You can find additional information on the HM Revenue and Customs website (https://www.gov.uk/government/organisations/hm-revenue-customs).

3.2 Her Majesty's Revenue and Customs

The Commissioners for Revenue and Customs administer Income Tax. They are responsible to HM Treasury and the Chancellor of the Exchequer, through the Financial Secretary to the Treasury.

HMRC is an executive agency of the UK Government, which operates through Revenue Officers.

HMRC Area and District offices are responsible for the issue and receipt of tax returns for income tax payers handled from that office. However, as taxpayers increasingly submit Income Tax returns online and central telephone call centres handle enquiries, the link to a specific tax district is not very significant for most people who complete income tax returns.

HMRC Accounts Offices are concerned with the collection of the assessed (usually, this means **self**-assessed) amounts of tax, and matching these to the liabilities shown by taxpayers' self-assessment returns.

HMRC Enquiry Centres give an initial point of contact for taxpayers with queries of any kind. It is possible for anyone to visit any Enquiry Centre in person, though HMRC handles an increasing number of enquiries by telephone and email.

HMRC also has dedicated telephone numbers and email addresses for the use of professional tax agents, such as accountants and chartered tax advisers acting for their taxpaying clients.

HMRC Specialist Offices and Agencies exist to handle specific administrative areas. Examples of these in the income tax field are the Charities Office, three Enterprise Investment Scheme (EIS) offices, the Employee Shares and Securities Unit (ESSU) and the Pension Schemes Office (PSO). The High Net Worth Unit deals exclusively with the wealthiest income tax payers.

A common tax tribunal system handles legal appeals in all tax disputes.

The Crown Prosecution Service in England, Wales and Northern Ireland (*the Crown Office and the Procurator Fiscal Service in Scotland*) handles criminal prosecutions in Income Tax matters.

3.3 Self-assessment

The following are the main administrative features of self-assessment.

(a) The Tax Return has a main return and varying supplementary pages.

(b) A separate Tax Return Guide, which anyone can view online, explains how to compute income and capital gains, where relevant, for each page of the tax return. The Tax Calculation Guide provides instructions for the self-calculation of income tax, capital gains tax and Class 4 National Insurance due, or income tax repayable. Helpsheets are also available explaining how to deal with specific types of income, and allowable deductions and reliefs including loss claims.

(c) There are two key dates for the filing of tax returns.
  (i) For taxpayers still filing a paper return, by 31st October following the end of the tax year;
  (ii) For taxpayers filing online, by 31st January following the end of the tax year.

(d) Thus for 2018/19 the two filing dates are 31st October 2019 and 31st January 2020.

(e) Failure to file a tax return for any year by the due date incurs an automatic fixed penalty of £100. A taxpayer who files the return more than 3 months late will face additional penalties of £10 per day up to a maximum of £900. If the return is still outstanding 6 months after the filing date a further penalty applies of 5% of tax unpaid at the original filing date, or £300, whichever is higher. For returns filed 12 months late there are further penalties, which are the greater of 5% of the tax unpaid or £300, or in cases of deliberate concealment, up to 100% of the tax due.

(f) All taxpayers are obliged to calculate and make the necessary tax payments based on his or her self-assessment. The taxpayer is liable to interest, and eventually surcharges, on any part of the tax liability that she or he does not pay on time. For payment more than 30 days late the penalty is 5% of the tax unpaid, 6 months late a further penalty of 5%, 12 months late a further penalty of 5%. Interest and penalties for late payment of tax are not allowable expenses in calculating trading profits or other assessable income for tax purposes.

(g) For taxpayers whose tax is not largely collected by deduction at source, two payments on account are required with a balancing payment to meet any tax outstanding at 31st January following the tax year-end.

(h) Based on the latest information submitted to them, the expected payments on account for the next tax year are notified by HMRC in regular Self-Assessment Statements of Account, addressed to the taxpayer. If the taxpayer has registered for online filing, then she or he can check these statements online. Paper Statements also contain a bank payslip for the next payment on account, but it can alternatively be paid online.

3.4 Self-assessment payments on account (POAs)

For self–employed taxpayers, POAs also operate for Class 4 National Insurance (see Chapter 17). You should note the following points:

(i) A taxpayer does not need to make POAs if either:
   (a) the self-assessment income tax (and class 4 NICs) due for last year was £1,000 or less; or
   (b) the amount payable by self-assessment for the preceding year was 20% or less of the total income tax and Class 4 NIC liability for that year. In other words, no POAs are required if more than 80% of the total income tax (and Class 4 NICs) liability last year was met by deduction of tax at source.

(ii) The ways in which income tax is deducted at source include Pay As You Earn (PAYE), the construction industry sub-contractors' (CIS) scheme (not discussed in this book), and other income paid to individuals, such as patent royalties, or some self-employment income.

(iii) It should be clear that income tax and Class 4 NIC liability (*net of tax deducted at source*) for the preceding year will determine whether payments on account are needed. If they are due, they are set at half the total income tax and Class 4 NIC payable for the preceding year, net of last year's tax deducted at source.

(iv) Where payments on account do not meet the entire tax (and Class 4 NIC) liability – net of tax deducted at source – for this tax year, a final payment will be due by 31st January after the end of the tax year. If payments on account are made more than the total tax payable, a repayment will be issued.

(v) If the taxpayer considers that standard payments on account for the current year are excessive (*because tax payable by self-assessment for the current year is reasonably expected to be less than for the prior year*), the taxpayer can make a formal application to reduce one or both payments on account. HMRC will revise the Self-Assessment Statement of Account to reflect the reduction(s). However, interest will be charged in due course from the original POA due dates, if reductions were applied for but later shown (*per the next year's tax return*) to have been unjustified.

3.5 Interim payments on account

To summarise, payments on account are due in the following circumstances:

Assessment to income tax – & Class 4 NIC 2017/18		Income tax deducted at source 2017/18	= 'Relevant amount' for 2018/19
Relevant amount	≥	£1,000	→ POA required 2018/19
		and	
Relevant amount	≥	20% of tax liability 2017/18	→ POA required 2018/19

Note that Capital Gains Tax for a tax year is also payable on the final tax payment date of 31st January. No payments on account are necessary for CGT.

Example

For 2017/18 Xan's self-assessment return showed the following:	£
Self-assessed income tax liability	10,000
Self-assessed Class 4 NICs (*see Chapter 17 for more on this tax*)	1,030
PAYE deducted at source (relating to 2017/18)	2,570

Required

Calculate the interim payments on account which Xan must make for 2018/19.

Solution

		£
Income Tax liability 2017/18		10,000
Less Income Tax paid at source under PAYE		(2,570)
2017/18 Income Tax paid by self-assessment		7,430
Class 4 NICs		1,030
Total IT and NICs paid by self-assessment 2017/18		8,460
		£
2018/19 Payments on account	31st January 2019 (50%)	4,230
	31st July 2019 (50%)	4,230

Example

Mrs Jackson has the following data on her self-assessment tax return for 2017/18:

	£
Full income tax liability	7,500
PAYE deducted at source	6,900

Required

Calculate the interim payments on account which Mrs Jackson must make for 2018/19.

Solution

Relevant amount 2017/18:	£
Income tax liability	7,500
Less PAYE	(6,900)
	450

As this is less than £1,000, no POAs are required for 2018/19.

Final payment (repayment) of tax

A final payment (or repayment) of income tax occurs in the following circumstances:

2018/19 self-assessment tax return

(Income tax liability + Class 4 NIC liability + Capital gains tax liability) – POAs
= Final payment or repayment due

Example

Padma has the following income tax and capital gains tax liabilities for the year ended 5th April 2019, based on her self-assessment tax return.

	£
Tax on Trade profits (*income tax and class 4 NICs*)	25,000
Capital gains tax	1,000

The relevant amount for 2017/18 was £18,000, all attributable to income tax on trade profits and NICs.

Required

Show the payments to be made in respect of the tax year to 5th April 2019, and the due dates.

Solution: Padma's tax and Class 4 NIC liability for 2018/19

		£
31st January 2019	50% × Relevant amount 2017/18 = 50% × 18,000	9,000
31st July 2019	50% × Relevant amount 2017/18 = 50% × 18,000	9,000
31st January 2020	Balance of tax and NIC due	8,000
		26,000

Note

The total tax due for 2018/19 is

	Income tax and Class 4 NIC	25,000
	Capital gains tax	1,000
		26,000
Less Payments on account (same as 2017/18 relevant amount)		(18,000)
	Balance due	8,000

Note: Payments on account are never required for Capital Gains Tax, so £1,000 of the final payment is a CGT payment (*see Part IV for more on CGT*).

3.6 Surcharges on income tax

In addition to the interest charged on any tax paid late, there is a system of penalty surcharges to encourage prompt payment. (See section 3.3.)

3.7 Interest on under and overpayments

A charge to interest will automatically arise on any tax paid late whether in respect of income tax, NIC or capital gains tax and can apply to:

(i) any payment on account;

(ii) any balancing payment;

(iii) any tax payable following an amendment to self-assessment, whether made by the taxpayer or by HMRC;

(iv) any tax payable following a 'discovery assessment' by HMRC. (*See 3.8 for more on discovery assessments.*)

Interest runs from the due date for payment to the date on which payment is finally made for payments on account and balancing payments.

For amendments to original self-assessments, the interest charge runs from the annual filing date for the income tax year, i.e. the 31st January following the end of the income tax year. Interest on any overpayments of tax is added automatically when the repayment is made.

3.8 HM Revenue and Customs enquiries

A Revenue Officer may carry out an 'enquiry' into any taxpayer's self-assessment tax return. Such returns may be selected on a sample basis, or because the Officer has concerns about some of the information returned. The enquiry system includes both powers for the Revenue Officer and rights for the taxpayer. For example, the Officer may request a meeting with the taxpayer, but the taxpayer has a right to representation, and to decline to attend. The enquiry should be restricted to a specified area of investigation and concluded within a regulated time limit.

The normal 'enquiry window' period is twelve months from the date of submitting the return. Formerly, it was twelve months from the latest date for filing (31st January) regardless of the actual filing date, but this was altered to encourage early filing.

The enquiry window is re-opened if the taxpayer submits an amendment to a submitted return. This includes the lodging of a further claim or withdrawal of a claim made on the original return. HMRC has up to twelve months to enquire into the amendment, or any related matter on the return.

After the enquiry window period has closed, HMRC can only reopen the return if there is a discovery of 'incomplete disclosure'. This means that HMRC finds out (*sometimes by reviewing information from a third party*) that something was omitted or concealed from the submitted return, causing a loss of tax to the Crown.

A discovery assessment can only be made if HMRC could not reasonably have been able to tell the true tax liability from the self-assessment return and any supporting information as originally submitted.

Incomplete disclosure that was not the result of fraudulent or negligent conduct by the taxpayer allows a discovery assessment by HMRC in the period up to five years after the original last filing date for the return (*i.e. nearly five years and ten months after the end of the tax year to which the incomplete return relates*).

Incomplete disclosure that was the result of fraudulent or negligent conduct by the taxpayer allows a discovery assessment at any time up to twenty years from the original last filing date. In addition to the additional tax due, and interest at normal rates, 'tax-geared' penalties can be imposed that depend on the taxpayer's behaviour (see 3.11).

3.9 Challenging the decisions of HM Revenue and Customs

Letters informing taxpayers of HMRC decisions will include information on the right of appeal. Appeals should be sent to HMRC in writing, within 30 days of the disputed decision. Some appeals may be settled by agreement with HMRC.

When agreement is not reached, HMRC may offer an internal review of the decision by another officer. The taxpayer may ask for an internal review if HMRC does not offer one. Whether or not a review takes place, a taxpayer may then appeal to the Tribunal Service.

3.10 Tribunal service

The tax appeals system is a two-tier tribunal system:

Most cases are heard by the First-Tier Tribunal (Tax Chamber).

The Upper Tribunal (Finance and Chancery Chamber) hears complex cases, plus all appeals from the First-Tier Tribunal. The Upper Tribunal is a court of record, whose decisions create binding precedents for the First Tier.

Appeals from the Upper Tribunal are to the Court of Appeal (Inner House in Scotland), and finally to the Supreme Court of the UK.

3.11 Penalties

Taxpayers are expected to take 'reasonable care' in making and keeping accurate records to enable them to provide a complete and accurate tax return. This principle applies to all income tax and national insurance contributions information in the self-assessment income tax return, along with return documents for other taxes (*principally Capital Gains Tax for individuals*).

Taxpayers can demonstrate they have taken reasonable care by: keeping accurate records, confirming the correct position when they do not understand tax issues, answering any enquiry questions raised by HMRC, and telling HMRC promptly about any errors discovered in tax returns after they have been sent.

Where taxpayers do not pay enough tax, and have not taken reasonable care, they may have to pay a penalty in addition to the tax due and any interest on late payment. The penalties can be reduced if the taxpayer makes an 'unprompted' disclosure of the underpayment, rather than one forced by the result of investigations by the tax authorities:

Taxpayer's approach to disclosure of underpayment	**Minimum penalty**	**Maximum penalty**
Reasonable care	No penalty	No penalty
Careless unprompted	0%	30%
Careless prompted	15%	30%
Deliberate unprompted	20%	70%
Deliberate prompted	35%	70%
Deliberate and concealed unprompted	30%	100%
Deliberate and concealed prompted	50%	100%

3.12 Error or mistake relief

The taxpayer can claim relief in writing against any over-payment of tax made due to an error or mistake (including an omission) in any return or statement.

The relief must be claimed within 4 years of the end of the tax year.

The claim in writing must be separate from a submitted self-assessment return and must provide the following information (Source HMRC Brief 22 / 2010):

- State that the person is making a claim for overpayment relief under Schedule 1AB TMA 1970
- Identify the tax year for which the overpayment or excessive assessment has been made.
- State the grounds on which the person considers that the overpayment or excessive assessment has occurred.

- State whether the person has previously made an appeal in connection with the payment or the assessment.
- If the claim is for repayment of tax, include documentary proof of the tax deducted or the tax being suffered in some other way.
- Include a declaration signed by the claimant, stating that the information given in the claim is correct and complete to the best of their knowledge and belief.

Student self-testing questions

Question 3.1, Arnie

Arnie has the following data relating to 2017/18 and 2018/19.

	2017/18	2018/19
	£	£
Total income tax liability	18,500	22,000
Capital gains tax liability	1,500	3,000
Total tax due by self -assessment	20,000	25,000

Calculate the tax payments in respect of 2018/19 and show the due dates for payments.

Solution to Question 3.1, Arnie

	2018/19 Payments		
	Interim Payments		Final Payment
	31-Jan-2019	31-Jul-2019	31-Jan-2020
1st Interim payment			
50% × 18,500	9,250		
2nd Interim payment			
50% × 18,500		9,250	
Final payment			
(25,000 – 18,500)			6,500
	9,250	9,250	6,500

Notes

(i) The interim payments are computed by reference to the tax liability for 2017/18, i.e. 18,500 excluding any Capital Gains Tax.

(ii) The final payment for 2018/19 includes all the capital gains tax liability for that year, i.e. £3,000, plus the balance of the other taxes not paid on account.

(For Capital Gains Tax generally, see Chapter 25 onwards.)

Question 3.2, Adam

The following concerns the tax payable by Adam for two successive tax years:

	2017/18	2018/19
	£	£
Total income tax payable	20,000	24,000
Tax deducted under PAYE	12,000	13,000

The income tax payable has been computed by self-assessment and is not disputed by HMRC.

Requirement: Show how Adam's income tax for 2018/19, to the extent not deducted at source, is required to be paid.

Solution to Question 3.2, Adam

Adam – total tax paid by self-assessment 2017/18:

	£
Tax liability	20,000
Less PAYE	(12,000)
Payable under self-assessment for 2017/18	8,000
(*this may have been met partly by payments on account, or met by a single payment if no payments on account were needed in 2017/18*)	

Adam - Tax payable by self-assessment for 2018/19:

	£
Tax liability	24,000
Less PAYE	(13,000)
Payable under self-assessment for 2018/19	11,000

Payments to be made under self-assessment for 2018/19:

	£	£
Total payable		11,000
Interim payments (*based on prior tax year's figures*)		
31st January 2019: £8,000 × ½	4,000	
31st July 2019: £8,000 × ½	4,000	
		(8,000)
Balancing payment due on 31st January 2020		3,000

4 Personal allowances and reliefs

4.1 Introduction

This chapter is concerned with the main features of the system of taxation in relation to the personal allowances and reliefs for individuals, blind persons, and married couples.

Note that it does **not** cover the 'personal savings allowance', which is really a nil rate savings income band available for basic- and higher- rate taxpayers (see section 2.4).

4.2 List of topic headings

Personal allowance
Husbands and wives /civil partners
Married couple's allowance
Blind person's allowance
Death of husband or wife

4.3 Personal allowance (PA) 2018/19 £11,850 (2017/18 £11,500)

This allowance is given automatically to all individuals, male or female, single or married, and set against UK net income, except for:

(a) non-domiciled UK residents who have elected to file on the remittance basis (*who are in general outside the scope of this book*); and

(b) taxpayers whose 'adjusted net income' exceeds £100,000, for whom the personal allowance is subject to gradual withdrawal ('abatement') above that level.

The normal Personal Allowance is reduced by £1 for every £2 excess of an individual's 'adjusted net income' over £100,000. For 2018/19, this means that it is removed completely once adjusted net income exceeds £123,700.

Unless withdrawn, the Personal Allowance is deducted from net income in arriving at taxable income, and thus receives relief at the taxpayer's highest marginal rate of tax.

Net income is defined as total income less any trading losses (see Chapter 14) and allowable payments (see Chapter 5). 'Adjusted net income' is the taxpayer's net income, less the gross amount of any Gift Aid donations (see Chapter 5) or personal pension contributions (see Chapter 16) which have received tax relief at source. Any relief given against employment income for subscriptions to trade unions or police organisations is added back in calculating adjusted net income.

The personal allowance is not transferable, except that a small amount may be transferred between husbands and wives or civil partners (see section 4.4).

Example

Abdullah (who lives in Northern Ireland) is single, has a salary income from employment for 2018/19 of £105,000 and no other income.

Compute his income tax liability for 2018/19.

Solution: Abdullah's Income tax computation 2018/19

	£	£
Income from employment (total income)		105,000
Personal allowance	11,850	
Restricted (105,000 – 100,000) × ½	(2,500)	
Remaining PA		(9,350)
Taxable income		95,650

Tax liability		£
	34,500 @ 20%	6,900
	61,150 @ 40%	24,460
	95,650	31,360

Note

Given high income from employment, most of this tax would already have been collected by PAYE (See Chapter 8), with any balance still owing being either paid by self-assessment or 'coded out' by adjusting the following year's PAYE code.

4.4 Husbands and wives/civil partners

Since the legalisation of same-sex civil partnerships in the UK from December 2005, all references to 'spouses' in tax legislation apply equally to registered civil partners from the tax year 2005/06. The following should therefore be read as applying also to registered civil partners, even where not mentioned.

For income tax purposes, to count as 'a couple' at a given date, a couple must be both legally married/in a civil partnership **and** living together. Living together means 'not separated in circumstances where the separation is likely to be permanent'. A mid-tax-year permanent separation terminates the relationship for income tax. (*The position is different for capital gains tax and inheritance tax; see Chapters 27 and 33 respectively*).

(a) Husband and wife/civil partners are treated as separate taxpayers, each completing his/her own tax return and responsible for his/her own tax liabilities.

(b) Each spouse receives a personal allowance. If one spouse does not have enough income to use their personal allowance, up to £1,150 may be transferred to the other spouse, if the second spouse is not a higher rate or additional rate taxpayer; relief is thereby given at the basic rate of 20%. This mechanism is called 'Marriage Allowance'.

(c) The married couple's age-related allowance (MCA) was phased out from 6th April 2000 but is still available (*at a 10% effective tax rate only*) for couples where one spouse or civil partner reached the age of 65 before 6th April 2000. Further details are in 4.5.

(d) Joint property giving rise to income is treated for income tax as belonging to spouses and civil partners in equal shares for income tax purposes, regardless of the true or beneficial ownership split. This applies for example to rent from a let property, or to a joint bank deposit. The income for income tax purposes is therefore allocated 50:50, even if the ownership is different for other legal purposes.

It is possible for spouses/partners to elect for a different split of the income arising from joint property, but they must when doing so declare that the proportions being specified reflect the true beneficial ownership of the underlying asset. The same division of ownership shares would then apply for CGT or inheritance tax calculations relating to the same asset.

4.5 Married couple's allowance (MCA) – 10% rate relief

Note that the 'Married Couple's Allowance' is something different from the 'Marriage Allowance' described at point (b) above.

	2018/19
Married couple's allowance	£8,695
Minimum amount	£3,360

a) The MCA is now a minor relief. It is only available where one or both spouses or civil partners was/were born before 6th April 1935.

b) A claim for the higher level of married couple's allowance is made by the husband for marriages before 6th December 2005, and by the partner with the higher taxable income (*which may vary year on year*) for marriages or civil partnerships started since 6th December 2005. In the rest of this section, for convenience, we assume the husband is the one claiming the MCA.

c) MCA is given relief at the 10% rate. So, if the MCA due after partial abatement (see below) is £4,500, then this allowance is given by an amount of £450 (10% of £4,500) being deducted from the tax liability of the husband.

d) If the husband cannot use all the MCA, the unused amount can be transferred to his wife. Note that for marriages before 6th December 2005, the wife's income, even if higher than the husband's, has no effect on the MCA available.

e) The full amount of MCA is reduced by ½ of the excess where the husband's adjusted net income exceeds £28,900.

f) Where the husband's MCA is reduced because his net income exceeds £28,900, it can never be reduced below a minimum of £3,360 (*which at 10% is a relief of £336 deducted from the tax liability on taxable income*).

Example

In 2018/19, Mr Zabir is aged 87 and his wife is aged 89. They have been married for 60 years. In the year 2018/19 Mr Zabir has pension income of £38,300 and Mrs Zabir has pension income of £28,000.

Compute the tax payable by Mr and Mrs Zabir for 2018/19.

Solution: Mr Zabir's Income tax computation 2018/19

	£
Pension income	38,300
Personal Allowance	(11,850)
Taxable income (non-savings, non-dividend)	26,450

	£
Tax liability:	
26,450 @ 20%	5,290
Less deduction for MCA:	
[8,695 – ½ × (38,300 – 28,900)] @ 10%	(399.50)
Tax payable	4,890.50

Mrs Zabir's income tax computation 2018/19

	£
Employment and pension income	28,000
Personal Allowance	(11,850)
Taxable income (non-savings, non-dividend)	16,150
	£
Tax liability: 16,150 @ 20%	3,230

Note that the level of Mrs Zabir's income has no effect on the MCA claimed by her husband.

4.6 'Blind person's allowance' £2,390 2018/19 (£2,320 2017/18)

This allowance is available to any person who is registered severely visually impaired. Where both husband and wife are registered severely visually impaired, each can claim the allowance. If either the husband or the wife (or one civil partner) cannot fully use the amount of their 'blind person's allowance' then the balance can be transferred to the other spouse. This rule applies whether or not the spouse receiving the transferred allowance is registered as severely visually impaired. A notice to transfer any unused allowance must be made in writing to HMRC within four years of the end of the tax year.

This allowance is deducted from net income to arrive at taxable income and is thus given relief at the taxpayer's marginal rate of tax. There is no income limit. It is given in addition to the PA, and the MCA if applicable.

Example

Kathy, who is a widow aged 55, is registered severely visually impaired. Kathy's income for the year 2018/19 consists of the following.

	£
Widow's pension	6,000
Wages for part-time employment (gross)	15,105
(PAYE deducted £900)	

Compute Kathy's income tax liability for 2018/19.

Solution: Kathy's income tax computation 2018/19

	£
Income from employment	15,105
Widow's pension	6,000
Net income (also total income)	21,105
Personal allowance	(11,850)
Blind person's allowance	(2,390)
Taxable income (all non-savings, non-dividend income)	6,865
	£
Tax liability at 20%	1,373
Less PAYE already paid	(900)
Tax payable	473

4.7 Year of death of either spouse

On the death of either spouse or civil partner:

(a) A full personal allowance for the deceased, and (if the age condition is met) a full MCA to either partner, is available in the tax year of death.

(b) Net income up to the date of death, less allowances and reliefs for the whole year, is ascertained and any remaining income tax due is payable by the personal representatives, out of the deceased's estate. If a tax repayment is due and made, this is an asset of the deceased's estate.

(c) The balance of any MCA not used against the husband's (*or higher earning partner's, for marriages/partnerships after 5th December 2005*) tax liability on the deceased's income up to the date of death is available for set-off against the surviving partner's own tax liability for the whole year.

Student self-testing question

Question 4.1, Barney

Barney was born on 1st February 1935. For the year to 5th April 2019 he has salary and pension income of £27,780 and has paid PAYE income tax of £3,000.

Required

Calculate the tax payable by Barney for 2018/19.

Solution to Question 4.1, Barney

Barney income tax computation 2018/19

	£
Income from employment and pension	27,780
Personal Allowance	(11,850)
Taxable income	15,930
	£
Tax borne at 20% =	3,186
PAYE already paid	(3,000)
Tax payable	186

5 Allowable payments and Gift Aid

5.1 Introduction

Allowable payments reduce total income but are not referable to any specific source of income – unlike for example the specific reliefs that are deductible only against income from employment (see Chapter 7).

Total income is reduced by allowable payments to give net income (see Chapter 2).

The concept of allowable payments remains that these costs have the character of 'annual payments'. Before the Income Tax Act 2007, 'charges on income' was the term used to describe all annual payments.

Gift Aid payments are dealt with by the 'extended basic rate band' method of tax relief.

For further comments on the present Gift Aid system, see 5.7.

5.2 Annual payments

These are payments which possess the quality of annual recurrence, are not voluntary transactions, and are usually supported by a legal obligation.

Annual payments are not allowable payments unless they fall within the following categories:

(a) payments of interest;

(b) other annual payments made for bone fide commercial reasons in connection with the payer's trade, profession or vocation.

5.3 Qualifying interest payments

Interest due in the UK on a loan used for any of the under-mentioned purposes is payable without deduction of income tax and is an allowable payment against total income.

(a) To purchase plant or machinery (but not a car) for use in a partnership or necessary for an employment.

(b) To purchase an interest in or make a loan to a partnership, where the taxpayer is a partner, but not a limited partner.

(c) Loans made in acquiring an interest in a co-operative enterprise as defined in section 2 of the Industrial Common Ownership Act 1976.

(d) To pay inheritance tax. Relief is available for one year only.

(e) To acquire ordinary shares or make loans to a close company, but not a close investment company. (*See Chapter 18 for what these are.*) The borrower must, with his or her associates:

(i) have a material interest in the company, i.e. more than 5% of the ordinary share capital or be entitled to more than 5% of the assets on a notional winding up; or

(ii) if having less than a 5% interest, work for the greater part of his or her time in the management of the company.

5.4 Business loan interest

Interest paid on loans taken out wholly for business purposes by traders is charged as an expense of trading, and not as a separate allowable payment. This applies to business bank loan or overdraft interest, providing the loan is used wholly and exclusively for the purposes of trade. Similarly, interest on a loan taken by an individual to buy property for letting is allowable for income tax as an expense of the letting, and not as an allowable payment against total income.

5.5 Gift Aid donations to charities

The present Gift Aid income tax system works as follows:

a) The donor must give the charity/CASC a Gift Aid declaration, either at the time of the donation, or at an earlier time (to cover future donations). This must state that the donor wishes Gift Aid tax relief to apply to the donation, and that the donor pays tax (*income tax and / or Capital Gains Tax*) each year of at least as much as the tax withheld from all Gift Aid donations. The required wording of all new Gift Aid declarations was amended in 2012 to make clear that council tax, VAT, and any other taxes, other than UK income tax and CGT, do not count as 'tax payable' in a Gift Aid declaration.

b) The declaration may be given in writing, over the phone or over the Internet, and the charity or CASC must keep a record of the date of the declaration and the donor's name and address.

c) The amount donated is treated for all tax purposes as paid net of 20% basic rate tax withheld by the donor. The charity / CASC can reclaim the tax on a quarterly or six-monthly basis but must preserve records of all Gift Aid donations received.

d) Donors who pay income tax at higher or additional rate may claim further higher or additional rate income tax relief for the gross donation. This is done on the self-assessment tax return by entering the amount of the gift-aided donations. It can be done by letter if the taxpayer is not within self-assessment.

e) Relief at the higher rate is given by extending the basic rate income band by the gross amount of Gift Aid payments. Relief at the additional rate is given by extending the higher rate band by the same figure.

f) Gift Aid payments made after the end of a tax year but before submission of the self-assessment return may, if the taxpayer wishes, be related back to the tax year of that return. If this is done, the same payment(s) cannot be claimed again in the tax year when paid.

g) Charities claim back basic rate tax withheld on their total Gift Aid income from HMRC Charities using Form R68. The names of all Gift Aid donors must be stated on the form or included in an attachment.

h) If a taxpayer does not pay enough income tax and CGT for a tax year to cover the total tax reclaimed by charities on his or her donations, then he or she must pay HMRC the difference, under section 424 ITA 2007. This situation could arise where trading losses of a later year are carried back against total income, so that an earlier year's tax liability is eliminated – see Chapter 14.

Computational rules for extending the basic rate band for Gift Aid payments

a) **Higher rate taxpayer:** Gross the gift aid payment up by the basic rate of income tax (ie multiply by $^{100}/_{80}$) and extend the taxpayer's personal basic rate band by that gross amount.

b) **Additional rate taxpayer:** Extend the basic rate band by the grossed-up amount of the gift aid payment as above and extend the top limit of the higher rate band by the same amount. This ensures that higher rate tax is paid in total on the same amount of income.

c) **Basic rate taxpayer**: Ignore Gift Aid altogether in the income tax computation, as full relief for the gross payment was given at source by the fact the payment was made net.

The gross amount of Gift Aid payments must also be considered for either a basic or a higher rate taxpayer, when computing the 'adjusted net income' for applying the Personal Allowance and Age Allowance income limits (see Chapter 4).

Example – Gift Aid

Terry, who is married and lives in England, has employment income of £49,000 for 2018/19. His wife Gloria has salary income of £15,000. They have no other income in 2018/19. Terry makes payments of £800 net (£1,000 gross) to a registered charity under Gift Aid. Gloria makes Gift Aid payments of £240 net (£300 gross) to the same charity.

Compute the income tax liabilities for 2018/19 for Terry and Gloria.

Solution: Income tax computations 2018/19

			Terry	Gloria
			£	£
Income from employment (= net income)			49,000	15,000
Personal allowance			(11,850)	(11,850)
Taxable income			37,150	3,150
Tax liability:			£	£
BR	34,500 or 3,150	@ 20%	6,900	630
Extend band 1,000		@ 20%	200	0
HR	1,650or 0	@ 40%	660	0
Tax liability			7,760	630

Notes:

Terry can claim higher rate relief at (40-20)% on his Gift Aid donation. This is given by extending the amount of income on which he pays basic rate tax by £1,000, the gross amount of his total donations (£800 × 100/80 = £1,000).

Therefore, Terry's basic rate band in 2018/19 becomes £35,500.

For Gloria, only basic rate tax relief is due on her donations: she has not enough income to pay tax at higher rate. Her tax saving has been received by her making the payment net, so there is no need to show the Gift Aid in her tax computation.

The charity meanwhile receives £1,300 in total: £800 from Terry, £240 from Gloria, and the other £260 on application to HMRC using Form R68.

5.6 Payroll giving scheme for charitable donations

Individual taxpayers who pay tax under PAYE (on employment or pension income) can give to charity with tax relief at their highest marginal rate via the 'payroll giving' scheme. The donations are deductible from employment income and relief is available up to the total of the money earnings from the employment. The employer or pension provider is responsible for making the payments to the charity and adjusts the employee's or pensioner's PAYE liability using the 'net pay arrangements' (see Chapter 8).

Student self-testing question

Question 5.1, Junaid and Sunita

Junaid and Sunita, who are married, both aged 55 and living in Wales, have the following income for 2018/19.

	£
Employment earnings Junaid	48,000
Employment earnings Sunita	29,200

On 1st February 2019 Junaid paid £960 (net) by way of a Gift Aid payment to a recognised charity.

During 2018/19 Sunita paid £100 per month to the same charity by payroll giving.

Compute the income tax liabilities of both Junaid and Sunita for 2018/19.

Solution to Question 5.1, Junaid and Sunita

Income tax computations 2018/19

	Junaid	Sunita
	£	£
Income from employment	48,000	29,200
Less allowable expense (payroll giving)		(1,200)
		28,000
Personal allowance	(11,850)	(11,850)
Taxable income (*all non-savings, non-dividend*)	36,150	16,150
Taxation liability	£	£
35,700* or 16,150 @ 20%	7,140	3,230
450 @ 40%	180	
36,150		
Tax contributions due	**7,320**	**3,230**

*** Note**

As the gift aid payment by Junaid is allowed at the higher rate, his basic rate income tax band is extended i.e. £34,500 + £1,200 = £35,700.

(Gross up donation: £960 × 100/80 = £1,200)

As both are employed, most or all of the tax liability would have been paid under PAYE before the end of the tax year.

6 Savings and investment income

6.1 Introduction

This chapter is mainly concerned with the taxation of savings and dividend income. It also covers the income tax relief available for investment in EIS shares, SEIS shares, and Venture Capital Trusts (VCTs). At the end of the chapter are brief notes about two kind of investment income which are classed as non-savings income under the ITA2007, namely income from patents or copyrights, and the charge on notional income from 'pre-owned assets'.

'Savings income' is basically interest income. The tax treatment of dividend income is dealt with in 6.4 and 6.5.

You will recall from Chapter 2 that different rates apply to different types of income:

Rate for non-savings, non-dividend income and for savings income		Band		Rate for dividend income
45%		Additional rate		38.1%
	£150,000		£150,000	
40%		Higher rate		32.5%
	£34,500*		£34,500*	
20%		Basic rate		7.5%
	£0		£0	

*£31,580 for Scottish Income Tax

When determining what rate of tax is payable, by reference to the basic, higher and additional rate tax bands, income must be 'stacked up' in a specific order, set out by the legislation. First comes non-savings, non-dividend income (*such as employment income, trading income and property income*), then savings income and then dividend income:

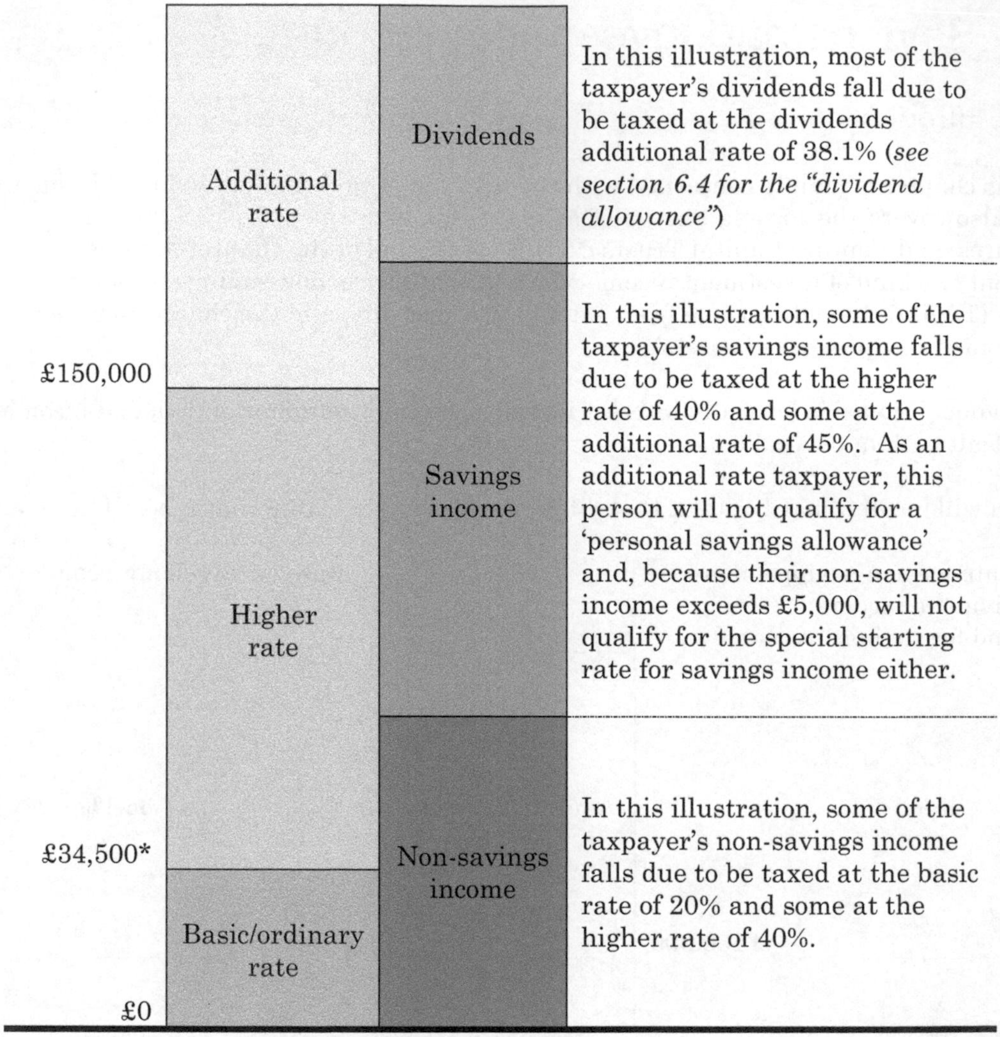

Additional rate

Dividends

In this illustration, most of the taxpayer's dividends fall due to be taxed at the dividends additional rate of 38.1% (*see section 6.4 for the "dividend allowance"*)

£150,000

Savings income

In this illustration, some of the taxpayer's savings income falls due to be taxed at the higher rate of 40% and some at the additional rate of 45%. As an additional rate taxpayer, this person will not qualify for a 'personal savings allowance' and, because their non-savings income exceeds £5,000, will not qualify for the special starting rate for savings income either.

Higher rate

£34,500*

Non-savings income

In this illustration, some of the taxpayer's non-savings income falls due to be taxed at the basic rate of 20% and some at the higher rate of 40%.

Basic/ordinary rate

£0

*£31,580 for Scottish Income Tax

6.2 Treatment of savings income

Starting rate for savings income

To the extent that savings income falls within the first £5,000 of taxable income, that savings income is subject to a 'starting rate' of 0%. This does not involve moving the tax bands or adjusting taxable income; rather, think of it as 'overlapping' with the other bands. Many taxpayers will not be able to benefit from this starting rate, as their non-savings income will already take them beyond £5,000 of taxable income.

E.g., someone working 40 hours per week on the Living Wage[1] of £8.75 per hour will have employment income of £18,200 (cf https://www.livingwage.org.uk/calculation) which, after deduction of their Personal Allowance, will be £6,350 and take them over the £5,000 starting band.

'Personal Savings Allowance'

Such a person would, however, be able to obtain some interest income free from income tax, as since 6th April 2016 a 'personal savings allowance' has been available for basic and higher rate (but not additional rate) taxpayers. This takes the form of a nil rate which 'overlaps' the tax bands (*ie. it is not a deduction from taxable income in the way the Personal Allowance is, nor does it extend the other tax bands*).

For basic rate taxpayers, the 'personal savings allowance' is £1,000. This means that the first £1,000 of savings income they have which is covered neither by their Personal Allowance nor by the 'starting rate band' referred to above will be subject to a nil rate of income tax.

For higher rate taxpayers, the 'personal savings allowance' is £500, and no 'personal savings allowance' is available for additional rate taxpayers.

Gross or net?

It used to be the case that most interest income had tax deducted at source, at the basic rate of income tax. For example, if a person earned £100 interest on a bank deposit account then the bank would pay £80 to the individual and £20 to the tax authorities, under the TDSI (Tax Deduction Scheme for Interest). The individual would then report interest income 'grossed-up' of £100 as part of her or his taxable income but would adjust her or his tax liability to take account of the fact that tax had already been suffered at source.

From 6th April 2016, banks and building societies no longer deduct tax from payments of interest to depositors. Instead they pay interest gross. Taxable savings income is included in the PAYE code and the associated tax collected via the PAYE system.

From 6th April 2017, the requirement for tax to be deducted at source is also removed in the case of interest distributions from open-ended investment companies, authorised unit trusts and investment trust companies (*these are all forms of collective investment funds*), and from interest on peer-to-peer loans.

---

[1] The 'Living Wage' means the amount which would be needed for a minimum acceptable standard of living, determined for the Living Wage Foundation by Loughborough University's Centre for Research in Social Policy. It should not be confused with the 'National Living Wage', which is the minimum wage an employer can pay under UK law. At £7.83 per hour for those aged over 25, the NLW falls well below the Living Wage, and which was renamed from 'National Minimum Wage' for political purposes.

In the short term, deduction at source will continue to apply in the cases of interest on corporate bonds and interest on some UK government securities acquired before 6th April 1998.

If the taxpayer is ultimately taxable on savings income at the basic rate of 20%, then any tax deducted at source will meet that income tax obligation.

A repayment can be claimed after the end of the tax year if tax was deducted at 20% from savings income that attracts the starting rate of 0%, or that falls within the saver's 'personal savings allowance'.

For a higher rate or additional rate taxpayer, the 40% or 45% rate applies to the gross savings income. Credit is given for any tax already paid. In general, savings income of individuals is treated for tax purposes as arising on the date of payment (receipts basis). There is an exception made by certain anti-avoidance legislation, not considered further here (the 'accrued income scheme').

6.3 Examples

Example 1

Alan has the following income for the tax year ended 5th April 2019:

- Income from property, net of expenses £16,000
- Interest on corporate bonds (net) £8,000

Compute Alan's income tax liability and income tax payable for 2018/19.

Solution: Alan's income tax computation 2018/19

	£
Income from property	16,000
Corporate bond interest income (8,000 × 100/80)	10,000
Total income / net income	26,000
Less PA	(11,850)
Taxable income (*analysed as £10,000 savings and £4,150 non-savings*)	14,150
Tax liability:	£
Non savings income 4,150 @ 20%	830
Savings income:	
Starting rate £850 @ 0%	-
'Personal Savings Allowance' £1,000 @ 0%	-
Basic rate on remaining £8,150 @ 20%	1,630
Tax borne	2,460
Less tax suffered at source	(2,000)
Tax liability	460

Notes:

(i) Tax of 20% was paid on the savings income at source;

(ii) Only £850 of Alan's savings income can benefit from the 0% starting tax rate, as his taxable non-savings income uses up most of the first £5,000 of income that would potentially qualify for the starting rate;

(iii) As a basic rate taxpayer Alan is entitled to a 'personal savings allowance', paying nothing on his first £1,000 of savings income.

Example 2

Bill (who lives in Northern Ireland) has the following income for the tax year ended 5th April 2019.

Income from property, net of expenses	£44,000
Interest on corporate bonds (net)	£8,000

Compute Bill's income tax liability and income tax payable for 2018/19.

Solution: Bill's income tax computation 2018/19

	Non-savings, non-dividend income	Savings income	Total income
	£	£	£
Property income	44,000		44,000
Interest on corporate bonds (8,000 × 100/80)		10,000	10,000
Total income	44,000	10,000	54,000
less Personal Allowance	(11,850)		(11,850)
Taxable income	32,150	10,000	42,150
Non-savings income:	£		£
basic rate 20% ×	32,150		6,430
Savings income:		£	
'personal savings allowance'		500	0
basic rate 20% × (34,500 – 500 – 32,150)		1,850	370
higher rate 40% ×		7,650	3,060
		10,000	
Tax borne			9,860
less Tax deducted at source			(2,000)
Tax liability			7,860

Note

Savings income is treated as the top slice of taxable income in this example.

6.4 Dividend income from UK and foreign companies

Dividend income received from companies, other than from UK real estate investment trusts (REITs – see 6.5), is not 'savings income' for individuals.

A "dividend allowance" is available at an amount of £2,000. As with the 'personal savings allowance', this takes the form of a nil rate band which 'overlaps' the basic/ordinary, higher and additional rate tax bands (*ie. it is not a deduction from taxable income, nor does it extend the other tax bands*). Unlike the 'personal savings allowance', the 'dividend allowance' is available at the same amount to all taxpayers, whether basic, higher or additional rate.

(a) The date when dividend income arises is the date when the dividend is received by the taxpayer.

(b) Dividend income is treated as the top slice of income, above savings income, when applying the UK income tax rate bands. However, the tax rate on dividend income is lower within every band than the rate on savings income.

(c) Dividend income falling in the basic rate income band, if not covered by the 'dividend allowance', is taxed at the 'ordinary dividend rate', which is 7.5%.

(d) Dividend income falling in the higher rate income band, if not covered by the 'dividend allowance', is taxed at the 'dividend upper rate', which is 32.5%.

(e) Dividend income falling in the additional rate income band, if not covered by the 'dividend allowance', is taxed at the 'dividend additional rate' of 38.1%.

Example

Rosie, who lives in England, has the following income for the tax year ended 5th April 2019.

Income from property	£24,000
Dividend income received	£1,800

Compute Rosie's income tax liability for 2018/19.

Solution: Rosie's income tax computation, 2018/19

	£
Income from property	24,000
Dividends received	1,800
Total income	25,800
Personal Allowance	(11,850)
Taxable income (£12,500 is non-savings, non-dividend)	13,950
Tax payable:	£
(i) 12,150 @ 20% on non-savings, non-dividend	2,430
(ii) 1,800 covered by dividend allowance	-
Tax payable by self-assessment	2,430

Example

Angus, who lives in England, has the following income for the year ended 5th April 2019.

Income from property, net of expenses	£30,000
Dividend income received	£40,000

Compute Angus's income tax liability for 2018/19 and the tax payable by self-assessment.

Solution: Angus, tax computation 2018/19

	Non-savings income	Dividends	Total income
	£	£	£
Property income	30,000		30,000
Dividends		40,000	40,000
Total income	30,000	40,000	70,000
Personal Allowance	(11,850)		(11,850)
Taxable income	**18,150**	**40,000**	**58,150**
			£
Non-savings income:	£		
basic rate 20% ×	18,150		3,630
Dividends:		£	
dividend nil band 0% ×		2,000	0
ordinary rate 7.5% ×		14,350	1,076
higher rate 32.5% ×		23,650	7,686
		40,000	
Tax contribution			**12,392**

6.5 Dividends from Real Estate Investment Trusts (REITs)

REITs are a special kind of corporate investment vehicle, which invests solely in property for letting. Individuals can buy shares in REITS and receive 'dividends' on them. They are not taxed on the individual as dividend income, but as property income. (See Chapter 9.)

6.6 Individual savings accounts (ISAs)

The main features of these tax-free investments are summarised as follows:

(a) ISAs can only be held by UK resident individuals over the age of 16, although a junior ISA exists for younger savers. All income received from an ISA, whether interest or dividends, is exempt from income tax. (*However, see final point (h) below, regarding dividends.*)

(b) Trustees cannot hold ISAs for other people.

(c) Annual limits set the maximum amount which an individual can invest in each tax year. For 2018/19, this is £20,000.

(d) Money may be withdrawn from an ISA, but if it is subsequently reinvested that counts as a fresh ISA investment and counts towards the annual maximum for that tax year. So, ISAs are not suitable for fluctuating savings or short-term deposits. They are intended for long-term saving.

(e) A junior cash ISA, in which up to £4,260 a year may be deposited, may be set up for any child not holding a Child Trust Fund.
(*A CTF is a special investment account which had to be started in early life for a child born in the UK between 1st September 2002 and 2nd January 2011. A CTF must currently remain invested until the child is 18.*)

(f) As ISAs with an annual subscription limit of several thousand pounds have existed since 1999, some individuals could by 2018/19 have large holdings built up in ISAs, and generating tax-free capital gains (for shares), interest or dividends. There is no overall lifetime limit on ISA holdings, but ISA status is lost on all investments held if the individual ceases permanently to be a UK resident or dies.

(g) ISA income does not have to be recorded in the self-assessment tax return. It is not included as income for the purposes of the calculations causing restriction (abatement) of the Personal Age Allowance and the Married Couple's Allowance for higher incomes.

(h) Dividend income from an ISA is exempt from income tax. In addition, the shares held in an ISA are exempt from Capital Gains Tax on their disposal.

6.7 Other exempt savings income, apart from ISAs

Interest on some 'National Savings and Investments' products is exempt from tax:

- Index-Linked Savings Certificates;
- Fixed Interest Savings Certificates;
- Children's Bonus Bonds; and
- Premium Bond prizes.

6.8 Enterprise investment scheme (EIS) shareholdings

Investments in EIS company shares attract UK income tax relief and other tax exemptions for the individual investor.

An EIS company must be an unquoted trading company (*or an unquoted company that is preparing to trade*), and other detailed conditions apply as to its maximum size and its permitted activities. Broadly, no activities that are 'asset-backed', such as leasing or agriculture, can qualify under current rules, and nor can activities that involve investing in other companies. EIS status is granted to a company by HMRC, and then notified to potential and existing investors by the company.
The maximum number of employees which an EIS company can have is 249 and the maximum amount of gross assets which it can have before the EIS share issue occurs is £15 million.

Cash subscribed for new EIS shares attracts income tax relief at 30% on the amount subscribed, if further qualifying conditions are met by the shareholder. Any income from EIS shares is taxable as dividend income. However, if EIS shares on which income tax relief has been claimed are held for more than three years, capital gains on disposal will be tax-free. (See Part IV, Chargeable Gains.)
EIS relief for income tax works as follows.

(a) An individual can subscribe for up to £1 million of EIS company shares in 2018/19 and obtain tax relief at the 30% rate. The relief is given 'in terms of tax', so 30% of the qualifying subscription cost is deducted from the tax liability of the individual. From 6th April 2018 the £1 million limit is doubled to £2 million if amounts exceeding £1 million are invested in knowledge-intensive companies (see section 6.12).

(b) To qualify for income tax relief,
   (i) the eligible shares must be held for at least three years from the date the company's trade started, or the date of the share subscription, if later;
   (ii) the individual and his or her associates (*this includes family, business partners, etc.*) must not be connected with the company as an employee, lender or a shareholder of more than 30% of the share capital at any time in the 2 years before the EIS subscription or the 3 years after it;
   (iii) the individual must not receive any value from the company, e.g. a loan or benefit in kind, during the qualifying 3-year shareholding period.

(c) The company must retain its EIS status throughout the qualifying 3-year shareholding period.

(d) Any part of the total amount invested by an individual in EIS shares in a tax year can be treated by election as if subscribed for EIS shares in the previous tax year, up to the maximum of EIS relief which could be claimed for that earlier year. So, in 2018/19, the maximum amount of EIS subscription that can be related back to tax year 2017/18 is equal to the 2017/18 EIS subscription limit, which was £1 million. This limit would then be reduced by any actual

EIS subscriptions made by the same taxpayer in 2017/18, for which relief had already been taken in 2017/18.

(e) If EIS shares are sold at a loss, the taxpayer can elect to claim that loss against total income of that or the preceding tax year, instead of as a capital loss. If this is done, they must deduct from the loss claimed the value of EIS relief already given against income tax.

There is a limit on the total amount of funding which a company can receive under the EIS and VCT (section 6.11) schemes, a maximum of £5 million per annum up to a total of £12million in the company's lifetime. The limit is higher for knowledge-intensive companies – see section 6.12.

6.9 The Seed Enterprise Investment Scheme (SEIS)

The SEIS is designed to assist small or early-stage enterprises to obtain equity finance, and offers a higher rate of tax relief than EIS investment, but otherwise complements the EIS.

The rules about qualifying trades mirror those for EIS, and it is envisaged that a company that starts up with the assistance of SEIS tax relief may well use EIS for later equity share issues.

UK income taxpayers who subscribe for equity shares in a SEIS company can claim income tax relief for 50% of the amount subscribed, by deduction from their UK tax liability. The annual limit for SEIS investment is £100,000 per year, giving a UK tax offset of £50,000. No capital gains tax is payable on SEIS shares held for more than 3 years.

SEIS share subscriptions can be carried back one year just like EIS subscriptions.

This gives greater flexibility for taxpayers to invest only once they know their final income tax position and tax relief capacity for a tax year.

Qualifying companies must obtain confirmation of their SEIS status from HMRC.

They must:

a) be undertaking or planning a new business (*if already trading, the trade must be less than 2 years old*);

b) have fewer than 25 employees;

c) have gross assets of less than or equal to £200,000;

d) raise not more than £150,000 in total under the scheme.

Directors, but not other employees, may invest under SEIS in the company for which they work. This allows 'business angels' to take a paid director's role in a company to which they have provided SEIS finance.

6.10 Social Investment Tax Relief

Individuals making an eligible investment can deduct 30% of the cost of their investment from their income tax liability. There is no capital gains tax liability when the investment is sold or redeemed. Individual investors can invest up to £1 million in qualifying social enterprises. There is a limit on the amount of SITR investment which a social enterprise can receive; £1.5million over its lifetime.

6.11 Venture capital trusts

The main features of this type of investment are as follow.

(a) The VCT scheme is designed to stimulate individual investment in a spread of unquoted trading companies, through the mechanism of quoted 'venture capital trust' companies. The type of companies that VCTs invest in is the same as under EIS (see 6.8), but by using a VCT the investor can choose a broader range of EIS-type investments while still obtaining income tax relief for the investment.

(b) Individuals can invest up to a maximum of £200,000 per tax year in VCT shares, attracting income tax relief at 30%, providing the shares are then held for five years. If the shares are not held for five years, the tax relief must be repaid.

(c) Dividends received from VCT shares are tax-free.

(d) VCT status is awarded to the VCT company by HMRC.

(e) There are also capital gains tax reliefs (not covered further here)

6.12 Knowledge-intensive companies

To qualify as a "knowledge-intensive company" under the various venture capital schemes, a company must – at the time the investment is made – meet at least one of the **operating** costs conditions:

- the company (or its subsidiary) must have spent at least **15%** of its operating expenses (excluding depreciation and amortisation) on research and development or innovation in **one** of the three years preceding the date of the investment; or
- the company (or its subsidiary) must have spent at least **10%** of its operating expenses (excluding depreciation and amortisation) on research and development or innovation in **each** of the three years preceding the date of the investment.

and at least one of:

- the **innovation condition** – the company or group is working to develop intellectual property with a reasonable expectation that it will exploit that intellectual property within 10 years (*this may require evaluation by an independent expert*); or

- the **skilled employees condition** – that at least 20% of the company's Full Time Equivalent employees must be skilled employees (*the company must continue to meet this condition for at least three years following the date of the investment*). A skilled employee is an employee who is directly engaged in the research and development or innovation activities, who has a master's degree or above and whose specific role requires them to hold a master's degree or above.

There is a limit on the amount of funding which a knowledge-intensive company can receive under the EIS and VCT schemes, of £10 million per annum (2017/18: £5 million).

6.13 Miscellaneous income

(a) **Patent royalties received.** These are normally received by individuals under deduction of basic rate income tax at source. The gross amount is treated as non-savings income under section 579 ITTOIA 2005. It is classed as 'miscellaneous income' for a third-party investor, and as trading income if the royalty recipient invented the patented process.

(b) **Copyright royalties received**. Copyright royalties are paid to authors or artists gross without deduction of income tax at source. Like patent royalties, they are taxable under section 579 as non-savings income (*miscellaneous income for an investor in the copyright, and trading income if the recipient is the original creator of the work*).

6.14 Pre-owned assets charge

Because of inheritance tax anti-avoidance legislation, an income tax charge may arise in respect of a deemed benefit which a UK resident receives by having free or low-cost enjoyment of an asset or assets which he or she formerly owned, but has given to another person, or has provided another person with the funds to purchase. The charge applies to both tangible (typically land and chattels) and intangible assets formerly owned by, and still enjoyed by, the taxpayer.

However, the pre-owned assets charge does not apply to the extent that:

(i) the property in question ceased to be owned before 18th March 1986;
(ii) property formerly owned by a taxpayer is now owned by their spouse;
(iii) the asset in question still counts within the taxpayer's estate for inheritance tax purposes, under the 'gift with reservation' rules;
(iv) the property was sold by the taxpayer at an arm's length price, and paid for in cash that was not indirectly supplied by the taxpayer;
(v) the taxpayer was formerly the owner of an asset only by virtue of a will or intestacy, which has subsequently been varied by agreement between the beneficiaries; or

(vi) any enjoyment of the property is no more than incidental, including cases where an outright gift to a family member comes to benefit the donor following an unforeseen change in circumstances. This exception was introduced to cover the situation where an individual contributes as a gift to the purchase price of accommodation for a family member, but later moves in to live there because of age or infirmity. The exception would not apply if the donor expected eventually to live in the accommodation at the time when the gift of money was made.

The pre-owned assets charge is calculated, broadly, for a house or a flat, as the rental income that could reasonably be expected from the property.

It is calculated on chattels and intangibles as notional income at a 'prescribed rate' of interest, applied to the market value of the 'pre-owned asset', which is re-valued for this purpose every five years.

The prescribed rate of interest currently matches the official rate of interest used for valuing certain employment benefits (see Chapter 7).

As no one is really paying this interest or rent, there is no matching deduction for any other taxpayer to match the notional income assumed to be received by the person who formerly owned the asset and is still 'enjoying' it.

The pre-owned assets charge is not a common item to see on real income tax returns or tax computations, because the main purpose of the 'pre-owned assets' income tax regime is deterrent, rather than to raise tax revenue.

If a taxpayer is caught by the pre-owned assets charge, he or she can escape it by electing instead to have the asset included in their estate for inheritance tax purposes, even if the exact circumstances of disposal were not caught by the normal 'gift with reservation' IHT rules (see Part V for these).

Student self-testing questions

Question 6.1, Abigail

The following relates to the self-assessment tax return of Abigail, who lives in Wales.

	Year ended 5th April 2019
	£
Salary (*gross before PAYE deducted of £25,000*)	91,000
Dividends	6,000
Bank interest	600
Gift Aid to Oxfam (cash amount paid)	1,600

Calculate the income tax liability and remaining tax payable by or repayable to Abigail for 2018/19.

Solution to Question 6.1, Abigail

Abigail, Income tax computation 2018/19

	Non-savings income £	Savings income £	Dividend income £	Total £
Salary	91,000			91,000
Bank interest		600		600
Dividends			6.000	6,000
Total income	91,000	600	6,000	97,600
Personal allowance	(11,850)			(11,850)
Taxable income	79,150	600	6,000	87,750

Tax liability:			£
On non-savings:	Basic rate	34,500 @ 20%	6,900
	Gift aid extension	2,000 @ 20%	400
	Higher rate	42,650 @ 40%	17,060
On savings:	PSA	500 @ 0%	-
	Higher rate	100 @ 40%	40
On dividends	Dividend nil rate	2,000 @ 0%	-
	Higher rate	4,000 @ 32.5%	1,300
Tax borne			25,700
Less tax paid under PAYE			(25,000)
Tax payable			700

Note
The basic rate is extended by (1,600 × $^{100}/_{80}$) = £2,000 to £36,500 to give relief for the Gift Aid at the higher rate.

Question 6.2, Emma

Emma lives in England and has business trading profits of £22,500 for the year ended 5th April 2019. She also receives bank deposit interest of £125 and dividends of £7,000.

What is her income after tax for 2018/19, ignoring National Insurance?

Solution to Question 6.2, Emma

	Non-savings Income	Savings income	Dividends	Total income
	£	£	£	£
Trading profits	22,500			22,500
Interest		125		125
Dividends			7,000	7,000
Total income	22,500	125	7,000	29,625
Personal Allowance	(11,850)			(11,850)
Taxable income	**10,650**	**125**	**7,000**	**17,775**
				£
Non-savings income:	£			
basic rate 20% ×	10,650			2,130
Savings income:		£		
'personal savings allowance'		125		0
Dividends:			£	
dividend nil band 0% ×			2,000	0
ordinary rate 7.5% ×			5,000	375
			7,000	
Tax liability				**2,505**

Calculation of income after tax but before NIC	£
Trading profits	22,500
Bank deposit interest	125
Dividends	7,000
Income Tax contribution for the year	(2,505)
Net income after tax	27,120

Question 6.3, Chris

Chris lives in Wales and has the following income and outgoings for the year ended 5th April 2019:

	£
Business trading profits	7,840
Salary	22,880
Bank interest	416
Building society interest	712
Rent receivable from let property (not in Chris's own home), net of expenses	1,890

Requirement: Calculate Chris's tax borne for 2018/19

Solution to Question 6.3, Chris

	Non-savings income	Savings income	Total income
	£	£	£
Employment income	22,880		22,880
Trading profits	7,840		7,840
Property income	1,890		1,890
Interest		1,128	1,128
Total income	32,610	1,128	33,738
Personal Allowance	(11,850)		(11,850)
Taxable income	**20,760**	**1,128**	**21,888**
Non-savings income:			
basic rate 20% ×	20,760		4,152
Savings income:			
'personal savings allowance'		1,000	-
basic rate 20% ×		128	26
		1,128	
Tax borne			**4,178**

Question 6.4, Pat

Pat lives in Northern Ireland and has the following income for 2018/19

	£
Trading profits	19,450
Dividends	2,160
Income from property (net of expenses)	1,000

Pat claims the personal allowance of £11,850.

Requirement:

(a) Calculate Pat's income tax payable by self-assessment for 2018/19

(b) How would your answer differ if Pat had £144,450 income from his business?

Solution to Question 6.4, Pat

(a) Pat's Income Tax computation with trading profits of £19,450

	Non-savings Income	Dividends	Total income
	£	£	£
Trading profits	19,450		19,450
Property income	1,000		1,000
Dividends		2,160	2,160
Total income	20,450	2,160	22,610
Personal Allowance	(11,850)		(11,850)
Taxable income	**8,600**	**2,160**	**10,760**
Non-savings income:			£
basic rate 20% ×	8,600		1,720
Dividends:			
dividend nil band 0% ×		2,000	-
basic rate 7.5% ×		160	12
		2,160	
Tax liability			**1,732**

(b) Pat's Income Tax computation with trading profits of £144,450

	Non-savings Income	Dividends	Total income
	£	£	£
Trading profits	144,450		144,450
Property income	1,000		1,000
Dividends		2,160	2,160
Total income	145,450	2,160	147,610
Personal Allowance	-	-	-
Taxable income	**145,450**	**2,160**	**147,610**
Non-savings income:			£
basic rate 20% ×	34,500		6,900
higher rate 40% ×	110,950		44,380
	145,450		
Dividends:			
dividend nil band 0% ×		2,000	-
higher rate 32.5% ×		160	52
Tax liability			**51,332**

Questions without answers

Question 6.5, Jacqueline

Jacqueline, who lives in Northern Ireland, has the following income for 2018/19:

	£
Salary (PAYE £5,000)	30,000
Bank deposit interest	7,000
Dividends	8,000
Gift aid donation (cash amount paid)	700

Requirement

Calculate Jacqueline's income tax payable.

Question 6.6, Jackie

Requirement

Jackie lives in England. Calculate her tax position in 2018/19 if her income was:

(a) trading profits of £150,500 and bank deposit interest of £3,000.

(b) trading profits of £15,500 and bank deposit interest of £3,000.

7 Income from employment I – general principles

7.1 Introduction

This chapter is concerned with the taxation of income from employment.

The major part deals with the taxation of earnings from employment and benefits treated as earnings.

The legislation is contained in the Income Tax (Earnings and Pensions) Act 2003.

7.2 Summary of taxable income

Tax under the ITEPA 2003 is charged in respect of the following income.

Employment income.
Pension income.
Social security income.

7.3 Employment

(a) Employment includes in particular:
   i) any employment under a contract of service;
   ii) any employment under a contract of apprenticeship;
   iii) any employment in the service of the Crown; and
   iv) any office, which includes any position that has an existence independent of the person who holds it and may be filled by successive holders.

(b) Employment is usually evidenced by a written contract of employment, or in older legal language, a 'contract of service'. UK employment law now provides that anyone employed for longer than a minimal period is entitled to a written statement of the terms of their employment.

   However, under income tax law, even if a written contract exists (*and even if it states that the engagement is not an employment*), the factual details of the worker's involvement, rather than the words of the contract, determine whether the engagement is an employment.

   In contrast to a '**contract of service**', a '**contract for** (particular) **services**' is associated with self-employment, the rewards of which are assessable as trading profits. For a leading case, see Hall v Lorimer 1992 CA STC 23.

(c) An office can be thought of as a position with duties attached to it which do not change with the holder, and which in a sense still exists between holders, even while the next holder is being chosen. It is the income of the office that is taxable as employment income. Examples of office holders are: a judge; a town clerk; a company director or company secretary.

7.4 Employment income

a) The legislation provides that earnings, in relation to employment, means:
   i) any salary, wages or fee;
   ii) any gratuity or other profit or incidental benefit of any kind obtained by the employee if it is money or money's worth; or
   iii) anything else that constitutes either general earnings or specific income of the employment.
   (*Before ITEPA 2003, the term 'emoluments' covered all the chargeable earnings of an employment. This word is still found in case law, but no longer appears in the statute.*)

b) For the purposes of (ii) above, 'money's worth' means something that is:
   i) of direct monetary value to the employee; or
   ii) capable of being converted into money or into something of direct monetary value to the employee.

7.5 Receipt of money earnings

a) Employment income is assessable in the tax year when it is received. General earnings consisting of money are to be treated as received at the earliest of the following times:
   Rule 1
   When the employee receives the money; or.
   Rule 2
   When the employee becomes entitled to receive the money; or
   Rule 3
   If the employee is a director of a company and the earnings are from employment with the company (*whether or not as a director*), whichever is the earliest:
   i) the time when the earnings are credited in the company's accounts or records (*whether or not there is any restriction on the right to draw the sums*); or
   ii) if the amount of the earnings for a period is determined by the end of the period, the time when the period ends; or
   iii) if the amount of the earnings for a period is not determined until after the period has ended, the time when the amount is determined.

b) Rule 3 applies if the employee is a director of the company at any time in the tax year in which the time mentioned falls.

c) In this section director means:
   i) in relation to a company whose affairs are managed by a board of directors or similar body, a member of that body;

ii) in relation to a company whose affairs are managed by a single director or similar person, that director or person, and

iii) in relation to a company whose affairs are managed by the members themselves, a member of the company,

and includes any person in accordance with whose directions or instructions the directors of the company (as defined above) are accustomed to act.

d) For the purposes of subsection (c), a person is not to be regarded as a person in accordance with whose directions or instructions the directors of the company are accustomed to act merely because the directors act on advice given by that person in a professional capacity.

7.6 Gifts and voluntary payments

In principle, gifts and voluntary payments unconnected with an employment are not taxable, but there is a presumption that payments from an employer to an employee are in return for service. A key test here is whether the employee would have reasonably expected the additional payment when they were originally carrying out the services to which the payment potentially refers. Case law and HMRC practice have established the following exceptions where the presumption that a payment was in return for employment services can be successfully defeated (rebutted) by factual evidence.

a) Reasonable gifts made by an employer in connection with an employee's marriage or retirement are not taxable.

b) Long-service awards in the form of gifts of objects or non-cash vouchers are not taxed, providing that: the award is in respect of not less than 20 years' service; no similar payment has been made during the previous 10 years; and the cost to the employer does not exceed £50 (previously £20) for each year of service. A cash award would be taxable.

c) The proceeds of a 'benefit' match for a sportsman were held not to be taxable as employment income if they were not part of the employment contract. However, transfer-signing fees received personally by footballers are taxable employment income.

d) A cash award of £130 (*at the time a significant amount*) to a bank clerk for passing his professional examinations was held to be a non-taxable gift. (*However, if such exam awards are included in the contract of employment, they will be taxable.*)

e) £1,000 paid by the English Football Association to each of the members of the 1966 England World Cup team for winning the tournament (not promised in advance) was held to be a gift, and not taxable employment income.

f) Tips of an employed taxi driver were held to be taxable in Calvert v Wainwright 1947 27 TC 475. ITEPA section 62 now confirms specifically that tips and gratuities received directly from customers by employed taxi drivers, postal workers, hairdressers, waiters, etc, in respect of services provided to the employer's customers, are in principle part of earnings.

g) The Easter offerings that a vicar received, being donations from his congregation following an appeal by his Bishop, were held to be emoluments (now employment income).

h) Gifts from third parties made to an employee in the course of employment costing not more than £100 in any tax year are not taxable, by concession.

i) A payment to a footballer by his old club to join a new club was held to be taxable as emoluments i.e. as a 'farewell' payment on retirement or removal from an office. The 'signing-on fee' paid by the new club on another footballer's transfer was held to be taxable as emoluments from the new employment.

7.7 Benefits treated as earnings – Benefits Code

Generally, all benefits provided by an employer are treated as earnings and valued under the Benefits Code. However, some benefits are specifically exempted.

The Benefits Code is now found in ITEPA 2003. It contains general rules for taxing any non-cash benefits for which no special rules exist, and specific rules dealing with specific types of benefit, e.g.,

Cars, vans and related benefits	Loans
Living accommodation	Cash equivalent benefits

7.8 The taxation of benefits as earnings

The taxation of benefits in kind as earnings depends upon placing a value on the goods and services that are provided to an employee.

For tax purposes, such benefits must be measured at the cost to the employer, unless another prescribed method is laid down (*for example as in the case of motor cars*).

Following the decision in Pepper v Hart HL 1992 STC 898, benefits provided 'in-house' in the form of the employer's own goods or services are valued at 'cost to the employer' on the marginal cost basis, not on an average cost basis including a share of overheads. In Pepper v Hart, it was held that if there were still places unfilled at the private school, the taxable value of the benefit of a free school place for a teacher's child was only the marginal cost of extra books, meals and laundry, less any such costs reimbursed by the employee.

7.9 Form P11D: end-of-year expenses and benefits

Employers must complete a return (form P11D) of all benefits in kind provided each year in respect of each employee", except for those which are 'payrolled' (*Although P11Ds must still be completed for employer-provided living accommodation and for beneficial loans – see 7.19-7.20 and 7.23 – whether or not these are 'payrolled'.*) Under 'payrolling', employers update the tax authorities as to employees' benefits and expenses in real time, and deduct the appropriate tax from their employees' salaries under PAYE.

Any benefits provided for the members of the family or household of an employee are treated as if they were provided for the employee personally. The term family or household covers the employee's spouse, children and their spouses, his or her parents, servants, dependants and guests.

Expenses paid or reimbursed to an employee which are deductible against earnings by the employee are exempt, as are allowances for travel and subsistence calculated and paid in an approved way.

7.10 Benchmark rates for day subsistence

HMRC has introduced advisory benchmark scale rates for day subsistence, which will not give rise to taxable benefits. The benchmark rates are:

- Five-hour rate – Up to £5 may be paid where the worker has been away from his or her home or normal place of work for at least five hours, and incurred cost for a meal.
- Ten-hour rate – Up to £10 may be paid where the worker has been away from his or her home or normal place of work for at least ten hours, and incurred cost for a meal, or meals.
- Breakfast rate (irregular early starters only) – Up to £5 may be paid where a worker leaves home earlier than usual and before 6.00 a.m. and incurs a cost on breakfast taken away from home.
- Late evening meal rate (irregular late finishers only) – Up to £15 may be paid where the employee finishes work late after 8.00 p.m. and buys a meal which he or she would usually eat at home.

7.11 Summary of benefits treated as earnings 2018/19

Benefit	Amount treated as employment income
Private use of employer's car	Car and fuel benefits (see below)
Private use of employer's van	Van and fuel benefits (see below)
Accommodation (see below).	Accommodation can be wholly or partly exempt, otherwise taxed on rent paid, or annual value if owned, plus expenses paid, plus an additional charge for accommodation costing more than £75,000. (see below)
Board and lodging	Taxed on cost to the employer
Suits and clothing	Taxed on cost to employer
Medical insurance	Premiums paid by employer taxable
Beneficial loans (see below)	Generally taxable at the deemed interest saving, with some exceptions
Cash vouchers, saving certificates	Full value taxable (even if employer pays less)
Assets loaned	20% of market value when first provided is taxable for each complete tax year
Assets transferred	Taxed on value increase enjoyed (see 7.22)

Season tickets and transport vouchers.	Taxed on cost to the employer
Sick pay	Taxed on amount received (*as it is cash, National Insurance Contributions on cash earnings will also apply, see Chapter 17*)
Scholarships provided by reason of employment	Taxed on cost to employer
Employer-subsidised nursery facilities	Taxed on cost to employer (*unless the nursery is at the workplace itself, in which case it is a tax-free benefit*)
Loan written off	Taxed on full value (*and as it becomes cash remuneration at that point it is also liable to National Insurance Contributions on cash earnings – see Chapter 17*)

7.12 Benefits with exemptions from Income Tax

Benefits with exemptions	**All employees**
Trivial benefits such as Christmas gifts	Qualifying benefits up to £50 are exempt
Electricity provided in workplace charging points for electric or hybrid cars owned by employees	Tax-exempt
'Green commuting' benefits, including: loan of cycling equipment, works buses, subsidised fares on public buses.	Tax-exempt
Mobile telephones with private use	One phone provided to employee personally is exempt; any further phones are taxed at cost to the employer
Job-related living accommodation (see below).	Either wholly or partly exempt (see 7.19 onwards)
Non-job-related living accommodation	Taxed on rental cost or annual value, plus any furniture loaned and expenses paid (see 7.19 onwards)
Industrial clothing	Tax-exempt (does not cover 'ordinary' clothing)
Approved share option schemes (See 7.35 onwards)	If the scheme is HMRC-approved, there is no income tax on the grant of share options nor on later exercise, if the exercise price is not less than the shares' market value when the option was granted. The employee is also liable to CGT and not income tax on gains on disposal of shares acquired via options.
Savings related approved share options	Not subject to income tax, CGT applies on final disposal

Free or subsidised meals in staff canteen	Tax-exempt if generally available to all employees
In-house sports facilities	Not taxable, if not available to the public
Overnight expenses	Up to £5 per night UK, £10 overseas, exempt
Workplace nurseries	Not taxable
Child-care vouchers which can be used to pay for childcare from various approved providers	Up to £55 per week per employee is exempt. The relief is limited to basic rate tax only. To give effect to this the limit is reduced to £28 for higher rate taxpayers and £25 for additional rate taxpayers.

7.13 Private use of employer-provided motor cars – benefit valuation rules

The benefit is calculated as follows:	£	£
List price of car and optional accessories when first provided	X	
Less capital contribution (if any) by employee	(X)	
= **Net Value**		X
Value of benefit = Percentage of net value based on		
CO_2 emissions (per table)		X
Less reduction for unavailability		(X)
Less payment by employee (if any) for private use		(X)
Car **Benefit treated as earnings**		X

Notes

i) The percentage to be applied to the net value of the car is determined from the CO_2 emission table, reproduced below.

ii) List price is the manufacturer's published price for that model when first registered, plus the list price of any optional accessories. HMRC obtains data on list prices from car manufacturers to check to Form P11D submitted information. Any purchasing discount received by the employer from list price is irrelevant for this purpose.

iii) Where the car is more than 15 years old at the end of the income tax year then its original list price, if more than £15,000, is taken as £15,000.

iv) The benefit for private use is reduced proportionally if the car is not available for any period of 30 days or more in the year. Periods of less than 30 days of unavailability are ignored. The benefit is also pro-rated in a tax year when the benefit started to be given for the first time or ceased to be given.

v) Where the employee makes a capital contribution to the cost of the car, then, subject to a maximum of £5,000, the amount is deducted from the list price.

vi) Where an employee is required to make a revenue contribution to the employer for private use of the car, the annual amount of this is deducted in arriving at the assessable benefit.

7.14 CO_2 emission table 2018/19

CO_2 emissions, grams per km	% of list price Petrol cars	CO_2 emissions, grams per km	% of list price Petrol cars
0 – 50	13%	140 – 144	29%
51 – 75	16%	145 – 149	30%
76 – 94	19%	150 – 154	31%
95 – 99	20%	155 – 159	32%
100 – 104	21%	160 – 164	33%
105 - 109	22%	165 – 169	34%
110 – 114	23%	170 – 174	35%
115 – 119	24%	175 – 179	36%
120 – 124	25%	180 or more	37%
125 – 129	26%		
130 – 134	27%		
135 – 139	28%		

A diesel supplement of 4% must be added to the percentages above (*but only to take the total percentage up to 37% at maximum*) in the cases of:

- Diesel cars registered from 1st January 1998 to 31st August 2017; and
- Diesel cars registered from 1st September 2017 not meeting the Real Driving Emissions Step 2 (RDE2) standard.

For the avoidance of doubt, diesel cars registered from 1st September 2017 which **do** meet the RDE2 standard are **not** subject to the diesel supplement.

Once determined, the same car benefit is used for Class 1A National Insurance contributions (see Chapter 17).

Example

Alex drives a petrol company car in 2018/19 with a list price of £26,000. CO_2 emissions are 162g/km.

Compute the assessable car benefit for 2018/19.

Solution: Cash equivalent benefit 2018/19

List price × 33% = 26,000 × 33% £8,580

7.15 Car fuel benefit

Fuel scale charges for employees receiving free fuel for private mileage in company cars are based on the same percentage as was calculated for the car benefit (*according to the car's CO_2 emissions*) which is applied to a scale charge of £23,400 (2017/18: £22,600).

Once determined, the same fuel benefit is used for employer's Class 1A National Insurance contributions (see Chapter 17).

The fuel benefit charge is proportionally reduced where an employee permanently stops receiving free fuel partway through the tax year. However, an employee opting out and then back into a free fuel benefit within the same year will result in a full year's charge with no reduction for non-availability.

(This rule was presumably designed to encourage employees to agree permanently to give up the benefit of employer-provided private fuel.)

Notes

i) The fuel benefit is reduced to nil if all private fuel is paid for or reimbursed (at approved rates) by the employee / director.

ii) The charge is not reduced at all if the employee / director reimburses only a partial amount of fuel provided by the employer for private journeys.

iii) Employers (not employees) are also required to pay NI at 13.8% on the assessable benefit value of cars/fuel provided for private use of employees. This NI is paid annually - see Chapter 17.

iv) Where one car is used jointly by two or more employees, a separate assessable benefit can arise in respect of each user.

Example

Ali is employed by Beta Ltd and is provided with a car (CO_2 emissions 200g/km) which cost £26,000 on 1st January 2012. Ali used the car during 2018/19 and Beta Ltd paid for all fuel, business and private. Ali pays £300 to the company each year for the private use of the car.

Calculate the value of any car benefit for 2018/19.

Solution: Ali – Value of car benefits

	£
Motor car benefit 37% × £26,000	9,620
Less contribution	(300)
	9,320
Motor fuel benefit £23,400 × 37% =	8,658
Total (*included in Ali's assessable employment income*)	17,978

7.16 Vans – benefit of private use of vans 2018/19 £3,350

Private use of a van with a vehicle weight up to 3,500kg is taxed at a fixed benefit value of £3,350 (2017/18: £3,230) for a full tax year (proportionately reduced for part-year). There is no taxable benefit where the employee is required to take an employer's van home overnight for reasons of either security or work efficiency, so long as there is no other personal use of the van. This is different from the rule for cars, where a private use benefit arises even if the only use of the car is for home to work commuting.

7.17 Vans – private fuel benefit 2018/19 £633

If an employee makes no reimbursement for fuel used during private use of a company van, there is a flat-rate fuel benefit of £633 (2017/18: £610).

7.18 Authorised mileage allowance payments

Where an employee uses his or her own vehicle to complete business journeys, mileage allowances are allowed by HMRC to be paid tax-free up to rates deemed not to involve a profit element for the employee. There are separate rates for cars and vans, motorbikes, bicycles and for carrying passengers.

An authorised mileage allowance payment must be:

a) paid to the employee, not to someone else for the employee's advantage; and
b) specifically for business mileage

The April 2018/19 maximum rates are as follows:

Cars and vans	
- First 10,000 miles	45p per mile
- Over 10,000 miles	25p per mile
Motorcycles	24p per mile
Bicycles	20p per mile
Carrying a passenger	5p per passenger

These permitted maximum rates may be varied at any time during a tax year by Statutory Instrument.

Where an employer has paid business mileage expenses of less than the statutory rate, the employee can claim an expense deduction against employment income for the difference. Payments more than statutory rates are liable to income tax.

7.19 Living accommodation

Cash-equivalent value of benefits

Where any employee is provided with living accommodation by an employer, then, subject to certain exemptions noted below, he or she is liable to tax on the 'cash equivalent value' of the benefit. This is defined as:

[Annual value + Cost of ancillary services – Employee's contribution – business use]

Annual value is the gross rateable value of the property, whether rented or owned by the employer. (*Gross rateable values can still be obtained from Government sources, although domestic rates are no longer based on them.*)

For a property rented by the employer, the annual value benefit is the greater of the annual value itself or the actual rent paid by the employer.

Cost of ancillary services is the total of any expenses incurred in providing services such as heating, lighting, rates, domestic services or gardening, and the loan value of any furniture provided by the employer.

Employee's contribution means any rent paid by an employee. Any payment by the employee towards expenses may also be deducted from the value of the taxable benefit.

Business use means the proportion of any benefit attributable to business use.

Total exemption from annual value charge - job-related accommodation

An individual is not taxed on the annual value of the accommodation if it is:

a) necessary for the proper performance of his or her duties, or
b) customary for the better performance of his or her duties, and in general provided for others in the same employment, or
c) required for security reasons.

A full-time working director with less than 5% interest in a company is eligible to claim exemption under (a) and (b), but not under (c). All other directors, whether or not they control the company, are ineligible for accommodation exemptions.

Partial exemption from the 'ancillary costs' benefit

If an individual is exempted from the annual value charge as noted above, then the taxable value of all ancillary services is limited to a maximum of an extra 10% of their net assessable earnings for the year.

Net assessable earnings for this purpose are computed as all income from the employment (ignoring the "ancillary costs" benefit), less allowable employment expenses, approved pension scheme payments and capital allowances.

Example

Quentin is an employee of Terruno plc, occupying a house with an annual value of £1,000, which is exempt job-related accommodation. The employer pays the following expenses in 2018/19:

	£
Heating and lighting (electricity bills)	1,200
Gardening	800
Domestic help's wages	500
New furniture, to be used in the house, costing	10,000

Quentin's salary for the year 2018/19 is £45,000. He pays Terruno £300 towards the running costs of the house and £5,000 of occupational pension contributions.

Calculate the value of the benefit for 2018/19.

Solution: Quentin, Cash equivalent value accommodation benefit 2018/19

		£	£
i)	Annual value of property (exempted as job-related)		–
	Ancillary services:		
	Heating and lighting cost	1,200	
	Domestic help cost	500	
	Gardening cost	800	2,500
	Use of furniture 20% × 10,000		2,000
			4,500
	less employee contribution		(300)
	Ancillary use benefit on normal terms		4,200

Compare:	£
Quentin – Net assessable earnings (45,000 – 5,000)	40,000
× 10% =	4,000
Less employee contribution	(300)
Maximum assessable cash-equivalent benefit	3,700

Notes

(i) The restriction applies in this case, so the assessable benefit is £3,700.

(ii) The furniture is valued as an asset loaned to an employee, at 20% of its market value when first provided, i.e. £10,000. (This assumes that there was no existing loaned furniture in the house at the start of the tax year.)

(iii) If Quentin's occupation were non-exempt, the value of his total accommodation benefits would be the annual value, plus the other benefits, i.e. £1,000 plus £4,500, less the contribution of £300, giving £5,200.

7.20 Living accommodation costing more than £75,000 ('expensive accommodation')

An extra taxable accommodation benefit arises if an employer owns rather than rents the accommodation and it is 'expensive accommodation' as defined.

This rule was added to the Benefits Code to deal with arrangements that had been adopted in cities such as London where the official 'annual value' of properties had diverged below the market rents. Without this additional 'deemed loan' benefit an employer could reduce the taxable benefit significantly by buying property rather than renting it.

The extra benefit applies if:

(a) living accommodation is provided by reason of an office or employment, and

(b) the cost of providing the accommodation was greater than £75,000, and

(c) the occupier is liable to a taxable benefit in respect of the provision of the accommodation. So, if the employee is exempt from the 'annual value' charge as noted above, s/he is also exempted from the expensive accommodation charge.

(d) The additional value is determined as:
ORI % × [cost or deemed cost – £75,000] less employee 'contribution', where:

ORI percentage	=	the **official rate of interest** in force on the 6th April of the tax year. For 2018/19 it is 2.50%.
Cost	=	capital cost of acquisition of the property, + cost of any capital improvements completed before the beginning of the current tax year. If the property was acquired more than six tax years before its first occupation by the employee, then the market value on first occupation is taken as the 'cost of providing' the accommodation.
'Contribution'	=	the amount by which any rent paid by tenant exceeds the annual value of the accommodation.

The £75,000 definition above which accommodation is classed as 'expensive' has not been increased since this legislation was first introduced. Thus, the charge now applies to a lot of employer-owned accommodation.

Example

Jura plc acquired a property in October 2014 for £265,000 which had an annual value of £10,000. In May 2017 improvements costing £25,000 were made. On 7th April 2018, Zack, the marketing director, occupied the property paying Jura plc a rent of £5,000 p.a. He paid £15,000 towards the original cost.

Calculate the value of the accommodation benefit in kind for 2018/19.

Solution: Cash equivalent value of benefit 2018/19

	£	£
2018/19 value of accommodation benefit:		
Annual value of property	10,000	
Less rent paid by director	(5,000)	5,000
Additional value charge for accommodation:		
Cost of accommodation + improvements	290,000	
Part of cost paid by director	(15,000)	
= deemed loan to director	275,000	
Less exempt amount	(75,000)	
	200,000	
Less 'contribution'	0	
	200,000	
2.50% × 200,000 =		5,000
		10,000

Notes

(i) £10,000 is Zack's benefit chargeable to income tax for 2018/19. This will be reported on his Form P11D by his employer (see Chapter 8).

(ii) As the rent paid by Zack is less than the annual value, there is no further deduction for this rent in the computation of the additional value.

(iii) The official rate of interest on 6th April 2018 was 2.50%.

(iv) Additional value charge, within the total benefit, is 200,000 × 2.50% = £5,000.

(v) If a property is not occupied throughout the year the charge is pro-rated.

7.21 Assets other than cars – private use

Where assets are made available for use by employees, then the annual benefit is calculated as follows.

(a) Land and property (other than accommodation) is valued at a market rent.

(b) Other assets e.g. a company motor cycle, are valued at 20% of the original market value when provided, or if higher, the rental paid by the employer.

7.22 Assets transferred to an employee

If an asset made available on loan to an employee is subsequently acquired by that person, then the assessable benefit on the acquisition is the greater of:

(a) the excess of the current market price over the price paid by the employee and,

(b) the excess of the market value when first provided for use by the employee, less any amounts assessed as annual benefits (at 20%) over the price paid by the employee.

When employees buy, from their employers, a previously loaned computer or bicycle for its full market value, no tax charge arises on the transfer of ownership.

7.23 Beneficial loans

Where an individual is provided with an interest-free or cheap loan, the financial benefit derived from such an arrangement is taxable. This exemption allows employers to offer 'season ticket loans' or other convenience loans of a relatively small amount to employees without income tax consequences.

The following are the benefit measurement rules:

(a) A loan to an employee, or to his or her relative, giving rise to an interest saving is a benefit in kind if obtained due to an employment.

(b) The assessable amount is calculated by two methods, (see below) in both cases using the **official rate of interest** less any interest paid by the employee.
(ORI at the start of 2018/19 = 2.50%)

(c) No benefit arises where the interest on the loan would normally qualify for tax relief, such as a loan for the purchase of plant or machinery (apart from cars) for use in the employment.

(d) If the value of all the loans outstanding at any time during the year does not exceed £10,000, there will be no charge.

7.24 Methods of calculation: Average method

(a) This method averages the amount of the loan for the whole tax year by reference to the opening and closing balances at the beginning of the year (*or the date of first advance if later*) and at the end of the year, and applies the official rate to this amount.

(b) Any actual interest paid is deducted from the amount computed in (a), to determine the benefit to be taxed.

(c) This method is applied automatically, unless an election is made by either the taxpayer or HMRC, to apply the second (precise) method.

Example

Zamarra Ltd makes an interest-free loan to Rachel, an employee, on 1st October 2018 of £24,000. It is repayable by eight quarterly instalments of £3,000, payable on 1st January, April, July and October. The first repayment is made on 1st January 2019.

Calculate the assessable benefit for 2018/19. Assume the official rate of interest is 2.50%.

Solution: Computation of interest benefit

		£
1-Oct-2018	Loan granted	24,000
5-Apr-2019	Balance of loan outstanding	
	(24,000 – (2 × 3,000))	18,000
		42,000
	Average loan outstanding	
	$\frac{42,000}{2}$	21,000

Period of loan
1-Oct-2018 – 5-Apr-2019 = 6 months. (i.e. complete tax months)

Notional Interest $2.50\% \times \frac{6}{12} \times 21,000 =$	262.50
Actual interest	Nil
Assessable benefit	262.50

7.25 Methods of calculation: Alternative method

(a) Under this method, the interest is calculated on the balance outstanding on a daily basis, at the official rate of interest.

(b) Any interest paid is deducted from the amount calculated.

Example

Using the data relating to Zamarra Ltd in the previous example, calculate the assessable benefit under the alternative method.

Solution: Computation of interest benefit – 2018/19

		£	£
1st Oct 2018	Loan granted	24,000	
1st Jan 2019	Loan repayment	(3,000)	
		21,000	
	Number of days from 1st Oct 2018 to 1st Jan 2019 = 92		
	Interest 92/365 × 2.50% × 24,000		151
1st Jan 2019	Balance outstanding	21,000	
1st Apr 2019	Loan repayment	(3,000)	
5th Apr 2019	Balance outstanding	18,000	

		£
No. of days from	1st Jan 2019 to 1st Apr 2019 = 90	
No. of days from	1st Apr 2019 to 5th Apr 2019 = 5	
Interest	90/365 × 2.50% × 21,000	129
	5/365 × 2.50% × 18,000	6
Assessable benefit 2018/19		286

Given these figures, the taxpayer will not elect for the precise method.

7.26 Deductions from earnings

The following may be deducted as expenses of the employment under ITEPA, if they are not reimbursed by the employer. If they are reimbursed, they are simply exempt; meaning that the expense is not treated as an allowable expense, the reimbursement is not treated as employment income and there is no requirement to report them on the P11D.

(a) Expenses falling within the general rule of Section 336. This states that a deduction from earnings is allowed for an amount if:

  (i) the employee is obliged to incur and pay it as holder of the employment, and

  (ii) the amount is incurred wholly and exclusively and necessary for the performance of the duties of the office or employment; for example, industrial clothing; tools of trade.
  Travelling expenses from the employee's home to the employer's place of business are not permitted expenses of the employment, see Ricketts v Colquhoun 1926 10 TC 118.

(b) Travel and subsistence costs incurred on the employer's business. Current rules can be checked on the HMRC website but in summary are as follows:

  (i) Site-based employees are employees whose duties require them to report for duty at a succession of workplaces, with no one 'normal place of work'. They can receive tax relief for expenses incurred on travelling from home to the site and for reasonable subsistence costs incurred (eg lunches) while working at a temporary site. The tax relief need not be claimed if the employer reimburses the expenses and has obtained a P11D dispensation in respect of the expenses. If no P11D dispensation is held, the expense reimbursement is taxable earnings but is separately covered by the deduction claimed.

  (ii) employees who do have a normal place of work cannot normally treat home-to work travel as an expense of employment. However, they can receive tax relief (or can be reimbursed without any net taxable earnings being identified) for the cost of business journeys which start from home, if these are no longer than the equivalent business journey starting from work.

  (iii) employees who are seconded by their employer to a temporary place of work can receive tax relief for subsistence and travel to the temporary workplace, providing there is the intention to return to the normal place of work within two years.

(c) ITEPA also permits specific deductions for fees and subscriptions to professional bodies, and contributions to exempt approved pension schemes.

(d) Capital allowances on plant or machinery necessarily provided by the employee to perform his duties may be deducted as an allowable payment, e.g. on the cost of office equipment, but not a private car.

(e) Payroll giving to an approved charity or charitable agency is an allowable expense of employment.

7.27 Employee liabilities and indemnity insurance

Income tax relief is available to employees and directors for payments they make to obtain indemnity insurance against liability claims arising from their job or to meet uninsured work-related liabilities. Relief is also extended to situations where the employer or a third party pays the insurance, which will not give rise to any benefit in kind. The cost of the insurance, if paid by the employee, is deductible as an expense from the earnings of the year in which the payment is made. Relief is extended to payments made by ex-employees for periods of up to six years after the year in which employment ceases.

7.28 Employees' incidental expenses paid by employer

Payments by employers of certain miscellaneous personal expenses incurred by employees are exempt from income tax and NIC.

The exemption covers round-sum allowances paid by employers for incidental expenses such as newspapers, telephone calls home and laundry bills incurred by employees when they stay away from home overnight on business.

Payments of up to £5 a night in the UK (£10 outside the UK) are tax-free.

However, if the employer pays round-sum allowances (without requiring receipts) which exceed these limits, the whole amount paid becomes taxable.

7.29 Removal expenses and benefits

The amount that can be paid tax-free to an employee as qualifying removal expenses has been greatly restricted since the 1990s and now stands at £8,000.
This figure has not been increased for many years. The low limit means that in 2018/19 relocating employees who are adequately reimbursed for genuine removal costs may find that part of the payment is liable to tax.

Within this limit, any of the following removal expenses may be paid tax-free in connection with moving his or her home (for work reasons).

(a) sums paid to an employee, or to a third party on behalf of an employee in respect of qualifying removal expenses, and

(b) any qualifying removal benefit provided for the employee or to members of his or her family or household (including sons and daughters in law, servants, dependants and guests).

(I) Qualifying removal expenses comprise the following.

(1) Expenses of disposal, i.e. legal expenses, loan redemption penalties, estate agents' or auctioneers' fees, advertising costs, disconnection charges, and rent and maintenance, etc. costs during an unoccupied period in the employee's former residence.

(2) Expenses of acquisition i.e. legal expenses, procurement fees, survey fees, etc. relating to the acquisition by the employee of an interest in his or her new residence.

(3) Expenses of abortive acquisition.

(4) Expenses of transporting belongings, i.e. expenses, including insurance, temporary storage and disconnection and reconnection of appliances, connected with transporting domestic belongings of the employee and of members of his or her family or household from the former to the new residence.

(5) Travelling and subsistence expenses during the travelling journey (subsistence meaning food, drink and temporary accommodation).

(6) Bridging loan expenses, i.e. interest payable by the employee on a loan raised at least partly because there is a time gap between paying for the new residence and the receipt of the proceeds of the old residence.

(7) Duplicate expenses, i.e. net expenses incurred because of the change in the replacement of domestic goods used at the former residence but unsuitable for use at the new residence.

(II) Qualifying removal benefits consist of benefits or services corresponding to the seven headings noted above, with the restriction that the provision of a car or van for general private use is excluded from category 5 above.

7.30 Payments on termination of employment

The provisions on taxation of payments for loss of office or employment are now in Part 6 of ITEPA, and they include the following rules:

(a) The first £30,000 is exempt, so long as it is compensation for the fact of being redundant, or for the stress of losing office. If the latter, it is only tax-free if paid 'ex gratia' and not if paid under the employment contract.

Any excess 'compensation for loss of office' over £30,000 is taxed by statute as employment income, even if it is awarded for the pain and distress of losing the job, and not as payment for past services.

(b) A general exemption applies to payments made:
   (i) on the death or permanent disability of an employee;
   (ii) as benefits due under a pension scheme;
   (iii) as terminal payments to members of the armed forces.

(c) Termination payments and benefits are taxed as income in the year in which they are received rather than the year of termination.

(d) A loss-of-office payment made to an employee who is at or near to retirement age may be rejected by HMRC as not genuinely paid to compensate for the pain and distress of becoming unemployed: HMRC have been known to argue that such payment is in reality an unapproved lump-sum 'pension', and taxable in full when received.

Example

Nina is dismissed as a director of Troncal Limited on 1st October 2018 and receives the sum of £35,000 by way of compensation. No loss-of-office compensation was provided for in Nina's service agreement.

Nina's other income for 2018/19 is a salary of £38,000, and bank deposit interest of £4,000.

Calculate Nina's taxable income.

Solution:

	£	£
Income from employment		38,000
Terminal payment - employment	35,000	
Less exempt amount	(30,000)	5,000
Bank interest		4,000
Net income (£4,000 savings, £43,000 non-savings)		47,000
Less Personal allowance		(11,850)
Taxable income		35,150

7.31 Outplacement counselling

This involves services paid for by the employer, for employees who are or become redundant, to help them find new work. Expenditure on this is exempt from tax and does not count towards the £30,000 limit for redundancy payments.

7.32 Pension income

Any pension paid to a former employee is taxable as earned income on the recipient. This includes payments from company-operated schemes, from schemes operated by assurance companies, and voluntary payments where there is no formal pension scheme.

If an occupational pension scheme is approved by and registered with HMRC then any contributions made by the employee into the pension scheme are deductible from taxable earnings. The employer's contributions to an approved scheme are tax-free benefits of employment (*as well as being allowed as a remuneration expense for the employer - see Chapter 10*).

Pensions paid by the state are taxable as social security income of the recipient.

Other pensions are taxed as employment income.

7.33 State Pension

The State Pension (*including Additional State Pension for people reaching State Pension age before 6th April 2016, and including Graduated Retirement Benefit*) is subject to income tax.

The full rate of state pension for a single person based on adequate contributions from a 35-year working life is £8,546 (2017/18: £8,297).

7.34 Social security benefits

The following benefits are taxable under this heading:

- Bereavement allowance (*excluding the lump sum bereavement payment – see section 2.8*);
- Carer's allowance;
- Employment and Support Allowance (contribution-based);
- Jobseeker's allowance – contribution-based;
- Jobseeker's allowance – income-based;
- Statutory adoption pay;
- Statutory maternity pay;
- Statutory paternity pay;
- Statutory shared parental pay;
- Statutory sick pay;
- Widowed parent's allowance

Note non-taxable social security benefits are listed in Chapter 2 section 8.

7.35 Company share option plans (CSOPs)

The UK government's policy is to encourage participation by employees as shareholders in the employing group or company. To obtain HMRC approval a CSOP must be open to all permanent employees on similar terms.

Under these schemes, an employee is given the option to buy shares at a fixed price in future. Any discount which the option exercise price represents on the future market value will not be subject to income tax as a benefit in kind if certain conditions are met by the option contract. The main conditions are:

i) The option must be held for a minimum to maximum period (3 to 10 years) before it can be exercised,

ii) The exercise price of the share option is fixed at not less than the market value, at the time the employee gets his or her option.

iii) The share option must relate to part of the ordinary share capital of the company.

iv) Employee participants in the scheme must work at least 20 hours a week for the company, and full-time working directors must work at least 25 hours a week.

If the conditions are met, then there is no income tax liability on the grant of the option or on any increase in the value of the shares up to the date of exercise.

On an eventual disposal of the shares by the employee the normal rules of capital gains tax apply, and the cost for CGT is the price the employee paid for the shares, which is normally the exercise price of the options (but could include any cost paid for the options).

Approved schemes are not limited to quoted shares but include shares in any company which is not controlled by other companies. If the shares are not quoted, the relevant market values must be agreed with HMRC's Valuation Office Agency.

7.36 Enterprise management incentive share schemes (EMI)

The main features of these schemes are:

(a) unlike CSOPs, they can be restricted to key employees and still get approval;

(b) employees can hold options over shares which at the time of grant of the option(s) had a market value of up to £120,000 – share options acquired on different occasions over 3 years are all combined to apply this limit;

(c) to be eligible, employees must work for the employing company for at least 25 hours per week or, if less, for 75% of their working time;

(d) only trading companies with gross assets equal to or less than £30m can participate in the EMI scheme;

(e) there is no income tax liability on the grant of the option or on any increase in the value of the shares between grant and exercise, providing that the option is only exercisable, and actually exercised, at least three years and no more than ten years after the grant;

(f) on the eventual disposal of the shares, normal CGT rules apply.

7.37 Share incentive plans (SIPs)

The rules for these Plans enable a company to give an employee free SIP shares worth up to £3,000 per tax year (for which performance targets may be set) and enable an employee to buy further SIP shares worth up to £1,500 per tax year (called 'partnership shares') by deduction of the cost from salary.

SIP shares are allocated by trustees of the SIP to funds on behalf of named employees. The company may also give the employee up to two additional free SIP shares for each partnership share he or she has purchased. The terms on which free shares match partnership shares must be the same for all employees.

The employee in the SIP leaves all shares for a specified period after purchase if the value awarded by the employer is to be free of tax and national insurance. The amount of dividends on SIP shares that can be reinvested in the plan tax-free on a participant's behalf are £1,500 per year.

8 Income from employment II – PAYE

8.1 Introduction

The Pay As You Earn system of deducting income tax at source applies to monetary employment income (see Chapter 7) from offices or employments such as wages, salaries, bonuses, taxable expenses and pensions, as well as (from 6th April 2016) any taxable savings income. The system is operated by employers who collect the income tax on behalf of HMRC.

National Insurance contributions payable by employees on money earnings (see Chapter 17) are also collected under the PAYE system.

As well as an organisation being required to operate PAYE in respect of its employees, from 6th April 2017, where a 'personal services company' provides services in the **public sector**, then the public-sector body, agency or third party paying them will be treated as an employer and must deduct income tax and Class 1 National Insurance Contributions in the same way as they would for an employee. A 'personal services company' is a company which sells the services of an individual or a small group of individuals, who are owner-managers of the company. Note that this requirement does **not** apply to the provision of services to **private sector** organisations.

PAYE operates on a 'real time information' (RTI) system, requiring information of individual employees' pay amounts, tax and NI deducted, current PAYE code, and other records such as employees leaving.

This allows more in-year adjustments of PAYE codings to keep the cumulative tax collected accurate even when a worker's circumstances change during the year.

The PAYE system does not apply to self-employed individuals. However, there is a system of deducting tax from payments to subcontractors in the construction industry, known as CIS (the Construction Industry Scheme), which for the principal contractor has some similarities to PAYE including the payment dates for the tax.

8.2 Taxable pay

For the purposes of tax deduction, 'pay' includes the following:

(a) salaries, wages, fees, bonuses, overtime, commissions, pensions, honoraria, etc. whether paid weekly, monthly or irregularly

(b) holiday pay

(c) Christmas boxes or other seasonal bonuses paid as cash

(d) termination payments, to the extent not exempt (see Chapter 7)

(e) statutory sick pay and statutory maternity/paternity pay.

The income tax liability on non-cash benefits in kind is, as far as practicable, taken into account by adjustment of the employees' PAYE code for either that year or the following year (see below), rather than HMRC expecting significant tax to be paid on benefits by self-assessment.

8.3 Net pay arrangements

In calculating taxable pay, the employer deducts any contribution to a pension scheme on which the employee is entitled to relief from tax as an expense. The agreement applies only to pension schemes which have been approved by the HMRC Pension Schemes Office.

8.4 Code numbers

(a) All employees, including Directors and private pensioners, are allocated a PAYE code number for each relevant employment. This code number is based on the personal allowances, other income, and reliefs available to individuals, as evidenced by the information contained in their last Tax Return or by the PAYE information submitted by the employer. In appropriate cases the code number also takes into consideration other factors such as tax underpaid or overpaid in previous years.
The PAYE code number is equal to the sum of expected tax allowances and reliefs, less expected non-cash benefits for the year, divided by 10, rounded down.
Other non-employment income such as casual profits, property income, interest and untaxed State pensions may be recognised in the tax code number, if the employee consents.
The resulting tax code tells the employer the periodic (weekly or monthly) amount of tax-free income an employee may earn and therefore the level of salary or wages at which income tax must start to be deducted in the current employment.

(b) Some of the letters used at present after a code number are as follows:

L Basic personal allowance
Y Personal allowance for those born before 6 April 1938
K see 8.6

(c) The following special codes are also used:

BR This means that income tax is to be deducted from all pay at the basic rate. It is also called the 'emergency code', because employers use it temporarily while waiting for evidence of the correct code to be received from the employee or from HMRC.

F This code, followed by a number, means that the tax due on a social security benefit, e.g. retirement pension, or widow's pension or allowance, is to be collected from the taxpayer's earnings from an employment.

NT This means that no tax is to be deducted when making payments.

D This code followed by a number means that the pension / benefit is more than the allowances.

OT This means that no allowances are allocated against earnings from this employment. (Usually because there is another pension or employment, against which all allowances have been provisionally set.)

8.5 Deductions from allowances in code numbers

The following items may be deducted in arriving at the code number:

(a) State benefits or pension

(b) Income from property

(c) Unemployment benefit

(d) Untaxed interest

(e) Taxable expense allowances and benefits in kind

(f) 'Excessive basic rate' adjustment where too much tax is paid at the basic rate and not enough at the higher rate

(g) Savings or dividend income taxed at the higher rate

(h) Allowance restriction. This is to compensate for allowances and reliefs that are due in terms of tax, at a lower rate than the marginal rate, e.g. MCA.

(i) Tax underpaid in earlier years: under self-assessment the balancing amount due for last year by a PAYE taxpayer may be 'coded out' up to £2,000. (See Chapter 3)

8.6 K Codes

'K' codes arise where there is a negative coding allowance, which usually occurs where the non-PAYE income, e.g. accommodation benefits in kind, are greater than the total allowances due.

The excess number shown is added to the taxable pay and taxed accordingly.

8.7 Statutory sick pay (SSP) and private sick pay

Where private or statutory sick pay is paid by the employer when an employee is unfit for work, this is part of gross pay for the purposes of both income tax and National Insurance.

An employer can recover some of the SSP paid if the SSP payments for an income tax month exceed 13% of the Employer's Class 1 contributions for that month. See 17.8 for more on Statutory Sick Pay and National Insurance generally.

8.8 Payment of tax

Income tax and National Insurance contributions (employer's and employee's) are due for payment not later than the 19th day of each month. Thus, the tax and NIC due for period 8, 2018, which covers the period from 6th November to 5th December, is payable on or before the 19th December 2018.

Employers whose average monthly payments of PAYE and NIC are less than £1,500 in total may pay the tax quarterly. Payments are due on the following dates: 19th July, 19th October, 19th January and 19th April. Similar arrangements apply to contractors in the construction industry.

8.9 Bonus and commission payments - timing

As a general principle, taxable pay is assessed in the year in which it is paid under the rules of the ITEPA, as outlined in Chapter 7.

Thus, for example, where Justine has a salary of £30,000 for 2017/18 and earns a commission of an additional £5,000 for that year which is only ascertained and paid in July 2018, then the commission is assessable in the tax year 2018/19.

8.10 Directors' remuneration

The rules of taxation under ITEPA apply to directors and all other employees or office-holders. (See Chapter 7)

8.11 PAYE regulations

Regulations for the operation of PAYE are provided under Part II of the ITEPA and embodied in The Income Tax (PAYE) Regulations 2003 (S.1 2003/2682). Where failure to operate PAYE takes place it is the employer who is primarily responsible for making good any deficit, and an assessment subject to appeal may be issued for recovery of PAYE not paid over.

If the determined amount is not paid within 90 days, then the tax may be recovered from an employee/director. This can arise where the employee/director received his or her employment income from the employer, knowing that the employer had wilfully failed to deduct tax. In general, wilful failure means 'with intention or deliberate' – see R v IRC Chisholm 1981 STC 253.

In R v CIR ex parte Keys and Cook 1987 QB. DT. 25.5.87 the controlling directors of a company which failed to deduct income tax under the PAYE system from their own remuneration were held to be liable for that tax.

Student self-testing question

Question 8.1, Tabitha

Tabitha's P60 from Premio plc for the year 2018/19 shows total gross pay of £31,500. She lives in Wales, where she is employed as a sales manager with a salary of £22,000 p.a. for 2018/19. In addition, she receives commission paid by reference to the profits shown by the company's accounts, amounting to:

Year ended 31st December 2017	£9,500	– confirmed and paid June 2018
Year ended 31st December 2018	£13,000	– confirmed and paid June 2019

Tax deducted under PAYE for the year 2018/19, according to her P60, amounted to £3,930. Tabitha has no other income.

Compute Tabitha's Income Tax liability for 2018/19.

Solution to Question 8.1, Tabitha

Tabitha, Income tax computation 2018/19.

		£
Income from employment	- salary	22,000
	- commission paid June 2018	9,500
		31,500
Less Personal allowance		(11,850)
Tax liability:		19,650
		£
	19,650 @ 20%	3,930
Tax liability		3,930
Less paid by PAYE		(3,930)
Amount still payable		nil

9 Income from UK land and property

9.1 Introduction

This chapter deals with the rules applicable to UK Property income, together with computational examples.

9.2 Basis of charge

a) The definition of 'property business income' is: 'the annual profits or gains arising from any business carried on for the exploitation, as a source of rents or other receipts, of any estate interest, or rights in or over land in the UK'. Receipts in relation to land include:
   i) any payment in respect of any licence to occupy or otherwise use any land, or in respect of the exercise of any further right over land.
   ii) rent charges, ground annuals and any other annual payments derived from land.

b) The following are not taxed as property income, but as trade profits:
   i) Profits or gains from the occupation of any woodland managed on a commercial basis;
   ii) Farming and agriculture;
   iii) Mines, quarries and similar concerns;
   iv) Hotels, serviced apartments, or bed-and-breakfast businesses.

c) The letting of furnished accommodation without meals or additional services is taxed as property income, with no separate assessment for the furniture hire; but there are special rules for furnished holiday lettings, which can be treated as a kind of a trading business for limited purposes (see 9.12).

d) The letting of caravans on fixed sites and houseboats on fixed moorings is chargeable as property income, while the hire or leasing of mobile caravans and boats is a trade.

9.3 Basis of assessment

The basis of assessment is the annual profits or gains arising in the income tax year. It is not possible to use an 'accounts basis' of taxation for property income tax.

Therefore, the income tax basis period runs from 6 April to 5 April even if the letting business draws up its balance sheet at some other date for business reasons.

9.4 Computation of taxable profits of a 'property business'

a) All profits or gains are computed in accordance with the rules applicable to a trading business (i.e. normal commercial accounting principles).

b) All property situated in the UK is to be treated as one letting business regardless of the type of lease or whether it is furnished accommodation.

c) Any business expenditure incurred in earning the profits from letting is to be deducted from the total pooled income, and is subject to the same rules for allowable expenditure as apply to trading income.

d) Capital allowances available (see (e)) are given as an expense chargeable against property income, so that the assessable property profits are after capital allowances. A landlord need not claim the allowances available.

e) Capital allowances are not generally available for plant and machinery (e.g. furniture) located in a let dwelling house. Instead, expenditure on **replacements** of furniture, furnishings, appliances and kitchenware is treated as allowable expenditure where the replacement is substantially the same as the item being replaced. Except for furnished holiday lettings (see 9.12), capital allowances are only available for plant and machinery used for estate management or for property maintenance (e.g. office equipment, or a garden lawnmower).

f) For 2018/19, interest payable on a loan to acquire assets for a property business is allowed as a deduction in calculating the profits of the business, as follows:

- 50% of the interest will be treated as an expense in calculating the taxable property income;
- 50% of the interest will attract relief only at basic rate, calculated as 20% multiplied by the lower of:
  - the finance costs not deducted as an expense,
  - the profits of the property business in the tax year, and
  - the total non-savings, non-dividend income in excess of the landlord's Personal Allowance plus Blind Person's Allowance.

For 2019/20, the interest split will be 25% expense, 75% tax reduction at basic rate;

from 2020/21 onwards, all finance costs will be relieved as a basic rate tax reduction.

Rental business losses must in general be carried forward and set against future profits from the same rental business. Where there are capital allowances due in respect of the rental business, that part of the loss attributable to capital allowances may be set against total income of the year as an allowable payment. The rest of the loss, if any, must still be carried forward.

Expenses of properties let on uncommercial terms (for example, at a nominal rent to a relative) can only be deducted up to the amount of the rent or other receipts generated by the uncommercially let property. The excess of the expenses over the receipts from an uncommercially let property cannot be deducted in the rental business, and therefore cannot create a loss.

Example

Zena purchased a freehold factory site on 6th April 2018, which she lets for an annual rental of £15,000 payable quarterly in advance. The first payment due on 6th April 2018 covered the period to 5th July 2018. Property expenses paid by Zena for the year to 5th April 2019 amounted to £2,500 and interest paid on a loan to purchase the factory was £3,500.

Landlord's capital allowances for the 12 months to 5th April 2019 have been agreed at £2,000.

Required:

(a) Compute Zena's property business income for 2018/19;

(b) Calculate the amount by which her income tax liability will be reduced because of relief for the loan interest which may not be claimed as a deduction from property income.

Solution

(a) Zena's property business income

		£	£
Rents receivable	- let for 12 months for £15,000		15,000
Less expenses: -			
	Property expenses	2,500	
	Loan interest (50%)	1,750	(4,250)
Adjusted profit			10,750
Less capital allowances			(2,000)
Property business income			8,750

(b) Zena will obtain a basic rate tax reduction on 50% of the loan interest, i.e. £3,500 × 50% × 20% = £350.

Notes

i) Rental income is always computed on an accruals basis.

ii) Property business income is not 'trading income'.

9.5 Lease premiums

A lease premium is a capital payment paid to the landlord by the tenant at the inception of a lease. Historically, UK law viewed it as a different type of payment from rent. Until special income tax rules were passed in the 1950s lease premiums were not liable to tax as income of the landlord, even though they could often be seen as a capitalised substitute for all or part of the future rent payments. The special capital-revenue splitting rules enacted for lease premiums in 1956 remain in force, even though the accounting treatment of premiums has become less variable.

The income tax system treats lease premiums paid by the tenant for a lease for up to 50 years as partly a payment of rental income and partly a capital payment. The capital / revenue split for income tax depends on the length of the lease in whole years. A lease premium includes any sum whether payable to the immediate or a superior landlord, arising in connection with the granting of a lease, but not arising from an assignment to a new tenant of an existing lease, with consent of the landlord.

Under an assignment, the new tenant takes the position of the original tenant, with the same terms and conditions.

Where a lease is granted (but not assigned) at a premium, for a period not exceeding 50 years, then the landlord is deemed to be in receipt of a rental income equal to the premium, less an allowance of 2% of the premium for each complete year of the lease remaining, excluding the first 12-month period. This deduction recognises what tax law treats as the 'capital element' of the premium.

Example

Bradley granted a lease for 24 years of his warehouse to a trader on the following terms:
A lease premium of £120,000 to be paid on 1st May 2018 and an annual rent of £72,000 payable monthly in advance from 1st May 2018.
Bradley's allowable letting expenditure for the year 2018/19 was £58,000.

Solution: Bradley Property business income 2018/19

Year ended 5th April 2019:	£
Lease premium received – 24-year lease	120,000
Less capital element 2% × 120,000 × (24 – 1)	
i.e. $^1/_{50}$ × 120,000 × 23	(55,200)
= rental income received in premium	64,800
Add rent receivable (11 months) 72,000 × $^{11}/_{12}$	66,000
	130,800
Less allowable expenses	(58,000)
Assessable property business income	72,800

In effect the lease premium is discounted by reference to its duration, and the longer the unexpired portion, the greater the discount. Thus, if a lease had 49 years to run, the discount would be:

(49 – 1) × 2% i.e. 96%.

A premium on a lease for a period greater than 51 years would not be taxed as property income at all. If the lease premium is paid by instalments, the full amount, less the discount, is taxable in the usual way. However, if hardship can be proved, the landlord's income tax on a premium received may be paid over a period not exceeding 8 years.

9.6 Lease premiums and the lessee

Where the lessee pays a lease premium on the granting of a lease, a proportion of that premium may be set against the following:

a) any trading income, if the leased premises are used for business purposes;

   The amount of the premium assessed as income on the lessor can be claimed as a deemed rental expense of trading by the lessee, but the tax deduction is spread evenly over the remaining lease, as illustrated below in 9.7.

b) any rental income or lease premium received from any sub-lease granted by the lessee, as illustrated below in 9.8.

9.7 Example of notional rental claimed by the lessee

Sabrina is granted a lease of premises to be used for trading purposes, for a period of 20 years, at an annual rent of £6,000 p.a. and an initial lease premium of £32,000.

Computation of income element of total premium:	**£**
Lease premium	32,000
Less capital element: 2% × 32,000 × (20 – 1) i.e. 38% × 32,000	(12,160)
= Lease premium charged on lessor as rental income	19,840

Additional rental relief available to Sabrina can be claimed over 20 years

The notional rental to include in Sabrina's trade expenses is $\frac{19840}{20}$ i.e. £992 p.a.

This expense claim is in addition to Sabrina's actual rental expense, of £6,000 per year.

9.8 Sub-leases and assignments

The creation of a sub-lease out of a head-lease for a premium can give rise to an immediate income tax liability on part of the premium for the intermediate lessee; but complete assignment of the existing lease could not as any proceeds received for an assignment for that are capital proceeds potentially liable to Capital Gains Tax.

Where a charge to income tax has already arisen when a head-landlord granted a lease at a premium, and this is followed by the intermediate tenant granting a sub-lease at a premium, then any liability arising on the intermediate landlord can be reduced, as shown in the example below.

Example

Janet granted a lease for 20 years to Martin for a premium of £10,000. After occupying the premises for five years (not for business), Martin granted a sub-lease to Roberta for a period of 10 years, at a premium of £6,000.

Required:
Show the computation of Janet's and Martin's assessable lease premium income.

Solution: Computation of Janet's liability (5 years ago)

	£
Lease premium (20-year lease)	10,000
Less 2% × 10,000 × (20 – 1) i.e. 38% × 10,000	(3,800)
	6,200

Computation of Martin's liability (now)

	£
Lease premium received (10-year lease)	6,000
Less 2% × 6,000 × (10 – 1) i.e. 18% × 6,000	(1,080)
Income element of premium received	4,920

Martin can then deduct from this deemed rental income 10 years' worth of the amount assessed on Janet as deemed rental income when Martin signed the 20-years head-lease.

$$\text{M's assessable premium income} = 4{,}920 - \frac{\text{Duration of sub lease}}{\text{Duration of head lease}} \times (\text{premium assessed on J})$$

$$= 4{,}920 - [10/20 \times 6{,}200] = 1{,}820$$

The amount of the new lease premium assessed on Martin is therefore £1,820. Martin has been able to claim tax relief for half of the amount of the premium taxed on Janet.

The above calculations are independent of any periodic rental also receivable under the new sub-lease granted by Martin. That rent would be true (*not deemed*) property income of Martin, and measured on the accruals basis.

9.9 Furnished accommodation

Rents from furnished accommodation are assessed as property income.

The former 'wear-and-tear allowance' for furnished lets is no longer available from 6th April 2016 (1st April 2016 for corporations); instead expenditure on replacements of furniture, furnishings, appliances and kitchenware is treated as allowable expenditure where the replacement is substantially the same as the item being replaced.

See 9.12 for special rules on Furnished Holiday Lettings.

It is possible for furnished letting income to be taxed as trade profits where the taxpayer provides substantial services in connection with the letting e.g. meals, cleaning, laundry, and other services of a similar nature. This is deemed to be carrying on a trade.

9.10 Rent-a-room: tax-free letting income

For 2018/19 the income tax exemption continues which allows any householder (including those who do not own their home) to let a room or rooms in their own home for up to £7,500 p.a. tax-free, provided it is let as furnished accommodation, and does not have its own entrance. The rules work as follows:

a) Gross rents up to £7,500 p.a. are exempt.
b) Gross rents greater than £7,500 are taxable as follows:
   i) either pay tax on excess rent i.e. (rent minus £7,500);
   ii) or pay tax on gross rents less expenses.

A claim must be made in writing for the Rent-a-Room exemption within one year of the end of the tax year to which it is to apply. The self-assessment tax return includes a tick-box to claim the exemption. If joint householders let a room or rooms in the same home, the exemption limit is split equally between them.

9.11 Real Estate Investment Trusts (REITs)

As already noted in 6.5, dividends from REITs are treated on the self-assessment return and in the tax computation as property rental income of the period in which they are received.

9.12 Furnished Holiday Lettings

The property income from a special class of letting called 'furnished holiday letting' is subject to additional rules giving semi-'trading' treatments such as the ability to treat Furnished Holiday Lettings property as a business asset for capital taxes purposes (see Parts IV and V), and to treat FHL income as net relevant earnings for pension contributions (see Chapter 16).

Losses from FHL businesses used to be claimable as trade losses but this has been abolished. Now FHL losses must be carried forward and set against future profits from FHLs. They cannot be combined with profits from non-FHL lettings.

It is possible to claim plant and machinery capital allowances (see Chapter 10) on the furniture and kitchen appliances etc installed in a FHL property. This contrasts with the treatment of furniture in other furnished lettings, which is not eligible for capital allowances, though plant used to maintain, but not located in, the let property is so eligible.

In summary, to be a FHL source of income, the property must be available for short lets (*up to 31 days to different tenants*) for at least 210 days of the year and actually let for at least 105. It can however be let 'out of season' (*i.e. during the rest of the year that it is not on short letting*) for a longer let and will not thereby lose its status as a FHL property.

If you need to remember the letting conditions for your course, it might help to note that the availability number 210, pronounced as "two-ten", sounds like the name of one of the authors of this book; while the actually-let condition is half that amount.

To the extent that the taxpayer uses a FHL property sometimes for private use, all general expenses of the year and any capital allowances must be time apportioned to remove the private use period(s). Private use incudes use by family or friends who do not pay a market rent for the property. However, specific expenses related only to the holiday letting business (e.g. advertising) need not be apportioned.

9.13 Rent paid to non-residents

Where UK rental profits are paid to a non-resident landlord, basic rate income tax must be deducted at source from the rent payments and accounted for to HMRC, unless a registered UK letting agent handles the collection.

9.14 Property allowance

The Finance (No. 2) Act 2017 introduced a "property allowance" of £1,000.
If an individual has total property income below £1,000 (excluding rent-a-room), then their relevant property business profits or losses are treated as nil (unless they elect otherwise). In the descriptions that follow, references to "relevant property income" or "relevant property profits" should be taken to exclude income or profits from a rent-a-room property business.

If the individual has total relevant property income greater than £1,000, then they may calculate their relevant property profits for tax purposes as either:

- Taxable receipts minus allowable expenses (ie. calculation in the 'normal' way); or
- Taxable receipts minus £1,000. The legislation refers to this as 'partial relief', and an election must be made. The property allowance cannot be used to create or increase a loss.

Individuals can decide on a year-by-year basis which approach to take.

An individual is excluded from claiming the property allowance if one of the following exclusions applies:

- any part of their property income is received from:
  - their employer (or the employer of their spouse or civil partner); or
  - a firm in which they are a partner (or connected with a partner); or
  - a close company in which they are a participator (or an associate of a participator); or
- they have a business which qualifies for rent-a-room relief, but they have chosen to disapply it (ie. to claim actual expenses instead).

Student self-testing question

Question 9.1, Geta and Raj

(a) Geta rents out a room in her house. In 2018/19 she received rent of £8,500 and incurred allowable expenses of £2,000.

Requirement: Calculate the amount of Geta's assessable income from property for 2018/19 assuming any necessary election is made.

(2 marks)

(b) Raj owns three flats which he lets out.

Flat 1. The flat was purchased on 6th September 2018 and let unfurnished from 29th September 2018. The new seven-year lease was at an annual rental of £7,000 payable on the usual quarter days. The incoming tenant was required to pay a premium of £5,000.

Flat 2. The flat was let unfurnished at an annual rental of £8,000 on a lease which expired on 23rd June 2018, the rent having been paid on the usual quarter days. The property was re-let on 30th September 2018 on the same conditions at an annual rent of £8,500.

Flat 3. The flat was let furnished for the full year on a weekly rental of £200. No furniture, furnishings, appliances or kitchenware were replaced during the year.

The usual payment dates are 25th March, 24th June, 29th September and 25th December.

Details of expenditure in the year ended 5th April 2019 were:

	Flat 1	Flat 2	Flat 3
	£	£	£
Insurance	400	200	600
Repairs	4,500	600	350
Water rates	-	-	400
Council tax	-	-	800

Notes

1. The amount of £400 insurance for Flat 1 was an annual premium for 12 months' insurance commencing on 6th September 2018.
2. Repairs shown for Flat 1 above include £4,000 spent on UPVC double-glazing on 10th September 2018 replacing leaking wooden window frames. The windows needed to be repaired to make Flat 1 habitable.

Requirement

(b) Calculate Raj's profit from property for 2018/19. (8 marks)
Note: Calculations may be made to the nearest month.

(c) State how loss relief is given where the loss is in respect of property let unfurnished. (1 mark)

(Total: 11 marks)

Solution to Question 9.1, Geta and Raj

(a) Geta

		£
(i)	Ordinary basis	£
	Rent	8,500
	Expenses	(2,000)
		6,500
(ii)	Alternative basis	£
	Rent	8,500
	'Rent a room' limit	(7,500)
		1,000

Assessment of income from property (lower figure) £1,000

(b) Raj: Income from property 2018/19

		£	£
Rent receivable	- Flat 1		3,500 (W1)
	- Flat 2		6,250 (W2)
	- Flat 3		10,400
Premium on lease	- Flat 1		4,400 (W3)
			24,550
Insurance	- Flat 1	233 (W4)	
	- Flats 2&3	800	
Repairs	- Flat 1	500 (W5)	
	- Flats 2&3	950	
Water rates and council tax	- Flat 3	1,200	(3,683)
Property business income			20,867

Working 1

$^{6}/_{12} \times$ £7,000	£3,500

Working 2

$^{3}/_{12} \times$ £8,000	£2,000
$^{6}/_{12} \times$ £8,500	£4,250
	£6,250

Working 3

Premium	£5,000
less (7-1) × 2% × £5,000	(600)
	£4,400

Working 4

$^{7}/_{12} \times$ £400	£233

Working 5

As the replacement of the window frames was necessary before Flat 1 could be let, the expenditure is deemed to be capital and not, therefore, allowable as an expense.

(c) If the expenses of letting property in a tax year exceed the income from property, the excess is carried forward to be set against the first available income from letting property in the future.

Question without answer

Question 9.2, Arthur Cook

Arthur Cook has two shops for unfurnished letting.

Shop 1. The annual rent was £4,500 on a lease which expired on 30th June 2018. Arthur took advantage of the shop being empty to carry out repairs and decorating. The shop was let to another tenant on a five-year lease at £6,000 per annum from 1st October 2018.

Shop 2. The shop was purchased on 10th April 2018 and required treatment to wood damaged by dry-rot before it could be let out. Arthur also undertook some normal re-decorating work before the shop was let on 1st October 2018 on a seven-year lease, at an annual rental of £6,000. A premium of £2,000 was received from the incoming tenant upon signing the lease on 1st October 2018.

The rent for both shops was due quarterly in advance on 25th March, 24th June, 29th September and 25th December.

The following expenditure was incurred for 2018/19:

	Shop 1	Shop 2
	£	£
Insurance	190	300
Repairs and decorating	3,900 (1) (Note 1)	5,000 (2) (Note 2)
Accountancy	260	290
Advertising for tenant	100	100

Notes:

(1) Includes £2,500 for re-roofing the shop following gale damage in February 2018. Because the roof had been badly maintained the insurance company refused to pay for the repair work.

(2) Includes £3,000 for remedial treatment to dry-rot damaged wood flooring discovered when the shop was bought. The floor needed to be repaired before the shop could be let out.

Requirement: Calculate the income assessable on Arthur for 2018/19 from the shops and explain how any losses would be dealt with.
(ACCA updated)

10 Income taxed as trade profits: I - general principles

10.1 Introduction

This chapter covers the measurement of the tax-assessable trading profits of an unincorporated business. The legislation and some of the case law and concessionary practice on this area was revised by ITTOIA 2005. A list of the main topic headings in this chapter is followed by an analysis of the main principles of tax law and practice coming under each heading. Questions and answers illustrating the adjustment of profit for tax purposes appear at the end of the chapter.

The 'basis period' rules for matching unincorporated trade profits to tax years are dealt with in the next two chapters. These basis period rules apply only to unincorporated traders, as companies have their own rules (see part III).

However, most of the principles discussed in this chapter, on determining trade profits, apply to both unincorporated and incorporated trades. If a rule differs when the trader is a company, the company rule is briefly noted here, then given more detailed coverage in Chapter 19 on corporation tax. In other cases, the trade profits rules may be assumed the same for sole traders, partnerships and companies. This chapter is therefore also relevant to answering exam questions on the trading profits of companies (see Part III for corporation tax in general).
Since 2013/14 an optional 'cash' or 'receipts and payments' basis of accounting for profit has been available for the smallest businesses, with turnover below the VAT registration threshold.

10.2 List of topic headings

Charge to tax on trade profits
The concept of trading
Simpler income tax for the simplest small businesses
Principles in computing profits of a trade
Capital receipts
General rules restricting deductions
Allowable expenditure
Non-allowable expenditure
Asset values for tax purposes
Other adjustment of profits

10.3 Charge to tax on trade profits

Income derived from a trade in the form of profits is chargeable to income tax where the trade is conducted by an individual, either as a sole trader or in partnership with someone else. Where the trade is undertaken by an incorporated person, typically a company, trade profits form part of the total taxable profit charged to corporation tax, not income tax.

> **Tax** under this heading is charged on the full amount of the profits or gains arising or accruing to any person residing in the UK from any trade, profession or vocation, whether carried on in the UK or elsewhere.
>
> **Trade** is defined to include any 'manufacture, adventure, or concern in the nature of trade'. All farming and market gardening in the UK are treated as carrying on a trade.

10.4 The concept of trading

As Lord Wilberforce pointed out in the case of Ransome v Higgs 1974 STC 539 'everyone is supposed to know what trade means so Parliament, which wrote this into the law in 1799, has wisely abstained from defining it'.

The Royal Commission on the Taxation of Profits and Income in 1955 looked at all the case law up to that time and listed 'six badges of trade' that are still used by the courts and HMRC in determining what is a trade, or an 'adventure in the nature of trade'. These are:

a) the subject matter of the realisation
b) the length of the period of ownership
c) the frequency or number of similar transactions by the same person
d) supplementary work on or in connection with the property realised
e) the circumstances that were responsible for the realisation
f) motive.

10.5 The meaning of 'trade'

The present day meaning of 'trade' must therefore be deduced from a mixture of previous and subsequent legal decisions, accepted practice and the 'badges of trade'.

The following is a summary of some general points.

a) Betting and gambling are not regarded as trading unless carried on by an authorised bookmaker. This is in HMRC's interest as statistically more losses than profits are made by gamblers.

b) The fact that a trade is illegal does not mean that it is not taxable.

c) Even where transactions are concluded within a year they may nevertheless be regarded as 'annual profits or gains'. See Martin v Lowry 1926 11 TC 297.

d) Isolated transactions can amount to trading if they are of a commercial nature. See Wisdom v Chamberlain 1968 45 TC 92 (buying gold bars short-term for profitable resale, using borrowed money, was a trade); and Rutledge v CIR 1929 14 TC 490 (buying far more toilet rolls than could possibly be needed for personal use suggested a commercial intention to resell them at a profit).

e) All farming and market gardening carried on in the UK is treated as a trade.

f) Changes in the activities or customer sector of a trade may amount to the establishment of a separate and different trade for tax purposes.

10.6 Simpler income tax for the simplest small businesses

Businesses with turnover up to £150,000 (as set by The Income Tax (Relevant Maximum for Calculating Trade Profits on the Cash Basis) Order, SI 2017/293) have the option to use a simplified method to work out their taxable profit. The simple method is based on money in and money out recording (the cash basis) rather than accounts prepared using the accruals basis required by normal generally accepted accounting principles, or practice (GAAP). They do not have to adjust for receivables, payables or inventory. Business receipts and payments are not generally distinguished between 'revenue' and 'capital' as they are in the paragraphs that follow, except that capital allowances (see Chapter 13) will still be applied to cars. Once registered, a business can stay in the scheme until their total business turnover reaches £300,000.

A person who has both trading income and property income may claim both the trading allowance and the property allowance referred to in section 9.2, if their levels of trading income and property income are sufficiently small.

10.7 Principles in computing profits of a trade

The detailed rules on what is included and excluded when calculating the profits of a trade are complicated and established by a variety of sources. However, some general principles in deciding whether an item is recognised in the calculation of trading profits may usually be seen operating in the detailed rules in the following ways:

- Recurring, day to day 'revenue' income and expenditure is recognised; but 'capital' transactions of acquisition or disposal of non-current (fixed) assets are not.
- Expenditure with a business purpose is recognised; but non-business expenditure is not.
- Expenses of running a business are a recognised deduction in calculating the value of trading profit; but appropriations of profits by the proprietor are not.

10.8 Capital receipts

Profits arising from 'capital transactions' are in principle not trade profits, although they may be taxable under some other tax, typically capital gains tax. A profit on the disposal of a fixed asset by an unincorporated business is not therefore subject to income tax, and conversely, the loss is not allowed as a business expense. Companies are treated differently from unincorporated businesses in respect of some such capital receipts – e.g. on sale of a trade intangible asset, the net profit or loss is a revenue item for corporation tax.

Where a person receives a sum of money which is paid under a legal obligation, in return for goods or services provided in the normal course of trade, this is clearly a trading transaction. However, where the receipt does not arise from any contractual obligation, and the person has given nothing in return, then it may be accepted as a non-taxable receipt. Some such transactions are considered below.

Foreign exchange profits and losses

For individuals, exchange profits arising from trading transactions are potentially chargeable to income tax, whereas those relating to capital or non-trading transactions will not be chargeable.

For companies all foreign currency exchange gains and losses fall under the corporation tax loan relationships rules and are thus part of the companies' total taxable profits for corporation tax. For a company, it is a trading loan relationship if the foreign currency was held for trading, and a non-trade loan relationship (but still not 'capital') if the foreign currency was held for investment.

Insurance claims

Insurance compensation received in connection with damage or loss to a fixed asset is not taxable as a trading receipt; it may be subject to CGT treatment instead. Claims for loss of profits under personal accident insurance, and claims relating to any loss suffered on a current asset, such as destroyed inventory, are taxable as trading receipts.

Damage compensation and voluntary payments

If these transactions arise in the ordinary course of a trade, then they are taxable on the recipient. If they are voluntary ex gratia payments, arising outside the domain of trading, then they are generally not taxable for the recipient or deductible by the payer.

10.9 General rules restricting deductions in computing profits of a trade (ITTOIA)

a) **First rule**: In calculating the profits of a trade, no deduction is allowed for items of a **capital** nature.

The concept of materiality applied by accounting standards is not formally incorporated into tax law and this causes differences when the question arises of whether to capitalise or expense certain regular purchases which may individually last the business for more than one year.

While an acceptable division between capital and revenue can normally be drawn on accounting principles, it does not follow that the accounting treatment is always conclusive for tax purposes as to what is definitely 'capital' and what is not. Case law has supplied most of the guidance on this matter, and the words of Viscount Cave in Atherton v British Insulated and Helsby Cables Ltd 1925 10 TC 155, are the most frequently quoted:

> 'when an expenditure is made not only once and for all but with a view to bringing into existence an asset, or an advantage for the **enduring benefit** of a trade, I think that there is a very good reason for treating such expenditure as properly attributable not to revenue, but to capital'.

b) **Second rule**

1) In calculating the profits of a trade, no deduction is allowed for:

   a) expenses not incurred **wholly and exclusively** for the purposes of the trade, or

   b) losses not connected with or arising out of the trade.

2) If an expense is incurred for more than one purpose, subsection (1) does not prohibit a deduction for the identifiable part or proportion of the expense which is incurred wholly and exclusively for the purposes of trade.

The following Court decisions provide some idea of the importance and range of the two important statutory rules noted above.

1. **Associated Portland Cement Manufacturers Ltd v Kerr 1946** 27 TC 103. Payments to retiring directors in consideration of covenants not to carry on a similar business in competition with the company were held to be capital, because they affected the longer-term future.

2. **The Law Shipping Co. Ltd v IRC** 1924 12 TC 103. 'Repair' expenditure required after purchase of a ship, necessary to enable it to be used as a profit-earning asset, was held to be capital expenditure and not 'repairs' for tax purposes.

3. **Odeon Associated Theatres Ltd v Jones 1972** 48 TC 257. Repair expenditure incurred some time after the purchase of a cinema was held to be an allowable repairs expense for tax. A significant point was that the

cinema had been successfully used for trading whilst in a state of disrepair during wartime conditions.

4. **Strong & Co (Romsey) Ltd v Woodfield 1906** 5 TC 215. Damages and costs of injuries to a guest, caused by a falling chimney were held to be non-revenue expenditure. This case would be unlikely to be decided in the same way today, due to occupier's liability laws, but it still contains judicial comments about the extent of a trading activity.

5. **Morgan v Tate & Lyle Ltd 1954** 35 TC 367. Expenses incurred to prevent the nationalisation of the sugar industry were held to be allowable deductions for a sugar refiner. This case is the exception to the rule that donations to political parties or campaigns are generally not accepted as allowable or trade-related.

6. **Copeman v Flood (William) & Sons Ltd 1941** 24 TC 53. Sums paid as director's remuneration are not necessarily expended wholly and exclusively for the purposes of trade, if the director is carrying out non-trade duties.

7. **ECC Quarries Ltd v Watkins 1975** STC 578. Abortive expenditure on planning permission was held to be capital expenditure hence not deductible against profits. (Moreover, it was not deductible as a cost for capital gains tax, because the planning permission was never obtained.)

8. **Tucker v Granada Motorway Services Ltd 1979** STC 393. A sum paid to a landlord to secure a favourable change in the formula for determining profit-related rents for the lease of a service station was held to be capital, because it affected many future years of the service station business, and the lease was viewed by the court as a capital interest in the property.

9. **C.S. Robinson v Scott Bader Co. Ltd 1980** STC 241. The salary, expenses and social costs of an employee, seconded to a foreign subsidiary, were held to be allowable trading expenses of the parent company.

10. **Dollar v Lyons 1981** STC 333. Payments made to a farmer's children for working on the farm were held to be pocket money, and not an allowable trading expense. It was significant that the children were too young to be legal employees of the farm.

10.10 Allowable expenditure – a summary

Subject to the general principles noted above, the following is a list of the most common items of expenditure that are allowed as an expense in computing taxable trading income. Except where noted otherwise, accruals accounting under UK or International GAAP applies. Some of these items are open, in the case of an individual trader or partnership, to proportionate disallowance for 'private use' under the 'wholly and exclusively' rule.

1. Advertising and promotional expenditure.
2. Bad and doubtful debts expenses; see below.

3. Cost of materials, components and goods purchased for resale.
4. Ex gratia payments and compensation for loss of office.
5. Flood defences - Contributions to partnership funding schemes for flood defences (see 10.21)
6. Fuel and power.
7. Gifts to educational establishments.
8. Hire purchase interest.
9. Incidental costs of obtaining loan finance; see below.
10. Insurance of assets, employees, goods etc.
11. Interest on bank loans and overdrafts, so long as the borrowing is wholly for trading purposes.
12. Interest on late paid tax and VAT is deductible for companies, but not for sole traders or partnerships.
13. Leasing payments (except leasing high emissions cars, see 13.18).
14. Legal expenses arising from trading, such as debt collection, see below.
15. Losses and defalcations of employees, except senior managers, see 10.20.
16. Patent renewal fees and expenses, see below.
17. Penalty payments for late delivery of goods.
18. Pension contributions to approved schemes – not deductible on an accounting basis, but rather based on what was actually paid in the year (see also 10.23).
19. Pre-trading expenditure of a revenue nature, incurred up to seven years before trading.
20. Printing and stationery.
21. Professional charges such as audit fees and consultancy charges, but not those ancillary to the acquisition of a non-current (fixed) asset.
22. Redundancy payments.
23. Rent business rates and telecommunication expenses.
24. Repairs and renewals; see below.
25. Research and Development expenditure (companies only) obtains special deductions: small or medium sized companies (according to EU definitions) may claim a 'super-deduction' of 230% of the expenditure (in other words, the allowable expense for tax purposes is 2.3 times the actual expenditure incurred). Large companies may not claim a super-deduction, but instead are able to claim from HMRC a (taxable) RDEC (Research and Development Expenditure Credit) calculated at 12% of the amount of qualifying research and development expenditure (so worth 9.72% after Corporation Tax at 19%). See Chapter 19.
26. Subscriptions and donations; see also 10.12 and 10.23.
27. Training expenditure incurred by an employer for staff. Where the trader is self-employed and incurs training expenditure for himself or herself, further questions must be asked about duality of purpose.
28. Travelling and accommodation expenses for business purposes, e.g. sales representatives, trade fairs and conferences.
29. Vehicle and aircraft running and maintenance expenses.
30. Wages and salaries, and employer's NI.
31. Waste disposal.
32. Welfare expenditure for employees.

10.11 Non-allowable expenditure – a summary

The following is a list of the most common items of expenditure that are not generally allowed as an expense in computing trading income.

1. Depreciation of, and losses on disposals of, property, plant and equipment. (Companies may deduct amortisation of some intangible assets; see Chapter 19).
2. Professional charges concerned with a taxation appeal.
3. General provisions against future expenditure such as those for doubtful debts, pension schemes, furnace relining, or for preventive maintenance. These costs are however potentially allowable once actually paid, i.e. when the provision set up in the accounts is applied.
4. Legal expenses on the acquisition of a capital asset.
5. Entertainment, except staff functions.
6. Losses and defalcations by directors.
7. Repairs which involve any improvement, or amount to a complete or substantial renewal.
8. Fines for illegal acts (except parking fines of employees in junior positions when on business, eg van delivery drivers: these fines may be reimbursed to the employees and claimed as an allowable business expense. The same rule does not apply to parking fines of business proprietors or directors).
9. Political donations (see exception in Tate and Lyle case, section 10.9).
10. Non-trading losses or non-trade costs of any kind.
11. Tax penalties for tax defaults (distinguish this from interest on late-paid tax, which is allowable for companies but not for sole traders or partnerships)
12. Surcharges arising from VAT late payments or returns (see part V).
13. Unpaid staff remuneration paid more than 9 months after an accounting date may only be deducted against profits once actually paid.
14. Council tax of proprietors or partners and other personal expenses of the same.
15. Crime-related payments – blackmail or extortion.
16. Criminal bribes paid either in the UK or overseas.

10.12 Business entertainment and gifts

Entertaining expenses are not allowed unless they are incurred for the entertainment of one's own staff, and this must be the main purpose of the function and not merely incidental to the provision of hospitality to others (e.g. clients).

Where an employer bears the cost of an annual Christmas party, or similar function such as a staff dinner and dance, which is open to the staff generally, then HMRC will not tax the staff on the benefit in kind, until it exceeds £150 per annum for each employee. Entertaining within this permitted limit need not be included on the employee's form P11D (see Chapter 8). In theory there is no limit to the amount of staff entertaining allowed to the employer as a business expense, but it will be taxed on the staff as earnings if it exceeds the annual exempt benefit limit.

Gifts of any kind given by way of entertainment are also disallowed, except small business gifts which:

a) carry a prominent advertisement;

b) are not food, drink or tobacco;

c) do not amount in value to more than £50 per person per year.

Modest donations or gifts to local charities or recreational associations are allowed, if they are incurred 'wholly and exclusively for the purposes of trade'.

This suggests that they must not be anonymous but must promote the business name or product.

10.13 Repairs and renewals

Improvements to premises are not allowable expenses, but repairs occasioned by normal wear and tear would be deductible. Repair is not defined but has been held to amount to 'restoration or replacement of subsidiary parts', whereas a renewal is the reconstruction of the entirety, meaning not the whole but substantially the whole. A renewal would therefore be regarded as capital expenditure and not allowed as a trading expense. As noted in the Odeon Theatre case above, repairs to newly acquired premises, necessary to make them usable, would also be disallowed.

10.14 Patent fees and expenses

Deduction as an expense is allowed for any fees paid or expense incurred in obtaining for the purposes of a trade:

a) the grant of a patent or extension of a patent period

b) the registration of a design or trade mark.

Expenditure on any abandoned or rejected application for a patent is also allowable.

10.15 Bad and doubtful debts (impairment of receivables)

Bad debts already proved to be irrecoverable are allowed as a deduction, and doubtful debts are also allowed, in so far as they are specifically and reasonably expected to go bad. Thus, a provision for specific bad debts is allowable, but a general provision based on some overall percentage of outstanding debtors, without any detailed consideration of the specific balances, is not allowable for tax purposes, as it is considered unreliable and potentially subject to manipulation.

Where a debt is incurred outside the trading activities of the business, e.g. loans to employees written off, then any loss arising will not be allowable. This would also apply to any bad debts arising from the sale of any fixed assets.

Any bad debts recovered are treated as trading receipts when received.

10.16 Pension scheme contributions

Sums paid to an approved retirement benefits (pension) scheme by an employer are allowed as a deduction. Approved in this sense means by the HMRC Office which deals with the approval of all schemes. The sums must be actually paid, not just accrued or set aside for future payment.

10.17 Redundancy payments / outplacement counselling

Payments made to employees under the Employment Rights Act 1996 are permitted deductions, and any rebates received are taxable as trading income. Payments made outside the provisions of the Act are also generally allowed.

10.18 Training costs

Expenditure on staff training related to the trade is allowable as a business expense. Expenditure by employers on training for new skills for employees who are about to leave, or those who have already left, is also allowed as a trading expense, if not already so treated. (This complements the outplacement counselling allowance.)

10.19 Legal expenses

Legal charges incurred in maintaining existing trading rights are allowable, and this would include costs of debt (receivables) recovery, settling disputes, preparation of service agreements, and defence of title to business property, and damages and costs arising from the normal course of trade.

As already noted, legal costs incurred in contesting an income tax appeal were held to be not allowable. However, accounting and legal expenses incurred in seeking taxation advice on matters relating to trading activities would normally be allowed.

Expenses concerned with the acquisition of an asset would not be allowed, but those arising in connection with the renewal (not acquisition) of a short lease (i.e. less than 50 years) are permitted.

The legal and professional costs of raising or altering any share capital of a company are disallowed, but costs relating to issuing loan capital are permitted as 'incidental costs of obtaining loan finance'.

10.20 Losses and defalcations

Any loss not arising from the trade, or not incurred wholly and exclusively for the purposes of trade, will not be allowable as a deduction in computing taxable profits.

Two categories give substance to this principle and indicate types of loss which are not deductible:

a) Any loss not connected with or arising out of the trade, profession or vocation.

b) Any sum recoverable under an insurance or contract of indemnity.

Regarding losses arising from the sorts of risks that are usually insured against such as fire, burglary, accident or loss of profits, then the loss sustained is allowable if arising from the trade, e.g. loss of stocks (inventory), and any compensation received must be treated as a trading receipt.

Where assets are involved then any loss arising would be of a capital nature and not allowable as a deductible expense.

Losses arising from defalcations or embezzlement by an employee would normally be allowable, but defalcations by a person having control over the business would not. See Curtis v Oldfield J & G Ltd 1925 9 TC 319.

10.21 Flood defence relief schemes

Contributions made from 1st January 2015 to partnership funding schemes for flood defences are deductible.

10.22 Post-cessation expenditure

For payments made in connection with a trade that has been permanently discontinued, relief is available for payments made wholly and exclusively

a) in remedying defective work done, goods supplied, or services rendered

b) in meeting legal and professional charges.

The relief is available within seven years of the discontinuance for self-employed individuals.

Relief is given primarily against an individual's total income for the year; but where this is insufficient, it may be set against any chargeable gains for that year.

10.23 Miscellaneous items

Unpaid remuneration

In calculating the profits of a trade, no deduction is allowed for employees' remuneration paid more than 9 months after the end of the period of account. A deduction is given instead in the period when the remuneration is paid.

Apart from this, all bona fide salaries to employees and directors, including commissions and bonuses, and including amounts paid after the period-end but accrued for at the period-end, are allowable if they are incurred for the purposes of trade. See Copeman v Flood 1941 24 TC 53.

Unpaid pension contributions

However, pension schemes contributions by employers are not allowed against trade profits as a deduction on an accruals basis. These may only be claimed as an expense once the cash has been paid to the scheme. There is a logical reason for this rule: the technicalities of accounting for employers pension contributions may be seen from a tax point of view as akin to 'general provisions'; also, the funds once paid to an approved pension scheme are in a tax-free growth vehicle (see Chapter 16), so HMRC will not give tax relief on the expense until funds have actually been transferred.

Subscriptions and donations

Subscriptions to trade associations or other bodies for the purposes of trade are allowable, but not those unconnected with trade, or involving entertainment.

Where the payment is for the benefit or welfare of employees it will usually be allowed, e.g. a donation to a hospital or convalescent home which is used by employees of the firm. Gifts to registered charities are allowed if made for the purposes of trade.

Where a donation is structured as a Gift Aid payment then it is not recognised as a business expense, and the taxpayer receives relief through another method (see 5.5).

Employees seconded to charities

When an employer seconds an employee temporarily to a charity, then any expenditure attributable to that employment by the employer is deductible as a business expense.

Costs of obtaining loan finance (rules for companies)

Incidental costs of obtaining loan finance (including convertible loan stock) are allowed as a deduction in computing trading income of a company, and this includes fees, commissions, advertising, printing and stationery (eg a debenture prospectus). This is a statutory deduction. By contrast any incidental costs of raising new equity finance for a company (even under EIS – see Chapter 6) are disallowable as capital costs.

Pre-trading expenses

Expenses incurred within seven years prior to the actual commencement of a trade is allowed as a trading expense of the first period of trading, if the expenditure would have been allowed as a trading expense had trading already been going on during that period. See also Chapter 14.

Gifts to educational establishments

Where a person carrying on a trade, profession or vocation makes a gift of business plant and machinery to an educational establishment, the proceeds of sale can be treated as zero. Thus, there is no loss of capital allowances.

Capital allowances

Capital allowances are claimed and deducted from the adjusted trade profits for the purposes of computing the net trade profits. See Chapter 13.

Simplified expenses

Unincorporated small business owners may choose to adjust, on a simplified flat rate basis: motoring expenses, business use of home and private use of business premises. The appropriate rates are:

Expenditure on motor vehicles -

First 10,000 miles at 45p per mile,
Excess over 10,000 miles at 25p per mile;

Expenses for use of home for business purposes –

25 to 50 hours a month at £10 a month,
51 to 100 hours a month at £18 a month,
Over 101 hours a month at £26 a month;

The flat rate expenses for use of home are to cover the costs of light power telephone and broadband. Additional expenses for council tax, insurance and mortgage interest may be recognised where an identifiable portion is available for business use.

Flat rate benefit from the private use of business premises may be used to measure the benefit from the non-business portion of expenditure on household services, rent utilities and food, in businesses such as guesthouses and small nursing homes:

1 person £350 a month,
2 people £500 a month,
3 or more people £650 a month.

The rate does not include council tax, mortgage interest or business rates.

10.24 Asset values for tax purposes

Property, Plant and Equipment

Non-current assets such as land and buildings or plant and machinery, fixtures and fittings etc, do not usually affect the determination of taxable trading income, except where the cost of an asset is charged against income, or in so far as there is a depreciation expense. In the former case, the cost would be disallowed as capital, whether or not capital allowances were available. Depreciation expenses are not allowed as business expenses, however computed.

Where a short lease of property is acquired by the taxpayer on payment of a premium, and the property is used for purposes of the trade, then an extra allowance based on the notional rental element of the premium is available, but must be spread over the lease term. See Chapter 9.

Intangible assets

Under this heading are included goodwill, patents and trademarks, licences of intellectual property, copyrights and know how. In the hands of an unincorporated trader these are viewed as capital assets and may give rise to a claim for capital allowances, see Chapter 13.

Different rules for the tax treatment of Intangible Fixed Assets (other than leases of premises) apply to companies, as explained in Chapter 19. Amortisation of patents, licences, purchased goodwill etc. may be deductible for a company on certain conditions.

Long-term investments

Long-term investments held as non-current assets do not give rise to any problems as they are normally non-trading assets, and any surpluses or deficits arising from annual revaluations are not brought into the computation of taxable income. Realisations would require capital gains tax consideration, however. For companies the 'loan relationships' regime, and not the chargeable gains regime, applies to any fixed or current assets defined as a loan relationship. See Chapter 19.

Where the investments are trading assets then they will be valued on the same basis as other current assets.

Current assets

Current assets held by a business for the purposes of its trade would normally be valued for accounts purposes at the lower of cost or net realisable value. The same principles are applied for taxation purposes, but there are some special factors relating to inventories.

Inventories

The following is a summary of the valuation of inventory and work-in-progress in a tax context.

1. In the absence of statutory authority inventories should be measured at the lower of cost or net realisable value. Net realisable value means selling price less selling expenses, and not replacement cost. See CIR v Cock Russell & Co. Ltd 1949 29 TC 287: BSC Footwear Ltd v Ridgway 1971 47 TC 495.

   Under the International Accounting Standard 2 (IAS 2), mandatory for UK listed companies from 1 January 2005, inventory needs to be measured in the financial statements at the lower of cost and net realisable value (NRV).

2. Consistency of method of valuation does not of itself guarantee that a correct method of valuation has been used. See BSC Footwear v Ridgway case noted above.

3. Overhead expenditure does not have to be included in the valuation of work in progress or finished stocks for tax purposes, even if this is done for accounting purposes. See Duple Motor Bodies v Ostime 1961 39 TC 537.
4. Standard cost values may be used but due allowance for variances from the standard must be made where they are material.
5. In general, neither the base stock method nor the LIFO method of stock valuation is an acceptable method of inventory valuation for tax purposes. See Patrick v Broadstone Mills Ltd 1953 35 TC 44; Minister of National Revenue v Anaconda American Brass Ltd 1956 AC.

   The LIFO method of valuation is also prohibited for accounts of listed companies under IAS 2.
6. Where there is a change in the method of inventory valuation from one valid basis to another, then the opening and closing stocks in the current period must both be valued on the same basis. A valid basis of valuation is one which does not violate the tax statutes as interpreted by the Courts, and which is recognised by the accounting profession.
7. Where a trade is discontinued, its stock must be valued at an open market price, or if sold to another trader, at realised selling price.

   Where the trade is discontinued, stock that is sold must be valued on an 'arm's length basis' if the purchaser and the vendor are connected persons.
8. Professional work in progress (e.g. solicitors' or accountants' professional work already completed, but unbilled) must be valued at recoverable selling price in the closing balance sheet, unless the receipt of fees is uncertain at the year-end. This recognises profit on the accruals principle.

Trading stock appropriated by traders for personal use

Where a trader takes goods from the business trading stock for personal consumption or consumption by his or her household, then it must be valued at its open market realistic value, and not at cost. Effectively the trader must sell himself the goods at selling price. This rule was established in the tax case of Sharkey v Wernher but has now been incorporated into ITTOIA. This is so even though accounting standards say that the cost price should be used – otherwise the proprietor is recognising a non-existent business profit from trading with himself or herself.

10.25 Tax and accounting principles

United Kingdom tax law requires that tax computations are prepared in accordance with generally accepted accounting practice subject to any adjustment required by law. Generally accepted accounting practice (GAAP) is defined as being the accounting practice that is used in preparing accounts which are intended to give a 'true and fair' view; either UK GAAP or International Financial Reporting Standards are acceptable for tax purposes under CTA 2010 subject to the adjustments required by corporation tax law.

As explained in 10.6, the smallest businesses may opt to produce accounts on a cash basis, rather than apply the accruals basis required by generally accepted accounting practice (GAAP).

10.26 Trading allowance

The Finance (No. 2) Act 2017 introduced a "trading allowance" of £1,000.
If an individual has total trading income plus miscellaneous income below £1,000, then their trading profits or losses are treated as nil (unless they elect otherwise).

If the individual has total trading income plus miscellaneous income greater than £1,000, then they may calculate their trading profits for tax purposes as either:

- Taxable receipts minus allowable expenses (ie. calculation in the 'normal' way); or
- Taxable receipts minus £1,000. The legislation refers to this as 'partial relief', and an election must be made. Note that the trading allowance cannot be used to create or increase a loss.

Individuals can decide on a year-by-year basis which approach to take.

Importantly, an individual is excluded from claiming the trading allowance if their trading income includes **any** income from:

- their employer (or the employer of their spouse or civil partner);
- a firm in which they are a partner (or connected with a partner); or
- a close company in which they are a participator (or an associate of a participator)

Note that the trading allowance applies to an individual's total trading activity.

That means that a person who already has trading profits and sets up a second trade is unlikely to benefit from the trading allowance, since claiming it would prevent them from claiming the expenses for their existing trade; whereas the same new trade set up by a person who already had employment income but no existing trade **could** benefit from the trading allowance.

This conflicts with Adam Smith's canon of horizontal equity, since people in similar situations in terms of taxable capacity would be treated differently.

Student self-testing questions

Question 10.1, Hilary

Hilary has been in business many years as a tile maker. Her Income Statement for the year ended 31st March 2019 was as follows:

	Notes	£	£
Revenue			900,000
Cost of sales			(553,795)
Gross profit			346,205
Less: Expenses			
Salaries and wages	1	55,000	
Rent & rates		8,500	
Motor expenses	2	12,000	
Legal expenses	3	13,000	
Advertising		5,500	
Loss on sale of plant an d machinery		150	
Depreciation		9,095	
Donation to Oxfam made with Gift Aid declaration (net amount paid)		50	
Employees' Christmas party		1,450	
			(104,745)
Net profit			241,460

1. Salaries and wages include Hilary's drawings of 'salary' of £24,000.
2. Motor expenses include Hilary's private use of the car amounting to 25%.
3. Legal expenses comprise the following:

Costs associated with Hilary's income tax appeal	3,000
Costs associated with the renewal of a short-term lease	5,000
Defending a legal case brought by a customer	5,000

Requirement: Calculate Hilary's income from trading for the year.

Solution to Question 10.1, Hilary

Adjusted trading profits calculation

	£	£
Profit per financial statements		241,460
Add: disallowable expenditure:		
Hilary salary	24,000	
Hilary motor expenses	3,000	
Legal costs: tax appeal	3,000	
Loss on sale of plant and machinery	150	
Depreciation	9,095	
Donation to Oxfam - Gift Aid scheme applies	50	
		39,295
Income from trading		280,755

Question 10.2, Mr S Eason

Mr S Eason has the following business accounting results:

		£
Income Statement for the year to 31st Dec 2018		
Gross operating profit		171,000
interest received		900
		171,900
Wages and salaries	48,000	
Rent & rates	2,500	
Depreciation	1800	
Bad debts written off	120	
Entertainment expenses	800	
Patent royalties	1250	
Bank interest	350	
Legal expenses on acquisition of factory	300	
		(55,120)
Net profit		£116,780

Notes:

(i) Salaries include £22,000 paid to Mrs R Eason who worked as an employee in the business

(ii) No staff were entertained

(iii) Patent royalties were paid net, as required by law, but are shown gross.

Requirement: Compute the assessable profit from trading for the year to 31st December 2018.

Solution to Question 10.2, Mr S Eason

		£
Profit per accounts		116,780
Add		
Depreciation	1,800	
Entertainment expenses	800	
Legal expenses (relating to non-current asset)	300	
		2,900
		119,680
less interest received (non-trading savings income)		(900)
Adjusted trading profit		118,780

Notes:

(i) Patent royalties are allowable gross as an expense in calculating income from trading, if wholly and exclusively for business purposes. The fact they were paid net means that the income tax withheld is added to Mr Eason's own tax borne on income, in his tax computation, to give a total personal liability that includes the income tax withheld on royalties paid. The additional tax liability calculation is not part of the answer above.

(ii) The adjustment for interest received is based on the figure included in the business income statement However, Mr Eason's self-assessment tax return must include the interest as savings income of the tax year when it is received.

11 Income taxed as trade profits: II - basis periods

11.1 Introduction

This chapter deals with the basis of assessment of income of a trade carried on by an individual. The rules applicable to a partnership are discussed in Chapter 15. The basis period rules are contained in ITTOIA 2005. A profits basis period is the period used for measuring the trade profit that is matched to a tax year.

11.2 Trade profit assessment for a tax year

We cover this topic under the following headings:

General rule
Commencement provisions
Cessation provisions

11.3 General rule

The general rule is that the basis period for measuring the trade profits of a tax year is the period of 12 months ending with the business's accounting date in that tax year. This is called the 'current year basis'.

The accounting date means the end of the period for which a business has prepared its annual accounts.

11.4 Commencement provisions

When an individual starts trading, the following rules apply for determining the profits of the first two or three tax years in which a continuing trade exists.

a) Profits of the first tax year are measured as the 'actual' profits of the period from the date of commencement of trading to the following 5th April. If the chosen accounting date is not 5th April (or 31st March), time- apportionment is used to measure assessable profit up to the end of the first tax year. This time-apportionment assumes that profits accrued evenly over the whole of the first period of account.

b) Profits of the second year are normally either:

   i) profits for the 12 months ending with the accounting date in that year; this basis applies if there is an accounting date in the second tax year, and it is the end of a trading period of twelve months or more; or

   ii) profits of the 12 months from the date of commencement. This applies if there is an accounting date in the second tax year, but it is not the end of a trading period of at least twelve months.

Where there is no accounting date in the second tax year, because the first period of account ends in the third tax year, then the second tax year's assessable profit is measured with hindsight, using time-apportionment of available accounts, for the period covering 6th April to 5th April.

c) For subsequent years the profits assessable for each tax year are the profits for the 12 months ending with the accounting date in the tax year.

Example

Tamsin commenced trading on the 1st June 2015 with the following tax adjusted profits for the first 3 periods of account:

	£
1st June 2015 – 31st May 2016	6,000
1st June 2016 – 31st May 2017	10,000
1st June 2017 – 31st May 2018	12,000

Compute the taxable profits for relevant tax years.

Solution

Tax year	Basis period	Assessed amount
2015/16	1st June 2015 – 5th April 2016 ($^{10}/_{12} \times 6{,}000$)	5,000
2016/17	1st June 2015 – 31st May 2016 (12 months to 31st May 2016)	6,000
2017/18	1st June 2016 – 31st May 2017 (12 months to 31st May 2017)	10,000
2018/19	1st June 2017 – 31st May 2018 (12 months to 31st May 2018)	12,000

Notes

i) The second year is assessed on the profit of the 12-month accounting period ending in the second year i.e. 12 months to 31st May 2016.

ii) The second tax year contains an 'overlap period' where profits are measured for a second time. This is the period 1st June 2015 to 5th April 2016 with overlap profit of $^{10}/_{12} \times 6{,}000 = 5{,}000$.

iii) The amount of overlap profits is recovered on the earlier of the following:

a) a change of accounting date that results in a period of account more than 12 months (see Chapter 12); or

b) the cessation of trading.

iv) Calculations should strictly be made in days and not months, although for the examinations of professional accounting bodies, calculations in whole months are usual.

HMRC has stated that an accounting date of 31st March may be treated as 5th April, so long as this rule is consistently applied for all tax years.

v) The assessed profits less the overlap profits to be recovered are therefore equal to the actual profits (33,000 – 5,000) = 28,000.

Example

Anna commenced trading on the 1st July 2015 and has the following tax adjusted results for the first 3 periods of account:

	£
1st July 2015 – 31st December 2016	24,000
1st January 2017 – 31st December 2017	30,000
1st January 2018 – 31st December 2018	40,000

Compute the taxable profits for all relevant tax years.

Solution

Tax year	Basis period	Assessed amount
2015/16	01-Jul-2015 – 05-Apr-2016 ($^{9}/_{18}$ × 24,000)	12,000
2016/17	01-Jan-2016 – 31-Dec-2016 ($^{12}/_{18}$ × 24,000)	16,000
2017/18	01-Jan-2017 – 31-Dec-2017 (12 months to 31-Dec-2017)	30,000
2018/19	01-Jan-2018 – 31-Dec-2018 (12 months to 31-Dec-2018)	40,000

Notes

i) The second year is assessed on the profits of the 12 months ending 31st December 2016.

ii) The overlap period is from 1st January 2016 to 5th April 2016, with profits of $^{3}/_{18}$ × 24,000 = 4,000.

iii) Assessed profits less the overlap profits to be recovered are thus equal to the actual profits.

(12,000 + 16,000 + 30,000 + 40,000) – 4,000 = 94,000

Example

Theo started business on the 1st January 2016 with first accounts for the 16 months to 30th April 2017 and thereafter:

	£
1st January 2016 – 30th April 2017	32,000
1st May 2017 – 30th April 2018	28,000

Compute the taxable profits for relevant tax years.

Solution

Tax year	Basis period	Assessed amount
2015/16	01-Jan-2016 – 05-Apr-2016 ($^3/_{16}$ × 32,000)	6,000
2016/17	06-Apr-2016 – 05-Apr-2017 ($^{12}/_{16}$ × 32,000)	24,000
2017/18	01-May-2016 – 30-Apr-2017 ($^{12}/_{16}$ × 32,000)	24,000
2018/19	01-May-2017 – 30-Apr-2018 (12 months to 30-Apr-2018)	28,000

Notes

i) There is no period of account ending in the second year 2016/17, therefore the actual basis applies.

ii) The overlap period is 1st May 2016 – 5th April 2017 i.e. 11 months

11/16 × 32,000 = 22,000

iii) Assessed profits less the overlap profits are thus equal to the actual profits (6,000 + 24,000 + 24,000 + 28,000) – 22,000 = 60,000

11.5 Cessation provisions

The profits of the tax year in which cessation takes place are measured as follows.

i) The final tax year has a basis period from the end of the previous basis period to the date of cessation.

ii) Any profits from the overlap period on commencement not previously recouped are deducted from the profits of the final basis period.

iii) The effect of the above is that over the life of a business only its actual taxable profits will be assessed.

Example

Qasim commenced trading on 1st June 2013 and sold the business on the 30th April 2018 with the following tax adjusted results.

	£
1st June 2013 – 31st May 2014	6,000
1st June 2014 – 31st May 2015	10,000
1st June 2015 – 31st May 2016	12,000
1st June 2016 – 31st May 2017	16,000
1st June 2017 – 30th April 2018	8,000

Compute the assessable trading income for all tax years of the trade.

Solution

Tax year	Basis period	Assessed am
2013/14	1st June 2013 – 05-Apr-2014 ($^{10}/_{12} \times$ 6,000)	5,000
2014/15	1st June 2013 – 31st May 2014	6,000
2015/16	1st June 2014 – 31st May 2015	10,000
2016/17	1st June 2015 – 31st May 2016	12,000
2017/18	1st June 2016 – 31st May 2017	16,000
2018/19	1st June 2017 –30th April 2018 (8,000–5,000 overlap)	3,000

Notes:

i) The overlap period is 1st June 2013 to 5th April 2014 i.e. 10 months.
Overlap profit = $^{10}/_{12} \times$ 6,000 = £5,000

ii) The final period of profits is from 1st June 2017 to 30th April 2018 assessed in 2018/19 i.e. £8,000. Overlap profits of £5,000 are deducted leaving a net assessment of £3,000.

iii) Total profits over the life of the business are £52,000 which is equal to the taxable profits assessed.

Student self-testing questions

Question 11.1: Hilary, Julia, James and Jeremy

(i) Hilary, who commenced business on 1st August 2014 and prepared her first accounts for the twelve months to 31st July 2015, had tax-adjusted profits of:

12 months ended 31st July	Adjusted profit, £
2015	24,000
2016	40,000
2017	32,000
2018	36,000

(ii) Julia commenced business on 1st January 2016, preparing her first accounts to 31st October 2016, then annually to that date. Her profits as adjusted for tax purposes were:

	£
10 months ended 31st October 2016	42,000
Year ended 31st October 2017	52,000
Year ended 31st October 2018	65,000

(iii) James began business on 1st September 2016 and made up his first accounts to 31st January 2017. His profits adjusted for tax purposes were:

	£
5 months ended 31st January 2017	24,000
Year ended 31st January 2018	60,000
Year ended 31st January 2019	72,000

(iv) Jeremy began business on the 1st February 2015 and made up his first accounts to 31st July 2016, eighteen months later. His profits adjusted for tax purposes were:

	£
Eighteen months ended 31st July 2016	56,000
Year ended 31st July 2017	40,000
Year ended 31st July 2018	45,000

Requirement

In each case, calculate the measured assessable trade profits in the first, second and third tax years and any overlap profits arising. You may make calculations in whole months.

Solution to Question 11.1: Hilary, Julia, James and Jeremy

i) Hilary

1st year	14/15	1st August 2014 – 5th April 2015 = 8 months 8/12 × 24,000	16,000
2nd year	15/16	Is there an accounting date ending in 15/16? Yes, 31st July 2015 The accounting period is greater than or equal to 1 year and therefore the basis of assessment is 12 months to the accounting date in the 2nd tax year. Year ended 31st July 2015	24,000
3rd year	16/17	As there was an accounting date ending in the 2nd tax year the basis of assessment is the year ended 31st July 2016	40,000
Overlap profit		01-Aug-2014 – 5th April 2015 = 8 months (8/12 × 24,000)	16,000

ii) Julia

1st year	15/16	1st Jan 2016 – 5th April 2016 = 3 months 3/10 × 42,000	12,600
2nd year	16/17	Is there an accounting date ending in 16/17? Yes, 31st October 2016 The accounting date is less than 1 year therefore the basis of assessment is the first 12 months of trading 10 months ended 31st October 2016 plus Nov & Dec 2016 Assessment is therefore: 10 months ended 31-Oct-2016 + 2/12 × 52,000	42,000 8,667 50,667
3rd year	17/18	As there was an accounting date ending in the 2nd tax year the basis of assessment is the year ended 31st October 2017	52,000
Overlap profits		01-Jan-2016 - 05-Apr-2016 01-Nov-2016 - 31-Dec-2016 (2/12 × £52,000)	12,600 8,667 21,267

iii) James

1st year	16/17	1st September 2016 – 5th April 2017 = 7 months (£24,000 + (2/12 × £60,000)	34,000
2nd year	17/18	Is there an accounting date ending in 17/18? Yes, year ended 31-Jan-2018 The accounting date is greater than or equal to 1 year after commencement therefore the basis of assessment is the year to the new accounting date	60,000

3rd year	18/19	As there was an accounting date ending in the 2nd tax year the basis of assessment is the year ended 31-Jan-2019	72,000
Overlap profits		01-Feb-2017 - 05-Apr-2017 ($^{2}/_{12}$ × 60,000)	10,000

iv) Jeremy

1st year	14/15	1st February 2015 – 5th April 2015 $^{2}/_{18}$ × 56,000	6,222
2nd year	15/16	Is there an accounting date ending in 15/16? No. Therefore the basis of assessment is profits from 06-Apr-2015 - 05-Apr-2016 $^{12}/_{18}$ × £56,000	37,333
3rd year	16/17	Basis of assessment for the 3rd tax year is 12 months to the accounting date in the 3rd tax year i.e. 31st July 2016 $^{12}/_{18}$ × £56,000	37,333
Overlap profits		The profits from 1st August 2015 to 5th April 2016 have been included in both 15/16 and 16/17. Overlap profits are thus £24,889 ($^{8}/_{18}$ × 56,000).	24,889

Question 11.2, Mr Elliott

In the spring of 2019, Mr Elliott was considering starting a new business and had prepared a business plan. This showed that the business would commence trading on 1st July 2019, and that the pattern of profits would be:

Period to 31st December 2019	£600 per month
Twelve months to 31st December 2020	£1,200 per month
Thereafter	£2,400 per month

Mr Elliott is considering two alternative dates on which to make up accounts each year, 31st March or 30th April.

(Note that he is not considering any other date and will not be making up accounts to 31st December.)

Required:

a) Compute the amounts which will be assessable as income from trading for each of the first three tax years under each of the two above alternative accounting dates. (10 marks)

b) Indicate the main advantages and disadvantages of each alternative. (5 marks)

(CIMA updated)

Solution to Question 11.2, Mr Elliott

(a) Accounting profits arising under the 2 proposed dates:

		£
31st March accounting date		
1st July 2019 – 31st March 2020	(6 × £600) + (3 × £1,200)	7,200
Year ended 31st March 2021	(9 × £1,200) + (3 × £2,400)	18,000
Year ended 31st March 2022	(12 × £2,400)	28,800
30th April accounting date		
10 months to 30th April 2020	(6 × £600) + (4 × £1,200)	8,400
Year ended 30th April 2021	(8 × £1,200) + (4 × £2,400)	19,200
Year ended 30th April 2022	(12 × £2,400)	28,800

Based on the accounting profits, the tax year measures of trading income will be as follows:

31st March accounting date:

	Basis period	Assessable profits £
2019/2020	1st July 2019 - 5th April 2020	7,200
2020/2021	12 months to 31st March 2021	18,000
2021/2022	12 months to 31st March 2022	28,800
		54,000

30th April accounting date:

	Basis period	Calculation	Assessable profit £
2019/2020	1st July 2019 – 5th April 2020	9/10 × 8,400	7,560
2020/2021	1st July 2019 – 30th June 2020	8,400 + (2/12 × 19,200)	11,600
2021/2022	Year ended 30th April 2021		19,200
			38,360

(b)

30th April

The 30th April accounting date gives a lower amount of total assessable profits for the first three years of assessment. There is a greater interval between earning profits and paying taxes.

(The difference in tax liability occurs because the business's profits are rising. If there were the same profit every month exactly, it would make little difference which accounting reference date was chosen.)

With the 30th April reference date, profits in the periods 1st July 2019 to 5th April 2020 (£7,560) and 1st May 2020 to 30th June 2020 (£3,200) are counted twice in the first three tax years – creating 'overlap profits' of (7,560+3,200) = £10,760.

Relief for overlap profits will be obtained either on cessation or on a change of accounting date.

31st March

The 31st March reference date gives no 'overlap' profits.

It has higher total assessable profits in early years giving rise to earlier tax liabilities on profits earned. The reason why it gives higher profits is that profits are rising over the first three years.

Hence there is a cash flow disadvantage compared to selecting a 30th April reference date.

Questions without answers

Question 11.3, Chatru

Chatru commenced trading on 1st November 2014. His first accounts were made up to 30th April 2016 and thereafter to 30th April annually. He ceased trading on 31st March 2019.

His trading results, adjusted for income tax purposes were:

	£
1st November 2014 – 30th April 2016	40,500
Year ended 30th April 2017	12,000
Year ended 30th April 2018	24,000
Period to 31st March 2019	46,000

Requirements:

Calculate the assessable income for all years in question

Calculate whether there would have been an income tax benefit in Chatru continuing to trade one extra month and making up final accounts to his normal accounting date, on the assumption that his tax-adjusted profit for April 2019 was £4,200.

11 marks
(ACCA updated)

Question 11.4, Nan and Arthur Pearson

Nan Pearson died on 30th June 2018. She had lived in Northern Ireland, where she was employed as a design engineer by Map plc, a company which specialises in the construction of motor bikes.

The following is supplied:

(1) Nan's salary, paid on the last day of each month, was £64,000 a year from which 5% was paid to an approved staff pension fund. The company's contribution was 8%. PAYE of £840 was deducted from the salary during 2018/19.

(2) Her other income for the tax year 2018/19 comprised bank interest of £2,000 and dividends received from UK companies of £7,000.

Arthur Pearson, Nan's husband, had been employed until his retirement in March 2014. Since that date, he undertook some self-employed bookkeeping activities in Northern Ireland and recent tax adjusted profits of this business are as follows:

	£
Year to 30th April 2015	5,000
Year to 30th April 2016	4,100
Year to 30th April 2017	5,900
Year to 30th April 2018	8,000

No tax has yet been paid on Arthur's income from trading for 2018/19.

Arthur received bank interest of £2,000 on 30th June 2018.

The following events took place after Nan's death.

(1) A payment of £140,000, being the sum assured on Nan's life under the Map plc's pension scheme, was paid to Arthur.

(2) A pension of £22,980 (gross) per annum, payable on the first day of each month, was paid to Arthur by Map plc. The first payment was made on 1st July 2018 and basic rate tax was deducted from the pension by Map plc.

Arthur used the £140,000 assurance policy receipt to acquire and furnish a small studio apartment on 1st February 2019. He let this apartment under a ten-year lease from 1st March 2019, the incoming tenant paying a premium of £4,000. The rent of £5,500 a year is payable quarterly in advance and was received when due. Arthur incurred the following expenses in connection with the letting:

	£
Interior decorating prior to letting	790
Year's insurance of premises and contents – 1st March 2019	384
Managing agent's fee (for tenancy agreement and March 2019 management)	250

Requirement:

Prepare income tax computations for 2018/19 for

(a) Nan Pearson, showing income tax payable or refundable [10 marks]

(b) Arthur Pearson, showing the final income tax position and indicating any final amounts of tax to be paid or repaid. [6 marks]

[Total: 16 marks]

12 Income taxed as trade profits: III - change of accounting date

12.1 Introduction

This chapter is concerned with the effects of a change of accounting date on the income taxed as trade profits for a tax year, under the basis period rules already described.

12.2 Detailed rules

An outline of the rules in respect of a change of accounting date follows:

a) HMRC will ignore any change of accounting date and require separate sets of financial statements as before for the original annual basis periods unless all the three undermentioned circumstances apply.

   i) The first period of account (i.e. period for which business accounts are made up) ending with the new date does not exceed 18 months.

   ii) Notice of the change is given to an officer of HMRC in a personal tax return on or before the day on which that return is required to be delivered.

   iii) Either

      1) no accounting change resulting in a change of basis period has been made in any of the previous five tax years; or

      2) the change is made for bona fide commercial reasons. In this case, notice in (ii) above must set out the reasons for the change and HMRC do not, within 60 days, give notice to the trader that they are not satisfied that the change is made for bona fide commercial reasons.

b) There is a right of appeal against HMRC's decision not to accept a second change in five years as being for commercial reasons.

c) Obtaining a tax advantage by an accounting date change is not accepted as a valid commercial reason for a change.

d) Where all the conditions are satisfied, or the accounting change is made in the second or third tax year of the business, the basis period for the tax year of the change is as follows.

   i) If the year is the second tax year of the business, the basis period is the 12 months ending with the new accounting date falling in that tax year (unless the period from commencement of the business to the new date in the second year is less than 12 months, in which case the basis is the first twelve months of the business). Overlap relief will arise to the extent that profits are brought into charge twice because of this rule.

ii) If the 'relevant period' is a period of less than 12 months, the basis period is the 12 months ending with the new date in the tax year. Further overlap profits will arise to the extent that profits are brought into charge twice because of this rule. These overlap profits will be added to any previous overlap profits

iii) If the 'relevant period' is a period of more than 12 months, the basis period consists of the relevant period, less any overlap relief available to deduct.

The 'relevant period' is the period beginning immediately after the end of the basis period for the preceding year and ending with the new date in the year.

In summary, when the accounting date change involves a move of the accounting date later in the tax year, previous overlap is released, and when it involves a move of the accounting date to earlier in the year, new overlap is created.

Difference between end of preceding basis period and new accounting date		**Basis period**
1st year	< 12 months	12 months to new A/C date
1st year	> 12 months	Period to new A/C date
2nd year	—	12 months to new A/C date

Profits for the period of overlap will need to be computed when a change of accounting date takes place.

Example

Axel starts in business on 1st July 2014 and produces accounts to 5th April until 5th April 2017, when a new date of 30th June 2017 is the next accounting date.

		£
Accounts	1st July 2014 – 5th April 2015	10,000
	6th April 2015 – 5th April 2016	12,000
	6th April 2016 – 5th April 2017	15,000
	6th April 2017 – 30th June 2017	2,000
	1st July 2017 – 30th June 2018	6,000

Compute the assessments.

Solution

			£
2014/15	1st July 2014 – 5th April 2015		10,000
2015/16	12 months to 5th April 2016		12,000
2016/17	12 months to 5th April 2017		15,000
2017/18	12 months to 30th June 2017		
	1st July 2016 – 5th April 2017 = 9 months		
	$^9/_{12} \times 15{,}000 =$	11,250	
	6th April 2017 – 30th June 2017 =	2,000	13,250
2018/9	1st July 2017 – 30th June 2018 =		6,000

Notes

i) Overlap Memorandum

There was no overlap profit arising on the commencement of the business, as a 5th April accounting date was adopted.

Overlap relief on change of accounting date:

Overlap period 1st July 2016 – 5th April 2017

= 9/12 × 15,000 = 11,250

Amount carried forward as overlap profits 11,250

ii) Total profit assessed less overlap relief

= £45,000: (10,000 + 12,000 + 15,000 + 13,250 + 6,000) – 11,250.

Example

Victoria started business on the 1st January 2014 with the following results.

6 months to 30th June 2014	20,000
12 months to 30th June 2015	40,000
12 months to 30th June 2016	50,000
18 months to 31st December 2017	75,000
12 months to 31st December 2018	60,000

Compute the assessable trading profits for all tax years, the overlap profit carried forward and the overlap relief.

Solution

Years	**Period**		**£**
2013/14	01-Jan-2014 – 05-Apr-2014		
	3/6 × 20,000 =		10,000
2014/15	First 12 months trading		
	20,000 + (6/12 × 40,000)		
	= 20,000 + 20,000		40,000
2015/16	CY 30-Jun-2015		40,000
2016/17	CY 30-Jun-2016		50,000
2017/18	01-Jul-2016 – 31-Dec-2017		
	total for period	75,000	
	less overlap released	(20,000)	55,000
2018/19	CY 31-Dec-2018		60,000

Notes

i) Overlap Memorandum

Original overlap profits
(01-Jan-2014 – 05-Apr-2014) + (01-Jul-2014 –31-Dec-2014) = 9 months

= 10,000 + 20,000 =	30,000
2017/18 overlap released 01-Jul-2016 – 31-Dec-2017 = 18 months	
18 – 12 = 6 months	
$6/9 \times 30{,}000$ =	(20,000)
Reduced overlap carried forward at 2018/19	10,000

ii) Total profit assessed less overlap relief
= £245,000
(10,000 + 40,000 + 40,000 + 50,000 + 55,000 + 60,000) – 10,000

Example

Bhavna has been in business for many years with the following results.

12 months to 31-Dec-2014	10,000
12 months to 31-Dec-2015	30,000
12 months to 31-Dec-2016	20,000
6 months to 30-Jun-2017	12,000
12 months to 30-Jun-2018	36,000

Compute the assessable trading profits for all tax years and the overlap relief arising on the change of accounting date and carried forward by the taxpayer.

Solution

Years	**Period**	**£**
2014/15	12 months to 31-Dec-2014	10,000
2015/16	12 months to 31-Dec-2015	30,000
2016/17	12 months to 31-Dec-2016	20,000
2017/18	12 months to 30-Jun-2017:	
	12,000 + (($6/12$) × 20,000)	
	= 12,000 + 10,000	22,000
2018/19	30-Jun-2018	36,000

Overlap relief 1st July 2016 to 31st December 2016

$6/12 \times 20{,}000$ = 10,000

Total assessed profits less overlap relief = (10,000 + 30,000 + 20,000 + 22,000 + 36,000) – 10,000 = £108,000.

Student self-testing question

Question 12.1, Aisling

Aisling starts in business on 1st May 2013 making accounts up to 5th April each year until 2017 when a new date of 30th November 2017 is chosen as the accounting date.

Business periods of account	**Adjusted profits (£)**
1st May 2013 – 5th April 2014	10,000
6th April 2014 – 5th April 2015	12,000
6th April 2015 – 5th April 2016	14,000
6th April 2016 – 5th April 2017	16,000
6th April 2017 – 30th November 2017	8,000
1st December 2017 – 30th November 2018	20,000

Compute the measured assessable trading profits for all tax years.

Solution to Question 12.1, Aisling

			£
2013/14	01-May-2013 – 05-Apr-2014		10,000
2014/15	12 months to 05-Apr-2015		12,000
2015/16	12 months to 05-Apr-2016		14,000
2016/17	12 months to 05-Apr-2017		16,000
2017/18	12 months to 30-Nov-2017		
	06-Apr-2017 – 30-Nov-2017	8,000	
	01-Dec-2015 – 05-Apr-2016 = 4 months		
	$^4/_{12}$ × 16,000 =	5,333	13,333
2018/19	01-Dec-2017 – 30-Nov-2018 =		20,000
Overlap relief			5,333
Carried forward			5,333
Total profits = 85,333 – 5,333 = £80,000			

Question without answer

Question 12.2, Lester

Lester started trading on 1st December 2014 with the following results:

	£
Period to 5th April 2015	7,000
Year to 5th April 2016	10,000
Year to 5th April 2017	15,000
6 months to 30th September 2017	8,000
Year to 30th September 2018	20,000

Compute the measured assessable trading profits for all tax years.

13 Capital allowances

13.1 Introduction

The chapter is about the allowances available to a taxpayer in respect of capital expenditure on fixed assets. These allowances, which are called capital allowances, consist of a mixture of annual and other allowances which are available in respect of qualifying expenditure incurred under the following headings.

Plant and machinery
Know-how (not available to companies)
Scientific research assets

The main statute is the Capital Allowances Act 2001, as amended by subsequent Finance Acts.

The UK government tends to alter capital allowances rules often, for reasons of economic policy. It is an area of law which is not subject to EU scrutiny as 'State Aid', which means changes can be given effect very quickly.

We divide the chapter into the following sections:

Part I	–	Plant and machinery
Part II	–	Other assets

Examples in this chapter which cover multiple periods of account may be projected into the future. This is to avoid confusion that could result from including obsolete allowances, or transitional rules of no future significance, in workings shown for earlier tax years.

Nearly all the capital allowance rules for plant and machinery, described in this chapter, apply in the same way for corporate taxpayers. Where there are differences, the difference is noted. (See Chapter 20 for more points on companies' capital allowances.)

For small businesses opting to adopt a 'cash' accounting basis from 2013/14, the distinction between 'revenue' and 'capital' business transactions will generally not apply. However, the capital allowances rules for cars will still apply to these businesses.

PART I – Plant and machinery

13.2 General conditions

a) Allowances are available under this heading if a person carries on a qualifying activity and incurs qualifying expenditure.

b) 'Qualifying activity' has the following meaning
   i) a trade, profession or vocation,
   ii) an ordinary property business,
   iii) a furnished holiday lettings business,
   iv) an overseas property business,
   v) the management of an investment company,
   vi) special leasing of plant or machinery,
   vii) an employment or office.

c) Expenditure is qualifying expenditure if:
   i) it is capital expenditure on the provision of plant or machinery wholly or partly for the purposes of the qualifying activity carried on by the person incurring the expenditure, and
   ii) the person incurring the expenditure owns the plant or machinery as a result of incurring it.

13.3 Qualifying expenditure

a) Plant and machinery is not conclusively defined in tax statute though Schedule AA1 to the CAA 2001 attempted to codify existing case law. The definition most frequently referred to is that contained in a non-tax case, Yarmouth v France 1887 QBD. The case was brought under the Employers' Liability Act 1880, and consideration given as to whether a horse was plant and machinery. During his judgement, Lindley LJ made the following statement:

   '... in its ordinary sense it includes whatever **apparatus** is used by a business man for carrying on his business, not his stock in trade which he buys or makes for sale, but all goods and chattels, fixed or moveable, live or dead, which he keeps for permanent employment in his business.'

b) In another important case it was stated that 'plant' **excludes** buildings and parts of buildings to the extent they are the '**setting**' of the trade, rather than the 'apparatus' of the trade.

c) Capital expenditure on alterations to an existing building, incidental to the installation of plant, may be treated as plant and machinery, where a qualifying activity is carried on.

d) Expenditure on the thermal insulation of an industrial building.

e) Fire safety expenditure.

f) Personal security expenditure.

g) Buildings and structures – see below.

13.4 Features integral to a building – the special rate pool

Since 2008 certain features integral to a building, thermal insulation and long-life assets (see 13.14) are placed for capital allowances purposes in a separate 'special rate pool'.

The writing down allowance is at a lower rate for this pool, compared to other items of plant and machinery.

The special rate pool also includes cars with carbon dioxide emissions exceeding 110g/km.

Features integral to a building are defined as: electrical systems; cold water systems; heating, ventilation, air cooling or purification systems including related floors and ceilings; lifts, escalators and moving walkways; external solar shading; active facades.

Allowances are available for both initial expenditure and replacement expenditure on integral features. 'Replacement' is expenditure on replacing or renewing over 50% of the asset within a 12-month period. Where capital allowances apply under this rule, a normal repairs deduction is not available as a deductible expense against profits.

13.5 Plant and machinery – buildings (to 5 April 2008 for Income Tax and 31 March 2008 for Corporation Tax)

Prior to the rules on 'features integral to a building' which could be included in the special rate pool, the following rules applied to distinguish trade plant and machinery from buildings in which that plant and machinery was incorporated:

Plant and machinery did not include:

i) buildings – see List A (references to Sch AAI CAA 2001)
ii) fixed structures – see List B
iii) interests in land.

Note The items included in list C could be claimed as plant and machinery of a trade, subject to the case-law criteria.

List A: Buildings

1. Walls, floors, ceilings, doors, gates, shutters, windows and stairs
2. Main services, and systems, of water, electricity and gas
3. Waste disposal systems
4. Sewerage and drainage systems
5. Shafts or other structures in which lifts, hoists, escalators and moving walkways are installed
6. Fire safety systems

List B: Structures

1. Any tunnel, bridge, viaduct, aqueduct, embankment or cutting
2. Any way or hard standing, such as a pavement, road, railway or tramway, a park for vehicles or containers, or an airstrip or runway
3. Any inland navigation, including a canal or basin or a navigable river
4. Any dam, reservoir or barrage (including any sluices, gates, generators and other equipment associated with it)
5. Any dock
6. Any dike, sea wall, weir or drainage ditch
7. Any structure not within any other item in this column

List C: Assets which can be included in buildings, but expenditure on which is unaffected by the buildings rules

i.e. These items could still be claimed **as plant and machinery**, subject to established case law principles. Note that some of these items are 'features integral to a building' which since April 2008 must get writing down allowance at the lower 'special' rate. The rest of the items on this list C remain potentially identifiable as plant and machinery in the general pool. Also, existing assets in these categories could still be included in the general pool brought forward, and account for some plant proceeds on disposal of a building.

1. Electrical, cold water, gas and sewerage systems –
   a) provided mainly to meet the requirements of the trade, or
   b) provided mainly to serve machinery or plant used for the purposes of trade
2. Space or water heating systems; powered systems of ventilation; air-cooling or air purification; and any ceiling or floor comprised in such systems
3. Manufacturing or processing equipment; storage equipment, including cold rooms; display equipment; and counters, checkouts and similar equipment
4. Cookers, washing machines, dishwashers, refrigerators and similar; washbasins, sinks, baths, showers, sanitary ware and similar equipment; furniture and furnishings
5. Lifts, hoists, escalators and moving stairways
6. Sound insulation provided mainly to meet the requirements of the trade
7. Computer, telecommunications and surveillance systems (including wiring or other links)
8. Refrigeration or cooling equipment
9. Sprinkler and other equipment for extinguishing or containing fire; fire alarm systems
10. Burglar alarm systems
11. Any machinery (including devices for providing motive power) not within any other item in this column
12. Strong rooms in bank or building society premises; safes

13. Partition walls, where moveable and intended to be moved during the trade
14. Decorative assets provided for the enjoyment of the public in the hotel, restaurant or similar trades. (The legal scope of this is clarified by court judgments, most recently in the J.D. Wetherspoon tax case of 2012 – see below.)
15. Advertising hoardings; signs, displays and similar assets
16. Alteration of land for the purpose only of installing machinery or plant
17. Provision of dry docks
18. Provision of any jetty or similar structure provided mainly to carry machinery or plant
19. Provision of pipelines
20. Provision of towers used to support floodlights
21. Provision of any reservoir incorporated into a water treatment works
22. Provision of silos used for temporary storage or on the provision of storage tanks
23. Provision of slurry pits or silage clamps
24. Provision of swimming pools, including diving boards, slides and any structure supporting them
25. Provision of fish tanks or fish ponds
26. Provision of rails, sleepers and ballast for a railway or tramway
27. Swimming pools
28. Cold stores
29. Any glass house with integral environment controls
30. Movable buildings intended to be moved during the qualifying activity

13.6 Cases on plant and machinery

The following is a summary of some of the cases concerned with the definition of plant and machinery. Cases prior to 2001 were influential in the drawing up of lists A B and C above:

1. **Jarrold v John Good & Sons Ltd 1962** CA 40 TC 681. In this case, movable metal partitioning used to divide office accommodation was held to be plant.
2. **CIR v Barclay Curle & Co. Ltd 1969** H.L. 45 TC 221. The company constructed a dry dock, the whole cost of which, including excavation, was held to be plant.
3. **Cooke v Beach Station Caravans Ltd 1974** CD 49 TC 524. The company constructed a swimming pool with an elaborate system of filtration, as one of the amenities at a caravan park. The cost, which included excavation, was held to be plant of the leisure business.
4. **St Johns School v Ward 1974** CA 49 TC 524. A special purpose prefabricated structure, for use as a laboratory and gymnasium in a school, was held not to be plant.

5. **Schofield v R & H Hall Ltd 1974** NI 49 TC 538. A grain importer built a concrete silo with gantries, conveyors and chutes, which was held to be plant.
6. **Benson v The Yard Arm Club Ltd 1978** CD STC 408. The purchase and conversion of an old ferry boat into a floating restaurant was held not to be plant, but the setting of the business.
7. **Dixon v Fitch's Garage Ltd 1975** CD STC 480. A metal canopy covering the service area of a petrol filling station was held to be a shelter, and not plant.
8. **Munby v Furlong 1977** CA STC 232. Books purchased by a barrister to create a library in his practice were held to be plant.
9. **Leeds Permanent Building Society 1982** CD Decorative screens incorporating the society's name in a building were held to be plant.
10. **Wimpy International Ltd v Warland 1988** CA Expenditure on items of decoration installed in the company's restaurants was held partly to be plant and machinery. However, item 14 in List C now expands the principles found in that case.
11. **J D Wetherspoon plc v HMRC 2012** UKUT 42 (TCC)– an important tax appeal case on what is 'plant' expenditure, and what is 'buildings', when refurbishing pubs. The Upper Tribunal (Tax and Chancery Chamber) issued judgment on 31 January 2012.

    The case at first instance was heard in 2007 and so the judgement relates to the 'plant' rules before the 2008 reforms, when the 'special rate pool' came in. The judgment includes useful guidance on the 'plant or buildings?' distinction for capital allowances on fitting out pubs and restaurants. For example, it was held that expenditure on new wall tiling is generally on buildings (so no capital allowances). However, tiling is plant where installed for a clear trading purpose - in this case, to protect the kitchen wall against splashes from cooking pans. In contrast, tiling in the customer toilets was held simply to be a general type of wall covering and not plant. In the pub itself, timber panelling on internal walls, which the taxpayer argued was plant installed for a trading reason - to create pub 'atmosphere', was held not to be plant, because it was not sufficiently special or distinctive to be distinguished from ordinary wall covering. The Wimpy case from 1988 (10 above) was referred to in detail.
12. **Hunt v Henry Quick Ltd: King v Bridisco Ltd CHD. 1992** STC 633. The construction of mezzanine platforms in a warehouse was held to be plant and machinery, as they had a trade function.
13. **Gray v Seymour's Garden Centre C.H.D. 1993**. The construction of a special horticultural greenhouse was held not to be plant and machinery.
14. **Attwood v Anduff C.A. 1997**. The expenditure on a purpose-built car wash site was held not to be plant and machinery. However, while structural expenditure on the site was not accepted as plant, car wash machinery clearly would be plant.
15. **Shove v Lingfield Park C.D. 2003**. An artificial all-weather track at a racecourse was held to be part of the premises and not plant.

13.7 When capital expenditure is incurred

The expenditure is normally treated as incurred on the date on which the obligation to pay becomes unconditional. However, if payment in whole or in part is not required until more than four months after the date on which the obligation to pay becomes unconditional, then so much of the amount as can be deferred is taken to be incurred on that later date when the obligation to pay becomes unconditional.

This is to prevent artificial acceleration of 'purchase dates' beyond a normal credit period, to obtain allowances in an earlier period.

Example

Kylie orders an item of plant from Gusto plc on the following terms:

31-Dec-2018	plant delivered and invoiced on same date to Kylie.
21-Jan-2019	due date for payment by Kylie, being the end of the month following date of delivery.
03-Feb-2019	Kylie makes payment.

The expenditure is deemed to have been incurred by Kylie on 31st December 2018.

Example

Lionel orders an item of plant from Tavola plc costing £50,000 as follows:

31st December 2018	plant delivered and invoiced on same date.
31st January 2019	90% of invoice amount due for payment.
30th June 2019	balance of 10% due for payment.

Lionel is deemed to have incurred the expenditure as follows:

31st December 2018	90% × £50,000 i.e. £45,000
30th June 2019	10% × £50,000 i.e. £5,000

13.8 Allowances available

The types of allowances which can be claimed in respect of expenditure on plant or machinery are:

- annual investment allowance (AIA)
- enhanced capital allowances (ECA) – also called 100% First Year Allowance (FYA) in the case of low emission cars
- writing down allowance (WDA)
- balancing allowance (BA)

Sometimes these are offset by a 'negative allowance' or balancing charge (BC).

13.9 Annual investment allowance £200,000

Annual investment allowance of 100% of expenditure up to £200,000 a year are available on any category of plant and machinery other than cars, for all categories of business.

The Annual Investment Allowance can be allocated to eligible assets in any order of the taxpayer's choice. The most efficient order of allocation is to the special rate pool first, then the general pool, then short life assets and lastly private use assets.

13.10 Enhanced capital allowances: 100% First Year Allowance for Energy/water saving plant

Enhanced capital allowances (ECAs) aim to encourage the use of energy efficient equipment by giving a 100% allowance on purchase. Only products included on the UK Energy Technology Product List approved by the Department of Energy and Climate Change qualify. The list is available at

https://etl.beis.gov.uk/etl/site/etl.html

The allowance, which is available to all businesses, is also extended to qualifying energy saving assets purchased for leasing or hire to others.

13.11 Enhanced capital allowances: 100% FYA for low-emission cars

a) A 100% FYA is available on the purchase of a new car if:
   i) it is a low-emission car i.e. emits not more than 50g/km of carbon dioxide, or
   ii) it is electrically propelled.

b) The 100% FYA is also available for plant and machinery to refuel vehicles with natural gas or hydrogen fuel, e.g. storage tanks, pumps, etc.

c) The allowance is extended to assets acquired to be leased, let or hired.

13.12 Enhanced capital allowances: 100% FYA for plant and machinery

Enhanced capital allowances (ECA or 100% FYA) are also available for plant and machinery, excluding cars (other than Low Emissions cars), for use primarily within an Enterprise Zone.

13.13 General pool plant and machinery WDA –18%

a) A writing down allowance (WDA) is available in respect of expenditure incurred in the capital allowances period of account (or the CT accounting period for companies), other than assets attracting ECA or FYA in that year.

b) The allowance is available whether the plant or machinery is brought into use for the trade by the end of the basis period, so long as it was acquired for the trade.

c) WDA is given on a reducing balance basis on the unrelieved general pool of plant expenditure, after adjusting for in-year additions and disposals, other than additions qualifying for FYA / ECA, as shown in the specimen computation below (13.16).

d) Before computing WDA, the pool is reduced by reference to the Total Disposal Receipts (TDR) (limited to the original cost) from any of the following events at any time during the chargeable period.
   i) The plant or machinery ceases to belong to the taxpayer.
   ii) The taxpayer loses possession of the plant or machinery in circumstances where it is reasonable to assume that the loss is permanent.
   iii) The plant or machinery ceases to exist because of destruction, etc.
   iv) The plant or machinery begins to be used wholly or partly for purposes other than those of the trade.
   v) The trade is permanently discontinued.

e) The balance remaining on the pool after deducting any proceeds of disposals is written down in the normal way. If the pool balance after deducting sale proceeds, and bringing in qualifying additions, is negative there is a balancing charge calculated to bring the balance on the pool to nil.

f) The taxpayer can claim any proportion of the allowances available, but must accept the full balancing charge arising on a disposal.

g) If a plant asset has any private use, the asset must be kept outside the pool. The 18% allowance is calculated in the normal way and deducted from the cost or written down value of the asset; the amount given as the full writing down allowance is then reduced accordingly for the private use element. A separate (single-asset) pool is required for each asset with a private use element so that private use can be accurately excluded from tax relief.

h) Companies do not have 'private use assets' as a company has no private identity. Assets used privately by directors or staff are in business use by the company and the private use is dealt with by the Benefits Code (see Chapter 7).

i) A writing down allowance is not available in the year of cessation of trading, though a balancing allowance may be.

j) If the balance remaining on the general pool before WDA in any year is less than £1,000, the taxpayer may take the whole amount remaining as WDA of that period, writing the pool down to nil.

k) A writing down allowance is not available in the same period as first year allowance on assets which received a partial first year allowance; but WDA is available in the same year as additional investment allowance, to the extent the asset expenditure is not already fully relieved by the allocated AIA.

l) Cars with CO_2 emissions of 110g/km or less qualify for the 18% writing down allowance and are added to the general pool, but do not qualify for any AIA.

13.14 Special rate pool - 8% WDA

Assets in the special rate pool attract a writing down allowance of 8%. These assets are:

a) Features integral to a building;

b) Thermal insulation in a building;

c) Cars with CO_2 emissions of more than 110 g/km;

d) 'Long-life assets' – ie Machinery or plant which has an expected working life when new of 25 years or more.

Expenditure on long-life assets which does not exceed a minimum limit is excluded from the rules requiring the assets to be put in the SR pool.

i) For companies, the minimum limit is £100,000 a year, divided by one plus the number of associated companies.

ii) The minimum of £100,000 a year also applies to individuals, and to partnerships made up of individuals.

iii) The exclusion for expenditure below the minimum limit does not apply to shared contributions to expenditure on machinery or plant, nor to expenditure on a share in machinery or plant, on machinery or plant for leasing, or on machinery and plant on which allowances have been given to a previous owner at the long-life asset rate.

The long-life assets category is not very significant for a small trader, because of the minimum value rules. It is more relevant for companies, which buy large assets such as ships, aeroplanes and helicopters, heavy cranes etc.

13.15 Separate pooling rules

A separate expenditure pool must be kept for each of the following classes of assets:

i) the general pool of plant and machinery (as detailed above);

ii) the special rate pool (as detailed above);

iii) assets with any private use (one pool per asset);

iv) short life assets where a de-pooling election has been made (one pool per asset, or per class of identical assets).

13.16 Specimen capital allowances computation – working layout

		General pool	Special rate pool
	£	£	£
Tax Written Down Value brought forward		X	X
Qualifying expenditure (not eligible for AIA =cars)		X	X
Qualifying expenditure (eligible for AIA, but not eligible for 100% FYA)	X		
Less: Annual Investment Allowance (£200,000 per annum from 1st January 2016 onwards; pro-rated for long or short period of account)	(X)*		
Excess of expenditure over AIA - taken to pool or special rate pool or both, depending on asset type		X	X
Available qualifying expenditure for WDA (before disposals)		X	X
Less: Total disposal receipts (limited to original cost of each asset, if this can still be traced)		(X)	(X)
		X	X
Less: Writing down allowances 18% or 8% (pro-rated for long or short period of account)		(X)*	(X)*
Qualifying expenditure for 100% ECA	X		
Less: Enhanced Capital Allowance at 100% (not pro-rated for a short or long period of account)	(X)*		
Tax Written Down Value carried forward		**X**	**X**

Notes

i) The total of trading capital allowances available for a period of account to a taxpayer is the sum of the items marked * in the computation layout above.

ii) The above computation omits a single-asset pool, but this would be set up in the same way as the multi-asset pools by entering the cost of the asset in its own column. The annual WDA is then deducted from the single asset pool WDV.

iii) For the operation of balancing charges and balancing allowances, which do not occur in the specimen layout above, see 13.21.

13.17 Capital allowances and accounts

For all businesses the following provisions apply.

1) Capital allowances are given for a 'chargeable period' which is based on the period of account for individuals, and on the corporation tax accounting period for companies.
2) Capital allowances are treated as a trading expense of the business in the chargeable period and any balancing charge is treated as a trading receipt. This means that the trade profit for tax purposes is after the deduction of capital allowances. However, the taxpayer is not obliged to claim the maximum allowances available. If lower capital allowances are claimed than are available, the unrelieved expenditure (written down values) carried forward to the next period will be correspondingly higher.
3) Where the period of account for income tax purposes is not a 12-month period, the writing down allowance and the annual investment allowance are contracted or expanded on a pro-rata basis. e.g.

Period of account, 8 months – writing down allowance	$^{8}/_{12}$ × 18%
Maximum AIA (e.g. April 2018 to November 2018)	$^{8}/_{12}$ × £200,000
Period of account, 15 months – writing down allowance	$^{15}/_{12}$ × 18%
Maximum AIA (e.g. April 2018 to June 2019)	$^{15}/_{12}$ × £200,000

4) The pro-rating rules above also apply to companies where the accounting period is shorter than 12 months. If a company has a period of account longer than 12 months, then this is split into one corporation tax accounting period of 12 months and one short period covering the rest of the period of account. Therefore, companies can never have WDAs and AIAs pro-rated upwards for long periods, but only downwards for short periods.
5) ECAs, FYAs, balancing allowances or charges are not adjusted for long or short periods.
6) On the commencement of a new unincorporated business, or on a change of accounting date, to deal with the taxable profits of the first and second years of assessment it will be necessary first to compute and deduct the capital allowances for the period(s) of account.

Example

Pedro started trading on the 1st May 2018 with the following results:

Adjusted profits 1st May 2018 to 30th April 2019	261,800
Adjusted profits 1st May 2019 to 30th April 2020	285,900
General plant and machinery purchased 10th April 2019	210,000

Compute the capital allowances available assuming current rules continue to apply in future years and show the assessable trading profits for the years 2018/19 to 2020/2021.

Solution

Capital allowances period 01-May-2018 – 30-Apr-2019		**General plant and machinery pool**
Opening WDV		0
10th April 2019 additions	210,000	
Less: Annual investment allowance – maximum	(200,000)	
Transfer unrelieved cost to pool		10,000
		10,000
Writing Down Allowance @ 18%		(1,800)
WDV 30th April 2019		8,200
Capital Allowances 01-May-2019 – 30-Apr-2020		
Writing Down Allowance @ 18%		(1,476)
WDV 30th April 2020		6,724

Period of Account	Adjusted Profits	Capital Allowances	**Taxable Profit**
	£	£	£
1.5.18 – 30.4.19	261,800	(201,800)	60,000
1.5.19 – 30.4.20	285,900	(1,476)	284,424

Assessments		£
2018/19 (1st May 2018 – 5th April 2019)	$^{11}/_{12} \times 60,000$	55,000
2019/20 (1st May 2018 – 30th April 2019)		60,000
2020/21 (1st May 2019 – 30th April 2020)		284,424

Note: The overlap period is from 1st May 2018 – 5th April 2019, i.e. 11 months, or profits of £55,000. When the business ceases trading, an adjustment for this amount will be made in the final self-assessment of trading profits.

Example

Quereshi started trading on 1st October 2018 with first accounts for the 15 months to 31st December 2019.

Capital expenditure of £265,000 on general plant and machinery was incurred on 1st October 2018. Capital expenditure of £24,000 was incurred on features integral to a building on 1st November 2018. Adjusted profits, before capital allowances, for the 15 months amounted to £333,525.

			General pool	Special rate pool
Capital expenditure General plant	01-Oct-2018	265,000		
integral features	01-Nov-2018	24,000		
Annual investment allowance	200,000×15/12	(250,000)		
Transfer unrelieved cost to pool			39,000	0
Writing down allowance	18% × 15/12		(8,775)	
Written down value carried forward			**30,225**	**0**

Assessments

	Adjusted profits 01-Oct-2018 – 31-Dec-2019	333,525
	Capital allowances (250,000 + 8,775)	(258,775)
		74,750
2018/19	01-Oct-2018 – 05-Apr-2019 74,750 × 6/15	29,900
2019/20	01-Jan-2019 – 31-Dec-2019 74,750 × 12/15	59,800

Notes

i) The capital allowances are computed for the period of account of 15 months.

ii) Capital allowances are deducted from the profits of the period of account before computing the profits assessed in different tax years, using the basis period rules.

iii) Overlap profits are January to March 2019: 74,750 × 3/15 = £14,950.

iv) If the first period of account had been less than 12 months in duration, the WDA and AIA would have been pro-rated down.

v) FYAs and ECAs are not scaled up or down for the length of a period of account.

13.18 Restriction on leasing costs for cars with high emissions

This is not strictly a capital allowances rule, but was introduced because of the capital allowances rules for cars. The legislators considered that, given the slower rate of writing down allowances for cars with high CO_2 emissions, businesses would lease these cars instead of buying them outright (obtaining a full expense deduction for the lease costs).

To discourage this, if a private car is leased or hired for trading purposes which emits more than 110 g/km of CO_2, then the hiring or leasing charge allowed as a business expense is restricted by 15%. This rule applies equally to incorporated and unincorporated businesses.

Example

Conrad hires a car for £3,200 p.a. which emits 190 g/km CO_2. Conrad uses the car 30% for private use.

	£
Total of hire charge	3,200
Restriction for high emissions 15%	(480)
	2,720
Restriction for private use 30%	(816)
Allowable expense	£1,904

13.19 Plant acquired by hire purchase

With this method of purchase, the interest element is allowed as an expense of trading. Regarding the capital element, capital allowances can be claimed:

a) Before the plant is brought into use, for any instalment due.

b) When the plant is brought into use, for all instalments outstanding, as if the whole of the balance of capital expenditure had been paid on at that date.

c) Where an HP agreement is not eventually completed after the plant has been brought into use, then an adjustment is made which claims back part of the allowance granted.

13.20 Leased plant and machinery

In general, a lessor of plant and machinery is entitled to the full amount of capital allowances on eligible expenditure, and the rental payments of the lessee are an allowable business expense on an accruals basis (*except for some cars, as noted in 13.18*).

Separate pooling arrangements apply to assets leased outside the UK, other than ships, aircraft and containers leased in the course of a UK trade.

13.21 Balancing charges and allowances: general rules

A balancing charge arises when the total disposal receipts (TDR) (limited to the original cost) of any pooled or non-pooled asset is greater than the amount of pool written down value existing for offset in the period of the sale.

Disposal value is the amount of the proceeds of sale, or where the asset is lost or destroyed, any insurance or compensation moneys received. In other circumstances, for example if plant is given away, the market price is used.

Where plant or machinery is demolished giving rise to a disposal treatment, the net cost of demolition can be added to the amount of unallowed expenditure at the time of the demolition.

A balancing allowance arises when the amount of pool written down value is greater than the total disposal receipts (TDR), but only in the following circumstances:

a) in the terminal period when trading permanently ceases;
b) when there is, or is deemed to be, a cessation of trade, see below;
c) when the asset has been de-pooled by election, or by reason of private use. (However, a balancing allowance is not available on a private use asset if it is sold to a connected person for less than its tax written down value.)

No balancing allowance is given on the sale of all remaining assets in the general or special rate pool unless the trade also ceases.

13.22 Deemed cessation of trading for capital allowances

For capital allowance technical purposes, the triggering of balancing adjustments is done by deeming the assets in 'special pools' as forming a separate notional trade to that of any actual trade undertaken, which is deemed to cease on disposal of the last item of plant/machinery features in that pool. This applies to the following categories:

a) private use assets
b) short life assets
c) ships
d) each letting of machinery otherwise than in the course of a trade of letting.

Example

Brian, who has been trading for many years, has the following data relating to his accounting year ended 31st March 2019.

		£
a)	Additions to general plant – 31st December 2018	12,000
	Proceeds of sale of plant (original cost £1,500)	2,500
	Purchase of red car for sales manager purchased 31-Jan-2019	14,000
	CO_2 emissions of red car 180 g/km	
	Sale of black car used by sales staff (original cost £9,000)	4,500
	CO_2 emissions of black car 105 g/km	

b) At 1st April 2018 the Tax Written Down Values of assets were:

	£
Plant and machinery	15,000
Grey car for B (private use 30%)	7,400
CO_2 emissions of grey car 105 g/km	

Compute the capital allowances claimable for the period of account to 31st March 2019.

Solution:

	General pool	Motor car (private use 30%)	Special rate pool
	£	£	£
TWDV at 31st March 2018	15,000	7,400	
Additions:			
Qualifying for AIA	12,000		
Not qualifying for AIA			14,000
Disposals:			
Plant (limited to original cost)	(1,500)		
Black car	(4,500)		
Annual Investment Allowance	(12,000)		
TWDV before other CAs	9,000	7,400	14,000
Writing Down Allowance at 18%	(1,620)	(1,332)*	(1,120)
TWDV at 31st March 2019	7,380	6,068	12,880

Capital Allowances claimable for the period of account to 31st March 2019 = 12,000 + 1,620 + 1,332×70% + 1,120 = **£15,672**.

Notes

(i) Notice that the car with private use forms a separate pool and the WDA is first computed at the 18% rate and deducted in full within that pool, then restricted as regards the actual allowance given. This method allows for varying proportions of private use over the life of the asset.

(ii) A car with CO_2 emissions of more than 110 g/km is entitled to WDA of only 8%.

(iii) Private use of cars by employees is irrelevant to the capital allowances position.

13.23 Plant and machinery – short-life assets

Short-life assets, other than cars, may be removed from the general pool ('de-pooled') at the option of the taxpayer. Generally, an election to de-pool will only be advantageous if the proceeds of sale are expected to be less than the written down value at the date of future disposal, so that the de-pooled treatment will give the chance of an immediate balancing allowance in the future chargeable period.

De-pooling can last for a maximum of nine accounting (or basis) periods, but sometimes for only eight, depending on how dates interact.

The provisions on short life assets are as follows.

a) The rules apply in respect of plant and machinery from the general pool, but do not apply to motor cars, ships or assets leased to non-traders, or assets already required to be pooled separately.

b) Where the taxpayer expects to dispose of an item of plant or machinery at less than its tax written down value, within eight years of the end of the period of acquisition, then they can elect to have the item extracted from the general plant pool, and a separate pool created. The plant is treated as being in use for a separate notional trade.

c) The election to de-pool a short life asset or class of assets must be made within two years of the end of the period of acquisition.

d) Any balancing adjustment arising on the disposal is calculated separately.

e) If the item of plant or machinery has not been sold or scrapped by the end of eight years from the end of the year of acquisition then its tax written down value is transferred back to the general plant pool on the day after the 8th anniversary.

Example

Tatiana, who has traded for many years, has an accounting year-end of 31st March. On 1st May 2014 she purchased equipment with a cost of £8,365 not relieved by AIA, electing for de-pooling.

Show the computations in the following circumstances:

a) The plant is sold in the year to 31st March 2019 for £2,000.
b) The plant is sold in the year to 31st March 2019 for £5,000.
c) The equipment is not sold by the 31st March 2019.

Solution: Capital allowances computation

		£
2014/15	Basis period to 31st March 2015: cost	8,365
	WDA @ 18%	(1,506)
	WDV 1st April 2015	6,859
2015/16	Basis period to 31st March 2016: WDA @ 18%	(1,235)
	WDV 1st April 2016	5,624
2016/17	Basis period to 31st March 2017: WDA @ 18%	(1,012)
	WDV 1st April 2017	4,612
2017/18	Basis period to 31st March 2018: WDA @ 18%	(830)
	WDV 1st April 2018	3,782

Scenario (a)		£
2018/19	WDV 1st April 2018	3,782
	Disposal proceeds	(2,000)
	Balancing allowance	1,782

Scenario (b)		
2018/19	WDV 1st April 2018	3,782
	Disposal proceeds	(5,000)
	Balancing charge	(1,218)

Scenario (c)

2018/19	WDV 1st April 2018	3,782
	Writing down allowance at 18%	(681)
	WDV 1st April 2019	3,101

Notes

i) Where short life assets of a similar nature are acquired in large numbers e.g. small tools or returnable containers, then the cost of the assets may be aggregated and treated as one sum.

ii) Where assets used in a trade are stocked in large numbers and individual identification is possible but not readily practicable, then the computation can be based on the number of each class of asset retained. Assets falling under this heading might be, for example, amusement machines or scientific instruments.

PART II – Other assets

13.24 Scientific research capital allowances

Allowances for capital expenditure on scientific research and development related to a trade carried on by a taxpayer are given against trading profits at 100% in the year the expenditure is incurred. The rules are as follows:

a) 'Research and development' means activities that fall to be treated as research and development in accordance with normal accounting practice.

b) Expenditure on research and development includes all expenditure incurred for:

   i) carrying out research and development, or

   ii) providing facilities for carrying out research and development.

   But it does not include expenditure incurred in the acquisition of rights in research and development, or rights arising out of research and development.

c) 'Normal accounting practice' means normal accounting practice in relation to the accounts of companies incorporated in a part of the United Kingdom.

d) Capital expenditure under this heading would include buildings and plant and machinery, but not land.

e) The amount of the allowance is 100% of capital expenditure.

Balancing adjustments can arise when assets representing research and development expenditure cease to be used for such purposes and they are either sold or destroyed.

Note Companies, but not income tax payers, can also get special allowances on research and development expenses that are revenue in character, equal to more than the total cost of that research and development expenditure. See Chapter 19.

Student self-testing questions

Note: These questions all relate to unincorporated taxpayers' capital allowances. You can find questions involving capital allowances for companies in and after part III.

Question 13.1, Ryan

Ryan incurred the following expenditure on plant and machinery in the year ended 31st December 2019:

		£
6th January 2019	New plant	36,000
11th February 2019	Second hand lorry	20,000
14th February 2019	Features integral to a building	196,500
17th July 2019	Ryan's car (30% private use)	13,000
14th August 2019	Car fleet for sales team (3 cars)	60,000

CO_2 emissions of all cars were 180 g/km.

Requirement

Calculate the capital allowances available to Ryan for the year ended 31st December 2019.

Solution to Question 13.1, Ryan

Year to 31st December 2019		General Pool	Special rate pool	Car,30% private, 180g emissions
	£	£	£	£
Qualifying expenditure incurred (not eligible for AIA) - cars			60,000	13,000
Qualifying expenditure (eligible for AIA but not 100% ECA)	252,500			
Less: Annual Investment Allowance (maximum)	(200,000)			
Transfer unrelieved cost to pool		52,500		
Less: Writing down allowance 18% or 8%		(9,450)	(4,800)	(1,040) 70% business
(WDV) carried forward		43,050	55,200	11,960

	£
Allowances: Annual investment allowance	200,000
Writing down allowance 18%	9,450
Writing down allowance 8%	4,800
WDA 13,000 @ 8% = 1,040 × 70% business	728
	214,978

Question 13.2, Tom

Tom commenced trading on 1st July 2018 and produced his first set of accounts to the period ended 30th September 2019. He purchased the following assets during this 15-month period:

		£
5th July 2018	Features integral to a building	249,250
10th July 2018	General plant	14,000
18th July 2018	Car (private use 25%)	16,000
20th July 2018	Van	18,000
30th July 2018	Office furniture	12,000
1st August 2019	Computer equipment	4,650

CO_2 emissions of the car were 180 g/km.

Requirement

Calculate the capital allowances available to Tom for the period of account.

Solution to Question 13.2, Tom

15-month period of account 1st July 2018 to 30th September 2019	£	General Pool £	Car (25% private) £
Qualifying expenditure incurred (car) (not eligible for AIA)		-	16,000
Qualifying expenditure - AIA (not eligible for 100% ECA)	297,900		
Less: Annual Investment Allowance – maximum (£200,000 × 15/12)	(250,000)		
Excess of expenditure over £250,000		47,900	
Less: Writing down allowances 15/12 × 18% or 8% [= 22.5% and 10%]		(10,777)	(1,600) 75% business
Written down value (WDV) carried forward		37,123	14,400

Allowances	Annual investment allowance	250,000
	Writing down allowance 18% × 47,900 × 15/12	10,777
	WDA 8% × 16,000 × 15/12 × 75%	1,200
		261,977

Questions without answers

Question 13.3, Wilton

Wilton starts a trade on 1st May 2018 and has the following results before capital allowances

Period of account	Profits
1st May 2018 – 31st July 2019	324,400
1st August 2019 – 31st July 2020	325,000
1st August 2020 – 31st July 2021	350,000

Plant is bought as follows:

Date		Cost
1st May 2018	Features integral to a building	154,750
30th June 2018	ICT equipment	14,000
1st December 2018	Other general plant	136,346
1st October 2019	Cars with 105 g/km CO_2 emissions	62,000
1st May 2021	Office equipment	4,000

On 1st May 2020 the ICT equipment which cost £14,000 was sold for £8,000

Requirement

Calculate assessments on profits from trading for the first four tax years. Assume no changes in future years to the plant and machinery capital allowance rules applying in 2.

Question 13.4, Homer

Homer started a business on 1st February 2018 and prepared accounts for the 18-month period to 31st July 2019, and then to 31st July each year. Between 1st February 2018 and 31st July 2020, he had the following capital expenditure and disposals.

Additions			**Disposals**		
01-May-2018	General plant	327,99 7			
01-May-2018	Grey car	11,000			
13-Jun-2018	Red lorry	9,000			
01-Oct-2018	Printer	7,000			
10-Nov-2019	Office equipment	5,000	30-Nov-2019	Printer (bought 01-Oct-2018)	9,300
15-Jun-2020	Machinery	2,000			
20-Jun-2020	Blue car	16,000			
30-Jun-2020	Yellow lorry	18,000	30-Jun-2020	Red lorry (bought 13-Jun-2018)	7,500

The private use of each of Homer's cars is 40%.
CO_2 emissions of the grey car purchased on 1st May 2018 were 190 g/km.
CO_2 emissions of the blue car purchased on 20th June 2020 are 105 g/km.

Requirement

Calculate the maximum capital allowances available to Homer for the periods ending 31st July 2019 and 31st July 2020.

Assume no changes to plant and machinery capital allowance rules applying in 2018/19.

14 Relief for trading and capital losses

14.1 Introduction

This chapter is concerned with the tax reliefs available to an income tax-payer who incurs a trading loss, and with the restricted circumstances in which 'capital losses' may be claimed against income. We cover losses by companies separately in Chapter 22.

14.2 List of loss reliefs

Trading loss set against total income of the same or prior tax year.	Section 64 ITA 2007
Trading loss carried forward and set against future trading income from the same trade.	Section 83 ITA 2007
Losses incurred in each of the first four years of trading set against total income of the three preceding tax years.	Section 72 ITA 2007
Terminal loss relief for losses of the last 12 months of a trade.	Section 89 ITA 2007
Relief for trading losses where a business is transferred to a limited company.	Section 86 ITA 2007
Relief for capital losses against income.	Section 131 ITA 2007
Relief for pre-trading expenditure (not technically a loss relief, but an expense relief, since 2005).	Section 57 ITTOIA 2005
Trading loss set against capital gains.	section 261B TCGA 1992
Property rental business losses.	Section 117 ITA 2007

14.3 Set against 'other income' Section 64 ITA 2007

The following points should be noted:

i) Capital allowances are deducted in computing adjusted taxable profits.

ii) Profits and losses are calculated by reference to periods of account, except the terminal loss computation for Section 89.

iii) The basis period rules apply to allocate losses to tax years, but there can be no 'overlap' so losses are only measured once. Thus, any loss which would otherwise count in two basis periods can only count in the earlier period.

iv) Relief against total income can be claimed in the tax year of the loss or the preceding tax year.

v) See 14.8 for the loss relief caps which apply to 'sideways' and carry-back claims against total income, for trade losses of tax year 2013/14 onwards.

vi) Where Section 64 total income claims are made in respect of both years the taxpayer can choose which claim should be taken in priority. Partial claims are not permitted.

vii) Any unused loss is carried forward under Section 83.

Example

Araminta, who has been in business for many years, has an adjusted loss from trading for the year ended 31st December 2018 of £12,000. Under the basis period rules this is a trade loss of tax year 2018/19.
For tax year 2017/18, Araminta's self-assessed taxable income, before any loss claims, was as follows:

	£
Trade profits year to 31st December 2017	10,000
Property business profit	30,000

Compute Araminta's income tax liability for 2017/18 on the assumption that she claims relief for the trading loss of 2018/19 in the previous tax year, under s64 ITA 2007.

Solution:

	£
Trading profits	10,000
Property income	30,000
Total income	40,000
Section 64 loss relief from 2018/19	(12,000)
Net income	28,000
Personal Allowance	(11,850)
Taxable income	16,150
Income tax contribution due @ 20%	**£3,230**

Notes

i) Personal allowances are claimed after relief for a loss, so that there may be wasted personal allowances if a large trade loss is carried back.

ii) The whole of the loss for 2018/19 has been used against total income of the tax year preceding the loss tax year, i.e. 2017/18.

14.4 Capital allowances

Capital allowances are deducted in computing trade profits, but the taxpayer does not have to claim the full allowances available in computing his or her taxable profits. Unusable losses can therefore sometimes be avoided by forgoing capital allowances in a period.

14.5 Tax planning considerations in making a Section 64 claim

The following points should be taken into consideration in deciding whether to make a claim for loss relief against total income under Section 64 for the current or prior year, or both, and in what order.

a) **Loss of personal allowance**: Cannot be carried forward, or back.

b) **Transfer of married couple's allowance, spouses aged 65 at 5th April 2000**: Can all be transferred to the spouse, on a joint election, although only obtaining relief at the 10% rate.

c) **Loss of personal pension plan relief** *(see Chapter 16)*: Net relevant UK earnings are after deduction of loss relief.

d) **Saving tax at higher rates**: A claim can be made for the tax year of the loss or the preceding year, or both in either order. The top tax rate of the taxpayer in these years may not be the same.

e) **Reduction in Class 4 NIC**: Profits for Class 4 National Insurance purposes (see Chapter 17) are after deduction of loss reliefs set against trade income (s83) but are not reduced by loss reliefs set against total income (s64).

14.6 Carried forward – Section 83 ITA 2007

To the extent that a trading loss has not been relieved by claims under section 64 or 72, which take priority, it may be carried forward and set against the first available profits of the same trade.

Any loss brought forward must be set off as soon as possible against trade profits, even where this causes a loss of personal allowances.

Example

Mr Rose has tax adjusted profits for the year to 31st December 2018 of £26,000, and no capital allowances. Trade losses brought forward under Section 83 amount to £3,105. Rose started in business on 1st July 2005 and has no other income.

Compute the income tax liability for 2018/19 of Mr Rose.

Solution: Income tax computation 2018/19

(basis period year to 31st December 2018)		£	£
Trade profits			26,000
Section 83 losses b/f			(3,105)
			22,895
Personal allowance			(11,850)
Taxable income			11,045
	£		£
Tax Liability	n/a	@ 0%	0
	11,045	@ 20%	2,209

14.7 Relief for losses in first 4 years of trading: Section 72 ITA 2007

The relief available under this section is in addition to that under Sec 64 or 83 but is only available in the first four tax years of a new trade. The relief is as follows.

a) Trading losses incurred in the first four tax years may be carried back and set against the total income of the taxpayer, in the previous three tax years in each case.

b) The set-off under section 72 is against income of an earlier year before a later year, i.e. on a FIFO basis.

c) The trade loss is calculated on the normal basis period rules for losses.

d) Each loss is set against income of the first available year in the order: non-savings income, savings income, and dividend income of the claimant.

e) A claim must be made by the filing date for the tax year after the loss is incurred.

f) Each claim is a separate claim for a separate tax year loss. It is not necessary to make the section 72 claim for all tax years if losses are incurred in all the first four years.

g) Where a claim is made for relief under Sec 64 and under Sec 72, then the loss cannot be apportioned between them. Butt v Haxby 1983 STC 239.

Example

Paul left his employment on 31st December 2015 and commenced trading on 1st January 2016 with the following results for tax purposes:

	£ (Loss)
12 months to 31st December 2016	(3,000)
12 months to 31st December 2017	(2,000)
12 months to 31st December 2018	(5,000)

Compute the losses available for set-off under section 72 and show the tax years in which they can be utilised.

Solution

2015/16	01-Jan-2016 – 05-Apr-2016 $^{3}/_{12} \times 3{,}000 =$			(750)
2016/17	Year ended 31-Dec-2016		(3,000)	
	Less allocated to 2015/16		750	(2,250)
2017/18	Year ended 31-Dec-2017			(2,000)
2018/19	Year ended 31-Dec-2018			(5,000)

Loss relief available is as follows:

	2015/16	2016/17	2017/18	2018/19
	£	£	£	£
	750	2,250	2,000	5,000
Set against total income				
2012/13	750	–	–	–
2013/14	–	2,250	–	–
2014/15	–	–	2,000	–
2015/16	–	–	–	5,000

Note: If the losses cannot be fully used by a section 72 claim then the balance can be carried forward in the usual way under Section 83.

14.8 Cap on income tax reliefs

From 6th April 2013 trade loss relief claimed against total income, and early years loss relief claims, are limited to the greater of £50,000 or 25% of adjusted total income. This limit applies separately for each tax year in which a trade loss is claimed against total income, i.e. under section 64 or 72.

Note that this restriction does not apply to loss relief against trading income arising from the same trade – only to relief against **other** income.

14.9 Terminal loss relief – Section 89 ITA 2007

Under this section relief is available where a cessation of trading takes place, and a loss arises attributable to all or part of the last 12 months of trading. The rules for computing the loss are designed to be fair to all traders, regardless of what point in the final tax year they cease trading.

A terminal loss may optionally be carried back and set against the trading profits (less capital allowances) of the three tax years prior to the tax year in which the trade ceases. The terminal loss is made up of 3 elements:

(a) The loss from 6th April to the date of cessation in the final tax year; plus

(b) The loss for the other part of the final twelve months of trading; plus

(c) Overlap profits.

Where part (b) of the calculation shows a profit, it is ignored in calculating the terminal loss.

Example

Sophia has overlap profits brought forward of £1,000, and ceased trading on 30th June 2018 with the following results:

Adjusted profits	**£**
9 months to 30th June 2018	(1,500)
12 months to 30th September 2017	1,200
12 months to 30th September 2016	1,600

Compute the terminal loss available for relief.

Solution: Calculation of terminal loss – 12 months to 30th June 2018

		£	£
2018/19	(06-Apr-2018 – 30-Jun-2018)		
$^3/_9 \times$ (1,500)		(500)	(500)
2017/18	(01-Jul-2017 – 05-Apr-2018)		
01-Oct-2017 – 05-Apr-2018 $^6/_9 \times$ (1,500)		(1,000)	
01-Jul-2017 – 01-Oct-2017 $^3/_{12} \times$ 1,200		300	(700)
Overlap profits			(1,000)
Terminal loss			(2,200)

14.10 Some further points on terminal losses

a) Capital allowances claimed are deducted before terminal loss relief is applied.

b) Terminal loss is computed after deducting capital allowances.

14.11 Transfer of a business to a limited company – Section 86 ITA 2007

If a sole trader or partnership transfers its business to a limited company, there is a cessation of trade. Accordingly, trading losses at the date of transfer are not available for set-off against any future corporation tax profits of the new company.

However, Section 86 provides some relief where the following conditions are met.

a) The consideration for the business consists wholly or mainly in allotted shares of the company. In this case 80% is often taken to satisfy ‘mainly’.

b) The shares are beneficially held by the transferor throughout the period of any tax year for which a claim under Section 86 is made.

c) The company carries on the same business throughout any tax year for which a claim is made.

Relief is available in respect of trading losses from a former business which can be carried forward and they can be set against income received by the transferor from the company. The losses must be set against earned income first, e.g. directors' fees or remuneration, and then investment income, e.g. dividends.

Example

Dinsdale transfers his business to a limited company on 1st August 2018 wholly for shares.

At that date the business has trading losses of £10,000. In the year 2018/19 Dinsdale receives director's remuneration of £8,000 and a dividend of £1,000 from the company.

Income tax computation 2018/19

	£
Income from employment	8,000
Less Section 86 loss	(8,000)
Dividend income	1,000
Less Section 86 loss	(1,000)

Notes

i) With this example there would be trade losses to carry forward to 2019/20 of £1,000 providing the conditions noted above are satisfied.

ii) In claiming the Section 86 relief for 2018/19 Dinsdale has lost his Personal Allowance which cannot be carried forward.

14.12 Relief against total income for capital losses on unquoted trading companies – Section 131 ITA 2007

Under this section a loss made by an individual on the disposal of any unquoted shares can be set against his or her income for income tax purposes. The loss must arise from the disposal of shares originally subscribed for on the formation of the company, and not from an inheritance or subsequent acquisition.

The claim is like a claim under Section 64 ITA 2007 but takes precedence over relief under that section. The company must be a UK trading company at the date of the disposal. A qualifying loss can only be claimed in the following circumstances:

a) on a disposal for full market value, or
b) on a winding up, or
c) on a claim that the shares have become of negligible value.

The loss is deducted from the taxpayer's income in the year in which the disposal takes place or in the preceding year.

This relief is also available where the unquoted shares sold at a loss were originally acquired under the Enterprise Investment Scheme (see also Chapter 6).

Example

Zahoor and his wife live in England and have the following relating to 2018/19:

	£
Zahoor Income from employment	54,000
Mrs Zahoor Income from employment	18,600
Zahoor bank deposit interest	1,000
Zahoor allowable loss under Sec 131 ITA 2007 arising from shares in Ashley Ltd	3,000

Compute the income tax liabilities for 2018/19 of Zahoor and his wife.

Solution: Income tax computations 2018/19

			Zahoor	Mrs Zahoor
			£	£
Non-savings income				
Income from employment Zahoor			54,000	–
Income from employment Mrs Zahoor			–	18,600
			54,000	18,600
Savings income:				
Bank deposit interest			1,000	–
			55,000	18,600
Less capital loss relief Sec 131			(3,000)	–
			52,000	18,600
Personal allowances			(11,850)	(11,850)
Taxable income			40,150	6,750
Tax liabilities:				
			£	£
Non-savings income:				
Basic rate	34,500 or 6,750	@ 20%	6,900	1,350
Higher rate	4,650	@ 40%	1,860	
Savings income:				
PSA	500	@ 0%	-	
Higher rate	500	@ 40%	200	
	40,150			
Tax liabilities			8,960	1,350

Notes

i) The relief for the capital loss is deducted from the earned income of Zahoor in the computation. If this is insufficient it is set against his unearned income.

ii) As Zahoor is paying tax at the 40% rate it would be tax efficient to transfer some of his investments to Mrs Zahoor, to generate additional income in her own right.

14.13 Pre-trading expenditure

Relief is available for expenditure incurred by a person in the seven years before he or she commences to carry on a trade.

a) The expenditure must be allowable trading expenditure which would have been deducted in computing trading profits if incurred after the commencement of trading.

b) Pre-trading expenditure is treated as an expense of the trade.

c) The relief does not apply to pre-trading purchases of stock.

d) A trading loss in the first tax year caused by pre-trading expenditure relief may be relieved under Section 64, 83 and 72 ITA 2007 in the normal way.

14.14 Restrictions on claiming loss reliefs

In addition to the restriction to £50,000 per year from 2013/14 for loss relief claims against total income or for early years losses, explained in section 14.8 above, the following restrictions apply:

a) A claim under Section 64 is only available to trades which were carried on with a view to profit, and on a commercial basis, in the tax year of the loss.

b) Farmers and market gardeners cannot obtain relief under Section 64 if in the previous five years their business has incurred successive trade losses, unless it can be shown that the trade is being carried on with a view to profit, and there is a reasonable expectation of profits in the future.

c) Loss relief under Section 83 is available in the earliest possible years only against the profits from the same trade, and not against total income or profits from any other trade.

d) Income Tax loss relief against total income under section 64 is restricted to a maximum of £25,000 offset in a tax year, if an individual does not spend more than 10 hours per week on average working in the trade which incurred the loss. There are also anti-avoidance rules, not covered in detail here, which restrict loss claims against general income, if the loss belongs to a film partnership, or to a trading partnership set up with an intention of tax avoidance. (See Chapter 15 for partnership taxation.)

14.15 Trading losses set against capital gains

Where a trading loss is incurred in a tax year, then to the extent that it has not been fully relieved by a total income claim under Section 64 ITA 2007, a claim for relief against net chargeable gains of the same year can be made. The amount set against capital gains cannot exceed the chargeable gains for the year, before deducting the CGT exemption amount of £11,700, for 2018/19.

Example

Nigella has the following data relating to the year 2018/19:

	£
Trade loss for year to 31st March 2019	(17,000)
Chargeable gains before exemption.	14,000

In the year to 5th April 2019 Nigella has other taxable income totalling £16,000.

Compute the income tax liability for 2018/19, assuming Nigella makes all possible current year loss claims.

Solution: Income tax computation 2018/19

	£
Total income	16,000
Less Section 64 claim	(16,000)
	–

CGT computation 2018/19	£
Chargeable gains	14,000
Less trading losses extended to gains (s280)	(1,000)
	13,000
Less annual exemption	(11,700)
Taxable chargeable gains	1,300

Notes

i) Nigella's personal allowance of £11,850 for 2018/19 would be wasted.

ii) The trading loss of £17,000 has been dealt with as follows:

		£
Section 64	2018/19	16,000
Capital gains	2018/19	1,000

iii) The CGT on the remaining £1,300 is taxable at the 10% rate (see Chapter 26)

14.16 Property business losses

1) Any rental business loss of an individual is automatically carried forward and set against rental business profits of the next year. It cannot be carried back or set against other income of the year.
2) Property business losses can only be set off against profits from property business (apart from (4) below).
3) Furnished holiday lettings losses may only be set against income from the same furnished holiday letting business.
4) Where a rental business loss is attributable to capital allowances then all or part of that attributable loss can be set against total income as relief for non-trade capital allowances against total income.

Example

Keith has a property business loss of £3,500 for the year 2018/19 after claiming landlord's capital allowances of £1,500.

Loss relief available against total income	£1,500

Notes

i) The £1,500 loss can be set against total income of 2018/19. The balance of £2,000 must be carried forward against future property business profits.
ii) Loss relief is limited to the smaller of the total property business loss and the capital allowances included in computing it.

Student self-testing questions

Question 14.1, James

James receives £3,000 per year income from property. He makes up business accounts for trading annually to 31st December. His recent tax adjusted results from trading have been:

Year to 31st December 2016	Profit	£42,000
Year to 31st December 2017	Profit	£48,000
Year to 31st December 2018	Loss	(£100,000)
Year to 31st December 2019	Profit	£58,000

Requirement

Show the net income before personal allowances in each of the years after making a tax effective claim for loss relief.

Solution to Question 14.1, James

Tax year	2016/17	2017/18	2018/19	2019/20
Period of a/c	31-Dec-2016	31-Dec-2017	31-Dec-2018	31-Dec-2019
	£	£	£	£
Income from trading	42,000	48,000	Loss	58,000
s83				(49,000)
				9,000
Income from property	3,000	3,000	3,000	3,000
Total income	45,000	51,000	3,000	12,000
s64		(51,000)		
Taxable total income	45,000	-	3,000	12,000

Loss Memorandum:

		£
2018/19	Loss arising	100,000
2017/18	s64 carry back against total income	(51,000)
2019/20	s83 carry forward against trade profit	(49,000)
c/fwd		0

Notes:

- A s64 claim against total income of the current year would not be tax effective, as the total income of 2018/19 is covered by the personal allowance;
- Carrying back £51,000 of the loss for offset against the total income for 2017/18 'wastes' the Personal Allowance for that year, which was £11,500, but generates a tax refund;
- Carrying forward the remaining £49,000 of the loss against future profits from the same trade leaves £12,000 of total income for that year. We don't yet know the Personal Allowance for 2019/20, but it's likely to be slightly higher than £12,000, meaning that there will be no tax to pay for that year either;
- Using only carry-forward relief would have wasted some (all but £3,000) of the 2019/20 Personal Allowance.

Question 14.2, Nathaniel

Nathaniel started trading on 1st October 2016 and prepared accounts to 31st December of each year from 2017.

His results for the first two accounting periods were: -

15 months to 31st December 2017	Loss 23,700
Year to 31st December 2018	Loss 19,320

Prior to becoming self-employed he had the following other income:

2013/14	12,200
2014/15	12,500
2015/16	12,800
6th April 2016 to 30th September 2016	6,900

Requirement

Calculate Nathaniel's net income for 2013/14 to 2016/17 using all available s72 claims.

Solution to Question 14.2, Nathaniel

Losses eligible for s72 Relief

Year	Basis period	Workings	Loss	Years for s72 claim
2016/17	1.10.16-5.4.17	23,700 × $^{6}/_{15}$	9,480	13/14 – 15/16
2017/18	1.1.17-31.12.17	23,700 × $^{12}/_{15}$ - 23700 × $^{3}/_{15}$	14,220	14/15 – 16/17
2018/19	y/e 31-Dec-2018		19,320	15/16 – 17/18

Using all possible s72 claims, total income is:

		2013/14	2014/15	2015/16	2016/17
Income from trade					0
Other income		12,200	12,500	12,800	6,900
s 72 relief	2016/17 loss	(9,480)			
	2017/18 loss		(12,500)	(1,720)	
	2018/19 loss			(11,080)	(6,900)
Total income		2,720	0	0	0

Carry forward loss of £1,340 for year 2018/19

Questions without answers

Question 14.3, Jensen

Jensen started to trade on 6th April 2017. Projected results are:

Year to 5th April		
2018	Profit	24,000
2019 (projected)	Profit	32,000
2020 (projected)	Profit	36,000
2021 (projected)	Profit	30,000
2022 (projected)	Loss	(56,000)

Jensen expects his business to be profitable thereafter.

Jensen also has rental income of £12,000 per annum. Using the 2018/19 loss relief rules:

a) **Outline alternative ways for Jensen to get relief for the loss of 2021/22;**
b) **Calculate the quickest way of relieving the loss.**
c) **How would the situation change if Jensen ceased trading on 5th April 2022?**

Question 14.4, Mr Yu

Mister Yu was employed as an auditor until 1st August 2017 and on that date started in business as a commodity dealer making up accounts to 30th June each year:

Income as auditor	£	Results as dealer (loss)	£
2014/15	30,000	1st August 2017 to 30th June 2018	(7,260)
2015/16	32,000	Year to 30th June 2019	(4,800)
2016/17	34,000	Year to 30th June 2020	(2,400)
2017/18	12,000	Year to 30th June 2021	nil

Requirement

Show the revised net income for all tax years if Mr Yu claims loss relief as early as possible.

Question 14.5, Finn

Finn's business ceased on 30th September 2018. Results were

	£
Year to 31st December 2015	24,000
Year to 31st December 2016	800
Year to 31st December 2017	600
9 months to 30th September 2018	(3,900)
Overlap profits on commencement (unrelieved)	900

Requirement

Calculate the terminal loss and show how it is relieved against earlier profits.

15 Partnership taxation

15.1 Introduction

A partnership exists where two or more persons join for business purposes forming an association which is not a separate legal entity for taxation purposes.

A trading or professional partnership is taxed as a collection of sole traders.

The main special features of partnership taxation relate to:

a) the allocation of profits for tax purposes,

b) the effect of changes in partnerships' members or profit-sharing arrangements, and

c) some loss restrictions for limited liability partnerships.

15.2 General rules

The following provisions apply to any new partnership that has a trade or profession.

(The partnership tax rules in this chapter do not apply to partners in investment activities, including letting of property. These are simply treated as joint owners of an investment asset, and taxed on their respective shares of the income, net of allowable expenses, for each tax year.)

a) For income tax purposes a partnership of two or more individuals is not treated as a separate legal entity distinct from the partners. The effect of this is that each partner is assessed for tax individually like a sole trader.

b) A 'partnership tax return' must also be completed for HMRC by the representative partner. This return is completed for a partnership period of account, not a tax year. It shows the adjustment of the firm's accounting profits for tax purposes, and the allocation of the adjusted profits to each partner, including capital allowances. The profits and capital allowances figures shown on the partnership return are then repeated as basis period data on the individual partners' self-assessment tax returns for a tax year.

c) Taxable profits of the partnership are calculated in the same way as for a sole trader, so that all partnership expenses and capital allowances are deducted from the profits before the allocation of net profits to the partners. Therefore, partners cannot individually decide whether to claim full or reduced capital allowances, or to de-pool a short life asset; such decisions must be the same for all partners, and notified on the partnership tax return.

d) Profits are assessed on a current year basis, with the normal basis period being the period of account for the twelve months ending in the tax year. The rules for determination of the assessable trade profits of each partner in the first two or three tax years, and last tax year, in which he or she is a member of the partnership are the same as the opening and closing tax years' basis period rules for a sole trader (see Chapter 11).

e) Partnership profits are allocated by reference to the partnership profit-sharing agreement applicable for the period of account, not the related tax year.

f) Where there is a change in the members of a partnership, so long as there is at least one partner carrying on the business both before and after the change, the change does not constitute a cessation of the partnership's trade for tax purposes (except for any partner who has left the partnership).

15.3 Adjustment and allocation of profits

As already noted, partnership accounting profits are adjusted for income tax purposes using the same principles as for a sole trader - see Chapter 10. Partners' 'salaries' and 'interest' earned on capital are taxed as trade income, affecting final shares of trade profits. So, partners' salaries (if any) and interest (if any) are allocated first, and the balance of tax-adjusted net profit is then divided between partners in the agreed profit-sharing ratio.

Example

Angus and Bruce formed a partnership in June 2010, sharing profits equally, after 'interest' of 5% per annum on their capital accounts of £160,000 and £100,000 respectively, and a 'salary' for A of £50,000. Tax-adjusted profits shown on the partnership return for the year ended 31st December 2018 were £150,000.

Show the allocation of profits for 2018/19.

Solution: Partnership computation 2018/19

Adjusted profits after capital allowances year to 31st December 2018 = £150,000

Allocation of profit 2018/19

	Total	A	B
	£	£	£
Interest on capital: 5%	13,000	8,000	5,000
Salary – A	50,000	50,000	–
	63,000	58,000	5,000
Balance shared equally	87,000	43,500	43,500
Share of trade profits	150,000	101,500	48,500

Notes

i) Each partner includes his share of profit, i.e. Angus £101,500, Bruce £48,500, in his personal self-assessment tax return, being trading profits measured for 2018/19 based on the year to 31st December 2018.

ii) All amounts shown in the partnership accounts for the year to 31st December 2018, for partners' salaries, share of profits already drawn, or interest on capital, will have been added back as proprietors' drawings in arriving at the taxable profit of £150,000 in the partnership tax return.

Example of opening year rules

Clive and Derek entered into partnership on 1st June 2014 with the following results:

	£ Adjusted profits	£ Capital allowances
1st June 2014 – 31st May 2015	20,000	2,000
1st June 2015 – 31st May 2016	30,000	5,000
1st June 2016 – 31st May 2017	40,000	15,000
1st June 2017 – 31st May 2018	50,000	10,000

The partners have agreed to share profits equally.

Show the individual partners' assessable trading profits for the relevant tax years.

Solution

	Partnership Clive and Derek	Assessments	Clive	Derek
2014/15	Period of account 1st June 2014 – 5th April 2015 10/12 × (20,000 – 2,000)	15,000	7,500	7,500
2015/16	Period of account 1st June 2014 – 31st May 2015 (20,000 – 2,000)	18,000	9,000	9,000
2016/17	Period of account 1st June 2015 – 31st May 2016 (30,000 – 5,000)	25,000	12,500	12,500
2017/18	Period of account 1st June 2016 – 31st May 2017 (40,000 – 15,000)	25,000	12,500	12,500
2018/19	Period of account 1st June 2017 – 31st May 2018 (50,000 – 10,000)	40,000	20,000	20,000

Notes

i) The overlap period is 1st June 2014 to 5th April 2015, with overlap profits of £7,500 being carried forward by each partner (this is counting in whole months, which is acceptable for accounting exams; the overlap figure is £7,595 each if one counts the exact days, which is the correct position in tax law). When the partnership ceases, or a partner leaves and is replaced by another, then the leaving partner's final profits assessment from the partnership will be reduced by his overlap relief.

ii) Paying income tax and class 4 National Insurance is the responsibility of the individuals in the partnership and not the partnership itself. However, many partnerships do account for, and pay, all income tax and class 4 NI for the partners, treating them as drawings from current account.

iii) We can check the overlap against total profits assessed for each partner:

Total profits assessed for 5 tax years (58 months of trading) = £61,500 based on £54,000 net assessable profits for 4 × 12 months to 31st May 2018.

Profits counted twice = first 10 months = £7,500

£7,500 = overlap carried forward by each partner (54000+7500 = 61,500)

15.4 Changes in a partnership

The basis period rules apply separately for each new partner who joins, and for each retiring (ceasing) partner. The trade is a source of income which is starting or ceasing for the individual, but the other partners are unaffected by a partner joining or leaving the partnership, so long as they themselves continue trading.

If there is a change in profit-sharing ratio during a period of account, for exam purposes it may be assumed that all income and expenses in that period of account accrued evenly. In practice, the final information about the allocated profit shares of partners, for a period of account when there is a change in either the partners or their profit shares, or both, will be effective as reported to HMRC on the partnership tax return.

Example

Max and Fay started in partnership on 1st July 2011, sharing profits equally.

Their accounts are made up to 31st December each year. On 1st January 2014, Caz was admitted as an equal partner, the profit ratio then becoming one-third each.

Tax-adjusted profits for the years to 31st December 2014 were as follows:

	£
1st July 2011 – 31st December 2011	20,000
12 months to 31st December 2012	40,000
12 months to 31st December 2013	50,000
12 months to 31st December 2014	60,000

Show the assessable trading profit of each partner for tax years 2011/12 to 2014/15. Calculations may be made to the nearest month.

Solution

Tax year	**Basis period**	**£**	**Total £**	**Max £**	**Fay £**	**Caz £**
2011/12	01-Jul-2011-31-Dec-2011	20,000				
	01-Jan-2012-05-Apr-2012 ($^3/_{12}$ × 40,000)	10,000				
			30,000	15,000	15,000	-

2012/13	12 months to 31-Dec-2012	40,000	20,000	20,000	-
2013/14	Max and Fay: 12 months to 31-Dec-2013	50,000	25,000	25,000	-
	Caz: opening year rules: 01-Jan-2014 - 05-Apr-2014 ($^3/_{12} \times 60{,}000 \times {}^1/_3$)	5,000			5,000
	Total for 2013/14	55,000	25,000	25,000	5,000
2014/15	12 months to 31-Dec-2014	60,000	20,000	20,000	20,000

Notes

(i) When Caz is admitted on 1st January 2014, there is continuation of the trade for the others.

(ii) The partners are assessed individually on their shares of the profits.

(iii) Caz is treated as starting in self-employment on 1st January 2014 and her individual overlap profit must be computed based on that start date. Her overlap will be the profits counted in both 2013/14 and 2014/15. This is as follows:

1st January 2014 to 5th April 2014 = 3 months

$^3/_{12} \times 60{,}000$ (i.e. profits to 31st December 2014) $\times \frac{1}{3}$ (Caz's share) = 5,000

(iv) When a partner leaves, his or her overlap profits are adjusted in his or her final assessment.

(v) Overlap carried forward by Max and Fay = £5,000 each: by Caz = £5,000

Basis periods	**Max + Fay**	**Caz**
2011/12	01-Jul-2011 – 05-Apr-2012	-
2012/13	01-Jan-2012 – 31-Dec-2012	-
2013/14	01-Jan-2013 – 31-Dec-2013	01-Jan-2014 – 05-Apr-2014
2014/15	01-Jan-2014 – 31-Dec-2014	01-Jan-2014 – 31-Dec-2014

Example

Using the data for Max, Fay and Caz in the above example, and the following further tax-adjusted results:

	£
12 months to 31st December 2015	80,000
12 months to 31st December 2016	90,000
12 months to 31st December 2017	100,000
12 months to 31st December 2018	140,000

Caz leaves the partnership on 30th September 2017.

Show the assessable trade profits of the partners for all tax years.

Solution

		Total	**Max**	**Fay**	**Caz**
		£	**£**	**£**	**£**
2015/16	12 months to 31-Dec-2015	80,000	26,667	26,667	26,666
2016/17	12 months to 31-Dec-2016	90,000	30,000	30,000	30,000
2017/18	Ratio changes when Caz leaves				
	01-Jan-2017 – 30-Sep-2017: $^9/_{12} \times 100,000$	75,000	25,000	25,000	25,000
	Less overlap relief Caz				(5,000)
	01-Oct-2017 – 31-Dec-2017: $^3/_{12} \times 100,000$	25,000	12,500	12,500	
	Max and Fay's assessable profit		37,500	37,500	
2018/19	12 months to 31st December 2018	140,000	70,000	70,000	-

Notes

i) Caz's assessment for the year 2017/18 comprises:

	£
9 months profit share from 1st Jan 2017 – 30th Sept 2017 =	25,000
Less overlap relief (see previous example)	(5,000)
	20,000

ii) Max and Fay do not cease trading on the retirement of Caz.

iii) **Basis periods**

	Max + Fay + Caz	**Max + Fay**	**Caz**
2015/16	1.1.15 – 31.12.15		
2016/17	1.1.16 – 31.12.16		
2017/18		1.1.17 – 31.12.17	1.1.17 – 30.09.17
2018/19		1.1.18 – 31.12.18	

15.5 Partnership taxed and untaxed income – notional business

a) Any other taxed or untaxed income of the partnership, after duly being allocated to individual partners, is treated as coming from a 'second notional business'. This second notional business commences when an individual becomes a partner and is treated as permanently discontinued only when the individual ceases to be a partner. It is taxed by applying the same basis period rules – including the possibility of 'overlap' profits – as apply to the principal partnership trade profits.

b) Where a partnership receives rents from subletting business accommodation, these rents can be treated as income of the primary trade (instead of forming income of a second deemed trade) in the following circumstances:

   i) the accommodation must be temporarily surplus to current business requirements;

   ii) the premises must be used partly for the business and partly let, in other words, rents from a separate property which is wholly surplus must be dealt with as property income;

   iii) the rental income must be comparatively small;

   iv) the rents must be in respect of the letting of surplus business accommodation only and not of land.

15.6 Partnership losses

a) Partnership losses as computed for tax purposes are apportioned between the partners in the same proportion as they share profits.

b) Where the overall partnership makes a profit as computed for tax purposes, but after allocation of prior shares (e.g. salaries) an individual partner makes a loss then this cannot be used for normal loss claim relief.

c) If the overall partnership a profit, but an initial allocation using the commercial profit sharing arrangement for all the partners produces a mixture of profits and losses for different partners, the actual total partnership profit (or loss) must be re-allocated so that only the net profit-making partners get any profit and no partners get a loss. The loss re-allocation is made in proportion to the notional profit (or loss) initially allocated to the profit-making partners.

d) If the overall partnership has a trading loss this may be shared between partners according to the profit (or loss) sharing agreement. The trade loss of each partner may then be dealt with as for a sole trader, i.e.:

   i) Set off against total income. Section 64 (but see 14.4).
   ii) Carried forward against share of future partnership profits. Section 83.
   iii) Used in a terminal loss claim. Section 89.
   iv) Used in an opening year's Section 72 claim by that partner (but see 14.4).
   v) Used in connection with the transfer of the partnership trade to a limited company. Section 86.

Example

Xue, Yuen and Zhang have been in partnership for many years with a regular accounting period to 31st December.

Profits are shared equally, after the provision of 'salaries' to Xue and Yuen of £50,000.

Adjusted profits for the year ended 31st December 2018, before salaries, amounted to £70,000.

Show the allocation of profits for 2018/19.

Solution: Xue, Yuen and Zhang partnership profit allocation 2018/19

Stage 1:

	Total	**Xue**	**Yuen**	**Zhang**
	£	**£**	**£**	**£**
Salaries	100,000	50,000	50,000	-
Balance of profit/(loss) (70,000 – 100,000)	(30,000)	(10,000)	(10,000)	(10,000)
Net allocation	70,000	40,000	40,000	(10,000)

As this gives Zhang a notional loss but the overall partnership did not make a loss, for tax purposes the loss is reallocated to the profit-making partners. i.e. Xue and Yuen take 40,000 / 80,000 or × ½ of the loss each.

In effect, Zhang's notional loss is allocated to Xue and Yuen proportionately, i.e. £5,000 each

	Total	**Xue**	**Yuen**	**Zhang**
	£	**£**	**£**	**£**
Original allocation (as above)	70,000	40,000	40,000	(10,000)
Re-allocation to remove Z loss	-	(5,000)	(5,000)	10,000
Net allocation for tax returns	70,000	35,000	35,000	-

A practical point for partnership accounting arises from this example, If the partnership accounts treat Zhang's partnership current account on the basis that he has taken a loss share of £10,000 for the year and Xue and Yuen have taken a profit allocation of £40,000 each, then Zhang may ask the other partners to make him a cash payment each. This payment would reflect the fact that they have each saved tax and NI at their marginal rates on £5,000 of actual partnership income, due to the loss reallocation rules. In effect, Xue and Yuen have had relief for Zhang's loss for tax purposes. If Xue and Yuen agreed to make such a payment (eg calculated at their marginal tax and NI rates), then that is a personal post-tax payment and not shown in any of the partners' tax returns or income tax computations.

Student self-testing question

Question 15.1: Mars, Venus and Pluto

Mars and Venus commenced in partnership on 1st July 2016 and decided to produce their accounts to 30th June annually. On 1st January 2018, Pluto joined the partnership. The partnership's accounts show the following adjusted profits:

	£
Year ended 30th June 2017	100,000
Year ended 30th June 2018	135,000
Year ended 30th June 2019	180,000

Requirement
Show the trading income assessable on the individual partners for all the tax years affected by the above information, assuming that profits are shared equally.

(11 marks)

Solution to Question 15.1: Mars, Venus and Pluto

		Mars	Venus	Pluto	TOTAL
		£	£	£	£
A/c to 30th June 2017		50,000	50,000	-	100,000
A/c to 30th June 2018	6/12	33,750	33,750	-	67,500
	6/12	22,500	22,500	22,500	67,500
		56,250	56,250	22,500	135,000
A/c to 30th June 2019		60,000	60,000	60,000	180,000

Mars and Venus will both be assessed as follows:

2016/17	£50,000 × 9/12	£37,500
2017/18	A/c to 30th June 2017	£50,000
2018/19	A/c to 30th June 2018	£56,250
2019/20	A/c to 30th June 2019	£60,000

Overlap profits carried forward are £37,500 for each of Mars and Venus.

Pluto will be assessed as follows:

2017/18	£22,500 × 3/6		£11,250
2018/19		£22,500	
	£60,000 × 6/12	£30,000	£52,500
2019/20	A/c to 30th June 2019		£60,000
Overlap relief on:	£11,250		
	£30,000		
	£41,250		

Question without answer

Question 15.2: Vera, Jack and Terry

Vera and Jack commenced in business on 1st October 2014 as hotel proprietors, sharing profits equally. On 1st October 2016 their son Terry joined the partnership and from that date each of the partners was entitled to one-third of the profits. The profits of the partnership adjusted for income tax, are:

Period ended	30th June 2015	£30,000
Year ended	30th June 2016	£45,000
Year ended	30th June 2017	£50,000
Year ended	30th June 2018	£60,000

Requirement

Calculate the assessable profits for each of the partners for all relevant tax years from 2014/15 to 2018/19. [7 marks]

Calculate the overlap profits for each of the partners. [4 marks]

16 Personal investment – pensions

16.1 Introduction

This chapter is concerned with the income tax aspects of a UK individual's saving towards a retirement pension.

A pension scheme is a separate legal entity, administered by trustees who hold assets in trust for the beneficiaries of the scheme and determine the funding strategy for those investments.

Where money is put aside to provide a retirement income, an individual is effectively sacrificing current income in exchange for future income. Tax system design in this area must consider at which of the following points tax should be levied:

- when contributions are made to the scheme;
- when income and capital gains accrue within the pension scheme;
- when income is taken in retirement.

In the UK we have an "EET" ("*Exempt, Exempt, Taxable*") approach – pension contributions are deductible for tax purposes when made (*so the current income sacrificed in exchange for future income is not taxed, subject to certain limits*), income and capital gains accruing within the pension scheme are exempt, and pension income in retirement is taxed as a form of employment income (*see Chapters 6 and 8*) and subject to PAYE.

To qualify for tax relief, a pension scheme must meet conditions which are considered socially desirable, for example regarding the maximum pension it offers and the way in which entitlements accrue. With exceptions for ill-health retirement and for certain specialised professions, a pension scheme will not be approved if its rules allow any value to be received by an individual member below the age of at least 55.

16.2 Workplace pension schemes

All employers must provide a workplace pension scheme, into which they must automatically enrol their employees aged between 22 and state pension age, earning more than £10,000 (*subsequent opt-out is possible by the employee, with protection in place to prevent employers from encouraging or forcing opt-out*).

Several schemes are available to employers to help them fulfil their obligations; for example, the National Employment Savings Trust (NEST) is a defined contribution workplace pension scheme set up by the UK government and available free to all UK employers (*members pay a 1.8% charge on contributions plus a 0.3% annual management charge on their total pot*). Some other schemes available to small employers are listed on the Pension Regulator's website.

The employer must contribute to a workplace pension. Employer contributions are allowable expenses for the employer in calculating trading profits, and they are **not** treated as income for the employee.

The employee must also contribute. Their contributions are deductible from gross pay when calculating income tax, but not when calculating National Insurance Contributions.

The minimum contributions are as follows as the workplace pension is implemented, the percentages being percentages of 'qualifying earnings' (*which includes bonuses and commissions*) between £6,032 and £46,350 a year.

Tax year	Employer contribution	Employee contribution*	Effective government contribution (via 20% tax relief)*	Effective total contribution
2017/18	1.0%	0.8%	0.2%	2.0%
2018/19	2.0%	2.4%	0.6%	5.0%
thereafter	3.0%	4.0%	1.0%	8.0%

* Employee contributions are paid from gross income, such that – after 2018/19 – the employee would see a minimum deduction of 5.0% of salary in their payslip. The table splits this between the net contribution and the tax relief.

To qualify as an automatic enrolment pension scheme, certain minimum requirements must be met, which depend upon the type of pension scheme. The specific requirements are not covered further here.

Defined contribution occupational pension schemes

"Defined contribution" ("DC") means that the employer and employee contributions are set, with the pension income in retirement depending upon the value of the investments when the beneficiary retires.

Each beneficiary has their own pension "pot", managed by the pension provider. Contributions are invested into a portfolio of investments, containing a mixture of equities, property, corporate bonds, cash and index-linked securities. As the beneficiary approaches retirement, the investment mix will usually be changed, moving towards a lower-risk portfolio to keep the investments 'safe' ready for the purchase of an annuity to provide a guaranteed income in retirement.

Defined contribution personal pension schemes

An employer may choose to fulfil its obligations by contributing to an employee's own personal pension scheme. This necessitates legally-binding agreements between the provider of the pension scheme and the employer, and between the provider of the pension scheme and the jobholder, to ensure that the minimum contributions are made.

Defined benefit pension schemes

"Defined benefit" ("DB") means that the pension income in retirement is promised in the scheme rules, based on the employee's final salary or average salary, with contribution rates adjusted as necessary during the beneficiary's working life to ensure sufficient funds were available to meet that promise during retirement.

For example, in the Universities Superannuation Scheme until 31st March 2016, a member's retirement income would be determined by a formula based upon their final salary at the point of retirement, the number of years they worked for a university and a fraction called the "accrual rate", which was 1/80 for USS:

Pension income = Final salary × number of years in scheme × 1/80

A Senior Teaching Fellow with a final salary of £55,000 who had built up 40 years of service would have an annual pension of:

£55,000 × 40 years × 1/80 = £27,500

Hybrid pension schemes

Defined benefit schemes are risky from the point of view of the employer and the pension scheme, since they involve promised pay-outs to pensioners but uncertain inflows from investments. On the other hand, defined contribution schemes are risky from the point of view of the jobholder because the income they will get in retirement is uncertain, depending upon the value if the investments.

Hybrid schemes have evolved as a way of sharing risk between employers and employees.

For example, the Universities Superannuation Scheme became a hybrid scheme from 1st April 2016, with employee income split into bands by a threshold. Up to that threshold, contributions build up a defined-benefit pension linked to career-average salary (*with the threshold serving as the maximum salary for the purposes of that calculation*); above the threshold, contributions go into a defined-contribution pot for the jobholder.

As was reasonably foreseeable, the January 2018 proposal to drop the DB/DC threshold to zero, thereby shifting all risk onto employees, was met with anger and strike action on a scale not before seen on UK campuses.

Collective Defined Contribution schemes

DB schemes require underlying investment portfolios with a sufficiently low level of risk to be able to meet pension promises, and to provide confidence to the Pensions Regulator that the scheme is being managed with sufficient prudence to limit the risk of claims being made of the Pension Protection Fund.

But when dealing with investments, lower risk means lower return. So, to secure a given amount of income is more expensive than would be the case with higher-risk investments; as such, DB schemes are expensive in terms of investment returns foregone.

DC schemes may take more risk, but because pension pots within those schemes are held individually rather than collectively, need to 'de-risk' as the individual beneficiary approaches retirement and will likely seek to purchase an annuity. That means losing out on potential investment returns. 'De-risking' will often start ten years away from retirement; out of a working life of 40 years or so, that is a substantial period of reduced returns.

Collective Defined Contribution ("CDC") schemes seek the best of both worlds, and are widespread in Canada, Denmark and the Netherlands. At the time of writing they are not permitted in the UK, new secondary legislation being required to make them possible. But the UK government is under pressure to pass such legislation quickly, following industrial action over pensions at Royal Mail and at pre-1992 universities. Indeed, Royal Mail has even offered to draft the required secondary legislation. We might expect to see CDC schemes available in the UK soon.

CDC schemes are similar to DB schemes, but with a **target** pension as distinct from a **promised** pension. As such they are sometimes referred to as "Defined Ambition" schemes. If something goes wrong, risk can be shared across all members – contributing jobholders and current pensioners – through adjustments to contributions and to pensions in payment.

Being collective rather than individual avoids the need for 'de-risking' – as a continuing long-lived scheme the pension fund can bear risks associated with short-term stock market volatility which an individual is not so able to bear. At the same time, being defined-contribution avoids the need for expensive 'backup' to guarantee pension promises, by way of some form of insurance or reliance on government or sponsoring employers.

Unfunded occupational schemes

One aspect of the universities pensions dispute in 2018 was comparability of pensions benefits of staff at pre-1992 universities and those at post-1992 institutions. The latter have their pensions provision not through the private Universities Superannuation Scheme, but rather through membership of the Teachers' Pension Scheme.

While the Universities Superannuation Scheme has an underlying fund of investments, the Teachers' Pension Scheme has no such fund. Rather, the pension payable from the unfunded public scheme is a promise by the Government, to be funded from future taxation.

Income tax relief is still given on an employee's contributions to unfunded public sector occupational schemes, such as schoolteachers' or police pensions. This relief is given even though such 'pension contributions', which earn future entitlement to a public-sector pension, are not being invested at all.

16.3 Personal pensions

A person may choose to arrange their own pension provision, for example if they are self-employed.

Stakeholder pensions

Stakeholder pensions are a form of defined contribution personal pension, with low and flexible minimum contributions, maximum charges set by the government and a default investment fund which the beneficiary can choose if they would prefer the pension provider to make investment strategy decisions on their behalf.

In these schemes, a specific fund is kept invested for each contributing member.

They are available to anyone and not attached to a specific employer, though an employer may contribute to a stakeholder pension on behalf of an employee. All contributions are treated as paid to the scheme's trustees net of basic rate tax. The value ultimately received by the scheme then includes an additional sum of 20/80 of the contribution, reclaimed by the pension provider from the Government, and representing the basic rate income tax relief due on all contributions.

Where the individual is a higher- or additional-rate taxpayer, the basic rate band (*and higher rate band if applicable*) is extended in a similar way as to give higher rates of relief on Gift Aid donations (*see Chapter 5*).

Up to £2,880 a year (*net*) - £3,600 a year (*gross*) is the maximum gross amount which may be saved in a stakeholder pension scheme by someone who has no 'relevant earnings'. The member does not even need to be a taxpayer to benefit from the £720 'tax relief top-up' that is added by the Government to a net contribution of £2,880 that is made to a stakeholder or personal pension scheme.

Self-Invested Personal Pensions ("SIPPs")

A Self Invested Personal Pension ("SIPP") is a normal personal pension plan (*so the member's contributions are again paid in net of basic rate tax*) but with a SIPP, the member can direct the fund manager where exactly to invest his or her fund (*subject to rules about suitable investments for approved pension funds*).

16.4 Contribution rules

The maximum allowable contribution payable by an individual contributing member of a pension scheme of any kind for each tax year is the greater of:

- £3,600 gross; or
- 100% of 'relevant UK earnings', but subject to the annual allowance maximum (see 16.5).

'Relevant UK earnings' are defined as:

- income from employment;
- chargeable income derived from the carrying on or exercise of a trade, profession or vocation (whether individually or as a partner acting personally in a partnership);
- earnings of overseas Crown employees that are subject to UK tax;
- income from furnished holiday lettings;
- patent or copyright income of the original artist, author or inventor.

There is no limit to the contributions that can be paid by an employer on behalf of a scheme member who is an employee, provided these meet the maximum annual allowance provisions (below). Employer contributions obtain tax relief for the employer as trade expenses only in the employer's accounting period in which they are paid.

16.5 Annual allowance

The maximum amount of pension contributions relievable for tax purposes in the tax year 2018/19 is £40,000 for basic and higher rate taxpayers (even if the relevant UK earnings are higher than this). The annual allowance includes both employee and employer contributions.

The annual allowance is reduced by £1 for every £2 of income above £150,000 (*where this figure includes pension contributions – ie. you do not deduct pension contributions made by the taxpayer to arrive at the income figure to be used for this purpose, and you* ***do*** *add any employer contributions*), until it reaches £10,000.

Individuals may carry forward any unused allowances, from years in which they were members of registered pension schemes, for up to four 'years'. For this purpose, the 2015/16 tax year is split into two 'years'; the 'pre-alignment tax year' (*6th April 2015 to 8th July 2015*), and the 'post-alignment tax year' (*9th July 2015 to 5th April 2016*).

So, for 2018/19, a taxpayer may use up any previously unused allowances from:

2017/18 (up to £40,000);

- 2016/17 (up to £40,000);
- the post-alignment tax year (*the annual allowance for this year is nil, unless the taxpayer was* ***not*** *a member of a registered pension scheme in the pre-alignment tax year, in which case the annual allowance is £40,000*); and

- the pre-alignment tax year (*the annual allowance for this 'year' is £80,000, but a maximum of £40,000 of unused allowance may be carried forward*).

Note that this has the effect of allowing somebody to make pension contributions of £160,000 in 2018/19 if they had not made any contributions in earlier years: £40,000 allowances from each of 2016/17, 2017/18 and 2018/19 plus £40,000 as an allowance from either the pre-alignment tax year (*if they were a member of a registered pension scheme then*) or the post-alignment tax year (*if they were not*).

16.6 Money Purchase Annual Allowance

Following changes introduced in 2015 to allow people to access their money purchase pension savings more flexibly, it was necessary to introduce a limit on the extent to which people could 'recycle' their pension savings to take advantage of tax relief. Therefore, individuals who have already flexibly accessed their money purchase pension savings have a lower contributions limit than other individuals, called the 'Money Purchase Annual Allowance'.

The MPAA was reduced from £10,000 to £4,000 with effect from 6th April 2017 by the Finance (No2) Act 2017.

Unlike the Annual Allowance, any unused MPAA cannot be carried forward.

16.7 Lifetime allowance

From 6th April 2017, the lifetime allowance limit is £1,030,000.

This is the amount against which the value of an individual's pension savings is tested each year, until pension payments begin.

For defined-benefit pension schemes, the value is determined by applying a standard valuation factor of 20:1 to the annual pension income which the pensioner would receive in retirement and adding any lump sum they would get at the point of retirement.

Example

Nikita Tin is a Senior Teaching Fellow at the University of Roter Ziegelstein, who has forty years' service in the Seniors Superannuation Scheme, a defined-benefit pension scheme in which her annual pension income is based on her career-average salary of £48,783, with an accrual rate of 1/75. As well as her annual pension income, she will be entitled to a tax-free lump sum on retirement equal to three times her annual pension income.

Alana Brushes is a Senior Lecturer at Tellerglas University, who has forty years' service in the Lecturers' Pension Scheme, a defined-benefit pension scheme in which her annual pension income is based on her average salary of £48,783, with an accrual rate of 1/57, but no entitlement to a lump sum.

Required

Calculate the value of each taxpayer's pension fund for the purposes of comparison against the lifetime allowance.

Solution

Nikita Tin: Fund value = 20 × annual pension + lump sum
= 20 × (48,783 × 40 years × 1/75) + 3 × (48,783 × 40 years × 1/75)
= £598,405 (well within the lifetime allowance)

Alana Brushes: Fund value = 20 × annual pension
= 20 × (48,783 × 40 years × 1/57)
= £684,674 (well within the lifetime allowance)

16.8 Consequences of a taxpayer exceeding the annual or lifetime allowance

Contributions (*either employer or employee*) in excess of the annual allowance are added to the employee's taxable income.

For the lifetime allowance, the amount of tax payable for exceeding the £1,030,000 limit depends upon how it is provided to the employee. The rates of tax, which apply at the point the individual takes money from their pension fund, are:

- 55% if taken as a lump sum; or
- 25% if taken as pension payments or cash withdrawals.

16.9 Unapproved pension schemes

Unapproved invested pension schemes also exist. One kind is simply a pay-as-you-go arrangement, where the employer pays a pension out of current profits to former employees. In this case the employer gets tax relief when the pension is paid and then the employee is taxed on the payment as pension income paid directly by the employer. The other kind is a funded arrangement known as an Employer-Financed Retirement Benefit Scheme (EFRBS for short). They have very different tax treatment from approved schemes.

(i) An employer's contributions to an EFRBS receive no tax relief when made and there is no tax relief on the funds invested.

(ii) Investment income and capital gains of an EFRBS are all taxable at the rate applicable to trusts. Trusts taxation is not covered in detail in this book.

(iii) When pension payments are made from an EFRBS, a tax credit for the income tax paid by the trust can be claimed by the pension beneficiary, so long as the pension clearly comes from UK taxed income of the trust.

However, contributions to unapproved schemes do not count towards the annual allowance, nor will the fund's accrued value count towards the lifetime allowance.

This exclusion may make an EFRBS attractive for very highly-paid employees who have already reached the lifetime limit for approved pension savings.

Student self-testing questions

Question 16.1, Christa

Christa lives in Wales and is sole proprietor of a beauty salon. Her tax adjusted trading profits for the year to 5th April 2019 are £180,000, and she has no other income. Christa makes net contributions of £14,400 to a personal pension during the year.

Required
Calculate Christa's income tax liability for 2018/19.

Solution to Question 16.1, Christa

First, we check whether there is any restriction to the maximum tax-exempt contributions which Christa may make, given that her income exceeds £150,000:

Maximum contributions = £40,000 – ½(180,000-150,000) = £25,000.

Christa's contributions fall below this limit, so qualify for tax relief in full.

Christa, Income tax computation 2018/19

	£
Income from trading (= total income/ net income)	180,000
Personal allowance (net income > £123700, so reduced to nil)	0
Taxable income (all non-savings)	180,000

	£	£		
Income Tax:				
Basic rate on non-savings		34,500	@ 20%	6,900
Extend basic rate band				
for gross PPPs: £14,400 $\times {}^{100}/_{80}$		18,000	@ 20%	3,600
Basic rate band limit		52,500		
Higher rate on non-savings		115,500	@ 40%	46,200
Extend higher rate band for	150,000			
PPPs as before: £14,400 $\times {}^{100}/_{80}$	18,000			
Higher rate band limit		168,000		
Additional rate on non-savings		12,000	@ 45%	5,400
		180,000		
Total income tax liability				£62,100

Question 16.2, Olivia

Olivia lives in Northern Ireland and is an employee whose only income during 2018/19 is a salary of £180,000.
She contributes 10% of her gross salary to an approved occupational pension scheme.

Required

Calculate Olivia's income tax liability for 2018/19.

Solution to Question 16.2, Olivia

Maximum contributions = £40,000 – ½(180,000-150,000) = £25,000.

Christa's contributions fall below this limit, so qualify for tax relief in full.

	£	£
Salary	180,000	
Less: pension contributions	(18,000)	
Income from employment		162,000
Personal allowance (fully abated)		0
Taxable income		162,000

Income Tax	£		£
Basic rate	34,500	@ 20%	6,900
Higher rate	115,500	@ 40%	46,200
	150,000		
Additional rate	12,000	@ 45%	5,400
	162,000		
Income tax liability			£58,500

17 National Insurance contributions and social security

17.1 Introduction

National Insurance is now essentially a tax on earnings, although in original concept it was a contribution towards State benefits, principally the State Pension.

This chapter is concerned with National Insurance and related aspects of the UK Social Security system, under the following main headings:

Classes of contribution	Statutory sick pay	Taxable state income
Gross pay	Statutory maternity pay	Non-taxable state income
Directors	Tax Credits	Class 4 contributions
Class 1 A NIC – benefits, cars and fuel		

Note The Contributions Agency, which collects some classes of National Insurance, is a branch of HMRC.

17.2 Classes of contribution

The classes of contribution payable are as follows:

Class 1 Paid by employed earners and their employers, based on earnings

Class 1A Employers' annual contribution paid on benefits-in-kind

Class 1B Employers' contribution paid on PAYE settlements

Class 2 Payable by self-employed workers at a flat rate

Class 3 Non-employed persons (voluntary NI)

Class 4 Self-employed persons, additional contribution, based on 'profits'

All employed persons and their employers must pay Class 1 contributions.
The weekly earnings thresholds and rates to find Class 1 NI contributions from 6th April 2018 are given below (see 17.4). Equivalent monthly thresholds apply to those paid monthly, and annual thresholds (equivalent to those for Class 4 NI) apply to company directors, whose NI earnings period is the tax year (see 17.5).

For simplicity, the accounting professional bodies allow thresholds for Class 1 to be applied on an annual basis in tax examinations (unless the employee changes job during the tax year).

An employed person is someone gainfully employed either under a contract of service, or as the holder of an office as defined for income tax purposes, e.g. a company director.

A self-employed person is liable for Class 2 and Class 4 contributions. The Class 2 contribution is a flat rate per week, but payable along with Class 4 contributions.

Class 4 NI is a percentage of the annual 'profits', as determined for income tax purposes. It is self-assessed on the tax return, and both Class 2 and Class 4 contributions are paid along with income tax.

Class 3 contributions are voluntary contributions, payable at a weekly flat rate. They preserve entitlement to some social security benefits including UK State Pension. Class 3 may be paid up to 6 years after the relevant tax year.

Employees must be aged 16 or over before any liability to National Insurance arises.

For employees who are over State pension age (currently 65 for men and 60 for women but due to equalise and then rise in stages to 68 in future) the NI position is as follows:

i) Primary contributions (employees' NIC) are not due on earnings paid after the 65th birthday, or state pension age if earlier;
ii) Secondary contributions (employers' NICs) continue as before even after state retirement age is reached.

Employer's Class 1A contributions apply to all taxable benefits in kind except where Class 1 NI contributions are already due (e.g. on cash vouchers) and those included in a PAYE settlement agreement.

17.3 Gross pay

Gross pay for Class 1 National Insurance purposes includes:

Wages/salaries
Bonus payments
Fees
Overtime pay
Sick pay and maternity /paternity pay
Petrol allowances - unless credited and charged to a company account
Cash allowances generally
Cash vouchers
Anything else readily convertible to money, e.g. quoted shares, or commodities that can be sold on a readily-traded market

As noted in the previous section, non-cash benefits are not part of Gross Pay for National Insurance, and are liable not to Class 1, but to class 1A National Insurance. Class 1A NI is paid on benefits in kind by the employer, at the end of the tax year. Non-cash benefits incur no NI liability for the employee.

17.4 National Insurance contributions - gross pay

Class 1 Employed earners from 6th April 2018

The following bands and rates apply for most employees.

Employee 'primary' Class 1 contributions

Up to £116 a week – lower earnings limit	exempt*
Between £116 and £162 a week – primary earnings threshold	0.0%*
Between £162 and £892 a week	12.0%
Over £892 a week	2.0%

Employer 'secondary' Class 1 contributions

Up to £116 a week – lower earnings limit	exempt*
Between £116 and £162 a week – secondary earnings threshold	0.0%*
Over £162 a week	13.8%
Class 1A on employment benefits	13.8%

As an incentive to employ and train more young people, different secondary Class 1 contribution bands apply for employees under 21 years old and for apprentices under 25 years old:

Employer 'secondary' Class 1 contributions for ...

... Employees under 21:

Up to £116 a week – lower earnings limit	exempt*
Up to £892 a week (UST, Upper Secondary Threshold)	0.0%*
Over £892 per week	13.8%

... Apprentices under 25:

Up to £116 a week – lower earnings limit	exempt*
Up to £892 a week (AUST, Apprentices UST)	0.0%*
Over £892 per week	13.8%

* The significance of the distinction between exemption and zero-percent contributions (around the 'lower earnings limit') is explained in the notes below.

As a measure to support small employers, An NIC 'Employment Allowance' is available to reduce an employer's Class 1 NICs by up to £3,000 per annum (2017/18: £3,000). It is not available to companies where the director is the sole employee, to employers whose work is mainly (more than 50%) of a public-sector nature, or to employers of domestic staff. It is, however, available to employers of care and support workers.

Notes on terms relevant to Class 1 calculations

(i) **LEL – Lower Earnings Limit**, £116 per week (which equates to £6,032 p.a.) This is enacted as an annual limit for company directors and a weekly limit for others. Earnings above LEL must be recorded on the employer's NI record, even though no NI is due by the employee or employer until pay exceeds the primary threshold. The reason there's a distinction between exemption from National insurance (below LEL) and being subject to National Insurance at a zero rate (between LEL and Primary threshold) is that certain benefits are available only where the person seeking to claim them has built up a certain number of years of National Insurance Contributions. Having a zero-rate band protects some low-paid workers without imposing a tax burden on them – they are building up entitlement to benefits by 'contributing' at a zero rate. The benefits concerned are contribution-based Jobseeker's Allowance, Incapacity Benefit, contributory Employment and Support Allowance, Bereavement Benefits, full State Pension and Maternity Allowance.

(ii) **Primary Threshold** (employees) – £162 per week (which equates to £8,424 per annum). The level at which main rate NI becomes payable by employees.

(iii) **Secondary Threshold** (employers) - £162 per week (which equates to £8,424 per annum). The level at which main rate National insurance becomes payable by employers.

(iv) **UEL –employee's Upper Earnings Limit** £892 per week (this equates to £46,384 per annum, but £46,350 may be used in exams which is the Upper Profits Limit for Class 4 contributions). This is the pay level at which a lower rate of NI becomes payable by the employee. The UEL is applied as a weekly or monthly figure to all employees except company directors.

Class 1A 13.8% on benefits in kind (paid by employers)

Class 2 Weekly rate £2.95 (2017/18 £2.85). Collected along with self-assessed income tax and Class 4 contributions. No liability if earnings are below £6,205 for the tax year, although contributions may be paid optionally to preserve entitlement to state social benefits.

Class 3 Weekly rate £14.65. (2017/18 £14.25)

Class 4 See below.

17.5 Directors

The National Insurance earnings period for employees is the interval at which regular payments are made, normally a multiple of weeks or months. For directors the earnings period is annual, whether they are paid weekly, monthly or at other intervals. The following rules should be noted.

i) For directors the earnings period runs from 6th April to the following 5th April.

ii) Directors in post at 6th April have an annual earnings period, even if they cease to be directors during the year.

iii) Where a director is appointed after 6th April then the earnings period is pro-rated using a 52-week period for the whole tax year.

Example

Algy is a Director of Kitsch Ltd. He receives a salary of £50,000 in 2018/19, paid six-monthly. Compute the primary and secondary National Insurance Contributions payable.

Solution: Algy National Insurance Contributions 2018/19

(Director, so annual earnings period)

			£
Primary contributions – employee			
ET	8,424	@ 0%	–
	37,926	@ 12.0%	4,551
	46,350		
	3,650	@ 2.0%	73
	50,000		4,624
Secondary contributions – employer			
	8,424	@ 0%	–
	41,576	@ 13.8%	5,737
	50,000		5,737

Note

Once the earnings paid in the tax year exceed the upper earnings limit, any additional cash remuneration paid to a director will incur all employee's Class 1 NI at the lower rate of 2%.

17.6 Class 4 contributions

The following are the main features of this class of contribution.

a) Contributions are calculated by the taxpayer on the self-assessment tax return and collected by HMRC together with all other self-assessed income tax.

b) Where a partnership exists, then each partner's liability is calculated separately and paid separately, as for income tax (see Chapter 15).

c) The contributions are based on the trade profits as determined in accordance with Chapter 11, with the following deductions:

 i) Capital allowances (balancing charges are added)

 ii) Loss relief under Sections 83 and 89, ITA 2007.

d) Personal allowances and pension payments of any kind are not deductible.

e) The rate of contribution is 9.0% of profits in between £8,424 and £46,350 for 2018/19, plus 2% on profits above £46,350.

f) Where the profits of farmers are averaged, the revised amounts are used for Class 4 purposes. However, when trading income or total profits are reduced by a trade loss carried back (see Chapter 14), the Class 4 NIC paid in the earlier year is unaffected.

g) Interest on late payment of Class 4 NICs is charged at the usual rate of interest for income tax paid late.

Where an individual is both employed and self-employed, Class 1 contributions will be paid on the employment earnings and Class 2 and Class 4 (in principle) are payable on the self-employed earnings. However, an individual should not pay more NI because income is split between employment and self-employment, than they would pay if all income came from employment.

Example

Xavier has been trading for many years with an accounting year-end to 30th June. He has the following data relating to the income tax year 2018/19:

	£
Trade profits to 30-Jun-2018, before deducting capital allowances	40,000
Capital allowances	2,065
Bank deposit interest	100

Calculate the income tax and Class 2 and 4 NI payable by self-assessment for 2018/19.

Solution: Xavier income tax, class 2 and 4 NI computation 2018/19

		£	£
Income taxed as trade profits		40,000	
Less capital allowances		(2,065)	37,935
Bank deposit interest			100
Net income			38,035
Personal allowance			(11,850)
Taxable income			26,185
Tax liability			
On non-savings	26,085 @ 20%		5,217
Personal savings allowance	100 @ 0%		0
Tax payable by self-assessment			5,217
Class 4 NIC contributions payable:			£
Trade profits			40,000
Less capital allowances			(2,065)
			37,935
Class 4 (£37,935 – 8,424) = 29,511 @ 9.0%			2,656
Class 2 NIC 52 @ £2.95			153
Total self-employed NI payable			£2,809

17.7 Directors liable for company's contributions

Where a company has failed to pay NICs on time and the failure appears to be attributable to fraud or neglect by one or more individuals who were officers of the company (culpable officers), the outstanding NICs may be sought from the culpable officers.

17.8 Statutory sick pay, statutory maternity pay, etc

Employers are responsible for paying statutory sick pay (SSP), statutory maternity, paternity, and adoption pay to their employees. The detailed rules for computing these entitlements change regularly. To qualify for SSP, a worker must be earning at least the lower earnings limit of £116 per week for 2018/19.

Employers can claim SSP reimbursement against their NI contributions payable if and to the extent that their SSP payments for an income tax month exceed 13% of their gross Class 1 contribution liability for that month. This can help a small business when a large proportion of the workforce is ill at the same time.

Both employers' and employees' Class 1 contributions count here.

Other payments like SSP work the same way in outline. Entitlement arises if earning above the LEL. Payments received are all subject to National Insurance and income tax, in the same way as wages and salaries. In addition, small employers can recover most of their SMP etc by setting it off against PAYE income tax and NI due.

17.9 Child benefit

Child benefit is a social security benefit paid to the person primarily responsible for caring for a child. The 2018/19 rate is £20.70 a week for the eldest child and £13.70 a week for each subsequent child. Children under 16 qualify automatically but this can be extended up to 19 if still in school education.

A taxpayer who has adjusted net income of over £50,000 a year is subject to a 'High Income Child Benefit Tax Charge', where they or their partner receive child benefit. If both partners have adjusted net income of over £50,000, only the partner with the higher income is liable for the charge.

The charge is 1% of the child benefit award for each £100 of income between £50,000 and £60,000. The charge on taxpayers with income above £60,000 will equal the amount of child benefit paid.

17.10 Child tax credit

Child tax credit is a separate social security benefit, based on income. It is non-taxable and has no effect on other income tax liabilities.

17.11 Working tax credit

Working tax credit is a social security benefit for people with low incomes from employment or self- employment. Again, this income does not have any effect on tax liabilities.

Student self-testing questions on employment income tax, PAYE and National Insurance

(These questions expect students to refer to Chapters 7-8 as well as 17.)

Question 17.1, William Wong

William Wong is the finance director of Glossy Ltd. The company runs a publishing business. The following information is available for the tax year 2018/19:

(1) William is paid director's remuneration of £2,400 per month by Glossy Ltd.

(2) In addition to his director's remuneration, William received two bonus payments from Glossy Ltd during the tax year. The first bonus of £22,000 was paid on 30th June 2018, in respect of the year ended 31st December 2017. William became entitled to this bonus on 15th March 2018.

The second bonus of £37,000 was paid on 31st March 2019 and was in respect of the year ended 31st December 2018. William became entitled to this second bonus on 15th March 2019.

(3) From 6th April 2018 until 31st December 2018, William used his private red motor car for business purposes. During this period, William drove 12,000 miles in the performance of his duties for Glossy Ltd, for which the company paid an allowance of 30 pence per mile. The relevant HMRC authorised mileage rates are 45 pence per mile for the first 10,000 miles, and 25 pence per mile thereafter.

(4) From 1st January 2019 to 5th April 2019, Glossy Ltd provided William with a diesel powered white company motor car with a list price of £46,000. The motor car cost Glossy Ltd £44,500, and it has an official CO_2 emission rate of 185g/km. Glossy Ltd also provided William with fuel for his private journeys.

(5) William was unable to drive his motor car for two weeks during February 2019 because of an accident, so Glossy Ltd provided him with a chauffeur, at a total cost of £1,800.

(6) Throughout the tax year 2018/19 Glossy Ltd provided William with a television for his personal use that had originally cost £3,825.

(7) Glossy Ltd has provided William with living accommodation since 1st January 2017. The property was purchased in 2000 for £90,000, and had a market value of £210,000 on 1st January 2017. It has an annual value of £10,400.

(8) Glossy Ltd pays an annual insurance premium of £680 to cover William against any liabilities that might arise in relation to his directorship.

(9) During May 2018 William spent ten nights overseas on company business. Glossy Ltd paid him a daily allowance of £10 to cover the cost of personal expenses such as telephone calls to William's family.

(10) William pays an annual professional subscription of £450 to the Institute of Finance Directors, an HMRC approved professional body, and a membership fee of £800 to a golf club. He uses the golf club to entertain clients of Glossy Ltd.

Required:

(a) State the rules that determine when a bonus paid to a director is treated as being received for tax purposes. (3 marks)

(b) Calculate William's taxable income for the tax year 2018/19. (15 marks)

(c) Calculate the total amount of both Class 1 and Class 1A national insurance contributions that will finally have been paid by both William and Glossy Ltd in respect of William's earnings and benefits for the tax year 2018/19. (5 marks)

(d) Advise William of the forms that Glossy Ltd must provide to him following the end of the tax year 2018/19 in respect of his earnings and benefits for that year, and state the dates by which these forms must be provided to him. (2 marks)

(25 marks)

(ACCA updated)

Solution to Question 17.1, William Wong

(a) The earliest of:

(1) The date that the bonus is paid.
(2) The date that entitlement to the bonus arises.
(3) The date when the bonus is credited in the company's accounts
(4) The end of the period of account if the bonus relates to that period and has been determined before the end of the period.
(5) The date that the bonus is determined if the period of account it relates to has already ended.

(b) **William – Taxable income computation 2018/19**

		£	£
Director's remuneration	(2,400 × 12)		28,800
Bonus (taxed when entitled)			37,000
			65,800
Benefits (see notes below):			
Car benefit (white car)	(note 2)	4,255	
Chauffeur	(note 3)	1,800	
Fuel benefit (white car)	(note 4)	2,165	
Television	(3,825 at 20%)	765	
Living accommodation			
– Annual value		10,400	
– Additional benefit		3,375	22,760
			88,560
Expenses claimed:			

Mileage allowance (red car)	1,400	
Professional subscription	450	(1,850)
Total / net income		86,710
Personal allowance		(11,850)
Taxable income		£74,860

(1) The first bonus of £22,000 will have been treated as income of 2017/18.

(2) The white company car was only available for three months of 2018/19, so the benefit is £4,255 (46,000 × 37% × 3/12). The list price must be used even though a lower amount was paid.

(3) The car benefit does not cover the cost of a chauffeur, so this is an additional benefit.

(4) The fuel benefit is £2,165 (£23,400 × 37% × 3/12).

(5) The living accommodation cost more than £75,000, so there will be an additional 'expensive accommodation' benefit. Since the property was purchased more than six years before first being provided to William, the benefit is based on the market value of £210,000.

(6) The additional benefit is therefore £3,375 (210,000 – 75,000) = 135,000 at 2.50%.

(7) The provision of liability insurance does not give rise to a taxable benefit, nor does the payment of the overseas overnight allowance, since it is not above the de minimis limit of £10 per night.

(8) The mileage allowance received will be tax-free, and William can make the following expense claim for the use of his own red car:

10,000 miles at 45p		4,500	
2,000 miles at 25p		500	
		5,000	
Mileage allowance	12,000 at 30p		(3,600)
			£1,400

(9) The golf club membership is not an allowable deduction despite being used to entertain customers.

(c) NIC (using annual equivalent thresholds)

Employee Class 1	(46,350 – 8,424) =	37,926 @ 12%	£4,551
	(65,800 – 46,350) =	19,450 @ 2%	£389
Employer Class 1	(65,800 – 8,424) =	57,376 @ 13.8%	£7,918
Employer Class 1A	(on benefits)	22,760 @ 13.8%	£3,141

(d) (1) Glossy Ltd must give Form P60, employee's certificate of pay, income tax and NIC deducted, to William by 31st May 2019.

(2) Glossy Ltd must give a copy of form P11D, detailing all reimbursed expense payments (other than those which are 'payrolled' or covered by a P11D dispensation), and the value of all benefits in kind provided by reason of employment, to William by 6th July 2019.

Question without answers

Question 17.2, Ali Patel

You should assume that today's date is 15th March 2018.

Ali Patel lives in England, has been employed by Box plc since 1st January 2014, and is currently paid an annual salary of £40,000. On 6th April 2018, Ali is to be temporarily relocated for a period of twelve months from Box plc's head office to one of its branch offices. He has been offered two alternative remuneration packages:

First remuneration package

(1) Ali will continue to live near Box plc's head office and will commute daily to the branch office using his private motor car.

(2) He will be paid additional salary of £500 per month.

(3) Box plc will pay Ali an allowance of 38 pence per mile for the 1,600 miles that Ali will drive each month commuting to the branch office.

HMRC authorised mileage rates are 45 pence per mile for the first 10,000 business miles driven each year, and 25 pence per mile thereafter. Ali estimates his net additional commuting cost for 2018/19 at £3,000.

Second remuneration package

(1) Box plc will provide Ali with rent-free living accommodation near the branch office.

(2) The property will be rented by Box plc at a cost of £800 per month. The annual value of the property is £4,600.

(3) Ali will rent out his main residence near Box plc's head office, and this will result in income from property of £6,000 for 2018/19.

Required:

(a) Calculate Ali's income tax liability and Class 1 national insurance contributions for 2018/19, if he:

(i) Accepts the first remuneration package offered by Box plc;

(ii) Accepts the second remuneration package offered by Box plc.

(b) Advise Ali as to which remuneration package is the most beneficial from a financial perspective. Your answer should be supported by a calculation of the amount of income, net of income tax and employee's Class 1 national insurance contributions, which he would receive for 2018/19 under each alternative.

(ACCA updated)

End of section questions without answers

Question 1

Evaluate the advantages, disadvantages and feasibility of replacing the taxation of income by: a direct expenditure tax; an annual wealth tax.

Question 2, Carol Courier

For the purposes of this question you should assume that today's date is 15th March 2018. Carol Courier lives in Wales, is employed by Quick-Speed plc as a delivery driver and is paid a salary of £26,000. She contributes 5% of gross salary into Quick-Speed plc's HMRC approved occupational pension scheme. As an alternative to being employed, Quick-Speed plc has offered Carol the opportunity to work for the company on a self-employed basis. The details of the proposed arrangement for the year ended 5th April 2019 are as follows:

(1) Carol will commence being self-employed on 6th April 2018.
(2) Her income from Quick-Speed plc is expected to be £38,000.
(3) When not working for Quick-Speed plc, Carol will be allowed to work for other clients. Her income from this work is expected to be £4,500.
(4) Carol will lease a delivery van from Quick-Speed plc, and 100% of the mileage will be for business purposes. The cost of leasing and running the delivery van will be £4,400.
(5) When she is unavailable Carol will have to provide a replacement driver to deliver for Quick-Speed plc. This will cost her £2,800.
(6) Carol will contribute the equivalent of £2,000 gross into a personal pension scheme during 2018/19. This will provide her with similar benefits to the occupational pension scheme provided by Quick-Speed plc.

Required:

(a) Assuming that Carol does not accept the offer from Quick-Speed plc and continues to be employed by the company, calculate her income tax and Class 1 NIC obligations for 2018/19. (5 marks)
(b) Assuming that Carol accepts the offer to work for Quick-Speed on a self-employed basis from 6th April 2018 onwards, calculate her income tax, Class 2 NIC and Class 4 NIC obligations for 2018/19. (6 marks)
(c) Advise Carol as to whether it will be beneficial to accept the offer to work for Quick-Speed plc on a self-employed basis. Your answer should be supported by a calculation of the amount by which her income for 2018/19 (net of outgoings, income tax and NIC) will increase or decrease if she accepts the offer. (4 marks)
(d) Critically comment on whether Carol would be considered an employee or self-employed under current HMRC policy. (5 marks)

(20 marks)

(ACCA updated)

Question 3, Foo Dee

On 31st December 2018 Foo Dee, who lives in Northern Ireland, resigned as an employee of Gastronomic-Food plc. The company had employed her as a chef since 2001. On 1st January 2019 Foo commenced self-employment running her own restaurant, preparing accounts to 30th September. The following information is available for 2018/19:

Employment

(1) During the period 6th April 2018 to 31st December 2018 Foo's total gross salary from her employment with Gastronomic-Food plc was £38,000. Income tax of £6,337 was deducted from this figure under PAYE.

(2) Foo used her private motor car for both business and private purposes during the period from 6th April 2018 to 31st December 2018. She received no reimbursement from Gastronomic-Food plc for any of the expenditure incurred. Foo's total mileage during this period was 15,000 miles, made up as follows:

Normal daily travel between home and permanent workplace	4,650
Voluntary travel between home and permanent workplace to turn off a fire alarm	120
Travel between permanent workplace and Gastronomic-Food plc's suppliers (part of employment duties)	750
Travel between home and a temporary workplace for a period of two months	3,800
Private travel	5,680
	15,000

The relevant HM Revenue & Customs authorised mileage rates to be used as the basis of any expense claim are 45 pence per mile for the first 10,000 miles, and 25 pence per mile thereafter.

(3) On 1st October 2018 Gastronomic-Food plc paid £12,900 towards Foo's removal expenses when she was permanently relocated to a different restaurant owned by the company. The £12,900 covered the cost of disposing of Foo's old property and of acquiring her new property.

(4) Foo contributed 6% of her gross salary of £38,000 into Gastronomic-Food plc's HMRC-approved occupational pension scheme.

Self-employment

(1) Foo's Income Statement for her restaurant business for the nine-month period ended 30th September 2019 is as follows:

		£
Gross profit		128,200
Depreciation	3,500	
Motor expenses (note 2)	4,200	
Property expenses (note 3)	12,800	
Other expenses (all allowable)	50,700	(71,200)
Net profit		£57,000

(2) During the period 1st January 2019 to 30th September 2019 Foo drove a total of 6,000 miles, of which 2,000 were for private journeys.
(3) Foo purchased her restaurant on 1st January 2019. She lives in an apartment that is situated above the restaurant, and one-quarter of the total property expenses of £12,800 relate to this apartment.
(4) On 1st January 2019 Foo purchased a motor car with CO_2 emissions of 105g/km for £16,667 (see note 2 above) and equipment for £3,600.

Other income

(1) During the tax year 2018/19 Foo received bank deposit interest of £2,000 and dividends of £7,000.

Other information

(1) Foo contributed £1,600 (net) into a personal pension scheme during the period 1st January 2019 to 5th April 2019.
(2) She did not make any income tax payments on account in respect of the tax year 2017/18.

Required:

(a) **Calculate Foo's tax adjusted trading profit for the nine-month period ended 30th September 2019.** **(6 marks)**

(b) (i) **Calculate the income tax payable by Foo for the tax year 2018/19.** **(13 marks)**

(ii) **Calculate Foo's balancing payment for the tax year 2018/19 and her payments on account for the tax year 2019/20, stating the relevant due dates.** (Ignore national insurance contributions.) **(3 marks)**

(c) **Advise Foo of the consequences of not making the balancing payment for the tax year 2018/19 until 31st May 2020.** (Assume the HMRC interest rate on late paid income tax is 3.00%)

(3 marks)

(25 marks)

(ACCA updated)

Question 4, Sue Macker

Sue Macker, who lives in England, was made redundant from her employment on 15th March 2018. She is a vintage motor car enthusiast, and so decided to take this opportunity to indulge her hobby.

On 6th April 2018 Sue took out a bank loan of £75,000 at an annual interest rate of 5%, rented a workshop for twelve months at a rent of £400 per month, and purchased equipment at a cost of £13,500.

On 10th April 2018 Sue purchased four dilapidated vintage motor cars for £8,000 each. The restoration of the four motor cars was completed on 10th March 2019 at a cost of £12,000 per motor car. Sue immediately sold all the motor cars for a total of £200,000.

Sue was then offered employment elsewhere in the country commencing on 6th April 2019. She therefore sold the equipment for £5,800 on 20th March 2019 and repaid the bank loan on 5th April 2019.

Because she has just been indulging her hobby, Sue believes that the disposal of the vintage motor cars during the tax year 2018/19 should be exempt from tax. She has done some research on the Internet and has discovered that whether she is treated as carrying on a trade will be determined according to the six following 'badges of trade':

(1) The subject matter of the transaction.
(2) The length of ownership.
(3) Frequency of similar transactions.
(4) Work done on the property.
(5) Circumstances responsible for the realisation.
(6) Motive.

Sue had no other income during the tax year 2018/19 except as indicated above.

Required:

(a) Briefly explain the meaning of each of the six 'badges of trade' listed above. (You are not expected to quote from decided cases.) (3 marks)

(b) Briefly explain why Sue is likely to be treated as carrying on a trade in respect of her vintage motor car activities. (3 marks)

(c) Calculate Sue's income tax liability and her Class 2 and Class 4 national insurance contributions for the tax year 2018/19, if she is treated as carrying on a trade in respect of her vintage motor car activities. (Ignore VAT.) (7 marks)

(d) Explain why it would be beneficial if Sue were instead treated as not carrying on a trade in respect of her vintage motor car activities. (2 marks)

(15 marks)
(ACCA updated)

Question 5, Tony Note

Tony Note is self-employed running a music shop. His Income Statement for the year ended 5th April 2019 is as follows:

	£	£
Gross profit		198,000
Expenses		
Depreciation	2,640	
Motor expenses (note 1)	9,800	
Professional fees (note 2)	4,680	
Repairs and renewals (note 3)	670	
Travelling and entertaining (note 4)	4,630	
Wages and salaries (note 5)	77,200	
Other expenses (note 6)	78,780	
		(178,400)
Net profit		19,600

Note 1 – Motor expenses

During the year ended 5th April 2019 Tony drove a total of 20,000 miles, of which 6,000 were driven for private journeys, and the remaining miles for business journeys.

Note 2 – Professional fees

The figure for professional fees consists of £920 for accountancy, £620 for personal financial planning advice, £540 for debt collection, and £2,600 for fees in connection with an unsuccessful application for planning permission to enlarge Tony's freehold music shop.

Note 3 – Repairs and renewals

The figure for repairs and renewals consists of £270 for a replacement hard drive for the shop's computer, and £400 for a new printer for this computer.

Note 4 – Travelling and entertaining

The figure for travelling and entertaining consists of £3,880 for Tony's business travelling expenses, £480 for entertaining suppliers, and £270 for entertaining employees.

Note 5 – Wages and salaries

The figure for wages and salaries includes a salary of £22,000 paid to Tony's wife. She works in the music shop as a sales assistant. The other sales assistants doing the same job are paid a salary of £18,000 p.a.

Note 6 – Other expenses

The figure for other expenses includes £75 in respect of a wedding present to an employee, £710 for Tony's health club subscription, £60 for a donation to a political party, and £180 for a trade subscription to the Guild of Musical Instrument Retailers.

Note 7 – Use of office

Tony uses one of the six rooms in his private house as an office for when he works at home. The total running costs of the house for the year ended 5th April 2019 were £4,320.

Note 8 – Private **telephone**

Tony uses his private telephone to make business telephone calls. The total cost of the private telephone for the year ended 5th April 2019 was £680, and 25% of this related to business telephone calls. The cost of the private telephone is not included in the profit and loss account expenses of £178,400.

Note 9 – Goods for own use

During the year ended 5th April 2019 Tony took goods out of the music shop for his personal use without paying for them, and no entry has been made in the accounts to record a sale. The goods cost £600 and had a selling price of £950.

Note 10 – Plant and machinery

The tax written down values for capital allowances purposes at 6th April 2018 were as follows:

	£	
General pool	9,250	
Motor car	15,000	CO_2 emissions 105 g/km

The car is used by Tony.

Required:

(a) Calculate Tony's tax adjusted trading profit for the year ended 5th April 2019. (16 marks)

(b) Calculate Tony's income tax liability for the tax year 2018/19. (2 marks)

(18 marks)

(ACCA updated)

[illegible]

Part III

Corporation Tax

18 General principles of corporation tax

18.1 Introduction

Corporation Tax is a direct tax on the income and capital gains of companies and other corporate bodies. In this chapter the main elements of the corporation tax system are outlined. It begins with some basic expressions, then forms of organisation liable and exempt from corporation tax are examined, followed by corporation tax self-assessment. The remainder of the chapter deals with the corporation tax accounting periods, and the rates of tax. A summary of corporation tax rates and a specimen computation are provided at the end.

Subsequent chapters in this part look in more detail at the measurement of the various categories of a company's income, and available reliefs, finishing with a chapter on special tax provisions for corporate groups and one summarising the most common international corporation tax issues which commonly affect a UK company which also has non-UK profits.

Detailed rules for computing the chargeable (capital) gains or allowable capital losses of a company are covered in Part IV, 'Taxation of chargeable gains'.

18.2 Development of Corporation Tax

Corporation tax as a separate form of business taxation was introduced by the Finance Act 1965. However, an entirely new set of rules for the determination of business income was not provided, and the substance of the income tax system was preserved, especially in the original rules for measuring companies' taxable income, and recognition of interest paid and received.

From the 1990s, company tax was reformed, so that the rules for certain types of transaction (such as borrowing for trade purposes) no longer mirror the income tax rules for the same type of transaction carried out by an individual. These corporate tax changes were influenced by several developments: partly by improvements in accounting standards, meaning that company directors had less choice about when to account for a company's revenue and expenses; partly by the UK's move to corporation tax self-assessment; and partly by the Government's wish to counter tax planning structures which exploited timing and measurement differences which existed under the previous systems for recognising financial profits and expenses (including cross-border tax differences, where transactions involved a non-UK counterparty).

Company tax rules on corporate finance, leasing and debt arrangements, including gains and losses on financial derivatives and foreign currency holdings, now follow, as far as possible, the required financial accounting treatment of such profits and losses (but with some restrictions for 'estimated' losses). There is a 'loan relationships tax regime' and a 'leasing tax regime' designed specifically for corporation tax. These rules cover financing transactions, other than those involving equity shares. The reformed system also covers profits and losses on foreign currency exchange transactions. Further reforms are still made periodically to the foreign currency, loan relationship and leasing tax regimes, if specific tax avoidance tactics are identified by HMRC.

For more on the loan relationships regime 19.10.

Also, companies are subject to a different tax regime from unincorporated businesses for intangible assets that are 'intellectual property', such as goodwill, patents, and know-how. (See 19.12.)

UK companies also qualify for extra tax reliefs for revenue expenditure on Research and Development ('R&D') compared to unincorporated businesses. (See 19.8 and 19.9).

The Corporation Tax Acts 2009 and 2010 changed some of the main terminology of corporation tax without changing the rules, and represent the first time in UK tax law that the corporation tax rules were placed in separate statutes on their own. (However, the term 'the Corporation Tax Acts' is defined, by CTA 2010, as also covering Income Tax statutes, so far as these contain rules that also apply to companies.)

However, rules for computing (though not for taxing) corporate capital gains are still contained in the Taxation of Chargeable Gains Act 1992, a statute which does still cover both individuals and companies, though for individuals it has been very significantly amended by subsequent Finance Acts. (See Chapters 25 to 32.)

The UK Government in November 2010 issued an important consultative policy document called 'Corporate Tax Reform: Delivering a More Competitive System' which set out further major reforms planned for the UK's corporate tax system. The reforms to the UK corporate tax system have included reducing the main rate of Corporation Tax to 19%, the lowest in the G20 group of nations, and exempting from UK tax foreign dividend income and, optionally, profits of foreign branches. In his 2016 Budget Speech the Chancellor announced further cuts in the rate of Corporation Tax to 17% by 2020.

Although the plan of the UK government is to make the UK competitive as an attractive country for multinational groups through low tax rates, the UK is a member of the OECD Base Erosion and Profit Shifting (BEPS) project to counter corporate tax avoidance by multinational enterprises. Corporate taxation has become a high profile political issue since media exposures claiming that multinational groups of companies with very high levels of business activity in the UK pay little or no UK corporation tax because of tax avoidance[1]. The new foreign profits regime is discussed in Chapter 24.

18.3 Basic expressions in corporation tax law

Financial year

A financial year runs from 1st April to the following 31st March, and each year is known by reference to the calendar year in which 1st April occurs. Thus, the Financial Year 2018 covers the period from 1st April 2018 to 31st March 2019. Corporation tax rates are fixed by reference to Financial Years.

Accounting period

Companies do not self-assess CT for financial years, but for corporation tax accounting periods, which are linked to their financial reporting periods. A CT accounting period can never exceed 12 months in length but can be shorter.

Close company

This is a company which is owned or controlled by a small number of persons (called participators) and their close family members. Private family companies usually fall into this category. The corporation tax consequences of a company being close are now quite limited. A loan by a close company to a participator that lasts past the year-end incurs a liability on the company to pay a temporary additional tax payment to HMRC which is refundable once the loan is repaid or replaced by a dividend. This provision is not discussed further here. Other special income tax and Capital Gains Tax rules on benefits received affect the participators in a close company, and they can obtain income tax relief for interest on a loan to purchase shares in a close company.

Close investment holding company (CIHC for short)

This means a close company, other than one whose business consists substantially of trading activities (for this purpose 'trading' includes acquiring and letting land or property to unconnected persons), except a company which is the managing or parent company of a group whose other companies all have a trade. The participators of Close Investment Holding Companies are excluded from any share tax reliefs that require the company to be a trading company.

18.4 Further key definitions

Total Profits

Paraphrasing slightly, the Corporation Tax Act 2010 defines 'total profits' as:

i) all a company's income from any source that is within the charge to Corporation Tax, after giving effect to specific expense reliefs available against specific sources of income, plus

ii) all a company's chargeable gains that fall within the charge to Corporation Tax, after giving effect to any specific deductions and tax reliefs available against chargeable gains.

Taxable Total Profits 'TTP'

This is defined as:

i) Total profits, less

ii) Amounts which can be relieved against total profits.

The term at (ii) covers certain loss reliefs, other special deductions, and qualifying charitable donations (see specimen computation at the end of this chapter). Where more than one such deduction is claimed, the order of set-off is usually fixed.

Note that dividends received from other companies are not taxable profits for Corporation Tax.

Group relief
This is the term used to describe the voluntary set-off of a trade loss, excess management expenses, excess charitable donations, a net non-trade loan relationship deficit, post 1 April 2017 property business losses, or certain other net outflows, of one member of a group of companies ('group' as specifically defined for group relief) against the profits of another member of the same group. See Chapter 23 for details.

'Related 51% group company'
For corporation tax purposes, this is a relationship where a company holds more than 50% of the ordinary shares of another company, or both are controlled by a common shareholder with a holding of more than 50%.

Main rate of corporation tax
This is set in the Finance Act each year. For Financial Year 2018 (FY2018) it is 19%. It is applied to taxable total profits to find the Corporation Tax liability for an accounting period. For Financial Year 2017 (FY 2017) also the rate was 19%. Further details on applying Corporation Tax rates are in 18.15 to 18.16.

18.5 Organisations liable to corporation tax (CTA 2009)

(a) Companies resident in the UK must self-assess and pay Corporation Tax on their 'Taxable Total Profits' (as defined for CT purposes), wherever in the world the profits arise. A company is resident in the UK if it is incorporated here. It is also UK resident if it is incorporated elsewhere but has its place of 'central management and control' in the UK.

The Finance Act 2011 contains an irrevocable opt-out election by which a UK resident company can choose to exclude the profits of an overseas branch or permanent establishment from inclusion in the UK company's worldwide profits charged to UK CT. The downside of this election is that net expenses / losses of the overseas branch cease to be allowed against UK profits, and UK capital allowances (see Chapter 20) are no longer available on plant and machinery of the overseas branch. This legislation implemented a stated policy of not taxing companies in the UK on profits not earned in the UK, abandoning the former 'worldwide' earnings approach to the scope of the charge to CT. See Chapter 24 for more on taxation of foreign branches.

(b) Companies not resident in the UK are chargeable to corporation tax on the profits of any UK 'permanent establishment' of that company which carries on a trade in the UK. See 18.6.

(c) 'Unincorporated associations' are liable to corporation tax. This term excludes partnerships and local authority associations but includes any form of club or society, including voluntary associations, if there is a trading or profit intention. If the club or society is non-profit-making or charitable, tax exemption may apply. See 18.7.

(d) Building societies, provident societies, and insurance companies. Special rules apply to these organisations.

(e) Corporate members of partnerships: If a company enters into a trading partnership, it is charged to **Corporation Tax** in respect of its share of the partnership profits, but partners who are individuals pay **Income Tax or Capital Gains Tax** on their shares of profits and gains. See Chapter 15 for taxation of partnerships in general.

18.6 Non-resident companies

a) A company not resident in the United Kingdom is within the charge to corporation tax if, and only if, it carries on a trade in the United Kingdom through a 'permanent establishment' in the United Kingdom.

b) If it does so, it is chargeable to corporation tax, subject to any exceptions provided for by the Corporation Tax Acts, on all profits, wherever arising, which are attributable to the UK 'permanent establishment'. These profits are the company's 'total profits' for the purposes of corporation tax.

c) CTA2009 provides that the UK 'permanent establishment's profits reported on its Corporation Tax self-assessment must be computed on the 'separate enterprise principle'. This means that all transactions between a UK branch operation and its foreign headquarters or parent group must be priced 'on arm's length terms', that is, at the same transfer prices as would have been agreed between unconnected parties.

d) If a foreign resident company has investment or property income derived from UK assets, but no UK trade through a 'permanent establishment', then it is liable only to basic rate income tax, not corporation tax, on its UK income only (subject to any Double Tax Treaty which may exempt this income from UK tax). A company with no trade in the UK is not liable to UK tax on its chargeable gains.

e) For the purposes of the Corporation Tax Acts a company has a **permanent establishment** in a territory if, and only if:

   i) it has a fixed place of business there through which the business of the company is wholly or partly carried on; or

   ii) an agent acting on behalf of the company has, and habitually exercises, in that territory authority to do business on behalf of the company.

f) A fixed place of business includes, according to the Finance Act 2003:

- a place of management;
- a branch;
- an office;
- a factory;
- a workshop;

- an installation or structure for the exploration of natural resources;
- a mine, an oil or gas well, a quarry or any other place of extraction of natural resources;
- a building site or construction or installation project.

The concept of a permanent establishment as a 'fixed place of business' was developed in intergovernmental negotiations in the early to mid-twentieth century, and is reflected in the OECD's current Model Tax Treaty. However, in 2012 the UK Parliament's Public Accounts Committee publicly examined some well-known global companies which claimed for tax purposes to have no 'permanent establishment' in the UK, despite having many staff and warehouses there. It has been concluded that the existing rules can be exploited by group structures which rely on modern means of communication, money transfer, and air travel, allowing controlling activities, staff knowhow, and intellectual property to be located outside a taxing jurisdiction where it could be argued that economic profits are 'made'. The OECD 'Base Erosion and Profit Shifting' project is working to develop a co-operative international response to international corporate tax avoidance. At present, the 'permanent establishment' rules operate to decide whether a given trade is liable to UK corporation tax.

18.7 Organisations exempt from corporation tax

(a) Partnerships (except for the profit share of a corporate partner – see above).

(b) Local authorities.

(c) Approved pension schemes.

(d) Charities. A charity, which is defined as 'any body of persons or trust established for charitable purposes' is exempt from corporation tax in so far as its income is applied to charitable purposes only. If a charity carries on a trade, then any profits arising will be exempt providing that:

  (i) they are applied solely for the purposes of the charity, and

  (ii) either the trade is exercised out of a primary purpose of the charity, or the work is mainly carried out by the beneficiaries of the charity.

(e) Agricultural and scientific societies.

(f) The Crown.

18.8 Notice of chargeability to corporation tax

A company must give notice to HMRC of the beginning of its first Corporation Tax Accounting Period which brings it into the charge to corporation tax. The notice must be given within three months of the beginning of the accounting period (henceforth 'AP' or 'CTAP'). For a new company, the information is given on form CT41G which is sent by HMRC to all newly-incorporated UK companies, acting on information from Companies House.

18.9 Self-assessment – CT return (Form CT600)

The main features of the corporation tax self-assessment (CTSA) system are:

a) The payment of CT and the filing of the company's tax return are separate activities. For required tax payment dates, see paragraph 10 onwards.

b) Between 3 and 7 weeks after the end of a company's AP (or what HMRC think is the end of an accounting period), HMRC issues a notice (form CT603) requiring the company to deliver a tax return for the specified period.

   The filing of the CTSA return (Form CT600), accompanying financial statements and computations must be done entirely online, using HMRC-approved software. Except for charities, the company's financial statements must be filed in iXBRL format. Charities may file their financial statements as a pdf file (Acrobat). Tax computations linking the financial statements to the figures in the Form CT600 must also be filed in iXBRL. This is a tagged electronic format readable by both humans and computers, and allows automated software to check key figures in the financial statements to the company tax computations and self-assessment return. HMRC provides free software to set up accounts and computations in iXBRL and approved commercial packages are also available which can be integrated with computerised accounting systems.

   There is an intention ultimately to combine the submission of company tax returns with the online submission of accounts to Companies House in the UK so that it is all achievable with a single online filing, but at present this is not yet the case. The date when accounts are required at Companies House is currently earlier than the date when Corporation Tax returns are required.

c) Whether filed in paper form or online, the CTSA return includes:

   i) a self-assessment of the CT payable for the accounting period

   ii) formal claims for allowances and reliefs

   iii) supplementary pages, if applicable, in respect of:

      loans to participators by close companies CT600A
      controlled foreign companies CT600B
      group and consortium relief CT600C
      insurance companies CT600D
      additional details where the taxpayer is a charity CT600E

   For limited companies, the financial statements must also be sent in iXBRL form together with any computations required to show how the financial statements link to the figures entered in the Corporation Tax return.

   Bodies that are liable to Corporation Tax, but are not limited companies, should send whatever form of accounts they are required to prepare. Any additional computations necessary to link these accounts to the Corporation Tax Self-Assessment return figures should also be provided.

d) The latest filing date for a Corporation Tax Self-Assessment return is 12 months from the end of the accounting period, or in the case of a period of account that covers more than one accounting period, twelve months from the end of the period of account. The directors are at liberty to file the Corporation Tax Self-Assessment return earlier than the latest filing date.

e) The company can amend its submitted Corporation Tax Self-Assessment return by giving a notice of amendment, within 12 months after the filing date. An amendment may include additional claims for relief, or the withdrawal of previously submitted claims.

f) HMRC can amend the submitted tax return to correct obvious errors or omissions, without launching a formal enquiry. This cannot be done more than nine months after the actual filing date, and the company may, if it wishes, appeal.

g) HMRC has up to twelve months from the actual filing date to raise an aspect enquiry (limited in scope), or a full enquiry, into a submitted Corporation Tax return and to propose its own amendments because of an enquiry. HMRC also has up to twelve months from the date of a submitted amendment to a return, to enquire into the amendment.

h) Penalties are automatically due if the Corporation Tax return is filed late. There are flat-rate and tax-related penalties depending on the extent of the delay in filing the corporation tax return:

Period of delay (months)	Penalties
1 – 3	£100
3 – 6	£200
6 – 9	£200 + 10% of tax unpaid
9 –	£200 + 20% of tax unpaid

For 3 or more late returns in a row, the flat rate penalties are increased from £100 and £200 to £500 and £1,000.

Penalties are also charged for an incorrect return, under the regime introduced in the Finance Act 2007, explained in 3.11

18.10 Corporation tax payments on account

a) 'Large profits' companies are still commonly referred to by accountants simply as 'large companies', although the official terminology changed in CTA2010. 'Large' (profits) companies are those whose profits exceed a given limit for an accounting period, providing the profits also exceeded the limit in the previous period. They are required to make quarterly instalment payments of their corporation tax liability for an accounting period. It is the responsibility of the company's management to estimate these payments on account.

b) A company is 'large' for a corporation tax accounting period (CTAP) if its Taxable Total Profits (TTP) are equal to or exceed the 'upper profits limit' – currently £1.5 million. However, this limit is reduced for related 51% group companies, and pro-rated for short accounting periods.

c) If there are related 51% group companies (see 18.4), then the £1.5m limit for profits is divided by the total number of companies in the 51% group, including the taxpayer company. Thus a parent company with 4 active subsidiaries has an upper relevant limit of £1,500,000 ÷ 5, i.e. £300,000. See

Chapter 23 for more on reducing the upper profits limit where there are group companies, or a short accounting period.

d) A company that becomes 'large' during a CTAP does not have to make Corporation Tax instalment payments for that period, provided:

   i) it was not a 'large' company in the previous CTAP, **and**

   ii) its taxable total profits for that CTAP do not exceed a £10 million 'maximum relevant amount' (this limit is divided where appropriate by the number of associated companies in the group, and apportioned for a short CTAP).

e) No company is required to make instalment payments if its Corporation Tax liability for the current CTAP is already known to be less than £10,000.

f) Subject to the exceptions above, Corporation Tax must be paid by 'large' companies in four quarterly instalments, based on anticipated current year's Taxable Total Profits, as follows:

Instalment	Due date
1st	6 months + 14 days after start of CTAP
2nd	9 months + 14 days after start of CTAP
3rd	14 days after end of CTAP
4th	3 months + 14 days after end of CTAP

Thus a company with a 31st March year end pays CT instalments on:

14th October, 14th January, 14th April and 14th July following the year end.

g) If management Corporation Tax estimates are accurate then 100% of the Corporation Tax liability is paid by four instalments of 25% each.

h) If management estimates are inaccurate, over- and under-payments are liable to interest at different rates, the differential acting as an incentive to make accurate estimates).

i) Interest arising on over- or under-payments of Corporation Tax is taxable/tax-deductible for the company as a non-trading loan relationship surplus/deficit for CT purposes. Interest on CT is regarded as normal commercial expense or receipt for the time value of the money, and does not count as a penalty or imply non-compliance by the company with its tax obligations.

j) Groups of companies are able to arrange to pay single Corporation Tax instalments on behalf of the whole group, without having to specify exactly which companies' final liability each instalment relates to. The allocation of the group's instalment payments to individual companies can be settled when the companies' individual Corporation Tax returns are finalised.

k) Companies which are not 'large' must pay all corporation tax by nine months and one day after the end of the Corporation Tax Accounting Period, and do not incur any interest on late payment until this date.

l) Note that for all companies, the Corporation Tax due payment date falls before the last submission date for the Corporation Tax return. A company whose directors cannot determine the expected Corporation Tax liability until the final

Corporation Tax return date should therefore either make an estimated overpayment of CT which can be refunded later, or accept the cost of interest.

m) From 1st April 2019 companies with annual profits of over £20m, 'very large companies' will be required to make earlier corporation tax payments on account, in months 3, 6, 9 and 12 of the Corporation Tax Accounting Period.

18.11 Interest on overpaid tax and on correct tax paid early

Interest paid by HMRC on overpaid Corporation Tax subsequently repaid is known as repayment interest. Interest paid by HMRC on overestimated quarterly instalments paid early (but not repaid because it is matched to a liability falling due later) is known as credit interest. Credit interest cannot be earned before, at the earliest, the first instalment payment date for an accounting period. Other than this rule, repayment and credit interest are computed from the date of actual payment to either the due date or the date of refund. All interest paid by HMRC to companies is taxable as income of a non-trade loan relationship.

18.12 Financial years and accounting periods

As already noted, Corporation Tax is charged on the profits of companies for the UK Government financial year which runs from 1st April. A UK Government financial year is known by the calendar year in which it begins, e.g.:

Financial year	Period
2017	1st April 2017 – 31st March 2018
2018	1st April 2018 – 31st March 2019

The corporation tax rate for a financial year (see more details in 18.15) is enacted in the Finance Act for that financial year.

The Provisional Collection of Taxes Act 1968, as amended in 2011, allows HMRC, and requires corporate taxpayers, to apply new tax rates and other rules in a Finance Bill that is still before Parliament, with those actions being legally ratified by legislation enacted by 6th October in that financial year.

18.13 Corporation tax accounting periods

(a) A corporation tax accounting period (CTAP) is the period for which the CT liability is computed, and can never exceed 12 months in length.

(b) A CTAP begins in the following circumstances:

- (i) When a company comes within the scope of UK Corporation Tax – for example, by starting a UK trade, acquiring its first source of taxable income (if incorporated in the UK), or becoming resident in the UK (if not previously so resident);
- (ii) immediately after the end of the last accounting period, provided the company remains within the scope of UK Corporation Tax.

(c) A CTAP ends when the earliest of the following events occurs.

- (i) The company reaches its reporting period end (i.e. its accounting reference date).
- (ii) The end of twelve months from the start of the current Corporation Tax Accounting Period.

(iii) The company starts or stops trading (a CTAP ends, and a new one begins, when all trade starts or stops, even if other business activities continue).

(iv) The company ceases to be within the scope of UK Corporation Tax e.g. by selling its trade and all its income-producing assets, or in the case of non-resident companies, by ceasing to trade in the UK or to carry on exploration/exploitation activities in the UK sector of the North Sea).

(v) The company goes into liquidation (once in liquidation, its CTAPs run for consecutive periods of 12 months until the completion of the winding-up).

(vi) The company starts or stops being resident in the UK.

18.14 Periods of account longer than 12 months

If a company's period of account (period for which it publicly files financial statements) is longer than 12 months, then it must be split into two or more CTAPs, for each of which a separate Corporation Tax return is submitted by the company. To find the total profits for each CTAP, the various types of taxable profits, gains, losses and reliefs must be allocated correctly under tax law to the CTAPs. For further details on these long-period rules, please see 19.4 and 19.5.

18.15 Corporation Tax rates

Until 31st March 2015 there were two rates of corporation tax, the small profits rate and the full or main rate. The level of augmented profits determined which rate applied, and there was marginal relief to smooth the average rate of CT between the small profits rate and main rate where profits fell in the intermediate zone.

This method was a form of progressive taxation varying the average rate of Corporation Tax according to how profitable the company was (including FII). The average rate of CT rose smoothly as taxable profits plus FII increased. Once the upper relevant profits amount was reached, the rate could not go up any more.

From 1st January 2016 there is an additional corporation tax 'bank surcharge' of 8% on banking sector profits, applied to profits exceeding £25million (on a group-wide basis). When Chancellor George Osborne introduced this surcharge in the Summer Budget 2015, he did so stating that it was important that banks 'help pay down the debts built up during the banking crisis.'

Financial years	FY14	FY15	FY16	FY17	FY18
Year to 31st March	2015	2016	2017	2018	2019
Full rate	21%	20%	20%	19%	19%
Small profits rate	20%				
Marginal relief fraction	1/400	-	-	-	-
Lower relevant amount	300,000	-	-	-	-
Upper relevant amount	1,500,000	-	-	-	-

Marginal relief formula: tax the company's profits at main rate first, then deduct:

(U – A) × N/A × the marginal relief fraction

where N = Taxable total profit, U = upper relevant amount, A = Augmented profits

18.16 Change in the rate of Corporation Tax part way through a CTAP

If a company's CTAP does not coincide with the financial year, and there is a change in the rate or rates of CT, the taxable total profits for the CTAP must be apportioned between the two financial years on a time basis, before adding on FII; then tax is computed at different rates for each fraction of a financial year.

The CT rate changed on 1st April 2017, so CTAPs that straddle that date are taxed by apportioning the taxable total profit between the two financial years, applying the correct rates of tax and treating the total as the single CT liability for the CTAP.

Example

Durata Ltd, a trading company, whose 12 month CTAP ended on 30th June 2017, had taxable total profits for that period of £2,000,000 and no associated companies. As the Corporation Tax main rate was 20% for FY2016 and is 19% for FY2017, Durata's Corporation Tax liability computation is as follows:

Taxable total profits	£	£
1.7.2016 to 31.3.2017 274/365 × 2,000,000	1,501,370	
1.4.2017 to 30.6.2017 91/365 × 2,000,000	498,630	2,000,000
Corporation tax payable		
Financial year 2016 to 31.3.2017 1,501,370 @ 20%		300,274
Financial year 2017 to 31.3.2018 498,630 @ 19%		94,740
Total CT liability		395,014

<u>Note</u> Although it is correct to apportion taxable profits of a CTAP to Financial Years using exact days, and this is done by commercial corporation tax software, it is acceptable to do the calculation in whole months for the tax exams of UK professional accounting bodies.

18.17 Specimen corporation tax computation (based on CT600 form)

INCOME AND GAINS	£	£
Tax-adjusted trading profits	–	
Less capital allowances	–	
Less Trade losses (pre 1st April 2017) brought forward against trading profits	–	
Subtotal: Net trading profits		–
ADD: Net non-trade loan relationship surplus * (typically interest receivable and similar income)		–
ADD: Overseas non-trading income	–	
ADD: Miscellaneous Income	–	
ADD: Income from which income tax has been deducted	–	
ADD: Non-trading gains on intangible fixed assets	–	
ADD: Income from UK land and buildings	–	
ADD: Chargeable gains, net of allowable capital losses	–	
SUBTOTAL – NON-TRADE PROFITS	–	
DEDUCTIONS SPECIFICALLY FROM NON-TRADE PROFITS:		
Non-trade loan relationship deficit (pre 1st April 2017)*	–	
Non-trade capital allowances	–	
		–
TOTAL PROFITS		–
LESS: DEDUCTIONS AND RELIEFS FROM TOTAL PROFITS:		
Losses set against total profits		–
Profit before qualifying charitable donations and group relief		–
LESS: Qualifying charitable donations paid		–
LESS: Group relief claimed		–
= TAXABLE TOTAL PROFITS		–
CORPORATION TAX :		
Financial year 2017 @ 19%		–
2018 @ 19%		–
Total corporation tax before reliefs and set-offs in terms of tax		–
LESS: Double taxation relief		–
NET CORPORATION TAX LIABILITY		–
Add Tax due on profits of Controlled Foreign Companies (see Chapter 24)		–
Less: relief for Income Tax suffered at source		–
CORPORATION TAX DUE		–

* non-trade loan deficits suffered are firstly netted against non-trade loan relationships income, and any negative balance is then taken to the non-trade loan deficit line.

18.18 Former small profits rate of corporation tax

For many years up to Financial Year 2014 this was a lower rate of CT payable by companies with 'augmented profits', as defined below, falling under certain levels. With the reduction of the main rate in Financial Year 2015 the main rate and the small profits rate merged at 20%, and are 19% for the Financial Year 2018.

Augmented Profits

This was the term used to determine whether a company paid corporation tax at the main rate, or a lower small profits rate. It was equal to:

Taxable Total Profits, plus FII, but excluding Group FII.

Franked investment income (FII)

When a UK resident company received a qualifying distribution (broadly, an income dividend) from another company, the amount of the payment was notionally increased by the UK dividend tax credit (1/9) which was available to individuals until 5th April 2016. The result of this calculation was known as 'franked investment income' (FII).

Student self-testing question

Tina Limited has Taxable Total Profits of £3,200,000 for the year ended 30th September 2018. In the year to 30th September 2017 the Taxable Total Profits were £3,500,000.

Requirement: Calculate Tina Limited's corporation tax liability for the year ended 30th September 2018, and state when the tax should be paid.

Solution

		£
FY 2017	3,200,000 × 6/12 × 19% =	304,000
FY 2018	3,200,000 × 6/12 × 19% =	304,000
		£608,000

With profits exceeding £1.5million in the year to 30th September 2018, and also in the preceding year, Tina Limited should make Corporation Tax payments on account as a 'large profits' company.

Corporation Tax must be paid by 'large' companies in four quarterly instalments, based on estimates of anticipated current year's taxable total profits, as follows:

Instalment	Due date	
1st	6 months + 14 days after start of CTAP	14th April 2018
2nd	9 months + 14 days after start of CTAP	14th July 2018
3rd	14 days after end of CTAP	14th October 2018
4th	3 months + 14 days after end of CTAP	14th January 2019.

References

1 http://www.thesundaytimes.co.uk/sto/news/uk_news/article1662903.ece (accessed 30th April 2016)

19 Computation of total profits

19.1 Introduction

This chapter is concerned with the determination of Corporation Tax total profits before deductions and reliefs, which is an important stage in the determination of taxable total profits.

The chapter examines the most important components of the Corporation Tax total profits computation as demonstrated in the specimen CT computation at the end of Chapter 18. The chapter concludes with a comprehensive example of the adjustment of accounting profits to trading profits for corporation tax purposes.

19.2 Generally accepted accounting practice

United Kingdom tax law requires that tax computations are prepared in accordance with Generally Accepted Accounting Practice. Generally accepted accounting practice is defined as being the accounting practice that is used in preparing accounts which are intended to give a 'true and fair' view (section 836A, Taxes Act 1988). The various accounting frameworks of the United Kingdom / international accounting bodies generally require that the relevant financial reporting standards need to be applied to all transactions of a reporting entity whose financial statements are intended to give a true and fair view.

19.3 Sources of income

Income is brought into Total Profits under the following headings:

- Trading profits
- Profits and gains from non-trading loan relationships
- Overseas non-trading income (under CTA2009 overseas trading income is included with UK trading profits)
- Other / Miscellaneous Income
- Income from which income tax has been deducted
- Non-trading gains on intangible fixed assets
- Income from land and buildings
- Chargeable gains, net of allowable capital losses

As noted in Chapter 18 dividends received are not taxable income for companies.

19.4 Long periods of account

Where a period of account exceeds twelve months, say 15 months, it is by law split into two accounting periods, the first CTAP being of the maximum length allowed, which is 12 months, and the second CTAP covering the balance of the statutory accounts, in this case three months.

Example

Koala Ltd has regularly prepared accounts to 31st December. On 1st January 2018 the directors decide that the year-end shall be 31st March, and the next set of accounts will be for the period of fifteen months to 31st March 2019.

Corporation tax accounting periods	Periods of account
12 months to 31st December 2017	12 months to 31st December 2017
12 months to 31st December 2018 3 months to 31st March 2019	15 months to 31st March 2019
12 months to 31st March 2020	12 months to 31st March 2020

19.5 Allocating income, gains and reliefs in a long period of account

The following rules apply to allocate income, capital gains, and reliefs to Corporation Tax Accounting Periods (CTAPs) in a long period of account

(i) Assessable (taxable) trading income / profit is computed by adjusting accounting profits for the whole period of account, **before** deducting capital allowances or adding balancing charges (see Chapter 20). The assessable trading income, before CAs, is then allocated to the CTAPs by time-apportionment, regardless of known fluctuations in sales or profitability.

(ii) Capital allowances, Balancing Allowances and Balancing Charges are calculated separately for each CTAP, and deducted in that period to the extent claimed.

(iii) Income from land and buildings (property business income) is computed for each CTAP on a business accounting (accruals) basis, applied for that period. Lease premiums received are treated on a receipts basis rather than an accruals basis.

(iv) Chargeable gains are assessable, and capital losses arise, in the CTAP in which the disposal contract was made. Capital losses of the later CTAP cannot be carried back and set against capital gains of the earlier one.

(v) Qualifying charitable donations are deducted from the total profits of the CTAP in which they were paid.

(vi) Surpluses and deficits on **non-trade** loan relationships, and other non-trading profits or expenses governed by special tax regimes reflecting financial accounting rules (see 19.10) are allocated to CTAPs on the same basis that they would be recognised in the company's financial accounts if financial accounts were drawn up for that same period. For example if an interest-bearing bank deposit account was closed after the first six months of a long period of account, the non-trading interest surplus arising would all be allocated to the first CTAP included and none of it to the second CTAP.

(vii) However interest payable on **trading** loan relationships follows the trade profits rules (covered at (i) above) and therefore is allocated pro rata to CTAPs as an expense of trading, regardless of when it was incurred.

19.6 Accounting periods of less than 12 months

As already indicated, for corporation tax purposes a company's accounting period cannot exceed 12 months in duration. If the CTAP is less than 12 months in length then the relevant profits amounts must be reduced accordingly.

Thus with an AP of nine months' duration ending in the financial year to 31.3.2019, the upper profit limit would be £1,500,000 × 9/12 i.e. £1,125,000. This would be used in determining whether the company needed to make corporation tax payments on account.

If the situation arises where a company has an AP of less than 12 months' length, and is a member of a 51% group with another company, then the respective profit levels are first divided by the number of companies in that group (including the company whose tax is being calculated now), and then reduced in proportion to the length of the short accounting period.

19.7 Trading profits

The following points should be noted under this heading.

a) The general principles of tax-deductible trading expenses for sole traders (see Chapter 10) also apply to companies; except where a specifically different rule exists for corporation tax. Profits and losses arising from trade loan relationships form part of trading profits. Companies do not have a private or personal existence and therefore there is not usually scope for expenses to be apportioned between private and business use. Expenses of providing benefits or assets for private use by staff or directors are allowable for the company as trade or management expenses, being part of allowable staff remuneration costs. (The private benefit element may be assessable on the director or employee as employment income under income tax rules – see Chapter 7.)

b) Costs of sponsorship paid to a charity, and the cost of seconding staff to a charity are allowable as part of normal business expenses. (See 21.5).

c) Petroleum revenue tax (a separate tax only paid by companies involved in UK oil extraction) is a deductible expense for corporation tax purposes, as are indirect taxes suffered on the company's costs (e.g. air passenger duty on air travel, import duty on goods, insurance premium tax on insurance, and employer's National Insurance on wages and salaries. Most of these taxes do not appear as 'tax' in the company's accounts, being included in the declared amount of the main expense. Irrecoverable input VAT is also an allowable cost for companies which suffer it (e.g. VAT-exempt traders, such as banks) - so long as the input VAT relates to business costs that are allowable for corporation tax purposes.

d) Incidental costs of obtaining loan finance, including costs in connection with the issue of convertible loan stock, are specifically allowed as a revenue deduction in computing trading income. This applies even to long-term non-trading loan finance. It includes such costs as professional fees, accountants' reports, commissions, advertising and communication costs related to bond or debenture issues, or to any other money borrowings, secured or not.

e) Pre-incorporation expenses incurred up to seven years prior to the actual commencement of trading are treated as normal expenses incurred on the first day of trading. Eligible expenditure includes all expenses which, had the company already been trading, would have been allowed as a trading expense, such as rent, rates, staff wages and salaries, but not initial company formation expenses, stamp duties, or capital expenditure (though capital allowances may be available on this in periods after the commencement of trading).

f) Unpaid remuneration:

   i) A deduction for employees' or directors' remuneration is not allowed in the computation of trading profits if the remuneration was paid more than nine months after the end of the period of account. Instead a deduction is allowed in the CTAP when paid.

   ii) 'Payment' in this case is based on the same rules used to determine when remuneration is received by the director or employee for the purpose of taxes on earnings (and PAYE). See Chapter 7 on this.

   iii) Where the corporation tax return is submitted less than nine months after the end of a period of account, any remuneration unpaid at that time should be added back in calculating the taxable profits. If the remuneration is subsequently paid before the end of the nine month period, an adjustment can be made to the submitted return within two years of the end of the period of account.

g) Just as for sole traders and partnerships that pay staff pension contribution for their employees (see Chapter 10), pension contributions paid by a company to a separate pension plan or fund on behalf of employees or directors may not be deducted on the accruals basis, but only when the payment has been made. This can also mean that a deduction is due in the tax computation of a company for employer's pension contributions that have been accrued in earlier years' accounts but were paid in the current AP.

h) A company's taxable profits are computed without any adjustment in respect of dividends paid or other distributions made out of its profits.

i) For tax relief on amortisation of intangible assets, see 19.11.

19.8 Research and development relief – small or medium sized companies (SMEs)

Relief is available for qualifying research and development expenditure (of a revenue nature) by UK companies, at an amount that is greater than the cost actually incurred. The rate is 230% (increased with effect from 1st April 2015 from 225%) for small or medium sized companies. Until 31st March 2016 a similar relief was available at a rate of 130% for large companies. Large companies now claim instead the 'above the line' tax credit explained below in 19.9. The terms 'large' and 'small or medium sized enterprises' are defined as for company law financial reporting purposes. The company law based limits for an SME are a maximum of: 500 employees; and either turnover of €100m; or assets of €86m. Note that those thresholds are measured in Euros rather than Sterling, as they derive from those found within EU regulations.

The following is an outline of the rules on R&D tax credits:

a) Rate of Research and Development Expenditure Credits: 230% of qualifying R&D expenditure for small or medium sized companies

b) A company's qualifying R&D expenditure is deductible in an AP if it relates to an actual trade or a future or potential trade. That is, either:
   i) it is allowable as a deduction in computing for tax purposes the profits for that period of a trade carried on by the company, or
   ii) it would have been allowable as such a deduction, had the company, at the time the expenditure was incurred, been carrying on a trade consisting of the activities in respect of which it was incurred.

c) '**Qualifying R&D expenditure**' of company means expenditure that meets the following conditions:
   i) it is not of a capital nature. Capital allowances for assets used in research and development may be claimed under the Research and Development Allowance (RDA), see 20.3.
   ii) it is attributable to relevant research and development directly undertaken by the company, or on its behalf.
   iii) it is incurred on staffing costs, or on consumable stores (including power, fuel, water, and software) or is qualifying expenditure on sub-contracted research and development.
   iv) any intellectual property created as a result of the research and development to which the expenditure is attributable is, or will be, vested in the company (whether alone or with other persons). This condition was removed for SME companies' R&D relief with effect from FY 2010.
   v) the expenditure is not incurred by the company in carrying on activities contracted out to the company by any person.
   vi) the expenditure is not subsidised.

d) Where:
   i) A company is entitled to R&D tax relief for an accounting period,
   ii) it is carrying on a trade in that period, and
   iii) it has qualifying R&D expenditure that is allowable as a deduction in computing for tax purposes the profits of the trade for that period, it may (on making a claim) treat that qualifying R&D expenditure as if it were an amount equal to 230% of the actual amount.

(e) As an alternative to claiming the 230% enhanced relief for qualifying R&D expenditure, loss making SMEs can claim a payable credit in cash at a rate of 14.5%.

Example

Piccolo Limited, an SME, has the following data relating to its CTAP ended 31st March 2019.

	£
Revenue	60,000,000
Research and development expenses	5,000,000
Other tax allowable expenses of trading	20,000,000

Compute the corporation tax liability for the CTAP to 31st March 2019, assuming the company claims R&D tax relief for an SME.

Solution

			£
Revenue			60,000,000
R&D expenses	(100%)	(5,000,000)	
Other expenses		(20,000,000)	(25,000,000)
Profit before tax			35,000,000
Taxation	(35m – (5m × 130%*)) @ 19%		(5,415,000)
Profit after tax			£29,585,000

* Note that the allowable deduction is 230% but 100% has already been included as an expense in calculating the profit before tax figure, so the extra amount to be deducted is 130%

19.9 Research and development 'above the line' (ATL) tax credit – large companies

As an alternative to the research and development credit large companies claim an 'above the line' (ATL) tax credit. Above the line tax credit is paid at a rate of 12% (increased with effect from 1st January 2018 from 11%), before tax, of qualifying expenditure on or after 1st April 2013. The ATL tax credit replaced the 130% super-deduction from 1st April 2016.

Example

Gemella plc, a large company, has the following data relating to its CTAP ended 31st March 2019.

	£
Revenue	600,000,000
Research and development expenses	50,000,000
Other tax allowable costs of trading	200,000,000

Compute the corporation tax liability for the CTAP to 31st March 2019, assuming the company claims 'above the line' ATL tax credit for R&D expenditure.

Solution

Revenue			600,000,000
R&D expenses		(50,000,000)	
ATL tax credit	12%	6,000,000	
Other costs		(200,000,000)	(244,000,000)
Profit before tax			356,000,000
Taxation	((356.0m @ 19%) – 6.0m)		(61,640,000)
Profit after tax			**£294,360,000**

19.10 Surplus on non-trading loan relationships

The income taxable under this heading is as follows.

a) Interest Income. Bank and building society interest is taxable under this heading on an accruals basis. If a company did receive UK deposit interest net of basic rate income tax, i.e. with 20% deducted at source before 31st March 2016, it is the gross amount (i.e. net interest plus associated income tax) which would be chargeable to corporation tax, and the income tax would be credited elsewhere (see below).

b) Other finance income from non-trade loan relationships. Measurement is based on the amount treated under GAAP (using either International Financial Reporting Standards or UK GAAP is acceptable) as the income amount for the CTAP (e.g. the gradual credits recognised each year under Accounting Standards as the redemption profit on a 5-year corporate bond redeemable at a premium). So there is no need for tax purposes to adjust finance income shown in the income statement for any such items.

   Upward revaluations of debt instruments recognised through profit and loss are also taxable as surpluses on loan relationships.

Loan receivables of companies are never chargeable assets for the calculation of chargeable gains for Corporation Tax. Thus for example the write-off or waiver of a non-trade loan to another company is a deficit on a non-trade loan relationship, not a capital loss.

Where income is received after deduction of income tax at source (such as patent royalties received from an individual), since the gross amount should be chargeable to corporation tax not income tax, the income tax deducted at source is recoverable as follows:

a) It can be set against any income tax payable in respect of payments made by the company under deduction of basic rate income tax at source – e.g. payment of patent royalties to an individual. (See Chapter 21.)

b) If relief is not fully available via quarterly income tax accounting returns as in (a), the excess income tax suffered may be deducted from the main corporation tax liability, or if this is exceeded, a cash repayment may be claimed.

Income tax that has to be deducted from payments of royalties etc. by companies, together with any related income tax claimed by offset under a) above, is accounted for under the 'quarterly return system' covered in Chapter 21.

19.11 Corporate loan relationships

a) In general a corporate loan relationship exists whenever a company is either creditor or debtor for a debt which is regarded as a loan under general law. A company-issued bond, other loan security or debentures would fall within this definition.

b) The definition in (a) above also covers company holdings of Government gilt-edged securities, building society PIBS (permanent interest-bearing shares), and corporate bonds and corporate debts. Bank interest receivable by a trading company (other than a company whose trade is banking) is taxed as a non-trading loan relationship credit, or 'surplus'.

c) In applying loan relationship tax rules there are two methods of accounting which companies are authorised to use, mirroring current accounting standards on financial instruments.

   i) an accruals basis;

   ii) a market-to-market basis – by which a loan relationship is accounted for in each CTAP at fair value in the Statement of Financial Position, and any movement is taken to the Income Statement.

   As a general rule, when reporting finance income and expenses, a company must follow its chosen accounting treatment for all taxation purposes.

d) Where a company enters into a loan relationship for the purposes of a trade, the recognised incomes and expenses relating to the loan relationship are treated as incomes and expenses of that trade and therefore included in the calculation of trade profits or losses.

e) Where a company enters into a loan relationship of a non-trade nature, i.e. it is not one in the course of activities forming an integral part of the trade, then incomes and expenses from all such relationships are netted off for tax purposes. Any net surplus is taxed, in effect as interest income, while any net deficit is dealt with as set out in 22.7. In summary this is as follows:
   i) by offset against the company's other income and gains chargeable to corporation tax for that accounting period; or
   ii) by surrender as group relief to other group companies (see Chapter 24); or
   iii) by carry-back against the company's previous three years' net surpluses (if any) from non-trade loan relationships, to the extent that such profits arise on a company's non-trading foreign exchange and financial instrument transactions; or
   iv) by carry-forward against future profits. For losses incurred up to 1 April 2017 the carry forward is against future non-trading profits, and for losses incurred from 1 April 2017 onwards the carry forward is against total profits.

f) The loan relationships rules apply to all UK companies within the charge to corporation tax, including UK branches of overseas companies.

19.12 Intangible assets

Companies (but not unincorporated businesses) are able to obtain tax relief for the cost of intangible assets / intellectual property, in most cases based on the expenses (including amortisation or impairment) charged in the accounts.

Costs of goodwill, and customer related intangible assets, acquired on or after 8th July 2015 are not eligible for tax relief as expenses of trading

Eligible intangible assets include:

i) patents, trademarks, registered designs, copyright or design rights;

ii) database rights, computers and software licences, know-how;

Intangible assets for this purpose do not include leases of property or land.

a) Expenditure on intellectual property is any expenditure incurred on the acquisition, creation, maintenance, preservation or enhancement of that property. It includes abortive expenditure and expenditure on establishing and defending title to that property. It also includes royalties paid for the use of the intellectual property. Whether or not the expenditure is treated as capital expenditure in the financial statements is irrelevant, except that capital expenditure on tangible assets is specifically excluded.

b) The system provides that a 'tax debit' (normally an item of tax deductible expenditure) in respect of intellectual property can arise in five ways:
   i. as expenditure written off as it is incurred;
   ii. as amortisation of capitalised intellectual property;

iii. as a write-down following an impairment review;
iv. as a reversal of a credit of a previous accounting period;
v. as a loss on disposal of intellectual property.

c) A 'tax credit' can arise on the following occasions:
   i. a receipt recognised in the Income Statement as it accrues;
   ii. a revaluation of intellectual property;
   iii. a credit in respect of 'negative goodwill' (indicative of a bargain purchase);
   iv. a reversal of a debit of a previous accounting period;
   v. a profit on disposal of intellectual property.

d) The rules only apply to assets created or acquired after the 31st March 2002. These assets are called chargeable intangible assets. All other intangible assets held by a company on 1st April 2002 called existing assets, continue to be dealt with under the previous rules so long as the assets remain in the hands of the same 'economic family'.

e) Where the intangible assets are not held for trade purposes, the taxable and relievable amounts are pooled to produce a net non-trading gain or loss.

19.13 Patent Box

The 'patent box' treatment allows qualifying companies with income directly earned from 'exploiting patented inventions' to pay a reduced rate of corporation tax of 10% on profits attributable to qualifying patents. Further details are not covered here as this is a specialist area of tax. Information is available online at https://www.gov.uk/corporation-tax-the-patent-box

19.14 Corporate Venturing Scheme

This scheme was an incentive to 'business angels' which worked for companies rather like the Enterprise Investment Scheme (EIS) works for income tax. It has been closed to new claims from 1st April 2011. Under this scheme, companies obtained 20% corporation tax relief on amounts subscribed for new ordinary shares in small higher-risk trading companies, if the shares were then held for at least three years. A loss on disposal of qualifying CVS shares (calculated net of the 20% upfront tax relief) can still be set against income.

Only investments in unquoted companies qualified for relief, but relief will not be withdrawn if the company later becomes quoted, provided there were no arrangements in place or planned, at the time the investment was made, for the company to seek a Stock Market listing.

Corporate Venturing Scheme relief is not withdrawn merely because the investee company goes into receivership.

19.15 Property income

Companies' property business income is measured on the same basis as the property income of individuals, except that companies do not deduct mortgage interest on loans to purchase letting property specifically against their rental income, but treat it as a general non-trade loan relationship deficit.

Also, a company accounts for its property business income in periods matching its CTAPs, and not (as individuals and trusts do) to a prescribed year-end of 5th April. The rules for offset of rental losses are also different – see 19.16, and Chapter 22.

Other rules are similar to those for property business income of individuals (see Chapter 9), but are summarised here for convenience.

a) Rental income and expenses are computed on an accruals basis, with a deduction for all expenditure wholly and exclusively incurred for the letting business.

b) Furnished lettings, holiday and non-holiday, are taxed as income from property. The replacement furniture relief is available for renewals of furnishings and kitchen utensils etc. in non-holiday furnished lets. Capital allowances may be claimed for this equipment in furnished holiday lettings, which are therefore excluded from replacement furniture relief.

c) Overseas property income is taxed as 'other' income, and available for double tax relief, but is measured using the same rules as for UK property business income.

d) Profits and losses on all lettings are pooled as the business is taxed as a single letting business.

e) The company intangible asset regime does not apply to intangible assets that bundle rights over land or buildings (i.e. typically leases, but also options over land): these assets have their own tax rules (see below).

f) Capital allowances where available are deducted as a business expense. These are not available on the property or let contents, except on furniture and kitchen appliances etc for qualifying furnished holiday lets. In other cases they are only available for the cost of plant and machinery used by the landlord to maintain the property.

19.16 Rental losses

Rental losses of a company are relieved against current period total profits. They may also be surrendered as group relief or carried forward against future total profits. This provides companies with a broader scope of property business loss relief than is available for individuals.

19.17 Lease premiums

The following paragraphs repeat points already made in Chapter 9, covering let property lease premiums which are liable partly as rental income if the related lease duration is 50 years or less. Companies are much more likely to receive (or pay) lease premiums in the current commercial environment than individuals are.

One way of looking at lease premiums is to regard them as a capitalised part of future rental income which would otherwise have been received by way of annual rent. They include any sum whether payable to the immediate or a superior landlord, arising in connection with the granting of a lease, but not arising from an assignment of an existing lease. (Under an assignment the lessee takes the position of the original lessee, with the same terms and conditions.)

Where a new lease is granted (but not when an existing lease is assigned) at a premium for a period not exceeding 50 years, then the landlord is deemed for income tax or corporation tax purposes to receive rental income equal to the premium, less an allowance of 2% of the premium for each complete year of the lease remaining, excluding the first 12 month period:

Income element of lease premium = $P \times (1 - (n-1) \times 2\%)$

where P = amount of premium

n = duration of lease in years

Example

Bruno Ltd granted a lease for 24 years of its warehouse to a trader on the following terms:

A lease premium of £12,000 to be paid on 1st January 2018 and an annual rent of £1,000;

Allowable letting expenditure for AP ended 31st December 2018 was £5,800.

Corporation Tax AP 31.12.2018	£	£
Lease premium received	12,000	
Less 2% × 12,000 × (24 – 1)		
i.e. 1/50 × 12,000 × 23	(5,520)	6,480
Annual rent		1,000
		7,480
Less allowable expenses		(5,800)
Property income liable to corporation tax		1,680

In effect the deemed rent amount of the lease premium is discounted by reference to its duration, and the longer the lease, the greater the discount. Thus if a lease had 49 years to run the discount would be:

$$(49 - 1) \times 2\% \text{ i.e. } 96\%.$$

19.18 Lease premiums and the lessee

Where the lessee makes a payment of a lease premium at the start of a lease, then a proportion of that premium may be set against the following:

a) any trading income, providing the premises are used for business purposes.

b) any rental income or lease premium received from any sub-lease granted by the lessee.

In effect the amount of the premium assessed as income of the lessor can be charged as an expense of trading by the lessee, the deductible expense being spread over the remaining life of the lease.

Example

Serra Ltd is granted a lease of premises to be used for trading purposes, for a period of 20 years, at an annual rent of £6,000 p.a. plus an initial lease premium of £32,000.

	£
Lease premium	32,000
Less 2% × 32,000 × (20 – 1) i.e. 38% × 32,000	(12,160)
Lease premium taxed on lessor as income	19,840

Relief available to Serra Ltd for notional rent as trade expense = $\frac{19840}{20}$ =£992 p.a.

19.19 Overseas income

Income from overseas activities of UK companies is computed on UK tax principles. Other awareness points on international issues for UK companies are covered in Chapter 24. The optional, but irrevocable, election to exclude the results of all a UK company's foreign branches from inclusion in the UK profits of the main company was mentioned in 18.5.

19.20 Capital gains tax

UK resident companies are not liable to capital gains tax as such, but they are liable to corporation tax on chargeable gains which must be computed in accordance with the appropriate Capital Gains Tax rules, covered in Part IV.

Net chargeable gains are taxed at the relevant corporation tax rate, as part of TTP.

Example

Knockout Ltd has net trading profits of £1,500,000 for its accounting year ended 31st March 2019, and a chargeable gain of £500,000.

Compute the corporation tax payable.

Solution: Knockout Ltd corporation tax computation. CTAP to 31.3.2019

	£
Net trading profits	1,500,000
Chargeable gain	500,000
Taxable total profits	2,000,000
Corporation tax @ 19%	380,000

19.21 Comprehensive example – adjustment of trading profit for a company

Note: In following the next example, refer to the foregoing sections and the contents of Chapter 10 on the adjustment of trading profits for income tax purposes.

For example, companies are subject to the income tax rules on allowable expenses of trading and on the disallowance of capital items and capital improvements included in repairs. They must also disallow certain business gifts, customer and supplier entertaining, illegal payments, some car leasing payments, and movements on general provisions.

Example

Stucco plc has the following results in respect of the year ended 31st March 2019.

		£	£
Revenue			283,165
Cost of sales			(127,333)
Gross profit			155,832
Expenses:	General administration	37,021	
	Marketing	28,197	
	Distribution	16,031	
	Financial	22,000	(103,249)
			52,583
Other income			14,723
Profit before tax			67,306

Additional information:		£
Cost of sales includes:		
Depreciation		17,832
Permanent partitioning of works office		3,179
Repairs to new premises to make usable		1,621
General expenses include:	Legal costs of tax appeal	627
	Legal costs of share issue	175
	Stamp duty – property	1,200
	Fines on employees for parking tickets	250
		£
Marketing expenses include:	Trade debts written off	1,211
	Loan to ex-employee written off	250
	Increase in general bad debt provision	5,000
	Increase in specific bad debt provision	1,000
	Promotional gifts (£45 each, not food or drink, and with company name on)	1,800
	Advertising on TV	6,000
Financial expenses include:	Bank interest on overdraft	1,100
	Bank charges	238

	Donation to political party	250
	Subscriptions to trade associations	1,250
	Redundancy payment to staff	11,000
Other income comprises:	Profit on sale of plant	323
	Bad debts recovered	1,700
	Agency commission income	12,700

Compute the adjusted profits for corporation tax purposes, ignoring capital allowances.

Solution: Stucco plc adjustment of profits. AP to 31st March 2019

	£	£
Profit before tax		67,306
Add back items disallowed(see notes 1 to 10):		
1. Depreciation	17,832	
2. Partitioning	3,179	
3. Repairs necessary to use premises	1,621	
General administration:		
4. Legal costs re tax appeal	627	
5. Legal costs re share issue	175	
6. Stamp duty – property	1,200	
Marketing expenses:		
7. Loan to ex-employee written off	250	
8. Increase in general bad debt provision	5,000	
Financial expenses:		
9. Political donation	250	
		30,134
Less		
10. Profit on sale of plant		(323)
Adjusted trading profits before Capital Allowances		97,117

Notes

1. Depreciation £17,832 – must be added back, capital allowances may be claimed in lieu.
2. Partitioning £3,179–plant and machinery; see Jarrold v Johnson & Sons 1962 40 TC 681. This is capital for tax purposes, even though treated as an expense in the accounts.
3. Repairs £1,621 – see Law Shipping Co. Ltd, and Odeon Theatres Ltd cases (Chapter 10).
4. Legal expenses £627 – expenses of a tax appeal are not allowed.
5. Legal expenses £175 – capital expenditure (as it relates to a share issue). This would be allowable as loan finance expenses if on a bond/loan stock issue.
6. Stamp duty £1,200 – capital expenditure not 'revenue expenditure'.
7. Loan to ex-employee written off £250 – making loans to individuals is not the company's trade so this is not a trading expense. (Customer bad debt write-offs are part of the trade, and loans to current employees that are waived

would fall under the category of staff pay, and the employees would be liable to income tax on them as earned income.)

8. Expenses arising from increases in general provisions are disallowed, while expenses arising from increases in specific provisions are allowed.
9. Donation to political party £250 – not an expense of trading.
10. Profit on sale of plant £323 – this is not a taxable item; in effect it is negative depreciation. No taxable capital gain will arise if the assets qualified for capital allowances and were sold for less than cost, or if they were chattels sold for below £6,000, or cars (see chapter 29 for details).

See also 10.9 for some case law on disallowable expenses.

Student self-testing question

Question 1: Trapunta Limited

Trapunta Ltd has the following results for the year ended 30th June 2018

	£	£
Revenue		160,000
Cost of sales		(40,000)
Gross profit		120,000
Wages and salaries	42,000	
Rent and rates	4,287	
Insurance and telephone	1,721	
Repairs and renewals	35,000	
Heating and lighting	2,897	
Professional charges	3,250	
Bank interest payable on business overdraft	1,155	
Subscriptions and donations	1,200	
Directors' remuneration	22,000	
Patent renewal fees	1,000	
Bad and doubtful debts	1,250	
Sales commission	5,680	
Loss on sale of assets	1,000	
Miscellaneous expenses	7,251	(129,691)
Net Trading loss		(9,691)
Other income:		
Discounts received	1,123	
Foreign exchange surplus (on trading account)	12,107	
Dividends received	1,620	
Rents receivable less outgoings	651	15,501
Profit before taxation		5,810

Additional information:	
Repairs and renewals:	£
Repairs to newly acquired premises of which £10,000 was necessary to make them usable	27,000
Furnace relining	8,000
Professional charges:	
Audit and accounting	1,250
Architect's fees for new factory design	1,750
Legal costs for renewal of short lease	250
Subscriptions and donations:	
Subscriptions to trade associations	150
Donation to a national charity	1,050
Wages and salaries of staff:	
Salaries and national insurance	32,000
Staff Bonuses (paid in May 2019)	10,000
Directors' remuneration:	
Salary paid in year	18,000
Pension scheme accrued payment due at year-end (paid 31.8.18)	4,000
Bad and doubtful debts:	
Trade debts written off	250
Increase in general provision	1,000
Miscellaneous expenses	
Office party	410
Theatre tickets for foreign customers	991
Removal expenses of new managing director	850
Compensation to customers for damage caused by company's product	5,000
Exchange surplus:	
Profit from currency dealings arising from trade	12,107
Rents receivable minus outgoings:	
Net rents from letting part of factory	1,000
Deficit on property let to retired employee at a nominal rent	(349)

Compute the trading profits for taxation purposes for the CTAP to 30th June 2018.

Solution to Question 1: Trapunta Limited

Trapunta Ltd, Accounting Period ended 30th June 2018

	£	£
Trading profit per accounts		5,810
Add items disallowed:		
Repairs and renewals	10,000	
Professional charges	1,750	
Donation to charity	1,050	
Pension provision unpaid at year end	4,000	
Bad debt provision (general)	1,000	
Loss on sale of asset	1,000	
Theatre tickets – entertaining	991	
Staff bonuses (unpaid after 9 months)	10,000	29,791
		35,601
Less dividends received (not taxable in hands of a company)	1,620	
Rents receivable (not trade income)	651	(2,271)
Trading profit for taxation purposes		33,330

Notes to answer

1. Repairs to make the premises initially usable are treated as capital expenditure, so not allowable.
2. Architect's fees for the new factory are capital expenditure on the factory building. (In general, building costs no longer get capital allowances, so there is no tax relief for these fees – except that they can be counted as part of the cost when computing the chargeable gain on a future factory disposal.)
3. There is insufficient information about trade connections for the donation to the charity to be allowed as a trading expense, but it can be deducted as a qualifying charitable donation in the taxable total profits computation.
4. Pension contributions are not allowed unless actually paid in the AP.
5. The increase in the bad debt provision is general and therefore not allowed: It will be allowed in future if applied to write off specific bad debts.
6. Losses on the disposals of property, plant and equipment are not allowed as trading expenses.
7. The theatre tickets are disallowed entertaining expenses, because they are for customers and not employees.
8. Dividends received by a company are not liable to corporation tax.
9. Rents receivable are taxable as income from property, not trading income.
10. The foreign exchange surplus has arisen through trading, so as a trading loan relationship it is allowed as a trading expense.
11. As the staff bonus was paid more than nine months after the year end, it is not allowed against taxable profits until the next accounting period.

Questions without answers

Question 2: Zia plc

Zia plc has the following results for the year ended 31st March 2019.

	£	£
Gross profit		1,900,000
Bank deposit interest receivable (gross)		3,200
		1,903,200
General operating expenses (all allowable)	50,000	
Director's remuneration	25,000	
Depreciation	8,000	(83,000)
Profit before tax		1,820,200

Compute the taxable total profit, showing each separate category of income, and the corporation tax payable.

Question 3: Carrot Limited

Carrot Limited, a company resident in the United Kingdom, makes up accounts annually to 30th September. The information listed below relates to Carrot Ltd's twelve month AP ended 30th September 2018.

INCOME	£
Trading profit (already adjusted for tax purposes)	1,320,000
Rents receivable	40,000
Dividends received from non-group companies	138,600
Bank interest receivable	48,000
Capital gains	148,000

Requirement: Compute the Taxable Total Profits for Carrot Ltd and the corporation tax payable.

Question 4: Profumo Limited

Profumo Ltd's accounts for the 12 months to 31st December 2018 showed the following:

	£	£
Revenue		442,100
Less: Cost of sales		(214,000)
Gross profit		228,100
Net rents receivable on property		750
Profit on sale of plant		5,500
		234,350

Expenses:		
Wages and salaries	90,500	
Rent, rates and insurance	6,000	
Motor expenses	2,000	
Legal expenses	2,000	
Directors' remuneration	35,000	
Audit charges	2,500	
Miscellaneous	1,300	
Depreciation	6,000	
Amortisation of software licences	14,000	
		(159,300)
Net profit		£75,050

Notes

i) Legal expenses comprise:

	£
Debt collection	600
Advice on staff service agreements	250
Issue of debentures	1,150
	2,000

ii) Miscellaneous expenses comprise:

		£
Subscriptions:	trade associations	150
	political party	440
Staff outing		710
		1,300

iii) On 1st January 2018 the company acquired software licences for £70,000, which it has decided to write off over 5 years (a treatment permitted by UK GAAP).

iv) Capital allowances for the CTAP to 31.12.2018 have been agreed at £33,230 and are deductible in computing trading income.

v) Gross profit has been computed after deducting £50,000 paid in November 2018 under a threat of blackmail of the chief executive.

Calculate the liability to corporation tax for the CTAP to 31st December 2018.

Question 5: Valerie Limited

Valerie Ltd's accounts for the 12 months to 31st December 2018 showed the following:

		£
Turnover		729,150
Cost of sales		(401,000)
Gross profit		328,150
Net rents		1,000
Profit on sale of plant (2)		2,500
		331,650
Less expenses:		
Wages & salaries	140,000	
Rent, rates and insurance	6,000	
Motor expenses	4,000	
Miscellaneous expenses (1)	2,000	
Director's remuneration	40,000	
Bad and doubtful debts (4)	3,650	
Audit fee	2,000	
Depreciation	5,000	
Premium on lease, written off (3)	14,000	
		(216,650)
Net profit		£115,000

Notes

(1) Miscellaneous expenses comprise:

	£
Staff outing	600
Penalty for late VAT return	400
Wine given to customers	1,000

(2) The profit on sale of plant relates to a disposal which gave rise to a chargeable gain of £1,600.

(3) On 1st July 2018 Valerie Ltd was granted the lease of additional factory premises for a period of 7 years on payment of a premium of £14,000.

(4) Bad and doubtful debts comprise:

	£
Increase in specific provision	2,000
Loan to an ex-employee, written off	650
Increase in general bad debt provision	1,000

Requirement: Calculate TTP for the CTAP to 31st December 2018.

Question 6: Argle Limited

Argle Ltd has the following income and chargeable gains for the 15 month period of account ended 31st March 2019:

		£
Trade profits before capital allowances (tax-adjusted)		330,000
Net property income from property letting at a monthly net rent of £10,000, from 1st July 2018 onwards		90,000
Chargeable gains realised on	(i) 30th Sept 2018	20,000
	(ii) 12th February 2019	400,000
Capital allowances computed for 12 months to 31.12.18		42,000
Capital allowances computed for 3 months to 31.3.19		36,000
Qualifying charitable donations:	paid March 2018	5,000
	paid September 2018	7,000
	paid March 2019	8,000

Requirement: Calculate Argle Ltd's corporation tax liability for the period of account, including both CTAPs, and state when this corporation tax is payable.

Question 7: Dilute Limited

Dilute Ltd is resident in the UK. It has one associated company. The board decided to alter the company's accounting date and prepared accounts for the 14 months from 1st April 2017 to 31st May 2018. The following relates to this period.

INCOME	£	£
Trading profit (before capital allowances)		420,000
Rents receivable		
- 24th December 2017 to 31st March 2018	52,000	
- 1st April to 31st May 2018	25,000	
		77,000
Bank interest receivable, all received July 2017*		48,000
Capital gains		
- October 2017	120,000	
- May 2018	150,000	
		270,000

The written down balances for capital allowances purposes brought forward at 1st April 2017 were:

	£
General pool	177,780
Special rate pool	22,500

Capital transactions during the above period were as follows:

Purchases:		
10/10/17	Lorry	24,000
05/05/18	Energy-saving machinery	12,033
Disposals		
02/05/18	A special rate pool asset sold (the asset had cost £12,200)	11,000

*The bank interest income wholly relates to the year ended 31/03/18.

Requirement: Compute the corporation tax liability payable in respect of the above accounting profits.

Question 8: Upbeat Ukuleles Limited

Upbeat Ukuleles Limited is a United Kingdom resident company, which has been manufacturing musical instruments for many years. It has no associated companies. The company has previously made up accounts to 30th June but has now changed its accounting date to 30th September.

The company's results for the 15 month period to 30th September 2018 are:

	£
Trading profits (as adjusted for taxation before capital allowances)	1,320,000
Corporate bond interest receivable (notes 3)	20,000
Bank interest receivable (note 4)	6,000
Chargeable gain (notes 5 and 6)	10,000
Gift aid payment (note 7)	5,000
Dividends received from UK companies (note 8)	30,000

Notes

1. **Capital allowances:** On 1st July 2017 the tax written-down value of the plant and machinery in the capital allowances pool was £100,000. There were no additions to, or disposals of, plant or machinery in the period of account to 30th September 2018.
2. On 1st July 2017 the company had trading losses brought forward of £800,000. These losses were made in the year to 30 June 2016.
3. The corporate bond was acquired in July 2018.
4. Bank interest receivable (non-trading loan relationship) accrued evenly over the period of account.
5. Chargeable gain. The chargeable gain of £10,000 is in respect of shares disposed of on 31st December 2017.
6. On 1st July 2017 the company had capital losses brought forward of £12,500.
7. A qualifying charitable donation of £5,000 was paid to a charity on 31st December 2017.

8. Dividends received

	£
25th April 2018	18,000
29th September 2018	12,000
	30,000

Requirement: Calculate the corporation tax liabilities for the 15 month period ended 30th September 2018. **(22 marks)**

Note. All apportionments may be made to the nearest month. (ACCA updated)

20 Capital allowances

20.1 Introduction

The capital allowance system, described in Chapter 13 in connection with income tax, is essentially the same for corporation tax. There is a difference in computing maximum writing down and annual investment allowances for a long period of account, as a CTAP cannot last longer than twelve months. Another difference is that companies do not have private use assets.

20.2 Main features

a) Capital allowances are available in respect of qualifying expenditure incurred in an accounting period.

b) Capital allowances are deducted as an expense in arriving at the trading income. A balancing charge is treated as trading income.

c) The pool system for plant and machinery and other assets is the same for companies as for individuals, but there is no de-pooling, or WDA disallowance, for private use made by staff or directors of a company asset.

d) A company need not claim all the capital allowances available, but it must accept any balancing charges that arise in a CTAP from the disposal proceeds of assets which have previously been included in a CAs claim.

e) If capital allowances claimed create or increase a trading loss then they are treated as an integral part of that trading loss for loss claims (Chapter 22).

f) Where a company's period of account is more than 12 months long (see 19.4), capital allowances are computed for each separate CTAP. WDA rates and limits are not 'scaled up' as they are for income tax purposes. However for short company CTAPs, the WDA rates and the AIA limits are scaled down.

g) A 100% Enhanced Capital Allowance (ECA) is available to certain environmentally-friendly assets of companies, just as for sole traders. This applies to the following expenditure:

- Approved Energy-saving and Water-saving plant and equipment (listed in Regulations);
- Low-emission cars – the limit is now set at 75g/km CO_2 emissions.

Unlike AIA, FYA or ECA is not reduced in short CTAPs – it remains at 100%.

h) The Writing Down Allowance (WDA) is 18% per year (reducing balance) on the general pool of plant and machinery, which includes cars with CO_2 emissions of 110g/km or less, if purchased on or after 1 April 2018, or 130g/km or less for cars purchased before 1 April 2018.

i) The WDA is 8% per year (reducing balance) in the special rate pool. This pool includes plant which qualifies as 'features integral to a building', 'long life assets', and cars with CO_2 emissions above 110g/km, if purchased on or after 1 April 2018, or above 130g/km for cars purchased before 1 April 2018. 130g/km.

'Features integral to a building' are items which are accepted as plant in nature but legally are part of a building. This includes expenditure on:

- electrical systems (including lighting systems);
- cold water systems;
- space or water heating systems, powered systems of ventilation, air cooling or purification, and any floor or ceiling part of such systems;
- lifts, escalators, and moving walkways;
- external solar shading; and
- active facades (which manage energy use)

A 'long-life asset' for capital allowances is a plant and machinery asset which has an expected useful economic life, when new, of more than 25 years. As a general rule, both companies and individuals are only obliged to treat non-fixtures with a life of over 25 years as 'long life assets' for capital allowances when total expenditure on the asset exceeds £100,000. However, this condition is ignored and the long life asset treatment is compulsory if the long life asset is shared or if it is to be leased to other traders.

j) Annual Investment Allowance (AIA) may be claimed by companies, as by sole traders, for expenditure on general pool or special rate pool assets, other than cars. Assets which have received 100% AIA in the year of purchase should still be tracked within their pool (either the general or special rate pool), as the proceeds of a future disposal must be allocated to the correct pool.

The AIA from 1st January 2016 is £200,000 for a full twelve month period. AIA has been changed frequently, and has varied between £50,000 and £500,000 a year.

Examples in this book adopt the approach of ignoring future changes until they are enacted, in order to keep the examples simple, and then focusing on the new rules rather than exploring the residual effects of the old ones.

If there is a group of companies under common control, sharing a similar trade or having the same trading premises, then only one AIA limit applies between them all. This is to prevent splitting of the same business across multiple companies to get better access to AIA. The AIA may be allocated to any company or companies but HMRC must be told how total AIA claims within the group have been allocated. In general in the examples in this book it may be assumed that AIA is available in full to the company being considered.

k) Like sole traders, companies can elect to 'de-pool' short life assets, namely plant from the general pool which will be used for less than 8 years in the trade, and where the directors expect the residual value to be lower than the tax written down value when the assets are sold or scrapped. The asset de-pooling election by companies must be made, specifying each relevant asset or asset class, within 2 years of the end of the CTAP in which the de-pooling is to apply.

De-pooled short life assets receive the same WDA during their ownership as they would have done if left in the general pool. The difference comes when they are sold or scrapped as the single-asset pool is deemed to relate to a separate trade, which comes to an end when the de-pooled asset is scrapped or sold. A balancing allowance or charge arises on the difference between the disposal proceeds and the written down value before disposal. A balancing allowance could not have been received if the asset had been in the general pool because the remaining pool of expenditure that qualified for capital allowances continues to be written down in each period, even if all the assets in that pool are sold or scrapped.

Example

Kevin plc has the following data relating to its CTAP ended 31st March 2019.

	£
Trading profits for tax purposes	1,865,550
Income from letting land and property	173,200
Plant and machinery pool at 1.4.2018	88,000
Additions 1.8.2018 (general plant and machinery)	24,000

Compute the capital allowances and the corporation tax liability for the CTAP to 31st March 2019.

Solution

Capital allowances: plant and machinery	**Pool**
	£
Written down value b/f	88,000
Additions qualifying for AIA	24,000
AIA within £200,000 annual limit	(24,000)
	88,000
Writing down allowance @ 18%	(15,840)
Written down value c/f in general pool	72,160

Total allowances (24,000 + 15,840) = £39,840

Corporation tax computation CTAP 31.3.2019

	£
Trading profits	1,865,550
Less capital allowances	(39,840)
Net Trading profits	1,825,710
Property business income	173,200
Taxable Total Profits	1,998,910
Corporation tax payable £1,998,910 @ 19% FY 2018	379,793

Example

Minty plc starts in business on 1st May 2018, prepare accounts to 31st December 2018.

Additions to plant and machinery:

		£
1st May 2018	White car CO_2 105 g/km	30,000
5th May 2018	General plant and machinery	128,333
6th May 2018	Approved water-saving plant	12,000
8th May 2018	Black car CO_2 45 g/km	15,000
9th May 2018	3-D printer	7,000
16th June 2018	Red car CO_2 210 g/km	53,333
10th October 2018	Yellow car CO_2 190 g/km	16,000

Required: Calculate maximum capital allowances for the CTAP 1st May to 31st December 2018.

Solution

		Workings	General pool	Special rate pool	Allowances
		£	£	£	£
Additions for AIA:					
General plant and machinery		128,333			
3-D printer		7,000			
		135,333			
Max £200k × $^8/_{12}$ = £133,333		(133,333)	2,000		133,333
Additions not for ECA or AIA:					
White car	<110g/km		30,000		
Red car	>110g/km			53,333	
Yellow car	>110g/km			16,000	
Subtotals			32,000	69,333	
WDA @ 18%	5,760 × $^8/_{12}$		(3,840)		3,840
WDA @ 8%	5,546 × $^8/_{12}$			(3,698)	3,698
Additions for 100% ECA:					
Water-saving plant		12,000			
Black car	(Low-emission)	15,000			
		27,000			
ECA 100%		(27,000)			27,000
Total allowances claimed					£51,205
WDV carried forward at 31/12/2018			28,160	65,635	

Example - continued

Minty plc (the same company) has the following disposals of plant and machinery for the year to 31st December 2019:

1st August 2019	Yellow car (cost £16,000)	£12,000
10th October 2019	3-D printer (cost £7,000)	£ 9,000

Required: Calculate maximum capital allowances for the year to 31st December 2019.

Solution			General pool	Special rate pool	Allowances
			£	£	£
WDV brought forward at 01/01/2019			28,160	65,635	
Disposals:					
Yellow car	proceeds			(12,000)	
3-D printer	proceeds	9,000			
	limit=cost		(7,000)		
Subtotals			21,160	53,635	
WDA @18% (full year)			(3,809)		3,809
WDA @8% (full year)				(4,291)	4,291
Total allowances claimed					£8,100
WDV carried forward at 31/12/2019			17,351	49,344	

Note: The proceeds received for the 3-D printer are not deducted in full from the relevant (general) pool because the amount deducted on disposal of an asset from a pool should never exceed the amount originally added to the pool when the asset was purchased. The deduction is limited to the original cost.

20.3 Research and Development Allowance (RDA) 100%

Research and development allowance (RDA) gives an allowance of 100% of expenditure on research and development assets other than land. If such an asset is disposed of, the proceeds create a balancing charge.

Student self-testing question

Question 1: Cinders Limited

Cinders Ltd has a general pool balance brought forward of expenditure of £200,000 at 1st May 2018, and prepares its accounts to 30th April each year.

On 5th June 2018 the company buys a laser cutter costing £270,000 and elects for it to be treated as a short-life asset.

On 30th September 2020 the laser cutter is sold for £24,000.

Required: Calculate capital allowances for the years ended 30th April 2019, 2020, and 2021.

Solution to Question 1: Cinders Limited

Capital Allowances computations for 3 successive CTAPs

Y/e 30-Apr-2019			General pool	Short-life asset	Allowances
			£	£	£
WDV b/f	1/05/18		200,000		
Addition	Cutter(SLA)	270,000			
AIA (max.)		(200,000)		70,000	200,000
WDA 18%			(36,000)		
WDA 18%				(12,600)	48,600
					248,600
WDV at	30/04/19		164,000	57,400	
Y/e 30-Apr-2020			General pool	Short-life asset	Allowances
WDA 18%			(29,520)	(10,332)	39,852
WDV	30/04/20		134,480	47,068	
Y/e 30-Apr-2021			General pool	Short-life asset	Allowances
Disposal proceeds - SLA				(24,000)	
Balancing Allowance				(23,068)	23,068
WDA 18%			(24,206)		24,206
					47,274
WDV at	30/04/21		110,274	0	

Questions without answers

Question 2: Wineglass Limited

Wineglass Ltd purchased the following assets in respect of the six-month accounting period ended 31st March 2019:

		£
1st October 2018	Office equipment	48,400
5th October 2018	Machinery	137,200
11th October 2018	Installation of cold water system	114,700
18th February 2019	Motor car (CO_2 emissions 105g/km)	20,600

The motor car purchased on 18th February 2019 is used by the sales manager, and 15% of the mileage is for private journeys.

The cold water system is a 'feature integral to a building'.

There were no pools of plant and machinery brought forward at 1st October 2018.

Required: Calculate capital allowances available to Wineglass Ltd for the period to 31st March 2019.

Question 3: Zebra Limited

On 1st April 2018 the tax written down values of plant and machinery of Zebra Limited were as follows:

	£
General pool	10,600
Special rate pool	16,400
Short-life asset	2,900

The following transactions took place during the year ended 31st March 2019:

		Cost/(Proceeds) £
1st May 2018	Sold office equipment	(12,800)
15th June 2018	Sold the short-life asset	(800)
8th July 2018	Purchased packaging equipment	194,200
14th July 2018	Sold plant from the special rate pool	(9,700)
26th August 2018	Purchased yellow car CO_2 emissions 105g/km	15,800
19th Nov 2018	Purchased black low emissions car CO_2 45g/km	19,700
15th December 2018	Purchased air cooling system (a feature integral to a building)	10,000

None of the assets disposed of were sold for more than their original cost.

Required: Calculate the maximum capital allowances available to Zebra Limited for the year ended 31st March 2019. (9 marks)

21 Quarterly returns and qualifying charitable donations

21.1 Introduction

For certain payments which a company makes, it has to withhold tax at source, to be paid across to the tax authorities later. You should ensure that you understand that the company is **paying** this tax but it is not **suffering** it. Rather, the company is effectively acting as a collector of taxes, splitting the relevant expense between 80% paid to main beneficiary (for example interest paid to an individual who has lent money to the company by purchasing a debenture) and 20% paid to the tax authorities on behalf of that beneficiary.

In this chapter we explain the quarterly returns system, which is the mechanism by which the company collects and accounts for income tax on behalf of the other taxpayers.

We also describe the tax treatment of qualifying charitable donations which companies make.

21.2 Collection of income tax on payments which are not distributions

The quarterly returns system operates as follows.

Return periods

a) A company must make returns to HMRC in respect of each of its accounting periods of any payments made to others (not accruals) subject to the deduction of income tax at source, and of any income received (not accrued) which has been taxed at source.

b) The returns must be made for a quarter and the dates prescribed are 31st March, 30th June, 30th September, and 31st December. These are known as standard return periods, and if a company's AP does not coincide with any of the quarterly dates, then an additional return is required at its year-end.

   Income tax is deductible from the following payments made by companies:

   - Loan interest paid to an individual (e.g. on debenture / loan stock)
   - Property Rents paid directly to non-UK resident landlords (including a non UK resident company): however, this requirement is lifted if the rent is paid via a UK agent
   - Payment to an individual of the income element of an annuity
   - Patent royalties paid to individuals

Note:

- Payments of interest, royalties, annual payments and annuities to companies by other companies are made gross without any tax deduction so long as the recipient company is within charge to corporation tax.

- From 6th April 2016 interest paid by financial institutions to individuals is paid gross, to coincide with the introduction of the income tax personal savings allowance
- From 6th April 2017 interest distributions by open ended investment companies (OEICs), authorised unit trusts (AUTs), investment trust companies (ITCs) and peer to peer lenders are also paid gross.

Example

Starnuto Ltd has an accounting year ending on the 30th November 2018. The return periods relating to that AP are as follows:

2017	1st December to 31st December
2018	1st January to 31st March
	1st April to 30th June
	1st July to 30th September
	1st October to 30th November

The company here has five return periods and each return must be submitted within fourteen days of the end of the return period. If there are no transactions in the period a nil return is not required.

c) The return forms must show particulars of payments made in the period, and income tax deducted is due on the return date without the making of any formal assessment. Particulars of any income must also be included on the returns, and any income tax suffered at source is offset, on the company quarterly returns, against any income tax the company has retained, under legal obligation, from payments.

d) It is now unusual for companies to receive income after deduction of income tax. However, this does apply to receipt of patent royalties from an individual.

21.3 The position at the end of a return period

a) If the income tax suffered in a return period exceeds the income tax retained from payments made then no income tax need be paid over for the quarter. The net excess of income tax suffered at source on income may be carried back and set against any income tax accounted for and paid on earlier quarterly returns in the same accounting period. This generates a repayment which cannot exceed the amount of income tax already accounted for and paid over relating to net-of-tax payments made in the accounting period.

b) If (as is generally the case) cumulative income tax suffered by the company on taxed income does not exceed its income tax retained on payments made, then the net amount of income tax withheld on payments, less any suffered on income, is payable to HMRC on the due date.

c) Once all quarterly returns required have been submitted, and if income tax retained by the company on payments to others has all been offset within the same CTAP against income tax suffered at source by the company itself, then any net income tax which the company has suffered on income received may be treated as CT already paid. Therefore, net income tax suffered is set off on the submitted CT return against the company's final CT liability for the AP (see last part of specimen computation at end of Chapter 18).

Example

Formaggio Ltd has a CTAP ended 31st March 2019 and during the year the following transactions took place.

2018	April 11th Debenture interest paid to individuals(net)	8,000
	June 30th Patent royalties received from individuals (net)	4,000
	August 7th Bank interest paid (gross – see note (ii))	12,000
	October 11th Debenture interest paid to individuals(net)	8,000
2019	January 1st Patent royalties received from individuals (net)	4,000

All transactions are shown as the amounts of the payment which left the company's bank account.

Show the quarterly returns for the year to 31st March 2019.

Solution

Quarter	Gross paid	Income tax retained (20%)	Gross received	Income tax suffered (20%)	Net income tax paid or repaid
	£	£	£	£	£
30.6.18	(10,000)	2,000	5,000	(1,000)	1,000
30.9.18	–	–	–	–	–
31.12.18	(10,000)	2,000	–	–	2,000
31.3.19	–	–	5,000	(1,000)	(1,000)
Total	(20,000)	4,000	10,000	(2,000)	2,000

Notes

i) In the fourth quarter, the excess of income tax suffered can be set against the payment made in quarter 1 or 3. This generates a repayment of £1,000 of income tax (previously accounted for and paid over) to the company for the 4th quarterly period.

ii) Interest paid by companies on bank borrowings is not subject to deduction of income tax and is, therefore, excluded from the quarterly return system.

iii) The 'total' line shows the company's cumulative position for the whole AP.

21.4 The position at the end of an accounting period

This may be summarised as follows.

(a) Income tax suffered on income received net exceeds income tax paid on outgoing net payments.

  i) Excess can be set against corporation tax payable on the profits of the accounting period.

  ii) If the excess is greater than the corporation tax payable then a cash repayment can be obtained.

(b) Income tax deducted from income received net does not exceed income tax paid on outgoing net payments.

  i) In this case since the excess has already been paid over within the quarterly return system, no further adjustment is necessary.

  ii) Note that as stated in Chapter 18, a UK trading company is not liable to Income tax (IT) on its own income, as it pays Corporation Tax.

So any basic rate income tax paid over by companies on the quarterly returns is income tax withheld out of gross payments, to meet income tax liabilities of the recipient, who is either an individual or a non-resident company.

That a company may deduct, from the basic rate income tax withheld and due on net payments it has made, any basic rate tax suffered at source on its own income in the same CTAP, is a cash flow convenience.

An individual, or a non-resident investment company, that receives interest, royalties or rents net from a UK company should also receive a tax certificate from the company showing the amount of tax withheld by law at 20%. This tax suffered is then creditable against the recipient's own income tax liability, whether the certifying company actually paid the tax over to HMRC or simply offset it against income tax suffered at source on its own income.

Example

Bosco Ltd has an AP ended 31st March 2019 and during that year, the following transactions took place.

2018	June 10	Interest on unsecured loan stock paid	
		– individuals (net)	1,600
	July 19	Patent royalties received from individuals (net)	2,000
	Aug 31	Bank deposit interest received (gross)	2,500
	Dec 10	Interest on unsecured loan stock paid	
		– individuals (net)	1,600
2019	Jan 19	Patent royalties received from individuals (net)	2,000

The adjusted trading profits for the year ended 31st March 2019 amounted to £1,795,300 before any adjustment for loan interest paid. The unsecured loan stock was issued for trade purposes. Property income in respect of the same period was £1,200 (received gross).

Show the quarterly returns for the year to 31st March 2019 and the corporation tax computation for the same period.

Solution

Quarter	Gross paid	Income tax retained (20%)	Gross received	Income tax suffered (20%)	Net tax paid/repaid	Net tax suffered at source, c/fwd
	£	£	£	£	£	£
30.6.18	(2,000)	400	–	–	400	–
30.9.18	–	–	2,500	(500)	(400)	(100)
31.12.18	(2,000)	400	–	–	300	–
31.3.19	–	–	2,500	(500)	(300)	(200)
Total	(4,000)	800	5,000	(1,000)	–	–

Corporation tax computation AP to 31.3.2019

	£
Trading profits (1,795,300 – 4,000)	1,791,300
Property income	1,200
Income taxed at source	5,000
Bank deposit interest	2,500
Taxable trading profit	1,800,000
	£
Corporation tax @ 19%	342,000
Less excess income tax as above	(200)
	341,800

Notes

The repayment of £400 for quarter 2 is limited to the amount of IT already paid for quarter 1. The £100 balance (500-400) of unrelieved tax suffered on net income in quarter 2 is carried forward to quarter 3. In quarter 3, this £100 is offset against the £400 of IT retained on net payments made; meaning that only £300 of tax has to be paid over with the 3rd quarterly return.

The £300 paid over for quarter 3 is then all refunded in quarter 4, following receipt of net-of-tax interest on which £500 of IT has been withheld. After the £300 repayment claimed for the fourth quarter, a net £200 of income tax suffered on income over the 4 quarters remains unrelieved. This net £200 is relieved by offset against the CT liability.

As there was an excess of taxed income suffered, the income tax unrecovered is set against the corporation tax payable. From a cash flow point of view, the benefit will not be felt until the corporation tax is due.

21.5 The treatment of payments to charities

Companies may obtain relief for charitable donations in one of two ways:

i) **Deduction as a business expense**
The cost of sponsorship or employees seconded to a charity is allowable as an ordinary business expense in calculating the income from trading of a company. Capital allowances may also be claimed on the cost of equipment donated to a charity.

ii) **Qualifying charitable donations**

Payments made by a company to a charity that do not meet the conditions for trading expense treatment are qualifying charitable donations.

21.6 Qualifying charitable donations

Qualifying charitable donations are allowed as a deduction in computing the taxable total profit for a CTAP. In equation form:

Taxable total profit	=	Total profits
		– Trading losses claimed against total profits
		– Qualifying charitable donations
		– Group relief claimed

Qualifying charitable donations are therefore deducted from total profits after same-company trading losses and before group relief.

Under current rules:

i) The company does not deduct basic rate income tax from the payment.

ii) The payment does not enter the quarterly CT61 scheme.

iii) The payment is treated as a qualifying charitable donation.

iv) The charity recipient cannot recover any income tax in respect of the amount it receives as this is the full amount of the donation.

v) There is no limit on the amount of charitable donations that could be made in this way by a company but if it pays more than its net total profits (after deductions and reliefs), the CT relief may be lost. Relief for charitable donations cannot be carried forward or back to another accounting period. However it can be surrendered as part of group relief (see Chapter 23). It is also likely under company law that a company would require the consent of its shareholders to any significant charitable donations.

21.7 Eligible payments

To be eligible for deduction from profits, qualifying charitable donations must comply with the following conditions.

a) They must be actually paid in the accounting period, and not accrued - except for a covenanted donation by a charity trading company to a charity which is its parent.

b) The payments must be ultimately borne by the company making the payment.

c) They must be paid out of the company's profits brought into charge to corporation tax.

d) They must be paid to a recognised charitable body.

21.8 Adjustment to accounts for charitable donations

Normal company accounts do not distinguish between qualifying charitable donations and other charitable expenses. Whereas trading expense relief is available for donations which are 'small', local to the company's trade, and have a demonstrable trade benefit, it is necessary to 'add back' qualifying charitable donations in the adjustment of trade profits.

In addition, only qualifying charitable donations actually paid in the CTAP are allowed in that CTAP, whereas for accounts purposes an element of accrual may have been made. If QCD payments were accounted for in an earlier period of account, they are nevertheless allowed as a qualifying charitable donation in the CTAP when the payments are made.

Student self-testing question

Kizzie Ltd has the following data relating to its AP ended 31st March 2019.

	£
Operating profits	1,550,000
Bank deposit interest receivable and received, non-trading	12,000
Qualifying charitable donation paid	40,000
Debenture interest payable and paid, to investors who are not individuals, on a trade loan	20,000

Compute the corporation tax payable for the CTAP to 31st March 2019.

Solution

Corporation tax computation AP to 31.3.2019

	£
Trading profits (1,550,000 – 20,000 trade interest payable)	1,530,000
Surplus on non-trade loan relationships: Interest receivable	12,000
Total profits	1,542,000
Less Qualifying charitable donation	(40,000)
Taxable total profit	1,502,000
Corporation tax liability 1,502,000 @ 19%	£285,380

Note A charitable payment by a company is made gross to the charity.

22 Relief for losses

22.1 Introduction

A company may obtain relief for losses by deducting them from income or gains of the company or other group companies. This chapter examines the various forms of loss relief available to a company which is not a member of a group, with group loss relief covered by Chapter 23. The main emphasis is given to loss reliefs available in respect of trading losses. Also covered, though in less detail, are relief for non-trading loan relationship deficits, relief for property business losses, relief for excess management expenses, and company capital losses.

Two major changes were introduced for Corporation Tax loss relief rules from 1 April 2017. One major change was the 'relaxation' of requirements to match losses against the same type of profit, so as to allow more types of loss to be set against total profit. This is a significant simplification. The other major change was a 'restriction' of the loss relief available, to companies making profits of more than £5 million, to a maximum relief of £5 million plus 50% of the total profits above £5 million, so as to ensure they pay some Corporation Tax in a profitable year. There was also a change to the rules for terminal loss relief on a company's cessation. Because of these changes some losses incurred before and after 1 April 2017 are dealt with differently.

A company can claim to set a trading loss against other income in several ways. In summary form these may be depicted as follows:

Set against profits (income and gains) of the same period.

Carried back and set against total profits (income and gains) of the previous year.

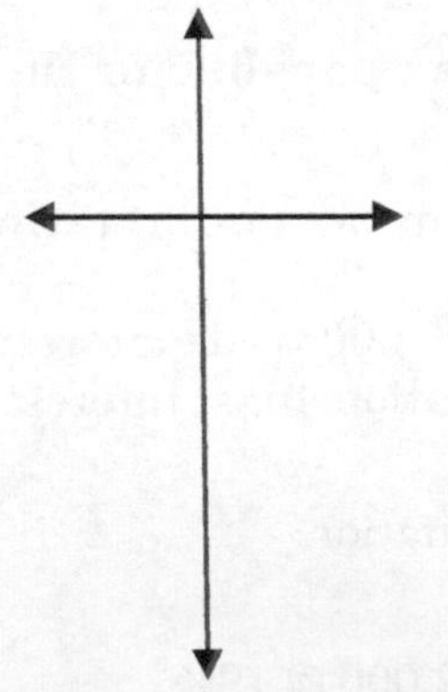

Carried forward and set against future income and gains.

For losses incurred before 1 April 2017 this set off may only be made against trading income from the same source.

Surrendered as group relief. (See Chapter 23 for group relief).

22.2 List of loss reliefs

i) Trade losses	–	Set against total profit of the same CTAP.
ii) Trade losses	–	Set against total profit of the CTAP(s) in the previous 12 months. (Only possible if a current period claim has been made first.)
iii) Trade losses	–	Carried forward and set against future total profits. (For losses made before 1 April 2017 the carry forward may only be set off against future trade income.)
iv) Trade losses	–	Carry back up to 36 months by terminal loss relief.
v) Trade losses	–	Surrender to a 75% fellow group member (or a consortium company) by way of group relief. See Chapter 23.
vi) Transfer losses with a trade (see 22.7)	–	Can transfer trade loss to successor company on a sale of the trade goodwill and trade assets.
vii) Non-trading loan relationship deficit (see 22.8)	–	Set loss against total profits. Set against non-trading loan relationship surplus of previous 12 months. Carry forward deficits of 1 April 2017 onwards against future total profits. (For losses made before 1 April 2017 the carry forward may only be set against non-trading profits). Group relief. See Chapter 23.
viii) Non-trading losses on intangible fixed assets (see 22.10)		Carry forward losses of 1 April 2017 onwards against future total profits. (For losses made before 1 April 2017 the carry forward may only be set against non-trading profits). Group relief. See Chapter 23.
ix) Excess management expenses (see 22.10)		As viii) above.
x) Property business loss (see 22.10)		Deduct in arriving at total profits. Carry forward against future total profits. Group relief. See Chapter 23.
xi) Net Capital losses (see 22.9-10)		Offset against future capital gains.

22.3 Trade losses

It is perhaps worth recalling that a trading loss is arrived at after deducting capital allowances, which very often differ from accounting depreciation expensed. Either large capital allowances, or interest costs arising from a **trading** loan relationship, may turn an 'operating profit' in the financial accounts (normally stated before any financial costs) into a trading 'loss' for tax purposes.

Trade losses set against total profits of the same period or previous 12 months

a) A company which has incurred a loss in its trade (excluding any loss brought forward) in any accounting period, may claim to set off that loss against total profits (i.e. including chargeable gains) of the same accounting period.

b) Any balance of loss remaining after this set off in the current period can be set off against total profits of APs falling within the previous twelve months.

c) A total profits claim for the current year must be made before claiming total profits relief for any preceding AP.

d) A claim under this section must be made within two years of the end of the AP in which the loss is incurred, or within such longer period as HMRC may allow.

e) Relief for the loss appears in the computation before QCDs donations and group relief are deducted. It may therefore displace QCDs which cannot be relieved elsewhere.

f) Even if the AP of the loss is less than 12 months' duration, the loss can nevertheless be carried back against total profits of the preceding 12 months, so long as a current period claim is made first.

Example

Questa Ltd has the following corporation tax profit / loss for its accounting years ended 31st March 2018 and 2019 and makes both the available claims for loss relief against total profit of the same period and previous 12 months.

Show the computations.

Questa Ltd

	31.3.18	**31.3.19**
	£	**£**
Trading profit/(loss)	80,000	(30,000)
Income from property	10,000	9,000
Chargeable gains	9,000	2,100

Solution

Claim for relief against total profit of the same period and previous 12 months

	£	£
Trading profit	80,000	-
Income from property	10,000	9,000
Chargeable gains	9,000	2,100
Total profits	99,000	11,100
Less loss claim	(18,900)	(11,100)
Assessment	80,100	-

Loss memorandum	£
The trading loss of £30,000 has been utilised as follows:	
Set against total profits for the year to 31.3.2019	11,100
Set against total profits for the year to 31.3.2018	18,900
	30,000

Notes

i) After making a claim for the year to 31st March 2019 it is not obligatory also to make the second claim to carry the losses back to the previous CTAP to March 2018.

ii) However, the carry-back relief, if claimed, is only available after a current period loss claim has been made.

iii) It is not possible to claim a partial relief for the year to 31st March 2019 and also claim relief for the period to 31st March 2018.

22.4 Trade losses carried forward against future profits

Where a company incurs a trading loss in an accounting period, if no other claim for relief is made by the taxpayer, the loss will be dealt with as follows:

a) It will be carried forward to succeeding accounting periods so long as the company continues that specific trade up to and including the period in which the losses are to be offset.

b) i) A trading loss incurred before 1 April 2017 carried forward is only deductible from future trading income arising from the same trade.

ii) A trading loss incurred after 1 April 2017 carried forward is deductible from total profits (income and gains).

c) A claim must technically be made within four years of the end of the AP in which the loss was incurred. In practice relief is given automatically by the self-assessment system, to the extent that no optional loss relief claims are submitted which take priority (including a group relief loss surrender – see Chapter 23).

d) Anti-avoidance legislation provides that there will be a disallowance of trading losses carried forward beyond the date of a change of ultimate ownership of the company, if there is also a major change in the nature or conduct of the trade within three years either side of the change of ownership. This is to prevent purchase of a company with existing trading losses, and then altering its trade, yet trying to keep the benefit of the unrelieved losses.

Example

Contadino Ltd has the following results for the two years ended 31st March 2019.

	31.3.18	**31.3.19**
	£	**£**
Trade profits/(loss)	(370,000)	140,000
Interest income (non trading)	60,000	80,000
Chargeable gain	120,000	20,000

The company makes loss claims against the same period and for carried forward losses.

Compute the taxable total profit after loss reliefs.

Solution

	31.3.18	**31.3.19**
	£	**£**
Trade profits	–	140,000
Interest income	60,000	80,000
Chargeable gain	120,000	20,000
Total profits	180,000	240,000
Less trade losses against total income of same period (first claim, in order of priority)	(180,000)	
Less trade losses carried forward against total income (second claim, in order of priority)		(190,000)
Taxable total profit	–	50,000

Notes

i) The trading loss of £360,000 incurred in the AP to 31st March 2018 has been utilised as indicated below.

	£
Accounting period to 31.3.18	180,000
Accounting period to 31.3.19	190,000
	370,000

ii) The trading loss carried forward to 31.3.18 is deducted from total profits because this loss was incurred after 1st April 2017.

iii) The company may choose how much, if any, of the post 1 April 2017 carried forward loss to set against the income of each future year.

Example

Dinamico Ltd has the following results for the two years ended 31st March 2018.

	31.3.17	31.3.18
	£	£
Trade profits/(loss)	(185,000)	70,000
Interest income (non trading)	30,000	40,000
Chargeable gain	60,000	10,000

The company makes loss claims against the same period and for carried forward losses.

Compute the taxable total profit after loss reliefs.

Solution

	31.3.17	31.3.18
	£	£
Trade profits	–	70,000
Less carried forward trade losses (second claim, in order of priority)	–	(70,000)
	–	-
Interest income	30,000	40,000
Chargeable gain	60,000	10,000
Total profits	90,000	50,000
Less trade losses against total income of same period (first claim, in order of priority)	(90,000)	
Taxable total profit	–	50,000

Notes

i) The trading loss of £185,000 incurred in the AP to 31st March 2017 has been utilised as indicated below.

	£
Accounting period to 31.3.17	90,000
Accounting period to 31.3.18	70,000
Unrelieved at 1.4.18 - carried forward to future years	25,000
	185,000

ii) The trading loss carried forward to 31.3.18 is deducted from trading profits only, and only from the same trade. Because this loss was incurred before 1st April 2017 it cannot be offset against any other future profits than those of the same trade.

22.5 Restriction to loss relief for companies with profits above £5million

From 1 April 2017 companies or groups with profits in excess of £5million will be subject to a restriction limiting the amount of carried forward losses which can be relieved against theses profits. The limit is 50% of profits in excess of the £5m 'allowance'.

For example, a company with £13million profits in a year could then relieve a maximum of £9million brought forward losses. This would be calculated as the £5million 'allowance' plus 50% of the £8million excess.

This may be seen as a reaction to public criticism of large multinational companies avoiding UK Corporation Tax by making losses through transactions which have been viewed as artificial tax avoidance. While a Diverted Profits Tax (see 24.15) has been introduced to counter such tax avoidance, the restriction on loss relief can limit the immediate use of losses built up through tax avoidance in previous years.

22.6 Terminal loss relief

Trading losses arising in the 12 months prior to a cessation of trading can be carried back against total profits of the CTAPs falling partly or wholly in previous 36 months (that is, the 36 months before the last 12 months), on a Last-In-First-Out basis.

A claim for relief must be made within two years of the end of the CTAP in which all or part of the terminal trade loss is made, or within such later period as HMRC may allow.

Note that:

(a) there is no limit on the amount of losses that can be carried back, provided that they relate to the last twelve months of trading;

(b) the company must have ceased trading before this claim can be made;

(c) the loss available for carry-back is computed for exactly twelve months, which may involve more than one CTAP, and apportioning the loss of the earlier one.

(d) Normal group relief or claims against total income and gains of the same period and previous 12 months may alternatively be made in respect of part of the qualifying terminal loss, leaving only some of it to be dealt with under terminal loss relief rules.

Example

Zampata Ltd has the following data for the four years ended 31st March 2019 when it ceased trading.

	31.3.16	31.3.17	31.3.18	31.3.19
	£	£	£	£
Trading profits	55,000	30,000	65,000	(180,000)
Income from property	7,000	8,000	9,000	9,000
Capital gains				1,000

The company makes a claim for loss relief first against income and gains of the current period and then for the remaining terminal loss.

Show the final taxable total profits for all relevant periods.

Solution: Zampata Ltd CTAPs ended 31st March

	2016	2017	2018	2019
	£	£	£	£
Trading profits	55,000	30,000	65,000	loss
Income from property	7,000	8,000	9,000	9,000
Capital gains	–	–	–	1,000
Total profits	62,000	38,000	74,000	10,000
Less loss against income of current period				(10,000)
Less terminal loss claim (LIFO)	(58,000)	(38,000)	(74,000)	-
Taxable total profits	4,000	–	–	-

Note

Loss Memorandum:	£	£
Trade loss to 31.3.2019		180,000
Used:		
Section 37 31.3.19	10,000	
Section 39 31.3.18	74,000	
Section 39 31.3.17	38,000	
Section 39 31.3.16	58,000	180,000

The terminal loss claims would generate a repayment of CT for earlier periods. No repayment interest arises on such repayments after the normal tax payment date for the accounting period of the terminal loss.

Note that the loss relief explained in 22.6 below does not affect Zampata Ltd, which does **not** have trade losses **brought forward into** the final period.

22.7 Amendment to terminal loss relief from 1st April 2017

An amendment to terminal loss relief applies from 1st April 2017, allowing companies to claim terminal loss relief for **trade** losses carried forward into the final accounting period. This is for the benefit of companies who have unrelieved trading losses brought forward as a result of the restrictions on loss claims for companies with profits in excess of £5million.

These trading losses may be relieved against total profits of three years ending at the end of the cessation period. Note this period does not match the period for the main terminal loss relief described in 22.6 above. The relief is only available for losses incurred after 1 April 2017 and can only be set against income and gains made after that date. Also, the losses cannot be claimed against income or gains of the original period in which the losses were made.

22.8 Non-trading loan relationship deficit

Interest incurred and receivable plus any other debits and credits relating to non-trade borrowing and lending must be pooled to produce either a non-trading credit or deficit for the period. This also includes any non-trading foreign exchange debt differences.
A net non-trading credit is included as interest income.

A net non-trading deficit is relieved by one or more of the following methods:

i) By offset against the company's taxable profits (in whole or part) for the same period. A current year non-trading deficit is deducted against taxable profits before: any current year trading loss offset; charges on income; and a non-trading deficit carried back from a subsequent period.

ii) Against the taxable profits of fellow group members under the group relief provisions.

iii) By carry-back (in whole or part) against the company's interest income loan relationships profits falling within the previous 12 months.

iv) By carry forward of deficits incurred from 1 April 2017 onwards against future total profits. (For deficits incurred before 1 April 2017 the carry forward may only be set against non-trading profits. For this purpose, non-trading profits represent the company's total profits except those constituting trading income.)

The above reliefs must be claimed within two years of the end of the relevant CTAP or such further period as HMRC may allow.

Example

Quando Ltd has this data relating to the year ended 31st December 2018.

	£
Adjusted trading profit	93,000
Income from property	5,000
Non-trade interest cost incurred	65,000
Non-trade interest received	15,000

Compute the taxable total profits for the CTAP to 31st December 2018.

Solution: Q Ltd corporation tax computation AP 31.12.18

	£
Trading profits	93,000
Income from property	5,000
	98,000
Non-trading deficit	(50,000)
Taxable Total Profits	48,000

Notes

i) The non-trade loan relationship deficit comprises:

non-trade interest paid	65,000
less non-trade interest received	15,000
	50,000

ii) The excess non-trade loan relationship deficit is deducted from total profits and taken off before group relief. (Refer to the specimen Corporation Tax computation at the end of Chapter 18)

22.9 Capital losses

The amount of any chargeable gain arising in a Corporation Tax Accounting Period is reduced by any allowable capital losses of the same Accounting Period and then by those brought forward from a previous period. A company can never carry capital losses back to an earlier accounting period.

Example

Robot Ltd has the following data relating to its CTAP to 31st March 2019.

	£
Capital losses brought forward 1.4.18	3,000
AP to 31.3.2019	
Trading profits	41,000
Chargeable gains	22,000

Compute the corporation tax payable.

Solution: Robot Ltd CTAP to 31st March 2019

	£	£
Trading profits		41,000
Chargeable gains	22,000	
Less capital losses b/f	(3,000)	19,000
Total profits/ Taxable total profit		60,000
Corporation tax payable: 60,000 @ 19%		11,400

22.10 Non-trading losses of a company – summary of the most important reliefs

Capital losses
are set against chargeable gains of same Corporation Tax Accounting Period, or carried forward. They cannot be set against total profits.

A company in a Capital Gains Group (see chapter 31) can additionally elect to transfer a capital loss to another group company in the same accounting period when the loss is made. Transferred capital losses can only be used by the receiving company against its own chargeable gains of that accounting period.

Other non-trading losses

The following non-trade deficits are reported on the Corporation Tax return and deducted directly in computing total profits. No formal loss claim is involved to obtain relief for them, if there are other profits to set them off against:

- Property business losses;
- Non trade loan relationships deficits;
- Non-trading losses on intangible fixed assets;
- Excess management expenses of an investment company.

If there are no other profits of the period these non-trading losses may be carried forward and set off in part or in full against future total profits of the company, or surrendered as group relief (see chapter 23).

Student self-testing questions

Question 1: Trailer Limited

Trailer Limited has the following results for the two years to 31st March 2019

	y/e 31-Mar-2018	y/e 31-Mar-2019
	£	£
Trading profit/(loss)	(42,000)	17,000
Interest income - non trade relationship	6,000	9,000
Capital loss	(2,000)	
Chargeable gains		7,000

Requirement: Calculate the Taxable Total Profits for the 2 periods, assuming that the trading loss is carried forward, and showing any remaining losses carried forward at 1st April 2019.

Solution to Question 1: Trailer Limited

	31/3/18	31/3/19
	£	£
Trading profit	-	17,000
Interest income	6,000	9,000
Chargeable gains (£7,000 - £2,000)	-	5,000
	6,000	31,000
Less: post 1 April 2017 loss carried forward		(31,000)
Taxable Total Profits	6,000	0

Loss memorandum

	£
Loss for year ended 31/3/18	42,000
Relieved year ended 31/3/19 (carried forward)	(31,000)
Available for further carry-forward at 1 April 2019	11,000

Question 2: Caravan Limited

Caravan Limited has the following results for the accounting years ended 31st March 2018 and 31st March 2019.

	Year to 31/3/18	Year to 31/3/19
	£	£
Trading profit/(loss)	39,000	(81,700)
Income from property	20,000	15,000
Qualifying charitable donations (gross)	500	500

Requirement: Calculate Taxable Total Profits for both periods, assuming that relief against total profits of the same period and previous 12 months is claimed for the loss in the period ended 31st March 2019. Show any losses available to carry forward at 1st April 2019.

Solution to Question 2: Caravan Limited

Caravan Limited: TTP computation for 2 years ending 31st March 2019

	Year ended 31/3/18	Year ended 31/3/19
	£	£
Trading profit	39,000	-
Income from property	20,000	15,000
Total profits	59,000	15,000
Loss relief against the current period and previous 12 months (the setoff for the current period must be claimed before the carry-back claim)	(59,000)	(15,000)
TTP	-	-
Unrelieved QCDs (Caravan loses tax relief, but the charity still gets the same donation)	500	500

Loss memorandum	£
Trade loss for the year ended 31/3/19	81,700
Relief against income of the current period ended 31/3/19	(15,000)
Relief against income of the previous 12 months ended 31/3/18	(59,000)
Trade loss carried forward at 1/4/19	7,700

Question 3: Buttercup Limited

Buttercup Limited made up accounts to 31st March and ceased to trade on 31st March 2019. Results have been as follows:

Year ended ...	31/3/16	31/3/17	31/3/18	31/3/19
Trading profit/(loss)	5,200	4,700	3,200	(76,500)
Income from property	20,000	10,800	10,900	10,500
Interest income - non trading	750	900	840	400
Chargeable gains	3,000	-	2,000	-
Qualifying charitable donations				
-amounts paid	300	300	300	300

Requirement: Show the Taxable Total Profits for all years, assuming the loss is relieved firstly under normal current period and previous 12 month rules, and for remaining losses under terminal loss relief.

Solution to Question 3: Buttercup Limited

Year ended ...	31/3/16	31/3/17	31/3/18	31/3/19
	£	£	£	£
Trading profit	5,200	4,700	3,200	-
Income from property	20,000	10,800	10,900	10,500
Interest income	750	900	840	400
Chargeable gains	3,000	-	2,000	-
Loss relief against profit of current period				(10,900)
Loss relief against profit of previous 12 months			(16,940)	
Terminal loss relief	(28,950)	(16,400)	-	
TP	0	0	0	0
QCDs	-	-	-	-
TTP	Nil	Nil	Nil	Nil
Unrelieved QCDs	300	300	300	300

Terminal trade loss of final 12 months	76,500
Current period ended 31/03/19	(10,900)
Previous 12 months ended 31/03/18	(16,940)
Terminal loss, LIFO	
Year ended 31/03/17	(16,400)
Year ended 31/03/16	(28,950)
Terminal loss remaining unrelieved	3,310

Questions without answers

Question 4: Uncut Undergrowth Limited

Uncut Undergrowth Limited (UUL) is a United Kingdom resident company which has been manufacturing garden machinery since 2001. It has no associated companies. The company results are summarised as follows:

	Year Ended 30/09/17	6 months to 31/03/18	Year Ended 31/03/19	Year Ended 31/03/20
	£	£	£	£
Trading Profit / (Loss)	25,000	(51,000)	(362,500)	87,000
Non-trade loan interest received (gross amount)	-	15,000	22,000	-
Bank interest received -non trade relationship	-	-	-	10,000
Income from property	25,000	-	-	-
Chargeable gains	-	-	30,000	-
Qualifying charitable donations	1,000	1,000	1,000	1,000

On 1st October 2016 there were no trading losses brought forward, but £40,000 of prior capital losses were still unrelieved.

Requirements

(a) Calculate the corporation tax liabilities for all years in the question, after giving maximum relief at the earliest time for the trading losses sustained and any other reliefs. (11 marks)

(b) Show any balances carried forward. (5 marks)

NB: All apportionments may be made to the nearest month.

Note: Assume FY 2018 tax rates will continue to apply for FY 2019.

(ACCA updated)

Question 5: Loser Limited

Loser Ltd's results for the year ended 30th June 2018, the nine month period ended 31st March 2019, the year ended 31st March 2020 and the year ended 31st March 2021 are as follows:

	Year ended 30 June 2018	Period ended 31 Mar 2019	Year ended 31 Mar 2020	Year ended 31 Mar 2021
	£	£	£	£
Trading profit/(loss)	90,200	(33,000)	34,600	(85,500)
Income from property	(3,600)	4,500	8,100	5,600
QCDs	(1,400)	(800)	(1,200)	(1,100)

Required:

(a) State the factors that will influence a company's choice of loss relief claims. You are not expected to consider group relief.

(3 marks)

(b) Assuming that Loser Ltd claims relief for its losses as early as possible, calculate the company's Taxable Total Profits for:

the year ended 30th June 2018,

the nine month period ended 31st March 2019,

the year ended 31st March 2020 and

the year ended 31st March 2021.

Your answer should show any amount of unrelieved losses as at 31st March 2021. (10 marks)

(c) Explain how your answer to (b) would have differed if Loser Ltd had ceased trading on 31st March 2021. (2 marks)

(15 marks)

(ACCA updated)

Student note: Some of these questions contain brief calculations of chargeable gains of companies, and this topic is covered fully in Part 4.

23 Groups

23.1 Introduction

This chapter considers extra corporation tax rules that apply where a company is a member of a group or consortium.

Where companies are related through shareholdings of more than 50%, the size limit for determining whether or not corporation tax payments on account are required is reduced as mentioned in section 18.10

Where companies are related through shareholdings of 75% or more, extra reliefs are available for sharing losses between companies, and extra provisions apply to the chargeable gains on transferring assets between group companies.

23.2 '51% group' companies

Company A is a related 51% group company to Company B if:

i) A is a 51% subsidiary of B; or

ii) B is a 51% subsidiary of A; or

iii) A and B are both 51% subsidiaries of the same company.

One company is a 51% subsidiary of another if the parent beneficially owns (directly or indirectly) more than 50% of the ordinary share capital of the subsidiary.

If a company has one or more subsidiaries in the accounting period, then both the upper limit and the £10m relevant maximum amount are divided equally between the companies in the 51% group. Thus a company with two subsidiaries would have to allocate the relevant amount threefold:

FY 2018, to 31.3.2019	**Upper limit**
	£
Parent company	500,000
First 51% subsidiary	500,000
Second 51% subsidiary	500,000
	1,500,000

In determining the number of group companies the following points should be noted.

(a) A group company which has not been active at any time in the accounting period (i.e. a dormant company) is disregarded.

(b) A company which is only a member of the group for part of an accounting period is counted.

(c) All active companies are counted separately in the total, even if they were group companies for different parts of the accounting period.

(d) Overseas companies are included in determining the number of group companies.

Example

Diverso Ltd, a company resident in the United Kingdom, owns 80% of the equity share capital of Secondo Ltd, 52% of the ordinary share capital of Judo Ltd and 25% of the ordinary share capital of Nonno Ltd.

The company prepares accounts to the year ended 31st December and provides the following information in respect of its AP of twelve months ended 31st December 2018:

INCOME	£
Trading profits net of capital allowances	260,000
Bank interest	140,000
Capital gains	50,000
Rental income net of allowable expenses	200,000

Requirement: Compute the corporation tax liability for Diverso Limited for the above accounting period.

Solution

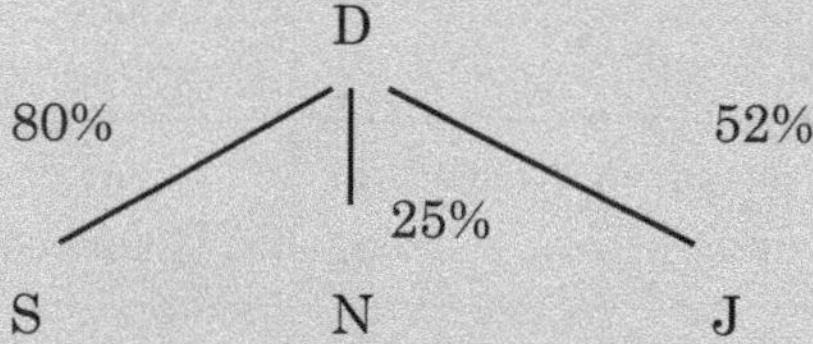

D, S & J are 51% group companies for the purposes of tax; N is not.

Divide upper limit by 3: £1,500,000 / 3 Upper limit £500,000

Calculation of Taxable Total Profits

Trading profits	260,000
Interest income	140,000
Income from property	200,000
Chargeable Gains	50,000
Taxable Total Profits	650,000

The Corporation Tax liability would be

Corporation Tax on TTP for CTAP 1.1.18 to 31.12.18:	£
FY17: 1.1.2018 to 31.3.2018 ($\frac{3}{12}$ × £650,000 × 19%)	30,875
FY18: 1.4.2018 to 31.12.2018 ($\frac{9}{12}$ × £650,000 × 19%)	92,625
Total corporation tax liability	**123,500**

23.3 '75% group' companies - Topics to be considered

a) Group relief (75% subsidiaries and consortia)	The offset of trading losses against the total profits (after QCDs) of another company under the same ultimate control
Group relief for carried forward losses	The carry forward of losses incurred after 1st April 2017 to a period in which they may be surrendered against the total profits of another company under the same ultimate control
b) Special rules for chargeable gains and losses involving companies in a CGs group (for main treatment, see Chapter 31)	The transfer of assets between group companies without a chargeable gain or loss arising; treatment of whole group trades as carrying on one trade for rollover relief; possibility to transfer chargeable gains / capital losses of the current CTAP to another group company for CT purposes.
c) Company reconstructions without change of ownership – e.g. divisionalisations, or 'hive-downs', 'hive-ups', etc., involving transfer of a trade, CAs-qualifying assets, or intangible assets (goodwill etc.) between different companies which are both under the same ultimate ownership	Capital allowances WDVs and WDAs continue as normal; no cessation of trade identified; no disposal of intangible fixed assets identified; past trade (not capital) losses can still be carried forward and used by the successor company.
d) Change in ultimate ownership of a company, accompanied within 3 years by a major change in the nature or conduct of its trade	Trade losses carried forward at the date of change of ownership can be disallowed against later trade profits.

23.4 Group relief (groups and consortia)

Group relief is a very flexible loss relief option within groups of companies. One company in a qualifying group of companies may surrender any specified amount(s) of its excess trading losses, charitable donations, or non-trade loan deficits, and other companies in the same group may claim the amounts to reduce their own taxable profits for UK CT.

23.5 Meaning of group – world wide

Two companies are members of the same group relief group if the following four conditions all prevail.

a) One is the 75% subsidiary of the other, or both are 75% subsidiaries of a third company. A 75% subsidiary is defined in CTA 2010 in terms of the direct or indirect beneficial ownership of not less than 75% of the ordinary share capital, ordinary shares meaning all shares other than 'restricted' preference shares.

b) The parent company is beneficially entitled to not less than 75% of the profits available for distribution to equity holders of the subsidiary company. An equity holder is any person who holds ordinary shares or is a loan creditor in respect of a loan which is not a commercial loan. Loan creditor has the same meaning as that used in connection with close companies except that the proviso in favour of bank normal borrowings is not excluded and therefore is within the definition for the purposes of these conditions. A normal commercial loan is one which carries a reasonable rate of interest, with no rights to conversion.

c) The parent company would be entitled beneficially to not less than 75% of any assets of the subsidiary company available to its equity shareholders on a winding up.

d) The meaning of 'group' for group relief includes non-UK subsidiaries, and UK branches of overseas companies. This means that control for group relief can be traced through non-UK intermediate companies.

   However in general there is no point in seeking to include non-UK companies in a group relief claiming relationship if they are not within the charge to UK corporation tax.

   As regards overseas companies surrendering losses to the UK, following the European Court of Justice Judgement in the Marks and Spencer case a small extension to the group relief rules was made from FY 2006. Relief may be claimed for losses from subsidiaries within the European Economic Area (EEA) or having a permanent establishment within the EEA (including indirectly held subsidiaries) if the tax loss cannot ever be relieved in the country of the loss. The loss surrender must be computed in line with UK tax rules. In practice few companies with loss-making overseas subsidiaries will satisfy these tight conditions (in the M&S case the loss-making Italian and French subsidiaries had actually closed and this made it impossible for them to relieve their losses by local carry-forward against profits).

Example of applying the 75% control rule to see if a GR relationship exists

Bianca Ltd owns 75% of the ordinary share capital of Watt Ltd, which in turn owns 75% of the ordinary share capital of Zuppa Ltd.

Since Bianca Ltd would only be entitled to 56.25% of the profits available for distribution by Zuppa Ltd the three companies do not constitute a group for the purposes of group relief. Bianca Ltd and Watt Ltd however would constitute a group, as would Watt Ltd and Zuppa Ltd. So Bianca Ltd cannot surrender losses to Zuppa and Zuppa cannot surrender losses to Bianca. But Watt can surrender or claim losses from either of the other two.

Example

Tino Ltd is the UK parent of two 100% subsidiaries, Alano Inc and Burro Inc, both being USA resident companies. Burro Inc owns 75% each of two UK companies, Diossina Ltd and Erboso Ltd.

T Ltd and its USA subsidiaries, and the sub-subsidiaries D and E, all constitute a group relief group for tax purposes. Therefore GR losses could be surrendered from T Ltd, D Ltd and E Ltd to either of the other two UK resident companies. As A Inc and B Inc are outside the European Economic Area they cannot partake in GR surrenders, even under the limited scope introduced after the Marks and Spencer case. However they are members of the group for control purposes.

23.6 What may be surrendered as group relief

Group relief changed from 1 April 2017, as part of the reform of Corporation Tax loss relief rules.

For losses made before 1 April 2017 the following losses could be given by a surrendering company as group relief, against income of a claimant company of the same period:

a) trading losses, excluding any losses brought forward, but after claims for capital allowances.

b) any excess of capital allowances normally given against income of a special class.

c) any charitable donations not relieved against total profits.

d) any excess of management expenses of an investment company, other than a close investment holding company.

e) a net loss arising from a loan relationship.

The surrendering company did not have to make any claim for loss relief before surrendering losses to GR claimants, although this was frequently done in practice.

For losses made after 1 April 2017 a company may surrender carried forward losses for group relief. The losses which may be surrendered are, carried forward:

a) trade losses.

b) non trading deficit from loan relationships.

c) non-trading losses on intangible fixed assets.

d) property business losses.

e) excess management expenses of an investment business.

These losses may only be surrendered if they cannot be used by the surrendering company in the accounting period.

23.7 The claimant

In the CTAP of the claimant company, the surrendered loss may be set against the claimant's total profits including chargeable gains determined as follows:

a) After taking into consideration any relief for losses brought forward from previous years.

b) After taking into consideration any loss relief against total income of the current accounting period, whether claimed or not.

c) Before any loss relief brought back from a subsequent accounting period.

d) After deducting qualifying charitable donations.

e) Group relief is only available to companies resident in the UK or trading here through a branch.

Relief may only be claimed to the extent it can be set against the current total profits of the claimant company.

23.8 General points

a) Group relief is limited to the smaller of the surrendering company's losses available for group relief, or the claimant company's profits available for group relief. This does not prevent any other form of loss relief being obtained by the surrendering company, e.g. carry forward against its future profit.

b) More than one company in the group may make a claim relating to the same surrendering company.

c) If any payment for group relief surrendered takes place between the claimant and the surrendering company, this transaction is:
   i) ignored for all corporation tax purposes, for both payer and recipient;
   ii) not treated as a distribution.

Example

Hobby Ltd has a wholly owned subsidiary company Merlo Ltd and the results of both companies for their current CTAP of the same 12 months to 31 March 2019 are given below:

	H Ltd	M Ltd
	£	£
Trading profits	(75,000)	70,000
Less pre 1 April 2017 trade loss b/f	–	(30,000)
	(75,000)	40,000
Interest income non-trading (NTLR)	15,000	–
Chargeable gain	10,000	5,000
Qualifying Charitable Donations	–	25,000

Hobby Ltd decides to make a claim for loss relief against total income of the current period and to surrender as much as possible of the balance of its loss to Merlo Ltd.

Show the effects of the claims on Hobby Ltd and Merlo Ltd.

Solution **Hobby Ltd**

	£
Interest income (NTLR)	15,000
Chargeable gain	10,000
Total profits	25,000
Less: claim against profit of the current period	(25,000)
Taxable total profit	–
Utilization of losses	
Available trade loss	75,000
Less Section 37 claim against total profits	(25,000)
Available for group relief	50,000
Less surrendered to M Ltd	(20,000)
Carried forward	30,000

Merlo Ltd

	£
Trading profits	40,000
Chargeable gain	5,000
Total profits	45,000
Less Qualifying Charitable Donations	(25,000)
Subtotal before group relief	20,000
Group relief claimed from H Ltd	(20,000)
Taxable total profits, after group relief	0

Smaller amount taken for group relief

Notes

i) In this example, group relief is limited to the Merlo Ltd profits of £20,000, as this is the maximum loss it is possible to use.

ii) Group relief is deducted from Merlo Ltd's total profits after qualifying charitable donations, so full Corporation Tax relief for those is preserved.

iii) As the carried forward losses of Hobby Ltd are incurred after 1st April 2017 they may be carried forward and relieved against its future profits, or surrendered for group relief for carried forward losses in the next accounting period.

23.9 Overlapping periods

Where the accounting periods of the surrendering company and the claimant company do not coincide, but they have been members of the same group throughout their respective accounting periods, maximum group relief is in effect restricted to the proportion of the loss/profit of the overlapping period. This may, in fact, cover more than one Corporation Tax Accounting Period of either company.

Example

Xu Ltd has a 75% subsidiary, Yang Ltd, and the results of both companies for the last two accounting periods are as follows:

X Ltd

AP to 31.3.2018 Trading profit	10,000
AP to 31.3.2019 Trading loss	(16,000)

Y Ltd

AP to 31.12.2018 taxable profits	6,000
AP to 31.12.2019 taxable profits	24,000

Compute the group relief available.

Solution

In this example the period of the loss by Xu Ltd covers two accounting periods of Yang Ltd and it will be necessary to determine the lower of the profit or loss in each corresponding period.

Group relief available

	£	£
Overlapping period 1.4.2018 to 31.12.2018		
X Ltd (3/4 × 16,000)	(12,000)	
Y Ltd (3/4 × 6,000)	4,500	
Restricted to the lower amount		4,500
	£	£
Overlapping period 1.1.2019 to 31.3.2019		
X Ltd (¼ × 16,000)	(4,000)	
Y Ltd (¼ × 24,000)	6,000	
Restricted to the lower amount		4,000
Total		8,500

a) An overlapping period is the period throughout which both the claimant and the surrendering companies meet the qualifying conditions for group relief (as to membership of the group or consortium) and which is a common period falling within the CTAP, or separate CTAPs, of both companies.

b) The maximum loss to be surrendered is the smaller of the unused part of the total GR loss available, or any unrelieved part of the total profits of the claimant company, in the overlapping period.

c) The unused part of the loss is the part remaining after prior surrenders or claims by the lossmaking company in respect of that CTAP and that loss. This assumes that the total trade loss (and other losses available for group relief) for the overlapping period is computed, and successive surrenders of loss, or loss claims by the loss-making company, are deducted from that total, until the whole of the loss relating to the overlapping period is exhausted.

d) The 'unrelieved part of the total profits' assumes a time-apportionment of the total profits for the entire CTAP, between the overlapping period and the remainder of the CTAP. The profit for the overlapping period is then taken and successive group relief claims are deducted from it until, cumulatively, the profit is exhausted. If it is not exhausted the balance of TTP will be added back the TTP of the non-overlapping part of the CTAP before CT liability is calculated for the single CTAP.

23.10 Companies joining or leaving a group

As already explained, group relief is only possible if the claimant and surrendering companies are members of the same group (or fulfil the conditions relating to a consortium) in at least part of a CTAP. When a company either joins or leaves a group or consortium, its profits for that CTAP need to be divided into the part relating to group membership and the part that does not. (This is broadly the same principle as is applied in accounting consolidations, when a subsidiary company joins or leaves a group)

Normally the total profits are apportioned purely on a time basis for group relief purposes. However, if it appears that such an apportionment would produce an unreasonable result, then a different 'just and reasonable' basis can be agreed with HMRC.

Example

Denaro Ltd, a trading company, acquires a 100% interest in Wu Ltd on 30th June 2018. Both companies have the same year end and the results for the year to 31st December 2018 are as follows:

	Denaro Ltd	**Wu Ltd**
	£	**£**
Trading profit	12,000	(40,000)
Interest income (non-trade loan relationship)	3,000	–
Chargeable gain (contract date pre 30.6.18)	15,000	–
Capital loss (contract date pre 30.6.18)	–	(10,000)

Compute the amount of group relief available.

Solution

On the acquisition of Wu Ltd who then with Denaro Ltd forms a group, there is deemed to be a commencement of an accounting period for group relief purposes.

	£
Loss to be surrendered by Wu Ltd	
Loss for 12 months to 31.12.2018	40,000
Proportion for deemed accounting period from	
1.7.2018 to 31.12.2018 $^{6}/_{12} \times 40,000$	20,000

Loss to be claimed by Denaro Ltd

Trading profit	12,000
Interest income (non-trade loan relationship)	3,000
Chargeable gain	15,000
	30,000
Proportion from 1.7.2018 $^{6}/_{12} \times 30{,}000$	15,000

Since this is smaller than the amount of the loss of the surrendering company, this is the maximum available for group relief.

The computations for the year ended 31st December 2018 are:

	£
Denaro Ltd	
Taxable profits as above	30,000
Less group relief claimed from Wu Ltd	(15,000)
Taxable total profit after group relief	15,000
Wu Ltd	
Trading loss	40,000
Less surrendered as group relief to Denaro Ltd	(15,000)
Balance of loss	25,000

Notes

i) As the balance of the loss of Wu Ltd was incurred after 1st April 2017 it would be available to be carried forward and surrendered for group relief for carried forward losses, or it can be used by Wu Ltd.

ii) The capital loss of W Ltd may not be set against the chargeable gain of any other company.

Similar provisions apply when a company leaves a group, and the profits and losses up to the date of the departure must be apportioned to determine the amount of any group relief available.

23.11 Group payments of interest etc. – intercompany transactions

Payments of interest, royalty payments and annual payments and annuities, are made by all UK companies to other companies without any deduction of income tax, so long as the recipient company is within charge to UK corporation tax, or in the case of interest and royalty payments, where the recipient is any EU company. Unlike the treatment of intra-group payments for consolidated accounting purposes, all companies in a group are charged to their own CT on an entity basis so income and payments which are intra-group (except dividends) must be included as either trading or non-trading items, when calculating total profits for the UK CT return. As regards intragroup sales, any unrealised intragroup profit, removed from group results for financial reporting, is already a realised profit for tax purposes in the company which made the sale. For this reason all calculations of a company's profits for CT begins from the entity's own filed statement of profit or loss, and not from consolidated accounts.

HMRC can apply transfer pricing reviews to payments of royalties, rent etc between UK companies under common control, unless the group is eligible for the SME exemptions for corporate reporting. For more on transfer pricing tax reviews, see 24.11.

23.12 Group Chargeable Gains rules including transfer of assets between group companies

a) The information below should be read in conjunction with similar coverage in Part IV, Chapter 31. See Part IV in general for the normal rules on computing a company's chargeable gain or capital loss.

b) The most important point to note on CGs and groups is that as a general rule, when a company disposes of a chargeable asset outside its CG group, it makes a chargeable gain or loss on normal principles. However, if a chargeable asset disposal is made by one member of a CGs group to another CGs group company, that transaction automatically takes place for tax purposes at **no gain and no loss**. This applies regardless of actual payment made for the asset by the acquiring company.

   Apart from the above key points, detailed tax rules for CG groups, as detailed below, are a specialist area of corporation tax outside the current syllabus of ACCA paper F6 (UK Taxation) and similar general accounting bodies, though they are in the syllabus for Chartered Institute of Taxation exams.

23.13 Companies defined as being in the same 'CG group'

a) A Capital Gains group comprises a 'principal company' and all of its '75% subsidiaries'. Unlike with section 130 group losses relief, a company cannot be a member of more than one 'CG group' at the same time.

b) A 75% subsidiary means a company whose ordinary share capital is owned by another company either directly or indirectly to the extent of at least 75%. Again ordinary share capital comprises all shares other than relevant preference shares.

c) A company which is itself a 75% subsidiary of another company cannot be the principal company of a CG group. It is the company which has no 75% parent above it which is the 'principal company' of a CG group. This may have an impact on which other companies further down a group are counted in the same CG group. A sub-subsidiary which is not in a ≥50% indirect relationship with the principal company (one particular company, as defined), as well as a $\geq$ 75% relationship with its own holding company, is excluded from the first CG group but may itself then be the principal company of another CG group.

d) Members of a consortium are not eligible for treatment as members of a CG group. Nor are close investment holding companies, unless the relevant chargeable asset (e.g. land) is transferred between two close investment holding companies which meet the tests for a CGs group relationship.

23.14 Assets available for group treatment

The disposal of any chargeable asset between group companies gets a no-gain-no-loss treatment, apart from exceptions given in the Act which are as follows.

a) Where the disposal is of redeemable preference shares (these would not be chargeable assets in the hands of a company anyway, but debts/ loan relationship assets, if accounted for as debt instruments and not equity).

b) Where the company is a dual resident member of a group of companies and any gain made by that company on the relevant disposal is exempt from UK tax under a double tax treaty.

If the transfer is of an asset which the recipient company appropriates to its inventory (trading stock), then that company is deemed to have received a capital asset and immediately transferred that asset to its inventory (trading stock). There would thus be no capital gain or loss arising on the inter-company transfer, as it would fall within the normal provisions covered above.

If the asset transferred to a group company was inventory (trading stock) of the transferor company, but has been treated as capital by the buyer, then the buyer is treated as having appropriated the asset as a capital asset immediately prior to the disposal. The value placed on the asset for trading purposes under Section 161 TCGA 1992 would be the transfer value from the 'no gain no loss' situation.

23.15 Other points

a) When an asset is disposed of by a group company to a company outside the group, capital allowances previously granted to any member of the group relating to the asset must be taken into consideration (ie excluded from allowable cost) when computing the chargeable gain or capital loss.

b) If a company to which an asset has been transferred at no-gain-no-loss ceases to be a member of a CG group within six years of the date of the asset transfer, there is the possibility of a 'de-grouping charge', which works as follows.

    i) At the date of the acquisition of the asset by the company leaving the group, or if later the beginning of the accounting period when the company left the group, it is deemed to have sold and reacquired the asset at its market value at the date when it acquired the asset from the other group member.

ii) There will therefore, be a chargeable gain or loss on the difference between the market value at the time of the intra-group asset transfer, and the original cost to the group of the asset.

Following recent reforms the de-grouping charge is longer a CT liability (on chargeable gains) for the company leaving the group. Instead it is treated as a separate chargeable gain arising to the immediate parent of the company which is leaving the group (i.e. the vendor of the shares in the departing company). The deemed chargeable gain is added to total profits of that company as a chargeable gain on the date of disposal. This is separate from any actual chargeable gain arising on the disposal of shares in the company which is departing (though in many cases that gain is covered by the corporate 'substantial shareholdings exemption' – see Part IV Chapter 31).

c) The provisions of Section 152 TCGA 1992 (rollover relief) are extended to CGT groups, which enables all trades carried on by the group to be treated as one for the purposes of the sale of assets 'used in the trade' and purchase of replacement assets 'used in the trade'.

For further details on this see Chapter 31.

Student self-testing question

The results of Atta Ltd and its wholly owned subsidiary Birra Ltd for the three years ended 31st March 2018 are as follows:

		31.3.2017	31.3.2018	31.3.2019
		£	£	£
A Ltd	Trading profit/(loss)	1,200	(7,500)	4,800
	Income from property	500	500	500
B Ltd	Trading profit	2,500	3,500	5,000

A Ltd makes a claim for loss relief against total profit of the same period and then claims group relief.

Show the computations of taxable total profit.

Solution:

	31.3.2017	31.3.2018	31.3.2019
A Ltd	£	£	£
Trading profit	1,200	–	4,800
Income from property	500	500	500
	1,700	500	5,300
Less: Claim against total profit of current period		(500)	
Against previous 12 months	(1,700)		
Post 1 April 2017 carry forward			(1,800)
Taxable total profit	–	–	3,500

B Ltd			
Trading profit	2,500	3,500	5,000
Less group relief	–	(3,500)	–
Taxable total profit	2,500	–	5,000

Loss memorandum		**£**	**£**
Loss year to 31st March 2018			7,500
Current period	31.3.2018	500	
Previous 12 months	31.3.2017	1,700	
Group relief	31.3.2018	3,500	
Carry forward	31.3.2019	1,800	
			(7,500)

Note. The maximum amount has been surrendered to B Ltd.

24 International aspects

24.1 Introduction

This chapter deals, at an awareness level only, with aspects of corporation tax arising from overseas or international operations of a UK resident company.

These are described under the following main headings:

Income from foreign sources

Relief for withholding taxes (WHT) suffered on income or gains

Double tax relief – general OECD principles

Foreign dividends

Foreign tax credit relief and other loss reliefs

The 'Patent Box' rules

Controlled foreign companies

Transfer pricing – awareness issues.

Differences between having a Foreign Branch and a Foreign Subsidiary

OECD Base Erosion and Profit Shifting (BEPS) project

Diverted Profits Tax

Restriction on UK allowable interest costs

Publication of large company tax strategies

24.2 Income from foreign sources

In principle, income from foreign sources is liable to CT in the same way as all other income of a UK resident company. Foreign interest receivable is within the loan relationship arrangements, and any profit on overseas loans is taxed as loan relationship surplus. Trading income from foreign branches (permanent establishments) is under the CTA2009 included in normal trade profits and not reported as a separate source of income (this was a minor legislative change).

However where double taxation credit relief is being claimed it is still necessary to identify accurately the amount of foreign-taxed branch income. Income from overseas rentals is treated in the same way as UK property income. Chargeable gains realised on overseas assets are computed in the same way as other gains and are liable to UK corporation tax if the owner is a UK resident company. All of these types of foreign profits may be referred to in a claim for double tax relief against the UK corporation tax liability.

Income from overseas sources that passes in cash payment may be subject to deduction of local withholding taxes (WHT) charged on certain payments leaving a tax jurisdiction (e.g. rents, royalties, licence fees or dividends). For all such receipts except dividends, the gross income is liable to UK corporation tax and so it must be grossed up for the foreign withholding tax suffered. Full relief is available for this withholding tax against UK CT, provided it has not been charged at a higher effective rate than the UK CT liability due on the same income. However, foreign dividends are not grossed up for actual foreign withholding taxes deducted, because they are not taxable income in the hands of a UK company. (See 24.4)

Example

Kudos Ltd has the following data relating to the 12 months Corporation Tax Accounting Period to 31st March 2019.

	£
Trading profits	1,280,000
Interest income receivable and received	
(net foreign interest after 15% withholding tax)	85,000
Chargeable gains	250,000

Calculate the UK Corporation Tax payable for the Accounting Period to 31st March 2018, assuming double tax relief is claimed.

Solution

Kudos Ltd corporation tax computation Accounting Period 31.3.2019

	£
Trading profits	1,280,000
Interest income (gross) £85,000 × 100/85	100,000
Chargeable gains	250,000
Total profits/taxable total profit	1,630,000
Corporation tax	£
1,630,000 @ 19%	309,700
Less double tax relief – withholding tax suffered	(15,000)
Corporation tax liability	294,700

Note

The double tax relief is the lower of the following:

	£
UK CT @ 19% on foreign income £100,000	19,000
Foreign tax	15,000

24.3 Double tax relief – general OECD principles

Double Taxation Agreements ('Tax Treaties') provide negotiated means of determining the taxing rights of any two competing Governments (Taxing States), where the domestic tax rules of both States charge tax on the same income or gains. The UK has an extensive network of Double Tax Treaties at Government level. These have been drafted so as to follow the OECD (Organisation for Economic Cooperation and Development) guidelines on Double Tax Treaties.

If there is no Double Tax Treaty with the relevant State, unilateral double taxation credit relief, which works on a similar basis to the commonest type of Tax Treaty credit relief, is given by the UK Taxes Acts for foreign tax shown to have been suffered on income or gains which are also liable to tax in the UK.

The OECD principles state that the profits of a permanent establishment in another Taxing State should be primarily taxable in that other Taxing State. A permanent establishment covers a branch operation if there is the capacity for employees to conclude contracts there which bind the UK company. It also covers an appointed general agent (i.e. not an employee of the UK company) who has authority to conclude binding contracts in the foreign territory on behalf of the UK company.

Another OECD principle of double tax relief is that, in giving relief in the second Taxing State for tax suffered in the first, the second State may limit that relief to the amount of tax that would be paid on the same income in the second country. This principle is illustrated by the Double Tax Relief calculations in the example at 24.2. If the foreign withholding tax had been 30% (£30,000), then only £19,000 of it would have been available for offset against the UK tax liability. The rest of the foreign tax would still be paid, but would be shown in the company's accounts as additional tax on the foreign activity.

24.4 Foreign dividends received

The dividends received by a UK company from companies resident outside the UK are treated the same way as UK dividends. Thus they are not taxable income in the hands of the UK recipient company.

24.5 Foreign tax credit relief and other loss reliefs

Where a UK company has foreign income, then in order to preserve the maximum amount of DT relief, loss relief claims should be considered carefully.

Example

Wombat Ltd and its wholly owned UK subsidiary Fax Ltd have the following results for the year ended 31st March 2019.

	Wombat Ltd	**Fax Ltd**
	£	**£**
Trading profits	(30,000)	80,000
Overseas Royalties	16,000	
(gross before withholding tax of 15%)		
Chargeable gains	2,000	1,000

Calculate the corporation tax payable in the following situations:

a) **Wombat Ltd claims loss relief against total profit of the current period and surrenders the maximum loss to Fax Ltd.**

b) **Wombat Ltd makes no claim for relief against total profit of the current period but surrenders as much loss as possible to Fax Ltd.**

Solution

(a) **Corporation tax computations Accounting Period 31.3.2019**

	Wombat Ltd	Fax Ltd
	£	£
Trading profits	–	80,000
Overseas royalties	16,000	–
Chargeable gains	2,000	1,000
	18,000	81,000
Less Current year offset	(18,000)	
Group loss surrender		(12,000)
TTP liable to CT	–	69,000
CT Payable @ 19%	–	13,110
Unrelieved foreign tax =	£2,400	

(b)

	Wombat Ltd	Fax Ltd
Trading profits	–	80,000
Overseas income	16,000	–
Chargeable gain	2,000	1,000
	18,000	81,000
Less Group loss surrender	–	(30,000)
TTP liable to CT	18,000	51,000
CT payable @ 19%	3,420	10,200
Less DTR	(2,400)	–
CT	1,020	10,200

Note: By Fax not claiming loss relief under Section 37 the full DT relief of £2,400 has been obtained by Fax.

24.6 The 'Patent Box'

Electing for 'patent box' treatment allows qualifying companies with income directly earned from 'exploiting patented inventions' to pay a reduced rate of corporation tax on profits attributable to qualifying patents. This applies also to profits earned outside the UK from holding the intellectual property in the UK. The patent box special treatment can be claimed on profits earned from 1st April 2013. To align the UK 'patent box' rules with international practice some revisions to the calculation of the relevant income are introduced for assets created from 1st July 2016, with existing assets continuing to benefit from the current calculations until 30th June 2021. Further details are not covered here as this is a specialist area of tax. Information is available online at:
https://www.gov.uk/government/publications/corporation-tax-patent-box-compliance-with-new-international-rules.

24.7 Controlled foreign companies (CFCs)

UK resident companies with interests (even non-controlling interests) in a profitable 'controlled foreign company' (CFC) that is resident in a 'low-tax area' (as defined) may have to self-assess UK corporation tax on an appropriate apportionment to the UK company of the profits of that CFC, on an arising basis.

The original rules about UK taxation on the profits of CFCs (commonly called 'tax haven subsidiaries') dated from 1984. They eventually ran into problems with the European Union Treaty principles on Freedom of Establishment. They were also rendered less effective by the corporation tax foreign dividend exemption introduced fully to the corporation tax system in FY2009. After a lengthy consultation, substantial reforms were enacted to the CFC tax rules in Finance Act 2012. The stated aim of the reforms was, in line with the Government's 2010 'CT Road Map', to make the UK a more attractive location for international headquarters companies.

The new CFC legislation is more clearly focused on 'artificial diversion of profits', specifically from the UK to a CFC (as defined), than were the old rules. Unfortunately the resulting legislative detail is very complex, and is not appropriate to an introductory textbook. In summary, if a CFC's profits are not economically attributable to any UK operations, then apportionment to a UK company for CT purposes should no longer be a risk.

Here is a very simple example: to the extent that a Bermuda company, which is part of a multinational group, has activities which generate profits economically 'belonging' to the group's trading presence in the USA, rather than the UK, the UK tax authorities will no longer seek UK CT on part or all of the CFC profits. (However, the US tax system may well have its own rules allowing the US Government to collect US tax on the Bermuda profits.) The old CFC rules contained no such 'economic substance' test for profits.

A Finance Company Regime has also been introduced as part of the new CFC rules. This offers either partial or complete exemption from UK CFC tax for the profits of a CFC whose main activity is 'overseas group financing'.

The next section explains what a UK company has to do in respect of CFC profits which are not exempted by the new rules, and therefore have to be apportioned to the UK company in proportion to its direct or indirect interest in the CFC.

24.8 Assessment in the UK of CFC profits

(a) If CFC exemption cannot be claimed, the CFC profit brought into UK taxable profits is the apportioned amount of the CFC's taxable total profit, computed on UK tax principles.

Any overseas taxes paid by the CFC which are attributable to these apportioned profits are eligible for Double Tax Relief, in the normal way.

(b) No self-assessment need be made unless the amount apportioned to a UK company and its associates of the CFC's chargeable profits amount to at least 10% of the CFC's chargeable profits.

24.9 CFCs – self-assessment

The Corporation Tax Self-Assessment rules – apply to CFCs. This means that UK companies have to include in their tax returns (Form CT600B) their share of a CFC's profits in accordance with the CFC rules. It is not necessary for HMRC to make a direction regarding a CFC, but HMRC do maintain information about possible CFCs and the UK companies believed to have controlling interests in them, so HMRC could initiate an enquiry into a CT return for the reason that CFC profits were omitted from a CT return.

24.10 Further reading on CFCs

For further discussion of the UK Government's current CFCs policy (and of other international aspects of UK corporation tax mentioned in this chapter), please see the companion volume which focuses more on tax policy questions: *Taxation Policy and Practice 2018/19*, by Andy Lymer and Lynne Oats (2018), Fiscal Publications.

24.11 International transfer pricing – tax issues

A UK company is required, when preparing its CT self-assessment, to consider all transactions with connected companies or businesses (e.g. a branch) and if necessary to revise the transfer prices used in those transactions and substitute an 'arm's length' basis, wherever this would increase the amount of UK taxable income.

The UK transfer pricing rules basically state that if

- a transaction occurs with a related company (whether a trading supply of goods, services or raw materials, a charge for rent, royalties or interest, or a charge for management services) at a price that is not the price which would be reached between two unrelated parties negotiating at arm's length, and
- as a result, the UK company (i.e. the company within the charge to UK tax) pays a higher amount in cost, or receives a lower amount in income, than would have arisen under an arm's length pricing basis,
- then, for corporation tax purposes an arm's length transfer price (as agreed with HMRC) must be substituted when computing taxable profits of the UK company.

The following additional rules apply here:

i) The transfer pricing tax rules do not apply to Small and Medium-sized Enterprises (as defined for corporate financial reporting law), except in relation to transactions with a related business in a territory which does not have a double tax treaty with the UK containing 'a suitable non-discrimination article'.

ii) For large groups (not SMEs), since 2004 the same transfer pricing tax rules apply between related group companies resident in the UK, as well as on cross-border international transactions.

iii) In exceptional circumstances, a 'medium-sized' company may be required by HMRC to apply transfer pricing adjustments.

In practice, HMRC is willing to enter into 'advance pricing agreements' with multinational companies, typically lasting six years at a time These will agree the basis on which work in progress, raw materials or components, or other goods or services are to be priced, when supplied to or purchased from a non-UK entity under the same ultimate control.

Advance pricing agreements are very important for multinational groups. They use them to minimise tax risk, and also to ensure that their methods of arriving at group internal prices, and entity profits on intra-group trading, are acceptable to the taxing authorities in all the countries involved (not just the UK).

All Governments worldwide with developed tax systems have introduced similar transfer pricing review rules to the UK's, in order to prevent the global profits of multinationals being disproportionately recognised, for accounting and tax purposes, in countries with the lowest tax rates.

The largest settlements of transfer pricing tax enquiries to date have been made by pharmaceutical companies. In June 2010, a transfer pricing out-of-court settlement with UK HMRC of £505 million in back taxes by Astra Zeneca plc was announced, covering Astra Zeneca's business in the years 1995-2010. Glaxo plc reached some very high-value transfer pricing tax settlements in both Canada and the US the previous year, though the US liabilities have since been reduced on appeal.

24.12 Foreign branches of UK companies

Where a UK company carries on part of its trade through a foreign branch then the following rules apply (unless the company has elected for the exclusion of all its overseas branches from UK taxation):

a) The trade of the overseas branch is subject to UK corporation tax: the branch profits are taxed as part of the company's trading profits.

b) If the overseas branch is subject to foreign taxation (i.e. direct tax on its profits) then this is taken into consideration for double tax relief against UK tax on total profits.

c) The OECD principles allow the other Taxing State to tax the branch profits first, if the branch is a permanent establishment, as defined.

d) The transactions of the foreign branch with the UK parent should be priced on a 'separate enterprise' principle when computing the profits of the branch, and of the UK parent, for the purpose of DTR, i.e. when comparing overseas tax on the branch profits with UK tax on the same profits.

e) Capital allowances are available in the UK tax computations for plant and machinery purchased by the overseas branch

f) Net trading losses of the overseas branch are in effect relieved against the UK profits without the need for a formal claim, since both results are combined.

g) The existence of a foreign branch does not increase the number of associated companies for the purposes of the small profits rate of CT.

h) It is generally straightforward for income flows to pass between the branch and the parent HQ, unless exchange control restrictions exist in the foreign country. There is no need for formal declaration of a dividend or any specific transaction for the branch to send profits to the UK.

i) Branch net profit is taxable in the UK, whether or not it is remitted to the UK.

As noted at 18.5, Finance Act 2011 contains an election allowing a UK company to opt out of having its overseas branches' income and expenses included in its taxable worldwide profits. If the opt-out is made it is irrevocable. It also means the losses of overseas branches can no longer reduce UK profits by aggregation and that overseas tax paid by the branch will not be available for DTR. Capital allowances will no longer be available on branch assets.

The availability of this election alters the commercial and financial choices available in 2012 onwards to companies that have to choose between expanding overseas using a branch, and expanding by means of a newly-incorporated or purchased subsidiary company.

24.13 Foreign subsidiaries of UK companies

The tax features of trading through a foreign branch, in the absence of an irrevocable exemption election, may be contrasted with the position where a separate foreign company is incorporated or acquired by a UK company to handle its trade in a foreign country. In that case:

a) The profits of the overseas company will not be subject to UK corporation tax, unless it establishes a taxable presence in the UK (or it is a CFC – see (h) below).

b) Any foreign taxation paid by the overseas company on its profits (i.e. direct taxes) is not relievable in the UK against UK tax.

c) Any dividends paid by the subsidiary out of taxed profits will be tax-free dividend income of the parent in the UK.

d) The transactions of the foreign subsidiary with the UK parent may be subject to tax transfer pricing rules to prevent suppression of profits that 'economically belong' in the UK. Foreign branches are of course subject to transfer pricing rules too. But in either case these rules do not apply if the UK company is an SME under financial reporting rules.

e) In contrast to a branch, capital allowances are **not** available in the UK for plant and machinery owned and used by the subsidiary company.

f) Net tax losses of the overseas subsidiary cannot be surrendered as group relief (except under the limited circumstances of the Marks and Spencer case if it is located in the EEA.) (See 23.5)

g) The subsidiary company will count as an extra associated company for the purposes of the small profits rate of CT.

h) Payments from the subsidiary company to the UK parent in the form of purchases of goods and services, management charges, rent or interest payments will be taxable income in the UK. However they will probably be allowable costs in the foreign country against profits taxed there.

i) If the subsidiary is located in a low tax area as defined, then it may be a CFC unless one of the exempting tests is satisfied.

24.14 Base Erosion and Profit Shifting (BEPS)

The UK is a member of the OECD G20 'BEPS' project against base erosion and profit shifting. For a multi-national enterprise a difference between national corporate profits tax rates will provide an incentive for planning its activities to maximise taxable profits in countries with a low tax rate and minimise taxable profits in countries with high tax rates.

The UK government has publicised a policy[1] to have a corporate profit tax level at the lowest rate charged in the G20, 20% being used by a number of the members. The UK government plans further reductions to a rate of 17% in 2020.

However, the UK's 19% rate is high compared to some other countries, such as Switzerland and the Republic of Ireland. This means the UK has experienced low corporate profits tax revenues from companies with activities such as:

i) Intra-group charges for use of intellectual property or brand names by UK group members, reducing UK profits;

ii) Restricting the operations in the UK to activities such as warehousing and distribution, which do not create a UK 'permanent establishment', and therefore not becoming liable to UK taxation;

iii) Using communications technology to record and process sales to UK customers in countries with low tax rates, and claiming these are not UK activities.

The OECD G20 BEPS Project member countries committed to promoting the 15 actions below to combat tax avoidance[2]:

1. Addressing the tax challenges of the digital economy.
2. Neutralising the effects of hybrid mismatch arrangements.
3. Designing effective controlled foreign company rules.
4. Limiting base erosion involving interest deductions and other financial payments.
5. Countering harmful tax practices more effectively, taking into account transparency and substance.
6. Preventing the granting of treaty benefits in inappropriate circumstances.
7. Preventing the artificial avoidance of permanent establishment status.

8-10. Aligning transfer pricing outcomes with value creation.

11. Measuring and monitoring BEPS.
12. Mandatory disclosure rules.
13. Transfer pricing documentation and country-by-country reporting.
14. Making dispute resolution mechanisms more effective.
15. Developing a multilateral instrument to modify bilateral tax treaties.

UK requirements in this chapter, such as those in the following sections demonstrate the practical steps taken to implement the actions above.

24.15 Diverted Profits Tax

Legislation was introduced in the (March) Finance Act 2015 to address erosion of the UK tax base by introducing a 'Diverted Profits Tax', effective for profits arising on or after 1st April 2015.

The Diverted Profits Tax is charged at a rate of 25% on profits which are diverted from the UK through:

i) a foreign company supplying goods or services in the UK through a separate person (the **'avoided PE'**), where it is reasonable to suppose that the arrangement was designed for the purpose of avoiding the foreign company having a 'permanent establishment' in the UK (see section 18.6); **or**

ii) a UK-resident company and another person engaging in transactions lacking economic substance.

Where such arrangements exist, the Diverted Profits Tax applies if:

- one of the main purposes of the arrangements is to avoid a charge to UK corporation tax (the **'tax avoidance condition'**); or
- the foreign tax liability arising on the diverted profits is less than 80% of the amount of Corporation Tax that would have arisen had those profits been included within UK Taxable Total Profits (the **'tax mismatch outcome'**), and the value of the reduced taxes exceeds any other economic benefit from the arrangement (the **'insufficient economic substance condition'**), and within six months of the arrangements being set up, one of the parties to the arrangements participated in the management, control or capital of the other (the **'participation condition'**)

It does not apply where both parties to the tax arrangements are Small- or Medium-Sized Enterprises, nor does it apply to profits relating to loan relationships.

The 'Diverted Profits' figure to which the tax applies is the increase in UK-tax-allowable expenses or reduction in UK-taxable-income of (in case i) the foreign company or (in case ii) the UK-resident company arising from the tax arrangements under review. These are calculated on the same basis as we have already seen in earlier chapters, except that, where HMRC believe that transactions have been recognised at an amount which does not represent an arms-length transaction, the diverted profit charge initially reflects a 30% disallowance of the relevant expenses. The business must pay the tax within 30 days of the charging notice and has a twelve-month review period during which the charge may be adjusted based on evidence.

24.16 Restrictions for UK companies on allowable interest

The UK tax authorities have become concerned that global groups can take advantage of the leading role of London as a centre for debt finance, and the higher rates of CT in the UK than in some other countries, to borrow money in London which the group does not actually need, viewed at the world level.

In theory, surplus funds could be borrowed in the UK, with full UK tax relief on the interest at 19%, and then advanced to group companies outside the UK at a lower rate of interest than is being paid in the UK. The borrowed funds, or the profits and trading returns that they generate, might never come back to the UK but might remain as group cash deposited in a low-tax country (a 'tax haven').

From 1st April 2017 a group's net interest deduction is restricted to a fixed 30% of earnings before interest, taxation, depreciation and amortisation (EBITDA) in the UK. A worldwide group ratio may be substituted, by election, for the 30% ratio. Worldwide groups with net interest expenses of less than or equal to £2 million will not need to apply these rules.

UK companies belonging to groups over a certain size had previously been subject to a 'worldwide debt cap' test on their UK interest costs since 1st January 2010. A version of this remains in force to ensure net UK interest deduction does not exceed the total net interest expense of the worldwide group.

24.17 Large businesses – requirement to publish tax strategies

For accounting years starting after 15th September 2016, large businesses must publish an annual tax strategy, made freely available online. The strategy must set out the business's approach to risk management and governance arrangements in relation to UK taxation; its attitude towards tax planning (so far as affecting UK taxation); the level of risk in relation to UK taxation that it is prepared to accept; and its approach towards its dealings with HMRC[3].

Student self-testing questions

Question 1: Dingbat Limited

Dingbat Ltd forecasts a tax-adjusted trading profit of £1,200,000 for the year ended 31st October 2018. Its directors are not expecting that it will earn any non-trading income or gains in the year. It has no associated companies.

Dingbat Ltd is planning to set up an overseas trading operation. The directors are unsure whether to set up a branch of Dingbat Ltd or a separate wholly-owned overseas company. In either case, the profit in the first accounting period would be the same, £140,000, and the overseas tax due on this profit would be £21,000. The overseas company would remit a dividend of half of its profit after tax.

Required:

Calculate the projected UK corporation tax liability of Dingbat Ltd and show the total tax paid out of the overseas profits (foreign and UK) for the year to 31st October 2018, after any available double tax relief:

(a) if the new operation is set up as an overseas branch, but no election is made by Dingbat Ltd to exclude the branch from UK taxation;

(b) if the operation is set up as an overseas subsidiary.

Solution to Question 1: Dingbat Limited

(a) Overseas branch: Corporation tax liability of Dingbat Ltd:

		£
Trading profits	UK operation	1,200,000
	Branch operation	140,000
Taxable total profit		1,340,000
Corporation Tax	At 19% × £1,340k	254,600
Less double tax relief :	Check : 21k/140k = 15% which is less than 19% so no restriction on DTR	(21,000)
UK CT liability		233,600
Additional overseas tax liability		21,000
Total tax on profits		254,600
Total tax on overseas profits	At 19% × £140k	26,600

(b) Overseas subsidiary: CT liability of Dingbat Ltd

		£
Trading profits	UK company	1,200,000
	[Foreign dividend income is exempted]	
Taxable total profit		1,200,000
UK Corporation Tax	19% × £1,200k	228,000
Additional overseas tax liability		21,000
		249,000
Total tax on overseas profits		21,000

Questions without answers

Question 2: Tartaruga Limited

Tartaruga Ltd, a UK company, owns 20% of Apatica Inc, a foreign resident company. Tartaruga Ltd has the following results for the year ended 31st March 2019:

	£
Operating profits	2,000,000
Chargeable gains	66,000
Overseas income:	
Dividend received from A Inc, (net of 15% withholding taxes)	85,000
Interest received from A Inc,	
(non-trading, net of 18% withholding taxes)	164,000
Debenture interest paid (trading, gross)	140,000
Dividend paid	500,000

Compute the CT payable by Tartaruga Ltd for the AP to 31st March 2019.

Question 3: Wash plc

Wash plc is a UK resident company that manufactures kitchen equipment. The company's trading profit for the year ended 31st March 2019 is £1,600,000. Wash plc has a 100% owned subsidiary, Dry Inc. that is resident overseas. Dry Inc. sells kitchen equipment manufactured by Wash plc. The results for Dry Inc. for the year ended 31st March 2019 are as follows:

	£	£
Trading profit		580,000
Corporation tax		160,000
		420,000
Dividend paid – net	270,000	
– withholding tax	90,000	360,000
Retained profits		60,000

Dry Inc.'s dividend was paid during the year ended 31st March 2018. The company's overseas corporation tax liability for the year ended 31st March 2018 was £8,000 more than that provided for in the accounts.

All of the above figures are in pounds sterling.

i) **Calculate Wash plc's corporation tax liability for the year ended 31st March 2019.**

ii) **Explain the tax implications if Wash plc were to invoice Dry Inc. for the exported kitchen equipment at a price that was less than the market price.**

(ACCA updated)

References

1 UK Trade and Investment, *A Guide to UK Taxation*. (2013) London, UK Trade and Investment [URN 13/663]

2 OECD, *Base Erosion and Profit Shifting Project 2015 Final Reports Executive Summaries* (2015)

3 https://www.cchdaily.co.uk/large-uk-businesses-must-publish-annual-tax-strategy-2017 (accessed 1st May 2016)

End of section questions and answers

Question 1: Tock-Tick Limited

Tock Tick

Tock-Tick Ltd is a clock manufacturer. The company's summarised profit and loss account for the year ended 31st March 2019 is as follows:

	£
Gross profit	822,280
Operating expenses	
Bad debts (note 1)	9,390
Depreciation	99,890
Gifts and donations (note 2)	3,090
Professional fees (note 3)	12,400
Repairs and renewals (note 4)	128,200
Other expenses (note 5)	426,920
Total expenses	679,890
Operating profit	142,390
Profit from sale of fixed assets	
Disposal of office building (note 6)	78,100
Income from investments	
Loan interest receivable (note 7)	12,330
	232,820
Interest payable (note 8)	48,600
Profit before taxation	184,220

Note 1 – Bad debts

Bad debts are as follows:

	£
Trade debts recovered from previous years	(1,680)
Trade debts written off	7,970
Decrease in specific bad debt provision	(3,100)
Increase in general provision for doubtful debts	6,200
	9,390

Note 2 – Gifts and donations

Gifts and donations are as follows:	£
Gifts to customers (pens costing £45 each displaying Tock-Tick Ltd's name)	1,080
Gifts to customers (food hampers costing £30 each)	720
Long service award to an employee	360
Donation to a national charity (made under the gift aid scheme)	600
Gift of wine to the agent representing an overseas supplier	250
Donation to a local charity (Tock-Tick Ltd received free advertising in the charity's magazine)	80
	3,090

Note 3 – Professional fees

Professional fees are as follows:	£
Accountancy and audit fee	5,400
Legal fees in connection with the issue of share capital	2,900
The cost of registering the company's trademark	800
Legal fees in connection with the renewal of a 35-year property lease	1,300
Debt collection	1,100
Legal fees in connection with a court action for not complying with health and safety legislation	900
	12,400

Note 4 – Repairs and renewals

The figure of £128,200 for repairs and renewals includes £41,800 for replacing the roof of an office building, which was in a bad state of repair, and £53,300 for extending the office building.

Note 5 – Other expenses

Other expenses include £2,160 for entertaining suppliers; £880 for counselling services provided to two employees who were made redundant; and the cost of seconding an employee to a charity of £6,400. The remaining expenses are all fully allowable.

Note 6 – Disposal of office building

The profit of £78,100 is in respect of a freehold office building that was sold on 20th February 2018 for £276,000. The office building was purchased for £197,900. You may assume the indexation allowance from the date of acquisition to December 2017 is £75,700.

The building has always been used by Tock-Tick Ltd for trading purposes.

Note 7 – Loan interest receivable

The loan interest is in respect of a loan that was made on 1st July 2018. Interest of £8,280 was received on 31st December 2018, and interest of £4,050 was accrued but not yet received at 31st March 2019. The loan was made for non-trading purposes.

Note 8 – Interest payable

The interest payable is in respect of a five-year debenture loan that is used for trading purposes. Fixed interest is paid six-monthly to debenture holders. £24,300 was paid on 30th September 2018 and again on 31st March 2019.

Note 9 - Plant and machinery

On 1st April 2018 the tax written down values of plant and machinery were as follows:

	£
General pool	12,200
Special rate pool	20,800
Short-life asset	3,100

The following transactions took place during the year ended 31st March 2019:

	Cost/(Proceeds)
	£
28th May 2018 Sold all the equipment from the special rate pool	(24,800)
7th June 2018 Purchased a grey car	14,400
1st August 2018 Sold the short-life asset	(460)
15th August 2018 Purchased equipment	6,700

The equipment from the special rate pool sold on 28th May 2018 for £24,800 originally cost £23,112. The grey car purchased on 7th June 2018 is a low emission motor car (CO_2 emission rate of less than 50 grams per kilometre).

Required:

(a) Calculate Tock-Tick Ltd's tax adjusted Trading profit for the AP (year) ended 31st March 2019. Your computation should commence with the profit before taxation figure of £184,220. (19 marks)

(b) Calculate Tock-Tick Ltd's taxable total profits for the AP (year) ended 31st March 2019. (5 marks)

(c) State the effect on Tock-Tick Ltd's taxable total profits for the year ended 31st March 2019 if Tock-Tick Ltd claims the maximum possible group relief that it can receive from a 100%-owned subsidiary company Buzz Ltd, which made a trading loss of £62,400 for its twelve month AP which ended on 31st December 2018.

(4 marks)

(28 marks)

(ACCA updated)

Solution to Question 1: Tock-Tick Limited

(a) Tock-Tick Ltd – Income from trading for the year ended 31st March 2019

	£	£
Profit before taxation		184,220
Depreciation		99,890
Bad debts – general provision		6,200
Gifts to customers – food hampers		720
Gift aid donation		600
Gift to agent of supplier - alcohol		250
Legal fees in connection with the issue of share capital		2,900
Legal fees in connection with the court action		900
Office extension		53,300
Entertaining		2,160
		351,140
Disposal of office building	78,100	
Loan interest received	12,330	
Capital allowances (working)	23,624	114,054
Trading profit		237,086

(1) Gifts to customers are an allowable deduction if they cost less than £50 per recipient per year, are not of food, drink, tobacco, or vouchers for exchangeable goods, and carry a conspicuous advertisement for the company making the gift.

(2) The long service award is deductible in calculating the trading profit.

(3) The gift aid donation is deducted in the corporation tax computation against total profits as a qualifying charitable donation, but is not an allowable trading expense in arriving at income from trading. The other national charity donation is not allowable because it was neither made under company gift aid declaration nor linked to local trade promotion.

(4) The gift to the supplier's agent is above the cost limit of £50 noted in (1), and also a gift of alcohol, and either of these make the cost disallowable for tax purposes.

(5) The legal costs of registering a trademark and of renewing a short-lease (less than 50 years) are allowable.

(6) The replacement of the roof is allowable since it amounts to repair and the whole structure is not being replaced. The office extension is not allowable, being capital in nature.

(7) The costs of counselling services for redundant employees and of seconding an employee to charity are allowable.

(8) Interest payable on a loan used for trading purposes is deductible in calculating the trading profit.

		General pool	Special rate pool	Short-life asset	Allowances
	£	£	£	£	£
WDV brought forward		12,200	20,800	3,100	
Proceeds of disposals (max. cost)			(23,112)	(460)	
			(2,312)	2,640	
Balancing charge (pool exhausted)			2,312		(2,312)
Balancing allowance (SLA disposal)				(2,640)	2,640
Additions qualifying for AIA					
Equipment	6,700				
AIA	(6,700)	0			6,700
Low emission motor car	14,400				
100% FYA	(14,400)	0			14,400
		12,200			
WDA 18%		(2,196)			2,196
WDV carried forward		10,004			
Total allowances CTAP to 31.3.19					£23,624

(1) The sale proceeds for the motor car sold are restricted to original cost.

(2) It is necessary to take a balancing charge on the special rate pool as this cannot go forward with a negative WDV.

(b) Tock-Tick Ltd – Corporation tax computation for the year ended 31st March 2019

	£
Trading profit	237,086
Interest income – non-trade loan relationship	12,330
Net Chargeable gains (276,000 – 197,900 – 75,700)	2,400
	251,816
Qualifying charitable donation – Gift Aid	(600)
Taxable total profit	251,216

(c) Group relief effect

(1) The accounting periods are not coterminous, so the claim in Tock-Tick Ltd's current period for group relief for losses made by Buzz Ltd would be restricted to the lower of £188,412 (£251,216 × 9/12) and £46,800 (£62,400 × 9/12).

(2) Tock-Tick Ltd's taxable total profit would therefore be reduced by £46,800 if that group relief claim were to be made.

(3) As the losses of Buzz Ltd were incurred after 1st April 2017, they may be carried forward into the next accounting period of Buzz Ltd and, if not set against the company's own profits for that period, then surrendered to Tock-Tick Ltd through group relief for carried forward losses.

Questions without answers

Question 2: Zoom plc

Zoom plc is a manufacturer of photographic equipment. The summarised draft profit and loss account of Zoom plc for the year ended 31st March 2019 is as follows:

	£	£
Operating profit (note 1)		813,980
Income from investments		
Bank interest (note 4)	26,820	
Loan interest (note 5)	22,500	
Net receipts from property (note 6)	29,480	
Dividends (note 3)	63,220	
Total other income		142,020
		956,000
Interest payable (note 8)		(46,000)
Profit before taxation		910,000

Note 1 – Operating profit

Depreciation of £48,100 has been deducted in arriving at the operating profit of £813,980.

Note 2 – Plant and machinery

On 1st April 2018 the tax written down values of plant and machinery were as follows:

	£
General pool	19,600
Special rate pool	20,200
Short-life asset (2 years old)	35,511

The following transactions took place during the year ended 31st March 2019:

		Cost/(Proceeds)
		£
15th April 2018	Purchased general equipment	7,100
19th June 2018	Purchased a computer	2,280
29th July 2018	Sold the equipment in the special rate pool	(24,200)
31st July 2018	Purchased motor car CO_2 105g/km (1)	16,600
3rd August 2018	Sold a lorry	(9,800)
22nd December 2018	Purchased motor car CO_2 100g/km (2)	10,800
1st February 2019	Purchased motor car (3)	14,200
28th February 2019	Sold the short-life asset	(8,000)

All the plant and equipment in the special rate pool was sold on 29th July 2018 for £24,200. It had originally cost £21,956. The lorry sold on 3rd August 2018 for £9,800 originally cost £17,200. Motor car (3) purchased on 1st February 2019 is a low emission motor car (CO_2 emission rate of less than 50 grams per kilometre).

Note 3 – Corporation Tax information

Zoom plc made quarterly instalment payments in respect of its corporation tax liability for the year ended 31st March 2019.

Zoom plc has is associated with three other companies in a '51% group'.

For the year ended 31st March 2018, Zoom plc had taxable total profits of £780,000.

Note 4 – Bank interest received

The bank interest was received on 31st March 2019 and there was no accrual brought forward or carried forward. The bank deposits are held for non-trading purposes.

Note 5 – Loan interest receivable

The loan was made for non-trading purposes on 1st July 2018. Loan interest of £15,000 was received on 31st December 2018, and interest of £7,500 was accrued at 31st March 2019.

Note 6 – Income from property

Zoom plc lets out two unfurnished office buildings that are surplus to requirements.

The first office building was let from 1st April 2018 until 31st January 2019 at a rent of £3,200 per month. On 31st January 2019 the tenant left owing two months' rent which Zoom plc was unable to recover. This office building was not re-let until May 2019.

The second office building was not let from 1st April 2018 to 31st July 2018. During this period Zoom plc spent £4,800 on advertising for new tenants, and £5,200 on decorating the office building. On 1st August 2018 the office building was let at an annual rent of £26,400, payable in advance.

Zoom plc insured its two office buildings at a total cost of £3,360 for the year ended 31st December 2018, and £3,720 for the year ended 31st December 2019. The insurance is payable annually in advance.

Note 7 –Interest payable

The interest is in respect of a debenture loan that has been used for trading purposes. Interest of £23,000 was paid on 30th September 2018 and again on 31st March 2019.

Required:

(a) (i) Calculate the amount of capital allowances that Zoom plc can claim for the year ended 31st March 2019. (12 marks)

(ii) Prepare a computation for the year ended 31st March 2019 reconciling Zoom plc's profit before taxation with its taxable total profits. Your reconciliation should commence with the profit before taxation figure of £910,000, clearly identify the tax adjusted trading profit and the amount of profit from land and property, and end with the figure of taxable total profits (TTP). (8 marks)

(b) Explain why Zoom plc was required to make quarterly instalment payments in respect of its corporation tax liability for the year ended 31st March 2019. (3 marks)

(c) Calculate Zoom plc's corporation tax liability for the year ended 31st March 2019, and explain how and when this will have been paid. You should assume the company's taxable profits accrued evenly throughout the year. (3 marks)

(d) Explain how your answer to part (c) above would differ if Zoom plc had no other group companies. (4 marks)

(30 marks)

(ACCA updated)

Question 3: Scuba Limited

Scuba Ltd is a manufacturer of diving equipment. The following information is relevant for the year ended 31st March 2019:

Operating profit

The operating profit is £162,400. The expenses that have been deducted in calculating this figure include the following:

	£
Depreciation and amortisation	45,200
Entertaining customers	7,410
Entertaining employees	2,470
Gifts to customers (diaries costing £25 each displaying Scuba Ltd's name)	1,350
Gifts to customers (food hampers costing £80 each)	1,600

Leasehold property

On 1st July 2018 Scuba Ltd acquired a leasehold office building that is used for business purposes. The company paid a premium of £80,000 for the grant of a twenty-year lease.

Plant and machinery

On 1st April 2018 the tax written down values of plant and machinery were as follows:

	£
General pool	47,200
White car CO_2 190g/km	22,400
Features integral to a building	276,900

The following transactions took place during the year ended 31st March 2018:

		(Cost/Proceeds) £
3rd July 2018	Purchased machinery	7,300
10th July 2018	Purchased a computer	1,400
4th August 2018	Purchased a blue car CO_2 180g/km	10,400
18th November 2018	Purchased machinery	4,800
1st December 2018	Purchased a ventilation system (a feature integral to a building)	10,150
29th December 2018	Purchased computer software	1,100
15th February 2019	Sold a lorry	(12,400)

The blue car purchased on 4th August 2018 for £10,400 is used by the factory manager, and 40% of the mileage is for private journeys. The lorry sold on 15th February 2019 for £12,400 originally cost £19,800.

Income from property

Scuba Ltd lets a retail shop that is surplus to requirements. The shop was let until 31st March 2018 but was then empty from 1st April 2018 to 31st July 2018. During this period Scuba Ltd spent £6,200 on decorating the shop, and £1,700 on advertising for new tenants.

The shop was let from 1st August 2018 to 31st March 2019 at a quarterly rent of £7,200, payable in advance.

Interest received

Interest of £435 was received from HMRC on 31st January 2019 in respect of the overpayment of corporation tax for the year ended 31st March 2017.

Profit on disposal of shares

On 18th April 2018 Scuba Ltd sold 5,000 £1 ordinary shares in Deep Blue Sea plc for £42,400. The shareholding had been purchased on 19th March 2007 for £26,900. The retail prices index (RPI) for March 2007 was 204.4, and for December 2017 it was 278.1.

Other information

Scuba Ltd has no subsidiaries.

Required:

(a) Calculate Scuba Ltd's tax-adjusted trading profit for the year ended 31st March 2019. (21 marks)

(b) Calculate Scuba Ltd's taxable total profits and corporation tax liability for the year ended 31st March 2019. (6 marks)

(c) State the date by which Scuba Ltd must pay its corporation tax liability for the year ended 31st March 2019, and explain the implications for the company if this liability is paid three months late.

(3 marks)

(30 marks)

(ACCA updated)

Question 4: Nugget Limited

Nugget Ltd has owned 60% of the share capital of Diamond Ltd for several years. Both companies are trading companies resident in the UK, but operate in different industries, in different geographical areas.

The following information relates to the ten month AP to 31st January 2019 of Nugget Ltd:

	£
Adjusted trading profit (before capital allowances)	177,000
Bank interest receivable – non-trading	5,000
Capital gains	10,000
Rental income	5,000

The balances brought forward at 1st April 2018 for capital allowances purposes were as follows:

General pool	Special rate pool
£58,887	£18,000

During the above period machinery was sold for £10,000 (original cost £11,000) and new desks were bought for £6,000 on 1st May 2018. A black car with CO_2 emissions of 165g/km was traded in for £10,000 against the cost of a new grey car with CO_2 emissions of 170g/km costing £12,000 on 1st June 2018. The proceeds of the black car were less than the original cost.

Requirement

(a) Compute the maximum capital allowances which Nugget Ltd may claim for the ten month accounting period to 31st January 2019.

(b) Compute Nugget Ltd's corporation tax liability for the ten month accounting period.

Part IV

Taxation of chargeable gains

25 General principles of taxation of chargeable gains

25.1 Persons chargeable to Capital Gains Tax (CGT)

The following classes of **UK-resident** person are liable to tax on their capital gains:

- **Individuals** – who pay Capital Gains Tax;
- **Trustees and personal representatives** – who also pay Capital Gains Tax, but CGT for trusts and estates is only very briefly covered in this book. Except where specifically noted, CGT computation rules for trustees follow the rules for individuals, but each Trust is a legally separate taxpayer.
- **Companies** – which compute their chargeable gains under the same legislation as individuals do (the Taxation of Chargeable Gains Act 1992), but which usually pay corporation tax rather than Capital Gains Tax on the resulting gains (*except that they pay ATED-related CGT on certain properties – see section 25.10*).

From 6th April 2015, non-UK residents are also liable to tax on capital gains arising from disposals of UK residential property (see section 25.10)

25.2 UK Taxation of capital gains – introduction

UK Capital Gains Tax began on 6th April 1965. However, due to subsequent reforms (*generally referred to as the '1982 rebasing' of Capital Gains Tax*), any part of a gain that is identified by CGT rules as having accrued before 1st April 1982 is now exempted from CGT. This date is the same for both individuals and companies. In some circumstances where an asset has been owned by a taxpayer since before April 1982, the asset's market value as at 31st March 1982 is still needed to compute the statutory chargeable gain on disposal of the asset.

Subject to the rebasing reform (*which was presented when it was begun in 1988 as compensation to taxpayers for no inflation relief being included in the CGT system prior to April 1982*), the basic principle of capital gains tax has always been that if value is derived from a capital asset by its owner – for example it is sold, given away, or exchanged for another asset – the excess of the realised value over the relevant (historic) cost of the asset is a 'capital gain' which may be liable to tax.

Although Capital Gains Tax has never raised a significant proportion of the tax take in the UK, the usual justification for the tax is behavioural. If income profits are taxable but capital gains are tax-free (*as was generally the case in the UK before 1965*), taxpayers have an incentive to structure transactions to make profits capital rather than revenue wherever that possibility exists.

Some capital gains are still exempt from tax, either because of the nature of the asset, or because of the circumstances of the disposal. Some other capital gains (*the rules as to which gains differ for individuals and companies*) are in principle taxable ('chargeable'), but not immediately so. The gain's effective date for Capital Gains Tax purposes may be deferred in various ways, such as by being treated as a cost reduction on the same asset, or another asset, in the hands of either the same or another taxpayer. These are classed as 'deferral reliefs' (*though each one has a specific name as well*). Deferral reliefs lead (in theory) to an equivalent gain arising later (*called 'crystallisation of the deferred gain'*), rather than on the original disposal.

Sometimes however, gains are legally deferred and then later events can lead to the deferred gain escaping tax altogether. For example, a business asset may be gifted with the benefit of gift holdover relief (see Chapter 32). But if the recipient of the gift dies still owning the asset, the deferred gain is never taxed.

Each chargeable (non-exempt) capital asset disposed of in a tax period (*tax year for individuals, Corporation Tax Accounting Period for companies*) generates a separate capital gain or capital loss for the same taxpayer.

To the extent that a realised capital gain of a tax year (*or of a Corporation Tax Accounting Period, for a corporate taxpayer*) is neither exempted nor deferred, it is a 'chargeable gain' for that taxpayer and must be reported under self-assessment.

Capital losses on chargeable assets are 'allowable capital losses' if a gain in the same circumstances would have been a chargeable gain.

For both personal taxpayers and companies, all separate chargeable gains of a tax year/corporation tax accounting period are added together, and allowable capital losses of the same tax year/CTAP are deducted from the total. The result is the 'net chargeable gains' of the taxpayer for that tax year or CTAP.

Net chargeable gains of an individual are liable to Capital Gains Tax, which is separate from Income Tax. Net chargeable gains of a company are reported as a separate category of profits in the computation of taxable total profits. Corporation Tax is then payable on them at the company's usual Corporation Tax rate.

All legislation on the detailed computation of chargeable gains for both individuals/trustees and corporate bodies is found in the Taxation of Chargeable Gains Act 1992, as amended.

It is important to recognise that currently the rules for computing chargeable gains of individuals differ in several ways from the rules for computing chargeable gains of companies – even though the rules for computing chargeable gains or allowable losses are all found in the same Act (as amended).

The biggest difference, in terms of the tax charge, is that individuals no longer get any kind of 'indexation allowance' added to the asset cost to reflect monetary inflation, even if they have owned the asset for a long time. Companies do still get inflation relief (for post-1982 ownership), in the form of the indexation allowance.

25.3 Indexation allowance

CGT indexation allowance (IA) was first introduced in 1982 and was made more generous in 1985. Its purpose was to reflect rising prices, which were causing nominal gains to be unfairly taxed rather than only real gains. For individuals, Indexation Allowance operated fully only until 1998, but for corporate taxpayers it is available for inflationary gains up to December 2017. It can by now add over 100% to the allowable cost of an asset when computing a chargeable gain.

However, Indexation Allowance cannot be claimed in full by a company if it exceeds the unindexed gain on the asset. So, IA (currently) can neither create nor increase an allowable capital loss.

When assets have been owned for a long time, and are worth more than their original cost, IA can make a significant difference to the amount of chargeable gain that is liable to tax. The Government has stated as its current policy that IA caused excessive complexity for individual taxpayers. It argues that, on average, the lower rates of CGT for individuals (*when compared to income tax rates*), compensate in a simple way for the absence of any inflation relief for individuals.

25.4 Brief history of CGT changes

From 1965 to 1988, capital gains were taxed at a flat rate of 30% for both individuals and companies. In April 1988 the tax rates on chargeable gains were aligned with tax rates on income for both individuals and companies.

From 1998 to 2008, individuals could no longer accrue new indexation allowance (*though Indexation Allowance that had accrued before April 1998 was still deductible in a disposal gain calculation*). A new Capital Gains Tax 'taper relief' reduced the amount of each personal chargeable gain by a set fraction, depending on the duration of ownership. Taper relief was made extremely generous if the asset was a 'business asset'. By 2007/08 the maximum business asset taper was 75% after 2 years of asset ownership, which reduced the real (or equivalent) rate of CGT on 'business' gains from the nominal 40% (the higher rate of income tax) to an effective 10%. This low rate of tax on business gains was widely believed to stimulate enterprise in small business start-ups.

Both Capital Gains Tax taper relief and the 'frozen' (pre-1998) indexation allowance were abolished for individuals (*but not for companies – see below*) from tax year 2008/09. To compensate, the personal CGT rate was reduced to 18% (for gains that can be matched against an individual's income tax basic rate band) and 28% on the balance of gains. That is, the rates of CGT depend on the income tax rates that would apply if the gains were taxed as the top slice of income (*as explained in 25.6 below*). The personal CGT rates were further reduced to 10% and 20% from 6th April 2016, although the earlier rates continue to apply to residential property that does not qualify for principal private residence relief, and to the annual tax for enveloped dwellings (see 25.10).

Many other complications (*mainly relics of '1982 rebasing' – see 25.2 above*) were removed from the personal Capital Gains Tax legal system in 2008/09.

However, some of the more technical 'rebasing' rules had to be kept for companies, because they still benefit from indexation allowance for UK inflation between 31st March 1982 and 31st December 2017. Apart from some mention in Chapter 30 on rules for shares and securities, this book ignores the technicalities on pre-1982 assets of companies.

2008/09 thus saw a major simplification of Capital Gains Tax for individual taxpayers, but at the expense of removing the taper relief on personal assets, notably the (exceptionally favourable) taper relief for shareholdings in private companies, and for goodwill of unincorporated businesses. Entrepreneur's relief was a somewhat last-minute response to critics of this reform.

25.5 Entrepreneurs' relief for certain business capital gains

To placate owners of private equity firms and small business owners, who had been expecting business asset taper relief to continue, the Government introduced a new CGT relief called 'entrepreneurs' relief' (ER) from 2008/09, which imposes a CGT rate of only 10% for gains on qualifying businesses and shareholdings.

ER was partly modelled on an earlier CGT relief that existed before 1998, called 'retirement relief'. ER does not cover all the types of disposal which up to 2007/08 obtained business asset taper relief. For the types of disposals which currently qualify for ER, see 31.7. ER is not available to corporate taxpayers.

25.6 2018/19 rates of Capital Gains Tax for individuals

In 2018/19, net personal capital gains, less allowable losses, are taxed:

	2018/19
On gains on which entrepreneurs' relief (ER) is claimed (and accepted by HMRC);	10%
Main rate on non-ER gains which can be matched against any remaining part of the individual's income tax basic rate band that remains after allocating the basic rate band first to taxable income, and then to ER gains	10%
Rates for individuals on residential property not eligible for private residence relief, on non-ER gains which can be matched against any remaining part of the individual's income tax basic rate band that remains after allocating the basic rate band first to taxable income, and then to Entrepreneurs' Relief gains	18%
Main rate on the balance of net chargeable gains.	20%
Rates for individuals on residential property not eligible for private residence relief on the balance of net chargeable gains	28%

The basic rate band limit for this purpose includes any extension for the gross value of Gift Aid donations or personal pension contributions paid in the year.

The Entrepreneurs' Relief rate of 10% must be claimed by the taxpayer, who must specify the relevant gains. This is done either on the self-assessment tax return or by a later amendment to that return. The usual time limit for a claim by amendment of a return is one year after the self-assessment submission deadline for the tax year (so for gains of tax year 2018/19 the time limit for claiming Entrepreneurs' Relief is 31st January 2021).

25.7 The CGT annual exempt amount for individuals

Every UK-resident individual (except those who are non-domiciled and claiming to be taxed on remittance basis) is entitled to a personal Capital Gains Tax annual exemption, officially now called the 'annual exempt amount' (AEA). Only net chargeable gains of each tax year more than the AEA are liable to CGT. The AEA for tax year 2018/19 is £11,700 (2017/18: £11,300).

25.8 Allocation of losses, Annual Exempt Amount and basic rate tax band to Entrepreneurs' Relief and non-ER gains

As ER gains are taxable at only 10%, it is necessary to have rules for priority of allocating allowable capital losses, the AEA, and any remaining basic rate band to ER and non-ER gains if the taxpayer has both types of gains. The current rules for allocating losses, the AEA and the basic rate income band are as follows:

(i) Both the annual exemption and any capital losses of the same year are set first against non-ER gains, if any, before Entrepreneurs' Relief gains.

(ii) Capital losses brought forward are also set first against the non-ER gains of a tax year, which is to the taxpayer's advantage. (*Also note that capital losses brought forward are not offset if they would offset gains already covered by the annual exemption.*)

(iii) Once non-ER gains have all been covered by losses/AEA, any balance of losses/AEA is set against ER gains of the current tax year.

(iv) Where the taxpayer has some remaining income tax basic rate band and has both ER and non-ER gains that are taxable, taxable ER gains are allocated against the remaining BR band before the non-ER gains. Of course, the CGT rate on ER gains is 10%, whether they are identified with the basic rate income band or not. But the allocation order has the effect of maximising the non-ER gains falling into CGT at the 20% and 28% rates.

(v) However, any remaining income tax basic rate band, after any ER gains, may be set off against other gains in an order chosen by the taxpayer.

The above rules give rise to annual tax planning activity for affected individuals around January to March, as the end of the tax year approaches. The question is whether to make asset disposals that will generate respectively capital losses and chargeable gains in this tax year or the next one, to benefit as much as possible from the annual exemption and from offsetting any brought-forward or foreseeable future capital losses against gains taxable at 20% or 28% rather than 10%. This is only practicable if the taxpayer has a choice over disposal timings.

25.9 Main post-1998 changes to tax on chargeable gains for companies

Corporation tax reforms from the 1990s onwards changed the tax framework for measuring company profits, moving the recognition rules much closer to Financial Reporting Standards. In particular the company loan relationships regime (1996-9) and the company intangible assets regime (2002) removed many categories of both financial and intangible assets from the scope of TCGA for companies. (*For corporation tax generally, see Part III.*)

The result of those changes is that the following types of asset are now outside the scope of TCGA for corporate taxpayers but are chargeable assets for personal taxpayers – unless specifically exempted (*eg UK gilts and some types of debt asset are specifically exempted by TCGA*).

- Intangible assets such as licences, copyrights and knowhow;
- Trade goodwill purchased or sold for valuable consideration;
- Debts of any kind - including foreign currency deposits, commercial loans, company bonds and debentures, and cash-settled financial instruments;
- Government stocks, such as gilts and Treasury Bonds – for individuals (and trustees), these are a CGT-exempt asset; For companies they create 'loan relationships' and the results are included in taxable total profits

25.10 Residential property

There are some important aspects to consider regarding disposals of residential property: Principal Private Residence; ATED-related CGT; and Non-UK-residents owning UK residential properties.

Principal Private Residence

A person's main home, their 'Principal Private Residence', is exempt from Capital Gains Tax – see section 29.5.

ATED-related CGT

'ATED' is the 'Annual Tax on Enveloped Dwellings', charged where a 'non-natural person' such as a company or trust owns residential property worth over £500,000 (unchanged from 2018/19):

ANNUAL CHARGE (£):

Property value	2013/14	2014/15	2015/16	2016/17	2017/18	2018/19
£20m+	140,000	143,750	218,200	218,200	220,350	226,950
£10m - £20m	70,000	71,850	109,050	109,050	110,100	113,400
£5m - £10m	35,000	35,900	54,450	54,450	54,950	56,550
£2m - £5m	15,000	15,400	23,350	23,350	23,550	24,250
£1m - £2m	n/a	n/a	7,000	7,000	7,050	7,250
£500k - £1m	n/a	n/a	n/a	3,500	3,500	3,600

This tax is an anti-avoidance measure whose objective is to tax property-holding structures used by wealthy individuals (*especially non-domiciled UK residents*) to own their UK residences through companies.

As such, a number of exemptions apply, allowing owners of residential properties to make a claim to be allowed not to pay ATED, such as where the property isn't at any time occupied by the owner or somebody connected with the owner and is:

- rented out on a commercial basis; or
- acquired as part of a property trading or property development business; or
- residential property acquired by a bank in the course of lending; or
- where the property is owned by a provider of social housing.

Entities liable to ATED also must pay ATED-related Capital Gains Tax, at a rate of 28%, on any chargeable gains arising on the disposal of the property. Any such gain is calculated in the usual way, except that where the entity owned the property before 1st April 2012, its market value at 1st April 2012 is used in place of its cost.

Non-UK-residents owning UK residential properties

Capital gains arising after 6th April 2015 on the disposal of UK residential property by a non-UK-resident are subject to Capital Gains Tax, calculated on the same basis as for UK residents.

Where the non-UK-resident owned the property before 6th April 2015, its market value at 6th April 2015 is usually used instead of its original cost when calculating the amount of the capital gain. However, the taxpayer can elect for the original cost to be used instead, with the gain time-apportioned between the pre-6th-April-2015 and post-5th-April-2015 periods. The taxpayer might wish to do that to avoid excessive gains being calculated where there has been a fall in the property's value between acquisition and 6th April 2015.

25.11 Summary of TCGA rules on Chargeable Assets

Students who are only studying the taxation of companies should read the following information about assets liable to CGT in the light of the important point noted at 25.9 that debts and foreign currency ('loan relationships'), and corporate intangible assets (*except leases of land*), have been excluded from the scope of TCGA by reforms to corporation tax during 1996-2002.

Under Sections 21 and 22 of TCGA, 'all forms of property are assets for the purposes of capital gains tax, whether situated in the UK or not', including:

(a) options, debts, and incorporeal property in general;

(b) currency other than sterling;

(c) any form of property created by the person disposing of it, or coming to be owned without being acquired;

(d) capital sums derived from assets.

25.12 Property

For individuals this term includes anything capable of being owned, such as freehold and leasehold land, shares and securities, and other tangible assets and intangible assets such as purchased and internally-generated goodwill. It also includes some legal claims that have a monetary value.

25.13 Options

Where a person (the grantor) grants an option over a chargeable asset to another person (the grantee) then this is a part-disposal by the first person of a chargeable asset, or alternatively the derivation of a capital sum from an asset. If the option is later exercised, any consideration received is added to any value given for the option, to form a single disposal transaction. If the option is allowed to expire (without being exercised), then any capital sum received for the grant of the option is treated as a taxable capital receipt from the asset.

When some types of option are abandoned, there is no disposal of an asset by the grantee, so that he or she cannot establish a capital loss. However, if the option is over equity shares, or is an exchange-traded option (*not held as part of a trading activity*), TCGA does allow a capital loss in certain circumstances.

For companies, any transactions in options or other derivatives (eg swaps) relating to underlying debt arrangements are taxed as loan relationships. However, where a company is the grantor or grantee of an equity share option, that asset still falls under TCGA, as it does for individuals.

25.14 Debts

The original CGT rules on debts now only apply to individuals (*a term which in this part of the book includes non-corporate trustees, unless otherwise stated*).

Since 1999 debts and loan relationships are not chargeable assets for companies. UK Government securities (*gilts, such as Treasury Stock*) that are owned by individuals or trustees are specifically exempted from CGT. Corporate bonds are also exempt from CGT if they are 'qualifying corporate bonds', which most are.

An ordinary debt is not a chargeable asset in the hands of the original creditor, his or her personal representative, or legatee. This means that a default on the debt is not a capital loss.

However, an individual who acquires an existing debt for value from another person (by legal assignment), obtains a chargeable asset. If it is later collected at a higher value than the cost given, a chargeable gain arises. If it is redeemed at a lower value, a capital loss may be claimed (*note that debt assignments usually involve a discount on face value*). Capital treatment does not apply if the individual trades in debts, e.g. a commercial debt factor.

Provided HMRC accept the commercial nature of the original loan, a loan made by an individual to a UK resident trader, or a loan guarantee that is called in, if proved irrecoverable, can be claimed by an individual as an allowable capital loss.

25.15 Currency

Foreign currency (*i.e. any currency other than sterling*) is capable of being a chargeable asset for an individual, if it was acquired for investment rather than trade purposes. However, there is a useful exemption for any gain realised on a holding of foreign currency 'acquired by an individual for personal use'. This covers currency acquired (typically) for use while travelling, even if any later surplus is reconverted to sterling realising a gain (*or a non-allowable loss*) due to exchange rate fluctuations.

25.16 Intangible assets

For individuals this term includes such assets as goodwill, copyright, trademarks or know-how as chargeable assets. For the corporation tax treatment of intangible assets see Chapter 19. Patents are not chargeable assets for individuals, since any profit over historic cost realised on a patent disposal is taxed as income under ITTOIA 2005.

For an individual, business 'know-how' is treated as a chargeable asset when it is disposed of along with any part of a trade, but not if disposed of alone, when it gives rise to a trading receipt under ITTOIA 2005.

25.17 Goodwill

'Goodwill' for CGT means any excess value of a business that is transferred as a going concern, which is not attributable to separable assets of the business. Both purchased goodwill and self-created business goodwill are chargeable assets for individuals. Self-created goodwill has a nil cost in the hands of the creator but is still a chargeable asset that generates a chargeable gain when disposed of for value with the rest of the business. The allowable cost of purchased goodwill for an individual trader is subject to further rules if acquired by a transaction with a connected person, on which, see 26.4.

For companies, goodwill acquired or created since 1st April 2002 is not a chargeable asset, as the corporate intangible assets regime takes priority. Goodwill acquired for value before 1st April 2002 is still a chargeable asset, until the company disposes of the relevant trade and its associated assets.

25.18 Capital sums

Capital receipts are defined by TCGA to include:

(a) Any capital sum received by way of compensation for damage or injury to assets, or for the loss, destruction or dissipation of assets, or for any depreciation of an asset;

(b) Capital sums received under a policy of insurance of the risks of any kind of damage or injury to, or the loss or depreciation of assets;

(c) Capital sums received in return for forfeiture or surrender of rights, or for refraining from exercising rights;

(d) Capital sums received as consideration for use or exploitation of assets.

When a person derives any capital sum from an asset without disposing of the asset itself, this is treated as a part-disposal of the chargeable asset. If any part of the amount received is used to restore or replace the original asset, then special reliefs apply. If the amount received is 'small', the taxpayer can elect to deduct the receipt from the cost of the asset instead of self-assessing a capital gain. (*See further, Chapter 29.*)

25.19 Non-chargeable assets and exemptions

The following assets are either exempt assets, or chargeable assets on whose disposal there is no chargeable gain or allowable loss because of specific circumstances.

(a) **Private motor vehicles**. This exemption includes private cars and vintage cars purchased for investment. It is however hardly necessary to note here that the downside of a gain not being taxable is that any loss incurred is not allowable, and in practice few private motor cars go up in value.

(b) **Savings certificates (irrelevant to companies).** All non-marketable securities are included under this heading, such as National Savings Certificates, and Defence Bonds.

(c) **Gambling winnings** - which covers football pools, lotteries, premium bonds and bingo prizes.

(d) **Decorations for valour (e.g. medals)** are exempt assets if disposed of by the individual to whom they were awarded, or by their heir or legatee. If purchased by anyone else, they become chargeable investment assets (but may still be low-value chattels – on which see Chapter 29).

(e) **Personal foreign currency** as noted at 25.15, foreign currency acquired by an individual for personal use, but subsequently changed back into sterling, is an exempt asset.

(f) **Compensation** No chargeable gain arises from compensation or damages obtained for any physical wrong or injury suffered by a person.

(g) **Life assurance and deferred annuities.** No chargeable gain arises on the disposal of any rights under a life assurance policy or deferred annuity, providing the disposal is made by the original owner. The acquisition of such rights from an original owner gives the next acquirer a chargeable asset (*unless acquired as part of a trade*).

(h) **British government securities (gilts) and 'qualifying corporate bonds' (QCBs)** are exempt from CGT when held by individuals. A QCB, to give a non-technical definition which will suffice for this book, is a bond or loan security issued by a company which is structured as a normal debt and is repayable in sterling.
(*Government securities, gilts, and QCBs held by corporate taxpayers count as corporate loan relationships. That means they fall outside CGT rules, but any net gains are liable to tax / net losses are deductible - as loan relationship surpluses or deficits. See Part III, Corporation Tax.*)

(i) **Wasting chattels**, i.e. Tangible movable property with a useful life of less than 50 years, not used for trade purposes. (See Chapter 29.)

(j) **Chattels bought and/or sold for less than £6,000**. (See Chapter 29)

(k) **Assets gifted to a recognised charity**.

(l) **Disposals conditionally exempted from IHT** e.g. artworks donated to public collections.

(m) The **principal private residence** of an individual, provided it has been occupied by them as such, or has been in deemed occupancy, throughout the period of ownership since 31st March 1982 or since acquisition if shorter. (See 29.5)

25.20 Exempt persons

The following persons are exempted by TCGA 1992 from CGT on their capital gains (*which typically arise on investments held in land or shares*):

(a) Pension funds approved by HMRC;

(b) Registered charities (*providing the gains are used for charitable purposes*);

(c) Registered friendly societies;

(d) Local authorities;

(e) Scientific research associations;

(f) Community amateur sports clubs.

25.21 Administration – CGT self-assessment

Companies report their chargeable gains on the CT600 company tax return and payment is made as part of the normal corporation tax payment system.

For individuals, Additional Sheet SA108 is a supplement to the usual self-assessment tax return, provided for individuals to notify HMRC of all chargeable gains and allowable losses of a tax year, to claim entrepreneur's relief, and to make other necessary CGT disclosures or notify exemptions and reliefs claimed. (*Sheet SA108: this may be viewed online at www.hmrc.gov.uk*)

There are also several CGT Help sheets available online (*or in hard copy by request from HMRC*), which personal taxpayers can use to work out their chargeable gains or check the rules about reliefs and exemptions.

Appeals against HMRC decisions on CGT are made in the same way as for taxes on income/profits of individuals. Disputes which end up in court now pass through the Tax Tribunal system (see 3.11).

If no self-assessment return has been issued, but the taxpayer made a gain in a tax year that gives rise to a CGT liability, it is the taxpayer's responsibility to notify the tax authorities of the gain by 31st October following the tax year.

25.22 Payment of CGT for individuals

The system of income tax payments was described in Chapter 2. An individual's CGT for a tax year is due by a single payment due on the same day as the final income tax payment for the tax year (if any), and also the following tax year's first payment on account (if any). The due dates for individuals are thus:

CGT for 2018/19 - 31st January 2020
CGT for 2017/18 - 31st January 2019

It is possible to apply to pay CGT by instalments if the disposal consideration is receivable over a period exceeding 18 months, and payment of capital gains tax in one sum would cause undue hardship.

Payment of tax by ten equal instalments is also available in respect of CGT due on any gifts not eligible for gift holdover relief (*see Chapter 32 for eligible gifts*).

Interest is charged on CGT instalments at the usual rate (*annual rate 3.00% at time of writing*).

Conventional layout for a capital gain/ loss computation (*each asset being dealt with separately*) for (I) an individual; (II) a company:

I. Chargeable disposals by individuals

[give details of asset and taxpayer number]	**Tax year 2018/19**	
	£	£
Gross proceeds of disposal (market value if non-arm's-length)		–
Less: Incidental costs of disposal		–
= Net proceeds of disposal		–
LESS Allowable deductions–		
Initial cost of asset	–	
Incidental acquisition expenses	–	
Enhancement expenditure (i)	–	
Enhancement expenditure (ii), *etc.*	–	
		–
= Capital gain / (loss)		– / (–)

Enhancement expenditure does not include maintenance expenses such as normal running repairs to a building. It does cover capital improvement expenditure.

Expenditure claimed as enhancing a capital asset must still be reflected in the condition of the asset at the date of the disposal.

After computing each capital gain as above, one must then consider whether:

- Any CGT deferral relief (automatic or optional) is available. If so, the gain still has to be computed and reported this tax year, but it will not be chargeable until a later occasion (see Chapters 31 -32);
- The gain qualifies for entrepreneurs' relief (*in which case it needs to be initially kept separate from non-ER gains when totalling net chargeable gains for the year, so that allowable losses, the AEA, and any basic rate income tax band can be correctly allocated using the rule given at 25.8*).

With due notification of any relevant claims as above, all chargeable gains and losses should be reported on the self-assessment tax return. 'Net chargeable gains' describes the sum of all chargeable gains of an individual for the tax year, less allowable capital losses.

Sheet SA108 Help Sheet instructs the taxpayer to append to the main return a separate computation of every individual gain or loss on all chargeable disposals made in the tax year, and to enter into the first boxes on sheet SA108 the total chargeable gains, and total allowable losses, for the tax year. There is then a separate box to enter the amount (*from within the total gains already declared*) of gains on which entrepreneur's relief is being claimed in this tax year.

II. Chargeable disposals by incorporated entities
[Name of asset] [Name of company]
– Capital Gain/(loss) for CTAP period ended xx/xx/201x

	£	£
Proceeds of disposal (use market value if non-arm's-length)		–
Less: Incidental costs of disposal		–
= Net proceeds of disposal		–
LESS: Allowable deductions:		
Initial cost of asset plus incidental purchase expenses	–	
Enhancement expenditure (i)	–	
Enhancement expenditure (ii), *etc.*	–	
		–
= Unindexed gain (or loss)		–/(–)
LESS: Indexation allowance		
– On initial cost plus purchase expenses	–	
– On enhancement expenditure (i),	–	
(ii) *etc*	–	
(note: limit IA to maximum of unindexed gain; no IA if loss)		–
= Chargeable gain / (allowable loss)		–/(–)

Like individuals, companies must provide a separate supporting computation of the chargeable gain or allowable loss arising on each separate chargeable disposal in the return period.
All the chargeable gains of a company are combined for each accounting period, and any allowable losses deducted, and the net total is shown as a separate category of the company's profits on the main CT self-assessment return (CT600).

There are further boxes on CT600 to enter gains set against capital losses brought forward, and gains covered by a claim for rollover relief (see 31.5-6)

25.23 Retail Prices Index – used for indexation allowance

The RPI figure is published monthly by the Office for National Statistics.

	Jan	Feb	Mar	Apr	May	Jun	Jul	Aug	Sep	Oct	Nov	Dec
1982	78.73	78.76	79.44	81.04	81.62	81.85	81.88	81.90	81.85	82.26	82.66	82.51
1983	82.61	82.97	83.12	84.28	84.64	84.84	85.30	85.68	86.06	86.36	86.67	86.89
1984	86.84	87.20	87.48	88.64	88.97	89.20	89.10	89.94	90.11	90.67	90.95	90.87
1985	91.20	91.94	92.80	94.78	95.21	95.41	95.23	95.49	95.44	95.59	95.92	96.05
1986	96.25	96.60	96.73	97.67	97.85	97.79	97.52	97.82	98.30	98.45	99.29	99.62
1987	100.0	100.4	100.6	101.8	101.9	101.9	101.8	102.1	102.4	102.9	103.4	103.3
1988	103.3	103.7	104.1	105.8	106.2	106.6	106.7	107.9	108.4	109.5	110.0	110.3
1989	111.0	111.8	112.3	114.3	115.0	115.4	115.5	115.8	116.6	117.5	118.5	118.8
1990	119.5	120.2	121.4	125.1	126.2	126.7	126.8	128.1	129.3	130.3	130.0	129.9
1991	130.2	130.9	131.4	133.1	133.5	134.1	133.8	134.1	134.6	135.1	135.6	135.7
1992	135.6	136.3	136.7	138.8	139.3	139.3	138.8	138.9	139.4	139.9	139.7	139.2
1993	137.9	138.8	139.3	140.6	141.1	141.0	140.7	141.3	141.9	141.8	141.6	141.9
1994	141.3	142.1	142.5	144.2	144.7	144.7	144.0	144.7	145.0	145.2	145.3	146.0
1995	146.0	146.9	147.5	149.0	149.6	149.8	149.1	149.9	150.6	149.8	149.8	150.7
1996	150.2	150.9	151.5	152.6	152.9	153.0	152.4	153.1	153.8	153.8	153.9	154.4
1997	154.4	155.0	155.4	156.3	156.9	157.5	157.5	158.5	159.3	159.5	159.6	160.0
1998	159.5	160.3	160.8	162.6	163.5	163.4	163.0	163.7	164.4	164.5	164.4	164.4
1999	163.4	163.7	164.1	165.2	165.6	165.6	165.1	165.5	166.2	166.5	166.7	167.3
2000	166.6	167.5	168.4	170.1	170.7	171.1	170.5	170.5	171.7	171.6	172.1	172.2
2001	171.1	172.0	172.2	173.1	174.2	174.4	173.3	174.0	174.6	174.3	173.6	173.4
2002	173.3	173.8	174.5	175.7	176.2	176.2	175.9	176.4	177.6	177.9	178.2	178.5
2003	178.4	179.3	179.9	181.2	181.5	181.3	181.3	181.6	182.5	182.6	182.7	183.5
2004	183.1	183.8	184.6	185.7	186.5	186.8	186.8	187.4	188.1	188.6	189.0	189.9
2005	188.9	189.6	190.5	191.6	192.0	192.2	192.2	192.6	193.1	193.3	193.6	194.1
2006	193.4	194.2	195.0	196.5	197.7	198.5	198.5	199.2	200.1	200.4	201.1	202.7
2007	201.6	203.1	204.4	205.4	206.2	207.3	206.1	207.3	208.0	208.9	209.7	210.9
2008	209.8	211.4	212.1	214.0	215.1	216.8	216.5	217.2	218.4	217.7	216.0	212.9
2009	210.1	211.4	211.3	211.5	212.8	213.4	213.4	214.4	215.3	216.0	216.6	218.0
2010	217.9	219.2	220.7	222.8	223.6	224.1	223.6	224.5	225.3	225.8	226.8	228.4
2011	229.0	231.3	232.5	234.4	235.2	235.2	234.7	236.1	237.9	238.0	238.5	239.4
2012	238.0	239.9	240.8	242.5	242.4	241.8	242.1	243.0	244.2	245.6	245.6	246.8
2013	245.8	247.6	248.7	249.5	250.0	249.7	249.7	251.0	251.9	251.9	252.1	253.4
2014	252.6	254.2	254.8	255.7	255.9	256.3	256.0	257.0	257.6	257.7	257.1	257.5
2015	255.4	256.7	257.1	258.0	258.5	258.9	258.6	259.8	259.6	259.5	259.8	260.6
2016	258.8	260.0	261.1	261.4	262.1	263.1	263.4	264.4	264.9	264.8	265.5	267.1
2017	265.5	268.4	269.3	270.6	271.7	272.3	272.9	274.7	275.1	275.3	275.8	278.1

26 The basic rules of computation

26.1 Introduction

This chapter is concerned with the basic rules of computation used in the taxation of capital or chargeable gains for both individuals and companies. In reading the various worked examples, it may also be found helpful to refer back to the standard computational layouts given at the end of Chapter 25.

26.2 Date of disposal

A disposal occurs for CGT on the date when the legal contract of disposal becomes unconditional. In the case of land and buildings, the disposal for CGT occurs on the unconditional contract date, and not on the (usually later) date when the full transfer of title is made (the completion date).

In the case of gifts, a disposal occurs on the effective date of transfer of ownership. If a gift is made by legal deed, the disposal date is the deed's execution date.

The date of disposal is important to determine in which tax year or CTAP a disposal occurs. For companies, it is also relevant to the indexation allowance.

26.3 Consideration/proceeds/deemed proceeds (market value)

Tax accountants generally speak of the 'proceeds' of a disposal as the starting point for a CGT computation, However, TCGA 1992 actually refers to the 'total consideration'. In the case of a market sale to an unconnected buyer, the total consideration is the gross sale price obtained, before allowing for selling expenses such as agents' fees, advertising etc.

If there is no actual market sale to determine the value obtained by the person making the disposal, then the 'consideration' (value obtained by the disposer) is assumed ('deemed') to be the current market value of the asset.

This happens in the following situations:

a) a disposal by gift;

b) a disposal by part-gift (i.e. a sale at under-value);

c) any other case where the transaction is 'not at arm's length'.

26.4 Connected persons and non-arm's length transactions

The term 'not at arm's length' is defined by TCGA to include any disposal between 'connected persons'.

Connected persons for an individual are his/her parents, children, siblings, grandparents, grandchildren, together with the parents, children, siblings, grandparents and grandchildren of his/her spouse or civil partner.

Connected persons also include business partners (in a commercial partnership) and fellow-shareholders in a close company.

Note that the definition of 'connected persons' in TCGA **excludes** spouses, civil partners, and companies in the same CGs group (see Chapter 31 for CGs groups). This is because in those three cases, asset disposals are by law deemed to occur not at market value but for deemed consideration giving a 'no-gain-no-loss' result.

Other chargeable disposals may also, on the facts, be 'not at arm's length'. This could cover family or personal relationships not defined by TCGA as 'connected persons', for example uncle and nephew.

26.5 Meaning of market value

Market value in the context of deemed proceeds for CGT, means the price which the asset in question might reasonably be expected to fetch in an unforced sale on the open market between a willing buyer and a willing seller.

For shares, the market value is determined as:

'(a) on any day the Stock Exchange is open, the lower of the two prices shown in the Stock Exchange Daily Official List for that day as the closing price for the shares, securities or strips on that day plus one-half of the difference between those two figures, and

(b) on any day the Stock Exchange is closed, that value on the latest previous day on which it was open.'

('The Market Value of Shares, Securities and Strips Regulations 2015')
This replaces the previous 'quarter-up' method.

There is a special department of HMRC called the Valuation Office Agency, which reviews, and if necessary challenge, and negotiate with taxpayers, the reasonableness of market values put forward for tax purposes. See Chapter 28 for specific statutory rules about the 'market value' of quoted shares for CGT purposes on any given day.

Whenever the law substitutes market value for the actual disposal proceeds for CGT purposes, then the person who acquires that asset is treated for all CGT purposes as acquiring the asset for a cost of (the same) market value.

It follows that for transactions between connected persons, the taxpayer submitting the disposal CGT computation knows that any market value he/she suggests will be subject to review by the HMRC Valuation Office Agency.

If an agreed figure cannot be reached for deemed proceeds / market value, the taxpayer can take the matter to the Tax Tribunal.

26.6 Allowable deductions from consideration

The allowable deductions set out in TCGA are:

a) The cost of acquisition, including incidental expenses (See 26.7);
b) Any enhancement expenditure, but not repairs or maintenance;
c) Expenditure incurred in establishing or protecting the title to an asset;
d) Incidental costs of disposal (see 26.7);
e) The indexation allowance, only for corporate taxpayers (see 26.10).

26.7 Incidental expenses

Incidental expenses include: fees, commission, or professional charges, such as legal, accountancy or valuation advice: costs of transfer and conveyance including stamp duty land tax: advertising to find a buyer or seller.

The following items of expenditure are specifically disallowed:

a) Costs of repair and maintenance;
b) Costs of insurance against damage, injury or loss of an asset;
c) Any expenditure allowed as a deduction in computing trading income;
d) Any expenditure recouped from the Crown or a public or local authority.

26.8 Part-disposals

On a part-disposal of an asset (other than a holding of shares), the attributable acquisition cost of the part disposed of is determined by the following statutory formula:

$$\text{Attributable cost} = \text{Cost of acquisition} \times \frac{A}{A+B}, \text{ where}$$

A is the proceeds for the part sold, excluding any expenses of sale, and

B is the market value of the part retained.

26.9 The basic computation for individuals

This section illustrates a basic computation for an individual.

Example 1: disposal not qualifying for Entrepreneurs' Relief:

Joshua purchased a house that was not his main residence, in January 1988 for £50,000. He incurred legal fees and survey fees of £500 on the acquisition of this property. In September 1992 Joshua added an extension to the property at a cost of £15,000. He sold the house on 1st May 2018 for £350,000, incurring legal fees and selling costs amounting to £2,000. Joshua has no other disposals for the tax year 2018/19. Joshua's taxable income for 2018/19 is £30,000, and he made net contributions of £1,600 to a personal pension scheme in the tax year.

Compute the chargeable gain and capital gains tax payable on the disposal.

Suggested solution

	£	£
Proceeds from sale		350,000
Incidental costs of disposal		(2,000)
Other allowable deductions:		
Initial cost	50,000	
Costs of acquisition	500	
Enhancement expenditure, September 1992	15,000	
		(65,500)
Chargeable gain		282,500
Less Annual Exempt Amount 2018/19		(11,700)
Gain subject to capital gains tax		270,800
		£
Capital gains tax @ 18% of £6,500 (see working)		1,170
Capital gains tax @ 28% of £264,300		74,004
Total CGT payable by Joshua		75,174

Working to support CGT rates above:	£
Income tax basic rate band 2018/19	34,500
Extension to basic rate band for Joshua (See Part 2 for income tax rules):	
Grossed up personal pension contributions £1,600 × 100/80	2,000
= Joshua's basic rate income tax band	36,500
Less Taxable income	(30,000)
= Basic rate band available for taxation of gains at 18%	£6,500

Residential property rates of 18% and 28% apply to this house.

Example 2: Disposal qualifying for Entrepreneurs' Relief:

Renitha purchased a retail shop selling electrical goods in October 1986 for £85,000. She incurred acquisition costs of £1,500. In September 2001 the shop was extended and structurally improved at a cost of £30,000. Renitha has been running this business as a trade since buying the shop. On 1st June 2018 Renitha sold the shop and the trade to an unconnected buyer for £750,000, incurring legal costs and other selling expenses of £3,500. Renitha has no other capital gains during the tax year, and has made no previous claims for entrepreneurs' relief. Compute the chargeable gains and the capital gains tax payable.

Suggested solution

	£	£
Proceeds from sale		750,000
Allowable deductions:		
Initial cost	85,000	
Costs of acquisition	1,500	
Enhancement expenditure, September 2001	30,000	
Incidental costs of disposal	3,500	(120,000)
Chargeable gain		630,000
Less Annual Exempt Amount		(11,700)
Gain subject to capital gains tax		618,300
Capital gains tax @ 10% (ER rate)		61,830

Notes:

i) This is a sale of a trade, together with the main chargeable asset used for the trade; therefore both disposals qualify for ER. It is assumed none of the sale proceeds stated were for non-chargeable trade assets such as inventory, or trade receivables.

From a CGT computational point of view it is not critical to separate the disposal into the separate assets of the shop and the trade goodwill, if both are sold together (though for stamp duty purposes it is likely that a clear price allocation must be set out in the legal documents).

ii) Renitha has now used up £630,000 of her lifetime allowance for capital gains tax ER purposes. She therefore has a lifetime balance left for ER of £9,370,000 at 2nd June 2018.

iii) The annual exemption has been set against ER gains as Renitha has no other chargeable gains to set it against.

26.10 Indexation allowance – Incorporated entities only

For incorporated entities, indexation allowance applies when computing their gains. The following are the current IA rules for company disposals.

a) The indexation allowance is calculated by reference to the change in the Retail Prices Index between the date of the disposal and:

   i) the date of acquisition, or

   ii) 31st March 1982, if that is later than the date of acquisition.

b) The indexation applies to the initial cost of acquisition and any enhancement expenditure but not to the incidental costs of disposal.

c) Where an asset was held on 31st March 1982 indexation is automatically applied to the market value at that date or the actual allowable expenditure, whichever is the greater.

d) On a part-disposal, indexation allowance is calculated based on the fractional part of the total cost that was used in the calculation of the unindexed gain.

The allowable cost carried forward for the part not disposed of is not indexed at that stage. For a part-disposal of shares acquired since March 1982, IA rules differ – see 30.4 to 30.6.

e) The indexation allowance cannot be used to create or increase a capital loss.

26.11 Calculation of indexation allowance

The 'indexation factor' is calculated according to the following formula, and is rounded by statute to three decimal places.

$$\frac{\text{RPI in month of disposal (or if earlier } 31^{st} \text{ December 2017)} - \text{RPI in month of acquisition}}{\text{RPI in month of acquisition}}$$

The official RPI table from the Office for National Statistics, covering March 1982 to December 2017, is provided at the end of Chapter 25. 31st March 1982 is substituted as the acquisition date for assets acquired earlier.

Example

Jay's Woodturning Ltd purchased a workshop for use in its trading business for £10,000 in January 1983. Legal charges and other allowable costs of acquisition amounted to £500. In January 1984 an extension to the property was built for £3,000, and major repairs undertaken amounting to £1,000. The whole property was sold for £100,000 on 28th January 2018, with incidental disposal expenses of £1,500.

RPIs: January 1983 = 82.61, January 1984 = 86.84, December 2017 = 278.1.

Required: Compute the chargeable gain arising to Jay's Woodturning Ltd on the disposal of the workshop. Jay's Woodturning Ltd's accounting period is the year ended 31st August 2018.

Suggested solution

CGT computation	£	£
Proceeds of sale		100,000
Less: Expenses of disposal		(1,500)
		98,500
Less: Cost of acquisition (1983)	10,000	
Expenses of acquisition (1983)	500	
Enhancement expenditure (1984)	3,000	
		(13,500)
Un-indexed gain		85,000
Indexation allowance to December 2017 (See working)		(31,449)
= Chargeable gain (with other net CGs, will be added to TTP)		53,551

Working: Indexation allowance:

On Cost (including acquisition expenses) January 1983 £10,500

			£
$\frac{278.1 - 82.61}{82.61}$ (rounded)	=	2.366 × 10,500 =	24,843
On Enhancement cost January 1984		£3,000	
$\frac{278.1 - 86.84}{86.84}$ (rounded)	=	2.202 × 3,000 =	6,606
Total indexation allowance			31,449

Note - The gain will be taxable at Jay's Woodturning Ltd's corporation tax rate, as part of Taxable Total Profits.

26.12 Indexation – losses

The indexation allowance claimed by corporations cannot be used to turn a gain into a loss or to increase a loss.

Example

B Ltd owns freehold property which was purchased for £20,000 in April 1982. The property was sold on 30th January 2019 for:

a) £300,000

b) £50,000

Compute the chargeable gain/loss.

Solution: B Ltd chargeable gain/loss computation

		£
a)	Proceeds of sale	300,000
	Cost April 1982	(20,000)
	Unindexed gain	280,000
Less IA: $\frac{278.1 - 81.04}{81.04}$ = 2.432 × 20,000 =		(48,640)
	Chargeable gain	231,360
b)	Proceeds of sale	50,000
	Cost April 1982	(20,000)
	Unindexed gain	30,000
	IA of £48,640, but restricted to	(30,000)
	No gain/no loss	nil

26.13 Disposals treated by law as no gain / no loss

The following transactions are treated as no gain/no loss disposals. This means that the proceeds of the seller and the cost of the acquirer are treated for all CGT purposes as whatever figure would give the seller no gain and no loss. (Other no gain/no loss transactions are outside the scope of this book.)

i) Disposals between spouses or civil partners who were not permanently separated throughout the tax year in question.

ii) Transfers of chargeable assets between companies in the same capital gains group (see 31.10).

26.14 Treatment of unknown deferred consideration

Even when consideration is payable by instalments, the whole of the consideration is treated as initial proceeds, so long as its value can be determined at the contract date.

However, the following rule applies if part of the consideration for an asset disposal is deferred, and its value is uncertain at the date of the original contract (eg an 'earn-out' payment which is based on the future profits of a company measured only after the shares have changed owners). This is a complex area of CGT law and not in the syllabus of the basic tax exams of accounting bodies. It is mentioned here as an example of the way that property case-law has refined the basic rules set out in TCGA about consideration, to deal with the real-life practice of contracts which include an unascertainable element of consideration in the original contract. This rule was established in 1980 by the leading CGT case of Marren v Ingles (54 TC 76).

In English law, a right to unascertainable consideration is viewed as intangible property (called a 'chose in action'). For CGT, this right to receive an (uncertain) additional amount at a later date is viewed as a separate asset created by the original sale contract. That asset (at its market value) is treated as part of the initial consideration, and is added to the value of the known consideration, to give the total consideration received for the original asset.

An estimated market value – defined as the amount which a third party would pay for an assigned right to all the deferred consideration – has to be agreed at the date of the original contract of sale. This part of the consideration is not treated as chargeable proceeds so the original cost is dealt with under the formula for part-disposals in 26.8.

Later, when the 'chose in action' becomes a cash debt (i.e. the deferred consideration value is known), that occasion is treated as the disposal of the 'chose in action' asset.

A problem may arise for the taxpayer if a capital loss is realised on the chose in action (i.e. the estimated value at the first disposal exceeded the final value). Capital losses cannot be carried back to an earlier tax year, so the taxpayer will need further capital gains (of that or a later tax year) to set the new loss against if it is to be of any value to him/her. However, provided this situation can be avoided, ie the chose in action can be prudently valued, the effect of Marren v Ingles is that two gains are made at different times, matching the dates of entitlement to known original and known deferred consideration, and the original cost is apportioned accordingly.

Student self-testing question

Question 1 Tariq

Tariq purchased a painting for £100,000 in August 1984, which he sold for £200,000 on the 3rd March 2019. Selling expenses amounted to £10,550.

Compute the capital gains tax payable on 31st January 2020, assuming no other chargeable disposals in the year, and that Tariq's 2018/19 taxable income is £49,000.

Question 1 suggested solution: Tariq's CGT computation 2018/19

	£	£
Proceeds of sale		200,000
Less Selling expenses		(10,550)
Net proceeds		189,450
Less Cost of acquisition		(100,000)
Chargeable Gain		89,450
Annual exemption		(11,700)
Gain subject to CGT		77,750
Capital gains tax @ 20%		15,550

Question without answer

Question 2 Anne

A shareholding qualifying for entrepreneurs' relief was acquired by Anne, an individual, in February 1989 at a cost of £70,000. Anne has not made any disposals since April 2009. The shareholding was sold in January 2019 for sale proceeds of:

i) £15,500,000

ii) £850,000

Requirement

Compute the capital gains tax payable in each case, assuming Anne has £50,000 of taxable income for 2018/19.

27 Chargeable persons

27.1 Introduction

This chapter is concerned with the persons liable to CGT (as opposed to corporation tax on chargeable gains).

The main category of taxpayer for CGT is an individual. However, CGT liabilities can also arise on an individual in the separate capacity of either a Trustee or a personal representative (this term means either an executor or an administrator of a deceased estate).

Individuals carrying on a trade in partnership (see Chapter 15) self-assess separately for CGT, each declaring the individual share of gains and losses on disposals of partnership business assets (e.g. goodwill).

27.2 Scope of liability - Individuals

An individual is liable to capital gains tax if he or she is resident in the UK in an income tax year, wherever he or she may be domiciled.

For persons legally domiciled in the UK as well as resident in the UK, all chargeable gains worldwide are taxed on the arising basis.

27.3 Remittance basis of assessment for non-domiciled individuals

An individual who is resident in the UK, but who is not domiciled in the UK, may elect to self-assess capital gains on foreign assets only to the extent that the proceeds from those gains are remitted to the UK. This is called the remittance basis. From 2008 a non-domiciled resident who claims UK taxation on the remittance basis does not benefit from a CGT annual exemption.

If the remittance basis is selected for CGT, many detailed rules define remittances and match them to gains (e.g. for double taxation relief). In general the gain made on an overseas-located asset is identified with the earliest possible remittance.

The CGT rate for gains taxed on non-domiciled residents on the remittance basis is 20% or 28% regardless of the taxpayer's taxable income.

In addition, as there is no concept of remitting loss, a non-domiciled individual who elects remittance basis obtains no relief for losses on foreign assets.

Therefore some non-domiciled residents who could choose remittance basis choose to be charged to CGT on the arising basis, in order to obtain relief for non-UK capital losses. For this purpose the terms residence and domicile have the same meaning as for income tax.

Non-domiciled individuals and the remittance basis

The remittance basis election is made separately for each tax year. It is important to remember that unremitted gains dating from earlier tax years, when remittance basis was chosen, must be self-assessed in the tax year of later remittance to the UK. This applies even if the gain is remitted in a tax year when the arising basis applies for current gains. Gains taxable on the remittance basis are computed at the date of disposal in accordance with normal UK rules.

Non-domiciled UK residents who have ever made the remittance basis election even just for one tax year, must be very careful with their financial record keeping as evidence of the source of remitted funds is crucial if tax is not to be payable.

'Remittance' of a past gain does not just include remittance of cash. For example a remittance can be triggered by buying an asset overseas (such as a yacht) which is later brought into the UK, or paying UK bills with an overseas credit card.

27.4 The CGT annual exempt amount (irrelevant to companies)

For individuals (except those taxed on the remittance basis), the first £11,700 of net chargeable gains in tax year 2018/19 is exempt from CGT (2017/18: £11,300). For trustees (who are assessed as a body to CGT on behalf of each trust they represent), the first £5,850 (2017/18: £5,650) of net gains in the year is exempt (this limit is subject to reduction for multiple trusts created on the same day).

You should note the following points:

(a) In principle, for each tax year, chargeable gains and allowable losses for the whole year are first added together. Any annual exemption is then deducted from the total net gains, before considering unrelieved capital losses brought forward, which may then be deducted. See 26.8 for the situation where there are both ER gains and non-ER gains in one tax year.

(b) If a taxpayer has no taxable income for the year, unused income personal allowances cannot be deducted from chargeable gains.

(c) Any CGT AEA unused by an individual or trust in a tax year is lost. It cannot be carried forward, or transferred to another taxpayer.

(d) The personal capital gains tax rate for 2018/19 is 10% (disposals qualifying for entrepreneurs' relief), with the main rates of 10% or 20% depending on the individual's income, and 18% or 28% rates retained for residential property not eligible for the principal private residence relief, as noted in Chapter 25.

(e) A capital loss can only be offset against a capital gain of the same or a later year. Losses of the current year must be set against gains of the current year before being carried forward. The annual exemption amount of £11,700 is deducted from the net gains.

   Losses brought forward can be set off against gains of the current year.

Losses brought forward are only utilised to the extent that they are used to reduce any gains to the £11,700 level.

The only time when capital losses can be carried back against gains of an earlier year is after death of the individual taxpayer. (See 27.7).

Example of current capital loss offset against gains

Barry makes a chargeable gain from shares of £20,000 on 3rd May 2018. He also incurred a capital loss in October 2018 of £2,500. The shares are not eligible for entrepreneurs' relief. Barry has taxable income of £48,000 for 2018/19.

Compute Barry's CGT liability for 2018/19.

Solution:	£
Chargeable gain	20,000
Less capital loss	(2,500)
Net Chargeable Gains	17,500
Less annual exempt amount	(11,700)
Taxable gains	5,800
CGT payable (£5,800 @ 20%) =	1,160

27.5 Spouses and civil partners

(a) Spouses or civil partners are treated as separate individuals, each with a CGs annual exemption of £11,700 for 2018/19.

(b) Chargeable gains are reported separately by spouses or civil partners in their respective Self-Assessment Tax Returns.

(c) The transfer of chargeable assets between spouses or civil partners in any tax year does not give rise to any CGT charge where they are living together in the tax year; however, the next owner takes on the previous one's exact CGT base cost at the date of transfer.

(d) Losses of one spouse or civil partner cannot be set against the gains of the other.

(e) Where assets are jointly owned, then in the absence of a declaration of beneficial interest, the 50–50 rule applies and each is treated as owning 50% of the assets.

(f) In a tax year when a married couple or civil partnership were living together on 6th April, they can have only one residence which qualifies as their joint principal private residence (see 29.5).

27.6 Trading losses set against chargeable gains

If a taxpayer incurs a trading loss for a tax year and makes a claim to set it against total income of the same or prior tax year (see 14.3), then to the extent that it has not been fully relieved against that total income, an optional claim is available for further relief of the trading loss against net chargeable gains of the same year. The amount claimed cannot exceed the net chargeable gains for the year, before deducting the AEA of £11,700. If made, this claim cannot be restricted to preserve AEA against net gains.

Example

Nick, who is single, has the following data relating to the year 2018/19:

	£
Trade profits 2018/19 (year to 31.3.2019)	45,000
Chargeable gains	25,500

In the year to 31st March 2020 Nick has a trading loss of £46,000, and no other income.

Compute Nick's income tax and CGT liabilities for 2018/19, if he makes all possible prior year claims in respect of the trade loss of 2019/20.

Solution

Nick Income tax computation 2018/19

	£
Total income (Trade profits)	45,000
Less loss relief	
– loss of 2019/20 against income of preceding year (see 14.3)	(45,000)
Assessable income 2018/19	nil

CGT computation 2018/19

	£
Net chargeable gains 2018/19	25,500
Less balance of 2019/20 loss set against prior year gains	(1,000)
Reduced Net chargeable gains	24,500
Less annual exemption 2018/19	(11,700)
	12,800
	£
CGT payable @ 10%	1,280

Notes

(i) Nick's personal allowance of £11,850 would be wasted in 2018/19.

(ii) The 2019/20 trading loss of £46,000 has been dealt with as follows:

	£
Carry-back against total income of 2018/19	45,000
Extend carry-back to cover 2018/19 capital gains	1,000

The trading loss for the year ended 31st March 2020 can be used in either 2018/19 or 2019/20. However, since there is no other income in the period to 31st March 2020, the carry-back has been used. Nick could also have decided to carry the whole trade loss forward against future trading income (see Chapter 14).

27.7 Asset transfers involving personal representatives and trustees

The executor or administrator of a deceased person's estate is deemed to have acquired all the chargeable assets at the market value at the date of death, but there is no disposal liable to CGT. Legatees are also deemed to have acquired assets passing to them from the executor or administrator, at their market value at the date of death, so that any transfer to a legatee is not a chargeable disposal.

Annual exemption for deceased estates. The first £11,700 of net gains on an estate under executorship is exempt in the tax year in which the death occurs, and also in the subsequent two tax years (if the estate remains under administration for so long).

The 2018/19 CGT rate for personal representatives (trustees administering the estate of a deceased person) is 20% with 28% for residential property.

The 2018/19 rate for Trustees who are not personal representatives of a deceased person is similarly 20% or 28%. (And the annual exemption is a maximum of £5,850.)

Capital losses of the deceased made in the tax year of his or her death can be carried back against that person's past chargeable gains of the previous three tax years. This carry-back requires an election by the personal representatives. Any tax repayment generated by such a carry-back is an asset of the deceased estate.

27.8 2013 Reform of overseas aspects of CGT for individuals

CGT is essentially a territorial tax based on residence. Overseas resident individuals and companies do not pay CGT on their gains on UK-situated chargeable assets, unless these are assets of a UK trading permanent establishment (or they are caught by the new CGT charge in FA 2013).

Since the 1990s there have been various reforms made to CGT to counter tax planning techniques used to avoid CGT on gains of individuals who had both a UK and an overseas connection.

After 1998, the technique of becoming 'non-resident' in the UK for a relatively short period, to avoid UK CGT on a specific planned asset disposal, was made more difficult by the CGT 'temporary non-residents' rule.

Temporary non-residents

The following rules apply to individuals who have been UK-resident, then become non-resident after 16th March 1998, but stay non-resident for less than five complete tax years. As a result these individuals are liable on their return to UK for CGT on certain gains made during temporary non-residence.

Chargeable gains (net of allowable losses) of the tax years falling between the tax years of departure and return ('the intervening years') are taxed as gains of the year of return, or allowed as a loss of the year of return, provided that:

(a) the individual was resident or ordinarily resident for at least four out of seven tax years before the tax year of departure; and

(b) the intervening years do not exceed five tax years; and

(c) the gain or loss arose on an asset acquired by the individual before actual departure from the UK.

27.9 Capital gains of partnerships

A partner is assessed individually in respect of his or her share of any chargeable gains accruing from the disposal of partnership assets. Therefore, other personal capital losses can be set against his or her share of any partnership capital gains, and vice versa.

Student self-testing question – married couples and CGT

Question 1: Roger

Roger bought a painting for £15,000 in June 2008 which he sold for £65,300 on the 8th May 2018. Costs of disposal amounted to £2,200. Roger has taxable income of £52,000 for 2018/19.

Roger's wife Vanessa has capital losses of £3,500 for 2018/19.

Compute Roger's 2018/19 CGT liability.

Solution to Question 1: Roger

CGT computation 2018/19

		£	£
Proceeds of sale 8th May 2018			65,300
Less	Cost	15,000	
	Cost of disposal	2,200	(17,200)
Gain			48,100
Less annual exempt amount			(11,700)
	Taxable gains		36,400
	CGT payable = £36,400 @ 20%		7,280

Note: Vanessa's capital losses are unavailable to Roger. They can be used only against her own future chargeable gains.

Questions without answers

Question 2: Frank

Frank has chargeable gains of £12,600 for the year 2018/19, and capital losses of £500. His wife Florence sold a piece of land for £10,000 on 10th May 2018, which was part of a larger plot purchased in 1995 for £3,000, and which was not used for a private residence. The remaining part of the land had a value of £30,000 on 10th May 2018. Frank's taxable income for 2018/19 is £21,300 and his wife Florence's is £12,000.

Compute the CGT liabilities of Frank and Florence for 2018/19.

Question 3: Arnold

Arnold purchased a painting in 2000 for £20,000 which he sells for £50,000 in January 2019.

Arnold's wife Patricia owned a small business including a goodwill intangible for which she paid £16,000 on 1st January 1989. On 1st January 2019 she sells the goodwill along with the business, to an unconnected person, for a price which valued the goodwill at £165,000, incurring disposal costs of £344.

Both Arnold and Patricia are higher-rate income taxpayers in 2018/19.

Compute the CGT liabilities of Arnold and Patricia for 2018/19.

28 Chargeable occasions

28.1 Introduction

A chargeable gain or loss arises on the disposal of a chargeable asset. For this purpose a disposal takes place in the following circumstances, each of which is examined in this chapter:

- on a sale by contract
- on the compulsory purchase of an asset by a local authority
- where capital sums are derived from assets which have been damaged, lost or destroyed - e.g. from insurance claims
- where an asset (typically a holding of equity shares in a company) has become of negligible value
- on the part-disposal of an asset (see also 26.8)
- by 'value-shifting' between related assets
- on a death
- when a gift is made (see also 26.3 onwards and Chapter 32)

28.2 Disposal by contract

Where an asset is disposed of by way of a contract, the date of the disposal is the time the contract is concluded and not, if different, the time when the asset is conveyed or transferred. For shares and securities the date of the contract note is the disposal date, and for land or buildings (real property), the date of the exchange of sale contracts is the relevant date, and not the date of completion.

28.3 Compulsory purchase

When there is a compulsory purchase of an interest in land, then the date of the disposal is the date when the amount of compensation is formally agreed.

28.4 Capital sums derived from assets

Compensation or insurance monies received in respect of an asset usually amounts to a disposal or part-disposal of it by the owner. Thus if a taxpayer has property which is damaged or destroyed by fire, any insurance money received constitutes a disposal for CGT purposes. However, this is varied to some extent where the capital sum is used for the following purposes:

a) to restore a non-wasting asset, or

b) to replace a non-wasting asset lost or destroyed.

For the meaning of wasting and non-wasting assets, see 29.8.

28.5 Restoration of a non-wasting asset

If a capital sum is received in respect of a non-wasting asset, which is not lost or destroyed, the taxpayer can claim to have the sum deducted from the cost of acquisition, rather than treated as a part-disposal. Such a claim can only be made if:

a) the capital sum is used wholly for restoration, or any amount not restored is small relative to the capital sum; or

b) the capital sum is small relative to the value of the asset.

Small is normally taken to be 5% or less.

Example

Terry purchased a picture for £35,000 in June 2009, which was damaged by fire in May 2018. Insurance proceeds of £1,000 were received in December 2018, the whole amount being spent on restoring the picture. Terry makes a claim to have the insurance receipt of £1,000 not treated as a disposal. The value of the painting after the fire was estimated at £8,000.

Show the computation of the Terry's CGT base cost carried forward.

Solution: Computation 2018/19

	£
Cost	35,000
Less insurance sum deducted from cost	(1,000)
	34,000
Add expenditure on restoration	1,000
Allowable expenditure c/f	35,000

Note

From a capital gains tax point of view, Terry is now in exactly the same position as he was before the picture was damaged.

If he had not made the election to deduct the insurance proceeds from the cost, he would have had to treat the receipt of £1,000 as a part –disposal and allocate it against an apportioned cost of 1,000 / (1,000+8,000) x £35,000 = £3,889 (using the A / (A+B) formula), and that would generate a capital loss of £2,889 - which might not be immediately of use to him.

Example

Sam purchased a piece of antique furniture for £12,000 in May 2008. The item was damaged by water in January 2018 for which £1,500 was received by way of insurance in July 2018. The amount spent on restoration was

(a) £1,500;

(b) £1,430.

Compute the allowable costs in each case, on the assumption that Sam claims to apply the insurance payment to restoration, rather than have it treated as a capital receipt on part-disposal.

Solution

(a) As the whole sum was spent on restoration there is no disposal if Sam claims, and no overall adjustment to the cost of the antique.

(b) In this case the whole sum was not spent, but the unused amount of £70 is less than 5% of the capital sum, i.e. £75. The £70 not spent on restoration need not be treated as a disposal, but may be deducted from the allowed cost.

Computation 2018/19

	£	£
Cost of antique		12,000
Less insurance claim:		
Spent on restoration	1,430	
Not spent	70	
		(1,500)
		10,500
Add expenditure on restoration		1,430
Allowable expenditure		11,930

Note: This is equivalent to the cost less the amount not spent on restoration, i.e. £12,000 – £70 = £11,930.

Example

Valerie has a collection of rare books purchased in February 2001 for £70,000 which were damaged by fire in May 2018 when they were estimated to be worth £100,000. The value of the collection as damaged by the fire was £60,000. In July 2018 Valerie received £30,000 insurance compensation and the collection was restored.

Compute the CGT effects of a) claiming for restoring and b) not claiming for restoring the book collection.

Solution

a) **Claiming:**

	£
Original cost of collection	70,000
Less insurance claim	(30,000)
	40,000
Add expenditure on restoration	30,000
Allowed expenditure c/f	70,000

As the whole sum has been spent on restoration there is no disposal if Valerie so claims, and no adjustment to the cost of acquisition.

b) **Not claiming: CGT computation 2018/19**

	£
Insurance proceeds	30,000
Apportioned cost $\frac{30{,}000}{30{,}000+60{,}000} \times 70{,}000$	(23,333)
Capital gain (take to net chargeable gains)	6,667
Balance of original cost carried forward (70,000 – 23,333)	46,667
Add enhancement cost - restoration expense	30,000
Total allowable expenditure c/f, if no claim is made	76,667

28.6 Replacement of non-wasting assets lost or destroyed

Where an asset is lost or destroyed and a capital sum is received by way of compensation, or under a policy of insurance, then if it is spent on a replacement asset within 12 months of the receipt of the sum (or such longer period as HMRC may allow), and the owner so claims, then:

a) the consideration for the disposal of the lost or damaged asset is taken to be such that neither a gain or loss arises.

b) the cost of the replacement asset is reduced by any excess of the capital sum received over the total of the consideration used in (a) above, plus any residual or scrap value of the old asset.

Example

Quentin purchased a picture for £8,000 in 2001 which was damaged by fire in July 2018. Insurance of £20,000 was received in December 2018 and Quentin decided to purchase another picture using the full amount of the insurance money. The scrap value of the picture was £100.

Show the computations, with and without a claim under Section 23.

Solution: CGT Computation 2018/19

a) If no claim is made

	£	£
Capital sum received December 2018	20,000	
Add residual value	100	20,100
Cost		(8,000)
Chargeable gain subject to CGT		12,100

b) If a claim is made

	£	£
Deemed proceeds of sale December 2018		8,000
Cost		(8,000)
No gain or loss		–
Replacement picture at cost		20,000
Capital sum received	20,000	
Less deemed proceeds	(8,000)	
	12,000	
Add scrap value	100	
Amount deducted from original cost		(12,100)
Allowable cost carried forward for replacement asset		7,900

Note

Where the whole sum is not spent on a replacement asset, then some relief is available providing that the amount not spent is less than the amount of the gain.

28.7 Assets whose value becomes negligible

The occasion of the entire loss, destruction, or extinction of an asset (wasting or non-wasting) amounts to a disposal of that asset, whether or not any capital sum is received. Where the value of an asset has become negligible, and HMRC accept that such is the case, then the owner may make a claim to the effect that the asset has been sold and immediately re-acquired for a consideration equal to the negligible value. Thus if a taxpayer owns a building which is destroyed by fire, and it was not insured, then he or she may claim to have made a disposal and re-acquisition at the scrap value, including the land. An allowable loss for capital gains tax purposes would arise in the tax year for which the claim was made.

28.8 The replacement of business assets

Where a qualifying 'business asset' is disposed of, including the occasion of the receipt of a capital sum, then special provisions apply if the gross proceeds are either wholly or partially spent on other qualifying business assets. This relief, which only relates to certain types of asset, is covered in Chapter 31.

28.9 Value shifting - shareholdings

Under special anti-avoidance rules, a disposal of shares may be deemed to occur where for example the value of a controlling interest in a company is 'watered down' in such a way that the value is passed into other shares or rights, without the occurrence of a legal disposal. These rules are complex and are not further considered here.

28.10 Hire purchase

Where a person enters into a hire purchase or other capital transaction, giving the hire and use of an asset for a period of time, at the end of which they become the owner of the asset, the acquisition for CGT is deemed to take place at the beginning of the period of use, even though it does not legally occur until a later date. However, if the contract ends before the property is legally transferred then no capital asset has been acquired, and it is simply re-characterised as a hire contract.

For individuals, most assets acquired on hire purchase are cars or other exempt personal chattels (e.g. low-value furniture, or mechanical items). For companies, capital losses are more common than gains on HP assets. The rules on wasting chattels qualifying for capital allowances (see Chapter 29) mean that losses are given relief via capital allowances only, though gains over cost are taxable (e.g. gains on aircraft).

28.11 Part-disposals

In general any reference to a disposal of an asset in CGT legislation also includes a part-disposal, and where this occurs it is necessary to apportion the allowable cost of acquisition. The detailed rules for this are covered at 26.8 and 29.3.

28.12 Death

On the death of a person there is no disposal of any chargeable assets for CGT purposes. The personal representative is deemed to have acquired any assets at their market value at the date of death, and any legatee also acquires the assets at the same market value, the date of acquisition being the date of death.

If a personal representative disposes of any assets other than to a legatee, e.g. in order to raise funds to pay any inheritance tax, then a chargeable disposal is made by the estate in administration. However, in the year of death and in the two following years of assessment, the personal representative is entitled (on behalf of the estate) to the same annual exemptions as an individual.

Losses incurred by a personal representative cannot be set against any previous gains of the deceased. However, if the deceased had incurred any losses in the year of his or her death, then if they cannot be relieved in that year, then they can be carried back and set against gains in the previous three years.

See also 27.7.

28.13 Gifts

A gift of a chargeable asset amounts in CGT law to a disposal for value. For more on gifts and CGT, see Chapter 32.

Student self-testing question

1. Jane has a collection of rare prints which cost £3,000 in May 1983. They were damaged by water in November 2012 and Jane received £17,000 by way of insurance compensation in May 2018. She spent £15,000 on restoration. The value of the prints in a damaged state was £6,000.

Compute any CGT liability arising and the amount of allowable expenditure carried forward if Jane claims to offset restoration costs against the total compensation received.

Solution: CGT computation 2018/19

	£
Capital sum received May 2018	17,000
Less spent on restoration of asset	(15,000)
Part-disposal proceeds	2,000
Proportion of cost allowable: $3{,}000 \times \frac{2{,}000}{2{,}000 + 6{,}000} =$	(750)
Capital gain (Add to net chargeable gains)	1,250
Allowable expenditure carried forward	
Cost of acquisition	3,000
Less part-disposal cost	(750)
Balance of cost carried forward	£2,250

29 Land and chattels

29.1 Introduction

This chapter deals with the CGT rules applicable to land and chattels under the following headings:

Freehold/leasehold land and buildings	Part-disposals of land
Small part-disposals of land	Private residences
Chattels	

29.2 Freehold/long leasehold land and buildings

There are no special rules for the computation of capital gains arising on the disposal of assets under this heading.

A long lease is a lease with more than 50 years to run at the date of the transaction.

Land includes houses, hereditaments and buildings.

Where the property is also the main residence of an individual owner or joint owners, the private residence exemption is normally available. See 29.5.

29.3 Part-disposals of land

Where there is a part-disposal of freehold or long leasehold land then unless the disposal is 'small' (see below), the normal part-disposal formula applies. This is in fact the CGT statutory formula used to apportion cost on a part-disposal of any chargeable asset, except holdings of shares and securities (see Chapter 30).

$$\textbf{Part disposal attributable cost} = \textbf{Cost of whole asset} \times \frac{A}{A+B}$$

Where A = gross disposal proceeds

B = Value of the part not disposed of at the date of the part-disposal

The 'cost of whole asset' figure used in the part-disposal cost formula:

(a) includes incidental purchase expenses, and also enhancements to the extent reflected in the nature and condition of the part being disposed of;

(b) is compared with 1982 value if rebasing applies.

Example

Graeme purchased a plot of land of 10 acres for £22,000 in May 1987, and an adjacent further 2 acres for £10,000 in June 2000. In December 2018 a sale of 5 acres was made for £60,000, from the original 10 acres, the remaining 5 acres being worth £75,000 at that time. The land was not used for business or residential purposes.

Compute the capital gains tax payable, assuming no other disposals during the year and a taxable income for Graeme of £55,000 in 2018/19.

Solution: CGT computation 2018/19

	£
Proceeds of sale	60,000
Cost $22{,}000 \times \dfrac{60{,}000}{60{,}000 + 75{,}000}$	(9,778)
Chargeable gain	50,222
Annual exemption	(11,700)
Taxable gain	38,522
Capital gains tax @ 20%	7,704

In this case, since the disposal was wholly out of the first identifiable plot, there is no need to combine the acquisition costs of the two plots. The two remain separate assets for CGT.

If title to the plots had been merged, with the sale being 5 acres out of the total of 12 acres and the remaining 7 acres being valued at £85,000 at the date of disposal then the computation would be:

	£
Proceeds of sale	60,000
Cost $32{,}000 \times \dfrac{60{,}000}{60{,}000 + 85{,}000}$ =	(13,241)
Chargeable gain	46,759
Annual exemption	(11,700)
Taxable gain	35,059
Capital gains tax @ 20%	7,012

29.4 Small part-disposals of land

There are some special rules which relate to land where:

a) the value of the part-disposal does not exceed £20,000; and

b) the part-disposal is small relative to the market value of the entire property, before the disposal. 'Small' in this context means 20% of the value immediately prior to the disposal.

Given these conditions, the taxpayer can claim to have the proceeds of part-disposal deducted from the allowable cost of the whole property carried forward for CGT. In that case there is no chargeable gain recognised on the part-disposal.

The taxpayer's total consideration for disposals of land in a tax year must not exceed £20,000, for him or her to be eligible to claim relief under this section.

Example

Zara owns 10 acres of land which she acquired in April 1992 for £20,000.

Incidental costs of the acquisition were £500. In August 2018 Zara sells 1.5 acres for £13,500, incurring disposal costs of £750. At the date of sale the remainder of the land had a market value of £135,500. The land was not used for business or residential purchases.

Compute the chargeable gain arising in 2018/19, showing the tax computations and the base cost carried forward:

(a) On normal principles;

(b) If Zara claims small part-disposal treatment under s.242 TCGA.

Solution:

(a) Zara, CGT computation 2018/19

	£
August 2018 proceeds of sale	13,500
Deduct – Incidental cost of part-disposal	(750)
	12,750
Deduct – allowable cost: $\frac{13,500}{13,500 + 135,500} \times (20,000 + 500)$	(1,857)
Gain 2018/19	10,893

Base cost carried forward = (£20,500 - £1,857) = £18,643

(b) Alternative treatment: Claim under Section 242 TCGA 1992

	£
Cost of acquisition	20,500
Less net proceeds of sale August 2018 (13,500 – 750)	(12,750)
Revised allowed cost on a future disposal (CGT base cost)	7,750

Notes

i) In this example, rather than claim relief under Section 242, it might well be better to accept the chargeable gain, since it falls within the annual exemption £11,700 for 2018/19, which might otherwise be unused.

ii) The election under Section 242 TCGA 1992 can be made where the proceeds of sale are less than £20,000 and less than 20% of the value of the entire property before the disposal. Check:

$$\frac{\text{Disposal value}}{\text{Total value before sale}} = \frac{13,500}{135,500} = 9\%$$

29.5 Private residence exemption

A gain accruing to an individual on the disposal of his or her private residence is exempt from capital gains tax. However, only one residence at a time qualifies for this treatment, so the relief is commonly referred to by tax practitioners as the **principal** private residence, or PPR, relief.

In some cases only a fraction of the total gain can benefit from the exemption. The rules about this are examined further below.

'Residence' includes a dwelling house (or part of one), or an apartment, together with associated garden land of up to half a hectare in area. A bigger garden can be included in a PPR if appropriate to the size and character of the house.

Full exemption is available where there has been a continuous period of ownership since 1st April 1982, or since purchase, whichever falls later, and the property has been occupied as the taxpayer's PPR for all of that ownership period.

If there have been identifiable periods when the owner's principal residence was elsewhere, all of the following are periods for which 'deemed occupation' may be claimed, and so can be included when determining how much of the time-apportioned gain qualifies for PPR exemption.

(a) Actual periods of occupation as PPR.

(b) Any period of absence during the **last 18 months** of ownership, provided that at some other time the residence was occupied as the principal private residence of the taxpayer. This deemed occupation period is the only one which applies even where the original PPR occupancy ended before 31st March 1982.

(c) Absences for any reason, for periods which in total do not exceed three years, and are both preceded and followed by occupation as the PPR (see comment below).

(d) Absence for any period of time during which the owner was in employment, carrying out duties abroad.

(e) Absences amounting in total to not more than four years, during which the owner:
   (i) lived elsewhere in the UK for reasons of employment because it was impossible to live at the property because of the distance to the place of employment, or
   (ii) lived away from home at the employer's request, in order to perform his or her employment more effectively.

Absences under items (c) to (e) above only qualify as deemed occupation if the owner actually occupies the home both before and after the period of absence, and if there is no other property which is claimed as an alternative PPR during the absence period. However, if the owner is unable to resume residence at the end of a (d) or (e) qualifying absence period for reasons of employment, periods of absence under (d) and (e) can still qualify as periods of occupation.

Where the maximum period of absence under (c) and (e) is exceeded, then only the excess is treated as a period of non-occupation giving rise to a chargeable gain for part of the ownership period.

Where the property qualifies as occupied for only part of the ownership period (or the period since 31st March 1982, if less), the exempt portion of the gain is:

$$\frac{\text{Period of exemption as main residence}}{\text{Total period of ownership}} \times \text{Gain}$$

29.6 Private residence exemption – additional points

You should note the following additional points:

(a) If part of any house (e.g. an office, or a consulting room) is used exclusively for business purposes, the part of any gain that relates proportionately to the business portion is not eligible for PPR exemption. Dual use of rooms for both business and private purposes however allows all rooms to be included in the property eligible for PPR exemption.

(b) If a house, or part of it, is let for residential purposes while the owner is not living there, then a further exemption called 'letting relief' can be claimed as deductible from the non-PPR portion of the gain. Letting relief is given up to the smallest of:

- (i) An amount equal to the gain already exempted by PPR rules;
- (ii) £40,000; and
- (iii) the remaining chargeable gain calculated as attributable to the let period or to the let proportion of the whole property.

(c) A husband and wife or civil partners can only have one residence between them for the purposes of the PPR and letting exemptions.

In a tax year throughout which spouses are permanently separated, or become divorced, each qualifies individually for the PPR exemption.

Example

Alex purchased a house on 1st July 1990 for £80,000, in which he lived until 31st March 1991. The property was then let for five years, followed by occupation by Alex until he sold the house for £720,000 on 31st March 2019.

Compute the chargeable gain.

Solution: Alex CGT Computation 2018/19

		£
Proceeds of sale		720,000
Cost of acquisition		(80,000)
Total gain before exemption		640,000
Less exemption:		
Proportion of total gain: 321/345 (see working) × £640,000		(595,478)
Subtotal –gain not eligible for PPR exemption		44,522
Less letting relief – Lowest of:		
maximum amount	40,000)	
gain otherwise exempt	499,626)	(40,000)
gain attributable to let period	44,522)	
= chargeable gain subject to CGT (before annual exemption)		4,522

Notes

		Years	Months	Total months
Period of occupancy	1.7.90 – 31.3.91	-	9	9
Period of absence	1.4.91 – 31.3.96	5	-	60
Period of occupancy	1.4.96 – 31.3.19	23	-	276
Period of ownership	1.7.90 – 31.3.19	28	9	345

	Months
Actual occupancy *	285
Maximum allowed absence preceded and followed by occupancy	36
Months qualifying for PPR exemption	321

* Note that the final 18 months of ownership would have been treated as a period of deemed occupancy anyway, even if Alex hadn't actually lived in that house at the time.

(d) In the absence of formal election, it is a question of fact which of several actual residences is the principal private residence of a couple, or of an individual. The taxpayer can make a formal election to specify which is to be regarded as the PPR but must do so within 2 calendar years of acquiring more than one possible PPR. If no election is made the decision as to which residence was the PPR can be made by HMRC when either property is later disposed of. It is not necessary that the taxpayer elects the property in which more time is spent as the PPR. However, residential properties are only eligible to be claimed as a PPR if there is the genuine character of a settled home, not an occasional and temporary residence, in the quality of the taxpayer's, or her family's, use of the property.

(e) Deemed occupation of a PPR can apply to an individual who lives in job-related accommodation (e.g. Army officers), but who intends in due course to occupy a house owned by that individual, as his or her main residence. This treatment also applies to self-employed people living in job-related accommodation.

29.7 Chattels

A chattel is a legal term for property that is tangible and movable. For CGT purposes, chattels fall into four categories:

a) Chattels which are specifically exempt from capital gains tax on disposal, e.g. private cars, and decorations for valour (medals etc).

b) Chattels which are 'wasting assets' (see 29.8).

c) Chattels, not being wasting assets, both bought and disposed of for £6,000 or less (the limit is applied to each chattel individually) (see 29.9).

d) all other chattels – which in general are subject to normal CGT rules.

29.8 Chattels which are wasting assets

A wasting asset is one with an estimated useful life of less than 50 years at the time of the disposal. A chattel which is a wasting asset is exempt from capital gains tax unless:

a) the asset has been used since first owned, for the purposes of a trade, profession or vocation, and capital allowances were available in respect of the expenditure, whether claimed or not, or

b) it consists of commodities dealt with on a terminal market.

Where capital allowances have been claimed, then no chargeable gain will arise unless the disposal value is greater than the original cost. If the proceeds are less than £6,000 then the exemption noted below can be claimed.

The rationale for this exemption is that wasting chattels will typically be sold at a loss due to their wasting nature. If the gains were taxable then the losses would have to be allowed as capital losses which could be set against other gains. But this does not reflect economic reality as wasting assets fall in value over time reflecting the fact that they have been used up in generating benefits for their owners, rather than because something has gone wrong. In other words, the decline in value represents not a loss to the owner, but rather the consumption of benefits by the owner. Therefore non-trade wasting assets are exempt.

Where a wasting chattel has received capital allowances, any excess of cost over proceeds is recouped through capital allowances given (see Chapters 13 and 20). Therefore there is another kind of tax relief given for the capital loss. It is therefore symmetrical to treat any gain on original cost as a non-exempt gain, but subject to other chattels reliefs than the wasting asset one. The cost that qualified for capital allowances is used as the cost in the final CGT computation.

29.9 Chattels disposed of for £6,000 or less

Any gain arising on the disposal of a chattel, not being a wasting asset, is exempt if the gross disposal value is £6,000 or less.

Relief where proceeds are up to £15,000 and the chattel cost under £6,000.

To avoid distortion of market pricing of chattels around the £6,000 CGT exemption limit, relief applies to limit the maximum gain if disposal proceeds are somewhat greater than £6,000 and cost was less than £6,000. This relief limits the maximum gain to:

$$\frac{5}{3} \times (\text{gross proceeds} - £6{,}000)$$

Thus the assessable gain on a chattel is always the **lower** of:

i) $\frac{5}{3} \times$ (gross proceeds – £6,000) or

ii) The actual gain i.e. gross proceeds less all allowable costs.

Some arithmetical checking shows that the maximum disposal proceeds where a marginal relief calculation and claim may save any CGT is just below £15,000. This is proved as follows: with £15,000 proceeds and a cost of nil, the marginal relief gain (5/3 x £9,000 = £15,000) equals the actual gain (£15,000 minus nil). Therefore for chattel proceeds above £15,000, the relief is never effective, even if cost was below £6,000.

Example – CGT marginal relief on chattels

Harry buys a piece of pottery for £800 in 1992, which he sells in October 2018 for (a) £4,800 or (b) £6,800.

Compute the chargeable gains in both cases.

Solution: Harry CGT computation 2018/19

a) As the proceeds of sale are less than £6,000 no chargeable gain arises.

b)	£
Proceeds of sale	6,800
Less: cost of acquisition	(800)
Chargeable gain on normal principles	6,000
But Chattel, so limited to a maximum of $\frac{5}{3}$ (6,800 – 6,000)	1,333
Chargeable gain (before annual exemption)	1,333

29.10 Restriction of losses on chattels sold for less than £6,000

If a chattel which cost more than £6,000 is sold for less than £6,000 then the allowable loss is calculated by reference to deemed gross proceeds of £6,000, and not the actual disposal value.

If both the disposal price and the cost price are less than £6,000 then any loss is not allowable for CGT.

Rules exist to prevent avoidance by claiming separate chattels reliefs or exemptions on two or more chattels that form part of a set, e.g. a set of matching chairs. Any successive disposals of part of the set to the same or connected persons have to be treated as a single transaction for the purposes of the chattels rules, even if done in different tax years. This means chattels relief and exemptions are not available if the cost and/or the disposal value of the whole set exceeds £6,000.

Student self-testing question

Question 1: Neil

In January 2019, Neil sells an oil painting, which he acquired in June 1992 for £10,000. He sells the painting for:

a) £7,200 b) £5,700

Compute the allowable loss in each of the above cases.

Solution to Question 1: Neil

a) The disposal is not exempt from CGT, as the proceeds exceed £6,000. The allowable loss is therefore calculated in the normal way as £2,800 (£10,000 – £7,200).

b) The asset was acquired for more than £6,000 and sold for less, therefore a restricted loss is allowed. The allowable loss is calculated by substituting £6,000 for the gross disposal proceeds. The allowable loss is therefore £4,000 (£6,000 – £10,000), not the actual loss of £4,300.

Questions without answers

Question 2: James

James purchased a house in Oxford, 'Millhouse', on 31st July 1988 and took up immediate residence. The house cost £50,000. On 1st January 1991 he went to work in the United States where he stayed until 30th June 1993. On 1st July 1993 James returned to the UK to work for his United States employers in Scotland, where it was necessary for him to occupy rented accommodation. He resigned from his job and returned to live in Millhouse on 1st June 1994. A month later, on 1st July 1994, his mother became seriously ill, and James decided to go and live with her. His mother died on 30th September 1995, leaving her house to James. James decided to continue to live in his mother's house. James sold 'Millhouse' on 30th June 2018 for £300,000.

Calculate James's self-assessed chargeable gain on the disposal of Millhouse in 2018/19. (ACCA)

Question 3: Mr and Mrs Scott

Mr and Mrs Scott had the following transactions in assets in the tax year to 5th April 2019.

Mr Scott

Sold an antique vase for £7,250, incurring expenses of £250, on 1st December 2018, which he had bought in April 1992 for £2,950, including expenses of purchase.

Sold a let residential property on 1st November 2018, which had been bought for £31,000 on 3rd April 1993. In May 1994 an integral garage costing £3,000 was added. The net proceeds of sale were £80,000.

Sold a vintage Rolls Royce car for £650,000 on 9th May 2018, which had cost £65,000 on 6th May 2002.

Mrs Scott

On 4th June 2018 sold an antique silver brooch for £4,200, incurring expenses of £54. It had cost £6,200, including expenses, on 5th April 2003.

Sold 5 acres of land on 14th October 2018 for £75,000, incurring expenses of £480. It was part of a 25 acre plot, which had been purchased on 14th March 1984 for £17,000, including expenses. The remaining 20 acres have been valued at £150,000.

Compute the capital gains accruing to Mr and Mrs Scott in each of the cases above.

Question 4: Lord Scarlet

Lord Scarlet carried out the following capital transactions in January 2019.

Sold a cricket bat, signed by the 1978 England test team, which he had bought at an auction in May 1992 for £1,400. The net proceeds, after paying auctioneer's fees of £520, were £11,520.

Sold for £12,000 medals awarded to his father for valour during the battle of Normandy in 1944. Lord Scarlet inherited these medals in 1996.

Sold an antique book for £3,000. He had bought it in May 1987 for £8,000.

Sold a one-third interest in a plot of agricultural land for £11,500. Lord Scarlet had acquired the land in June 1984 for £15,000. The value of the remaining two thirds interest in January 2019 was £28,000.

Compute the total capital gains tax payable by Lord Scarlet for 2018/19, if his taxable income for the year is £46,000.

30 Shares and securities

30.1 Introduction

This chapter is concerned with the CGT rules applicable to shares and securities. From 6th April 2008, following removal of CGT indexation allowance and taper relief for individuals, apportionment of cost of shares of the same class became much simpler. For corporate taxpayers, gains and losses on transactions in stocks and securities still require a calculation of indexation allowance using the weighted average cost of the shareholding.

This chapter commences with an overview of the current rules on calculating the CGT cost of holdings of shares or securities of the same type and class acquired at different times. It then examines bonus and rights issues and takeover bids.

30.2 Individuals

Since the simplification of CGT (6th April 2008), the following rules apply to compute the capital gains and the tax liability on disposals of shares and securities by individuals.

(Note that the pooling rules below have not applied at all times since 1965. For instance, when taper relief was part of CGT, share purchases were not pooled, due to the need to track the exact length of ownership for each share disposal).

a) Unless shares are bought and sold within a very short period (see (d) below), a taxpayer's entire shareholding of the same type of shares in the same company is treated as a single asset for CGT. Its statutory name is 'the section 104 holding' and its informal name is 'the share pool'. Matching rules apply to determine how many of the shares sold on a part-disposal come from the section 104 holding/ share pool – see 30.3.

b) The cost of shares added to the section 104 holding (by purchase, subscription, inheritance, rights issue etc) increases the total allowable cost of the share pool. On a disposal of less than the whole holding, the allowable cost is apportioned on a weighted average basis to the proportion of the shares leaving the pool.

c) If a shareholding qualifies for entrepreneurs' relief (see 31.7) the gain on disposal is taxed at the reduced rate of 10%. Shares qualify for ER if throughout a one-year qualifying period, the individual making the disposal:

    i) is an officer or employee of the company, or of a company in the same group of companies; and

    ii) owns at least 5 per cent of the ordinary share capital of the company and that holding enables the individual to exercise at least 5 per cent of the voting rights in that company.

d) Shares and securities held at or prior to 31st March 1982 are valued at their 31st March 1982 market value for the computation of the capital gain on disposal.

e) Shares that meet the income tax relief criteria as investments in the 'risk capital' schemes Enterprise Investment Scheme ('EIS'), Seed Enterprise Investment Scheme ('SEIS'), Venture Capital Trusts ('VCT'), Community Investment Tax Relief ('CITR') and Social Investment Tax Relief ('SITR') are exempt from capital gains tax.

30.3 Share matching rules for individuals

When there is a part-disposal of some of the shareholding of a particular type of share in a given company, the following matching rules apply to decide which shares were sold, and therefore what they cost:

1) Against any shares acquired on the same day as the disposal;

2) Against any shares acquired within the following 30 days, taking the earlier acquisitions before the later;

3) Against all past share acquisitions, with the cost calculated on a weighted average basis (this refers to the main pool of shares, known as the 's104 holding').

These matching rules prevent a taxpayer triggering an artificial gain by share disposals with very quick repurchase, to make use of the annual CGT exemption.

Before the thirty-day matching rule was enacted for individuals, 'bed and breakfasting' shares used to be a standard tactic in share portfolios, mainly in March before the end of the tax year. The taxpayer sold selected shares, whose market value was sitting above their averaged CGT cost, to trigger gains up to the CGT annual exemption, and then repurchased the same type of shares, typically the next day (as same-day share matching applied since 1965). The chargeable gains were covered by annual exemption, and the share pool's average cost was increased, thus saving CGT in future (or increasing allowable losses in future).

The Government decided this 'bed and breakfasting' was unacceptable tax planning, and so passed new matching rules to make it only work if the shares are not repurchased for 31 days thus exposing the taxpayer to genuine market volatility. (Though shares in another company in the same market sector can be purchased the same day, instead.)

Companies have no counterpart to the 'shares of the same type bought within 30 days later' share-matching rule, as they do not get an annual exemption.

Examples of pooled shares weighted average cost - individuals

Example 1

Denis has the following transactions in the 25p ordinary shares of Zephyr plc, a quoted trading company.

				£
6th May 1982	purchased	3,500	shares at cost	2,500
31st March 1984	purchased	1,000	shares at cost	1,500
3rd April 1998	purchased	2,000	shares at cost	7,500

Calculate the value of the section 104 holding at 6th April 2018.

Suggested solution

S.104 holding – (share pool) Denis ordinary shares in Zephyr plc

		Number of shares	Qualifying expenditure
		£	£
6th May 1982	Purchased	3,500	2,500
31st March 1984	Purchased	1,000	1,500
3rd April 1998	Purchased	2,000	7,500
Pool at 6th April 2018		6,500	11,500

Notes:

i) If all the shares were sold the qualifying expenditure would be the full £11,500.

ii) The average cost per share at this point is 11,500÷6,500 = £1.77. However, using a per-share average cost for CG computations involving many shares introduces rounding errors. Also, TCGA 1992 technically deems the whole of the s.104 holding to be a **single asset** for CGT. This means that the proceeds and cost of a single share are not the relevant legal values for CGT, unless only one share was sold. Therefore, in tax exams, accounting students should use the statutory method, which deals with the whole pool together as one asset, and the shares sold as a part-disposal. Students should not work out a gain per share and then multiply by the total number of shares, even though it may give the same answer where rounding is minor.

iii) If part of the holding is disposed of, the allowable cost is always allocated pro-rata. For example, if 1,625 of the 6,500 shares are sold now, the apportioned cost of these for CGT is £2,875 (1625/6,500 × £11,500). The balance of cost (£8,625) is carried forward and averaged with future acquisitions (except any acquisitions not becoming part of the s.104 holding, because they are matched with recent disposals under the matching rules).

Example 2

Colin has the following transactions in the 25p ordinary shares of Kodiak plc, a quoted trading company.

				£
1-Jun-1990	purchased	1,000	shares at cost	525
1-Sep-2000	purchased	500	shares at cost	575
2-Jan-2003	purchased	2,500	shares at cost	3,500
10-Oct-2018	sold	3,000	shares, proceeds	36,000

Calculate the chargeable gain for 2018/19 before annual exemption.

Suggested solution

General pool K plc		**Number of shares**	**Qualifying expenditure**
			£
1-Jun-1990	Purchase	1,000	525
1-Sep-2000	Purchase	500	575
2-Jan-2003	Purchase	2,500	3,500
	Total	4,000	4,600
10-Oct-2018	Disposal	3,000	3,450
11-Oct-2018	Balance remaining in pool	1,000	1,150

Colin CGT computation 2018/19

		£
10-Oct-2018	Proceeds of sale of 3,000 shares	36,000
	Allowable cost	(3,450)
	Chargeable gain before annual exemption	32,550

30.4 Share matching rules - incorporated entities

The following matching rules apply to companies' shareholdings when deciding which shares out of one type of share in a given company were sold:

1) Against any shares acquired on the same day as the disposal;
2) Against a pool of any shares acquired in the previous 9 days, on a first-in-first-out (FIFO) basis;
3) Against the pool of shares acquired on or after 1st April 1982 (the s104 pool or the 'indexed pool');
4) Against the pool of shares acquired between 6th April 1965 and 31st March 1982 ('the 1982 holding');
5) Against any shares acquired before 6th April 1965, unpooled, on a last-in-first-out (LIFO) basis.

Pooling rules - incorporated entities

The following are the main provisions which apply to working out the cost and the indexation allowance on cost for part-disposals from holdings of shares or securities of the same class by an incorporated entity.

a) Shares or securities acquired on or after the 1st April 1982 form '**the section 104 holding**' for a company.

   This is not the same definition as the section 104 holding for individuals, which since 2008 extends back to shares acquired from 6th April 1965 (though any shares held at 31st March 1982 count in the section 104 holding at their 1982 value, if greater than their original cost).

   The section 104 shareholding pool of a company is indexed for inflation continuously, indexation allowance being added before every 'operative event' (either when its cost increases or when some shares leave the pool). To prevent rounding error the indexation factor calculated at each step is specifically not rounded to 3 decimal places like all other CGT indexation calculations, but is left as an unrounded fraction.

   Shares or securities acquired from 1965 to 31st March 1982 by a corporate taxpayer are called 'the 1982 holding'. This is treated for chargeable gains calculations as a single asset, separate from the single asset that is the section 104 holding.

b) Disposals or part-disposals from the 1982 holding qualify for indexation allowance, calculated once the disposal is made (exactly as for non-share assets of companies). The indexation calculated applies only to the proportion of the pool disposed of at that time, and to the apportioned cost, not to the whole 1982 holding.

c) The re-basing rules apply to shares and securities held at the 31st March 1982. The rebased cost of the 1982 holding for company tax computations in FY2017 or FY2018 is the market value at March 1982 of all remaining shares in the 1982 holding at 1st April 1985, less any shares from that holding which were matched against part-disposals since April 1982.

d) After checking for the same-day and nine-day prior purchases, share disposals by a company are matched first to the Section 104 Holding, until it is exhausted, and then to the 1982 Holding.

Example – share transactions and matching – incorporated taxpayer

Volta Ltd had the following transactions in the quoted shares of Zeal plc, a quoted trading company.

31-Jan-1983	Bought	8,000	shares costing	£15,600
31-May-1998	Bought	12,000	shares costing	£36,000
28-Jan-2019	Sold	15,000	shares for	£176,000

Compute the chargeable gain (RPI table is at the end of Chapter 25).

Suggested solution

The first step is to construct the section 104 holding. In documenting a company's section 104 holding, 3 columns are required for the pooled cost records: an 'indexed cost' column is required as well as one for (historic) 'cost'. Indexation must be calculated in the 'indexed cost' column between each pair of successive 'operative events'. An operative event means not only a chargeable disposal of any shares from the s. 104 holding, but also any addition of more shares to the holding - except an addition involving no actual or deemed cost to the shareholder (i.e. a bonus issue).

Section 104 holding	Number of shares	Cost	Indexed pool
		£	£
31-Jan-1983 Pool starts	8,000	15,600	15,600
IA to 31-May-98 (operative event):			15,275
$\frac{163.5-82.61}{82.61} \times 15{,}600$ (do not round)			
31-May-1998 Purchase	12,000	36,000	36,000
			66,875
IA to 31-Dec-2017 (end of indexation):			46,874
$\frac{278.1-163.5}{163.5} \times 66{,}875$			
(remember not to round the adjustment factor for shares disposals)			
Total in pool 28-Jan-19	20,000	51,600	113,749
28-Jan-2019 Disposal (15/20)	(15,000)	(38,700)	(85,312)
	5,000	12,900	28,437

Volta Ltd CG computation – disposal on 28th January 2019

	£
Sales proceeds (15,000 shares)	176,000
Allowable deductions:	
Cost (from s.104 pool working)	(38,700)
Un-indexed gain	137,300
Indexation from s. 104 pool working (85,312 – 38,700)	(46,612)
Chargeable gain included in Taxable Total Profits	90,688

Notes:

i) The remaining cost and indexed cost balance in the pool will be held until the next 'operative event'.

ii) The unindexed gain should be shown separately, in case a loss on disposal is incurred. In the case of a loss the indexation allowance is restricted so as not to create or increase a loss. Thus if the shares in this example were disposed of for £50,000, the indexation allowance deduction would be restricted to £11,300 (equal to the unindexed gain, or the sale proceeds less the apportioned historic cost). A capital loss can only be allowed when the shareholding is sold for less than its historic cost.

30.5 Bonus issues of similar shares

When a company makes a bonus (or 'scrip') issue of shares of the same class to existing members, then the cost (or market value at 31st March 1982) of the shareholder's total holding is unchanged, but the shares number in the holding is increased. So the average cost per share is reduced. For an individual taxpayer the number of shares additionally received is simply added to the total holding giving a reduced average cost per share to allocate to future part-disposals.

For corporate taxpayers, the number of shares in the first column of the s.104 share pool working is increased by the bonus issue number, but no change is required to the value of the other two columns (for total share cost and 'indexed cost'.)

No new indexation allowance needs to be computed on a bonus issue, as there is no change to cost, and no shares are yet leaving the pool. To use the legislative language, a bonus issue is not an 'operative event' requiring any indexation uplift to the pool cost.

Example

T Ltd makes a bonus issue of 1 for 5 in respect of its ordinary shares on 1st August 2004. Alex had acquired 500 ordinary shares in T Ltd on 1st May 2002 at a cost of £1,250. In January 2019 Alex sells 250 of the shares for £650. The holding does not qualify for entrepreneurs' relief.

Compute the chargeable gain to Alex on the share sale.

Suggested solution – individual CG computation for Alex

Cost of shares

		£
1-May-2002 cost for	500 ordinary shares	1,250
1-Aug-2004 cost for	100 bonus shares	–
	600	1,250

The deemed date of acquisition of the bonus shares for CGT purposes is the date of the original purchase of the shares which gave entitlement to the bonus issue.

Alex chargeable gain computation 2018/19	**£**
Proceeds of sale January 2019	650
Cost of 250 shares sold:	
$\frac{250}{600} \times 1,250$	(521)
Alex's Chargeable gain (to add to other gains of 2018/19)	129

Notes

i) The whole section 104 holding, or share pool, of identical shares in the same company is a **single asset** for CGT and any disposal of less than the entire holding is technically a part-disposal of one chargeable asset. It is therefore not correct in tax law to work out a share disposal CGT computation on the basis of the proceeds per share and a pool cost per individual share. There is one single asset before the sale, of which 250/600 was sold. The holding sold is by tax law allocated a fractional proportion of the total asset's cost, which in this case is £521.

ii) The CGT cost of the 350 shares retained (pool cost carried forward) is £1,250 – 521 i.e. £729.

Comparative pool working and CG computation on same facts, if Alex were a company

For the purposes of illustrating how indexation on the share pool cost works for a corporate taxpayer entitled to indexation allowance, imagine now that Alex (in the previous example) is a corporate body, Alex Ltd. As a bonus issue is not an operative event, no indexation allowance should be calculated on the holding until 31st December 2017 when indexation ends. The indexation is calculated on the whole holding, not just on the part sold. This is different from the part-disposal rules for all other types of asset, in particular for part-disposals of land.

The RPI for December 2017 is 278.1. The RPI for May 2002 was 176.2 (see table at end of Chapter 25).

TCGA s. 104 holding of T Ltd ordinary shares	**Working**	**No. of shares**	**Cost £**	**Indexed cost £**
Purchased 1.5.02		500	1,250	1,250
Bonus issue 1.8.04		100	-	-
Subtotal		600	1,250	1,250
Indexation allowance May 02 to December 17	$\frac{278.1 - 176.2}{176.2} \times £1,250$ (no rounding of factor)			723
Pool cost at January 2019		600	1,250	1,973
Shares sold	(250/600)	(250)	(521)	(822)
Pool carried forward		350	729	1,151

Alex Ltd CG computation (for CTAP covering January 2019)	**£**
Proceeds of sale of 250 shares, January 2019	650
Less share of cost – from pool working	(521)
= Unindexed gain	129

Less share of indexation allowance – from pool working

Use statutory method $\frac{(278.1-176.2)}{176.2} \times 521 = 301$

But IA cannot exceed the unindexed gain, so only deduct	(129)
= Alex Ltd's chargeable gain on the T Ltd shares sale	**NIL**

(For inclusion in total profits with all net chargeable gains)

Further example: a bonus issue followed by part-disposal

AB Ltd made a bonus issue of 1 for 10 on 30th June 2007. John had acquired 10,000 ordinary shares in AB Ltd in April 2000 at a cost of £15,000. John sells 2,000 shares in January 2019 for £8,000. The shares do not qualify for entrepreneurs' relief.

Compute the chargeable gain.

Solution: John CGT computation 2018/19	**£**
Proceeds of sale – 2,000 shares	8,000
Apportioned cost on part-disposal (see pool working):	
$\frac{2000}{11000} \times 15,000 =$	(2,727)
Chargeable gain	5,273

Notes

(i) John's Pool:

Section 104 holding of AB Ltd shares:	Number	Cost £
April 2000 cost	10,000	15,000
June 2007 bonus issue	1,000	Nil
Pool at January 2019	11,000	15,000

ii) The pool cost carried forward by John for the remaining 9,000 shares is (£15,000 – £2,727) = £12,273

Comparative computation if John were a company (for RPIs used, see Chapter 25)

TCGA s. 104 holding of T Ltd ordinary shares		Number of shares	Cost £	Indexed cost £
April 2000 cost		10,000	15,000	15,000
Bonus issue June 2007		1,000	-	-
Subtotal		11,000	15,000	15,000
Indexation allowance April 00 to Dec 17	$\frac{278.1 - 170.1}{170.1} \times £15,000$ (no rounding of factor)			9,524
Pool at January 2019		11,000	15,000	24,524
Shares sold	(2,000/11,000)	(2,000)	(2,727)	(4,459)
Pool carried forward		9,000	12,273	20,065

John Ltd CG computation (for CTAP covering Jan 2019)	**£**
Proceeds of sale of 2,000 shares, January 2019	8,000
Less share of cost – from pool working	(2,727)
= Unindexed gain	5,273
Less share of indexation allowance – from pool working	
Use statutory method (4,459-2,727) = 1,732	
Does not exceed the unindexed gain, so deduct full IA	(1,732)
John Ltd chargeable gain on AB Ltd shares sale	£3,541
(For inclusion in Taxable Total Profits with all net chargeable gains)	

Both of the above workings, for an individual and a company selling shares at the same price and the same historic cost profit, illustrate the general point that (for all chargeable assets, not just shares, the longer an asset has been held the greater the tax advantage of being a corporate body and not an individual, due to indexation allowance wiping out inflationary gains. But companies have no equivalent of the CGT annual exempt amount and are not eligible for Entrepreneurs' Relief.

30.6 Rights issues of the same class of share

Where a company makes a rights issue of the same class of shares as existing ones and they are taken up, then for CGT purposes the following rules apply.

a) The consideration paid for the shares by way of the rights issue is deemed to take place at the time when the cost of the rights becomes due.

b) For corporate taxpayers, the rights shares are allocated to the 1982 holding and the section 104 holding in proportion to the shares already in each holding. Each pool cost is increased accordingly.

If some of the rights shares are issued in proportion to shares held since before 1965, these rights shares and the rights cost must be separately allocated to the pre-1965 holding. For individuals the rights shares and cost will either increase the section 104 holding or increase the pre-1965 holding. There is no separate '1982 holding' share pool for individuals since April 2008 (following the removal of indexation allowance for individuals).

c) For corporate taxpayers, indexation allowance calculated on a disposal from the 1982 holding, when dealing with cost added to the 1982 holding by a post- March 1982 rights issue, only counts the time since that rights issue.

Example: Rights issue followed by part-disposal of shareholding – individual

(Note, this only involves a post-1982 shareholding; pre-1982 shareholdings are excluded from most UK professional bodies' basic tax syllabuses)

Jack acquired 1,000 ordinary shares in Roxy plc for £1,300 on 1st October 2002. Roxy plc made a rights issue on the 7th February 2004 of 1 new ordinary share for every 2 held, at a price of 125p per share. Jack sold 750 shares for £10,000 on 25th January 2019.

Compute the chargeable gain.

Solution: Jack's CG computation 2018/19

S.104 holding	**Number of shares**	**Cost £**
1-Oct-2002 First acquisition	1,000	1,300
7-Feb-2004 Rights issue	500	625
Pool value @ 25th January 2019	1,500	1,925
25-Jan-2019 Disposal of 750 shares	(750)	
Cost apportioned $\frac{750}{1,500} \times 1,925$		(963)
Balance of pool c/f	750	962

Jack, CGT computation 2018/19

	£
750 R plc shares Proceeds of sale	10,000
Cost – from pool working	(963)
Chargeable gain (to add to other net gains before deducting annual exemption)	9,037

Note

The rights issue cost of 1 for 2 is 500 new shares at £1.25 per share i.e. £625

Comparative computation if Jack were a company, Jack Ltd (for RPIs, see Chapter 25. The RPI for December 2017 was 278.1)

TCGA s. 104 holding of R plc ordinary shares	Working	Number of shares	Cost £	Indexed cost £
October 2002 cost		1,000	1,300	1,300
Operative event Feb 2004 (rights issue):				
Indexation allowance Oct 02 to Feb 04	$\frac{183.8 - 177.9}{177.9} \times £1{,}300$ (no rounding of factor)			43
Rights issue Feb 2004		500	625	625
Subtotal		1,500	1,925	1,968
Indexation allowance Feb 04 to Dec 17	$\frac{278.1 - 183.8}{183.8} \times £1{,}968$ (no rounding of factor)			1,010
Pool at January 2019		1,500	1,925	2,978
Shares sold	(half of holding)	(750)	(963)	(1,489)
Pool carried forward		750	962	1,489

Jack Ltd CG computation (for CTAP covering January 2019)	**£**
Proceeds of sale of 2,000 shares, January 2019	10,000
Less share of cost – from pool working	(963)
= Unindexed gain	9,037
Less share of indexation allowance – from pool working	
Use statutory method (1,489 – 963) = 526	
Does not exceed the unindexed gain, so deduct full IA	(526)
Jack Ltd chargeable gain on Roxy plc shares sale	£8,511

(For inclusion in Taxable Total Profits with all net chargeable gains)

30.7 Takeover bids

When a company succeeds in a bid for the shares of another company, one of the following disposal situations will arise for shareholders in the target company:

a) The consideration is satisfied entirely by cash. In this case any shareholder who accepts the takeover offer has made a chargeable disposal of all their shares. CGT computations will be done on that basis, allocating proceeds pro rata between different CGT share pools or holdings, if more than one class of share is received on the takeover.

b) The consideration is satisfied in shares, ie a share for share exchange. In this case an accepting shareholder is deemed to have acquired the new shares at the cost of the original shareholding(s) now given in exchange for the new shareholding. In this case no disposal arises for CGT as no cash has been received – the replacement shares 'stand in for' the old shares and inherit their base cost, including accrued indexation allowance.

c) The consideration is partly in cash and partly in shares, or it consists of two or more different shares or securities issued in exchange for the target shares. In both these cases, it is necessary to use the market value of the separate components of the takeover consideration, in order to apportion the original cost between those new assets. If part of the consideration is cash, that part of the transaction represents a chargeable part-disposal of the original shareholding.

Example

Arthur owns 10,000 ordinary shares in Poppy Ltd which he acquired for £15,000 on 27th June 2003. On 30th May 2018 Zentral plc makes a bid for P Ltd on the following terms:

For every 2 shares in P Ltd: 80p in cash, 1 ordinary £1 share in Zentral plc. The market value of Z plc shares when first quoted after the takeover is 375p.

Compute the base cost of the Zentral plc shares received by Arthur, and the chargeable gain or allowable loss in 2018/19.

Solution

Working:	**Market value**	**Apportioned cost (4:18.75)**
	£	**£**
Cash (10,000/2) × 80p	4,000	2,637
Ordinary shares (10,000/2) × 375p	18,750	12,363
	22,750	15,000

Arthur – P plc shares CGT computation 2018/19

Disposal cash receipt	4,000
Less apportioned cost of part-disposal for cash	(2,637)
Chargeable gain (before annual exemption)	1,363

CGT base cost of 5,000 Zentral plc shares carried forward (from working) = £12,363.

Arthur then sells all his 5,000 ordinary shares in Zentral plc for £100,000, on 1st December 2018.

Compute the chargeable gain before annual exemption.

Solution: Arthur – Zentral plc shares CGT computation 2018/19	**£**
Proceeds of sale 5,000 shares in Zentral plc	100,000
Less cost of acquisition (as above)	(12, 363)
Chargeable gain (before annual exemption)	87,637

30.8 Small capital distributions Section 122 TCGA 1992

Where a person receives cash by way of a capital distribution, e.g. on a takeover bid, in the course of a liquidation, or by the sale of rights, then there is normally a part-disposal for capital gains tax purposes.

However, if the cash received is small relative to the value of the total shareholding at the time, and does not exceed the CGT allowable base cost, then the cash received may be deducted from the acquisition cost. 'Small' here is defined as the higher of £3,000 or 5% of the value of the shares immediately after the capital distribution.

Example

Terry acquired 5,000 ordinary shares in Albatross Ltd at a cost of £3,750 on 8th February 2008. On 12th June 2017 the company made a rights issue of 1 for 10 at a price of 25p. Terry sold his rights for 60p each on the 1st August 2018, when the market value of the 5,000 ordinary shares was £7,000.

Compute the allowed cost carried forward for Terry's Albatross Ltd shares and any CGT liability for 2018/19, if he makes a claim for small capital distribution treatment.

Solution: Terry CGT computation 2018/19

	£
Proceeds of sale of rights 500 × 60p	300

As this is less than 5% of the market value of the shares of £7,000, the cost of acquisition can be reduced instead of computing a gain on a part-disposal:

Cost of 5,000 ordinary shares	3,750
Less sale of rights August 2018 - proceeds	(300)
Allowed cost carried forward	3,450

Notes

i) As there is no part-disposal there is no CGT liability for 2018/19.

ii) 5% of MV of £7,000 = £350.

Example

Andy holds 100,000 ordinary shares in Beta plc, which he bought in September 2008 for £50,000. In May 2018 there was a rights offer of 1 for 10 which Andy did not take up. Instead he sold his rights for £20,000. The ex-rights price of the whole shareholding on the first day the shares went ex-rights was £120,000.

Compute Andy's chargeable gain for 2018/19.

Solution:	**£**
Proceeds of sale of rights	20,000
Allowable cost (use part-disposal formula)	
$50{,}000 \times \dfrac{20{,}000}{20{,}000 + 120{,}000}$	(7,143)
Chargeable gain subject to capital gains tax before annual exemption	12,857

Note: 5% × ex rights price £120,000 = £6,000, which is less than the proceeds of sale from the rights, therefore this gain cannot be deducted from the cost of the original acquisition under section 122. Instead it must be treated as a capital sum derived from the holding, using the part-disposals statutory formula to find the relevant allowable cost.

Student self-testing questions

Question 1: Felipe

Felipe acquired the following shares in Hirst plc.

Date of acquisition	No. of shares	Cost
9-Nov-90	17,000	£25,000
4-Aug-05	7,000	£19,400
15-Jul-09	6,000	£19,000

He sold 24,000 shares on 20th July 2018 for £80,000.

Calculate the chargeable gain arising.

Solution to Question 1: Felipe

S.104 holding	Number of shares	Cost £
9-Nov-90 Acquisition	17,000	25,000
4-Aug-05 Acquisition	7,000	19,400
15-Jul-09 Acquisition	6,000	19,000
Total	30,000	63,400
20-Jul-2018 Sale (24/30)	(24,000)	(50,720)
Balance to carry forward	6,000	12,680

Felipe CG computation 2018/19	£
Sale proceeds	80,000
Cost (from working)	(50,720)
Chargeable gain	
(Add to net chargeable gains)	**29,280**

Question 2: Paul

Paul had the following transactions in shares of Super Ltd, in which he holds the position of Finance Director.

1-Oct-95	Bought 20,000 shares (10%) holding for £30,000
11-Sep-03	Bought 4,000 shares for £10,000
1-Feb-04	Took up rights issue 1 for 2 at £2.75 per share
14-Oct-18	Sold 10,000 shares for £40,000

Compute the gain arising in October 2018 and the capital gains tax payable, assuming Paul has no other gains during the year and a taxable income of £75,000 for 2018/19.

Solution to Question 2: Paul

S.104 holding – Super Ltd shares	Number	Cost £
1-Oct-95 purchase	20,000	30,000
11-Sep-03 purchase	4,000	10,000
Pool at 1-Feb-04	24,000	40,000
Rights issues 1-Feb-04	12,000	33,000
	36,000	73,000
14-Oct-2018 sale	(10,000)	(20,278)
carried forward	26,000	52,722

Paul CGT computation 2018/19	£
Sale proceeds	40,000
Cost	(20,278)
Chargeable gain	19,722
Annual exemption	(11,700)
Chargeable gain subject to CGT (qualifying for ER)	8,022
CGT payable @ entrepreneurs' relief rate (10%)	802

Question 3: Tony

Tony has the following transactions in the 10p ordinary shares of Walrus plc, a quoted trading company.

30-Apr-2002	purchased	1,500	shares cost	£2,475
20-May-2003	sold	500	shares for cash	£1,000
25-Oct-2009	purchased	500	shares cost	£1,000
30-Mar-2019	sold	1,200	shares for cash	£10,000

Compute the chargeable gain for 2018/19.

Solution to Question 3: Tony

Section 104 Holding: Pool working	Number of shares	Qualifying expenditure £
30-Apr-2002 Purchase	1,500	2,475
20-May-2003 Sale (500/1,500)	(500)	(825)
25-Oct-2009 Purchase	500	1,000
	1,500	2,650
30-Mar-2019 Sale (1,200/1,500)	(1,200)	(2,120)
s 104 holding Pool carried forward	300	530

CG computation:

Sale proceeds	10,000
Allowable cost:	
Section 104 holding	(2,120)
Chargeable gain before annual exemption	**7,880**

Note: If Tony had been an incorporated taxpayer Tony Ltd, the pool working would have involved an extra column to calculate the indexation allowance within the share pool, and claim the appropriate share of this in the chargeable gain computation.

Questions without answers

Question 4: Frank

Frank acquired 10,000 ordinary shares in Trent plc on 12th May 2002 for £1,500. On 15th December 2003, T plc made a rights issue of 1 for 5 at a price of 130p. Frank took up the rights and then sold half of his total holding on 10th May 2018, for £16,000.

Compute the CGT liability of Frank for 2018/19, if he had no other capital transactions and his taxable income is £65,000, with no Gift Aid or personal pension payments. The shares do not qualify for entrepreneurs' relief.

Question 5: Trevor

Trevor has the following transactions in the 10p ordinary shares of Baker plc, a quoted company. Trevor has taxable income of £38,000 for 2018/19.

4-May-02	purchased	5,300	@	100p	£5,300
16-May-02	purchased	1,000	@	104p	£1,040
30-Apr-03	purchased	3,000	@	125p	£3,750
5-Sep-10	purchased	2,000	@	150p	£3,000
31-Mar-19	sold	9,000	@	300p	£27,000

Compute Trevor's CGT liability for 2018/19. The shares do not qualify for Entrepreneurs' Relief.

Question 6: Claudius

Claudius had the following share transactions in 2018/19.

(1) Sold 2,250 quoted ordinary shares of Nero plc for £23,150 in March 2019. Before making the sale he owned 6,750 shares, of which 4,500 were purchased in December 1988 for £4,599 and 2,250 were acquired in August 1992 on the occasion of the company's rights issue of 1 for 2 at 160p per share.

(2) Sold 2,550 quoted shares of Livia plc for £12,375 on 10th June 2018. His previous transactions in those shares had been as follows.

April 1988	Purchased	1,500	cost	£3,093
August 1990	Purchased	900	cost	£2,700
May 1992	Bonus issue	1 for 2		

(3) Sold 13,500 units of the Tiberius Unit Trust for £11,480 on 15th June 2018, which had cost £3,450 upon their original offer to the public in June 1987.

(4) Gave his brother 12,000 quoted shares in Augustus plc out of his holding of 30,000 shares in March 2019. He had originally purchased 22,500 shares in January 1989 at a cost of £49,500 and received a scrip issue of 1 for 3 in June 1991. At the date of the gift the shares were quoted at 150p each.

Claudius's taxable income for 2018/19 is £55,000.

Requirement:

Calculate Claudius' liability to capital gains tax for the tax year 2018/19. None of the transactions undertaken qualifies for Entrepreneurs' Relief.

31 CGT special reliefs and CGs groups

31.1 Introduction

This chapter discusses various important CGT reliefs. Most of them are given specifically to businesses or on chargeable assets of a business, but a minority (mainly EIS reinvestment relief) can also be used to defer gains on non-business assets. The first reliefs discussed, rollover / holdover reliefs on asset replacements, is available for both companies and individuals. The next few special reliefs only apply for individuals. (Trustees' CGT is outside the scope of this book.) At the end of the chapter, further special rules and reliefs available only to companies, especially in capital gains groups (CG groups) as defined by TCGA, are outlined. Few illustrative worked examples are given on CGs group rules, as this is beyond the scope of an introductory textbook.

The holdover relief available (by election) to individuals, to defer (or transfer) the capital gain made upon gifting a business asset is covered in Chapter 32.

The rationale for most CGT reliefs is either fairness or convenience (or both). Some of them are designed to reward 'entrepreneurship' or to assist succession planning in family businesses.

31.2 Deferral reliefs

The earliest CGT business asset reliefs deferred a gain to a later occasion while preserving its taxable value. These can be categorised as 'deferral reliefs'. Some of these reliefs were automatic; some had to be claimed (so were optional).

The attraction of some deferral reliefs for individuals has been changed by the advent in 2008 of entrepreneurs' relief (ER). ER offers the certainty of a low (10%) CGT rate, but requires tax to be paid up front, with no opportunity to put off the assessment of the tax to a later tax year. To get the certainty of the benefit of ER, a taxpayer must forgo the option to defer the gain to a later date. On the other hand, claiming a deferral relief, such as gift or incorporation relief, runs the genuine risk that the present low general CGT rates may rise again before the gain becomes chargeable.

31.3 Reliefs for corporate taxpayers

Corporate taxpayers do not have the option of the personal CGT reliefs designed for individuals, though they can get the rollover relief or holdover relief on replacement of business assets. Perhaps the biggest recent change to company capital gains taxation was the introduction in 2004 of the 'substantial shareholdings exemption', discussed at Section 31.13. This removed the kind of double taxation that used often to apply when companies sold shares in their subsidiaries or associates.

31.4 Topics in this chapter

In this chapter the following topics will be examined, in the order shown:

a) Rollover and holdover relief on replacement of business assets (available to both individuals and companies, including groups of companies);

b) Entrepreneurs' relief (for individuals);

c) Incorporation relief for individuals (on transfer of the assets of an unincorporated business into a company in return for shares);

d) Capital Gains groups for companies (outline only);

e) The Substantial Shareholdings Exemption (SSE) for companies;

f) CGT treatment of capital assets transferred to or from a business's trading stock (inventory).

31.5 Rollover relief on replacement of business assets

The rollover relief provisions (sections 152-158 of TCGA) allow a taxpayer to 'roll over' a gain, or part of a gain, arising on the disposal of a qualifying business asset, by reinvesting the proceeds in a replacement qualifying asset and reducing the base cost of the new asset by the amount of the gain deferred. It is not necessary that the asset disposed of, and the asset(s) specified in the claim as its qualifying replacement(s), be the same type of asset.

Further rules are as follows:

a) A 'business asset' for this purpose is a chargeable asset that is used wholly for the purposes of a trade, and falls within the following classes, listed in the Act:

- land and buildings;
- fixed plant and [fixed] machinery;
- satellites, space stations, space craft;
- ships, aircraft and hovercraft;
- goodwill *;
- EU agricultural quotas *.

The last two items, being intangible assets, are not chargeable assets for corporate taxpayers, and so cannot support a replacement asset deferral claim for a company. They remain qualifying assets for individuals.

b) If the new asset is not a 'depreciating asset', (see below) the gain is deferred indefinitely, which is called 'full rollover'. The gain is deducted from the CGT cost of the replacement asset(s), in proportion to the proceeds reinvested in each one.

If the new asset is a 'depreciating asset', the gain is technically only 'held over,' and can only be deferred for a maximum of ten years. See 31.6 for more on this.

c) The asset disposed of ('the old asset') must have been used for a trade throughout the period of ownership, measured only from 31st March 1982 if owned before then. Use for a trade includes, in the case of an individual, the use of personal assets (such as a building) by the taxpayer's personal company so long as no rent is charged.

d) The replacement asset acquired ('the new asset') must be brought into immediate use in the taxpayer's trade. Where a 'new asset' is not, on acquisition, immediately taken into use for the purposes of a trade, it will nevertheless qualify for relief provided:

   i) the owner proposes to incur capital expenditure for the purpose of enhancing its value;

   ii) any work arising from such capital expenditure begins as soon as possible after acquisition, and is completed within a reasonable time;

   iii) on completion of the work the asset is taken into use for the purpose of the trade and for no other purpose; and

   iv) the asset is not let or used for any non-trading purpose in the period between acquisition and the time it is taken into use for the purposes of the trade.

e) The new asset must be acquired within 12 months before the date of disposal, or three years after. HMRC has power to extend these limits.

f) Where a trader closes one trade and re-invests in business assets to be used in a new trade, relief is available providing the interval between the two trades is not greater than three years.

g) Only partial relief is available where the whole of the proceeds of sale are not used in the replacement. In these circumstances, the gain is restricted to the extent that the disposal proceeds are not reinvested. That is, the gain immediately charged to tax is the lower of:

   i) the proceeds not reinvested, and

   ii) the chargeable gain (in which case the claim has not been effective).

   By concession HMRC regard proceeds net of disposal costs for this purpose.

h) Where the proceeds from the disposal of an asset are used as capital expenditure to enhance the value of existing assets, that can be treated as acquisition of a new asset, provided:

   i) the other assets are used only for the purposes of the trade, or

   ii) on completion of the work on which the expenditure was incurred, the assets are immediately taken into use and used only for the purposes of the trade.

Example – rollover relief for an individual

Peterkin purchased the freehold land of a retail business in 1989 for £15,000 and sold it on 1st December 2018 for £40,000. On 31st December 2018 Peterkin purchased the freehold building of a new business for £60,000.

Compute the chargeable gain.

Solution: Computation 2018/19	£
Proceeds of sale of land	40,000
Less original cost	(15,000)
Chargeable gain eligible for rollover relief	25,000
Cost of new building	60,000
Less rolled over gain from land	(25,000)
Reduced CGT base cost of new building carried forward	35,000

Notes:

i) The base cost on any subsequent disposal of the new business asset is £35,000.

ii) There is no charge to CGT on the first disposal as all of the proceeds have been re-invested.

Example

Karen purchased a freehold factory for her business use in 1992 for £75,000. This was sold for £250,000 on 31st May 2018, and a new factory acquired for £230,000.

Compute the chargeable gain.

Solution: Computation 2018/19	£	£
Proceeds of sale		250,000
Less cost		(75,000)
Potential chargeable gain		175,000
Less rollover relief:		
Gain	175,000	
Less amount of consideration not reinvested	(20,000)	(155,000)
Gain chargeable immediately		20,000

Notes

i) The base cost for subsequent disposals would be £230,000 – £155,000 i.e. £75,000.

ii) The rolled over gain is restricted by any part of the consideration not reinvested, i.e. (250,000 – 230,000) = 20,000.

31.6 Replacement with a 'depreciating asset'

Where either the old asset or the replacement asset (or both) is a depreciating asset, the gain is not used to reduce the base cost of the replacement asset, but is instead 'held over' until the earliest of the following events:

a) disposal of the replacement asset (e.g. sale, gift or scrapping), or

b) the replacement asset ceases to be used in a trade, or

c) the expiry of 10 years from the date of the replacement.

A 'depreciating asset' is defined as one which will be a wasting asset for CGT within 10 years from the date of acquisition, i.e. will last less than 60 years at the date of acquisition.

This effectively covers all assets on the approved rollover list except

i) land and buildings held on freehold or long-leasehold (an over 60 year lease);
ii) exceptionally long-life fixed plant (such as certain fixtures in buildings);
iii) goodwill (for individual taxpayers only).

Where a gain on a disposal is initially held over against a depreciating asset, and a suitable non-depreciating asset is bought later, before the held-over gain on the depreciating asset crystallises, it is possible to 'roll over' the held-over gain a second time, into a non-depreciating replacement.

Depreciating asset holdover relief is often called 'temporary rollover' by tax practitioners, in order to distinguish it from other CGT reliefs known as 'holdovers', principally the holdover relief on a gift of a business asset (see Chapter 32).

Example of holdover relief – depreciating asset

Johnny sold his freehold shop property, which he had used wholly for trade purposes, for £120,000 on 1st August 2009. The property was bought for £50,000 on 1st May 2001. In December 2009 Johnny acquired plant for £130,000, which he used immediately for trade purposes until he ceased trading altogether on 31st January 2019, when all plant was scrapped. He had no other gains in the year 2018/19.

Compute the chargeable gain arising when the plant was scrapped.

Solution

Johnny's CG computation 2009/10 (required to compute held-over gain):

	£
1st August 2009 Proceeds of sale of property	120,000
1st May 2001 Cost of acquisition	(50,000)
Chargeable gain	70,000
Less amount held over	(70,000)
Chargeable gain after holdover relief	Nil

Johnny's CGT computation 2018/19 (when held-over gain crystallised):

	£
Held-over gain crystallising	70,000
Less annual exemption	(11,700)
Gain subject to CGT	58,300
CGT at 10%	5,830

Notes

i) As the business ceased to trade the held-over gain has crystallised. Entrepreneurs' relief (see section 31.7) is available to Johnny on this gain, as the trade has ceased, and he has owned the business for over one year.

ii) No further gain arises on the scrapping of the plant, as original cost is assumed to exceed any sale proceeds (given that the word 'scrapped' is used and no proceeds are stated). No capital loss is claimable for this scrapping as the net economic cost is already relieved by way of capital allowances (see Chapter 13).

iii) The held-over gain is not deducted from the cost of the replacement depreciating asset(s) for CGs purposes, but is 'held in suspense' until the plant is all scrapped.

31.7 Entrepreneurs' relief (ER) for individuals

Entrepreneurs' Relief was introduced to compensate business owners who were disadvantaged by Business Asset Taper Relief being abolished. However ER does not cover all the disposal types where BATR was given pre-2008/09. In particular, ER applies to the disposal of a business or part of a business but does **not** cover gains on **single** business assets that are sold or gifted by the owner.

ER is not automatic: it must be claimed. It is claimed on sheet SA108, which is a supplement to the annual self-assessment tax return (see 25.21 and 25.22).

ER is available in respect of gains made by individuals on the disposal of:

a) all (or a complete separately-functioning part) of a trading business which the individual carries on alone or in partnership (but note that, a claim for ER is **not** available in respect of any gain arising from the disposal of goodwill to a limited company in which the individual holds 5% or more of the shares, or 5% or more of the voting rights (unless the transfer of the business to the company is part of arrangements to sell the business to a new, independent owner));

b) individual assets of an individual's or partnership's trading business, following the cessation of that business for income tax purposes (the relief is available for one year after cessation);

c) shares in (and securities of) the individual's 'personal' trading company (or the personal holding company of a trading group). The relief is given in this case only if throughout a one-year qualifying period before the share disposal, the individual making the disposal:

   i) is an officer or employee of the company, or of another company in the same group; and

   ii) owns at least 5 per cent of the ordinary share capital of the company, and that holding enables the individual to exercise at least 5 per cent of the voting rights in the company.

d) assets owned by an individual personally and provided rent-free for trade use by his/her 'personal' trading company (or personal trading group), or by his or her trading partnership, provided that they are associated with a disposal of at least a 5% shareholding in the company or a 5% share in the assets of the partnership. [Note that this 5% condition does not apply to the disposal of the whole of an individual's interest, if it previously formed part of a larger stake]

e) The above rules for ER extend to assets of the same types legally owned by trustees and personal representatives. In the case of (c) the beneficiary of the trust, or the deceased person in the case of personal representatives, should meet the employment condition if shares are to qualify.

It is also worth noting that a gain on any property used for qualifying furnished holiday lettings qualifies for ER once the business ownership period exceeds twelve months. Compared with a potential CGT liability at 28% on let properties, this is a substantial incentive to landlords to run a qualifying FHL business rather than an ordinary letting business.

In contrast to unincorporated business disposals (generally no ER unless there is a disposal of the whole business), a shareholding can be reduced in stages by successive part-disposals, each still qualifying for ER, so long as the owner continues to meet the ER requirement of still holding the shares in a 'personal trading company'. This requires both employment by the company and a holding (before each disposal) of at least at least 5% of shares by voting control.

The 'lifetime limit' for ER gains per individual is now £10 million. It is a cumulative limit for the ER gains of all tax years since 2008/09 inclusive. Once a taxpayer's cumulative ER gains have exceeded £10 million any further chargeable gains are taxed at the ordinary rates – currently 10% and 20%.

31.8 Entrepreneurs' relief – extension to long term investors

Entrepreneurs' relief was extended in the 2016 Budget to external individual shareholders in unlisted trading companies. The extension applies to shares issued on or after 17th March 2016, which are held for a period of at least three years starting from 6th April 2016. 'Investors' relief' is subject to a similar (but separate) lifetime cap of £10 million as entrepreneurs' relief.

31.9 Transfer of a business to a company – incorporation relief (Section 162 TCGA)

The transfer of a business to a company is a disposal of the assets of the unincorporated business and can therefore give rise to more than one chargeable gain (or allowable capital loss).

A form of long-duration deferral relief exists where an individual transfers the whole of his or her business to a company in exchange for shares, wholly or partly. The whole gain is rolled over by deduction from the CGT 'base cost' (i.e., allowable cost) of the shares acquired.

The gain(s) to which this section relates is/are that or those gain(s) arising on the transfer of chargeable business assets, and the amount deferred is equal to:

$$\text{The net gain} \times \frac{\text{Value of shares received}}{\text{Total value of consideration, e.g. shares and loans and cash}}$$

All assets of the business (except cash) must be transferred to the company. Cash balances and any non-business assets may be retained by the taxpayer.

The taxpayer can elect for the incorporation relief *not* to apply, which may be advantageous in terms of his/her entrepreneurs relief entitlement - for instance if he/she will not be a future employee of the company which acquired the business.

Example

Andrea transfers her established sole-trade business to Trent Ltd on 6th April 2018 in exchange for 100,000 ordinary shares of £1 each fully paid, having a value of par, and a loan declaration document promising to pay her £25,000 cash once the company can do so. The only chargeable business asset involved was goodwill on which a capital gain was realised of £75,000. Andrea has been in business since 1990.

Compute the chargeable gain if Andrea accepts incorporation relief.

Solution: Calculation of Andrea's s.162 rolled-over gain 2018/19

	£
Total chargeable gain	75,000
Less s. 162 incorporation relief (gain related to share proceeds):	
Gain $75{,}000 \times \frac{100{,}000}{100{,}000 + 25{,}000} =$	(60,000)
Gain immediately chargeable (before annual exemption)	15,000

Deemed base cost of shares carried forward	£
Value of shares at issue	100,000
Less rolled-over gain under s. 162 incorporation relief	(60,000)
Net base cost of shareholding on a future CGs computation	40,000

31.10 Capital Gains Groups

If a company's chargeable asset transactions involve other members of the same CGs group, special rules apply. The main rules and reliefs are outlined below, but this is by no means a full coverage of all the rules about CGs groups.

This section explains how a corporate CGs group is defined by TCGA. CGs groups are not optional, but depend on the legal and voting control within the group.

No company can be in two different CGs groups at the same time (unlike group relief groups where a company can have a GR connection with each of two other companies which may not themselves share a GR relationship – see Chapter 23).

a) A CGs group comprises a principal company and all of its 75% subsidiaries.

b) A 75% subsidiary means a company whose ordinary share capital is owned by the other company, either directly or indirectly, to the extent of at least 75%. Ordinary share capital comprises all shares other than fixed interest preference shares.

c) A company is not a member of a given CGs group unless the principal member of the group holds either directly or indirectly a more than 50% interest in the other company's profits, voting control, and assets.

d) Chargeable assets can be passed around within a CGs group without immediate tax implications, but no company can be in two different CGs groups at the same time so there is a boundary outside which assets cannot pass without triggering a full disposal of the chargeable asset.

e) The principal company of a CGs group defines how the 75% ownership boundary is drawn for all the others in that group.

   For example, if A plc owns 75% of B Ltd and B Ltd owns 75% of C Ltd, then there is a > 50% indirect relationship between A and C, as A's ownership of C is 56.25% (75% x 75%).

   So A, B and C are in the same CGs group (assuming no other company owns > 75% of A plc, which would alter the position).

   However, if C Ltd now owns 80% of D Ltd, A's ownership interest in D Ltd is only 80% x 56.25%, which is 45%. So D Ltd cannot be included in A plc's CGs group.

   In this example, A, B and C will form the A plc CGs group, with A plc defined as the principal company of that CGs group.

   D Ltd is not in the A plc CGs group, (through D Ltd could in theory be the principal company of a different CGs group, consisting of itself and its 75% subsidiaries).

   D Ltd also cannot be in the same CGs group with its direct parent, C Ltd - even though C owns 80% of D Ltd. This is because C Ltd cannot be principal company of a group, if it already belongs to the CGs group where A plc is the principal company.

f) A CGs group can include a direct or indirect control link through a company not resident in the UK. But a non-UK company cannot itself be one of the two companies involved in a chargeable asset transaction eligible for group treatment, unless the asset involved belongs to a trading branch (permanent establishment) of the non-resident company which is within the charge to UK corporation tax.

31.11 Effect of CGs groups on the tax treatment of transactions

It can be seen from above that the definition of a group for corporate capital gains is different from that for group loss reliefs (covered in Chapter 23.)

The presence of a CGs group can alter the deemed proceeds, chargeable person, or chargeable occasion relating to a chargeable asset transaction by a company. Key points are as follows:

(a) For rollover relief on replacement of assets, the trades of all companies in the CGs group are deemed by law to be a single trade. Thus the gain on an asset disposal by one group company can be reinvested in an asset or assets acquired by another group company.

(b) When a group company disposes of a chargeable asset to any other company in the CGs group, this asset disposal takes place for tax purposes at no-gain-no-loss. This treatment is automatic for companies in the same CGs group. Any actual payment made is irrelevant for tax purposes.

The no-gain-no-loss treatment is achieved by deeming the consideration for the transfer (regardless of actual payment) to be equal to all allowable deductions available to the previous owning company for CG purposes. Those deductions include indexation allowance up to the month of transfer. This deemed consideration then becomes the allowable cost of the asset for the next company in the CGs group to own the transferred asset.

When such an asset is ultimately disposed of outside the group, the gain calculated on normal principles (using the NGNL cost as the allowable base cost) forms part of the taxable profits of the disposing company; unless it elects to treat the final disposal as made by another group company – see (c).

(c) Any two UK-resident companies in a CGs group can elect within 2 years of the end of a CTAP that a chargeable asset disposal physically and legally made by one of them is to be treated, for all corporation tax purposes, as if it were made by the other company. This can be done whether the disposal gives rise to a chargeable gain or an allowable loss.

(d) Members of a consortium are not eligible for treatment as a group for the purposes of this section, nor are close investment holding companies, unless the transfer is made between close investment holding companies.

Example of transfer of a capital loss between CGs group members

Zodiac Ltd (Z Ltd) and its 75% subsidiary company Burnham Ltd (B Ltd) had the following results for the year ended 31st March 2019.

	Z Ltd	B Ltd
Trading profits	125,000	80,000
Chargeable (loss) / gain	(75,000)	100,000

Zodiac Ltd and Burnham Ltd jointly elect that the capital loss of £75,000 arising in the year to Z Ltd is to be treated as a disposal by B Ltd.

Show the effects of the election.

Solution: Corporation tax computations for CTAP ended 31st March 2019

	Z Ltd	B Ltd	Total
Trading profits	125,000	80,000	
Chargeable gains (100,000 – 75,000)	NIL	25,000	
	125,000	105,000	
Corporation tax @ 19%	23,750	19,950	43,700

Notes

i) It is not necessary for Z Ltd actually to transfer the asset, giving rise to the loss of £75,000, to B Ltd before the disposal takes place. Especially in the case of land sales, this greatly simplifies the legal aspects of the disposal.

ii) The gain or loss transfer election must be made by both companies jointly, within two years of the end of the AP when the gain-producing asset was disposed of outside the group, i.e. in this case by 31st March 2021.

iii) The election can be made in respect of part of an asset.

iv) Assuming there are no other associated companies, without the election to transfer, B Ltd would be taxed at 19% on Taxable Total Profits of £180,000 and Z Ltd would have to pay tax at 19% on all £125,000 of its trade profits because its capital loss cannot be used against trading profits.

v) Group cash savings:

		£
CT before the election = Z Ltd (125k × 19%)	(unchanged)	23,750
B Ltd (£180k × 19%)		34,200
	Total	57,950
CT after the election = (as above)		(43,700)
		14,250

Capital loss value to B Ltd = 75,000× 19%) = £14,250

OR (simply comparing B's CT) (34,200 – 19,950) = £14,250

31.12 Miscellaneous points

(a) When a chargeable asset that has qualified for capital allowances is disposed of by a group company to a party outside the group, then any net capital allowances granted to any member of the group relating to the asset must be taken into consideration as non-deductible cost when computing the net chargeable gain or loss.

(b) If a company to which an asset has been transferred intra-group at no-gain-no-loss ceases to be a member of a group within six years of the date of that asset transfer, the following tax consequences arise.

  (i) the company now leaving the group is deemed to have sold and reacquired the asset at its market value on the date of the past intra-group transfer of the asset;

  (ii) As a result, a chargeable gain arises on the difference between the market value at the time of the intra-group transfer, and the original cost (plus indexation) of the asset to the group. That gain crystallises in the company which is selling its shareholding and causing the asset-holding company to leave the CGs group.

  This provision does not apply if a company ceases to be a member of a group by being wound up (though logically in that case it must have made a disposal of the chargeable asset to another owner, in the course of the winding-up).

  There is no charge on the intra-group deferred gain if the departing company leaves the group more than six years from the intra-group no-gain-no-loss transfer.

(c) When a company is a dual-resident member of a CGs group, detailed provisions exist which are designed to prevent:

  (i) the transfer of assets at a no-gain-no-loss value where the dual resident company would be exempt from UK corporation tax on a later disposal, under a Double Tax Treaty

  (ii) the granting of rollover relief for the replacement of business assets where the replacement assets were acquired by a dual-resident company.

(d) 'Pre-acquisition' capital losses brought into a group, when a company joins with its own brought-forward capital losses from past transactions, are not available to set against future group gains even if the necessary election is made to transfer the disposals to the company with the pre-acquisition losses. In effect such capital losses are only available for unrestricted set-off against gains on:

  (i) assets already held by the same company at the date that it joined the group, or

  (ii) assets acquired from outside the new group by that company after joining the group, and used by it in a trade that was already carried on by that company before it joined the group.

31.13 Substantial shareholdings exemption for companies

Disposals by companies of 'substantial shareholdings' in other companies are exempt from UK corporation tax on chargeable gains, provided that certain conditions are met.

i) The relief is available for disposals by a trading company or a member of a trading group (the 'investing' company).

ii) It applies to gains on the disposal of a 'substantial shareholding' in another trading company, or holding company of a trading group (the 'investee' company).

iii) A substantial shareholding means at least a 10% interest.

iv) The substantial shareholding must have been held for a continuous period of at least 12 months falling within the two years immediately before the date of the disposal.

In order to hold a substantial interest, the investing company needs to be beneficially entitled to at least 10% of the investee company's:

i) ordinary share capital; and

ii) profits available for distribution to equity holders; and

iii) assets available for distribution to equity holders in the event of a winding-up.

In determining whether a holding amounts to a substantial shareholding, any shares held by other group members are aggregated over the world-wide group.

31.14 Trading stock

'Trading' stock (inventory) is not a CGT chargeable asset – it is sold to generate taxable trading income.

Where an asset, originally held for continuing use in the business, is transferred into trading stock, there is a deemed disposal at its market value at the date of the appropriation. An election can be made to have the resulting capital gain deducted from (or the loss added to) the base cost of the asset in inventory, so that the ultimate profit is all taxed as trading income when the asset is sold and not before.

If the reverse happens, and an asset is appropriated from trading stock to non-current assets for any purpose (eg a builder who decides to retain and let a constructed block of flats, instead of selling them), the asset is deemed to be acquired for CGT purposes at the disposal value that was taken into account in computing the trader's assessable trading profit.

Example

Keith purchased an asset in October 1986 for £20,000 which he held as an investment until 31st July 2018 when it was transferred to trading stock. Market value at 31st July was £45,000. It was sold as trading stock in December 2018 for £60,000.

Show the effects of the above, both with and without an election to aggregate the capital gain on appropriation into trading stock value.

Solution

a) Without election: Keith's CGT computation 2018/19

		£
July 2018 market value of asset (= deemed proceeds)		45,000
Less cost of acquisition		(20,000)
Chargeable gain to Keith in 2018/19		25,000
Keith's Tax-adjusted trading profits (extract)		£
Sale of inventory (trading stock)		60,000
Less cost (= deemed cost/ market value)		(45,000)
Taxable profit		15,000

With election: Keith's CGT computation 2018/19

		£
July 2018 market value of asset (= deemed proceeds)		45,000
Less cost of acquisition		(20,000)
Potential capital gain on appropriation		25,000
Less gain deducted from cost of inventory		(25,000)
Chargeable gain		nil
Keith's Tax-adjusted trading profits (extract)	£	£
Sale of inventory (trading stock)		60,000
Less cost:		
Market value on appropriation	45,000	
Less gain deducted (as above)	(25,000)	
		(20,000)
Taxable trade profits		40,000

Notes

i) The asset must be of a kind sold in the ordinary course of trade.

ii) The appropriation must be made with a view to resale at a profit.

iii) An election is only available to a person who pays income tax on trade profits.

Student self-testing questions

Question 1: Alfie

Alfie, a sole trader, bought a freehold factory in October 1998 and sold it for £340,000 on 18th May 2018 giving a gain of £135,900. He bought a replacement factory on 6th June 2018 for £320,000.

Requirement: Assuming a claim for rollover relief was made, what is the base cost, going forward, of the new factory?

Solution to Question 1: Alfie

	£
Total gain	135,900
Less Amount not reinvested (340,000 - 320,000) (taxed immediately)	(20,000)
= Gain eligible for roll-over	115,900
Cost of new factory	120,000
Less Gain rolled over by claiming under section 152	(115,900)
Base cost of new factory	204,100

Question 2: Linda

Linda is a sole trader who bought a qualifying business asset for £341,250 on 5th November 1991 and sold it for £982,800 on 31st December 2018. A replacement business asset was acquired on 1st November 2018 at a cost of £1,092,000. This asset was sold on 3rd September 2021 for £1,829,100. A rollover claim was made on the first sale only. Assume existing CGT rules will still apply in 2021.

Requirement: Calculate Linda's expected capital gain on the sale of the second asset.

Solution to Question 2: Linda

Working 1: 2018/19 disposal (needed to find the rollover relief amount)

	£	£
Sale proceeds 31-Dec-2018		982,800
Less Cost		(341,250)
= potential capital Gain		641,550
– Rollover relief claimed (no restriction, as all proceeds reinvested in qualifying asset within the required time-frame)		(641,550)
Chargeable gain in 2018/19		NIL

Linda's capital gain on the 2021/22 disposal

Sale proceeds		1,829,100
Less Cost (1st November 2018)	1,092,000	
Less Rollover relief claimed 2018/19	(641,550)	(450,450)
Chargeable gain 2021/22		1,378,650

Question 3: Hadley Limited

Hadley Limited purchased a factory in November 1989 for £250,000. Not needing all the space, the company let out 15% of it. In January 2019 the company sold the factory for £800,000 and bought another in the same month for £900,000. Assume an indexation factor of 1.347 from November 1989 to December 2017.

Requirement: Calculate:

(a) The chargeable gain or allowable loss, if any, arising on the disposal in January 2019

(b) The base cost of the new factory.

Solution to Question 3: Hadley Limited

(a) Split the old factory & the new factory into qualifying and non-qualifying parts and compute the gains on them separately:

	Qualifying	Non qualifying
	£	£
Disposal proceeds (85%/15%)	680,000	120,000
Less cost	(212,500)	(37,500)
Unindexed gain	467,500	82,500
Indexation allowance		
(212,500 × 1.347) and (37,500 × 1.347)	(286,238)	(50,513)
Indexed gain	181,262	31,987

The gain of £31,987 will be taxed immediately as it does not qualify for rollover relief.

(b) The base cost of the new factory is reduced by the amount of the gain rolled over. It is therefore:

	£
Purchase cost	900,000
Less gain rolled over	(181,262)
Base cost of new factory	718,738

Question 4: Harold

Harold bought a freehold shop for use in his business in June 2010 for £150,000. He sold it for £175,000 on 1st August 2018. On 8th July 2018 Harold bought some plant and machinery to use in his business costing £178,000. He will sell the plant and machinery for £192,000 on 20th November 2019.

Show Harold's CGT position in 2019/20 assuming 2018/19 rules will continue unchanged.

Solution to Question 4: Harold

2018/19:	£
Proceeds of shop disposal	175,000
Less cost (no other details available)	(150,000)
= Capital Gain 2018/19	25,000
Less holdover claim	(25,000)
Chargeable gain 2018/19	NIL

The gain is deferred by a holdover claim in relation to the plant and machinery.

2019/20	
Disposal of plant and machinery:	£
Proceeds	192,000
Less cost	(178,000)
Gain	14,000
Add held-over gain now crystallising	25,000
Total chargeable gains from sale in 2019/20	39,000

Questions without answers

Question 5: Anthony

Anthony purchased a grocery business on 1st June 1988 which he is considering selling, to an unrelated purchaser, in December 2018 for an estimated price of £400,000. The sale price is allocated between the business assets as follows:

	Consideration
	£
Freehold premises	275,000
Flat above premises (occupied by Anthony since acquisition as his only residence)	40,000
Goodwill	50,000
Inventory	20,000
Shop fixtures	15,000
	400,000

The cost of the business at 1st June 1988 was £150,000 comprising the following:

	£
Freehold premises	60,000
Flat above premises	30,000
Goodwill	40,000
Inventory	15,000
Shop fixtures	5,000

The shop fixtures are a number of 'wasting assets' and none were sold for more than their original cost.

Calculate the CGT liability which would arise should Anthony sell the business in 2018/19 and retire. He expects no other chargeable gains to arise in 2018/19 and has taxable income of £45,000 for 2018/19.

Question 6: Chandra Khan

Chandra Khan disposed of the following assets during 2018/19:

a) On 15th June 2018 Chandra sold 10,000 £1 ordinary shares (a 30% shareholding) in Universal Ltd, an unquoted trading company, to her daughter for £75,000. The market value of the holding on this date was £110,000. The entire shareholding was purchased on 10th July 1997 for £38,000. Chandra and her daughter have elected to defer the gain as a gift of a business asset.

b) On 8th November 2018 Chandra sold a freehold factory for £146,000. The factory was purchased on 3rd January 1997 for £72,000. 75% of the factory has been used in a manufacturing business run by Chandra as a sole trader. However, the remaining 25% of the factory has never been used for business purposes. Chandra has claimed to roll over the gain on the factory against the replacement cost of a new freehold factory that was purchased on 10th November 2018 for £156,000. The new factory is used 100% for business purposes by Chandra.

c) On 8th March 2019 Chandra incorporated a wholesale business that she had run as a sole trader since 1st May 2003. The market value of the business on 8th March 2019 was £250,000. All of the business assets were transferred to a new limited company, with the consideration given to Chandra consisting of all the 200,000 £1 ordinary shares in the company valued at £200,000 and £50,000 in cash. The only chargeable asset of the business was goodwill, and this was valued at £100,000 on 8th March 2019. The goodwill had a nil cost to Chandra.

Calculate the capital gains arising from Chandra's disposals during 2018/19. You should ignore the annual exemption. (ACCA updated)

Question 7: Astute Limited

Astute Ltd sold a factory on 15th January 2019 for £420,000. The factory was purchased on 24th October 1997 for £164,000, and was extended at a cost of £37,000 during March 1999. During May 2000 the roof of the factory was replaced at a cost of £24,000 following a fire. Astute Ltd incurred legal fees of £3,600 in connection with the purchase of the factory, and legal fees of £6,200 in connection with the disposal.

Astute Ltd is considering the following alternative ways of reinvesting the proceeds from the sale of its factory:

(1) A freehold warehouse can be purchased for £440,000.

(2) A freehold office building can be purchased for £375,000.

(3) A leasehold factory on a 40-year lease can be acquired for a premium of £450,000.

The reinvestment will take place during May 2019.

All of the above buildings have been, or will be, used for business purposes. Astute Ltd prepares annual accounts to 31st December.

The RPI table is available at the end of Chapter 25.

Required:

(a) State the conditions that must be met in order that rollover relief can be claimed. You are not expected to list the categories of asset that qualify for rollover relief. (3 marks)

(b) Before taking account of any potential rollover relief, calculate Astute Ltd's chargeable gain in respect of the disposal of the factory. (5 marks)

(c) Advise Astute Ltd of the rollover relief that will be available in respect of EACH of the three alternative re-investments. Your answer should include details of the base cost of the replacement asset for each alternative. (7 marks)

(15 marks)

(ACCA updated)

32 Gifts and CGT gift holdover relief

32.1 Introduction

This chapter is concerned with CGT treatment of gifts of chargeable assets. It begins with a list of exempt gifts and then examines the optional gift 'holdover' relief, which can only be claimed on gifts of **business** assets (as defined).

No coverage is given here of the other CGT gift holdover relief which is available on gifting a chargeable asset to a relevant property trust in circumstances which create a chargeable lifetime transfer for IHT. Trusts in general are outside the scope of this book (other than a brief mention in Part V basic inheritance tax).

Gift holdover relief works by deducting the capital gain realised by the gift of a business asset from the deemed (market value) acquisition cost of the person receiving the asset, instead of the gain being immediately chargeable for the donor (the giver of the gift). By doing this the person making the gift avoids a charge to capital gains tax and instead the recipient takes on the expectation that he or she instead will suffer a higher gain on eventual disposal. The relief can be valuable and provide scope for succession planning (including Inheritance tax planning) for family businesses.

It is also worth considering in any other situation where an individual is thinking of disposing of a business asset in a 'non arm's length' transaction (a sale at undervalue)

Gift relief is technically not a full 'rollover' but a holdover relief, because there is one circumstance in which the held-over gain can become chargeable on its own, without any further disposal of the asset. (See 32.4.) However in most cases gift relief operates like a normal rollover relief and the gain is taxed when the relevant asset is disposed of by the donee.

If no chargeable disposal is ever made by the donee (typically, if the donee dies while still owning the asset; death being an exempt disposal for CGT), gift relief can become a permanent CGT relief rather than a deferral relief.

This can also happen if CGT law is reformed after a holdover has been made and before the gain crystallises. For example, when universal CGT rebasing to 1982 occurred in April 1988, as-yet-untaxed held-over gains made before April 1982 fell out of the charge to CGT.

32.2 Gifts and bargains

As stated in Chapter 25, a gift of a chargeable asset amounts to a disposal for capital gains tax purposes. Any disposal by bargain not at arm's length (not just a gift, but equally a sale at undervalue to a favoured friend) is deemed for CGT to be made for consideration equal to market value.

32.3 Exemptions

The following gifts do not give rise to any chargeable gain or loss.

a) A gift to a charity or other approved institution such as the National Gallery, or the British Museum. Such a transfer is deemed to take place on a no gain or loss basis.

b) Gifts of works of art, manuscripts, historic buildings, scenic land etc., if the conditions required for inheritance tax exemption are satisfied.

c) A gift of a chattel with a market value of less than £6,000. See Chapter 29.

d) A gift of an exempt asset such as a private motor car, or the principal private residence of the taxpayer, unless otherwise taxable.

32.4 Gifts of business assets – Section 165

The following are the main provisions relating to gifts of business assets.

a) Gift holdover relief is available to an individual who makes a transfer, for consideration at less than market price, of:

   i) business assets used for the purposes of a trade, profession or vocation carried on by:

      1. the transferor, or
      2. his or her personal company
      3. a member of a trading group, of which the holding company is his or her personal company.

   ii) Shares or securities of any trading company, or of the holding company of a trading company where:

      1. the shares are neither quoted on a stock exchange nor dealt in on the AIM, or,
      2. the trading company or holding company is the transferor's personal company.

   iii) agricultural property qualifying for 100% IHT relief.

b) A personal company is one in which the individual is entitled to exercise 5% or more of the voting rights. (Note that this is not the same as the 'business asset' definition for entrepreneur's relief because the taxpayer can claim gift relief on a company's shares without having to be an officer or employee of the company as well)

c) The relief must be claimed jointly by the transferee and the transferor, within four years of the date of transfer.

d) The relief is only available in respect of a business asset.

e) Holdover relief is not available:

   i) if the donee is non-resident, or is exempt from CGT by reason of a double tax treaty;

   ii) if the recipient is a company controlled by non-residents who are connected with the donor.

f) The held-over gain (in isolation) becomes chargeable on the donee, if the donee emigrates permanently from the UK within six tax years of a gift being made on which holdover relief was claimed. If this happens the held-over gain 'crystallises' as a gain realised by the new owner of the asset at the date of permanently ceasing UK residence and ordinary residence. If the donee becomes non-resident after more than six tax years, there is currently no crystallisation of the held over gain.

Example of gift holdover relief

Beryl purchased the goodwill and freehold property of a retail business for £90,000 in 1990 and gave it to her son in May 2018 when it was worth £200,000.

Compute the chargeable gain that can be held over.

Solution: Computation 2018/19	**£**
Disposal at market price	200,000
Less Cost	(90,000)
Chargeable gain held over by gift relief	110,000

Acquisition by Beryl's son – base cost £	
Market value of assets received by gift	200,000
Less held-over gain	(110,000)
Adjusted base cost on a future disposal	90,000

Example

Cyril purchased freehold business premises in September 1988 for £40,000, and gave the asset to his son Ricky in May 2000 when it was worth £120,000. An election for gift holdover relief was made and accepted.

On 2nd June 2018 Ricky sold the premises for £200,000. Ricky had been running his own business from the premises for five years at the date of the sale.

Compute the chargeable gain to Ricky for 2018/19, and any earlier chargeable gain to Cyril, on the business premises.

Solution: CGT 2000/2001	£
Value of premises	120,000
Cost of acquisition	(40,000)
Held-over gain	80,000
Chargeable gain to Cyril	NIL

CGT 2018/19

Proceeds of sale	200,000
Base cost (120,000 – 80,000)	(40,000)
Chargeable gain to Ricky, subject to CGT at 10%	160,000

Note

i) The gain in 2018/19 is chargeable at 10% as the asset qualifies for entrepreneurs' relief for Ricky.

ii) The annual exemption of £11,700 is still available to Ricky, unless he has other net gains in the year not qualifying for ER, which would take the annual exemption in priority to the ER gain.

32.5 Gift of shares in personal company

If the transfer by an individual is of shares in his or her personal company then the held over gain is restricted, where there are any non-business assets in the company. The gain is restricted where either:

a) at any time within 12 months of disposal not less than 25% of the company's voting rights were exercisable by the transferor, or

b) the company is his or her personal company at any time within that period.

The amount of gift relief available will be calculated as:

$$\text{Chargeable gain} \times \frac{\text{Chargeable business assets of the company at date of disposal}}{\text{Chargeable assets of the company at date of disposal}}$$

$$= \frac{\text{CBA}}{\text{CA}}$$

Example

Stella acquired all the shares of Horton Ltd, a trading company, for £9,000 in March 1994, and transferred them by way of a gift to Phil in May 2018 when they were worth £140,000. At the date of the gift the company's assets were valued thus:

	£
Freehold land and buildings	30,000
Goodwill	30,000
Plant and machinery – all items > £6,000	25,000
Investment in quoted company	60,000
Inventory (stock), receivables (debtors) and cash	18,750

Requirement

Calculate the chargeable gain arising on Stella's gift to Phil for the tax year 2018/19, if both parties agree to claim Gift Relief.

Solution: Computation 2018/19	**£**
Proceeds of sale of shares	140,000
Less cost of acquisition	(9,000)
Potential chargeable gain	131,000
Held over gain: $\frac{85}{145}$ × 131,000 (see working)	(76,793)
Chargeable gain	54,207

Working	**Chargeable business assets** (open market value at date of disposal)	**Chargeable assets**
	£	£
Freehold land	30,000	30,000
Goodwill	30,000	30,000
Investment	–	60,000
Plant and machinery	25,000	25,000
	85,000	145,000

Notes

i) The deemed cost to Phil is £(140,000 – 76,793) i.e. £63,207

ii) Chargeable business assets are any assets on the disposal of which a gain would be a chargeable gain, and excludes, therefore, motor cars and items of moveable plant and machinery sold for £6,000 or less.

iii) Inventory, receivables and cash are exempt from capital gains tax, thus these are not chargeable business assets.

iv) A business asset for gift relief purposes is an asset used for the purpose of trade.

v) Goodwill counted in the business's or company's net asset value is a chargeable business asset for an individual therefore any amount paid for the business / the shares that exceeds the value of identifiable assets can be deemed to relate to goodwill which is a chargeable business asset.

vi) The investment held by the company is not a chargeable business asset.

32.6 Gifts of non-business assets, works of art etc.

Holdover relief is also available on gifts, where both the transferor and the transferee are individuals or trusts for:

i) gifts which are immediately chargeable transfers for IHT purposes i.e. gifts to relevant property trusts (see Part V).

ii) gifts which are either exempt or conditionally exempt for IHT purposes e.g. gifts to political parties or gifts of heritage property, but not PETs.

32.7 Payment of tax by instalments

a) Capital gains tax on gifts not eligible for full holdover relief may be paid by ten equal annual instalments where an election is made. This only applies to the following assets:
   i) Land or any interest in land.
   ii) Shares or securities in a company which immediately before the disposal gave control to the person making the disposal.
   iii) Shares or securities of a company not falling in (ii) and not quoted on a recognised stock exchange nor dealt in on the USM/AIM.

b) Where the gift is to a connected person, tax and accrued interest become payable where the donee subsequently disposes of the gift for a valuable consideration.

c) The first instalment is due on the normal due date. Instalments are not interest free unless the gifted property is agricultural land qualifying for IHT agricultural property relief.

Student self-testing questions

Question 1: Karen

Karen purchased a business in 1990 which she gave to Mark in May 1999 when the market value was £125,000. Both Karen and Mark elected to hold over the computed gain. Mark sold the business in May 2018 for £180,000. The cost in May 1990 was £40,000. The business qualifies for entrepreneurs' relief.

Show the CGT computations.

Solution to Question 1: Karen

Karen CGT Computation 1999/2000	**£**
Deemed proceeds of sale (May 1999)	125,000
Cost (May 1990)	(40,000)
Gain held over (note (i))	85,000
Mark CG Computation 2018/19	**£**
Proceeds of sale (May 2018)	180,000
Deemed base cost to Mark (125,000 – 85,000)	(40,000)
Mark's chargeable gain	140,000

Mark's gain appears eligible for entrepreneurs' relief (and a 10% CGT rate), as Mark is disposing of his whole business.

(Note that Karen could not claim ER on her gift made in 1999 as ER did not exist before 2008.)

No CGT is payable by Karen upon the gift of the asset to Mark in 1999/2000, as no chargeable gain arises to Karen then, due to full gift relief claimed.

Question 2: Michael and Simon

On 5th December 2018, Michael sold to his son Simon for £75,000 a freehold shop, valued at £250,000, from which Michael had previously run his business. Michael and Simon agreed to claim gift relief. Michael had originally purchased the shop in July 2001 for £45,000. Simon initially continued to run his own business from the shop premises but decided to sell the shop in May 2019 for £230,000.

Compute any chargeable gains arising. Assume the rules of CGT in tax year 2018/19 will continue to apply in May 2019.

Solution to Question 2: Michael and Simon

Michael's Chargeable gain position, 2018/19	£
Deemed proceeds (= market value)	250,000
Less cost	(45,000)
Potential capital gain	205,000
Less gain deferred by gift relief claim	
£205,000 – (£75,000-£45,000)	(175,000)
Gain left in charge for 2018/19 (subject to ER claim, & annual exemption)	30,000
Simon's CG position in 2019/20	**£**
Proceeds	230,000
Less base cost: MV £250,000 – £175,000 gift holdover	(75,000)
Simon's Gain subject to CGT	155,000

Notes:

i) In this case, for Michael in 2018/19 the excess of consideration received over his original cost (£30,000) is a gain immediately chargeable to CGT.

ii) Michael's disposal of the shop will only qualify for entrepreneurs' relief if he closed or disposed of his own business (or a complete separately-functioning part) at the same time as he disposed of the shop to Simon.

iii) Simon is deemed to have purchased the shop for £75,000. ER will apply to Simon's gain if he disposes of his own current business along with the shop, but not if he merely relocates it to other premises;

iv) Simon is assumed to meet the ER qualifying condition of having owned and run his business for more than twelve months before disposal.

Questions without answers

Question 3: Penny

Penny purchased a controlling shareholding in Nominal Ltd, a trading company, for £100,000 in 1991 and gave it to her son on 1st April 2004 when she was 48 years of age. The market value of the shareholding at the gift date was £500,000. A joint gift relief claim under Section 165 TCGA 1992 was made. Penny's son sold the shareholding for £650,000 in June 2018.

There were no non-business, chargeable assets owned by Nominal Ltd.

Compute the chargeable gains arising in 2018/19.

Question 4: Jack Chan

Jack Chan, aged 45, has been in business as a sole trader since 1st May 2001. On 28th February 2019 he transferred the whole business to his daughter Jill, at which time the following assets were sold to her by Jack:

(i) Goodwill with a market value of £60,000. The goodwill had been built up since 1st May 2001, and has a nil cost. Jill paid Jack £50,000 for the goodwill.

(ii) A freehold office building with a market value of £130,000. The office building was purchased on 1st July 2003 for £110,000, and has always been used by Jack for business purposes. Jill paid Jack £105,000 for the office building.

(iii) A freehold warehouse with a market value of £140,000. The warehouse was purchased on 1st September 2003 for £95,000, and has never been used by Jack for business purposes. Jill paid Jack £135,000 for the warehouse.

(iv) A motor car with a market value of £25,000. The motor car was purchased on 1st November 2005 for £23,500, and has always been used by Jack for business purposes. Jill paid Jack £20,000 for the motor car.

Wherever possible, Jack and Jill have elected to hold over any gains arising.

Jack has unused capital losses of £6,400 brought forward from 2017/18.

Required: Calculate Jack's capital gains tax liability for 2018/19 and advise him by what date he must pay this tax. (15 marks)

(ACCA updated)

Part V

Inheritance tax

33 General principles of Inheritance Tax

33.1 Introduction to Inheritance Tax

Inheritance tax arises on a '**transfer of value**' (see section 33.2) by a person who is UK domiciled.

It also arises on transfers of property located in the UK by a person who is not UK domiciled. From April 2017, this includes all UK residential property even when held indirectly by a non-domiciled person through an offshore structure (*although where the UK property makes up 5% or less of the person's total property interests, such 'minor interests' are disregarded*).

The tax rates and bands for Inheritance Tax are as follows:

	2017/18	**2018/19**
Rate (for estates)	40%	40%
Reduced rate (*for estates leaving 10% or more to charity*)	36%	36%
Rate (*for* ***Chargeable Lifetime Transfers*** *– see section 33.6*)	20%	20%
Nil rate band limit (see section 33.8)	£325,000	£325,000
Residence nil rate band limit (see section 33.9)	£100,000	£125,000

33.2 Transfers of value

A transfer of value occurs where an individual's estate (*ie property of any kind*) is reduced in value because of a gift or disposition. The amount of the reduction in the donor's estate value is the 'transfer of value' for IHT purposes. This may not always be the same value by which the donee's estate is increased by the gift. For example, a gift of one third of a 60% shareholding in a private company to a person who had no prior holding in the company reduces the donor's estate by the difference between a 60% and a 40% shareholding, whereas it increases the donee's estate by the market value of a 20% holding in isolation.

In the case of transfers on a death, the whole estate is a transfer of value and the value transferred is the value of the individual's whole estate immediately prior to the death. It should be noted that investments in ISAs and PEPs (*Private Equity Plans, the predecessor of ISAs*), which are outside the scope of income tax and capital gains tax during life, are included in the death estate for IHT.

33.3 Exempt transfers, Chargeable Lifetime Transfers, Potentially Exempt Transfers and the Death Estate

Transfers of value are of the following types:

- Lifetime transfers:
    - Exempt transfers (see section 33.4)
    - Potentially Exempt Transfers (see section 33.5)
    - Chargeable Lifetime Transfers (see section 33.6)
- Death estate transfers (see section 33.7)

Transfers of value made during a person's life may be exempt transfers (*in which case they are not subject to Inheritance Tax*), Potentially Exempt Transfers (*in which case they are provisionally exempt from Inheritance Tax, but may become chargeable if the person transferring the property dies within seven years of the transfer*) or Chargeable Lifetime Transfers (*which are subject to Inheritance Tax at the point of the transfer*).

33.4 Exempt transfers

The following are the main exemptions and reliefs available:

		LT	DT
(a)	Transfers between husband and wife or registered civil partners.*	✓	✓
(b)	Annual exemption: transfers each year up to £3,000.** *(An unused annual exemption may be carried forward for one year only, and must be used up before the annual exemption of that year)*	✓	
(c)	Small gifts to any one person not exceeding £250.	✓	
(d)	Transfers by way of normal expenditure out of taxed income.	✓	
(e)	Gifts in consideration of marriage: £5,000 max: donor is parent to one of the people getting married; £2,500 max: donor is grandparent / great grandparent; £1,000 max: donor is in any other relationship.	✓	
(f)	Gifts to charities.	✓	✓
(g)	Gifts to political parties.	✓	✓
(h)	Gifts for national purposes or for public benefit.	✓	✓
(i)	Gifts made during lifetime for family maintenance including the education of children.	✓	

LT = Lifetime Transfers; DT = Death Transfers

* There is no limit to the value which may be transferred between a husband and wife or civil partners, except where the donee is not domiciled in the UK, in which case the exempt amount is limited to an amount equal to the nil rate band. A legally non-UK-domiciled spouse /CP of a UK-domiciled person can also elect, for IHT only, to be deemed domiciled. If this election has been made, then normal unlimited spouse/CP transfers can be made by the UK-domiciled partner to the other.

** Any unused annual exemption from one tax year may be carried forward to the next tax year, but not beyond that. The current tax year's annual exemption must be used up first before any leftover exemption from the prior year.

The following types of property are not liable to IHT on a lifetime transfer, and do not form part of an individual's estate on death:

(a) property situated outside the UK where the owner is non-UK domiciled.
(b) reversionary interests in a settlement, except those acquired for money or money's worth or those where either the settlor or his or her spouse/CP is beneficially entitled to the reversion.
(c) any income entitlement/life interest in a Relevant Property Trust created on or after 22 March 2006.
(d) any life interest in a settlement made by a non-UK domiciled person and comprising only non-UK property.
(e) property of individuals whose death was caused or hastened by injury on active service (*members of the armed services, emergency services and humanitarian aid workers. This includes serving and former police officers and service personnel targeted because of their status*).

To qualify as excluded property owned by a non-UK domiciled person, the assets must be situated outside the UK. The location of assets is determined in accordance with the general principles of property and land law as follows:

Land	Land, including leasehold property is situated where the land is physically located.
Tangible moveable property	Assets such as furniture and paintings are situated where they are located. Coins and bank notes are situated where they are at the time of the transfer.
Shares/ securities	These are situated where the company share register is kept.
Bearer shares	These are situated where the certificate of title is kept.
Debts	These are located where the debtor resides.
Business assets	Assets of a business are located where the place of business is situated. An interest in a partnership is located where the head office is found.
Goodwill	This is located where the business is carried on.
Trademark	This is situated where it is registered.

33.5 Potentially exempt transfers

A potentially exempt transfer is a lifetime transfer of value made by an individual:

(i) to another individual, or

(ii) to a trust primarily for the benefit of a disabled person (as defined).

Although a PET is a transfer of value, no inheritance tax is due when the transfer is made.

If the transferor dies within seven years, the PET becomes a chargeable lifetime transfer. Otherwise, it becomes wholly exempt.

When a PET becomes chargeable on the death of the donor, it is very common for there to be no actual IHT liability on the PET itself, because the PET (*being earlier in date*) will rank before later transfers in taking the benefit of the donor's available nil rate band.

However, the inclusion of earlier 'failed PETs' in the cumulative lifetime transfers reduces the nil rate band available to the death estate and thus causes a higher tax liability on death.

In the less common situation where actual IHT (*at a positive rate*) becomes payable on a PET that 'fails' (*ie becomes chargeable on death within 7 years*), the IHT liability on that PET falls by default on the PET recipient.

If the recipient cannot be traced, or the gift was declared net of IHT when made, then the tax authorities will require the IHT on the PET to be met from the estate of the donor.

If IHT on a PET is paid out of the donor's estate, it is necessary to 'gross up' the value of the PET to find the IHT due on it.

33.6 Chargeable Lifetime Transfers (CLTs)

A **chargeable transfer** is any transfer of value which is not an exempt transfer (section 33.4) or a potentially exempt transfer (section 33.5). It is chargeable to Inheritance Tax at the time it occurs. The main type of chargeable lifetime transfer is a transfer of value by an individual to a 'Relevant Property Trust' (*this term covers all trusts created by lifetime transfers, except qualifying disabled persons' trusts*). Transfers by individuals to companies are also CLTs.

A liability to Inheritance Tax arises on a Chargeable Lifetime Transfer at the time the transfer is made, at a rate of 20%. If the donor dies within seven years of a chargeable lifetime transfer then the transfer is charged additional IHT to bring the tax up to the death rate, but (a) the nil rate band that applies to the further liability calculation is the one applying at date of death, not date of transfer; and (b) any further IHT is subject to taper relief where the interval between the CLT and the death is three years or more (see section 33.10).

CLTs covered by the nil rate band (see section 33.8) are not the same as exempt transfers: exempt transfers are ignored when comparing the cumulative total of previous chargeable transfers with the current IHT nil rate band to find whether a liability at 20% or 40% arises on the latest transfer.

The chargeable value of transfers in life or on death may be reduced by business and agricultural property reliefs (see Section 33.14).

33.7 Death Estate transfers

The total amount which is liable to IHT on death consists of:

i) all chargeable transfers in the seven years before death (*including 'potentially exempt transfers' brought into charge upon death*), plus

ii) all the chargeable estate at death, plus

iii) any property given away before death, but which was subject to a 'reservation' in favour of the donor, or the donor's spouse or civil partner, during any time within seven years of the donor's death.

The tax due on a death transfer may be reduced by Quick Succession Relief to the extent that IHT was paid on the same property on another person's death within the past 3 years (see Section 33.15).

IHT that is due on lifetime gifts because of the death of the donor within seven years may be reduced by taper relief if more than 3 years have elapsed between the relevant gift and the death (*see Section 33.10 below for rates, and Sections 34.3 to 34.6 for worked examples*). Only the final tax liability (if any), not the chargeable value of the original lifetime transfer (*which also affects the tax rate on later transfers*) is reduced by taper relief.

33.8 Nil rate band

When a transfer is made which is subject to Inheritance Tax, a nil rate band is available. The nil rate band is not an annual allowance, but rather is a band applied to chargeable transfers of value made in the last seven years from the date of the transfer currently being considered, applied on a cumulative basis to the earlier transfers first. For 2018/19 the nil rate band is £325,000.

A surviving spouse or civil partner's IHT representatives on death may claim the unused **proportion** of a previously deceased spouse's or civil partner's nil rate band. Effectively this means that the nil rate band is to some extent now transferable between spouses and civil partners from the first to the second death.

The system works as follows: Personal representatives (*i.e. executors, or intestacy administrators*) of the estate of a deceased individual can claim up to the whole of a second nil rate band in addition to the normal one, if they can reasonably show that part or all of another person's nil rate band was not used against any chargeable estate on their earlier death, and that when the first person died, he or she was married to (*or in a civil partnership with*) the later deceased person, whose IHT return has now to be completed.

The main purpose of this reform was to negate the need for complicated trust structures allowing spouses / civil partners to ensure that one nil rate band was not 'wasted' on the first death if (as is common) the bulk of the first to die's property was left to the survivor – an exempt transfer for IHT, but potentially pushing the widow or widower's estate up to a level where higher IHT would be payable on the second death.

For people who have had more than one predeceasing spouse or civil partner before their own death, **all** the available unused nil rate bands from all those other people's death estates may be combined, but the absolute maximum enhanced nil rate band available on the second death is double the normal nil rate band for an individual (*measured at the date of the second death*).

Extra unused nil rate band from a predeceasing partner is only available if the marriage/partnership still existed at the time of the first death. So it does not apply if the partners dissolved the partnership or divorced before the first death.

In general, for all IHT purposes, 'married' means legally married or in a civil partnership, and all spouse / civil partner treatments for IHT continue until the marriage or partnership is legally ended by divorce or dissolution, regardless of the parties' living arrangements.

In addition to this general nil rate band, a residence nil rate band is available.

33.9 Residence Nil Rate Band (RNRB)

The Residence Nil Rate Band (RNRB) applies where an individual dies on or after 6th April 2017, leaving a home or a share of a home to their direct descendants.

The amount of RNRB which may be claimed will be equal to the value of the home left to the direct descendants on the individual's death, plus any 'downsizing addition', up to a combined total for 2018/19 of £125,000. The RNRB tapers away by £1 for every £2 by which the value of the estate exceeds £2million.

So, for an estate worth £2,250,000 or more there will be no RNRB available (*assuming no unused RNRB transferred from a predeceased spouse*).

The 'downsizing addition' arises where the deceased had downsized to a less valuable home, or ceased to own a home, on or after 8th July 2015, and is measured as the difference between the value of the former home and the replacement home. It applies only where the former home would have qualified for the RNRB if it had been kept until death, and at least some of the estate is inherited by the deceased's direct descendants.

For deaths in subsequent tax years the RNRB will be:

- £150,000 in 2019 to 2020;
- £175,000 in 2020 to 2021;
- for later years, it will increase in line with CPI inflation.

As with the general nil rate band, when a person dies, the proportion of any unused RNRB can be transferred to their spouse's or civil partner's estate.

33.10 IHT Taper relief - PETs becoming chargeable, and CLTs taxed further on death

Any inheritance tax payable upon death in respect of chargeable transfers made within seven years of the death of the donor (*including PETs that have become chargeable*) is reduced by reference to the following table:

Years between date of transfer and date of death	% of normal tax charged	% reduction in tax
0 - 3	100	-
3 - 4	80	20
4 - 5	60	40
5 - 6	40	60
6 - 7	20	80

33.11 Gifts with reservation

Where an individual makes a transfer of value but still retains some interest in the property, then on death he or she is deemed to be beneficially entitled to the whole property and it is taxed together with the rest of the estate. Examples of gifts with reservation are:

(i) a gift of a house where the donor or their spouse or civil partner remains in residence – unless a 'full market rent' is paid;

(ii) a gift to a trust where the donor or their spouse or civil partner is a beneficiary (*even a remote beneficiary*).

33.12 Property subject to reservation

Property is subject to a reservation if:

(i) possession and enjoyment of the property is not bona fide assumed by the donee at or before the beginning of the 'relevant period', or

(ii) at any time in the 'relevant period' the property is not enjoyed to the entire exclusion, or virtually so, of the donor and of any benefits to him or her by contract or otherwise.

The 'relevant period' is the period ending on the date of the donor's death and beginning seven years before then, or the date of the gift, if later.

33.13 General scope of IHT

If the individual making the transfer of value is domiciled in the UK, IHT applies to all his or her property wherever it is situated. This applies even if the person is not UK-resident for income tax and capital gains tax purposes.

Where the transferor is domiciled outside the UK, then only property situated in the UK is chargeable to IHT . This would include shares in companies whose registered office/share register is located in the UK, but not shares in an offshore company, even if that company owned property in the UK.

For IHT purposes there are special rules by which an individual who has strong or recent UK residence connections is deemed to be domiciled in the UK for IHT purposes, even if legally domiciled elsewhere:

(i) a deemed UK domicile is acquired for IHT purposes once a person has been resident (*for income tax purposes*) in the UK for 17 of the last 20 tax years. Legal domicile is then irrelevant.

(ii) when someone formerly domiciled in the UK changes their legal domicile (*eg by permanent emigration*), their deemed domicile for IHT purposes remains the UK for another 3 tax years after the year of change of legal domicile.

33.14 Business and agricultural property reliefs

These important reliefs are available in respect of both transfers during lifetime (*both PETs and immediately chargeable transfers*) and on death. They are given effect to by a reduction in the value transferred.

(a)	Relief for business property Percentage reductions available are as follows: (i) Transfers of a business or partnership interest (ii) Transfers of business assets (iii) Transfers of shares in unquoted companies including AIM (iv) Transfers of a controlling interest in a quoted company	 100% 50% 100% 50%
(b)	Relief for agricultural property Percentage reductions available are as follows: (i) Where the transferor has the right to vacant possession or could obtain it within 12 months after a transfer (ii) Where the transferor does not have the right to vacant possession or cannot obtain it within 12 months of the transfer	 100% 50%

See 34.11 to 34.13 for more details of on business property relief rules and an example computation for a PET of business property that becomes chargeable on the death of the donor.

33.15 Quick succession relief

This is available in respect of property transferred by inheritance from a person whose estate was liable to IHT, if the same property is again charged to IHT on the death of the next owner within five years. The relief is given by a reduction in the IHT on the second death, equal to a percentage of the IHT (at the estate rate) paid on the same property on the first death, as follows:

Death within	Reduction
1 year	100%
2 years	80%
3 years	60%
4 years	40%
5 years	20%

33.16 Sale within 1 or 4 years of death (*Fall-in-value relief*)

Where shares are sold at arm's length within one year of death, or land is sold within four years of death, and the proceeds of sale are less than the probate value (*value for Inheritance Tax purposes*) at the date of death, then relief may be claimed for any reduction in the price achieved below the amount treated as originally liable to Inheritance Tax, and a refund of Inheritance Tax paid on the difference in value may be obtained.

33.17 Liabilities and expenses

In general, liabilities are taken into account in computing the value of an estate for Inheritance Tax purposes insofar as they have been incurred for a consideration in money's worth or imposed by law. Liabilities forming a charge on any property, such as a mortgage on a house, are deducted from the value of that property.

33.18 Intestacy

Where a person dies without making a will then there are rules of intestacy which prescribe the way an estate must be distributed.

33.19 Post-death variations

The beneficiaries under a will or intestacy can vary the terms of the Will or the standard intestacy rules regarding who gets what, so long as all of them are of full legal capacity (*so minor beneficiaries cannot have their shares of the estate altered or reduced in this way*).

The legal document doing this is known as a 'Post-Death Deed of Variation' and to be effective for Inheritance Tax it must satisfy the following conditions.

(a) The instrument in writing must be made by the persons or any of the persons who benefit or would benefit under the dispositions of the property comprised in the deceased's estate immediately before his or her death.

(b) The instrument must be made within two years after the death.

(c) The instrument must clearly indicate the dispositions that are the subject of it, and vary their destination as laid down by the deceased's will or under the law relating to intestate estates, or otherwise.

(d) A notice of election to vary the Will for Inheritance Tax and Capital Gains Tax purposes must be given within six months of the date of the instrument, unless HMRC sees fit to accept a late election.

(e) A Deed of Variation will automatically replace the Will for capital tax purposes (CGT and IHT) if the Deed itself states that it is to have that effect.

Any liability to IHT on death will be calculated based on the revised estate distribution resulting from the Deed of Variation.

Deeds of Variation have no effect for income tax until the estate is distributed under the revised terms of the Deed. Therefore income (eg rents) may accrue during an estate administration period and be taxed on the previous estate beneficiary as income, even if they have given away the capital entitlement in a Deed of Variation. A Deed of Variation is not an IHT transfer of value or a CGT chargeable disposal by any person entering it who gives away property or inheritance rights to others by means of it.

33.20 Administration and payment

(a) Reporting lifetime transfers to HM Revenue and Customs is carried out as follows.

    (i) In the case of a chargeable lifetime transfer, the transferor must report it, unless some other person such as the donee liable for the tax has already done so. The account must be delivered within 12 months of the transfer or, if later, three months from the date on which he or she first becomes liable for the tax.

    (ii) In the case of a PET that becomes chargeable, it is the transferee's duty to report the transfer and pay any tax within 12 months after the end of the month in which death occurs. The Personal Representatives are also responsible for listing the recipients of PETs that have become chargeable, and chargeable lifetime transfers that are liable to further tax on death, on the IHT return.

(b) Appeals against an IHT assessment should initially be made to HMRC, then if dissatisfied with their response to the First-tier Tribunal (Tax Chamber).

(c) For transfers on death, a grant of representation (sometimes called 'probate' or 'letters of administration') for the legal right to access things like the deceased person's bank account will not be given until an IHT account (provisional, if necessary) has been rendered and any IHT due paid (*subject to the provisions for paying by instalments*).

(d) Where the estate is 'excepted' (small in value), then there is no duty to make an IHT return on death. This applies where:

(i) the gross value of the property at death + relevant life time-transfers ≤ the basic nil rate band, and the deceased died domiciled in the UK; or

(ii) The aggregate gross value of the estate + relevant lifetime transfers ≤ £1.0m, and the aggregate value less any deductible liabilities and less transfers to spouse and charity) ≤ the basic nil rate band, and the deceased died domiciled in the UK; or

(iii) The deceased was never domiciled in the UK and the value of all UK estate ≤ £100,000.

(e) Payments of IHT may be made by instalments for these transfers on death:

(i) land and buildings (freehold and leasehold wherever situated);

(ii) a controlling interest in a company, quoted or unquoted;

(iii) unquoted shares and securities where the value transferred exceeds £20,000, and the shares represent at least 10% of nominal share capital;

(iv) the net value of a business, profession or vocation;

(v) timber where the proceeds of sale basis of valuation is not used.

(f) Instalments are payable by 10 equal yearly amounts. Interest on IHT due on land other than land used for business or agricultural purposes is calculated on the whole amount outstanding and added to each instalment.

IHT due on other property payable by instalments only incurs interest when an instalment is in arrears.

The payment of tax by instalments is available on lifetime transfers of the appropriate property where the IHT is paid by the donee.

(g) IHT is due for payment as follows:

(i) On a transfer on death – six months after the end of the month in which the death takes place.

(ii) On a lifetime transfer – six months after the end of the month of transfer.

33.21 IHT and Trusts – outline

A trust is an arrangement whereby legal ownership of an asset or cash is vested in one or more persons (the trustee(s)) but all the benefit or income from the assets is passed on to other named person(s) (*known as the trust beneficiaries*).

There are many choices available to the creator (*known as the settlor*) of a property trust or settlement. The terms on which the trust property is to be managed and held must all be set out in the Trust Deed: the settlor cannot vary them later as he or she relinquishes control of the assets when the trust is created. The Trust deed may be part of a Will if the trust is created on a death.

The income benefit and capital benefit in a trust can be awarded differently. The destination of the various benefits can be laid down in ways which trustees cannot alter, or the trustees can be given discretion as to the final allocation of income and/or capital among various possible classes of beneficiary.

The trustees may also have power to accumulate income and add it to capital rather than paying it out to income beneficiaries as income.

In the case of 'Disabled Person's Trusts', the disabled beneficiary is treated as owning the underlying property for Inheritance Tax purposes, and all gifts into the trust are treated as PETs to that person.

Other trusts, 'Relevant Property Trusts' (*which covers other discretionary trusts, interest-in-possession trusts and pre-2006 'Accumulation and Maintenance' Trusts*) are separate IHT taxpayers and the trustees must keep their own IHT cumulative transfer records. IHT arises on capital transfers of value out of an RPT, and also at ten-year intervals on property within an RPT. The details of IHT for RPT trustees are not considered further here.

34 IHT computations

34.1 Introduction

In this chapter we consider the following:

- Death with no chargeable transfers within seven years of death
- Grossing up procedures
- Taper relief
- Chargeable lifetime transfers
- Potentially exempt transfers
- Transfers of value made within seven years of death and earlier transfers.
- Business Property Relief

34.2 Death after no chargeable transfers or PETs within 7 years

On the death of a person who has not made chargeable transfers within the previous seven years, the death rates and nil rate band are simply applied to the value of the death estate, subject to any exemptions and reliefs.

Example

Monty died on 14th June 2018, leaving a chargeable estate of £485,000 to his children, including a house worth £179,000. He had made no lifetime transfers and was divorced from his previous spouse before she died. Compute the IHT payable.

Solution: Monty deceased IHT computation 14th June 2018

				£
Total value of estate				485,000
Tax payable:		£		£
	NRB	325,000	@ 0%	-
	RNRB	125,000	@ 0%	-
		35,000	@ 40%	14,000
		485,000		14,000

Note Estate rate of IHT = $\frac{14,000}{485,000} \times 100 = 2.89\%$

The estate rate is relevant where there is any IHT payable by instalments e.g. UK land, or by different persons. It is also relevant where Double Tax Relief is claimed for overseas IHT.

34.3 Grossing up procedures

Where a lifetime transfer is made and IHT is to be paid by the donor, e.g. on a transfer to a Relevant Property Trust, then it is necessary to 'gross up' the net transfer as IHT is payable on the gross amount. The donor can specify that any gift, including a PET, is to be a transfer net of IHT. If no such direction is made then a transfer bears its own IHT (*ie the donee pays the IHT*), and no grossing up is required.

Grossing up is also necessary, at death rates, where a death estate is divided in such a way that legacies of set amounts are chargeable to IHT but the residue (*the balance of the estate*) is left to one or more exempt beneficiaries eg. a charity, surviving spouse or civil partner.

Example

Amy makes a net chargeable lifetime transfer to a Relevant Property Trust of £340,000 on 15th May 2018. Amy has never been married, has used all her annual IHT exemptions, but has not made any previous chargeable lifetime transfers or PETs.

Compute the amount of the gross chargeable lifetime transfer by Amy.

Solution

	£
15th May 2018: Net gift	340,000
Add IHT paid by Amy as donor: 20/80 × (340,000 – 325,000) =	3,750
Gross transfer by Amy	343,750

		£
Check:	Gross transfer	343,750
	IHT (343,750 – 325,000) × 20%	(3,750)
	Net transfer	340,000

34.4 Potentially Exempt Transfers

For potentially exempt transfers no chargeable transfer arises unless death occurs within seven years of the date of the transfer. When this happens, IHT is calculated on the now non-exempt (i.e. chargeable) transfer using the death rate and nil rate band at the date of death, but using the value of the transfer at the date it was made. The IHT on a 'failed PET' is payable by the donee, unless the transfer was stated to be a transfer net of any IHT becoming due in future, in which case grossing-up applies and the death estate bears the tax.

34.5 Chargeable lifetime transfers (non-PETs)

These transfers are chargeable at half the death rate at the time of the transfer, and where necessary must be grossed up.

Example

Mike makes a cash transfer of £400,000 to a relevant property trust on 1st December 2018, agreeing to pay any IHT. All annual IHT exemptions had been used but Mike had made no previous IHT-chargeable transfers of value.

Compute any IHT payable by Mike because of this gift.

Solution:

	£
1st December 2018 Gift to relevant property trust	400,000
Available NRB (*no previous chargeable transfers*) = £325,000.	
Lifetime IHT on a net CLT of £400,000:	
First £325,000 (NRB) × nil rate	-
Next £75,000 (400,000 – 325,000) × 20/80 (*as 20% lifetime rate for net CLTs*)	18,750
Gross chargeable transfer by Mike at lifetime rate on gift	418,750
	£
IHT immediately payable by Mike at lifetime rate on gift	18,750
	£
Check (418,750 – 325,000) = 93,750 excess value over Mike's NRB £93,750 × 20% (*lifetime IHT rate on gross CLT*) =	18,750

If death occurs more than seven years after the date of the transfer, then the position is as follows.

(i) The chargeable transfer is ignored in computing the IHT payable on the value of the estate.

(ii) There is no additional tax payable by the donee.

(iii) IHT already paid when the transfer was made is not recoverable.

Taper relief (see section 33.10) does not affect the amount of inheritance tax payable on an estate by the executors.

34.6 Chargeable lifetime transfers – death within seven years

When the transferor dies within seven years of making a chargeable transfer then the gift is re-taxed at the death rates, net of any taper relief. Any IHT payable when the gift was first made is then deducted in arriving at any additional tax due by the donee.

The value of the transfer is taken at the date of the gift but, if it is to the donee's advantage, any additional tax arising on the death of the donor can be calculated by reference to the lower of:

(i) the market value at date of donor's death, or

(ii) the proceeds of an earlier sale by the donee.

Example

Noel died on 11th June 2018 leaving an estate valued at £194,000 to his children. This comprised his home worth £184,000 and other assets worth £10,000.

On 1st June 2015 he made a gift of £350,000 (gross) to a relevant property trust, inheritance tax of £5,000 being paid by the trustees on this lifetime transfer. Noel had never been married and the gift to the trust was of cash (*so there is no question of its value having changed between the gift and Noel's death*).

Calculate the IHT due in respect of Noel's estate, and any additional tax payable on his death relating to the chargeable lifetime transfer.

Solution

	£
11th June 2018 Value of Noel's death estate	194,000

Calculate nil rate band available on death:

	£
Nil rate band 2018/19	325,000
Gross chargeable transfers within previous 7 years	(350,000)
Nil rate band available to death estate	nil

IHT payable on death estate at 2018/19 death rates:

	£
RNRB 125,000 @ 0% =	0
69,000 @ 40% =	27,600
Death estate Inheritance Tax	**27,600**

Additional tax payable on lifetime gift:

	£
1st June 2015 Gross transfer	350,000

	£
IHT due on this at 2018/19 death rates:	
NRB 325,000 @ 0% =	0
Balance 25,000 @ 40% =	10,000
Less taper relief (3-4 years) 20% × £10,000	(2,000)
IHT liability after taper relief (*borne by original donee, ie trust*)	8,000
Less IHT paid by trustees on original gift by Noel	(5,000)
Additional tax due by trustees on Noel's death	**3,000**

Notes

(i) If the additional tax payable calculation gave rise to a 'negative amount', none would be recoverable.

(ii) The death nil rate band is allocated first to CLTs within seven years of death, in chronological order, then to the death estate.

(iii) Where the cumulative CLTs exceed the nil rate band on death, and there are no exempt legacies, then the estate IHT is the value of the whole death estate at the 40% (or 36%) death rate.

(iv) The lifetime gift IHT originally paid by the trustees has been computed as (350,000 – 325,000) @20% = £5,000. £325,000 was the nil rate band in 2015/16. If NRBs increase year on year (*not currently the policy of the Government*), then lifetime IHT in an earlier year may exceed the equivalent IHT on the same transfer that is re-computed at death rates after taking account of an increased NRB available on death.

34.7 Potentially exempt transfer within seven years of death

There is no inheritance tax payable when a PET is made, since a potentially exempt transfer is by law assumed to be exempt, until proved otherwise by death of the donor within seven years. Upon death within seven years of the transfer, the PET is taxable at the death rate, subject to taper relief if the interval is more than three years. In addition the PET (now a CLT) ranks with other CLTs to reduce the nil rate band available to the estate when calculating the IHT payable on the death transfer.

As with all lifetime transfers brought into charge on death, the estate is treated as the last transfer, and the cumulative transfers in the previous seven years as earlier transfers, to be allocated against the nil rate band on death, in date order.

34.8 Calculating IHT payable on death by a lifetime donee

Example

Eddie died on 10th October 2018, leaving to his daughter a net estate valued at £250,000, including his home worth £188,000. On 1st December 2013 Eddie had made a gift to his son with a value of £400,000, after having used all relevant lifetime IHT exemptions. Eddie had made no other transfers of value and divorced his wife many years ago.

Calculate the IHT payable on Eddie's death.

Solution

	£
10th October 2018 value of Eddie's estate at death	250,000

Nil Rate Band available against estate:	£
NRB 2018/19	325,000
Cumulative transfers in previous 7 years	(400,000)
Remaining NRB	Nil

Inheritance Tax on death estate:		£
RNRB	125,000 @ 0% =	-
Remaining estate	125,000 @ 40% =	50,000
IHT payable out of death estate by executors		50,000
(borne by Eddie's daughter as sole beneficiary)		

Computation of additional tax payable by son on failed PET 01-Dec-2013 (*Use death year NRB and death year tax rates*)

	£		£
NRB	325,000	@ 0% =	-
balance	75,000	@ 40% =	30,000
	400,000		
Less taper relief: (4-5 years) 40% × £30,000			(12,000)
Tax payable by Eddie's son			**18,000**

Further example – fall-in-value relief

Using the data in the previous example, compute the IHT payable, if the PET to Eddie's son was not cash, but an asset worth £400,000, which was only worth £350,000 at the date of Eddie's death.

Solution

	£
10th October 2018 Value of Eddie's estate	250,000
IHT payable on estate	**£50,000** (as above)

IHT payable by Eddie's son on Eddie's death:

	£
1st December 2013 Value of gift	400,000
Less fall in value relief (£400,000 - £350,000)	(50,000)
10th October 2018 Value of gift retrospectively	350,000

IHT on £350,000	
(350,000 – 325,000) × 40%	10,000
Less taper relief: (4-5 years) @ 40%	(4,000)
IHT payable by Eddie's son	**£6,000**

Notes

(i) The value of the original gift is included in calculations of IHT on the death estate. In other words, it is still 'cumulated' at the original value.

(ii) The fall-in-value relief only affects the amount of any tax or additional tax due when a PET becomes a CLT on death, or a CLT becomes liable at death rates (*less taper relief if any*).

(iii) Additional tax due on earlier lifetime transfers because of a death is in principle a cost borne by the donee. If it is borne by the donor's estate (*which could only be by specific direction of the donor*) then the tax on the gift (at grossed-up rate) is an additional transfer of value under the will.

(iv) In practice, the donee or the donor of a lifetime gift can often without difficulty, and at modest cost, insure the donor's life for the next 7 years, to cover the cost of an extra IHT liability arising within 7 years of a lifetime gift. This is done using a single-premium seven-year term life insurance policy, the proceeds of which can be used by the donee to pay the estimated maximum IHT. If the donor does not die within 7 years no insurance money is repayable to the donee but there is no IHT to pay either. If the donor pays the insurance premium and writes the proceeds of the policy in trust for the donee, this is not itself a chargeable transfer of value.

(v) There is no taper relief for tax computed at death rates on a chargeable lifetime transfer less than three years before death (see 33.10).

34.9 Transfers of value made within fourteen years of death

Transfers of value made more than seven years before the date of death are not accumulated to arrive at the NRB usage and effective IHT rate at the date of death.

However, where a chargeable lifetime transfer (*including a failed PET*) was made within seven years before death, then in determining any additional IHT payable on death by the recipient of that transfer, all now-chargeable transfers (including original CLTs and any failed PETs) made in the full seven years before the date of that transfer must be considered when deciding how much NRB can be allocated to that transfer in taxing it retrospectively at death rates.

Example

Kate, who is divorced, made a gross chargeable transfer of £300,000 (*after lifetime IHT exemptions*) to a discretionary trust for her adult children on 1st February 2007. On 1st November 2012, Kate gave her stepson cash of £81,000 (*value stated before annual IHT exemptions*). Kate died on 30th August 2018, leaving an estate of £500,000 to her 3 adult children, including her home which was worth £193,000.

Required

(a) Calculate the IHT payable by the Executors out of Kate's death estate; and

(b) Calculate the IHT payable by her stepson on the 2012 cash gift of £81,000, because of Kate's death in 2018.

Solution

(a) IHT payable by executors:

	£
30th August 2018 Value of Kate's estate	500,000
Check on nil rate band available to death estate:	
Compute Kate's IHT transfers of value made within previous 7 years:	
1st November 2012 Gift to son – gross transfer of value	81,000
Less Kate's IHT annual exemptions for 2011/12 and 2012/13	(6,000)
= Gross chargeable transfer (*was PET, now CLT*) taxed on death	75,000

Therefore Kate's nil rate band available to death estate:
(*£325,000, less £75,000 set against PET now chargeable as CLT*) = £250,000
IHT payable on death estate: (2018/19 rates)

	£		£
NRB remaining	250,000	@ 0%	0
RNRB	125,000	@ 0%	0
Remaining estate	125,000	@ 40%	50,000
	500,000		**£50,000**

IHT payable by executors out of death estate (borne by heirs) **£50,000**

(b) Tax payable by Kate's son on failed PET:

We must consider whether there is enough NRB available to cover the whole life-time gift made on 1st November 2012. When taxing a lifetime gift on death we always use the death-date NRB (*the 2018/19 NRB, not the NRB that applied on deaths occurring in 2012/13*). But it is necessary to allocate that NRB only after taking into account the cumulative record of previous CLTs made by Kate in the whole 7 years before the lifetime gift now being taxed (*the PET that has failed*).

There was a CLT in 2007 and even though this was made more than 7 years before Kate's death, it was not made more than 7 years before the 2012 gift to the stepson.

Thus, the calculation of tax on the failed PET is:

		£
01-Feb-2007	Chargeable lifetime transfer (CLT)	
2018/19 NRB allocated	to 2007 CLT (as at 01-Nov-2012)	325,000
	(Gift to discretionary trust)	(300,000)
2018/19	NRB remaining to cover CLT in 2012	25,000

So, there is only £25,000 of death NRB left to cover the cash gift made in 2012 when it is retrospectively charged to IHT on Kate's death.

01-Nov-2012 PET to son is now a CLT of £75,000, with £25,000 NRB available

		£
IHT at 2018/19 death rates	(0% × £25,000)	nil
	(40% × £50,000)	20,000

Less taper relief, because gift made >3 years before death:

Taper relief for 5-6 years (01-Nov-2012 – 30-Aug-2018) = 60% × £20,000	(12,000)
IHT payable by stepson on failed PET	**£8,000**

Notes

i) The failed PET must be retrospectively taxed on death using 2018/19 IHT rates and 2018/19 IHT NRB. Death tax is calculated using the cumulative total of chargeable lifetime transfers made in the 7 years before the original PET date. Taper relief then reduces the IHT.

ii) Thus, the CLT in 2007 still affects the IHT cost of the later PET if death occurs within 7 years of the PET. The earlier CLT is not itself further taxable on death, as it was made more than 7 years before 30th August 2018.

iii) A professional IHT adviser, if aware that an earlier CLT had preceded Kate's 2012 PET, might well have advised Kate in 2012 to take out term life insurance for the maximum foreseeable death-rate IHT cost (*as suggested at 34.8*).

iv) The taper relief for a chargeable lifetime transfer made between five and six years before death is 60% (see 34.10).

34.10 Business Property Relief (BPR)

Business Property Relief is available to reduce the chargeable amount of transfers of value, either during the lifetime or on the death of an individual, of relevant business property.

The relief is given by way of a percentage reduction from the valuation of the property:

Type of property	Valuation reduction
a) Property consisting of a **business** or interest in a business such as a partnership or sole trader. A business includes total assets including goodwill, less liabilities.	100%
b) Shares or securities in **unquoted** companies: for BPR this term includes shares listed on the Alternative Investment Market (AIM).	100%
c) Shares or securities of a **quoted** company which gave the transferor **control** of the company immediately before the transfer.	50%
d) **Business assets** (*such as land, buildings, plant and machinery*) owned by the transferor as a sole trader, partner, or as a controlling director of a company, and used in that business.	50%
e) **Business assets** (*such as land, buildings, plant and machinery*) used by the transferor in a business which was settled property in which he or she had an interest in possession.	50%

34.11 Relevant business property

In addition to the summary above, the following should be noted.

(a) To qualify for relief, the property must have been owned by the transferor for at least two years immediately prior to the transfer. Where property directly replaced other business property, and the two years' ownership requirement cannot be met on the second asset, BPR is still available provided aggregate ownership of both qualifying assets is greater than two years out of the previous five.

(b) Assets not used wholly or mainly for the purposes of the business within the two-year period noted in (a) above are 'excepted assets' of the business (*e.g. investments, or surplus cash*) and BPR is not available for those items.

(c) Relief is not available for a transfer of business property which is used wholly or mainly for the following purposes:
   (i) Dealing in stocks, shares or securities.
   (ii) Dealing in land or buildings.
   (iii) Making or holding investments.

(d) The expression 'business' includes a profession or vocation but does not include a business carried on otherwise than for gain.

(e) Shares in a non-trading holding company qualify for BPR if all its trading subsidiaries would qualify for the relief if held directly by the individual. If some of them would not so qualify, those subsidiaries are 'excepted assets' within the value of the parent company.

(f) To retain the benefit of BPR when retrospectively taxing a failed PET of business property, the original property (*or if sold, its replacement – see next point*) must have been owned by the donee throughout the intervening period from the chargeable lifetime transfer up to the donor's death, unless the donee predeceased the donor.

(g) If the original property is disposed of before the donor's death and the proceeds are used by the donee to purchase replacement business property full BPR is available if:
   (i) the whole of the proceeds is used to purchase a replacement; and
   (ii) the sale and purchase take place within three years of each other.

(h) If only part of the original property (or its replacement) is in the donee's possession on the death of the donor, only that part is eligible for relief.

34.12 Excepted assets for BPR

The BPR will be restricted on a transfer of shares if the company owns 'excepted assets'. An 'excepted asset' is an asset that is not used for business purposes throughout the two years immediately preceding a transfer, or is not required for future use in the business. The amount of the transfer qualifying for BPR, is the value of the shares gifted multiplied by the fraction below:

$$\text{Qualifying transfer} = \text{Gift} \times \left(\frac{\text{Total assets - excepted assets}}{\text{Total assets}}\right)$$

If the company has no excepted assets, all of the value of the shares will qualify for BPR. If non-trading assets make up more than 50% of total assets, HMRC may deny any BPR, on the grounds that the company is not substantially a trading company.

34.13 PETs and Business Property Relief

If the property eligible for business property relief is transferred by a PET, it follows that tax will only be payable on the death of the transferor within seven years of the date of the transfer. BPR which has been assumed at the time of a lifetime gift (PET) to reduce the chargeable value of the PET may be lost because of events after the PET. BPR is not available when a PET becomes chargeable (*ie on the donor's death within 7 years*) unless either:

(a) the property (or its identifiable replacement) is still held by the donee as relevant business property at the donor's death, or

(b) the donee has died before the donor.

This rule can cause an unwelcome IHT exposure for the donee of business property. The risk of the donor's death should be covered by term life insurance if the donee does not intend to retain the gift as his or her own relevant business property for 7 years.

Example involving BPR on shareholding

Larry, who had made no previous chargeable transfers (*and who had divorced his wife years ago*), gave his controlling shareholding in Zoot Ltd, a private company, to his son on April 12th 2012. The shareholding was valued at £440,000 on that date. Larry's shares were acquired for £50,000 in 1993. Larry died on 10th August 2018, leaving an estate of £500,000, including his home worth £198,000, to his two grandchildren. Larry's son still held the shares in Zoot Ltd as a controlling interest when Larry died.

Compute the IHT arising on Larry's death.

Solution

	£	£
10-Aug-2018 Value of Larry's death estate		500,000
Check transfers of value made within previous 7 years		
12-Apr-2012 gift to son (PET, now chargeable)	440,000	
Less business property relief (100% × 440,000)	(440,000)	
		£ nil

No nil rate band is required to cover the PET (now CLT), because of 100% BPR.

IHT payable on death estate at 2017/18 rates:

	£		£
RNRB	125,000	@ 0%	0
NRB	325,000	@ 0%	0
Remaining estate	50,000	@ 40%	20,000
Total estate	500,000		
IHT payable by executors out of the estate			**20,000**

Notes

(i) No IHT was payable in 2012 as the transfer of value was then a PET.

(ii) Business property relief at 100% applies to the gift, so there is no IHT payable by Larry's son on the death of his father, as he has retained the gifted shares as qualifying business property. However the PET is no longer exempt but has become chargeable; and BPR needs to be claimed when reporting the failed PET in the IHT return submitted on Larry's death.

(iii) The original cost of Larry's controlling interest is irrelevant to the IHT position, though it was relevant to Larry's Capital Gains Tax liability in the tax year when he made the shares gift. (*See section 32.4 for CGT and Gifts.*)

Student self-testing questions

Question 1: Zeb

Zeb, a widower, died on 22nd October 2018, leaving a net estate of £600,000 to his children and grandchildren, including his home worth £203,000. His wife died in 2004 leaving everything to him. During his lifetime he had made the following transfers of value:

1st December 2011	Cash Gift to his daughter of £130,000.
20th June 2013	Cash Gift to a relevant property trust of £245,000 gross. No Lifetime IHT was paid by Zeb on this transfer.

Compute the IHT payable on the death of Zeb.

Solution to Question 1: Zeb

	£
Lifetime transfers made in the previous 7 years:	
01-Dec-2011 Gift to daughter (PET, now failed) – gross	130,000
Less IHT annual exemptions for 2010/11 and 2011/12	(6,000)
	124,000
20-Jun-2013 Gift to trust (*CLT covered by nil rate band in life*), gross	245,000
Less IHT annual exemptions for 2012/13 and 2013/14	(6,000)
= Transfers now allocated against Zeb's NRB on death	363,000
	=========

Remaining NRB available to Zeb's death estate:	£
Zeb's own nil rate band	325,000
Add predeceasing wife's unused proportion of NRB	325,000
less lifetime chargeable transfers in 7 years before death (above)	(363,000)
NRB available for death estate	287,000
	=========

Residence Nil Rate Band available to Zeb's death estate:

	£
Zeb's own RNRB	125,000
Add predeceasing wife's unused proportion of RNRB	125,000
Potentially available RNRB	250,000
But value of home at death is only	203,000

IHT payable on death estate (2018/19 rates):

	£		£
Remaining NRB	287,000	@ 0% =	0
RNRB limited to value of home	203,000	@ 0% =	0
Remaining estate	110,000	@ 40% =	44,000
Total estate	600,000		
IHT payable on death estate			**44,000**

IHT payable by donees of lifetime gifts on death (2018/19 rates apply):

	£	£
01-Dec-2011 – failed PET covered by NRB at death	124,000	
IHT payable by daughter:		nil
20-Jun-2013 Gift to relevant property trust (CLT) – covered by (increased) NRB at death	239,000	
IHT payable by trustees:		nil

Notes

i) Due to the availability on Zeb's death (*though not during his lifetime*) of the unused NRB of his predeceasing wife, on Zeb's death there is enough combined NRB to cover both the 2011 failed PET and the 2013 Chargeable Lifetime Transfer.

ii) Details of the claim to use a predeceasing spouse's unused NRB at death were covered at 33.8.

iii) Taper relief makes no difference to the chargeable amount of a lifetime transfer taxed on death, but only to any death tax falling due on the donor's death within 3-7 years. If the 2011 failed PET were liable on death to a positive sum of IHT, taper relief would reduce that tax (*a period of 6-7 years between a CLT and death = 80% taper relief*). But as the available NRB covers the whole failed PET, death IHT is nil, and taper relief is also nil.

Question 2: Bert

Bert never married. He died on 7th April 2018 leaving the following estate:

	£
20% interest in Underpass Ltd, an unquoted private company	125,000
Freehold land used by Underpass Ltd	35,000
Shares in Yo plc, a quoted company (< 1% holding)	15,000
Home	208,000
Other property (net)	312,500

Three years before his death, Bert transferred a 15% interest in the shares in Underpass Ltd to his nephew. Bert has made no other transfers but has used all his lifetime IHT annual exemptions. Bert's nephew has retained his interest in Underpass Ltd, valued at £40,000 at the date of the gift, and worth £280,000 on Bert's death. Bert leaves all his estate to his nephew.

Calculate the IHT arising on Bert's death.

Solution to Question 2: Bert

	£	£
7th April 2018 value of Bert's estate:		
20% interest in Underpass Ltd	125,000	
Less business property relief 100% × 125,000	(125,000)	–
Freehold land used by Underpass Ltd		35,000
Shares in Yo plc (no BPR)		15,000
Home		208,000
Other property		312,500
		570,500

Nil rate band available on death:
Chargeable lifetime transfer (failed PET) in previous 7 years

Gift of shares in Underpass Ltd	40,000	
Business property relief 100% × 40,000	(40,000)	= nil

Remaining Nil rate band available on Bert's death estate:
(£325,000 – nil) = £325,000.

IHT on death estate at 2018/19 rates:

325,000 @ Nil	Nil	
245,500 @ 40%	98,200	
570,500		
IT payable by executors		**£98,200**

Notes

(i) No Residence Nil Rate Band is available, because Bert left all his estate to his nephew, not to a direct descendant.

(ii) A BPR rate of 100% applies to the gift of shares in Underpass Ltd to Bert's nephew, but even if it had failed to retain BPR, in this case it would be covered by the nil rate band available when the PET failed on Bert's death.

(iii) The knock-on effect of this transfer losing BPR (*if the nephew had not kept the shares*) would be to reduce the balance of nil rate band available on the death estate by £40,000 (*causing additional IHT of £16,000 (£40,000 × 40%) to be due on the death estate*).

(iv) No BPR is available for the freehold land used by Underpass Ltd as Bert did not have a controlling interest.

(v) The failed PET is valued at the date of the lifetime transfer and not the date of Bert's death for IHT purposes. (*However, BPR reduces that value to nil in any case.*)

Question 3: Jamie

Jamie, a generous uncle, made a PET of £200,000 by a cash gift to his nephew Tom in October 2017, and suddenly died one year later, in October 2018.

Due to previous chargeable transfers by Jamie (*earlier PETs which have become chargeable on Jamie's death*) only £50,000 of Jamie's nil rate band is available to cover Tom's PET. The IHT rate applicable to the rest of Tom's PET is 40% (*death rates apply to lifetime transfers taxed on death*).

Calculate the IHT payable on the 'failed' PET to Tom as a result of Jamie's death, if:

(a) Tom pays the IHT on the failed PET

(b) Jamie's estate pays the IHT on the failed PET.

Solution to Question 3: Jamie

(a) If Tom pays the IHT on the 'failed' £200,000 PET (the normal/default situation) then Tom would pay IHT of (0% × £50,000 + 40% × £150,000), i.e. £60,000.

This obligation and the tax liability would be notified to him by the Executors of Jamie's estate.

(b) If the PET to Tom was stated by Jamie at the time it was made to be 'made net of Inheritance Tax', or if for some other reason Jamie's estate ends up paying the IHT on the failed PET (*eg Tom is now insolvent*), then the value to be taxed at 40% must be **grossed up** for the tax liability taken on by Jamie.

Thus the gross transfer becomes (retrospectively)

Value taxed at nil IHT	£50,000
Value taxed at 40% (£200,000 gifted - £50,000 nil rate band) × 100/60 =	£250,000
Gross transfer value of gift to Jamie, total	£300,000
IHT due on this gross value (40% of £250,000) =	£100,000

This £100,000 is payable out of Jamie's estate, and the grossed up amount of £300,000 is recorded in the record of chargeable PETs reported by Jamie's Executors as the gross value of the original lifetime gift made to Tom.

Question without answer

Question 4: Jimmy

Jimmy died on 14th May 2018. His first wife survived him. He had made the following gifts during his lifetime:

(1) On 2nd August 2013 Jimmy made a cash gift of £50,000 to his grandson as a wedding gift when he got married.

(2) On 14th November 2014, Jimmy made a cash gift of £800,000 to a relevant property trust. Jimmy paid the inheritance tax on this gift.

At the date of his death Jimmy owned the following assets:

(1) His main residence, valued at £260,000.

(2) Building society deposits totalling £515,600.

(3) A life assurance policy on his own life, written in trust for his widow. Proceeds of £210,000 were received from this following Jimmy's death.

The cost of Jimmy's funeral amounted to £5,600.

By the terms of his will, Jimmy left £300,000 to his wife (including his main residence), leaving the residue of his estate to his daughter.

Required:

(a) Explain why it is important to differentiate between potentially exempt transfers and chargeable lifetime transfers for inheritance tax purposes. (2 marks)

(b) Calculate the inheritance tax payable because of Jimmy's death. (12 marks)

(c) State by when the personal representatives must pay the inheritance tax due on Jimmy's estate. (1 mark)

(Total: 15 marks)
(ACCA updated)

Part VI

Value added tax

35 General principles

35.1 Introduction

Value Added Tax is a tax on the supply of goods and services made by a registered taxable person, in the course of business, within the UK. Prior to 2008 the UK's VAT rates had been constant for many years. In response to the financial crisis of 2008, the Government announced a temporary reduction in VAT standard rate in November 2008, cutting it by 2.5% from 17.5% to 15% for a period of 13 months. From 1st January 2010 the standard VAT rate reverted to 17.5%.

Following the change of Government in May 2010, it was announced that the UK's standard rate of VAT would be 20% from 4th January 2011.

Unlike the 2008 VAT rate change, the 2011 change is not 'temporary', so may be assumed a long-term policy. Other EU countries have also recently raised their standard rates of VAT, in response to well-publicised public spending deficits.

This chapter begins with a summary of the sections in which the basic rules of VAT will be described.

35.2 Summary of sections

Legislative background

VAT rates

Classification of goods and services

Zero-rated goods and services

Reduced rate goods and services

Exempt goods and services

Land and buildings

Taxable persons

Business splitting

Compulsory registration

Voluntary registration

Voluntary de-registration

Group registration

Divisional registration

Accounts and records

Administration

Late registration

Default surcharge

Errors on VAT returns

Tax avoidance schemes

35.3 Legislative background

Value added tax was introduced in the UK with effect from 1st April 1973, superseding purchase tax and selective employment tax. The main provisions of VAT law are now contained in the Value Added Tax Act 1994, as amended by subsequent Finance Acts and expanded by Regulations. Many UK VAT law changes since 1973 have implemented VAT Directives issued by the European Union. Governments of all Member States are obliged to implement these Directives, as a condition of membership, with the aim of maintaining a common VAT system in the European Economic Area.

The general principles of VAT are thus common to the whole EU fiscal area. VAT is levied on goods and services on a common basis of charge, but domestic VAT rates may be varied, within limits, by individual Member-states. The maximum rate of VAT that is currently allowed under EU law is 25% and the minimum reduced or lower rate that is allowed for social reasons is 5%.

The UK's zero-rate of VAT, which still applies to certain goods and services, is a historical anomaly dating from before the UK's accession to the European Community in 1973. In terms of VAT law any transaction that is zero-rated for VAT is still a 'taxable supply' and fully part of the VAT reporting system.

Also, any reference in the VAT Acts to 'zero-rated goods and services' covers reduced-rate goods and services as well, even if not separately specified.

In VAT law, all supplies are taxable supplies unless they are either exempt supplies or supplies outside the scope of VAT. Supplies outside the scope of VAT include employment services performed in return for a wage or salary, supplies within a VAT group (see 35.16), and any supply by a non-taxable person. Exempt supplies are defined in Schedule 9 of the VAT Act (see 35.8).

35.4 VAT rates and the VAT fraction

VAT has to be charged on the taxable supply of goods and services within the UK by a taxable person. VAT is charged at the following rates:

Standard rate	20.0%
Reduced rate	5.0%
Zero rate	0.0%

In the UK, consumer protection law requires that prices quoted directly to consumers by VAT-registered traders, such as retailers, are stated inclusive of VAT. The invoice or retail receipt should however identify the amount of VAT separately.

UK traders who sell to both consumers and businesses, or only to businesses, may quote prices net of VAT and add the VAT later on the invoice.

Since the current standard rate is 20%, it follows that the VAT element of a price stated inclusive of VAT is $^{20}/_{120}$, or $^{1}/_{6}$. This is known as 'the VAT fraction', and can be applied to any VAT-inclusive price for a standard-rated supply to find the VAT amount contained within it.

When the standard rate was 17.5% before January 2011, the VAT fraction was $^{17.5}/_{117.5}$ or $^{7}/_{47}$. While standard rate of VAT was temporarily 15%, the VAT fraction was $^{15}/_{115}$ or $^{3}/_{23}$.

The VAT fraction for reduced-rate goods and services at 5% is $^{5}/_{105}$ or $^{1}/_{21}$.

35.5 Classification of goods and services

A taxable supply is a supply of goods or services made in the UK in the course of business by a VAT-registered trader, other than an exempt supply.

For VAT rating purposes, goods and services are classified into four groups as listed below, but as noted above the zero-rated and reduced-rate group are for legal definition purposes treated as one single group.

Standard-rated supplies	All goods and services not specifically listed as zero-rated, reduced-rated or exempt
Zero-rated supplies	Goods and services which are subject to a zero rate of VAT, e.g. printed matter, public transport (see 35.6).
Reduced-rated supplies	Goods and services which are subject to the reduced (currently 5%) rate of VAT (see 35.7). These are mainly items which were formerly standard-rated but for social or welfare reasons have been reduced to the lowest possible rate that can now be imposed.
Exempt supplies	Goods and services which are not subject to VAT, e.g. healthcare, education, banking and insurance (see 35.8).

Definitions of zero-rated, reduced rate and exempt supplies are set out in the VAT Act, and summarised below.

Standard-rated supplies are not defined in the VAT Act but this is the default classification of any goods or service supplied for a consideration in the course of business, if none of the other specified descriptions applies.

Since the UK's accession to the European Community in 1973, it is not possible to introduce new categories of zero-rated supply, but the previous ones continue until amended. For example, the Conservative government in the 1990s removed the VAT zero-rating of domestic fuel and power (ie home electricity and gas bills). When Labour came to power in 1997, despite a manifesto promise to reverse this VAT increase, they could not reduce the rate on domestic fuel and power to less than 5% (which it still is).

35.6 Zero-rated (ZR) goods and services

Particulars of the goods and services which are zero-rated are contained in Schedule 8 to the VAT Act 1994 and there are sixteen groups each containing separate listed items, as follows.

Group 1: Food. Most food for human consumption is Zero-Rated, unless supplied as a restaurant meal or catering service, when it is standard-rated (SR). Cold takeaway food sold for consumption off the promises is Zero-Rated, but hot takeaway food is Standard-Rate. Cold food and beverage products not sold in the course of a catering service are in principle Zero-Rated but there is a long list of exceptions to this rule, meaning that certain foodstuffs and drinks are SR.

The policy rationale given for excluding certain foods and beverages from zero-rating is that such items are 'non-essential' or 'luxuries'. Examples of items not eligible for zero-rating include ice cream, sweets and chocolate, potato crisps, alcoholic drinks, fruit juices and chocolate-covered biscuits (but chocolate-covered cakes are ZR). Pet foods are also SR, but general animal feeding stuffs are ZR.

Group 2: Sewerage services and water. The supply of water and sewerage to domestic customers is Zero-Rated, but not distilled and mineral water. The supply of water and sewerage services to industry is Standard-Rated.

Group 3: Books and printed matter. The supply of books and magazines, newspapers, music, maps and charts is ZR. Diaries and printed stationery (ie printed items intended to be written in or on by the purchaser) are SR. E-books supplied electronically to be printed out by the customer are SR services not ZR goods, as are online journals or newspapers supplied for consideration, unless a printed version of the publication is also included in the supply.

Group 4: Talking books for people with disabilities, and wireless sets for blind people. Zero-Rated items include magnetic tapes, tape recorders and accessories, if supplied to approved agencies such as the Royal National Institute for the Blind and similar charities.

Group 5: Construction of buildings. The position under this heading may be summarised as follows.

Zero-rated

i) Construction of new domestic buildings, buildings used for non-business purposes by a charity, village halls or similar buildings for community use.

ii) Approved alterations to listed buildings, used for the domestic, charitable or community purposes noted above.

iii) Alterations to suit the condition of people with disabilities.

Standard-rated

i) Construction of new buildings, other than domestic charitable or community use buildings noted above.

ii) Repair, maintenance or alteration of existing buildings.

iii) Civil engineering services or new work.

iv) Civil engineering services or repair, maintenance or alteration of existing buildings.

v) Demolition of domestic and non-domestic buildings.

vi) The construction of a building for own use in business.

Group 6: Protected buildings.

Group 7: International services.

Group 8: Transport. Zero-rating applies to the supply of passenger transport both inland and international, international freight transport, and the supply, repair and maintenance of certain ships and aircraft. Standard-rating applies to taxis (if the provider is VAT-registered), transport in cars or aeroplanes carrying fewer than six people, hire cars, car parking and luggage storage.

Group 9: Caravans and house-boats. Caravans above the maximum size permitted for use on UK public roads (7 metres in length and 2.3 metres in width) were ZR on sales and non-holiday lettings before 6th April 2013. From that date, they are only ZR if they meet the British Standard (2632:2005) for caravans used as dwellings. Where they do not meet that British Standard, supplies (other than holiday lettings) of such caravans are liable to VAT at the reduced rate from April 2013. Smaller towable caravans are SR, as is the supply of caravan holiday accommodation. House-boats, if suitable for permanent habitation, are ZR.

Group 10: Gold. The supply of gold coins which are legal tender is taxable at the standard rate. The supply of gold held in the UK, by a central bank to another central bank or a member of the London Gold Market, and reciprocal transactions, are Zero-Rated.

Group 11: Bank notes. The issue of bank notes payable to bearer is zero-rated.

Group 12: Drugs, medicines, aids for people with disabilities etc. The following supplies are Zero-Rated: goods dispensed by a registered pharmacist on prescription, medical and surgical appliances, electrical and mechanical appliances for a person with a disability. Other drugs and medicines sold or dispensed without prescription are Standard-Rated.

Group 13: Imports, exports etc. The transfer of goods from the UK, without a legal sale taking place, by a person carrying on a business both inside and outside the EU, to the non-EU located business is also Zero-Rated. This would cover, for example, the transfer of parts to be assembled into products from a UK VAT-registered company to its non-EU branch.

Group 14: Tax-free shops. This covers any shop situated in an airport, port or Channel Tunnel terminal approved by HMRC for the purposes of this Group, and also sales of limited amounts of goods by the providers of air or sea transport or Channel tunnel shuttle trains to passengers who have purchased transport services from them.

Group 15: Charities etc. Zero-rating applies to the supply by a charity established primarily for the relief of distress or the benefit or protection of animals, of goods donated for sale, any exports, medical or scientific equipment used solely in medical research, and appliances for people with disabilities. The supply by a charity shop of goods purchased for resale is standard-rated - there is no general exemption for charity shops (though a small charity shop may be able to keep total taxable turnover below the registration limit).

Group 16: Clothing and footwear. Children's clothing and footwear are Zero-Rated. Protective boots and helmets are Standard-Rated when supplied to a person for use by his or her employees. Supplies of protective boots and helmets to any other person for industrial use remain zero-rated. Also zero-rated are motor cycle helmets. Other clothing is Standard-Rated.

35.7 Reduced rate goods and services

Particulars of goods and services which are reduced-rated supplies are contained in the Schedule 7A to the VAT Act 1994, and there are 11 groups.

Group 1: Fuel and power supplied for domestic and charity use.

Group 2: Installation of energy-saving materials.

Group 3: Grant-funded installations of heating or security equipment.

Group 4: Women's sanitary products

Group 5: Children's car seats and car seat bases

Group 6: Certain residential conversions

Group 7: Certain residential renovations and alterations

Group 8: Contraceptive products (unless exempt from VAT i.e. NHS or private healthcare)

Group 9: Welfare advice supplied by charities/ state-regulated private welfare institutions

Group 10: Installation of mobility aids for the elderly

Group 11: Smoking cessation products.

Reduced-rate supplies can in general be characterised as those on which a previously higher applicable rate of VAT has been reduced, as a deliberate policy, for social or welfare reasons.

35.8 Exempt goods and services

Particulars of goods and services which are exempt supplies are contained in Schedule 9 to the VAT Act 1994 and there are 15 groups, classified as follows.

Group 1: Land. See 35.9 for more details.

Group 2: Insurance. All forms of insurance are exempted and this includes insurance broking and agency services.

Group 3: Postal services. The conveyance of postal packets other than telegrams, by the Royal Mail was exempted up to 31st January 2011. Postal services rendered by persons other than the post office were taxable. However, as part of EU policy to reduce distortion of competition between state and private providers, the UK Royal Mail lost its exemption in respect of parcel services and certain other postal services, and from 31st January 2011 these are standard rated.

Group 4: Betting, gaming and lotteries. Examples of exempt services under this group are bookmakers, charges for bingo and profits from casino games. Admission charges to any premises where betting or the playing of games of chance takes place are however taxable at Standard Rate, as are takings from gaming or entertainment machines.

Group 5: Finance. In general, banking services relating to the borrowing or lending, receipt and transfer of money are exempt. Specific services offered by banks such as executorship and trustee work, portfolio management etc. are taxable at Standard Rate, as are the commissions from stockbroking, and management fees of unit trusts.

Group 6: Education. Non-profit educational services provided by schools, colleges, universities and youth clubs are exempt, as are the supply of goods and services to those establishments. However, services provided by organisations selling training or education with a view to profit, such as correspondence courses, are taxable at standard rate. Where training or education is SR, printed learning materials are SR if supplied exclusively for the training course, but are ZR if they are also available to buy alone, without buying the training course.

Group 7: Health and welfare. The supply of goods and services by registered healthcare providers such as doctors, dentists, opticians, occupational therapists etc. is exempted. Goods supplied under a prescription by a pharmacist are ZR.

Group 8: Burial and cremation. The services of undertakers in connection with a funeral or cremation are exempt, and within limits this includes charges for the supply of a coffin, shroud etc. but not flowers.

Group 9: Trade unions and professional bodies. VAT exemption is given for membership fees and other mutual services, and related goods supplied by a trade union and most non-profit-making professional, learned or representational bodies.

Group 10: Sports competitions. The grant of a right to enter a competition in sport or physical recreation, where the consideration for the grant consists in money which is to be used wholly for the provision of prizes, is exempt.

Group 11: Works of art etc. The disposal of works of art in circumstances where there is no liability to inheritance tax or capital gains tax (broadly, sale to public collections for the public benefit) is exempt.

Group 12: Fund raising activities by charities.

Group 13: Cultural services etc.

Group 14: Supplies of goods where input tax cannot be recovered.

Group 15: Investment gold.

35.9 Land and buildings

The VAT treatment of supplies of land and buildings is complex. Details may be found in VAT Notice 708 'Buildings and construction' which may be downloaded from the HMRC website.

Where stamp duty land tax is payable on the sale or lease of land or buildings, the consideration liable to VAT is the sale price plus the stamp duty land tax.

35.10 Taxable persons

A taxable person is any person who is, or should be, registered for VAT. Person includes an individual, partnership, company, club, society or trust. Any person may register for VAT who is carrying on a business that involves making taxable supplies for a consideration. The business in question need not be a profit-making or profit-seeking business. VAT registration is compulsory once turnover of taxable supplies exceeds a set level (See 35.13).

35.11 Business splitting

If the same person carries on two businesses then both businesses have to be registered under the same registration and have to be considered as one when applying the VAT registration limits. HMRC is alert to the possibility that to keep turnover under the VAT registration threshold, two members of a family, or two individuals, sometimes operate two apparently independent businesses from the same premises, or one business is run by a partnership alongside a connected business operated by one of the partners as a sole trader. HMRC has indicated that the following factors will be taken into consideration in deciding whether or not a genuine independent business exists for VAT registration purposes.

(i) Appropriate premises and equipment for each business should be provided by the person carrying on the business.

(ii) Day-to-day records identifying each business should be kept and where appropriate separate annual accounts.

(iii) Purchase and sales invoices for each business should be in the name of the person carrying on the trade who should be legally responsible for all trading activities.

(iv) A separate bank account should be opened for each business.

(v) All payroll payments should be paid by the person carrying on the business.

(vi) Each business should be treated as an independent business for income tax purposes.

35.12 Artificial separation of business activities

Formerly, HMRC could not require separate businesses to register as a single trader for VAT purposes unless it could show that the main reason (or one of the main reasons) for keeping those businesses separate was to avoid a liability to be VAT-registered.

This limitation has been removed, and connected businesses which have avoided liability for VAT by artificially separating will be liable to be treated as one, whatever the purported reason for the separation. For example, HMRC can direct that a series of limited companies running a pub, launderette or other retail outlet for only one month a year each, in order to keep the turnover of each company below the registration threshold, will be treated as one business.

According to HMRC it is impracticable to give a complete list of all the circumstances in which a separation will be artificial, as each case will depend on its own facts. However, HMRC 'would at least make further enquiries' where:

(a) Separate entities supply VAT-registered and non-VAT-registered customers.

(b) The same equipment and/or premises are used by different entities on a regular basis – this may be particularly relevant where an ice cream van (for example) is used by traders in rotation.

(c) A supply, which is usually a single supply, is split into separate parts – for example, a bed-and breakfast establishment where the bedroom is said to be supplied by the husband and the breakfast by the wife.

(d) Where the separated parts retain the appearance of a single business: the example given being that of pub catering where 'in most cases the customer will consider the food and the drinks as bought from the pub and not from two independent businesses'. However, franchised 'shops within shops' will usually be accepted as truly independent businesses.

(e) One person has a controlling influence in two or more businesses which make the same type of supply at separate locations.

35.13 Compulsory registration

VAT registration is compulsory once a business's turnover of taxable supplies exceeds a threshold set out in the legislation, which is usually increased each year on 1st April (occasionally on 1st May). However, the thresholds were not increased in 2018, so the latest thresholds are as follows:

	from April 2018	from April 2017
VAT registration threshold	£ 85,000	£ 85,000
VAT deregistration threshold	£ 83,000	£ 83,000

Notes

(i) "Taxable supplies" comprises all non-exempt supplies, including those which are zero-rated.

(ii) Registration is mandatory in the following circumstances:

  a) At the end of any month, if the value of the taxable supplies in the past year has exceeded the past turnover limits.

  b) At any time, if there are reasonable grounds for believing that the value of the taxable supplies in the next 30 days will exceed the turnover limit.

(iii) For (ii) a) notification to HMRC must be made within 30 days of the end of the relevant month. Registration is effective from the end of the month following the relevant month, or such earlier date as may be mutually agreed. The relevant month is the month at the end of which historic 12-month turnover exceeds the threshold, so that a liability to register arises.

(iv) For (ii) b) notification must be made before the end of the 30 day period. Registration is effective from the beginning of the 30 day period.
Notification of registration is now dealt with online at www.gov.uk/vat-registration

35.14 Voluntary registration

Where a person who is not required by law to be registered satisfies HMRC that he or she:

(i) makes taxable supplies; or

(ii) is carrying on a business and intends to make such supplies in the course or furtherance of that business;

then, if the person so requests, he or she can be voluntarily registered, with effect from the day on which the request is made or such earlier date as may be mutually agreed.

35.15 Voluntary de-registration

A registered person may apply for de-registration if in the next year his or her taxable turnover excluding VAT is not expected to exceed £83,000.

De-registration in principle requires the trader to account for output VAT on a self-supply of all inventory and fixed assets, on which input VAT was previously recovered, which are still on hand at deregistration. However, if the amount of VAT involved in the self-supply charge on deregistration is less than £2,000, the liability is ignored, being deemed 'de minimis' (too small to matter).

35.16 Group registration

Under Section 43 VATA 1994, as amended, two or more companies or limited liability partnerships (collectively referred to as corporate bodies) may register as a single taxable person, known as a VAT Group, if

(i) each body has a permanent establishment in the UK;

(ii) they are under common control, for example one or more company is a subsidiary of a common parent company, or both/ all of them are controlled by a business partnership, or by an individual.

A restriction applies where the turnover of a prospective VAT group is over £10 million per year and the group is partly owned or managed by a third party (e.g. a joint owner owning 50% of the parent company but not itself in the VAT group).

This entity can only register as a group for VAT if:

i) no more than 50 per cent of benefits generated by the business go to third parties;

ii) under GAAP the whole VAT group uses consolidated accounting;

iii) no third party consolidates the VAT group into its accounts.

The effects of a group registration are as follows.

(i) The VAT administration is handled by one group company, known as the representative member, and only one VAT return is required for all transactions by the group. All group companies use the same VAT number;

(ii) Intra-group supplies are outside the scope of (ie not subject to) VAT;

(iii) All members of the group are jointly and severally liable for the VAT due from the representative member; and

(iv) Turnover limits for registration, deregistration, and special schemes and partial exemption methods (see Chapter 36 for these two) are based on the group figures.

35.17 Companies organised into divisions - Divisional registration

A company carrying on UK business in several divisions may register its divisions separately as unincorporated traders, as follows.

(i) All divisions of the company must be registered separately. It is not possible to exclude certain divisions from registration e.g. where they fall below the registration limits.

(ii) A separate VAT return is made by each division.

(iii) However, the separate divisions are not separately taxed persons and the company remains liable for the whole VAT.

(iv) Inter-divisional transfers are not subject to VAT.

(v) Each division should be an independent unit with its own accounting and administration, carrying on business activities in separate locations.

(vi) Input tax attributable to exempt supplies (exempt input tax) by the corporate body as a whole must be less than the partial exemption de minimis limits given at 36.17.

Divisional registration is subject to the approval of HMRC.

35.18 Accounts and records

Almost all VAT returns must be submitted online and VAT payments made online.

Paper records may still be kept supporting input and output VAT, though electronic records are equally acceptable.

(a) Any taxable supply of goods or services must be supported by a 'tax invoice', the details of which are described in 36.9;

(b) At regular intervals, usually quarterly, a VAT return must be completed showing the amounts of output and input tax for the period, and the net amount payable to or receivable from HMRC. The period covered by a VAT return is known as a tax period and each online return must be submitted not later than one month and seven days after the end of that tax period;

(c) Adequate records and accounts of all transactions involving VAT must be maintained to support both the amount of output tax chargeable, and the claims for deductible input tax. To support input tax claims the primary requirement is keep valid tax invoices received from suppliers. These records are checked on control visits by HMRC officers;

(d) Books and records, including electronic records, must be kept for a period of six years. Business records include the following:
   - Orders and delivery notes
   - Relevant business correspondence
   - Purchase and sales books
   - Cash books and other account books
   - Purchase invoices and copy sales invoices
   - Records of daily takings e.g. till rolls
   - Annual accounts – Statements of Financial Position and Comprehensive Income
   - Import and export documents
   - Bank statements and paying-in-slips
   - Any credit/debit notes issued or received; and

(e) There are some optional special schemes for retailers to simplify record keeping for VAT purposes and these are covered in Chapter 36.

35.19 Administration

HM Revenue and Customs is the government department responsible for the administration and collection of VAT.

Dispute and appeals procedure

In the event of a dispute between a taxable person and the VAT office, there is first an optional internal review procedure in which a Revenue Officer who has not been involved in the case before is asked to review the complaint and respond within 45 days. If this review supports the decision of the original Revenue Officer, or if there is no internal review, the taxpayer can appeal within 30 days to the Tax Chamber of the First-Tier Tribunal. Appeals to the First-tier Tribunal might cover matters such as:

(a) Registration or cancellation of registration.

(b) Assessment of tax.

(c) Amount of tax chargeable.

(d) Amount of input tax deductible.

(e) Bad debt claims.

(f) Group registration matters.

(g) Matters concerned with the value or categorisation of supplies.

On questions of law a further appeal can be made to the Upper Tribunal (Tax and Chancery Chamber) from which further appeal lies to the Court of Appeal (Inner House in Scotland) and ultimately to the UK Supreme Court.

As VAT is European Law, questions of the interpretation of EU Directives or Regulations, and of whether domestic VAT legislation or HMRC practice is compatible with EU law, can be referred by the judge directly from any UK Court or Tribunal to the European Court of Justice, for a definitive ruling on the relevant point of European Law. The UK courts are obliged to follow this court's rulings in applying VAT law to cases before them and if anything in the UK VAT legislation is found incompatible with the EU VAT Directives then the UK Government is obliged to change the law. In deciding UK VAT cases the UK courts also take account of similar decisions on VAT matters from the courts and VAT tribunals of other EU Member States.

35.20 Late registration penalty

(a) Failure to notify HMRC at the proper time that a business should be registered for VAT purposes may incur a tax-based penalty:

Type of behaviour	Unprompted or prompted disclosure	Penalty range as a percentage of potential lost tax revenue
Non-deliberate	Unprompted – within 12 months of tax being due	0% to 30%
	Unprompted – 12 months or more after tax was due	10% to 30%
	Prompted – within 12 months of tax being due	10% to 30%
	Prompted – 12 months or more after tax was due	20% to 30%
Deliberate	Unprompted	20% to 70%
	Prompted	35% to 70%
Deliberate and concealed	Unprompted	30% to 100%
	Prompted	50% to 100%

The penalty is not due if the trader can satisfy HMRC that there was a reasonable excuse for the failure.

The following do **not** amount to reasonable excuse:

i) insufficiency of funds to pay the tax

ii) reliance on a third party to pay the tax

iii) ignorance of the law relating to registration.

(b) HMRC has indicated that the following guidelines show circumstances where there might be a reasonable excuse for late registration.

(i) **Compassionate circumstances** where an individual is totally responsible for running a small business and he or she, or a member of the immediate family, was seriously ill or recovering from such illness at the time notification was required.

(ii) **Transfer of a business as a going concern** where such a business is taken over with little or no break in the trading activities and returns have been submitted and tax paid on time under the registration number of the previous owner.

(iii) **Doubt about liabilities of supplies** where there is written evidence of an enquiry to HMRC about the liability of supplies and liability has remained in doubt.

(iv) **Uncertainty about employment status** where there are genuine doubts as to whether a person is employed or self-employed or where correspondence with HMRC can be produced about these doubts.

(v) **Effective date of registration earlier than required** where a person has requested registration from an earlier date than was legally required in the mistaken belief that he or she had to do so to recover input tax on inventories and other assets for the business. This excuse could only apply if there was no reason to believe that taxable turnover would exceed the registration threshold from the required date.

35.21 The default surcharge – Section 59 VATA 1994

The default surcharge regime has been in place for many years but its details have changed with the 2011 change to online VAT reporting. Online VAT returns and electronic VAT payments are now required for all traders with a VAT-exclusive turnover exceeding £100,000, and all newly registered traders, since April 2011.

The due date for both online payments and returns is one calendar month and seven days after the end of the return period. The rules about VAT default surcharge work as follows:

(a) A person is in VAT default if a return is not submitted on time, or if a payment is made late;

(b) A trader can be in default for one return period without incurring a monetary penalty. However, the first time the taxpayer is in default, HMRC serve a surcharge liability notice. The surcharge liability notice once issued remains in force for a period of 12 months, during which time there must be no further default;

(c) While the notice is in force, a default surcharge liability arises for any period in which there is another default. In addition, each time there is a default in an existing notice period (surcharge period), the current surcharge period is extended for a further 12 months;

(d) The penalty is based on the amount of VAT due and unpaid at the time when the default occurred. The percentage penalty goes up the more defaults there are in the same surcharge period. The surcharge period continues until there have been twelve months with no default;

(e) The rates of surcharge are:

	% of VAT
1st default	2%
2nd default	5%
3rd default	10%
4th and subsequent	15%

(f) Surcharge assessments at rates below 10% will not be issued if the calculated penalty is £400 or less;

(g) Once the rate reaches 10% (third default), an assessment will be issued for £30 minimum, or the calculated surcharge if greater;

(h) The above surcharge regime takes effect more slowly for businesses with an annual turnover of less than £150,000. On the first default (late return or late tax payment) by such a trader, HMRC will send a letter offering help and support. If the business, having either received or declined the help and support service, is late with another VAT return or tax payment in the next twelve months, a surcharge liability notice will then be issued, and a normal surcharge period will then commence;

(i) **Reasonable excuses:** A person is not liable to a surcharge if he or she satisfies the Commissioners that in the case of a default:
   (i) the return, or as the case may be the tax, was despatched at such time and in such manner that it was reasonable to expect that it would be received within the appropriate time limit, or
   (ii) there is a reasonable excuse for the return or the tax not having been despatched.

   The following are not reasonable excuses (section 71 VAT Act):
   (i) Insufficiency of funds to pay any tax;
   (ii) Where reliance is placed on any other person to perform any task, the fact of that reliance or the fact of any other dilatoriness or inaccuracy on the part of the person relied upon.

After April 2011 it would seem that the 'despatched on time' argument, dating from when VAT returns were all submitted by post, can now apply only to traders who do not have to submit online. However it is conceivable that an IT problem might arise such that a trader could prove that an online return or payment was correctly sent, despite failing to reach HMRC on time.

35.22 Errors on VAT returns

Where a VAT error is made, it can be corrected in one of two ways:

Method 1

Provided that the following conditions are satisfied:

(i) the error has a net value which is below £10,000, or which is both below £50,000 and below 1% of total 'outputs' for VAT purposes in the return period; **and**

(ii) the error was not deliberate

then the error may be corrected on the next VAT return ("Method 1").

Alternatively, Method 2 may be used if the taxpayer so chooses (see the note after the penalties table below).

Method 2

If

(i) the error has a net value which is more than £50,000; **or**

(ii) the error has a net value which is both greater than £10,000 and greater than 1% of total 'outputs' for VAT purposes in the return period; **or**

(iii) the error was deliberate

then Method 2 **must** be used, which is to notify HM Revenue and Customs of the error using VAT Form 652, instead of including correction of the error within the next VAT return.
Penalties for such errors would be as shown in the following table.

Type of behaviour	Unprompted disclosure	Prompted disclosure
Reasonable care	No penalty	No penalty
Careless	0% to 30% of PLR	15% to 30%
Deliberate	20% to 70% of PLR	35% to 70%
Deliberate and concealed	30% to 100% of PLR	50% to 100%

Note that for careless errors, it might (depending upon the size of the error) be sensible for the taxpayer to choose Method 2 – notification by VAT form 652 – so as to seek a reduction in penalty from the top end of the range shown. This is because merely making a correction through the next VAT return does not constitute a 'disclosure' under the penalties regime.

35.23 Tax avoidance schemes - VAT

Businesses making taxable supplies ≥ £600,000 must disclose their use of specific VAT avoidance schemes, which HMRC publishes in a statutory list. This must be done within 30 days of the date when the first return affected by the scheme becomes due. Failure to disclose incurs a penalty of 15% of tax avoided for the use of such 'listed schemes'.

In addition, businesses with taxable supplies > £10m must disclose the use of any schemes that have 'the hallmarks of avoidance'. A penalty of up to £5,000 may be imposed for the use of such 'hallmarked schemes'.

Student self-testing questions with answers

Question 1: Mitch's Mining Limited

Mitch's Mining Ltd owns a quarry. It extracts stone from this quarry and sells the stone to Reece's Rockware Ltd for £10,000 plus VAT. Reece's Rockware Ltd converts all the stone into paving slabs and sells these slabs to Tina's Tulips Ltd for £18,000 plus VAT. Tina's Tulips Ltd owns and runs a garden centre, where the slabs are sold to the general public for a total of £32,000 plus VAT.

Requirement:

Show how VAT is charged and collected at each stage of the process. (Assume that VAT is to be accounted for at 20% throughout).

Solution to Question 1: Mitch's Mining Limited

	Cost price before VAT	Input tax	Selling price before VAT	Output tax	Paid to HMRC
	£	£	£	£	£
Mitch's Mining Ltd	-	-	10,000	2,000	2,000
Reece's Rockware Ltd	10,000	2,000	18,000	3,600	1,600
Tina's Tulips Ltd	18,000	3,600	32,000	6,400	2,800
					6,400

Question 2: Farm Crafts Limited

Farm Crafts Ltd commences in business on 1st July 2018. Every month, Farm Crafts Ltd receives: £18,000 from sales of food which would be zero-rated if the company was VAT-registered; £12,000 from sales of furniture; and £7,500 rent.

Requirement:

Demonstrate the date by which Farm Crafts Ltd will pass the VAT registration threshold, and state the date by which the company should register for VAT, and the date from which registration would be effective.

Solution to Question 2: Farm Crafts Limited

	Furniture taxable at standard rate	Food taxable at zero rate	**Total taxable supplies**	Rent exempt
	£	£	**£**	£
July	12,000	18,000	30,000	7,500
Cumulative to 31st July	12,000	18,000	30,000	7,500
August	12,000	18,000	30,000	7,500
Cumulative to 31st August	24,000	36,000	60,000	15,000
September	12,000	18,000	30,000	7,500
Cumulative to 30th September	**36,000**	**54,000**	**90,000**	22,500
October	12,000	18,000	30,000	7,500
Cumulative to 31st October	48,000	72,000	120,000	30,000
November	12,000	18,000	30,000	7,500
Cumulative to 30th November	60,000	90,000	150,000	37,500

The VAT threshold is reached when the net taxable supplies exceed £85,000. For Farm Crafts Ltd this is at the end of September 2018, when the cumulative supplies which would be taxable if the company was registered total £90,000 (£36,000 standard-rated furniture, plus £54,000 zero-rated food).

The exempt supplies are not counted, and nor is any VAT which would be added to taxable supplies if the company was registered.

The need to be registered should be notified by 30th October 2018, and the registration would be effective from 1st November.

36 The VAT system in more detail

36.1 Introduction

This chapter covers further features of the VAT system under the following main headings:

The VAT return	Imports
Zero rated and exempt supplies	Exports
Taxable supply of goods and services	Goods for private use
Taxable persons	Bad debts
The supply of goods and services	Transfer of a business as a going concern
Place of supply	Sale of business assets
Tax point	Business assets – capital allowances
Tax invoice/credit notes	Opting to tax non-domestic land and buildings
Value of goods and services	Changes in tax rates
Mixed supplies/composite supplies	Cash/annual accounting schemes
Input tax – deductions	Flat rate scheme – small firms
Input tax – no deduction	Special retail schemes
Fuel for private motoring	Miscellaneous
Partial exemption	

36.2 The VAT return

A taxable person is required to charge VAT on taxable supplies to customers, which is called output tax. He or she is also able to claim credit for the tax paid on business purchases and this is known as input tax.

At the end of a VAT accounting period, usually a month or three months, the trader has to submit a VAT return to HMRC. This must show the total taxable supplies made and the VAT charged (output tax), together with the VAT on all purchase and expense invoices received (input tax), but excluding any input VAT that is blocked from recovery (see 36.15). If the tax charged exceeds the amount paid then the balance is payable to HMRC. Where the output tax is less than the input tax then a repayment can be claimed.

Example

	£	£
Total taxable turnover (SR) for the quarter	100,000	
Output tax @ 20%		20,000
Total taxable inputs (SR) for the quarter	80,000	
Input tax @ 20%		(16,000)
Balance of VAT payable to HMRC		4,000

36.3 Zero-rated and exempt supplies

Goods or services which fall within the zero-rated (ZR) or exempt categories do not include any VAT at all in the total invoiced price, and for this reason are often thought by students to be similar. However, there is an important difference between zero-rated and exempt supplies.

(a) Zero-rated goods or services are taxable outputs, but liable at a nil rate of output tax. It follows that any input tax incurred in providing those outputs can be reclaimed by the supplier, and will be repaid in full, since there is no output tax collected from customers to give a normal means of recovering the supplier's input VAT.

(b) Supplies of exempt goods and services are made outside the VAT system and therefore, in principle, any input tax incurred in making such supplies cannot be reclaimed by the trader. Such irrecoverable input VAT is an allowable business cost for income or corporation tax (unless the related cost is disallowable for direct tax purposes, eg customer entertaining).

36.4 Taxable supply of goods and services

VAT is chargeable on any supply made in the UK, or imported, where the supply is taxable under VAT law. The supply must be of non-exempt goods or services made for consideration by a taxable person in the course of business.

36.5 Taxable persons

A taxable person is any person who has registered for VAT, as described in Chapter 35. All business activities must be aggregated in order to determine whether or not a person must register. Registration can be for an individual, partnership or limited company. The total of taxable business supplies made (excluding VAT charged) is called taxable turnover.

36.6 The supply of goods and services

The supply of goods can include any of the following:

(a) sale by ordinary commercial transaction;

(b) sale by auction or through agents;

(c) sale under a credit sale agreement or by hire purchase;

(d) goods supplied for further processing;

(e) goods supplied for personal use.

The supply of services covers any which are provided for money or money's worth, and includes the hire, lease or rental of any goods. Services which are ancillary to the supply of goods, such as postage and packing and delivery, are normally treated as services and not as part of the goods sold, if they are shown separately on the sales invoice.

36.7 Place of supply

In principle only goods and services supplied in the UK are chargeable to UK VAT so that the determination of the place of supply is important.

Goods

If the goods to be supplied are physically located in the UK then they are within the scope of UK VAT even if they may be subsequently exported. Goods that are located wholly outside the EU fiscal area and remain so are not subject to UK VAT at any time during the course of their supply. They are outside the scope of VAT, even if a UK trader enters into business transactions involving these goods.

This could arise, for example, where a shipping company arranges for a consignment of goods to be sold and transferred from one country to another, but they never enter the EU Fiscal Area.

For VAT purposes the UK includes the Isle of Man, but not the Channel Isles.

For VAT treatment of imports and exports of goods to/from the UK, see 36.18 – 36.22.

Services

For VAT purposes, the place where a service is treated as being supplied is the only place where it is liable to VAT (if any). A particular service can have only one place of supply.

Where both the supplier and the customer are in the UK then there is no problem about deeming the place of supply of services as this will (on basic principles) be the UK.

The problems of competing places of supply arise when the customer is not in the UK and the supplier is, or vice versa. The rules are different depending on whether the customer is a business customer or a non-business customer.

Both situations are covered at 36.22.

36.8 Time of supply – tax point

The tax point determines the period in which a supply falls, therefore when the supply should be included on the next VAT return and what rate of VAT applies if there is a change in rate. As with place of supply, the tax point rules differ depending on whether a supply is one of goods or of services.

For goods the basic tax point is the date when the goods are delivered or made available, and for services the basic tax point is the date of performance. However, there are two key exceptions.

(a) If an invoice is issued within 14 days after the time when goods are delivered or made available, then the date of the invoice becomes the tax point. This practice is widely followed and enables the VAT return to be completed from invoice records. A longer period than 14 days between delivery and invoice may be agreed with HMRC if the business has a regular invoice billing cycle eg on the last day of the month,

(b) If payment of consideration for the supply is made in advance of the date when goods are delivered or made available, then it is the earliest of the invoice, delivery or payment date which determines the tax point.

The same rules apply for deciding the period in which taxable inputs of goods arise.

The most common tax point is the invoice date. If credit is taken on business purchases, relief for input tax may well be obtained in an earlier VAT quarter than the time when the supplier is paid.

36.9 Tax invoice

A tax invoice is a sales invoice issued by a registered person in respect of any goods or services supplied by him or her to another taxable person. The invoice must contain:

(a) supplier's name, address and VAT registration number;

(b) customer's name and address;

(c) type of supply i.e. whether a sale, sale by HP, hire or rental;

(d) description of goods or services supplied, together with the amount payable for each excluding VAT; items chargeable at different VAT rates must be shown separately, and the exact number of items of each type must be stated;

(e) total amount payable without VAT;

(f) particulars of any discounts offered; and

(g) total amount of VAT.

A less detailed invoice, omitting the customer's name and address, may be used where individual supplies by a retailer amount to less than £250, including VAT.

36.10 Credit notes

Regulations require all registered traders to show the related VAT on credit or debit notes, whenever a price adjustment alters the amount of VAT due on a previous invoice.

36.11 Value of goods and services

The general rule is that the value on which VAT is chargeable is the amount of money (excluding VAT) which a customer has to pay for the goods or services supplied. This is known in VAT law as the consideration. The following should be noted.

(a) Price discounts (e.g. for customer loyalty) must be deducted from the invoiced amount to determine the VAT value.

(b) In the case of prompt payment discounts, VAT must be charged on the amount the customer actually pays. This can be achieved in either of two ways:

  (i) By issuing an invoice for the full (undiscounted) amount, then if the customer earns the discount issuing a credit note for the amount of the discount. In both cases (invoice and credit note), the price/discount should be split between the net and VAT components; or

  (ii) By issuing an invoice which includes the terms of the prompt payment discount plus a statement that the customer can only recover as input tax the VAT paid to the supplier. HMRC has recommended the use of wording along the lines of "A discount of X% of the full price applies if payment is made within Y days of the invoice date. No credit note will be issued. Following payment you must ensure you have only recovered the VAT actually paid."

  [Note that prior to 1st April 2015, VAT was charged on the discounted amount irrespective of whether or not the customer earned the discount].

(c) If a supply is not made for money consideration then the open market value of the supply, less any VAT included in that value, should be taken as the value of the supply, and VAT computed on it. This would apply for example on a part-exchange transaction.

(d) The cost of the goods to the supplier may be used to determine the value of a taxable supply. This would apply to goods appropriated from trading stock for personal use, and to the trader's own built plant and machinery, on which input VAT is accounted for under the 'self-supply' rules.

36.12 Mixed supplies

A mixed supply occurs where a single inclusive price is charged for a number of separate supplies of goods and services. Where all the supplies are taxable at the same rate, then the normal rules of VAT can be easily applied to compute the VAT element. However, where different rates apply then an apportionment must be made which is 'fair and justifiable'. (See Card Protection Plan V CIR. 2001 STC)

Example

B makes a mixed supply of goods at a VAT-inclusive price of £160. The product costs show zero-rated goods costing £30 and standard-rated goods costing £50 (exclusive of VAT).

Solution

Computation of VAT

Proportion of total cost at SR $\frac{50 + \text{VAT}}{(50 + \text{VAT}) + 30}$ = 60/90

VAT inclusive price of standard-rated goods 60/90 × £160 = £106.67

VAT included = £106.67 × 20/120 = £17.78

Sale value of zero-rated supply = (160 – 106.67) = £53.33.

Analysis of total price as apportioned

	£
Value of standard-rated supplies (£106.67 - £17.78)	88.89
VAT on standard-rated supplies 20% × £88.89	17.78
Zero-rated supplies	53.33
Price of mixed supplies	160.00

Other methods of apportionment e.g. based on market values, can be used.

Apportionment must not be made where the supply is a composite supply (see next section). Examples of a mixed supply are:

- Annual subscription to the AA (C & E v AA QB 1974 STC 192)
- Fees for correspondence courses (Rapid Results College Ltd 1973 VAT TR 197). (Books are zero rated. Tuition is standard rated).

36.13 Composite supply

This occurs where goods and services supplied together make up a single indivisible supply, and apportionment must not be made for VAT rating purposes as the components cannot be viewed as separable. The VAT treatment of a composite supply depends on the judgment as to what is the principal supply, with the other parts of a different type being classed as ancillary. If the composite supply, as a whole package, does not clearly qualify for exemption or zero-rating then it must be standard-rated. Examples of supplies that have been held in decided cases to be composite supplies include:

Services of a launderette (supplies of water, heat, use of machinery)	Mander Laundries Ltd 1973 VAT TR 136
A course in dress design (material and guidance notes)	Betty Foster (Fashion Sewing) 1976 VAT TR 229

36.14 Input tax – Deduction

Input tax is the VAT suffered on business purchases and expenses, including imported goods, goods removed from an import warehouse, and capital expenditure.

To be deductible, the input tax must be in respect of goods and services for the purposes of the business, and not of a class where the tax is specifically not recoverable.

Input tax can be reclaimed providing that it is attributable to the making of:

(i) standard- or zero-rated supplies (which term includes reduced rate supplies);

(ii) supplies made in the course of business which are outside the scope of UK VAT, but would have been subject to standard or zero rate if made in the UK

(iii) supplies of warehoused goods.

Input tax incurred in respect of any other activity not covered by (i) to (iii) above is not reclaimable.

Input tax on business overheads or research and development expenditure can be claimed as input tax provided that the overheads or R&D are attributable to the three activities noted above. If the overhead or R&D expenditure is partially attributable to exempt supplies or to activities outside the three categories above, then only the part of the input tax that can be attributed to the three listed activities is reclaimable.

Input tax incurred in relation to making exempt supplies may however be recoverable where after calculating the total amount for a period, it is found to fall under a specified de minimis level. (See partial exemption, 36.17.)

36.15 Input tax – Blocked deduction

Input tax charged in respect of the following is non-deductible.

(a) The purchase of private motor cars, except:

 (i) Cars purchased for use exclusively for business purposes, and not being capable of additional private use by the trader.

 (ii) Cars used solely for business such as taxis, self-drive hire cars.

 (iii) New cars purchased for resale by a car dealer.

 VAT on the purchase of commercial vehicles such as vans is deductible.

(b) To mirror the rule that input VAT on purchased cars is usually blocked, only 50% of the input VAT incurred on leasing any private car(s) is deductible on a fully taxable trader's VAT return. The VAT-exclusive rental, plus 50% of the VAT incurred, is therefore charged in the accounts as an allowable expense for direct tax purposes. This rule does not apply to very short hires.

(c) Motor accessories. When a motor car is purchased, VAT on the accessories provided at first registration is not reclaimable, even if invoiced separately.

VAT on accessories purchased and fitted later is deductible, provided that the car is still in business use.

(d) Business entertainment expenses. Input tax on this kind of expenditure is only allowable where it is incurred for staff entertainment for the purpose of the business, eg provision of meals and seasonal staff entertainment. In principle, VAT cannot be reclaimed on the entertainment of customers, suppliers or prospective customers/members of the public.

(e) However, in 2010 in the case of Danfoss/AstraZeneca (C-371/07), the European Court of Justice held that VAT on the cost of 'basic' meals provided to overseas business contacts to facilitate sales meetings should be recoverable, as it had a clear business purpose. HMRC then issued guidance that VAT recovery would now be allowed for such entertainment costs (the guidance notes suggested this only covered 'necessary' meals and transport). This change was confirmed by Finance Act 2011, but the relaxation only applies to non-UK customers, and only where the entertaining is reasonable, and has a clear business purpose.

36.16 Fuel purchased by a business and used by staff or proprietor for private motoring – the scale charge

Input tax on all road fuel purchased by a VAT-registered trader which is then applied for business and private use is reclaimable, so long as the business is making taxable supplies to which the fuel purchases can be attributed. However, if exempt supplies are made, part of the input tax on fuel may not be recoverable. If there is any onward supply of fuel to proprietors or employees for private motoring (i.e. they do not fully reimburse the business for the cost of any fuel used for private mileage), a flat rate 'fuel scale charge. must be accounted for per car /employee. This charges VAT on an assumed or notional amount of fuel that is deemed to be supplied onwards for private use to the employee(s) or the business proprietor(s) out of the VAT registered business's fuel purchases. Output tax is charged on this notional supply, and must be paid by the business, by reference to the fuel scale charge rates.

VAT fuel rates 2018/19

Like car income tax benefit in kind charges, VAT scale charges are based on the CO_2 emissions of the car. A separate output VAT scale charge must be entered on each VAT return for every car that had use of business fuel for private motoring. For monthly or annual VAT return periods, pro-rate the charges accordingly.

HMRC has confirmed that a trader who does not wish to reclaim any input tax at all on car fuel is permitted to treat it all as wholly irrecoverable and then there is no need to account for the output tax scale charge. VAT fuel rates for VAT accounting periods starting on or after 1st May 2018 are as follows:

CO_2 band	VAT fuel scale charge, 3 month period	VAT on 3 month charge	VAT exclusive 3 month charge
120 or less	£140	£23.33	£116.67
125	£210	£35.00	£175.00
130	£224	£37.33	£186.67
135	£238	£39.67	£198.33
140	£252	£42.00	£210.00
145	£266	£44.33	£221.67
150	£280	£46.67	£233.33
155	£295	£49.17	£245.83
160	£309	£51.50	£257.50
165	£323	£53.83	£269.17
170	£336	£56.00	£280.00
175	£351	£58.50	£292.50
180	£365	£60.83	£304.17
185	£379	£63.17	£315.83
190	£393	£65.50	£327.50
195	£407	£67.83	£339.17
200	£421	£70.17	£350.83
205	£436	£72.67	£363.33
210	£449	£74.83	£374.17
215	£463	£77.17	£385.83
220	£477	£79.50	£397.50
225 or more	£491	£81.83	£409.17

36.17 Partial exemption

A trader who makes supplies of taxable goods and/or services, and also makes supplies of exempt goods and/or services, is referred to as a partially exempt trader.

The special rules about input VAT recovery by partially exempt traders are outlined below. (Note that the term 'exempt input tax' is used in the VAT legislation to refer to input tax attributed to the making of exempt supplies rather than taxable supplies.)

(i) Where a business makes exempt supplies of financial or land-related services, and these are not incurred in the course of carrying on a business in the financial sector, then all exempt input tax can be recovered provided it has been incurred in relation to any of the following supplies:

  a) the granting of any lease or tenancy of land, or any licence to occupy land (provided that the exempt input tax related to all such supplies made by the business is less than £1,000 per tax year, and that the business does not incur any exempt input tax other than that related to those supplies listed in this paragraph);

  b) any deposit of money;

  c) any services of arranging insurance;

  d) any services of arranging mortgages;

  e) any services of arranging hire-purchase, credit sale or conditional sale transactions;

  f) the assignment of any debt in respect of a supply of goods or services by the assignor.

If the exempt input tax is incurred in relation to supplies other than those listed above, then the tax must be taken into consideration 'in comparing the trader's total exempt input tax with the statutory disregard or 'de minimis limit', as described below.

(ii) A business can be treated as fully taxable (ie can recover all its input VAT) providing its exempt input tax is not more than £625 per month on average.

  This de minimis test applies for the business's VAT year (equating to £7,500 over a VAT year) but is provisionally applied to each return separately with adjustment at the end of the year if necessary.

  In addition businesses must satisfy the condition that the exempt input tax disregarded must be no more than 50% of total input VAT.

(iii) Exempt input tax is not recoverable where financial businesses are carried on, such as a bank, building society, money lender, credit card company etc.

(iv) The standard method of calculation to be used to apportion input VAT between taxable and exempt supplies, where the business is making partially exempt and partially taxable supplies in the period, is as follows.

(a) Identify the input tax that is directly attributable to taxable supplies

(b) Identify the input tax that is directly attributable to exempt supplies.

(c) The balance of input tax is input tax that is not attributable to any particular supplies (non-attributable input tax)

(d) Calculate the percentage, rounded up to the next whole number, of such non-attributable input tax which is equal to:

$$\frac{\text{Value of taxable supplies (excl. VAT)}}{\text{Value of taxable supplies (excl. VAT)} + \text{Value of exempt supplies}}$$

(e) Add the percentage obtained at (d) to the input tax already attributed to taxable supplies at (a). This input tax can all be treated as relating to taxable supplies.

(f) Add the remainder of the non–attributable input tax [(c) less (d)] to the exempt input tax already attributed to exempt supplies, at (b)

(g) If the total of exempt input tax at (f) is below the de minimis limit of £625 per month AND 50% of all input tax, then it can be reclaimed. If it exceeds the de minimis limit, it is irrecoverable.

(v) The standard method is the default method provided by the VAT Act but it is not mandatory: a trader can apply to use any other special method more suited to its business, provided advance agreement is obtained from HMRC. Commonly used special methods to allocate input tax between taxable and exempt supplies include methods based on staff numbers, floor-space occupied, relative purchases (whereas the standard method uses sales) or transaction counts. Any VAT partial exemption method approved by HMRC has to be 'fair and reasonable'.

(vi) For convenience, it is possible for an established business to use last year's overall partial exemption fraction as an estimated apportionment method for the first three quarters of its next VAT year, and only carry out a detailed annual calculation in the final VAT quarter of that year.

Example – Partial exemption calculation

Appear Ltd had the following transactions in the quarter to 31st December 2018:

Supplies made:	£
Standard-rated supplies (excluding VAT)	150,000
Zero-rated supplies	50,000
Exempt supplies	100,000

Input tax has been paid on input costs attributable to the following outputs and activities:

	£
Standard-rated supplies	12,000
Zero-rated supplies	–
Exempt supplies	17,000
General overheads	4,000

The general overhead input tax cannot be directly attributed to any of the listed supplies.

Compute the VAT payable for the quarter to 31st December 2018.

Solution:

		£	£
Output tax 150,000 @ 20%			30,000
Input tax:	Attributable to SR supplies	12,000	
	Attributable to ZR supplies	–	
	Overheads (see note (i))	2,680	(14,680)
VAT due			15,320

Notes

(i) VAT attributable to overheads:

$$\frac{150{,}000(SR) + 50{,}000(ZR)}{150{,}000(SR) + 50{,}000(ZR) + 100{,}000(EX)} \times 4{,}000 = 67\% \times 4{,}000 = 2{,}680$$

(ii) 67% (rounded up from 66.7%) of the non-attributable input tax on overheads can be apportioned to taxable supplies and recovered along with the input tax attributed to taxable supplies. The other 33% of the VAT on overheads, added to the £17,000 of input tax directly attributed to making exempt supplies, clearly exceeds the de minimis levels for exempt input tax, so the rest of the input VAT is irrecoverable.

(iii) An annual computation is not required to decide the final position in this case because the exempt input tax in this one quarter (£18,320) exceeds even the annual de minimis level, which is £7,500 (12 × £625).

36.18 Imports of goods

VAT on Imports of goods

There are many special rules about import of goods to the UK, especially from outside the EU Fiscal Area. This is an outline of the basic VAT rules only.

VAT is charged at the appropriate rate (zero, reduced or standard) on goods imported into the UK (including business acquisitions both from within the EU and from outside the EU). Private individuals also have to pay VAT on personal imports of goods into the UK (subject to certain personal exemptions).

Payment of VAT on imported goods is due at the time of importation, or removal from a bonded customs warehouse, unless deferment arrangements have been made. A registered trader approved by HMRC may defer payment of tax on goods imported in the course of business during a calendar month until the 15th of the following month (or the next working day after the 15th if that day is a holiday). The VAT is normally collected by a direct debit mandate which forms part of the application for deferral.

VAT on imported goods can be reclaimed by UK traders as normal input tax, subject to the normal rules. (This does not apply to imports in a private capacity, even if the importer also has a business VAT registration). The claim for the VAT as input tax must be made in the return for the accounting period during which the importation or removal from the relevant warehouse occurred.

Warehoused goods

When goods are warehoused for customs and excise purposes, payment of import VAT is usually suspended. VAT becomes payable when the goods are removed from the warehouse for use in the UK.

36.19 Imports of services – Reverse charge procedure

Where services are received from other countries outside the UK by UK businesses, and do not have any VAT applied in the state of the supplier or in the UK by the supplier, this means the supplier has classed the place of supply of the services as the UK, and not being VAT-registered in the UK they have treated the service as outside the scope of VAT on their own home-country VAT return.

In this situation, the UK-registered trader (who is the customer) must operate the **reverse charge** procedure. This means he/she/it must account for both UK output VAT on the imported services (as though self-supplied – see section 37.23) and also UK input VAT of the same amount, which it has in effect 'charged itself' and now seeks to recover. Both figures (input VAT and output VAT) will be the same figure, and appear on the same VAT return - unless partial exemption restricts input tax recovery.

So long as the UK purchasing business is making fully taxable supplies, there is no net VAT cost from operating the reverse charge on imports, as the same amount is added to input VAT and output VAT in the same period. This puts it in the same cash position as if it had used a UK supplier for the services – i.e. it pays VAT on the services, but the input VAT is all recovered against its own taxable supplies.

However, if the UK trader is partially exempt, and the service purchased related wholly or partly to its exempt supplies, then some input VAT will be irrecoverable.

The same amount of UK VAT would have been irrecoverable if the services had been purchased in the UK, and normal UK VAT had been paid. One purpose of the reverse charge procedure (which works the same way across the European Economic Area) is to remove the unfair pricing advantage that non- UK businesses would otherwise enjoy over UK sellers, when selling their services to partially-exempt UK businesses.

This example also shows how the reverse charge prevents a loss of tax to the UK Government, by ensuring that VAT recoverable in the UK, on imported services treated as supplied in the UK, has been paid in the UK.

36.20 Overseas businesses selling goods to UK customers using online market places

HMRC may direct an overseas business to appoint a VAT representative with joint and several liability. The Finance Act 2016 introduced a provision to enable HMRC to hold an online marketplace jointly and severally liable for unpaid VAT of an overseas business selling goods in the UK using that marketplace. The policy objective is to tackle non-compliance which is estimated to have cost £1billion to £1.5billion in unpaid VAT in 2015/16.

(see https://www.gov.uk/government/publications/vat-representatives-for-overseas-businesses-and-joint-and-several-liability-for-online-marketplaces)

36.21 Exports of goods from the UK

In summary, for exports of goods from the UK:

- Exports to EU non-business customers are liable to VAT at the normal rate;
- Exports to EU business customers are zero-rated; and
- Exports outside the EU are zero-rated.

More detail:

Supplies of goods to non-business customers in the EU are liable to UK VAT at the appropriate rate.

Exports (technically called Intra-Community Supplies) to business customers in the EU are zero-rated, but the business customer has to pay VAT in their own country.

Exports of goods to an overseas customer outside the EU Fiscal area are zero-rated. Where goods are sent to a final exporter in the UK then they will not be zero-rated by the UK supplier, as there is a supply in the UK being made; but they can be if there is delivery to a port or a central clearance depot for shipment.

36.22 Export of services from the UK to business and non-business customers

In summary, the usual situation for exports of services from the UK is:

- Exports to **non-business** customers are treated as having their place of supply where the **supplier** is based; so exports from the UK are liable to **UK VAT** at the normal rate;
- Exports to **business** customers are treated as having their place of supply where the **customer** is based; so exports from the UK are **outside the scope** of UK VAT; and
- The situation is different for digital services supplied within the EU – see 36.23

More detail:

The rules are different depending on whether the customer is a business customer or a non-business customer.

If the customer belongs outside the UK, and provides evidence to the UK supplier that it is in genuine business in its own country, then the supply of services is treated as taking place where the customer belongs, not where the supplier belongs.

For UK VAT purposes, the supply of services to business customers outside the UK is outside the scope of UK VAT and so no UK VAT should be charged on it. (Note that the supplies do not count as exempt or zero-rated supplies – 'outside the scope' means they are not taxable supplies at all.)

However, if the business customer belongs in another EU state, and the UK supplier also has its own VAT registration in that other state (which is possible; a trader can register for VAT in any number of different EU states where it does business), the supplier should charge VAT at the rate applying in that other state and show it as Output VAT on the VAT return in the other state.

If the business customer belongs in another EU member state but the UK supplier has no VAT registration in that other EU state, and therefore has treated the supply as outside the scope of VAT, the customer must account for output VAT itself in its own state, using the reverse charge procedure (see 36.19).

If the customer is not in business, the UK supplier should charge VAT at the UK rate on the services and issue a UK VAT invoice.

36.23 Supplies of digital services within the EU

From 1st January 2015, supplies of the following services ('BTE') within the EU are treated as having their place of supply where the **customer** is located:

- Broadcasting services;
- Telecommunications services; and
- Electronic services (fully automated internet-reliant services with minimal human intervention, such as downloads of music, games and other 'apps')

This does not represent a change for business-to-business ("B2B") supplies, which are already treated as occurring where the customer is based; but it **does** mark a change for business-to-consumer ("B2C") supplies of BTE services, the general rule for B2C supplies of services being that they are treated as occurring where the supplier is based (see 36.22).

A UK supplier exporting BTE services to other EU countries must therefore account for VAT at the overseas rate in each of those countries.

To save the administrative burden of submitting VAT returns in every EU country where a business has customers, it may instead register with a VAT 'Mini One-Stop Shop' (MOSS), allowing a single quarterly VAT MOSS return and payment to be made to HMRC. Each EU state has its own VAT MOSS, and the tax authorities of member states pass on appropriate returns and payments to each other.

36.24 Goods put to private use

Where goods which belong to a business are put to private use outside the business, then a taxable self-supply is being made and output tax is chargeable. Thus if trading stock is withdrawn from the business for private use, or an employee uses a business asset for private purposes, in principle a taxable supply occurs.

VAT is chargeable on the **cost** to the business (for income tax purposes it is the market value in the case of trading stock withdrawn from a business by a sole trader) of the supply, and the tax point is the time when the goods are made available for non-business use.

The special rules for the private use of fuel for motor cars were covered at 36.16.

36.25 Bad debts

VAT relief is available for irrecoverable bad debts suffered by a taxable person, and a claim can be made for a refund of the appropriate output tax previously reported and paid (in effect as if it were new input tax suffered). The conditions for a claim (VATA 1994, s36(1)) are that:

(a) the taxable person has supplied goods or services and has accounted for and paid VAT on the supply;

(b) the whole or any part of the consideration for the supply has been written off in the taxable person's accounts as a bad debt; and

(c) a period of 6 months (beginning with the date of the supply) has elapsed.

In theory a debtor who has made a claim for input tax on a supply which was never paid for, and on which the supplier has claimed bad debt relief, should repay to HMRC the VAT previously reclaimed. In order to assist this, a business claiming bad debt relief is asked to state the VAT number of the customer on the claim, if the customer was a VAT registered trader. However if the customer is insolvent, HMRC may not be able to enforce the repayment in practice.

The amount of the claim will usually be readily ascertainable by reference to the actual debt outstanding. However, where there are payments on account (not allocated by the debtor to any particular supply) these are allocated to the earliest supplies in the account after adjusting for any mutual supplies ie contra items.

Example

Retro Ltd is registered for VAT. One of its customers, Fax Ltd, went into liquidation on 31st July 2018.

The sales ledger account for the last two months to 31st July 2018 was as follows:

Retro Ltd sales ledger control account for Customer Fax Ltd

		£			£
1.5.18	Balance b/f	12,000	30.6.18	Cheque May a/c paid	12,000
25.5.18	1. Goods (incl. VAT)	36,000	23.7.18	Cheque payment on a/c	10,000
15.6.18	2. Goods (zero rated)	9,000	31.7.18	Balance c/f	50,000
20.7.18	3. Goods (incl. VAT)	15,000			
		72,000			72,000

Required: Compute the bad debt relief available to Retro Ltd.

Solution

Amount due from Fax Ltd at 31st July 2018 £50,000

		Gross	VAT
		£	£
Invoice	No. 3	15,000	2,500
	No. 2	9,000	–
	No. 1 (part)	26,000	4,333
		50,000	6,833

Notes

(i) VAT on Invoice No.1 36,000 × $^{20}/_{120}$ = 6,000

Proportion $\frac{26,000}{36,000}$ × 6,000 = 4,333

(ii) The VAT recoverable by bad debt relief is the net VAT included in the debts written off, which is £6,833.

(iii) Assuming VAT at 20% standard rate.

36.26 Transfer of a business as a going concern

(a) The sale of the assets of a business as a going concern is not a supply of goods or services and is outside the scope of VAT, provided that:

- i) the assets are to be used by the purchaser in carrying on the same kind of business, whether as part of an existing business or not;
- ii) in a case where the seller is a taxable person, the purchaser if not already registered must register for VAT immediately; and
- iii) there is no break in trading between business owners.

(b) A sale of part of a business may be treated as a sale of a going concern, provided that the part sold is capable of separate operation.

(c) The purchaser cannot claim any input tax in respect of the purchase of the business, even where this has been incorrectly charged to him or her.

(d) The provisions do not apply where the business is a different one after the transfer to that carried on by the seller.

(e) The transfer of a sole trader's business to a limited company, or into partnership with one or more other persons falls within these transfer provisions, and is therefore outside the scope of VAT.

(f) Where the business is transferred as a going concern, it is possible for the VAT Registration number of the vendor to be transferred to the purchaser, subject to certain conditions, and the approval of HMRC.

(g) Where a business carried on by a taxable person is transferred to another person who is not registered at the time of the transfer, the new owner must register for VAT immediately if the treatment as outside the scope of VAT is claimed on the business sale.

A business sale that does not meet the above conditions (for instance, the purchaser is not going to register for VAT) is standard-rated in respect of the price paid for all goods (inventories or other assets) transferred by sale, except those that are exempt, (e.g. second hand cars, or buildings).

36.27 Sale of business assets

The sale, other than transfer as a going concern, of assets used by a person in the course of business, e.g. plant and machinery, is subject to VAT as a taxable supply.

This also applies where a VAT-registered person ceases to trade or deregisters for VAT (even if the assets are not immediately sold).

VAT is not chargeable on the disposal of a motor car second-hand unless input VAT was reclaimed on the purchase of the car. The circumstances when this can be done are limited to businesses where there is no possibility of private use of the car.

Other assets sold by a registered trader which have been used in the business (e.g. computers) are generally subject to standard rate VAT on the price charged when sold.

36.28 Business assets – cost for Capital Allowances

In general there is no difference between the treatment of capital goods and other inputs for VAT purposes, and if the input tax is recovered by the trader it does not qualify as part of the cost for capital allowances. However, where a trader's supplies are exempt, or partially exempt, or the trader is not VAT-registered, then they will not be able to recover all or part of the input tax on the capital goods. In such cases the VAT not recovered is added to the cost of the asset for capital allowance purposes.

For most motor cars the VAT is not recoverable input tax, and VAT is therefore added to the cost of cars for capital allowance purposes.

36.29 Opting to tax non-domestic land and buildings

A supply consisting of the hire or sale of land or a building is VAT-exempt, unless **either** the building is a newly-constructed commercial (non-domestic, non-charitable) building, *or* a hire period is for less than 24 hours. In both of these cases, any supply of land or a building is standard-rated.

However, under schedule 10 VATA 1994, the owner of a commercial building, or a piece of land (which may include a building or buildings), can elect to waive the default VAT exemption. This decision is now officially referred to in Schedule 10 by its former nickname which is that the owner is 'opting to tax' the land or the building(s).

Opting to tax means that all future supplies of the land/building will be standard-rated (for that owner). The decision whether to 'opt to tax' a specific building or piece of land requires careful consideration by the owner. Apart from a 'cooling–off period' of six months (during which a submitted election can be withdrawn), an option to tax cannot be varied by the owner for (usually) a minimum of 20 years, and even then HMRC can refuse permission for the building to become again VAT-exempt if tax avoidance is suspected.

A landlord's most common reason for opting to tax a building is to avoid having VAT-exempt rental income, which could limit recovery of input VAT on the landlord's costs. It is not possible to waive VAT exemption for domestic or charitable buildings, or for any building (or part of one) that is used as a residence.

If the landlord has opted to tax a building, then a VAT-registered tenant who makes fully taxable supplies will be able to recover the VAT charged on the rent. However, tenants who are unregistered, exempt or partially exempt (for example, insurance or healthcare providers) will not be able to recover all their VAT on rents (unless they are only partially exempt and keep their own exempt input tax under the de minimis level - see 36.17).

The election to waive exemption is made on a building-by-building basis. It is common for a landlord of several buildings to opt to tax some buildings, seeking VAT-registered tenants for those, while keeping other buildings VAT-exempt and therefore cheaper for tenants who cannot recover VAT on rents.

Further details of this area of VAT are beyond the scope of this book but can be consulted online in HMRC VAT Notice 742 (June 2013).

36.30 Changes in the tax rates

When a change in the standard rate of VAT occurs, the following rules apply.

(a) Output tax is calculated under the normal rules i.e. by reference to the tax point - unless the special change of rate provisions are applied;

(b) Under these provisions, where the rate goes up, the tax at the old rate can be charged on goods removed or services performed before the date of change, even though a tax invoice would normally have been issued after the date of change;

(c) Where a supply of services takes place which crosses the threshold date of change in rate, then the supply can be apportioned by reference to normal costing or pricing procedures. Tax at the old rate may be charged on services performed before the date of the change if the supplier apportions the total bill. However the supplier may choose not to do an apportionment; and

(d) It is generally the supplier's decision how to apply the tax point rules at a change in rate. The amount of input tax paid by the purchaser following a change in rate is obtained from the supplier's invoice, and only the amount actually charged can be reclaimed. For less detailed tax invoices which do not show the VAT separately, the amount of input tax can be computed at the rate appropriate at the stated tax point of the whole invoice.

36.31 Cash accounting scheme

The cash accounting scheme is optional for all businesses with a taxable supplies turnover of less than £1,350,000. It achieves a cash flow benefit for businesses whose customers take longer credit periods than the business takes against its own trade creditors. The main features of the scheme are;

(a) VAT on inputs and outputs is included in the VAT return for the period when cash was received or paid to settle the invoice, rather than on the basis of the usual tax point (under the rules given at 36.8).

(b) Applications for the scheme, once approved, remain in force for two years.

(c) The problem of obtaining relief for VAT on bad debts does not arise since output VAT is not paid before the customers have paid. However, the business will not be able to reclaim input VAT until it has actually paid the relevant business cost.

36.32 Annual accounting scheme

This scheme is available to traders who have been VAT-registered for at least one year, and whose estimated VAT taxable turnover in the next 12 months is £1,350,000 or less. The main features of the scheme are:

(a) Businesses choosing annual accounting make only one VAT return a year instead of the usual four. It is submitted two months after the VAT year-end.

(b) They make nine equal payments on account by direct debit during the year, which are each set as 10% of the total VAT paid for the previous year. A tenth, balancing, payment is made with the annual return to make up the correct amount of VAT actually due for the year.

(c) Businesses already using the scheme will be able to continue until their turnover reaches £1,600,000.

36.33 Flat rate scheme – small firms only

The flat-rate VAT scheme is available by application, and suits very small businesses. The scheme is available to traders whose annual taxable turnover, including reduced and zero-rated supplies, does not exceed £150,000 in the year of entry to the scheme. The purpose of the flat-rate scheme is simplification (it greatly simplifies accounting for net VAT due, by ignoring the details of actual input tax incurred and assuming an average) rather than to provide a cash benefit – hence the introduction of a different rate for limited cost businesses as described at item (v) below, to counter tax avoidance.

(i) Under the flat-rate scheme, traders avoid having to account internally for input VAT on all their purchases and output VAT on their supplies. Instead they calculate the net VAT liability as a flat rate percentage of their total **VAT inclusive** turnover (including standard-rate, reduced-rate, zero-rate and exempt supplies);

(ii) Traders using the flat-rate scheme issue invoices to their customers showing normal VAT details i.e. at the standard, reduced or zero rates, or that the sale is VAT-exempt. The flat rate percentage is merely used to simplify the calculation of the net VAT payable on the trader's own VAT return. The flat-rate scheme does not affect the customers, who receive normal VAT invoices to support their own VAT reclaims (if registered).

(iii) Once operating a flat-rate scheme the trader merely applies the standard quoted percentage to all business turnover, including exempt supplies, to arrive at the 'net amount of VAT' due for the period. The flat rate percentage reflects a notional average for the net output tax due after offsetting input tax on expenses (the amount actually incurred will not be relevant) and is the only calculation needed to operate the scheme. Actual input tax suffered is not reported on the trader's VAT return;

(iv) The flat rate percentage applied to turnover depends on the trade classification set by HMRC. These vary between 4% for retailing food, confectionary, tobacco, newspapers or children's clothing to 14.5% for accountancy or book-keeping. There is a 1% discount on each flat rate percentage in the first year when a trader is within the flat rate scheme;

(v) From 1st April 2017 a flat rate of 16.5% applies, regardless of sector, to "limited cost businesses" – those which only spend a small amount on goods (as distinct from services). A limited cost business is one whose goods cost less than

a. 2% of turnover; or

b. £1,000, if more than 2% of turnover.

Expenditure on **goods** includes inventory purchased for resale, materials purchased for use in a manufacturing process, office supplies used for administration and goods purchased for use in the supply of services, such as shampoo and conditioner purchased by a hairdresser for use in his or her business. However, capital expenditure, vehicle parts, fuel and certain other items are specifically excluded from the measure.

Examples of **services**, which would **not** be included in expenditure on goods, include digital software, payroll costs, postage stamps (Royal Mail delivery being a service) and expenditure on subcontractors.

Notice that a business making standard-rated supplies and having zero expenditure on inputs would pay VAT at an amount of 20% of its turnover, which equals 16.7% of its VAT-inclusive turnover (20 ÷ 120 = 16.7%). That indicates how the 16.5% rate was probably chosen as suitable for businesses with only limited costs.

(vi) The rates for the flat rate scheme allow for low value capital expenditure purchases. However, input VAT on VAT-inclusive capital expenditure over £2,000 can be recovered outside the flat rate scheme. Such separate treatment does not cover cars, since input VAT recovery on these is generally excluded. Where VAT recovery on larger capital purchases has been dealt with outside the flat rate scheme, output tax on their later disposal (or deemed disposal, in the case of de-registration) is also dealt with separately;

(vii) For businesses using the VAT flat rate scheme, business accounts will be prepared using gross receipts less flat rate VAT percentage for turnover, and expenses will include irrecoverable input VAT. Limited companies are required by law to show their turnover net of VAT, therefore the cost of irrecoverable input VAT in a company's accounts should be reduced by the flat rate VAT applying on total turnover. Note that the percentage is applied to VAT inclusive turnover. For example, 14% flat rate scheme VAT is calculated as (14% × 120% × sales value), and not (14% × sales value).

36.34 Special retail schemes

(a) There are five standard retail schemes:

- Point of sale scheme
- Apportionment scheme (2 schemes)
- Direct calculation scheme (2 schemes)

Details may be found at http://www.gov.uk/vat-retail-schemes

(b) No trader will be allowed to use any retail scheme if it is reasonably practicable for them to account for VAT in the usual way.

(c) Retail schemes can only be used for retail sales. If a trader makes some retail sales and others to VAT-registered traders than the usual VAT procedures must be applied to the latter.

(d) Turnover limits of £1m and £130m restrict availability of the retail schemes. Details may be found on the HMRC website.

The purpose of these schemes is to simplify output VAT calculations for traders making combined supplies at 0%, 5% and 20% rates to non-business customers.

36.35 Miscellaneous

(i) **Pre-registration expenditure.** Input tax on pre-registration business expenditure can be included in the first VAT return after registration. In the case of input tax on goods (as distinct from services) the goods must either be still retained at the date of first registration, or have been converted into other goods still retained. For services, the expenditure must have been incurred (tax point of the invoice) within the six months prior to the date of first registration.

(ii) **Business gifts**. In general traders are not required to account for VAT as a taxable supply on the value of small business gifts such as diaries and calendars. The limit on such goods is £50 per item. The treatment of a series of business gifts in any 12 month period to the same person is aligned with that of a single gift. Where the limit is exceeded, output tax is due on the value of all the gifts made up to that point.

Student self-testing question with answer

Question 1: Octavius Limited

Octavius Limited is a fully taxable trader and does not operate the flat rate or cash accounting VAT scheme. You are provided with the following information relating to Octavius Limited for the quarter ended 31st August 2018:
The VAT-exclusive accounts show the following

	£	£
Sales		165,000
Sales returns		(11,000)
		154,000
Purchases	96,000	
Purchases returns	(3,000)	
Bad debts written off	15,000	
Other expenses	24,000	
		(132,000)
Profit		22,000

The sales, purchases and 'other expenses' are all standard-rated for VAT.
All input VAT is reclaimable.
The sales and purchases returns are all evidenced by credit notes issued and received.
The bad debts were written off in August 2018. The time of supply of the original sales was 16th April 2018.
A sales invoice for £3,000, excluding VAT, had been omitted in error from the VAT return for the quarter to 28th February 2018.
Included in the expense figure is the cost of both business and private petrol for Managing Director's car, which had CO_2 emissions of 210g/km.

Requirement

(a) **For the three-month period ended 31st August 2018, calculate how much VAT is payable to HM Revenue and Customs. (7 marks)**

(b) **When is the tax shown by (a) above payable? (1 mark)**

(c) **State the course of action is open to a taxpayer who disagrees with a decision by HMRC on the application of VAT. (1 mark)**

(d) **What are the consequences of any action taken by the taxpayer in part (c) above? (2 marks)**

(ACCA updated)

Solution to Question 1: Octavius Limited

(a)

			£
Output tax :			£
On Sales (165,000 × 20%)			33,000
On Car fuel scale charge (see table given at 36.16)			75
Less refunded on sales returns (11,000 × 20%)			(2,200)
Adjust output tax error on February VAT return	(3,000 × 20%)		600
			31,475
Input tax:		£	
On purchases and expenses (96,000+24,000) × 20%		24,000	
(must be supported by tax invoices)			
Less refunded on purchase returns (3,000 × 20%)		(600)	
			(23,400)
Net VAT due to HMRC for quarter			8,075

Note: The bad debts written off this quarter are not yet eligible for relief, as the time of supply was less than six months ago.

(b) The VAT is payable within one month and seven days of the end of the quarter, i.e. by 7th October.

(c) A trader who disagrees with a decision by HMRC on the application of VAT may apply within 30 days to the local VAT office asking them to re-consider their decision.

(d) After re-considering their decision HMRC will either:

Confirm their original decision. The trader then has 21 days to submit an appeal to the First-Tier Tax Tribunal; or

Revise their original decision. If the trader still disagrees, he/she/it has 30 days to submit an appeal to the First-Tier Tax Tribunal.

Questions without answers

Question 2: Portia Limited

You are provided with the following information relating to Portia Limited, a consultancy company, for the quarter ended 30th November 2018:

	£
Fees (standard-rated and exclusive of tax)	60,000
Rent received from sub-letting part of the company's offices	6,000
Car purchase (exclusive of VAT)	18,000
Overheads (standard-rated and exclusive of VAT)	9,000
Input VAT attributable to taxable supplies	2,000

Notes

The car was purchased on 1st September 2018 and had CO_2 emissions of 200g/km.

Petrol for both private and business motoring was charged through the business with no adjustments being made for private mileage.

A bad debt of £550 (exclusive of VAT @ 20%) was written off during November 2018; payment was due in February 2018.

Portia has not made an election to waive VAT exemption for the office rental income, and has not joined the Flat Rate Scheme.

Requirement:

Calculate the VAT payable for the quarter ended 30th November 2018, and state when this will be payable to HMRC. (9 marks)

(ACCA updated)

Question 3: Antrobus Limited

Antrobus Limited had the following transactions in the quarter to 30th June 2018:

Sales:	£
Standard-rated supplies (excluding VAT)	150,000
Zero-rated supplies	50,000
Exempt supplies	100,000

Input tax on expenses had been paid as follows:

Standard-related supplies	13,500
Zero-related supplies	5,000
Exempt supplies	9,000
General overheads	4,000

The general overhead input tax cannot be directly attributed to any of the listed supplies.

Requirement:

(a) Calculate the VAT payable by Antrobus Limited for the quarter

(6 marks)

(b) State the records and accounts which must be kept for VAT purposes and state for how long they must be retained by the trader.

(5 marks)

Total: 11 marks

(ACCA updated)

Part VII

Tax Planning

37 Elements of tax planning

37.1 Introduction

This chapter is concerned with some of the basic principles of tax planning which can be applied where a taxpayer has a choice of alternative courses of action. The chapter starts by defining tax planning and outlining some of the objectives involved in this process. Some basic tax planning caveats are then considered followed by a tax planning summary table. The focus of the chapter is on the taxation consequences of the choice between operating a business as a sole trader or as a limited company. This area of taxation has generated considerable interest over the years, and as you have seen from the sections on both income tax and corporation tax is subject to change on an annual basis.

37.2 What is tax planning?

Given a set of circumstances or a situation where a decision is to be made which involves the incidence of taxation, then tax planning is concerned with achieving the best result with respect to that decision from the taxation perspective. The 'best result' is usually taken to mean achieving the least amount of tax payable consistent with any cash flow advantages which are also often important.

An exercise in tax planning involves the following.

(a) Identification of the specific problem to be considered.

(b) Identification of the parts of tax law which are relevant to the problem.

(c) Application of the tax rules identified to the problem.

(d) Evaluation of the various options available to minimise the incidence of taxation.

(e) Identification and examination of any other factors of a legal, commercial or financial nature which should be taken into consideration.

37.3 Objectives of tax planning

Tax planning objectives for individuals may be summarised as follows.

(a) To reduce taxable income and/or chargeable gains falling to be assessed.

(b) To lower the rate of tax which is applicable to taxable income or chargeable gains.

(c) To defer the date on which tax becomes payable, thereby gaining a cash flow/interest advantage.

For companies in general, similar objectives can be applied. However, for family companies with shareholder directors/employees, tax planning for the individual must inevitably be considered together with that for the family company. This arises because in many cases most of the income of the family director/employee shareholder is in fact derived from family company sources, in the form of remuneration, benefits in kind and dividends.

37.4 Tax planning caveats

The following points should be borne in mind when undertaking any tax planning exercise.

(a) Tax planning (*such as investing in environmentally-friendly plant and machinery to obtain 100% Capital Allowances*) should not be confused with tax evasion. The latter, which is unlawful and may lead to criminal prosecution, is associated with fraudulent or dishonest plans to avoid taxation (*such as failing to declare income to the appropriate tax authorities*).

(b) Commercial factors should not be ignored just for the sake of a business tax planning exercise. For example, there is no point in investing in additional capital expenditure to obtain capital allowances if the capital project itself shows negative returns on investment.

(c) Future financial security should not be put at risk. The making of substantial lifetime gifts to mitigate IHT on the death of the donor should be balanced against the possible shortfall in annual income which might result.

(d) Possible changes in the law in the future may render current tax planning exercises less advantageous.

(e) Tax plans should be flexible to accommodate, if possible, changes in circumstances.

(f) Packaged 'tax avoidance schemes' offered by any organised promoter must be disclosed to HMRC as soon as the first offer of the scheme is made to the public. HMRC maintains a register of such schemes. Taxpayers utilising any such registered scheme must disclose this fact and the scheme number in the self-assessment tax return. Advising individuals how to re-arrange their personal or business affairs with tax benefits, such as the examples below, do not count as 'tax avoidance schemes' under this heading, so long as the steps involved have a main purpose and commercial effect beyond just the tax saving.

(g) A 'general anti-abuse rule' (GAAR) has existed in legislation since 2013/14 to counteract advantages arising from any tax avoidance schemes seen as abusive.

37.5 General Anti-Abuse Rule ("GAAR")

The General Anti-Abuse Rule was introduced as part of Finance Act 2013 and is significant in some important respects:

- it marks a distinct shift away from a specific-rules-based approach in the UK to a more principles-based approach;
- it gives substantial power to the HMRC GAAR Guidance;
- it effectively prohibits the use of loopholes; and
- in a sense it resets the clock so far as UK taxation case law is concerned, in that legal cases where the courts previously ruled in favour of the taxpayer might now, on similar facts, rule in favour of the tax authorities.

Principles

Tax avoidance has long been a problem for governments, with specific/targeted rules drawn up to deal with tax avoidance activity considered unacceptable. A flaw of that approach is that governments were always 'playing catch-up', with new rules required to deal with each new avoidance strategy encountered.

A purpose of a general anti-avoidance rule is to set in place principles-based regulations which have general (rather than specific) applicability to prevent new schemes which try to avoid tax from being effective in the first place.

The GAAR aims to counter abusive tax arrangements:

> "(1) Arrangements are '**tax arrangements**' if, having regard to all the circumstances, it would be reasonable to conclude that the obtaining of a tax advantage was the main purpose, or one of the main purposes, of the arrangements.
>
> (2) Tax arrangements are '**abusive**' if they are arrangements the entering into or carrying out of which cannot **reasonably** be regarded as a **reasonable** course of action in relation to the relevant tax provisions, having regard to all the circumstances including—
>
> (a) whether the substantive results of the arrangements are consistent with any principles on which those provisions are based (whether express or implied) and the policy objectives of those provisions,
>
> (b) whether the means of achieving those results involves one or more contrived or abnormal steps, and
>
> (c) whether the arrangements are intended to exploit any shortcomings in those provisions."
>
> *section 207, Finance Act 2013* (**emphasis added**)

The core principle here is the 'double-reasonableness' test; that if a reasonable person would not view the tax arrangements as a reasonable course of action, then they are abusive and so fall due to be countered under the GAAR.

Where tax arrangements are held to be abusive, HM Revenue and Customs may recalculate the taxable income of the individual or company to reverse the effect of those arrangements.

By including as an explicit circumstance for consideration of "whether the arrangements are intended to exploit any shortcomings in [tax] provisions", the GAAR has effectively shut down the use of loopholes. Going through the detail of tax legislation trying to find a clever way around it by making use of unintended gaps won't work because seeking to exploit such a gap would itself constitute an indication of abuse.

In the UK, new legislation automatically supersedes previous law, such that if inconsistencies arise then the new legislation takes priority. This means that there's a very real sense in which past case law in the area of taxation cannot necessarily be relied on to anticipate outcomes under the new regime – had the GAAR been in force at the time of the case under consideration, the outcome might have been different.

GAAR Guidance

HM Revenue and Customs has issued guidance which sets out the purpose and operation of the GAAR, as well as examples to indicate what might and might not be considered abusive under the GAAR.

Although strictly this is 'mere' guidance and not legislation, note the requirement in the legislation to have "regard to all the circumstances" – circumstances which include, of course, the tax authorities' guidance.

Part D of HMRC's GAAR Guidance comprises examples to indicate what might and might not be considered abusive under the GAAR, including examples of previous cases which HMRC lost in the courts but would expect to win if they occurred today.

Categories of tax arrangements

The GAAR Guidance categorises tax arrangements as follows, to help taxpayers and their advisors understand what is, and what is not, acceptable:

First, tax arrangements which would usually be considered acceptable:

- **Intended legislative choice**
  This refers to situations in which legislators intentionally created the possibility of choosing a course of action to reduce one's tax liability, for example using a salary sacrifice arrangement in return for enhanced pension rights.

- **Established practice**
  This refers to arrangements which have become normal and accepted practices for taxpayers to adopt, for example giving choice when a listed company is returning funds to shareholders as to whether those funds come out in capital or in income form.

- **Situations where the law deliberately sets precise rules or boundaries**
  Where the law sets precise boundaries, a taxpayer should reasonably suppose that "staying the correct side of the boundary" would not be considered abusive. For example, a taxpayer selling shares on the last day of the tax year to crystallise a capital gain (*so as to use up his or her Annual Exempt Amount*) then buying them back 31 days later (*with a higher base cost so as to give lower capital gains in future*) has gone beyond the 30-day period for share-matching purposes (*see section 30.3 of this book*) so can be assured that the transaction will be accepted as legitimate by the tax authorities.

Next comes a category of tax arrangements which could be acceptable or unacceptable, depending upon the facts and circumstances of the case:

- **Standard tax planning combined with some element of artificiality**

Finally, tax arrangement which would be considered abusive:

- **Transactions that are demonstrably contrary to the spirit (or policy and wider principles) of the law;**
- **Exploiting a shortcoming in legislation whose purpose is to prevent a form of activity; and**
- **Arrangements that are contrived or abnormal and produce a tax position which is in no way consistent with the legal effect and economic substance of the underlying transaction.**

Being aware that tax arrangements must not be abusive, we can now move on to consider some legitimate areas of tax planning advice which could be given to individual and corporate taxpayers.

37.6 Tax planning summary: Individuals

I	Income tax	Employees	Self-employed	Directors
1.	Claim expenses of employment	✓	–	✓
2.	Claim capital allowances for privately owned asset/ Authorised mileage rates	✓	✓	✓
3.	Company pension scheme: consider AVC	✓	–	✓
4.	No company pension scheme: maximise contributions up to 100% of net relevant earnings, but subject to annual maximum of £40,000.	✓	✓	✓
5.	Inter-spouse transfers of assets to use PAs, lower rate tax bands, and MCA where available	✓	✓	✓
6.	Car fuel benefit/payment business mileage	✓	–	✓
7.	Phase capital expenditure to save Class 4 NIC/income tax	–	✓	–
8.	Employ staff with earnings below NI thresholds	–	✓	–
9.	Consider ISA – tax-free	✓	✓	✓
10.	Consider investment schemes (EIS / SEIS / SITR) – see sections 6.8 – 6.10	✓	✓	✓
11.	Consider Venture Capital Trust	✓	✓	✓

II	Capital gains tax	Employees	Self-employed	Directors
1.	Consider entrepreneurs' relief on business or share disposals	-	✓	✓
2.	Inter-spouse transfers of assets to minimise CGT	✓	✓	✓
3.	Phase chargeable asset disposals between tax years to use Annual Exemption, and the lower CGT rate band	✓	✓	✓
4.	On a takeover, consider cash/shares split and available reliefs to minimise or defer CGT	✓	✓	✓

III	Inheritance tax				
1.	Maximise use of general exemptions –	£250	✓	✓	✓
		£3,000	✓	✓	✓
	Normal expenditure out of taxed income		✓	✓	✓
	Marriage		✓	✓	✓
	Inter-spouse		✓	✓	✓
	Charitable bequests		✓	✓	✓
2.	Consider lifetime gifts/PETS –	personal assets	✓	✓	✓
		business assets	–	✓	–
3.	Deeds of Variation to change distribution of a death estate to save IHT / maximise use of nil rate band		✓	✓	✓
IV	**VAT**				
1.	Consider voluntary registration to claim input tax		–	✓	–
2.	Phase capital expenditure to benefit cash flow from input tax recovery		–	✓	–
3.	Consider payment for private fuel rather than scale charge		–	✓	–
4.	Monitor turnover level as it approaches compulsory registration point		–	✓	–
5.	Consider Flat Rate, Annual Accounting and/ or Cash Accounting scheme – small firms		–	✓	–

37.7 Tax planning: Companies

1. Extended account period: 18 months, or 2 periods of 6 and then 12 months?

2. Phasing capital expenditure to maximise Annual Investment Allowance.

3. Consider whether additional payments to shareholder directors should be made as directors' remuneration or dividends – there is a National Insurance saving for the latter.

4. Consider dividend payments in place of normal salary.

5. Maximise pension contributions made through the company as employer.

37.8 The choice of business form

A person running a business may choose to operate the business as:

- a sole trader; or
- a company

If the person goes for the incorporation option, then there is a choice as to how they will extract the profits generated by the business – as some combination of:

- Salary;
- Dividends;
- Interest (*under certain circumstances – more on this later*);
- Pension contributions.

Pension contributions are the most tax-efficient way to extract profits: they will be an allowable expense for the company and not subject to income tax for the individual. But of course there is a limit to how much may be contributed each year while remaining tax-exempt (see Chapter 16). For the rest of this section, we will focus on salary, interest and dividends.

With the incorporation option, there is also a choice as to **when** the individual may extract the profits. The trader may choose to have the company distribute some profits as dividends (*in which case the company will pay Corporation Tax and the shareholder will be subject to further tax on dividend income*) and to retain some profits (*in which case those profits, although still subject to Corporation Tax, are 'protected' from further tax in the hands of the shareholder until such future date as they are distributed as dividends or crystallised through sale of shares giving rise to a capital gain*).

The HMRC General Anti Abuse Rule Guidance makes clear (at section B4) that these decisions are, in normal circumstances, outside the target area of the GAAR – they fit into the "intended legislative choice" category.

It used to be the case that, purely from a taxation perspective, it was always advantageous to trade as a company rather than a sole trader – largely because rates of income tax on dividends were lower than for other forms of income and the tax credit associated with dividends mitigated the impact of double taxation of corporate profits (*taxed in the hands of the company then again in the hands of the shareholders when distributed as dividends*).

However, since the 2016 reforms, that is no longer always true. To see why this should be the case, consider the **marginal** tax effect of earning an extra £1,000 of trading profits for three different taxpayers:

Sole trader option			
	Basic rate taxpayer £	Higher rate taxpayer £	Additional rate taxpayer £
Trading profits	1,000.00	1,000.00	1,000.00
Income Tax	(200.00)	(400.00)	(450.00)
National Insurance	(90.00)	(20.00)	(20.00)
Post-tax income	**710.00**	**580.00**	**530.00**

Company option – dividends			
	Basic rate taxpayer £	Higher rate taxpayer £	Additional rate taxpayer £
Trading profits	1,000.00	1,000.00	1,000.00
Corporation Tax	(190.00)	(190.00)	(190.00)
Post-tax profits distributed as dividends	810.00	810.00	810.00
Income Tax on dividends (7.5% or 32.5% or 38.1%)	(60.75)	(263.25)	(308.61)
Post-tax income	**749.25**	**546.75**	**501.39**

This shows that, **at the margin**, higher-rate and additional-rate taxpayers who choose the corporate option pay more tax than sole traders, if they extract the marginal profits as dividends.

In advising a client as to the choice of business form and how to take profits from the business, the following are some of the important points we ought to consider:

Non-tax aspects

As the marginal analysis shows, for an individual **who intends to take all the profits from her or his business**, up to a certain level of income, the best result (*purely from a taxation point of view*) would be to set up a company rather than operate as a sole trader, and extract profits from the company by way of dividends. But beyond some level of business profits (see section 37.11) it might be better, purely from a taxation point of view, to operate as a sole trader facing Income Tax and National Insurance on trading profits (*though bear in mind that incorporation allows ownership of a business to be shared between a husband and wife or civil partners, such that the income can be split (by way of dividends) across two sets of Personal Allowances and tax bands*).

However, a sole trader's personal assets are at risk. If the business goes bankrupt, creditors can require the individual's own assets, such as their house and car, to be sold to pay off debts. Whereas in the case of a company, the individual benefits from limited liability; her or his personal assets are protected, and she or he can only lose the money invested in the business.

A company also has access to more sources of finance than a sole trader. It is able to issue shares to other individuals.

So, for somebody anticipating a high level of business profits, the tax advantages of operating as a sole trader must be weighed against the advantages of limited liability. The choice made by the individual should depend upon the nature of the business, the individual's attitude to risk, and the plans for the future regarding possible expansion.

Further, the "retained earnings shield" should be considered. To the extent that profits are retained within the company, current year tax will be lower operating as a company, because the rate of Corporation Tax is lower than the higher and additional rates of Income Tax.

If the individual does choose to operate using a company, then a decision must be made as to what combination of salary, interest and dividends should be used to extract the business profits.

Salary

A salary of £116-£162 per week (£6,032-£8,424 per year) falls between the lower earnings limit and the primary threshold for National insurance purposes, such that the earner is deemed to have made contributions for the purposes of protecting contributory benefit entitlement, even though the amount of National Insurance Contributions is zero. This level of salary would also, for many individuals, be covered by their Personal Allowance, so no income tax would be payable either.

Notice that these amounts would, for a person working full-time, fall below the "National Living Wage". Minimum wage legislation applies to workers but not to office-holders, so does not automatically apply to company directors. The government has made clear that "if there is no written employment contract or other evidence of an intention to create an employer/worker relationship they will not seek to contend that there is an unwritten or implied employment relationship between a director and his company"[1]

The salary would be an allowable expense for the company in calculating its trading profits, so would reduce the Corporation Tax liability.

The company could pay the salary irrespective of the level of profits; whereas dividends may only be paid out of retained earnings and so may not be paid in the early years of a company which is loss-making (*from the point of view of accounting calculations rather than taxable profit calculations*).

---

1 *(Institute of Chartered Accountants in England and Wales, TAXGUIDE 7/00, "National Minimum Wage", September 2000)*

Interest

Ideally, the person would wish to extract much of the business profits by way of interest: interest for trading purposes would be an allowable expense to the company, would allow basic-rate and higher-rate taxpayers to make use of their personal savings allowances, and would not give rise to National Insurance Contributions. Using the same approach as on the previous page, we would have the following **marginal** effects (*ignoring the Personal Savings Allowance for this calculation*):

Company option - interest

	Basic rate taxpayer	Higher rate taxpayer	Additional rate taxpayer
Corporation:	£	£	£
Trading profits before interest	1,000	1,000	1,000
Interest	(1,000)	(1,000)	(1,000)
Taxable Total Profits	-	-	-
Individual:	£	£	£
Savings income	1,000	1,000	1,000
Income tax on savings income	(200)	(400)	(450)
Post-tax income	**800**	**600**	**550**

Remember the sole trader option gave post-tax income of £710, £580 and £530 for basic, higher and additional-rate taxpayers, respectively, while the company options with dividends gave £749.25, £546.75 and £501.39.

This is clearly a substantial improvement on the sole trader or dividends options (*and note that extracting profits as employment income would be worse than those options, due to employer's National Insurance being payable and employee's National Insurance being higher than sole trader's National Insurance*).

So why not advise clients to take all profits out of their companies as interest?

There are two very important aspects which prevent this being possible.

First, if the interest expense of the company was, in terms of economic substance, really a distribution of profits to the owner of the company rather than servicing of loan finance, then HM Revenue and Customs would be able to treat it as such. The interest would then not be an allowable expense of the company, and would be treated as dividend income in the hands of the shareholder. For it to be a legitimate interest expense, there would need to be a loan agreement between the company and the individual, with interest charged on commercial terms, for actual lending (*ie. the individual has provided money or assets to the company to be repaid under the terms of the loan agreement*).

Second, the lending must be genuinely needed by the company. Remember that, for an expense to be allowable as a trading deduction, it must be for trading purposes. So there must be a legitimate trade purpose to the lending, such as the company needing to borrow the money to invest in plant and machinery for the trade. Simply lending money to the company when it doesn't need it would result in the interest expense not being allowed for the company (*which would then get taxed on higher profits*) and being taxed in the hands of the individual.

In advising a client, we therefore might wish to recommend that they give a loan to the newly-formed company, but only where:

- There is a legitimate business need (*e.g. purchase of machinery*); and
- The individual has sufficient funds to lend the money to the company, without causing herself or himself undue financial stress; and
- A formal loan agreement is put in place, with a clear repayment schedule on commercial terms (*using HMRC's Official Rate of Interest would ensure that it would not be challenged*)

Dividends

Any further funds the individual wishes to extract from the company can be by way of dividends, which as we have seen is superior (*from a tax point of view*) to taking employment earnings, due to lower tax rates and no national insurance.

Dividends give more flexibility than interest (*there is a choice as to how much to pay, subject to there being sufficient retained earnings*), but are not an allowable expense for the company; thus, they will, to some extent, be double-taxed. That is, the company will be taxed on its profits, then will distribute dividends from its post-tax profits which will be taxed again in the hands of the shareholder.

Retained earnings

To the extent that the business owner wishes to leave profits in the company rather than distribute them, there will be less tax to pay. Recall the comparison we made of operating as a sole trader with operating as a company which distributes dividends. If we run the same calculations again, but this time assuming that no profits are distributed, then we have:

Sole trader option

	Basic rate taxpayer	Higher rate taxpayer	Additional rate taxpayer
	£	£	£
Trading profits	1,000	1,000	1,000
Income Tax	(200)	(400)	(450)
National Insurance	(90)	(20)	(20)
Post-tax income	**710**	**580**	**530**

Company option – retaining profits

	Basic rate taxpayer	Higher rate taxpayer	Additional rate taxpayer
	£	£	£
Trading profits	1000	1000	1000
Corporation Tax	(190)	(190)	(190)
Post-tax profits retained	**810**	**810**	**810**

In this case, the company option looks superior.

Bear in mind, however, that tax is effectively deferred rather than avoided here – eventually there will be income or gains arising in the future. If the profits are distributed in the future, the dividend income will be subject to income tax. If the company shares are sold in the future, the disposal will be subject to capital gains tax. If the shareholder dies without taking any further income or gains, her or his estate will be subject to Inheritance Tax.

Reliefs may be available for all of these, for example dividends may be distributed so as to fall within the individual's Personal Allowance and "dividend allowance"; shares may be sold in stages so that gains fall within the individual's Capital Gains Tax Annual Exempt Amount; gift relief may be available to defer any capital gain arising; shares may be gifted so as to fall within the Inheritance Tax annual exemption.

It is clear just from identifying those tax consequences and potential reliefs that it is crucial to discuss with the client their plans.

The future

The future is, of course, uncertain. Any advice we give a client should depend not only upon their future plans, but also the future tax environment. As noted in section 37.4, changes in the law in the future may render current tax planning exercises less advantageous.

In advising a client as to the best course of action, we should take account of known and expected changes to tax law, making it clear that those changes form the basis of our advice.

For the next sections, we will calculate tax based on the following assumptions, based on detail of forthcoming tax changes as shown at page xx:

- The rate of Corporation Tax will be 17%;
- The Personal Allowance will be £12,500;
- The Basic Rate band will be £37,500;
- Class 2 NICs will be abolished;
- The Class 4 band at which NICs drop to 2% will be £50,000, in line with the Income Tax level for moving to higher rate; and
- Other rates and bands will remain unchanged from 2018/19.

37.9 Tax planning example: Sole trader vs incorporation (1)

This section provides an example of a small business and the choice of whether to incorporate or not. Remember that there are many factors to consider depending on the circumstances and this section provides simply a basic comparison.

Example

Peter is a self-employed electrical engineer and makes profits of £80,000 each year. He pays £8,000 net per year into an HMRC-approved personal pension scheme. He is considering whether he should incorporate his business and pay himself a minimal £12,000 salary and the balance in dividends, with a non-contributory director's occupational pension scheme; or continue as a sole trader.

A possible approach: Compare net disposable income (*Anticipated 2020/21 tax bands and rates*)

Sole trader:			£	£
Profits				80,000
Total income				80,000
Personal Allowance				(12,500)
Taxable income (all non-savings)				67,500
			£	£
Tax liability:	BR £37,500	@ 20%	7,500	
(pens. conts. relief) extend	BR £10,000	@ 20%	2,000	
	HR £20,000	@ 40%	8,000	
	67,500			
Total income tax				17,500
NIC:				
Class 4	(50,000 – 8,424) @ 9%		3,742	
Excess Class 4	(80,000 – 50,000) @ 2%		600	
Total national insurance contributions				4,342
Total income tax and NIC				21,842

Disposable income – sole trader	£
Profits	80,000
Less pension contributions (net amount paid)	(8,000)
less Income Tax and National Insurance Contributions	(21,842)
Disposable income	**50,158**

Incorporation:	£
Profit before proprietor's pay (company)	80,000
Salary (cost to company)	(12,000)
employer Class 1 secondary NI (cost to company) (12,000-8,424) @ 13.8%	(493)
Pension contribution (cost to company) (Assumed)	(10,000)
Company's taxable profit	57,507
CT @ 17%	(9,776)
After-tax profit for distribution – say distributes £47,731.	47,731

Director income:

	Non-savings income	Dividends	Total income
	£	£	£
Employment income	12,000		12,000
Dividends		47,731	47,731
Total income	12,000	47,731	59,731
Personal Allowance	(12,000)	(500)	(12,500)
Taxable income	-	**47,231**	**47,231**
Dividends:		£	£
dividend nil band 0% ×		2,000	0
ordinary rate 7.5% ×		35,500	2,663
higher rate 32.5% ×		9,731	3,163
		47,231	
Income tax liability			5.826
Add Employee's class 1 NIC on salary – annual earnings period for director (12,000-8,424) @ 12%			429
Net employee income tax and primary NIC			**6,255**

Net disposable income - Director	£
Salary	12,000
Dividends	47,731
less IT and NIC paid	(6,255)
Disposable income	**53,476**

Total application of £80,000 profits:

	Incorporation £	Sole trader £
HMRC: Company tax and NI (9,776 + 493)	10,269	0
HMRC: Peter's personal tax and NI	6,255	21,842
Transfer from HMRC to pension fund to top up net pension contributions received of £8,000	n/a	(2,000)
Net inflow to HMRC	16,524	19,842
Pension savings - total cash received by pension fund of some kind (*in sole trade, £8,000 from Peter and £2,000 from HMRC; under incorporation, all £10,000 from the company*)	10,000	10,000
Peter's net disposable income	53,476	50,158
Retained earnings left in company	-	
Total pre-tax earnings	80,000	80,000
Less HMRC's 'take' (net tax and NIC)	**(16,524)**	**(19,842)**
Total value retained by Peter (including pension contributions)	**63,476**	**60,158**

Notes

(i) This example produces a saving of £3,318 (19,842 – 16,524) in total taxation for the incorporation model when compared with a sole trader.

(ii) This example assumes that under incorporation, Peter will make use of a non-contributory occupational director's pension scheme, with all contributions paid by the company, to save NIC.

The tax comparison above includes the £2,000 "basic rate tax refund" benefit that is paid by HMRC into Peter's personal pension under the sole trader route; this has been set against his personal tax bill, even though it is not legally done in that way under current tax legislation.

(iii) The difference in disposable income is significant. There is a very clear NI cost saving from incorporation because of the very low salary paid (*£922 of NI contributions, compared with £4,342 as a sole trader*).

(iv) There is also an income tax saving by the dividend route.

To the £5,826 of net tax paid by Peter on dividends must be added the company's CT payable on its pre-dividend profits, 17% of £57,507 = £9,776.

The NIC and income tax savings from incorporation are slightly offset by the fact that the company gets tax relief on the pension contribution at only 17%, which therefore costs it £8,300 net, whereas Peter obtained 40% tax relief on this payment (costing him £6,000 net) when he made it personally as a sole trader. 20% of this income tax relief was given within his tax computation, by extending the basic rate band, and the other 20% by HMRC augmenting his pension contribution by £2,000, claimed by the pension provider.

(v) There are many other factors to consider in choosing to incorporate a sole trade, especially in terms of personal preferences for the pension contribution, dividend and salary (or benefits) combination; and also, the Capital Gains Tax implications of company ownership, if assets are to be held or profits retained long-term in the company. This example provides a useful basic comparison only if the choice is made not to place significant assets or retain earnings in the company.

37.10 Tax planning example: Sole trader vs incorporation (2)

Mr Smith has a chain of shoe shops and expects trading profits of £200,000 per annum. He is currently operating as a sole trader and is considering whether he should incorporate his business or not. He informs you that he currently contributes £16,000 (net) each year into an approved personal pension plan. He also advises you that if he were to incorporate his business he would require a director's salary of £60,000 per year gross and that he would like the company to pay his pension for him with a non-contributory arrangement.

Required:

Compute the total income tax and national insurance as a sole trader and the total income tax, corporation tax and national insurance as an incorporated entity, which Mr Smith should expect to incur each year, using the rates and allowances listed at the end of section 37.8.

Solution:

Sole trader			£	£
Tax-adjusted trading profits (*assumed no other income. No personal allowance as > £125,000*)				200,000
			£	£
Tax liability	BR 37,500	@ 20%	7,500	
	extend BR 20,000	@ 20%	4,000	
	HR 112,500	@ 40%	45,000	
	AR 30,000	@ 45%	13,500	
	£200,000			
Total income tax				70,000
NI				
Class 4	50,000 - 8,424	@ 9%	3,742	
excess	200,000 - 50,000	@ 2%	3,000	6,742
Total Income Tax and NICs				**76,742**

Incorporation				£
Profit (company)				200,000
Salary cost to company				(60,000)
Employer NI (60,000-8,424) @ 13.8%				(7,117)
Pension contribution				(20,000)
Taxable profit of company				112,883
CT @ 17%				(19,190)
Profit after tax				93,693
Director's income:				£
Salary				60,000
Personal Allowance				(12,500)
Taxable income (non-savings, non-dividend)				47,500
			£	£
Tax liability	BR 37,500	@ 20%	7,500	
	HR 10,000	@ 40%	4,000	
Total income tax				11,500
Employee's NI (50,000 - 8,424) @ 12%				4,989
(60,000 - 50,000) @ 2%				200
Total income tax and NICs				16,689

Summary : Total tax costs compared

Incorporation:	£
Director's tax and NI	16,689
Company's tax and NI (19,190 + 7,117)	26,307
Total tax and NICs	**42,996**
Sole trader:	**£**
Total Income Tax and NICs	**76,742**

Notes:

(i) In this example, the owner is not extracting all the profits from the company, therefore a tax saving has arisen and incorporation results in an effective total tax saving on profits earned for the year of £33,746 (£76,742 - £42,996).

(ii) Mr Smith could extract additional funds out of the business either in the form of an increase in salary or by dividends (*or a combination of the two*) if he required, but this would impact upon the tax saved by operating through a company.

(iii) Mr Smith could also consider increasing his pension provision if he wished.

(iv) It may be more efficient for Mr Smith to draw out a dividend payment instead of part of the salary of £60,000.

37.11 Tax planning example: Sole trader vs incorporation (3)

Mr Ahmed is a self-employed professional business advisor who has asked you to prepare calculations to compare his tax position if he were to continue to operate as a sole trader with the position if he were to offer his services through a company, Waseem Consultancy Limited, on the basis of expected business profits of £338,900 (*not including any expenses arising from salary or interest paid to Mr Ahmed*). Mr Ahmed does not have sufficient funds to make a long-term financial commitment to the company. He would like to extract all the profits from the business each year in the most tax efficient way he can, subject to ensuring that he preserves his National Insurance contributory benefits entitlement. He has already used up his pensions lifetime allowance, and has no other sources of income.

Required

Advise Mr Ahmed on the most appropriate business form for him to choose. Use calculations to support your answer, showing the tax consequences of each choice.

Mr Ahmed: Illustrative Solution

"*Mr Ahmed does not have sufficient funds to make a long-term financial commitment to the company*" indicates that Mr Ahmed is not able to make a loan to Waseem Consultancy Limited. Therefore he will not be able to extract business profits as interest.

"*... subject to ensuring that he preserves his National Insurance contributory benefits entitlement*" indicates that Mr Ahmed requires a salary from the company which reaches the lower earnings limit for National Insurance purposes.

"*He has already used up his pensions lifetime allowance ...*" indicates that further pension contributions would not be tax efficient.

Mr Ahmed: sole trader option

	£
Trading profits	338,900
Personal Allowance	-
Taxable income	**338,900**

	£
Non-savings income:	
basic rate 20% × 37,500	7,500
higher rate 40% × (150,000 – 37,500)	45,000
additional rate 45% × (338,900 – 150,000)	85,005
Total Income Tax	137,505

	£
Class 4 NICs:	
(50,000 – 8,424) @ 9% =	3,742
(338,900 – 50,000) @ 2% =	5,778
Total National insurance	9,520

	£
Business profits	338,900
Income Tax	(137,505)
National Insurance	(9,520)
Post-tax income	**191,875**

Mr Ahmed: company option

Profits extracted as:

- £8,424 salary;
- £274,295 dividends

Corporation:

	£
Profits before salary and interest	338,900
Salary expense	(8,424)
Taxable Total Profits	**330,476**
Corporation Tax at 17%	56,181

Individual:	Non-savings income	Dividends	Total income
	£	£	£
Employment income	8,424		8,424
Dividends		274,295	274,295
Total income	8,424	274,295	282,719
Personal Allowance	-	-	-
Taxable income	**8,424**	**274,295**	**282,719**

	£	£	£
Non-savings income			
Basic rate 20% ×	8,424		1,685
Dividends:			
dividend nil band 0% ×		2,000	0
ordinary rate 7.5% × (37,500 – 2,000 – 8,424)		27,076	2,031
higher rate 32.5% × (150,000 – 37,500)		112,500	36,562
additional rate 38.1% ×		132,719	50,566
		274,295	
Total income tax			**90,844**

Overall:	£
Business profits	338,900
Corporation Tax	(56,181)
Income Tax	(90,844)
National Insurance	0
Post-tax income	**191,875**

Mr Ahmed: Conclusion

We can see that this example gives rise to exactly the same post-tax income result whether Mr Ahmed chooses to operate as a sole trader or as a company.

Therefore, we could not give advice purely based on taxation using this static calculation. We would need to consider Mr Ahmed's situation in more dynamic terms, and to consider non-tax aspects. We might consider such aspects as:

- **Growth:** How does Mr Ahmed expect his business to perform over the next few years? If profits are likely to fall, Mr Ahmed's income would fall into the region for which incorporation would give him the best tax outcome. If profits are likely to rise, Mr Ahmed would end up in a position where operating as a sole trader would give the best tax result (*assuming he wishes to continue extracting all the profits from his business*);
- **Risk:** Would Mr Ahmed be happy to continue operating with unlimited liability, or would he prefer the protection of limited liability? As a professional business advisor, it may be that he doesn't have much in the way of financial commitments, particularly if he works from home – so being able to meet his obligations as they fall due might not cause a problem for him. With either business form, he ought to have professional indemnity insurance to protect him against claims by clients for loss or damage;
- **Long-term plans:** Does Mr Ahmed intend to expand the business to bring in new advisors? If so, he might wish to incorporate as a way to make it easier to access finance and (through limited liability) to mitigate the risk which might come from spreading duties across a number of people;

- **Mrs Ahmed:** Is Mr Ahmed married? If so, does Mrs Ahmed have lower taxable income than him? Waseem Consultancy Limited could be established with shares issued to both Mr and Mrs Ahmed. For example, if Mrs Ahmed has no other taxable income and the shares were split 50:50 between them then their dividends from the previous calculation would have been split £137,148.50 each and neither of them would have income falling into the additional-rate tax band (*Mr Ahmed would have taxable income of £8,424+£137,148.50 = £145,572.50*).

37.12 Tax planning example: dividend or salary?

Parmar is the 100% owner of Alpha Ltd, an unquoted trading company with a reporting date of 30th June.

Trade profits of Alpha Ltd are £280,000 for the year ended 30th June 2018 after director's remuneration to Parmar of £60,000. There were no dividend payments.

Parmar would like to have available cash of about £25,000 by December 2018 and requests advice as to the tax costs of extracting this sum from the company.

Advise Parmar, if he will be a higher-rate taxpayer.

Solution

Cash required of £25,000 – Dividend Route	**£**	**Tax cost £**
Dividend required (25,000 × 100/(100-32.5))	37,037	12,037
Cash of £25,000 – Salary Route	£	£
Gross salary required (see note) 25,000 × 100/58	43,103	18,103
Employer's NIC 13.8% × 43,103	5,948	
Net Corporation Tax saving (43,103 + 5,948) × 19%	(9,320)	(3,372)
Net tax cost of payment to both director & company, after company tax relief		14,731
Total profits used up in profit extraction:		£
Salary: Cash received by director		25,000
Tax and NIC received by HMRC		14,731
Total		39,731
Dividend: Cash received by director		25,000
Tax received by HMRC (no NIC)		12,037
Total		37,037

The total tax cost is £2,694 higher for the salary route than the dividend.

Extracting £25,000 from the company is therefore more costly to Parmar if it is done by way of additional salary than if it is done by way of a dividend payment.

This is due to dividends being subject to a lower rate of income tax than earnings, and being exempt from National Insurance – whereas earnings give rise to both employee and employer National Insurance contributions being required.

Note: An employee who is a higher rate taxpayer faces marginal tax rates of 40% income tax plus 2% National insurance Contributions; therefore their after-tax marginal earnings are 58% of their pre-tax marginal earnings.

The gross marginal earnings are therefore × $^{100}/_{58}$ of the pre-tax marginal earnings.

Question without answer

Mr Chapman, a single man, is about to start a business which will be engaged in the repair of domestic appliances. His starting date is 1st April 2018 and he will make up accounts to 31st March each year.

His business plan shows that he is likely to make a taxable profit in the first few years, before any salary for himself, of approximately £80,000 per annum.

He is uncertain whether he should set up the business as a sole trader or as a limited company and seeks your advice. He has advised you that, if the business is run as a company, he will require a gross salary of £45,000 per annum.

Mr Chapman has no other sources of taxable income.

Required:

Draft a report for Mr Chapman, indicating the important differences from a tax and NIC point of view, of the two alternative methods of running the business.

Your answer should contain, as an appendix, computations showing the overall tax and NIC burden which will arise in each case.

Assume that the rates and allowances listed at the end of section 37.8 apply throughout.

[15 marks]

[CIMA updated]

38 Additional questions

Exam–type Questions and Answers on Personal Taxation

Question 1

Fred lives in Wales and is employed as a manager by Textile Importers plc, at a salary of £100,000 a year, and contributes 6.25% of his salary to the company's occupational money purchase pension scheme. During the year to 5th April 2019 he is provided with a black car producing 157 g/km CO_2, which has a list price of £30,000. The company pays all running costs of the car, and all fuel, including fuel for private use by Fred.

Fred is also provided with a mobile phone, on a contract costing the company £200 a year. Fred also receives free leisure clothes, at a cost to the company of £800, which would have a retail price of £1,600.

Karl lives in England and is a self-employed clothes importer, who runs his own business with the assistance of two employees. The draft income statement for his business for the year to 31st March 2019 shows:

		£	£
Revenue			376,000
Less: Cost of sales	(note 1)		(188,800)
Gross profit			187,200
Less:			
Staff expenses	(note 2)	50,000	
Rent		26,000	
Insurance		1,300	
Telephone		200	
Motor expenses	(note 3)	4,000	
Depreciation	(note 4)	6,000	
Overdraft interest		500	
			(88,000)
Net profit			£99,200

Notes

1. Cost of sales includes £800 for sports clothing taken from the business by Karl for his personal use. If the clothing were sold to customers, the sale price would be £1,600.

2. Staff costs are the wages, employer's National Insurance and pension contributions relating to the two employees: Vladimir and Leon.

3. Motor expenses are the running costs of Karl's car. One quarter of the expenses shown relate to private use of the car by Karl.

4. Depreciation is charged for Karl's car, which cost £30,000 new on 6th April 2018, and has CO_2 emissions of 173 g/km.

Karl pays £5,000 cash (net amount paid) in contributions to a personal pension scheme during the tax year 2018/19.

Required

(a) Calculate Fred's Income Tax and National Insurance liabilities for the tax year 2018/19. (9 marks)

(b) Calculate Karl's tax-adjusted profit from trading, after maximum capital allowances, for the year to 31st March 2019. (5 marks)

(c) Calculate Karl's Income Tax and National Insurance liabilities for the tax year 2018/19. (7 marks)

(d) Advise Fred and Karl of the factors which cause differences in their Income Tax and National Insurance liabilities as employed and self-employed individuals respectively; and evaluate the significance of these differences for their decision to be employed or self-employed. (9 marks)

(Total 30 marks)

Question 1 - Solution

(a) Fred, Income tax and employee's National Insurance, 2018/19

			£
Employment income:			
Salary			100,000
Less pension contributions	6.25% × salary		(6,250)
Car benefit	157 g/km	32% × list price £30,000	9,600
Fuel benefit		32% × £23,400	7,488
Phone	Exempt		0
Clothing	Cost to employer		800
			111,638
Adjusted net income exceeds £100k so PA is withdrawn (111638-100k) = 11638 × ½ = 5,819 (11,850-5,819)		reduced PA= £6,031	
		LESS personal allowance	(6,031)
			105,607

Income (non-savings, non-dividend)	Tax		£
34,500	@20%	6,900	
71,107	@40%	28,443	

105,607			35,343
Employee's Class 1 NICs			
(46,350 - 8,424) @ 12%		4,551	
(100,000 - 46,350) @ 2%		1,073	
			5,624
Fred's total Income Tax and NIC liabilities			40,967

(b) Karl

				£
Reported accounts profit				99,200
Add:				
Depreciation				6,000
Private use expenses	Car	£4,000 × ¼		1,000
Clothes taken for own use / consumption	@ Selling price			1,600
				107,800
Less:				
Capital allowances – car (>110g)	Cost £30k × 8%		2,400	
	Less 25% private		600	
	= WDA deduction			(1,800)
Adjusted profit				106,000

(c) Karl Income tax and NI liabilities

			£
Income from trading			106,000
Personal allowance	*(not restricted because gross PPCs of £6,250 reduce Adj. net income to £99,750)*		(11,850)
Taxable income (non-savings, non-dividend)			94,150
£	Tax	£	
34,500	@ 20%	6,900	
Extend BR band by gross PPCs			
6,250	@ 20%	1,250	
53,400	@ 40%	21,360	£
94,150			29,510
NI class 2	52 @ £2.95		153
NI class 4		£	
(46,350 -	8,424) @ 9%	3,413	
(106,000 -	46,350) @ 2%	1,193	4,606
Karl's total Tax and NIC liabilities			34,269

(d) Advise Fred and Karl of the factors which cause differences in their Income Tax and National Insurance liabilities as employed and self-

employed individuals respectively; and evaluate the significance of these differences for their decision to be employed or self-employed.

A good answer would adequately make points such as:

- Note the similarity of Fred and Karl's affairs: They both receive an income of approximately £100,000, clothing which costs £800, and a fully expensed car; and both make pension contributions worth £6,250 a year.
- Fred's benefits in kind as valued for income tax increase his income past the point where he suffers part-withdrawal of personal allowance in 2018/19, increasing the difference between his tax liability and Karl's. This point is **not** however a particular feature of the tax and NI differences between employment and self-employment: Karl would also suffer withdrawal of PA if his adjusted net income were > £100k.

Differences in income tax and NI are that:

- Fred's taxable income as an employee is increased by over £15,000 car and fuel benefits. This is much higher than the private use of the car and petrol disallowed in Karl's self-employed adjusted profits calculation (*£1,000 for motor expenses, plus private use depreciation, as the rest of the depreciation add back is compensated by capital allowances given over the car's useful life*).
- Fred's clothing is valued at cost to his employer of £800. Karl's own consumption of clothing from his business is valued at selling price of £1,600.
- Rates of class 4 NI for self-employed on (£46,350 – £8,424) = £37,926 are 9%, compared to 12% class 1 NI employees contributions, saving Karl £1,138 a year. However, self-employed people also pay class 2 NI contributions costing £2.95 a week, totalling another £153. Earnings as measured for class 4 self-employed NI includes the value of private use adjustments and own consumption added back; employees do not have to pay class 1 NI on benefits in kind. Class 1 NI contributions currently give better entitlement to certain social security benefits (eg statutory sick pay) than Class 2 NI.
- The calculations in (a) to (c) above show (£40,967 – £34,269) = £6,698 lower income tax and NI payable by Karl, the self-employed trader.
- Both have received the same value of higher rate tax relief on pension contributions, but the tax relief is given in a different way.

Other significant issues exist in choosing employment or self-employment:

- Levels of responsibility for generating the individual's, and any employees', work;
- Employees' entitlement to limited hours of work, reasonable workload and paid holidays;
- Reliance for income on a single employer;
- Better social security benefits available for sickness and unemployment if Class 1 NIC has been paid than Class 2; and

- Whether £6,698 (above) more or less tax and NI is significant compared to the other differences between employment and self-employment is a personal choice.

Question 2

Dave, who was born on 1st April 1934, retires as a director of Palaeolithic Limited on 6th April 2018. Dave is entitled to a pension of £1,250 gross each month, from his company occupational pension scheme. PAYE (Pay As You Earn) income tax at the basic rate is deducted by the pension scheme before making a net payment to Dave. Dave also receives a state pension of £691 gross each month, and this is paid without any deduction of tax.

Dave owns two properties:

A shop, 1 Armley Arcade, has been owned for many years. The shop is rented out unfurnished for the whole of 2018/19 at a rent of £1,200 per month. A new tenancy started on 6th April 2018, and Dave received a premium of £15,000 for a 5 year lease.

A house, 2 Birstall Brow. The house was bought at the beginning of April 2018 and rented out furnished for April, May and June 2018 at a rent of £650 per month. The house was empty from 1st July to 31st December, as no tenant could be found. A new tenant rented the house for January, February and March 2019, at a rent of £650 per month.

The costs associated with the properties for 2018/19 are:

	1, Armley Arcade	2, Birstall Brow
Letting agent's fees	£2,500	£1,450
Insurance	£1,100	£550
First set of furniture for house, bought in April 2018		£2,000
Painting external woodwork in May 2018	£600	
Chemical treatment to remove woodworm from floors and roof timbers in October 2018		£4,880
New conservatory added in November 2018		£14,000
Furniture bought in December 2018 to replace sofa damaged by first tenants		£420

Other information relating to Dave's financial affairs is:

- Interest received from Hellifield Building Society £100 cash.
- ISA (Individual Savings Account) interest received from the Iceland Volcanic Bank £300.
- Dividends received from Palaeolithic Limited £5,050 cash.
- Dave paid Gift Aid donations to Oxfam, £80 cash per month, in tax year 2018/19.

- Based on Dave's tax return for the tax year 2017/18, HM Revenue and Customs expect a total of £3,000 in payments on account of Dave's self-assessment Income Tax liability for 2018/19.

Required

(a) Calculate Dave's income from property for 2018/19. [11 marks]

(b) Calculate Dave's Income Tax payable for 2018/19. [15 marks]

(c) (i) State the due dates and amounts of Dave's 2018/19 income tax payments on account;
(ii) Calculate Dave's tax income tax balancing payment for 2018/19, and state the date when this is due;
(iii) Calculate Dave's first payment on account for 2018/19.
[4 marks]
Total 30 marks

Question 2 – Solution

(a)		Property 1 Armley Arcade shop	Property 2 Birstall Brow house
Rent receivable			
12 months@ £1,200		14,400	
6 months @ £650			3,900
Premium received			
	15,000		
Capital element for tax:			
15,000 × 2% × (5-1) = 1,200			
Income element = balance		13,800	
		28,200	3,900
Expenses:			
Agents' fees		2,500	1,450
Insurance		1,100	550
Repairs and maintenance		600	4,880
Replacement furniture		-	420
Conservatory & first furniture- not allowable expenses (no CAs)		-	-
		(4,200)	(7,300)
Profit / (loss)		24,000	(3,400)
Loss set off by netting all results		(3,400)	
Assessable Property income		20,600	

(b) Dave's income tax computation 2018/19

	Non-savings, non-dividend income	Savings income	Dividends	Total income
	£	£	£	£
Pension income	15,000			15,000
Property income (a)	20,600			20,600
State Pension (£691 × 12)	8,292			8,292
Interest		100		100
Dividends			5,050	5,050
Total income	43,892	100	5,050	49,042
less Personal Allowance	(11,850)			(11,850)
Taxable income	32,042	100	5,050	37,192

				£
Non-savings income:	£			
basic rate 20% ×	32,042			6,408
Savings income:		£		
"personal savings allowance"		100		0
Dividends:			£	
dividend allowance 0% ×			2,000	0
ordinary rate 7.5% × (34,500	- 32,042	- 100) =	2,358	177
higher rate 32.5% ×			692	225
			5,050	
Tax borne				6,810
less PAYE (£15,000 @ 20%)				(3,000)
Tax liability				3,810

Payments made for 2018/19 by Dave		£
(c) Payments on account – per HMRC requirement (i)	31st Jan 2019	1,500
(ii)	31st July 2019	1,500
Balancing payment (to settle 2018/19 liability)	31st Jan 2020	810
		£3,810

Payment on account for 2019/20 (£3,810 × ½) £1,905

Question 3

(a) The following information relates to Nurul, a self-employed trader, who has been in business since 2004:

Accounting period to 31st March:	2016	2017	2018	2019	2020
Profit from trading	£50,000	£30,000	£60,000	Loss (£120,000)	£20,000
Year to 5th April:	**2016**	**2017**	**2018**	**2019**	**2020**
Income from property	£6,000	£6,500	£7,000	Loss (£2,000)	£5,000
Bank interest received	£2,600	£2,800	£2,400	£2,000	£1,200

Requirement (a)

Assuming Nurul claims relief for losses as soon as possible, calculate his taxable income, after loss reliefs, for the tax years 2015/16 to 2019/20.

Finally, state the amount of trade losses remaining for Nurul to carry forward at 5th April 2020. (12 marks)

(b) The UK income tax system restricts tax-deductible expenses for a self-employed trader. For example, expenses are disallowed if they relate to:

(i) repairs which are capital improvements (enhancing the original asset);

(ii) business entertainment;

(iii) costs which have some business purpose but are not 'wholly and exclusively' incurred for a business purpose (*e.g. normal clothes, chosen and worn only for business meetings*).

Requirement (b)

Critically evaluate whether the rules disallowing some business expenses from tax relief satisfy the accepted criteria for a good tax system, in particular fairness (equity), simplicity, certainty and convenience.

(8 marks)

(Total 20 marks)

Question 3 - Solution

	2015/16	2016/17	2017/18	2018/19	2019/20
Trading	50,000	30,000	60,000	Loss	20,000
Trade loss b/f (s83)					(20,000)
Property	6,000	6,500	7,000	Loss	5,000
Property loss b/f					(2,000)
					3,000
Interest	2,600	2,800	2,400	2,000	1,200
Total income	58,600	39,300	69,400	2,000	4,200
S 64 loss claims					
– current year				(2,000)*	
- prior year			(69,400)		
Total income	58,600	39,300	0	0	4,200

Loss memorandum working:

		£
Trade loss of 2018/19		120,000
Set against 2018/19 total income	(s 64, optional)	(2,000)
Set against 2017/18 total income	(s 64, optional)	(69,400)
s 83 loss Carried forward from 2018/19		48,600
Used 2019/20 (automatic)		(20,000)
Still available for future set-off against profits of the same trade		28,600

(b)

A good answer would adequately make points such as:

Capital in repairs

- fairness - capital assets last for more than one year, but income tax is an annual tax.
  - which only allows costs of ONE year, not costs relating to 'enduring assets'
  - but capital allowances may be available under tax law (not always)
  - also, cap. enhancement expenditure is allowable cost for CGT (where applicable):
    => fair not to give deduction twice
- simplicity - it is not simple - need to understand rules
- if all bills clearly linked to only wear and tear / maintenance, can be claimed as revenue

Entertaining

- business entertaining may be an effective promotional tool and genuinely for business purposes;
- but not fair if entertaining is cheaper when done through business than when done personally;
- VAT has the same rule - to promote fairness, as entertaining is also benefiting someone personally;
- simplicity - at least if ALL non-staff entertaining is disallowable that is easy to understand

Wholly and exclusively rule

- Not fair if traders can get a subsidy from the tax system for private 'perks' such as nice clothes;
- Mallalieu case - dual (simultaneous) purpose of clothes in providing warmth and decency cannot be ignored;
- Similarly, not fair to allow tax-deductible private use of business assets if cheaper than incurring the same expense in private capacity

Question 4

Columbus commences as a self-employed proprietor in business on 1st January 2019 and has the following transactions in property, plant and equipment, all of which qualify for capital allowances:

For the period of account 1st January 2019 to 30th September 2019:

15th April 2019	Bought plant and equipment	£18,000
20th April 2019	Bought black car with CO_2 emissions 105g/km	£29,000

For the accounting year ended 30th September 2020:

31st January 2020	Sold plant (*the plant had cost £9,000 in April 2019*)	£10,000
31st March 2020	Bought water saving plant and equipment	£158,266
30th June 2020	Bought red car with CO_2 emissions 190g/km, and 25% private use	£17,000

For the accounting year ended 30th September 2021:

30th September 2021	Red car sold for	£10,787
	All other plant and equipment sold for (*none of this was sold for more than cost*)	£14,130

Columbus always claims the maximum capital allowances available.

The income from trading before capital allowances for the periods of account is:

Period 1st January 2019 to 30th September 2019	£ 27,193;
Year ended 30th September 2020	£170,925;
Year ended 30th September 2021	£ 92,678.

Columbus closed the business on 30th September 2021.

Required:

(a) Calculate Columbus's capital allowances for the periods of account shown, assuming the rates and allowances for 2018/19 continue unchanged for the years 2019/20 to 2021/22.

(10 marks)

(b) Calculate Columbus's adjusted income from trading, after capital allowances, for all the periods of account shown.

(3 marks)

(c) Calculate assessable income from trading for Columbus for all relevant tax years.

(7 marks)

Total 20 marks

Question 4 – Solution

			General pool	Car>110g 25%PU	Allowances
9 month period 01-Jan-2019 to 30-Sep-2019					
Additions		18,000			
AIA		(18,000)			18,000
Car <110g/km			29,000		
WDA 18%	× $^{9}/_{12}$		(3,915)		3,915
					21,915
WDV			25,085		
y/e 30-Sep-2020					
Car > 110g/km				17,000	
Addition for ECA					
		158,266			
ECA 100%		(158,266)	0		158,266
Disposal	10,000 proceeds	Max cost			
			(9,000)		
			16,085		
WDA:					
18%			(2,895)		2,895
8%				(1,360)	75% 1,020
					162,181
WDV			13,190	15,640	

y/e 30-Sep-2020					
Disposal	Proceeds	< cost	(14,130)	(10,787)	
Cessation of Trading			(940)	4,853	
Balancing charge			BC940		BC(940)
Balancing allowance				BA(4,853)	BA 3,640
BC / BA				Net	BA 2,700

(b)	Adj. Profit per accounts £	Capital allowances £	Trading profit after CAs £
1-Jan-2019 -30-Sep-2019	27,193	(21,915)	£5,278
y/e 30-Sep-2020	170,925	(162,181)	£8,744
y/e 30-Sep-2021	92,678	(BA) (2,700)	£89,978

(c) Assessable income from trading

Tax year	**Basis rule**			£	**Assessable** £
2018/19					
First	'Actual' (apportioned)	$^3/_9 \times 5{,}278$			1,759
2019/20					
Second	First 12 months:	$^9/_9 =$		5,278	
		Plus ($^3/_{12} \times$ 8,744)		2,186	
					7,464
2020/21					
CYB	y/e 30-Sep-2020				8,744
2021/22					
Final	All to end			89,978	
	LESS overlap				
		First 3 months	(1,759)		
		Other 3 months	(2,186)		
	Total overlap			(3,945)	
	Assessable trading profit final tax year				86,033

Question 5

(a) Barbara made the following asset disposals in 2018/19.

(i) On 9th July 2018 she sold an antique dresser for £9,900. She had bought it in 1989 for £2,500.

(ii) On 1st March 2019 she sold a speedboat for £15,000, which she had bought in February 2010 for £12,500.

(iii) On 5th December 2018 she sold part of a piece of grazing land for £30,000. The original piece of land had cost her £10,000 in August 1987. The market value of the unsold part of the land at the disposal date was £40,000. Barbara did not use the grazing land for business purposes.

Barbara has a taxable income of £52,500 in 2018/19 after deducting her personal allowance. She has capital losses brought forward from 2017/18 of £1,420.

Required: Calculate Barbara's Capital Gains Tax payable for 2018/19.
(7 marks)

(b) Shahid purchased a shop building to use as his business premises in 1990, paying £25,000. In May 2008, he gave the shop building to his son Hassan. At that time the property's market value was £90,000. The appropriate joint election for CGT gift relief was made to hold over Shahid's capital gain. Shahid continued to carry on his business in a different building.

After renting it out for some time, Hassan sold the building in December 2018 for £120,000.

Required: Calculate Hassan's chargeable gain for 2018/19 on disposal of the shop building, before any annual exemption.

(5 marks)

Question 5 – Solution

		£	£	£
(a)	Barbara			
	Antique dresser			
(i)	Proceeds	9,900		
	Cost	(2,500)		
	Gain	7,400		
	Restricted to max			
	(9,900 – 6,000) × 5/3	6,500	6,500	
	Motorboat			
	Is a Wasting chattel			
(ii)	(almost certainly)			
	So, Exempt			
	Part-disposal of land			
(iii)	Proceeds	30,000		
	Acquisition Cost:			
	10,000 × 30,000 / (30,000 + 40,000)	(4,285)		
			25,715	
			32,215	
	Losses b/f		(1,420)	
	Net gains		30,795	
	Annual exemption		(11,700)	
	Taxable net gains		19,095	
	CGT @ 20%		**£3,819**	

				£
(b)	Deemed proceeds - market value 2008			90,000
		Shahid's cost		(25,000)
	no proceeds - full holdover elected for			65,000
		held over gain		(65,000)
	Shahid's gain in 2008			NIL
	Hassan's disposal in 2018		Proceeds	120,000
	less cost (deemed)		90,000	
		'cost' reduced by held-over gain	(65,000)	
				(25,000)
		Hassan's Gain before AEA		95,000

Exam–type Questions on Personal Taxation, excluding IHT, without answers

Question 6

Assad is aged 35, lives in Northern Ireland and was employed as a mechanic until April 2018. His last salary payment, received on 30th April 2018, was £2,000 gross, from which PAYE tax was deducted of £320. Assad then decided to become a self-employed taxi driver, commencing business on 1st May 2018.

For the first 3 months he leased a car (Car 1) for business use. He made no private journeys in Car 1, which had a CO_2 emissions rating of 180g/km. In return for the monthly lease charge of £600 the lease company met all the car 1 running expenses except insurance and fuel. On 1st August 2018 Assad terminated the Car 1 lease, having purchased a new car (Car 2) for £20,000, which had a CO_2 emissions rating of 172g/km. From the time of purchase, Car 2 was used in the business, and also 20% privately by Assad.

Assad used his business mobile phone 40% for private purposes.

Assad has drawn up his first accounts to 30th April 2019, showing the following results for the twelve month period:

	£	£
Taxi fares collected		46,200
Tips received		4,100
		50,300
Commissions paid to taxi booking company	2,850	
Car expenses (see analysis below)	6,900	
Taxi operating licence (12 months)	1,980	
Traffic Speeding fine (incurred while working)	80	
Mobile phone contract (£40 a month)	480	
Meals / drinks while working at night	750	
Depreciation of Car 2	6,000	
Training course in computing	250	
		(19,290)
Net trading profit		31,010

The analysis of the Car expenses account is as follows:

	Car 1 £	Car 2 £
Petrol	750	2,500
Leasing cost of car 1 (3 months)	1,800	
Running costs for car 2 (9 months) (servicing, car tax etc)		850
Car insurance – Car 1 (May to August)	250	
- Car 2 (September to April)		750
	2,800	4,100
Total		6,900

From 6th June 2018, Assad rented out a bedroom in his house for £300 per month. Assad has calculated that the fair share of house bills (heating, electricity, etc) relating to the let bedroom is £25 a month.

Assad also received dividend income of £6,300 in January 2019.

Required:

(a) Calculate Assad's adjusted trading profit, after claiming any available capital allowances, for the period of account to 30th April 2019.

(11 marks)

(b) Write brief notes explaining to Assad your treatment of the following expenses as allowable / disallowable against his business income in the tax-adjusted profits computation:

(i) Car 2 running expenses and depreciation
(ii) Speeding fine incurred
(iii) Car 1 leasing costs
(iv) Computer training course (6 marks)

(c) Calculate Assad's taxable income and income tax liability for the tax year 2018/19, and the amount of tax still due. (9 marks)

(d) Calculate Assad's Class 4 national insurance liability for 2018/19.

(2 marks)

(e) Either calculate the amount, or if preferred, describe how you would calculate it if you had the necessary information, that should be paid by Assad as the first payment on account of income tax and class 4 NIC due for the tax year 2019/20. (2 marks)

(Total 30 marks)

Question 7

Simon, aged 45, is employed as a Public Relations consultant by Bogota Ltd. For the year ended 5th April 2019, he has provided the following information:

1. His basic annual salary was £38,000.
2. He received a performance bonus of £2,728 on 31st October 2018. This related to the six months ended 30th September 2018. On 1st April 2019 he was notified that he was entitled to a bonus of £1,250 for the six months to 31st March 2019, and this was paid to him on 30th April 2019.
3. He had the use of a company diesel car from Bogota Ltd from 6th May 2018 (date of first registration) until after 5th April 2019. The car's list price was £22,500 but the company negotiated a 15% discount from a dealer. All business and personal fuel was paid for by the company and Simon uses the car privately every week. The car has a CO_2 emission rating of 147g/km and did not meet the Real Driving Emissions Step 2 standard. Simon did not have a company car for the first month of tax year 2018/19.
4. Simon had a company mobile phone, on which he was allowed to make private calls. The phone cost the employer rent and charges of £360.
5. He was reimbursed £275 by Bogota Ltd during the year for expenses incurred entertaining clients.
6. Simon received an interest-free loan of £15,000 from Bogota Ltd on 6th June 2018, which he repaid on 6th December 2018.
7. Simon paid £200 per month into the Bogota Ltd occupational pension scheme, by direct deduction from his salary. This pension scheme is not contracted out of the state second pension.

Assume that the official rate of interest is 2.50%.

Simon had no other income in the year 2018/19, but he sold a painting in November 2018 for £18,300. He had purchased the painting in 1998 for £2,500. He had no personal capital losses brought forward at 6th April 2018.

Simon tells you in July 2019 that he plans to leave his employment and become a self-employed Public Relations consultant. He plans to advertise his services widely, and has already identified potential new clients.

He also hopes to sell some of his self-employed services to Bogota Ltd after he leaves their full-time employment. His current manager is willing to offer him some short-term tasks on a 'freelance' basis, working with teams he knows.

Required:

(a) Calculate Simon's assessable employment income for 2018/19. **(12 marks)**

(b) Calculate Simon's Class 1 NIC liability, and his employer's total NIC liability, in respect of earnings and benefits in 2018/19. **(3 marks)**

(c) Calculate Simon's Capital Gains Tax liability for 2018/19, and state when he must pay the capital gains tax. **(5 marks)**

(d) **Advise Simon how he should carry out his self-employed activities, including any services provided for a fee to Bogota Ltd, if he wishes to resist any suggestion from the tax authority that he is still an employee of Bogota Ltd. (7 marks)**

(e) **Explain how it would alter Simon's UK tax position if occasional work that he did for Bogota Ltd after he left his present employment were viewed as a return to employment, not as self-employment. (3 marks)**

(Total 30 marks)

Question 8

(a) Lydia Smith has an established trading business and also lets 2 properties. Her income and losses for the five years to 31st March 2019 are as follows:

Year ending	31/03/15 £	31/03/16 £	31/03/17 £	31/03/18 £	31/03/19 £
Trading profit	28,000	25,000	10,000	Loss (65,000)	43,000
Bank deposit interest	240	320	400	NIL	NIL
Property letting:					
16 Park Row	-	Loss (4,000)	10,500	Loss (5,000)	NIL
12 Highfield Grove	-	7,600	Loss (3,000)	11,000	6,500

Lydia always claims relief for losses as early as possible.

Required: Calculate Lydia's taxable income for each of the five years to 31st March 2019, showing appropriate claims for loss relief. (10 marks)

(b) Ron is a higher rate taxpayer and has the following disposals of assets during 2018/19, which were his only transactions relevant to Capital Gains Tax:

(i) Sold a fish and chip shop for £250,000 in October 2018, from which £12,500 selling commission was deducted. The shop cost £160,000 in August 1997. Ron claims Entrepreneurs' Relief on the disposal.

(ii) Sold part of a plot of land in February 2019 for £40,000. The whole piece of land had cost £25,000 in November 1997. The value of the part retained was £30,000 in February 2019.

(iii) Sold a sculpture for £10,000 in March 2019. The sculpture cost £18,500 in January 1991, with an additional £1,500 of acquisition costs.

Required: Calculate Ron's Capital Gains Tax liability for 2018/19. (10 marks)

(Total 20 marks)

Question 9

(a) Gareth commenced business as a landscape architect on 1st November 2016 and prepared his first accounts to 30th April 2018. He purchased office equipment costing £11,500 on 1st November 2016, on which he claimed an Annual Investment Allowance equal to its full cost.

His tax-adjusted trading profit for the period ended 30th April 2018, before deducting the above capital allowances claim, was £67,500.

Required

(i) Calculate the trading profits assessable for income tax purposes on Gareth for the tax years 2016/17, 2017/18 and 2018/19. (7 marks)

(ii) State the amount of Gareth's overlap profits and show how you have calculated this figure. (2 marks)

(iii) Is there anything which Gareth could have done to avoid having overlap profits arising in his business? (2 marks)

(b) Mary-Anne was born in 1936 and is registered severely visually impaired. She has the following income in 2018/19:

State pension (*no tax deducted at source*)	£8,546
Private pension (*before £1,044 tax deducted at source under PAYE*)	£10,680
Income from dividends	£9,792
Income from Cash ISAs	£780
Interest income from bank deposit accounts	£4,000

Required

Calculate Mary-Anne's income tax liability for tax year 2018/19, showing how much tax is still payable or reclaimable after the end of that year. (9 marks)

(Total 20 marks)

Question 10

(a) Sam Street commenced trading on 1st May 2018 and prepares business accounts to each 31st December thereafter. In May 2018 she bought the following assets:

	£
Plant and machinery	141,850
Office furniture	4,500
3 Computers (*3-year useful economic life*)	2,300
Photocopier/printer	5,500
A car which she uses privately for 25% of its annual mileage (CO_2 emissions, 106 g/km)	15,000

In the year to 31st December 2019 the following transactions in plant and equipment took place:

- Sold an item of machinery for £3,500 which had originally cost £2,600.
- Bought a van costing £11,500 to use for business deliveries.
- Sold the 3 computers when they were 18 months old in November 2019, for £150 in total.

Required

Calculate the capital allowances available to Sam for her first two periods of account, assuming that she always claims the maximum allowances and makes elections to get quicker relief wherever possible. Assume that capital allowances **rates** for 2018/19 will continue unchanged in 2019/20. **(12 marks)**

(b) Roberta has been a sole trader since 1990. On 31st March 2019 she transferred her business to her daughter Jill, which included the following assets:

- A shop with a market value of £150,000. It had been purchased on 1st August 2004 for £80,000 and has always been used for Roberta's business. Jill paid Roberta £50,000 for the shop.
- A warehouse with a market value of £120,000. It had been purchased in 1995 for £45,000 and has never been used for business purposes by Roberta but rented out. Jill paid Roberta £40,000 for the warehouse.

Wherever possible, Roberta and Jill have elected to hold over the gift element of the capital gains arising to Roberta on these sales.

Required

Assuming that gift holdover claims are made where possible, calculate Roberta's capital gains, before annual exemption, for 2018/19. Ignore Entrepreneur's Relief. **(8 marks)**

(Total 20 marks)

Exam–type Questions and Answers on Corporate Taxation and VAT

Question 11

(a) The financial controller of Otto Ltd is new and has no recent experience of UK Corporation Tax. He has prepared a draft of the income statement for Otto Ltd, a company which has one subsidiary company Roxy Ltd, for the eight month accounting period from 1st April to 30th November 2018. He would like you to work out your best estimate of the company's corporation tax liability for the period. His draft income statement currently looks like this:

		£
Turnover		300,000
Operating expenses	(note 1)	(196,930)
Operating profit		103,070
Interest income	(note 3)	30,000
Dividends income	(note 4)	12,600
Profit for the period		£145,670

Notes

1. Operating expenses include:
   - Depreciation of Property, Plant and Equipment £15,987
   - Amortisation of intangible asset (registered design) £8,433
   - Amortisation of 2012 lease premium (see Note 2) £2,000
   - Legal fees for letters chasing slow-paying debtors £1,250
   - Legal fees for drawing up financial controller's contract £500
   - Surcharge incurred for a late VAT return £650
2. A lease premium of £30,000 was paid on 1st August 2012 on commencement of a new ten-year lease of trade premises. This premium is being amortised in the income statement of Otto Ltd over ten years on a straight-line basis, at £250 per month.
3. Interest income was all from Roxy Ltd and arose on a non-trading loan relationship. The loan of £1.5 million was outstanding throughout the whole period of account and carries a 4% annual interest rate. The £30,000 received represents the gross interest charged from 1st April to 30th September 2018. No inter-company charge has yet been raised for the period since 1st October.
4. Dividend income comprised:

		£
30th June 2018	Dividend received from non-group company Poppy plc	4,500
30th September 2018	Dividend received from subsidiary company Roxy Ltd	8,100
		£12,600

5. There was no pooled plant and machinery expenditure that had qualified for capital allowances brought forward at 1st April 2018.

Additions to general plant and machinery during the period were:

Lorry (*or 'truck', a commercial vehicle*)	£16,667
Car (with CO_2 emissions 105g/km)	£ 3,333

(a) Required: For the Corporation Tax Accounting Period 1st April to 30th November 2018, and using all the above information:

(i) Calculate Capital Allowances, assuming Otto Ltd claims the maximum allowances available; (3 marks)

(ii) Calculate the tax-adjusted trading profit of Otto Ltd, after capital allowances; (5 marks)

(iii) Calculate the taxable total profits of Otto Ltd, and Otto Ltd's expected Corporation Tax liability for the accounting period. (8 marks)

(b)

Misto Ltd is required to prepare a Value Added Tax return for the period 1st July to 30th September 2018. The company sales records show:

Standard-rated outputs, net of VAT	£24,000
Zero-rated outputs	£ 7,000

The company purchase and expense invoice records for the quarter show the following totals:

	Net	VAT	Gross
Purchases and expenses relating to:	£	£	£
Standard-rated business	11,500	1,825	13,325
Zero-rated business	2,350	270	2,620
Car petrol costs incurred (overhead)	800	200	1,000
Car leasing costs incurred (overhead)	900	180	1,080

Misto Ltd provides its sales manager with a fully expensed company car with CO_2 emissions of 145g/km. The fuel scale charge for the car is £266 gross per quarter. A bad debt of £720 gross of VAT at the standard rate was written off during the period, having been due for payment since January 2018.

(b) Required:

(i) Calculate Value Added Tax payable or reclaimable by Misto Ltd for the period 1st July to 30th September 2018; (6 marks)

(ii) Advise the directors of the requirements for input VAT incurred to be reclaimable which you have applied in part (i), and evaluate the extent to which these rules demonstrate a clear principle; (5 marks)

(iii) Advise the directors of any benefits which Misto Ltd might obtain by joining the VAT Annual Accounting Scheme, and note any possible drawback of joining this scheme, for companies in general. (3 marks)

Total 30 marks

Question 11 – Solution

(a)(i)

			Additions £	Main pool £	Allowances £
Plant additions			16,667		
Annual Investment Allowance (AIA)			(16,667)		16,667
Car < 110 g/km				3,333	
WDA (8 months)	18%	× $^8/_{12}$		(400)	400
					£17,067
				2,933	

(ii) Tax-adjusted trading profit		£	£
Reported operating profit			103,070
Add back:			
Depreciation		15,987	
VAT surcharge		650	
Lease amortisation		2,000	
Legal fees chasing debtors	*allowable*	0	
Legal fees re staff contract	*allowable*	0	
Design licence amortisation	*allowable*	0	18,637
			121,707
Less 2012 lease premium "deemed rent" claimable: Matches Deemed rent for 10 years taxed on landlord = £30k × (100% - (2% × 9)) = £30k × 82% = £24,600; spread over 120 months at £205/month = for 8 months			(1,640)
Less:			
Capital allowances		(from (i))	(17,067)
= Income from trading			**103,000**

(iii) Taxable total profits

		£
Trading profit	As above	103,000
Non-trade loan relationship surplus (*interest receivable, taxed on accruals basis*): £1.5m × 8/12 × 4% *[the 2 months accrued income* ***is*** *taxable, even though (by taxpayer error) omitted from the draft income statement]*		40,000
Taxable Total Profits		**143,000**
CT at 19%		**£ 27,170**

(b)(i)

VAT return for quarter to 30th September 2018					£
Output VAT:					
Standard rate		£24,000	× 20%		4,800
Zero rate					0
Fuel scale charge	145g/km	£266	× 20/120		44
					4,844
Input VAT:					
Purchases	for SR output			1,825	
	For ZR output			270	
Car leasing	£180 × 50%			90	
Car fuel	Full reclaim			200	
Bad debt relief claimed	£720 × 20/120			120	
					(2,505)
					£2,339

(b)(ii) Advice on reclaimability of input VAT suffered by the business

A good answer would make points such as:

The general principle: the related input tax on all costs incurred in making taxable (VAT-able) supplies can be reclaimed by a registered trader, unlike the input tax incurred in making VAT-exempt supplies. Both standard and zero rate supplies made are theoretically liable to VAT, and therefore in principle Misto Ltd can reclaim all input VAT.

- However , input VAT is only reclaimable on inputs used **for business**
- 50% of the VAT on car leasing is deductible, which recognises an element of business and non-business use can be present in a car motoring cost.

- Also, input VAT on **purchase** of cars is not reclaimable by most businesses - unless non-business use of the car is impossible.
- The 50% car leasing VAT rule is an example of simplicity over accuracy - it assumes that on average, around 50% of the lease cost of a car is the purchase cost and the rest covers business-related use.

Another example seen in this situation (*again not strictly following the principle of <u>accurate</u> calculation of non-business proportion*):

- Even if some private fuel is supplied via the business to the proprietor or to staff, input tax on all business fuel purchases can be reclaimed
- But instead an output is recorded (*as if the business sold private fuel to itself*) to give a similar economic result to disallowing input VAT
- The value of the output is determined by a scale, related to the car's CO_2 emissions. It is not related to the actual private versus business usage of the car in the period, or nor to actual petrol cost recorded.
- To this extent the rule about not reclaiming input VAT on private purchases is being applied in general terms but not accurately.
- One economic effect of the fuel scale charge table is to encourage affected businesses to run lower emission cars.

(b)(iii) Advantages /possible disadvantages for Misto Ltd of joining Annual Accounting Scheme

SIMPLICITY is the key word here

Advantages:

- trader only must do one detailed VAT return annually;
- trader has longer to finalise the year's annual VAT return (*due 2 months after the end of the VAT year*);

Disadvantage:

- may result in temporary overpayment of VAT during the on-account payment phase, if actual turnover is decreasing, or if recoverable input VAT on costs is rising more than sales are rising (*since instalments are usually based on the prior year's actual VAT liability*),

Question 12

(a) The income statement of Minnie Ltd, a single company, for the 16-month period from 1st July 2017 to 31st October 2018 shows:

		£
Revenue		1,777,650
Operating costs	(note 1)	(1,066,700)
		710,950
Profit on disposal of land and buildings	(note 2)	420,000
Loss on disposal of investments	(note 2)	(4,600)
Financial income	(note 3)	111,000
Profit before tax		**£1,237,350**

Notes

1. Operating profit is calculated after the following expense deductions:

	£
Depreciation	152,033
Entertaining customers at £30 each	8,250
Entertaining staff at £40 each	800
Political donation	3,000
Qualifying charitable donations - £1,500 per month from 1st January 2018 onwards	15,000
Staff bonuses:	
- For the year to 30th June 2017, paid on 31st May 2018;	8,000
- Accrued for the period to 31st October 2018, to be paid and made available on 30th September 2019.	14,000
Repair expenditure includes:	
Replacing 75% of the air conditioning system (*a feature integral to a building*) during September 2018	8,333
Purchasing a car with CO_2 emissions of 135g/km on 1st October 2018	33,767

2. The disposal of the land, buildings and investments on 21st August 2018 gave rise to net chargeable gains for tax purposes of £260,000.

3. **Financial income** comprises:

Interest receivable on a £1.2 million non-trading loan at 5% annual interest, from 1st May 2018.	30,000
Cash dividends received from Babbers plc	
- 1st August 2017	54,000
- 1st February 2018	27,000

4. Minnie Ltd had no expenditure brought forward on any plant and machinery capital allowances pools at 1st July 2017.

Required:

(a) **Calculate the tax-adjusted income from trading of Minnie Ltd for the 16 month period of account from 1st July 2017 to 31st October 2018.**

(6 marks)

(b) **Calculate Minnie Ltd's Corporation Tax liabilities for the relevant Corporation Tax Accounting Periods.**

(12 marks)

(c) **Evaluate the recent policy of the UK government of decreasing the main rate of Corporation Tax, while maintaining or increasing the rates of VAT, national insurance and personal income tax.**

(8 marks)

(Total 26 marks)

Question 12 - Solution

(a) **Minnie Ltd Tax-adjusted trading profit for 16 months to 31st October 2018**

	£	£
Reported profit		1,237,350
Add:		
Depreciation		152,033
Loss on sale of investments		4,600
Entertaining		8,250
Political donation		3,000
Property, plant and equipment included in repairs expense		42,100
Qualifying charitable donation		15,000
Remuneration unpaid within 9 months		14,000
		1,476,333
Less:		
Dividends receivable	81,000	
Interest receivable	30,000	
Profit on sale of property	420,000	
		(531,000)
Tax adjusted trading profit		**£945,333**

(b) Calculate Corporation Tax liabilities for the relevant Corporation Tax Accounting Periods

Capital allowances:

Short period ended 31-Oct-2018		Special Rate pool £	Allowances £
WDV b/fwd at 01-Jul-2018	£	0	
Additions qualifying for AIA	8,333		8,333
Car > 110 g/km		33,767	
WDA 8% × $^4/_{12}$		(900)	900
Total allowances (period 2)			**£9,233**
WDV c/fwd		**32,867**	

		Y/e 30-Jun-2018	4 mths to 31-Oct-2018
Trading profit	£945,333		
	$^{12}/_{16}$ + $^4/_{16}$	709,000	236,333
Capital allowances	From working	0	(9,233)
		709,000	227,100
Interest (6 months)	$^2/_6$ + $^4/_6$	10,000	20,000
Chargeable gain	Date of disposal	0	260,000
		719,000	507,100
Qualifying charitable donation	Date paid	(9,000)	(6,000)
Total Taxable Profits		**710,000**	**501,100**
Corporation tax :			
FY 2017		£	£
CT @ 19 % × $^9/_{12}$ × £710,000 TTP		101,175	
FY 2018			
CT @ 19% × $^3/_{12}$ × £710,000 TTP		33,725	
		£134,900	
CT @ 19%	× £501,100 TTP		**£95,209**

(c) Evaluate the policy of the UK government of decreasing the main rate of Corporation Tax, while maintaining or increasing the rates of VAT, national insurance and personal income tax.

(8 marks)

- The reduction of national tax rates on company profits is a common phenomenon across the OECD;
- Full rate of Corporation Tax is being reduced to make UK a competitive tax regime to attract and retain companies in the UK;
- It is easy for international companies to move to another country to avoid high levels of taxation, which poses a challenge to governments trying to tax them;
- UK employment prospects will be enhanced by the presence of companies whose employees will pay UK personal income tax and national insurance;
- Both these taxes produce more government revenue (proportionally) across the UK economy than corporation tax does;
- And in recessionary conditions it is important for the government to try to maintain sources of revenue to fund public expenditure;
- Note that employers' national insurance increases staff costs, and is a disincentive for companies to employ more UK staff.
- VAT – Governments can collect increased revenues fast by raising VAT as it is collected continuously and not on an annualised basis;
- On the whole most businesses do not directly bear VAT themselves on their profits or turnover – strictly they collect VAT but pass the cost on to their customers. (*Exceptions: healthcare, finance, insurance, and education – all big sectors of the UK economy*);
- BUT a rise in VAT rates can discourage consumer spending thus reducing retail and service sector profits on which CT is collected;
- A rise in VAT also imposes cost rises on exempt businesses and thereby reduces the profits on which Corporation Tax is collected;
- In general VAT is a regressive tax; Corporation Tax used to be a progressive tax when there were different full and small rates, but is now a proportional tax.

Question 13

Blackbird Ltd produces accounts showing these results:

	Year to 31st July 2016	8 months to 31st March 2017	Year to 31st March 2018	Year to 31st March 2019
	£	£	£	£
Trading profit / (loss)	210,000	6,000	Loss (184,000)	490,000
Property Income	27,600	20,000	10,000	-
Chargeable gains / (losses)	Loss (16,000)	-	80,000	-
Dividends received from Non-group quoted share investments	-	-	-	18,000
Qualifying charitable donations	36,000	24,000	36,000	36,000

Blackbird Ltd has a policy of claiming tax relief for all losses as soon as possible.

Required:

(a) Calculate the Total Taxable Profits of Blackbird Ltd for each of the Corporation Tax accounting periods shown above, assuming that loss reliefs are claimed as early as possible, and identifying any amounts unrelieved by the end of the final accounting period; (12 marks)

(b) Evaluate the directors' policy to claim loss reliefs in the earliest period possible. (6 marks)

(c) Advise the directors of alternative tax relief opportunities that might be available if Blackbird Ltd was a wholly owned subsidiary of a UK company which paid Corporation Tax. (2 marks)

Total (20 marks)

Question 13 - Solution

a) Blackbird Ltd: Loss allocations and final TTP:

	Y/e 31-Jul-16	P/e 31-Mar-17	Y/e 31-Mar-18	Y/e 31-Mar-19
Trading profits	210,000	6,000	Loss	490,000
Property profits	27,600	20,000	10,000	-
Chargeable gains			80,000	
Less cap. losses	Loss		(16,000)	
			64,000	
Total profits	237,600	26,000	74,000	490,000
Less current year trading loss claim (W)	-	-	(74,000)	-
Less prior year trading loss claim (W)	(79,200) Max $^4/_{12}$	(26,000)	-	-
Less loss carried forward				(4,800)
Total Profits	158,400	0	0	485,200
Qualifying Charitable Donations	(36,000)	-	-	(36,000)
Taxable Total Profits	122,400	0	0	449,200
Unrelieved QCDS		24,000	36,000	

Loss memorandum working:

	£
Trading loss for year ended 31st March 2018	184,000
Claimed against current year total profits	(74,000)
Claimed against prior 8 month period total profits	(26,000)
	84,000
Claimed against $^4/_{12}$ × previous year total profits	(79,200)
Available to carry forward to y/e 31st March 2019	4,800
Used by carry forward claim in y/e 31st March 2019	(4,800)
Remaining unrelieved by 31st March 2019	NIL

(b) Evaluate the directors' policy to claim loss reliefs in the earliest period possible. (6 marks)

- There is a cash flow advantage to the business in claiming loss reliefs earlier rather than later,
- through tax liabilities being reduced in earlier years, delaying cash outflows of tax from the business until later years.
- However, the tax relief on QCDs of periods ending 31st March 2017 and 2018 above is wasted;
- totalling (24k + 36k) = 60k @ 20% = £12,000 of potential tax savings against the taxable total profits of the year.
- The policy may not therefore be tax-efficient in this case.

(c) Advise the directors of alternative tax relief opportunities that might be available if Blackbird Limited was a wholly owned subsidiary of a UK company which paid Corporation Tax. (2 marks)

- To the extent the accounting periods match, losses of Blackbird could be claimed against the profits of its parent.

- It is possible for companies to make intra-group payment for CT losses transferred but this is not absolutely necessary if the relationship is a 100% parent-subsidiary one. If there is some outside holding in the subsidiary company a payment would be normal.

- Any payment for group relief is ignored for CT purposes in both companies as long as it does not exceed the gross value of the losses. It is usually accounted for via the Tax line in the income statement.

Question 14

(a) Hopkins Ltd had a general pool of plant and machinery with a written down value of £14,695 on 1st April 2018. Hopkins Ltd has a policy of claiming the maximum capital allowances available. The following transactions in non-current assets took place during the 16 month period of account from 1st April 2018 to 31st July 2019:

	Additions	**Cost**
1st July 2018	General plant and machinery	£201,000
1st August 2018	Grey car with CO_2 emissions of 105g/km	£10,000
15th August 2018	ICT equipment to be treated as a short life asset	£5,000
1st May 2019	White car with CO_2 emissions of 190g/km	£21,000
15th May 2019	Black 'low emissions' car	£24,000
	Disposals	**Proceeds**
6th May 2019	ICT equipment bought for a cost of £5,000 in August 2018	£2,000
30th June 2019	Machine bought for a cost of £16,000 in December 2016.	£18,000

(a) Required: Calculate the capital allowances on plant and machinery available to Hopkins Ltd for the relevant Corporation Tax accounting periods. Assume the same rates and allowances for capital allowances apply unchanged in FY19, the same as in FY18. **(10 marks)**

(b) Thompson Catering Ltd bought a hotel for use in its business for £2,600,000 in September 2001. The hotel was sold for £3,200,000 in August 2007. Thompson Catering Ltd elected to claim rollover relief for the replacement of business assets against the cost of a restaurant bought for £3,130,000 in June 2008. The restaurant was sold for £3,700,000 in January 2019. The Retail Prices Index was 278.1 at December 2017.

(b) Required: Calculate the immediately taxable chargeable gains arising on the disposals of the hotel in August 2007, and of the restaurant in January 2019. **(10 marks)**

Total (20 marks)

Question 14 - Solution

a)		General pool	Special rate pool	Short life asset	Allowances
Y/e 31st March 2019					
WDV b/fwd		14,695			
Plant					
	201,000				
	201,000				
AIA					
	(200,000)	1,000			200,000
Car <110g		10,000			
Short life asset				5,000	
WDA		18%		18%	5,525
		(4,625)		(900)	
					£205,525
WDV c/fwd		21,070		4,100	
P/e 31st July 2019					
Cars >130g/km			21,000		
Low emission car					
	24,000				
ECA					
	(24,000)	0			24,000
Disposals		Max cost (16,000)			
				(2,000)	
Balancing Allowance				(2,100)	2,100
		5,070	21,000		
WDA × $^{4}/_{12}$		18%	8%		304
		(304)	(560)		560
					26,964
WDV		4,766	20,440		

(b) Thompson Catering Ltd
Chargeable gain computations 2007 and 2019

Hotel August 2007

		£	£
Proceeds			3,200,000
Cost			(2,600,000)
Unindexed gain			600,000
Indexation	Aug 07-Sep 01		
Round to 3 decimal places	(207.3 – 174.6) / 174.6	2,600,000 × 0.187	(486,200)
Indexed Gain			113,800
Max gain for roll over		113,800	
Restricted by proceeds not reinvested			
(3,200,000 - 3,130,000)		(70,000)	
Rolled over			(43,800)
Chargeable gain			**£70,000**

Restaurant January 2019		£	£
Proceeds			3,700,000
Deemed cost	Actual	3,130,000	
	Less Rolled-over gain	(43,800)	
			(3,086,200)
Unindexed gain			613,800
Indexation	Dec 17 – Jun 08		
(Round to 3 decimal places)	(278.1 – 216.8) / 216.8	3,086,200 × 0.283*	(613,800)
Chargeable gain			**£ nil**

* Remember that indexation cannot create, or increase, a chargeable loss. Hence the indexation allowance has been restricted here to match the unindexed gain (*the calculated indexation allowance would have been £873,395*).

Question 15

(a) Clare Ltd acquired 4,500 shares in Nehal plc in December 1988 at a cost of £10,845. In August 1992 Clare Ltd bought its share of a 1 for 3 rights issue at a price of £2.50 per Nehal plc share. In January 2019, Clare Ltd sold one half of its shareholding in Nehal plc for a price of £23,150. Clare Ltd has never owned a substantial shareholding in Nehal plc. The Retail Prices Index at December 2017 was 278.1.

(a) Required: Calculate the chargeable gain or allowable loss on disposal of Nehal plc shares in January 2019.

(8 marks)

(b) The directors of Code plc, the UK parent company of an international group, have asked for advice on the tax implications of their decisions on the level of transfer prices to be charged when goods and services are supplied between group companies resident in different states.

(b) Required:

(i) Briefly advise the directors why intra-group transfer pricing is an important tax issue for the UK, and for foreign governments. (6 marks)

(ii) What must a large UK company confirm on each year's Corporation Tax self-assessment return, regarding all trade prices paid or charged to connected companies? (2 marks)

(iii) Suggest practical steps which the Board of a UK company can sensibly take, to minimise risk of a detailed enquiry by the UK tax authorities (HMRC) into the transfer prices used for intra-group transactions in its company accounts and Corporation Tax return. (4 marks)

Total 20 marks

Question 15 - Solution

a) Clare Ltd's chargeable gain on Nehal plc share sale

Section 104 holding – share pool	Number	Cost £	Indexed cost £
Bought Dec 1988	4,500	10,845	10,845
Indexation to Aug 92 (138.9-110.3)/110.3 × 10,845			2,812
			13,657
Acquired From rights issue Aug 92	1,500	3,750	3,750
			17,407
Indexation to Dec 2017 (278.1 - 138.9)/138.9 × 17,407			17,445
Pool cost at Jan 2019	6,000	14,595	34,852
Sold 3,000 shares (½)	(3,000)	(7,298)	(17,426)
Pool cost remaining	3,000	7,297	17,426

Computation of gain on disposal of shares January 2019

	£
Proceeds	23,150
Cost (from pool cost column)	(7,298)
Unindexed gain	15,852
Indexation (17,426 - 7,298)	(10,128)
Chargeable gain	5,724

(b) (i) Briefly advise the directors why intra-group transfer pricing is an important issue for the UK, and foreign governments. (6 marks)

A good answer would adequately make points such as:

- Companies and governments use accounts to determine taxable profit reported in each territory but in the case of intragroup transactions, business income of the group entity in one country is the business cost in another.
- For group accounting purposes, all intragroup transactions are ignored or cancelled out, but transfer prices matter when companies under common control located in different taxing states have to declare and pay tax on profits arising in each state.
- As companies do not return taxable profits on a consolidated basis, prices charged between companies under common control can be influenced to shift taxable profits into a different territory with lower profits taxes. If total group consolidated profit remains the same, the

group as a whole gains. Tax authorities may therefore question transfer prices within groups.

(ii) What must be confirmed on each Corporation Tax return of a large UK-resident company, regarding transfer prices charged or paid to connected companies?

(2 marks)

That the profits reported on the CT return have not involved under-pricing of sales to, or overpricing of purchases from, any company under the same control;

OR

That the company has made any adjustments that are required by the UK transfer pricing rules so that intragroup prices used to compute taxable profits have been set on an "arm's length" basis.

(iii) Suggest practical steps which the Board of a UK company can take to reduce the risk of a later enquiry by the UK, or foreign, tax authorities into the figures used in its CT returns for intra-group cross-border transfer prices. **(4 marks)**

- It can enter into an Advance Pricing Agreement for up to 6 years
- to obtain agreement that the basis of its transfer pricing is acceptable to HMRC
- and will not be challenged retrospectively.
- An APA may be done in conjunction with the other taxing state involved, for maximum administrative efficiency.

Exam–type Questions on Corporate Taxation and VAT, without answers

Question 16

MJL Ltd is a small manufacturing company and has prepared the following income statement for the 18-month period to 30th September 2018.

		£
Revenue		481,045
Cost of Sales	(note 1)	(199,655)
Gross profit		281,390
Distribution costs	(note 2)	(13,124)
Administrative expenses	(note 3)	(154,800)
Operating profit		113,466
Profit on sale of car park land	(note 7)	45,800
Interest expense on business overdraft		(2,800)
Dividends from unconnected UK companies	(note 8)	18,000
Rent receivable on car park land	(note 7)	3,500
Profit before taxation		177,966

Further notes to the Income Statement:

(1) Cost of Sales includes
- Depreciation of £7,800
- Cost of refurbishment of a machine which was purchased for £1,200 (pre-owned) from a bankrupt competitor in July 2017, but which turned out to be completely unusable in MJL Ltd's trade until it had been adapted at a cost of £3,750

(2) Distribution costs include
- A car leasing payment of £3,467 incurred on a 3 year operating lease, taken out in January 2018, of a car emitting 175g CO_2/km

(3) Administrative expenses include:
- Depreciation of £4,000;
- A charitable donation of £750 to the UK central office of Oxfam, paid on 1st September 2018;
- A closing accrual of £10,750 for employer pension contributions to top up the staff occupational retirement pension scheme, which had not yet been paid to the pension provider by 30th September 2018; and
- Legal fees of £800 related to sale of land in November 2017.

(4) At 1st April 2017 MJL Ltd has unrelieved trading losses of £27,500 and a capital loss of £4,500 agreed and brought forward from prior periods.

(5) MJL Ltd has a capital allowances general pool written down value brought forward of £28,467 at 1st April 2017.

(6) There were no additions to Property, Plant and Equipment in the period other than the second-hand machine bought in July 2017 (see Note 1) and no disposals of Property, Plant and Equipment other than the land sold in November 2017 (see Note 7).

(7) The profit on sale of land recognised in the accounts related to a car park area that the company had originally used for its own business but had ceased to need, so it was rented out to a public car park operator at £500 per month from 1st April 2017 to 31st October 2017.
This car park land was sold outright to the car park operator (the former tenant) in November 2017 for £65,000, realising a chargeable gain of £18,600 for corporation tax purposes.

(8) Dividends were received as follows:

May 2018	£13,500
August 2018	£ 4,500

Required:

(a) Compute the tax-adjusted trading profits of MJL Ltd, before capital allowances, for the 18 month period of account to 30th Sept 2018. **(9 marks)**

(b) Compute maximum capital allowances claimable by MJL Ltd for the corporation tax accounting periods covered by this 18 month period of account. **(6 marks)**

(c) Compute MJL Ltd's taxable total profits for the relevant corporation tax accounting periods, assuming that maximum capital allowances and loss reliefs are claimed. **(7 marks)**

(d) Compute MJL Ltd's corporation tax liability for the relevant accounting periods. **(2 marks)**

(Total 24 marks)

Question 17

Cardigan Cars Limited has 3 activities: new cars, children's car seats and finance. The VAT records for the quarter to 30th September 2018 show the following:

Activity⇨	New cars £	Children's car seats £	Finance £	Head office £
Sales turnover, net of any VAT	675,000	195,000	90,000	
Rate of VAT	20%	5%	Exempt	
VAT on divisional purchase and expense invoices	97,500	8,250	11,750	
VAT on general overhead expense invoices				5,000

On 30th September 2018 Cardigan Cars Limited wrote off a bad debt due from Idle Interiors Limited of £12,000 inclusive of VAT at the standard rate of 20%.

The debt was in respect of one £5,000 invoice for a car which had a due date for payment of 1st February 2018 and a second invoice of £7,000 for another car dated 2nd July 2018.

(a) Required: Calculate the VAT payable or refundable for the quarter ended 30th September 2018. (9 marks)

Archway Garages, the first land and buildings used by Cardigan Cars Limited, were bought in January 1995 for a price of £390,000, with a further £2,500 of professional fees as expenses of the acquisition.

The land and buildings were sold in February 2001, when the company moved to new premises. The sales proceeds of the old Archway land and buildings in February 2001 were £575,000. The proceeds were used to buy the new land and buildings at Bath Buildings in February 2001 for £550,000, and to pay for a magazine advertisement costing £25,000. The company claimed rollover relief for the replacement of business assets on the change of business premises.

In January 2019 the new land and buildings at Bath Buildings were sold for gross proceeds of £738,000, incurring selling commission of £3,000.

(b) Required: Calculate the Corporation Tax payable as a result of the disposal of the new land and buildings, assuming Cardigan Cars Limited pays Corporation Tax at 19%. *(You will need to use the RPI information at the end of Chapter 25 for this question.)* **(12 marks)**

(c) Evaluate the extent to which Value Added Tax (VAT) contributes to desirable characteristics of the UK tax system (9 marks)

(Total 30 marks)

Question 18

(a) Splash Ltd is a UK resident company that manufactures hot tubs. It prepares financial statements to 31st March each year.

On 1st April 2018 the tax written down values of Splash Ltd's plant and machinery were as follows:

	£
General pool	144,280
Single short-life asset (2 years old)	13,440

During the year to 31st March 2019, Splash Ltd made the following purchases and sales of plant, equipment and motor vehicles.

		Cost/ (proceeds)
		£
14th April 2018	Purchased energy-saving plant	64,500
15th April 2018	Sold a lorry	(14,160)
5th May 2018	Purchased general plant and machinery	19,000
15th May 2018	Purchased white car CO_2 105 g/km	15,800
12th June 2018	Sold the short-life asset	(5,520)
22nd Sept 2018	Purchased blue car CO_2 180 g/km	23,760

The plant purchased in April 2018 was certified energy-saving plant which appeared on the UK government's Energy Technology Product List.

The lorry sold on 15th April 2018 had originally cost £21,600.

Required

(a) Calculate the maximum plant and machinery capital allowances available to Splash Ltd for the year ended 31st March 2019.

(10 marks)

(b) Dixon Limited is a successful UK trading company selling office equipment.

Its directors are considering expansion overseas to carry on the same trade in a non-UK country where the managing director has good business contacts.

They propose to do this either by setting up either a branch operation (*a non-UK branch of the existing company*) or a wholly-owned subsidiary company (*a separate company, incorporated and resident in the non-UK country*).

They have tested the overseas market, and consider there is a good chance that the overseas operation would be profitable from the start. However there is also a possibility that it will incur losses in at least the first two years of operation.

The overseas country in question charges a direct tax of 10% on the profits of all businesses located there and has a double taxation treaty with the UK.

Note: For the purposes of this question you should assume the directors of Dixon Ltd do not intend to make an irrevocable election to exclude the new foreign branch from UK Corporation Tax.

Required (b):

Advise Dixon Limited's directors, in connection with the choice between setting up the overseas operation as a branch or as a subsidiary:

(i) How UK tax is charged on the profits of an overseas branch of a UK company and how the UK tax position differs if the same net profits are made in a non-UK subsidiary company, which later pays a dividend to its UK parent company. (4 marks)

(ii) Whether net trading losses of the overseas branch can be set against UK profits for tax purposes, and how this situation differs if the overseas operation is a wholly-owned subsidiary company. (3 marks)

(iii) In what circumstances the UK tax authorities can seek to adjust the transfer prices charged for goods sold from a UK company to an overseas subsidiary company and why they might choose to use this power. (3 marks)

Total 20 marks

Question 19

Shelby Limited acquired 15,000 shares in Tobacco Exploitation plc in January 1995 at a cost of £29,000. In October 2000 Tobacco Exploitation plc made a bonus issue of 1 new share for every 2 held. In May 2004 Shelby Ltd bought its share of a 1 for 4 rights issue at a price of £1.60 per Tobacco Exploitation plc share. In January 2019 Shelby Limited sold one third of its shareholding in Tobacco Exploitation plc for a price of £13,000.

(a) **Required: Calculate the chargeable gain or allowable loss on disposal of Tobacco Exploitation plc shares in January 2019.** (*You will need to use the RPI information at the end of Chapter 25 for this question.*) **(9 marks)**

(b) The managing director of Shelby Ltd also requires advice on the tax treatment of certain proposed payments that will be made by the company in the next accounting period.

These payments are:

(i) A political donation to the UK Liberal Democrats of £5,000.

(ii) The cost of taking 10 key sales staff and directors to an important sales conference in Morocco (*cost per head, £2,000 including flights, hotel, conference fee and meals*).

(iii) A fine of £3,500 for exceeding the axle weight permitted for the company's delivery lorries.

(b) **Required: Advise the managing director whether or not each of the proposed payments (i) to (iii) can be treated for tax purposes as a trading expense of the next corporation tax accounting period by Shelby Ltd. Give reasons for all your answers, either from specific rules of tax law or from general principles of the UK tax system.** **(6 marks)**

(c) **Required: Using examples from the UK tax system, evaluate the extent to which the government is attempting to affect taxpayers' behaviour with respect to cars.** **(5 marks)**

(Total 20 marks)

Index

The index numbers refer to chapters or to chapter sections.

administration of income tax, 3
allowable payments, 5.1–7, 10.10
appeals, 3.2, 3.9, 10.11, 10.19, 35.19
authorised mileage allowances, 7.18
avoided permanent establishment, 24.16

bad debts, 10.15, 36.25
bank surcharge, 18.5
base erosion and profit shifting (BEPS), 24.14
bases for tax, 1.6
beneficial loans, 7.23-7.25
benefits code, 7.7–27
blind person's allowance, 4.6
bonuses, 8.9
bonus issues, 30.5
broadcasting, communication and electronic services, 36.23
building society interest, 6.2
business assets, 27.1, 28.8, 31.1-7, 33.1-5
business form, 37.8
Business Premises Renovation Allowance (BPRA), 13.24
business splitting, 35.11

capital allowances, 10.23, 13, 14.4, 20, 36.28
Capital Gains groups, 31.10-31.11
capital sums, 25.18
car fuel benefit, 7.15
chargeable assets, 25.11-17
chargeable occasions, 28.1–13
chattels, 25.19, 29.7-10
consideration, 26.3-5
Chargeable Gains, 25-33
    death, 27.4, 27.7, 28.1, 28.12
    entrepreneurs' relief, 25.5, 26.9, 30.2, 31.2, 31.7
    exemptions, 25.19-20, 31.4, 31.13
    gifts, 32.1–6
    gifts of business assets, 32.4-5
    holdover relief, 32.1-6
    husband and wife, 27.5, 29.6
    indexation allowance, 25.3, 25.23, 26.10-12
    indexation allowance (shares), 30.4
    land, 29.2–6
    market value, 26.5
    overseas aspects, 19.19, 27.8
    part-disposals, 26.8-10, 28.4, 28.11, 29.3-4
    persons chargeable, 25.1,25.10,27.1-9
    personal representatives, 27.7, 31.7
    private residences, 29.5–6
    replacement of assets, 28.6, 31.3
    restoration of assets, 28.5
    Retail Prices Index, 25.23
    rights issues, 30.6
    shares and securities, 30.1–8
    substantial shareholdings exemption, 31.13
    takeover bids, 30.7
child benefit, 17.9
civil partners, 2.9, 4.4, 27.5, 29.6
close company, 18.3
Collective Defined Contribution (CDC) pension schemes, 16.2
commission, 8.9
communication services, 36.23
company, 37.8
copyright royalties, 6.13
Corporation Tax, 18–24
    accounting periods, 18.12–14
    bank interest, 19.10-11
    capital allowances, 20
    capital gains, 19.5, 19.20, 23.11, 25.10
    change in rate, impact, 18.16
    computation of total profits,19
    corporate venturing scheme, 19.14
    controlled foreign companies, 24.7–10
    double tax relief, 24.3–5
    financial year, 18.3, 18.12
    foreign branch, 18.5, 24.2, 24.12
    G.A.A.P, 19.2, 19.10
    groups, 23.1–15
    group relief, 22.1, 23.1–15
    income tax collection / offset, 21.1-4
    intangible assets, 18.2, 19.12-19.13, 23.3
    interest deductibility restriction, 24.16
    international aspects, 24.1–16
    loan relationships, 19.9-10, 25.9
    loss relief, 22.1–10
    non-resident companies, 18.6, 18.13
    management expenses, 22.10

marginal relief fraction, 18.15
marginal rate,18.15
organisations liable, 18.5
patent box, 19.13
payment of tax, 18.9-10
qualifying charitable donations, 21.5-8
rates of tax, 18.15-16
R&D reliefs, 18.2, 19.8-9
self-assessment, 18.9
specimen computation, 18.17
trade losses, 22
transfer pricing, 24.11
worldwide debt cap, 24.16
current year basis, 2.5, 11.3

death, 4.7, 28.12, 33, 34
deduction at source, 2.2, 3.3-4, 6.2, 8
defalcations, 10.20
Defined Ambition (DA) pension schemes, 16.2
Defined Benefit (DB) pension schemes, 16.2, 16.7
Defined Contribution (DC) pension schemes, 16.2
diesel supplement, 7.14
digital services, 36.23
directors, 7.5, 8.10, 17.5
disallowable expenditure, 3.4, 10.11
Diverted Profits Tax, 24.15
dividends, 6.4, 18.4, 24.4, 37.8
donations, 5.5-5.6, 10.9, 10.11, 10.22

employment income, 7
employment, 7.3
Enterprise Investment Scheme, 6.8
errors on VAT returns, 35.22
e-services, 36.23
excise duties, 1.11
externalities, 1.2

foreign subsidiaries, 24.13
fuel scale charge, 36.16

G.A.A.P, 10.24, 19.2, 19.10
General Anti-Abuse Rule, 1.15, 37.5, 37.8
Gift Aid, 5.1, 5.5
gifts – CGT, 7.6, 10.22, 32.1–7
group relief, 23.1–15

horizontal equity, 1.5, 10.26
husband and wife, 4.4, 27.5, 29.6
hypothecated taxes, 1.10

imputation system (CT), 1.14
income from employment, 7
Income Tax, 2–17
administration, 3
allowable payments, 5, 10.10
annual investment allowance, 13.9
annual payments, 5.2
assessments, 2.5, 3.3, 3.8
asset values, 10.24
badges of trade, 10.4-5
benefits code, 7.7–31
building society interest, 6.2
business entertainment, 10.10, 10.12
capital allowances, 13
capital receipts, 10.8
car benefit rules, 7.13
change of accounting date, 12
child benefit, 17.9
child tax credit, 17.10
classification of income, 2.3
CO_2 emission table, 7.14
computation layout, 2.2
deduction of trading expenses, 10.9–22
dividend income, 6.4
due dates for payment, 3.5
extended basic rate band, 5.5, 16.9
furnished holiday lettings, 9.12
furnished lettings, 9.9
gift aid, 5.5–7
income assessed as trade profits, 10
- basis periods, 11
- change of accounting date, 12
income from employment, 7
interest on overdue tax, 3.7
investment income, 6
lease premiums, 9.5-8, 19.17-18
leased cars, 13.18
leased plant, 13.20
leases, 9.5–8, 13.20
loss reliefs, 14
net pay arrangements, 8.3
non-taxable income, 2.8
official rate of interest, 7.20, 7.23
partnership taxation, 15
PAYE system, 8
payroll giving, 5.6
pensions, 10.16, 16
personal allowances and reliefs, 4
plant and machinery, 13.2–23
post-cessation expenditure, 10.22
pre-owned assets charge, 6.14
property business losses, 14.16
property income, 9, 19.15-18

qualifying loans, 5.3-4
rates of tax, 2.4
REITs, 6.5, 9.11
savings income, 6
stakeholder pension, 16.3
tax rate bands, 2.4
trade profits, 10, 11
transfer of business to company, 14.11
van benefits, 7.16-7.17
working tax credit, 17.11
Incorporation relief, 31.9
Inheritance Tax, 33–34
administration, 33.20
agricultural property relief, 33.14
annual exemption, 33.4
business property relief, 33.14, 34.10-13
chargeable transfer, 33.6
deeds of variation, 33.19
exempt transfers, 33.4
gift with reservation, 33.11-12
gifts to charities, 33.4
gifts to political parties, 33.4
grossing up procedures, 34.3
intestacy, 33.18
liabilities, 33.17
lifetime transfers, 33.2-33.6, 34
location of assets, 33.4
payment, 33.20
pre-deceasing spouse's NRB, 33.8
pre-deceasing spouse's RNRB, 33.9
quick succession relief, 33.15
rates, 33.1
small gifts, 33.4
taper relief (IHT), 33.10
transfers of value on death, 33.7
transfers of value in lifetime, 33.2-33.6
intangible assets, 10.24, 18.2, 19.12, 23.2
interest, 37.8
inventories, 10.24
Investors' relief, 31.8
ISAs, 6.6

knowledge-intensive companies, 6.12

leased cars, 10.10,13.18
leased plant, 13.20
leases, 9.5–8, 13.20, 19.17-18
legal expenses, 10.19
limited liability, 37.8
living accommodation, 7.19-7.20
living wage, 6.2, 37.8
losses
trading (income tax), 14
trading (corporation tax), 22
capital, 25.2, 25.8, 27.4

management expenses, 23.6
merit goods, 1.2
Money Purchase Annual Allowance, 16.6
motor vehicles, 13.11–14

National Employment Savings Trust (NEST), 16.2
National Insurance, 17.1–7
National Living Wage, 6.2, 37.8
Nil Rate Band (NRB), 33.8
negligible value claims, 28.7
non-tax aspects, 37.8, 37.11

opt to tax, 36.29
outplacement counselling, 2.8, 10.17

patent fees and expenses, 10.14
patent royalties, 6.13
Pay As You Earn, 8
payments on account, 2.7, 3.5
pension contributions, 10.16, 10.22, 16, 37.8
permanent establishment, 24.3, 24.14-15
personal pensions, 16.3
personal reliefs, 4
personal savings allowance, 2.4, 6.2
plant and machinery, 13.2–23
pre-trading expenses, 10.22, 14.13
prompt payment discounts, 36.11
property allowance, 9.14
property income, 9
public goods, 1.2

quarterly returns, 21

redistribution, 1.2
redundancy payments, 10.17
removal expenses, 7.29
rent, 9
rent-a-room, 9.10, 9.14
repairs and renewals, 10.13
Residence Nil Rate Band (RNRB), 33.9
Retail Prices Index (RPI) 25.23
retained earnings, 37.8
royalties, 6.13

salary, 37.8
secondments, 10.22
Seed Enterprise Investment Schemes (SEIS), 6.9
Self-Invested Personal Pensions (SIPPs), 16.3
self-supply, 36.24
shares and securities, 30.1-8
sick pay, 8.7, 17.8
simplified expenses, 10.22
Social Investment Tax Relief (SITR), 6.10
social protection, 1.2
social security income, 1.2, 17.9-11
sole trader, 37.8
stabilisation, 1.2
statutory maternity pay, 17.8
statutory paternity pay, 17.8
statutory sick pay, 17.8
stakeholder pensions, 16.9
subscriptions, 10.22

taper relief (IHT), 33.10
tax avoidance, 1.15, 24.14-16, 35.23, 37.5
tax bases, 1.6
tax, definition, 1.1
tax evasion, 1.15
tax gap, 1.16
tax, incidence, 1.9
tax planning, 37.1-12
taxation, desirable characteristics, 1.5
taxation, direct, 1.7
taxation, indirect, 1.8
terminal losses, 14.9–10, 22.6-7
termination payments, 7.34
trading, 10.4–5
trading allowance, 10.26
training costs, 10.18

unpaid remuneration, 10.22

vans, 7.16-7.17
Value Added Tax (VAT), 35-36
  accounting for VAT, 35.18
  administration, 35.19
  annual accounting scheme, 36.32
  appeals, 35.19
  artificial separation, 35.12
  bad debts, 36.25
  cash accounting scheme, 36.31
  change in the rate of VAT, 36.30
  default surcharge, 35.21
  exempt goods and services, 35.8
  flat-rate scheme, 36.33
  fuel scale charge, 36.16
  group registration, 35.17
  imports and exports, 36.18–22
  input tax, 36.14–15
  mixed / composite supplies, 36.12-13
  partial exemption, 36.17
  place of supply, 36.7
  rates of tax, 35.4
  reduced-rate goods and services, 35.7
  registration, 35.13–17
  special schemes for retailers, 36.34
  tax point, 36.8
  zero-rated goods and services, 35.6, 36.3
VAT avoidance schemes, 35.23
Venture Capital Trust (VCT), 6.11
vertical equity, 1.5

withholding tax, 1.12, 24.2-3
worldwide debt cap, 24.16

Tax rates 2018/19

Income tax

Starting rate 0% Savings income £0 – £5,000 band

Savings nil rate 0% £1,000 of savings income for basic rate taxpayers; £500 of savings income for higher rate taxpayers; not available for additional rate taxpayers

Dividend 'allowance' 0% on first £2,000 of dividend income

UK rates and bands (except Scotland):

	£				
Basic rate	0 – 34,500	NSND*/ savings	20%	Dividends	7.5%
Higher rate	34,501 – 150,000	NSND*/ savings	40%	Dividends	32.5%
Additional rate	150,000+	NSND*/ savings	45%	Dividends	38.1%

Scotland rates and bands:

	£		
Starter Rate	0 – 2,000	NSND*	19%
Basic Rate	2,001 – 12,150	NSND*	20%
Intermediate Rate	12,151 – 31,580	NSND*	21%
Higher Rate	31,580 – 150,000	NSND*	41%
Top Rate	150,000+	NSND*	46%

Residents of Scotland pay the same income tax on savings income and dividends income as other UK residents.

* NSND = Non-Savings, Non-Dividends income

Personal reliefs 2018/19

	£
Personal allowance	11,850
Abatement income level	100,000
Marriage allowance: Both born after 5th April 1935	*1,190
*Relief at 20%	
Allowances: Born before 6th April 1935	
Married couple's allowance (65 before 6th April 2000) min **£3,360	**8,695
Abatement income level for married couple's allowance	28,900
Blind person's allowance	2,390
**Relief only at 10%	

National Insurance

Self-employed

Class 2 contributions		£2.95 per week
Class 4 contributions	9.0% of profits between	£8,424 – £46,350
	2.0% above	£46,350

Class 1 Employed earners from 6th April 2018

£ per week earnings

Employee £ per week earnings	
Earnings up to £162 a week – ET	Nil
Earnings between £162 and £892	12.0%
Earnings over £892 a week	2.0%
Employer	
Earnings up to £162 a week	Nil
Earnings over £162 a week	13.8%
Class 1A on Benefits in Kind	13.8%

Apprenticeship levy: Rates and allowances

	2017/18	**2018/19**
Apprenticeship Levy allowance (per employer)	£15,000	£15,000
Apprenticeship Levy rate	0.5%	0.5%

Benefits in kind

Employees' Car Benefit	Employees' Car Fuel Benefit
List price × CO_2 emission% • 13% for a car with up to 50g/km CO_2 emissions; • Cars with emissions of 51 to 75g/km incur a benefit of 16%; • Cars with emissions of 76 to 94g/km incur a benefit of 19%; • Cars with emissions of 95g/km and above incur an additional 1% for every 5g/km to a maximum of 37%. • 3% supplement for some diesel cars (see section 7.14), up to a maximum of 37%.	£23,400 × CO_2 emission % for the car (as determined at left)
Employees' Van Benefit	**Employees' Van Fuel Benefit**
£3,350	£633

Capital allowances

Plant and machinery

Annual investment allowance:
100% on £200,000 of expenditure per 12 months

Enhanced capital allowances	FYA 100%
Low Emission Cars (< 50g/km CO_2)	FYA 100%
Writing down allowance (WDA):	
General pool of plant and machinery and cars with CO_2 emissions of 110 g/km or less	18% per year
Special rate pool: features integral to a building, long life assets, and cars with CO_2 emissions of more than 110 g/km	8% per year

Lease premia

Capital element of a premium received on a lease of less than 50 years (*the rest of the premium is income*):

P × 2% × (n – 1), where P = premium amount and n = life of lease in years

Capital gains tax

	2017/18	2018/19
Standard rate	10%	10%
Higher rate and trust rate	20%	20%
Surcharge on residential property *	+8%	+8%
Annual exemption		
For individuals, PRs and some trustees	£11,300	£11,700
For most trustees	£5,650	£5,850
Entrepreneurs' relief rate	10%	10%
Entrepreneurs' relief lifetime limit of gains	£10m	£10m
Investors' relief rate	10%	10%
Investors' relief lifetime limit of gains	£10m	£10m

Investors' Relief applies to disposals of shares in unlisted companies, where those shares were newly issued to the investor seeking relief, after 17th March 2016, and were held for a continuous period of at least three years.

* (excluding Principal Private Residence, which remains exempt)

Inheritance Tax

	2017/18	2018/19
Rate (for estates)	40%	40%
Reduced rate *(for estates leaving 10% or more to charity)*	36%	36%
Rate (for Chargeable Lifetime Transfers)	20%	20%
Nil Rate Band	£325,000	£325,000
Residence Nil Rate Band	£100,000	£125,000

Corporation tax

	Years to 31st March	
	2018	2019
Financial year	FY17	FY18
Corporation Tax main rate	19%	19%

Value added tax

Standard rate	20% (1/6 × gross)
Reduced rate	5%
Zero rate	0%

Registration threshold (from 1st April 2017) — £85,000 taxable turnover in cumulative 12 month period, **or** in next 30 days

Deregistration threshold — £83,000 (from 1st April 2017)